LANGUAGE ARTS
IN CANADIAN CLASSROOMS

ANNE ELLIOTT
Brock University (Emeritus)

VERA WOLOSHYN
Brock University

TORONTO

Vice-President, Editorial Director: Gary Bennett
Editor-in-Chief: Michelle Sartor
Acquisitions Editor: David S. Le Gallais
Marketing Manager: Kathaleen McCormick
Supervising Developmental Editor: Suzanne Schaan
Developmental Editor: Megan Burns
Project Manager: Ashley Patterson
Manufacturing Manager: Susan Johnson
Production Editor: Susan Broadhurst
Copy Editor: Susan Broadhurst
Proofreader: Susan Bindernagel
Compositor: Cenveo Publisher Services
Photo Researcher: Diane Hartmann
Permissions Researcher: Joanne Tang
Art Director: Miguel Acevedo
Cover Designer: Shawn Lambino
Cover Image: Shawn Lambino

Credits and acknowledgments for material borrowed from other sources and reproduced, with permission, in this textbook appear on the appropriate pages within the text and on page 507.

10 9 8 7 6 5 4 3 2 1 [EB]

Library and Archives Canada Cataloguing in Publication

Elliott, Anne E. (Anne Elizabeth), 1943–
Language arts in Canadian classrooms / Anne Elliott, Vera Woloshyn.

Includes index.
ISBN 978-0-13-800387-6

1. Language arts (Elementary)—Canada. 2. English language—Study and teaching (Elementary)—Canada. I. Woloshyn, Vera Ella, 1965– II. Title.

LB1576.E435 2012 372.6'044 C2011-906900-8

ISBN 978-0-13-800387-6

Brief Contents

Contents

Preface

These are exciting times in education! Teachers and students are rising to the challenge of using their reading and writing skills to communicate effectively and skilfully across a variety of forums. In these times of adaptation and change, however, some things remain the same: Teachers still make a significant and often profound difference in their students' lives.

This text is constructed to help teacher candidates meet this expectation by becoming effective language arts teachers. We have drawn on current research and coupled it with practical examples of how research can be applied effectively in classrooms. We have also included profiles and words from exemplary classroom teachers who understand how to connect theory and practice to maximize student learning. Finally, we have included student perspectives throughout the text.

Reading this text will reveal several dominant and recurring themes. First, we believe that literacy learning is a dynamic, interactive, constructivist process built on students' existing experiences and serving to open their minds to new worlds, possibilities, insights, knowledge, and imaginative ideas. We also believe it is imperative that teachers promote literacy learning as pleasurable while they provide students with the necessary literacy skills. We challenge our readers to become highly engaged in the learning process and to continue to develop professionally throughout their careers, thus serving as models for their students.

This text is not merely a "how-to" book. Rather, we focus on cognitive and social processes throughout, as we believe that all teachers need to understand the theory underlying the development of language skills and the acquisition of the reading and writing processes. We also believe that the choices teachers make about the strategies, resources, and literature they bring into their classrooms significantly affect student learning, and we provide comprehensive discussion on how to meet individual differences among students. We believe that the "what" of language arts is as important as the "how." Finally, we have shared the techniques and resources that we love and we encourage beginning teachers to build their own instructional repertoires and collections of valued resources and children's literature.

During the writing of this book we faced the conundrum of having to present in successive chapters components of a balanced language arts program that occur simultaneously and interactively. We have tried to make connections throughout and we encourage our readers to remain aware of this reality while reading this text.

Chapter 1: Discovering Yourself and Your Students as Language Learners

- Description of the four cueing systems for language learning
- Description of students' cognitive development
- Discussion of how to identify the zone of proximal development
- Description of scaffolding to support student learning
- Examples of how to use information processing theory to enhance instruction
- Description of how to use explicit strategy instruction
- Description of literature circles
- Identification of the components of a balanced language arts program

Chapter 2: Listening, Speaking, and Beyond

- Description of family literacy's influences on early reading and writing experiences
- Identification of school readiness factors
- Description of accommodations for gender differences in young children
- Discussion of creating a literate kindergarten environment
- Examples of how to conduct conversations in the classroom
- Description of how to integrate drama into the language arts curriculum
- Examples of how to integrate activities that combine listening and speaking
- Description of how to conduct a Readers' Theatre

Chapter 3: Assessing and Evaluating Your Students as Language Users

- Discussion of how to recognize and distinguish the various purposes of assessment
- Discussion of the reconceptualization of the role of assessment in student learning
- Discussion of how to administer and interpret standardized assessments across the language arts
- Discussion of controversies associated with the use of high-stakes assessment
- Description of general assessment techniques for determining students' beginning to read skills and abilities
- Instructions for completing miscue analyses, running records, and informal reading inventories
- Description of a response to intervention model for working with students who have reading and writing difficulties
- Description of how to develop and implement classroom-based assessments for students' reading comprehension

Chapter 4: Word Learning

- Description of how to develop students' phonological and phonemic awareness
- Instructions for assessing phonological and phonemic awareness skills
- Instructions for teaching phonics
- Instructions for teaching sight words
- Discussion of methods for creating an interest in word learning
- Description of how to help students develop skills for identifying unfamiliar words
- Description of how to assess reading fluency
- Identification of how to work with students who are experiencing fluency difficulties

Chapter 5: Comprehension of Narrative Text

- Instructions for implementing Read Aloud programs
- Discussion of how to select appropriate reading resources

- Discussion of how to teach story structure elements to improve comprehension
- Discussion and examples of how to structure questions that encourage students to think about and comprehend what they read
- Examples of comprehension strategies for narrative text
- Discussion and example of a guided reading lesson

Chapter 6: Reading Comprehension Strategies for Non-Fiction: Reading in the Content Areas

- Discussion of the differences between narrative and expository text structures
- Suggestions for selecting non-fiction for the classroom
- Discussion of the challenges associated with content area reading
- Examples of how to address the challenges associated with content area reading
- Instructions for teaching vocabulary associated with content area reading
- Examples of how to provide explicit strategy instruction for reading expository text
- Example of reciprocal teaching instruction
- Instruction about how to teach study skills and report writing

Chapter 7: Writing: Exploring the Reading and Writing Connection

- Discussion of the connections between reading and writing
- Discussion and examples of how to implement the writing process
- Instructions for implementing a variety of writing formats in the classroom
- Discussion of how to use technology to enhance student writing
- Instructions for assessing students' writing
- Instructions for conducting a student-teacher writing conference
- Instructions for establishing a writers' workshop
- Discussion of how to create a community of writers

Chapter 8: Teaching the Writing Tools: Spelling, Grammar, Mechanics, and Handwriting

- Description of how to conduct an effective spelling program
- Discussion of teaching spelling strategies using auditory, visual, and kinesthetic methods
- Examples of how to teach the use of prefixes and suffixes
- Discussion of how to help students use Standard English
- Examples of how to conduct grammar mini-lessons
- Examples of how to use a literary context to teach grammar
- Discussion of how to teach the mechanics of writing

Chapter 9: The Role of Children's Literature

- Discussion of the history of children's literature
- Discussion of the beginning of Canadian children's literature
- Discussion and examples of how to choose literature that will attract children
- Discussion and examples of how to choose literature about diversity
- Examples of promoting discussions about diversity in the classroom
- Discussion of the importance of including Canadian literature in the literacy program
- Discussion of how to include poetry appreciation in the classroom
- Examples of how to help students write poetry
- Discussion and examples of how to be a good storyteller

Chapter 10: Refining Literacy: Integrating the New Literacies and a Critical Response to Popular Culture in Your Classroom

- Discussion of the scope of the "multiliteracies"
- Discussion of literacy in the future
- Discussion and examples of how to use digital tools in literacy learning
- Instructions for conducting a webquest
- Discussion and examples of how to bring critical literacy into the classroom
- Discussion and examples of how to help students become critical consumers
- Discussion of graphic novels and instructions for using them in the classroom

Chapter 11: Working with Students with Diverse Learning Needs

- Discussion of how some Aboriginal communities have overcome educational limitations
- Discussion of the characteristics of inclusive classrooms
- Discussion and examples of how to instruct students who are learning English as a subsequent language
- Examples of how to work with students who are at risk
- Examples of how to work with students who are living in poverty
- Instructions for providing programs for students with learning disabilities
- Discussion of methods for working with students with attention deficit hyperactivity disorder (ADHD)
- Examples of how to work with slow and reluctant learners
- Discussion and examples of how to differentiate instruction to meet all students' needs

Chapter 12: Creating Your Language Arts Classroom: How Do You Begin?

- Discussion of planning the physical set-up of your classroom
- Discussion and examples of how to set up special spaces for language arts
- Instructions for setting up a classroom library
- Examples of how to create an independent reading centre using levelled texts
- Instructions for planning a daily and weekly schedule
- Discussion of how to plan a balanced literacy program
- Discussion of how to create a positive classroom atmosphere
- Instructions for getting started effectively in September
- Discussion of how to be an effective substitute teacher
- Examples of how to communicate effectively with parents
- Examples of how to continue your professional development

TEXT FEATURES

MyEducationLab (www.myeducationlab.com)

Throughout the printed text you will find the following icons that link you to related content on MyEducationLab. In the Pearson eText, these icons are hyperlinked directly to the online resources:

Watch See video clips of real classroom scenarios. If you are a visual learner, this is for you!

Explore Dive into a deeper understanding of critical concepts by exploring a variety of links, activities, and artifacts.

Teacher and Student Voices

To present a truly Canadian orientation to teaching the language arts, we invited teachers, students, and professors from across Canada to contribute to this book. These individuals represent the diversity of regions, grade levels, and classroom configurations that comprise teaching in Canada. Their voices are featured in the Opening Vignettes, Teacher Voices, and Student Voices contained within each chapter. These features provide thought-provoking considerations for classroom practices and are intended to form the basis for informed discussion.

Opening Vignette Each chapter begins with a vignette that features a Canadian teacher. The vignettes provide real-world context for the information contained in the chapters, with teachers elaborating on their personal orientations and the techniques and instructional strategies they use in their classrooms.

Teacher Voice Practising teachers from across the country provide thought-provoking comments and instructional recommendations in each chapter.

Student Voice Students from across the grades and across the country provide frank and open responses about their experiences in language arts classrooms.

Pedagogical Tools

To assist readers in applying the information contained in each chapter, a number of pedagogical features have been included. These features provide exemplars of outstanding classroom practice and are intended to form the basis for informed discussion.

Lesson Plans To assist readers in applying the information contained in the book to their classroom teaching, extended lesson plans have been provided in several chapters. These lesson plans provide readers with step-by-step instructions for completing targeted learning activities and instructional units.

Tables and Figures To facilitate and enhance the reading of this book, numerous tables and figures have been inserted in each chapter. While some of these tables and figures synthesize critical information contained in the text, others provide lists of high-quality children's and young adult literature or instructional resources and materials. Reference to these books, resources, and materials will be especially beneficial as readers begin their classroom practice. Teaching strategy tables have also been incorporated in each chapter. These tables provide readers with concise, practical pedagogical recommendations with respect to implementing effective instructional practices in their classrooms.

Cautions Effective language arts teachers are able to adjust their instructional practices to meet the needs of their students and the demands of their programs. These teachers recognize the limits associated with various teaching techniques, instructional approaches, and learning contexts. The cautions outline specific pedagogical considerations and constraints.

Learning Aids

Each chapter contains features intended to assist the readers in processing and comprehending text information.

Chapter Objectives Taking the form of "how to" statements, several learning objectives are provided at the beginning of each chapter. These "how to" statements are intended to assist readers in bridging theory and practice by outlining how they can demonstrate their learning of information contained in each chapter.

Suggestions for Professional Development The teaching profession is not static. Rather, it is a dynamic, ever-changing profession that requires ongoing personal and professional growth. Effective teachers are problem solvers who are able to initiate and reflect on their own teaching and learning. Recognizing that effective teachers are those who embrace lifelong learning and that readers' understanding of each chapter will be enhanced by the completion of authentic activities, suggestions for professional development are provided at the end of each chapter. Many of these suggestions require readers to interact with colleagues, students, and other professionals in the education field.

As you pursue your goal of becoming a language arts teacher, we hope that this text will provide you with a solid understanding of the relevant theories of instruction and that the classroom examples will enable you to walk across the bridge from theory to practice with confidence. We also hope that the teachers whose practices we have featured will inspire you to apply your unique skills creatively and knowledgeably. We anticipate that you will challenge your language learners to attain higher-order thinking skills so that they can become critical thinkers in all aspects of their learning.

Our ultimate goal is to provide you with a blueprint for language arts instruction that you can employ, integrate, and modify for the students you teach so that they experience success in language learning and both you and them enjoy the journey. Finally, we issue a challenge to you to take control of your professional development, so that you can become a dynamic classroom teacher whose students will observe a model of ongoing enthusiasm for continuous learning.

SUPPLEMENTS

Student Supplements

MyEducationLab

The moment you know.

Educators know it. Students know it. It's that inspired moment when something that was difficult to understand suddenly makes perfect sense. Our MyLab products have been designed and refined with a single purpose in mind—to help educators create that moment of understanding with their students.

MyEducationLab delivers **proven results** in helping individual students succeed. It provides **engaging experiences** that personalize, stimulate, and measure learning for each student. And, it comes from a **trusted partner** with educational expertise and an eye on the future.

MyEducationLab can be used by itself or linked to any learning management system. To learn more about how MyEducationLab combines proven learning applications with powerful assessment, visit **www.myeducationlab.com**

MyEducationLab will help students improve their understanding of the concepts taught in this text. This online tool includes videos of real classroom experiences, sample lesson plans, simulations, case studies, and links to important educational and teaching websites to help students make the transition to teaching.

With access to MyEducationLab, students also have the opportunity to use the virtual classroom management resource "Managing to Teach." This learning tool is based on a broad conception of classroom management and encompasses the multi-faceted dynamics of the student-teacher relationship and the organization of the physical classroom space. "Managing to Teach" uses a modular structure and includes:

- Introduction to a virtual school
- Developing constructive expectations
- Preventing and pre-empting problems through prior planning
- Creating positive personal interactions by exhibiting desired modes of behaviour

MyEducationLab—the moment you know.

CourseSmart for Students CourseSmart goes beyond traditional expectations, providing instant, online access to the textbooks and course materials you need at an average savings of 60 percent. With instant access from any computer and the ability to search your text, you'll find the content you need quickly, no matter where you are. And with online tools such as highlighting and note taking, you can save time and study efficiently. See all the benefits at **www.coursesmart.com/students.**

Instructor Supplements

Instructor's Manual The Instructor's Manual contains a wealth of resources for instructors, including chapter overviews, outlines, teaching suggestions, and further readings. A very practical resource, the Instructor's Manual will help teachers create engaging lesson plans and an environment of literacy for their students.

Pearson MyTest MyTest from Pearson Canada is a powerful assessment generation program that helps instructors easily create and print quizzes, tests, and exams, as well as homework or practice handouts. Questions and tests can be authored online, allowing instructors ultimate flexibility and the ability to efficiently manage assessments at any time, from anywhere. These questions are also available in Microsoft Word format (see Test Item File, below).

Test Item File Each question in this test bank is referenced to the corresponding text page number, topic, and skill level. The test bank is available both as a Test Item File in Microsoft Word format and in MyTest format (see above).

The above supplements can be accessed through Pearson Canada's online catalogue (www.pearsoncanada.ca/highered). Navigate to your book's catalogue page to view a list of those supplements that are available. See your local Pearson representative for details and access.

Pearson Custom Library For enrolments of at least 25 students, you can create your own textbook by choosing the chapters that best suit your own course needs. To begin building your custom text, visit www.pearsoncustomlibrary.com. You may also work with a dedicated Pearson Custom editor to create your ideal text—publishing your own original content or mixing and matching Pearson content. Contact your local Pearson representative to get started.

Technology Specialists Pearson's Technology Specialists work with faculty and campus course designers to ensure that Pearson technology products, assessment tools, and online course materials are tailored to meet your specific needs. This highly qualified team is dedicated to helping schools take full advantage of a wide range of educational resources, by assisting in the integration of a variety of instructional materials and media formats. Your local Pearson Canada sales representative can provide you with more details on this service program.

CourseSmart for Instructors CourseSmart goes beyond traditional expectations, providing instant, online access to the textbooks and course materials you need at a lower cost for students. And even as students save money, you can save time and hassle with a digital eText that allows you to search for the most relevant content at the very moment you need it. Whether it's evaluating textbooks or creating lecture notes to help students with difficult concepts, CourseSmart can make life a little easier. See how when you visit **www.coursesmart.com/instructors.**

About the Authors

Anne E. Elliott developed her teaching skills during several years working in the inner city of Toronto and in Peterborough, Ontario. She subsequently completed her Master of Education at Brock University and obtained a doctorate from the Ontario Institute for Studies in Education at the University of Toronto. Beginning her academic career at Brock University's Faculty of Education, she specialized in the teaching of language courses to beginning teachers for many years. Always an avid reader herself, she promoted the power of children's literature with a focus on Canadian authors as a motivator to help children develop reading skills and a love of reading. Later, she became intrigued by the changing patterns of communication that brought the "new literacies" into education and her research focused on the patterns and habits of children as they interact with media. A recently retired professor, she has been named as a Professor Emeritus at Brock University.

Vera E. Woloshyn, Ph.D., is a professor in the Faculty of Education and the former director of the Reading Clinic at Brock University. She teaches courses in reading development, instruction and assessment, cognition and learning, language arts, and research methodology. Her research interests include promoting the use of effective learning strategies and instructional techniques, especially for students who struggle with reading and writing. She has written numerous research articles and books pertaining to the use of evidence-based learning strategies and instructional techniques and has been an expert member on several Ministry of Education and community panels. She believes that with appropriate instruction, guidance, and support, all students can become proficient readers and writers and develop a lifelong love of reading. Like Anne, she has become interested in the role of the new literacies in the daily lives of students, including those who struggle with reading and writing.

Acknowledgments

As in teaching, the writing of this book has been a collaborative endeavour. We have talked to and consulted with many education professors, teachers, and students across Canada, which provides this book with its strong Canadian focus. We are grateful for the time, expertise, and experience shared by all contributors.

We would particularly like to thank the following expert contributors:

- Dr. Debra McLauchlan is a well-known drama specialist and educator who is a professor at Brock University. Her contributions to Chapter 2 enhance the readers' understanding of the creative role of drama in the classroom. The classroom-based activities she describes and outlines in great detail make her contribution a valuable one for the readers of this book.
- Cathy Miyata is an internationally known storyteller, an award-winning author, and an active literacy specialist. She shares her extensive knowledge of storytelling in Chapter 9 and provided many specific examples of ways to incorporate this motivational tradition into the classroom. She has also shared her favourite resources with our readers.
- Mira Bajovic is a lecturer in education specializing in educational psychology, assessment and evaluation, and literacy courses. She shares her knowledge and insights in Chapter 3. Mira is currently a Ph.D. candidate.

We are also grateful to our colleagues who reviewed both our initial proposal and several draft chapters of this book and provided thoughtful feedback that helped us gain new insights on our project:

Deborah Berrill, Trent University

Dorothea Bryant, University of Windsor

Mary Clare Courtland, Lakehead University

Jackie Eldridge, University of Toronto at Mississauga

Janette Hughes, University of Ontario Institute of Technology

Carol Leroy, University of Alberta

Sandra Martin-Chang, Concordia University

Rosamund Stooke, University of Western Ontario

In addition, we would like to extend a heartfelt thank you to our Developmental Editor, Megan Burns; our Production Editor and Copy Editor, Susan Broadhurst; our Proofreader, Susan Bindernagel; and our Project Manager, Ashley Patterson, whose diligence, attention to detail, and unfailing support were integral to the success of this project.

Chapter 1

Discovering Yourself and Your Students as Language Learners

Learning Objectives

In this chapter you will discover

- How to identify the four cueing systems for language learning.
- How to recognize students' cognitive development.
- How to identify the zone of proximal development.
- How to use scaffolding to support student learning.
- How to use information processing theory to enhance instruction.
- How to use explicit strategy instruction.
- How to use literature circles.
- How to identify the components of a balanced language arts program.

LIZ MCANANAMA: CREATING A BALANCED LANGUAGE ARTS PROGRAM

For the past seven years, Liz McAnanama has taught junior grades in four different schools. She has also participated in an extensive array of professional development activities, including obtaining her Master of Education degree. She believes that understanding of student development and the learning process is increasing rapidly, as is our understanding of effective instruction and technologies. These developments can inspire teachers to review their teaching practices.

Liz also believes that every child can be successful, although children's experiences in school are unique and varied. For some, school is an enjoyable experience; for others, it is not. This is especially true in junior grades, when many students become self-conscious about their social status. Liz is intent on making her classroom a safe, comfortable, and positive place and spends considerable time learning about individual students and their strengths. More importantly, she expends considerable effort ensuring that students recognize their own strengths and appreciate those of others. She encourages students to make mistakes: "big" mistakes that create great learning opportunities. In support of this idea, Liz often tells students about her own errors. Although the students often laugh at her stories, she believes that she is modelling risk taking and the belief that individuals can hold multiple viewpoints. When students acknowledge alternative viewpoints and ways of thinking, they become more caring and respectful of each other.

Liz believes that discrepancies in students' skills, abilities, development, and experiences are magnified in the junior grades. She relies extensively on modelling, scaffolding, and guided practice to ensure that all students receive appropriate programming, even when presenting skills and strategies that have been taught earlier. The challenge is to recognize students to whom she can release responsibility early versus those who need continued support and scaffolding.

Liz reflects on a recent newspaper unit that she completed with her grades 5 and 6 split class. The focus of the integrated unit was on making connections and on personal safety. The unit was inspired by a recent event featured in several local newspapers in which a young driver lost control of his vehicle while text messaging and driving. The accident happened close to the school and several of the students had witnessed the event.

Liz transferred the articles from various newspapers to an overhead and read them aloud to the class. As part of this process, she shared her thoughts about how the articles differed across the newspapers as well as how the events related to her own life, her concern for her children's safety, and her own cellphone habits. She provided a commentary about the pictures that accompanied the articles, which showed extensive damage to the car. She then invited the students to respond to the articles, providing them with guiding questions and prompts that would help them connect the event to their own experiences in a meaningful way. While students who had witnessed the accident spoke about the driver's response, others extended the conversation to the use of cellphones and text messaging in their own lives, including the dangers associated with text messaging and walking.

After the discussion, Liz led the students in developing a summary of the articles and introduced them to the larger task of composing an article with the intent of publishing a class newspaper focusing on personal safety. They continued the conversation the next day by discussing the intended audience, the content criteria (i.e., what, who, when, where, why, and how information), and the importance of the title, hook, and illustration. Finally, they brainstormed possible topics.

Liz then assigned students to small groups, carefully considering the grade level, strengths, and needs of each student. She tried to ensure that the groups were balanced with respect to individuals with strong reading, writing, or visually representing skills. The latter was particularly important, as students were required to include an image to accompany their article. As students completed their articles over the next several classes, Liz moved between the groups, assessing students' understanding of the task and the quality of their work. She provided leading questions to groups that appeared to be experiencing difficulties (e.g., "Tell me more about your hook? How do your words represent your intentions as authors?") and revisited the focal article with those that needed redirection and greater support. The remaining students completed the task independently. These sessions also provided Liz with critical assessment information, including insights about the quality of intrapersonal group interactions.

Once students completed a draft of their article, they exchanged copies with another group and followed the Two Stars and a Wish feedback protocol (i.e., two areas of strength and one recommendation for improvement). They then submitted their final draft to Liz, who reviewed the papers for content and mechanics. Students then published their articles using the computer and posted their final products. They shared their articles, explaining the rationale for their images and elaborating on the connections they made with themselves and the world.

At this point, Liz guided the students in the final component of the newspaper project: selecting the one story and illustration that would be on the front page. Students were given the option of selecting one of the articles completed by their classmates or creating a new one. To guide them in this process, Liz shared the front pages of popular magazines and used Think Aloud again. Conversations unfolded about why the magazine editors might have selected these images and how the images captured the essence of the related print articles and piqued the readers' interest.

Overall, Liz was very pleased with the students' final products and with their ability to make connections with themselves and the world. Students selected from a wide range of topics related to personal safety, from simple topics such as pool safety or home-alone safety to more complex topics such as internet and identity safety. Liz believes that providing students with choice within a commonly defined task allowed them to draw on a range of previous experiences while also allowing her to accommodate instruction to meet their learning needs. She was pleased that the unit provided students with the opportunity to engage in all elements of language arts, including reading, writing, listening, speaking, viewing, and visually representing.

Before reading this text, we challenge our readers to complete two distinct tasks.

REFLECTIVE ACTIVITY 1

Reflect on the three most important characteristics of a good teacher. When you have identified three characteristics, force yourself to rank them in order of highest importance.

You might consider the following characteristics:

- Consistent and fair
- Knowledgeable
- Good sense of humour
- Organized
- Flexible
- Likes children
- Large repertoire of teaching strategies
- Allows for individual differences
- Calm and kind
- Effective classroom management skills

Share your ranked list with another person, providing a rationale for your selections. Negotiate a new list of three items. Share your revised list with another pair and negotiate a new list that satisfies all four of you.

REFLECTIVE ACTIVITY 2

Select a children's book that has been made into a movie. Examples include *Madeline, Charlotte's Web, Stuart Little, The Secret Garden*, the Harry Potter books, *Beauty and the Beast, The Little Mermaid*, other fairy tales, *Mrs. Frisby and the Rats of NIMH, Anne of Green Gables, Charlie and the Chocolate Factory, The Lion, the Witch and the Wardrobe, Mary Poppins, Matilda*, and *Tuck Everlasting*. Read the book and watch the movie.

When comparing the two experiences, think about the similarities and differences between viewing and reading. Watch to see if the theme, characters, plot lines, or ending have changed.

Reflect on (and discuss with your peers) which you prefer and how you might use one in a class to enhance understanding of the other. Confront your prejudices one way or the other.

INTRODUCTION

Infant language and literacy development

FEW OF US REALLY REMEMBER HOW WE LEARNED TO READ OR THE EXACT MOMENT when we began to identify ourselves as readers and writers. Regardless, reading and writing are transformative and magical experiences that serve simultaneously as a rite of passage and as a window to the world beyond our immediate selves. Built on existing listening and oral language skills, the development of reading and writing skills furthers opportunities for critical comprehension, vocabulary development, media use, and research skills. In order for teachers to assist students in joining the language users club or to enhance and elaborate students' existing skills, it is imperative that they understand student development and the basic processes involved in learning.

Four Cueing Systems

Language is organized around four cueing systems: phonological, syntactic, semantic, and pragmatic. Proficient communication involves the integration of information across these cueing systems, with each system complementing its counterparts. Most proficient language users access these interrelated systems simultaneously and unconsciously, with parents passing this knowledge to their children seamlessly as part of their early language experiences. As children's knowledge of oral language develops, so does their implicit understanding of these cueing systems, which, in turn, enhances their listening, reading, and writing abilities. Although the systems are interdependent and interactive, we provide a brief description of each below. More detailed descriptions of each system are also provided in the remaining chapters of this text.

The **phonological system** refers to the 44 speech sounds that constitute the English language. As children begin to speak, they learn to pronounce the sounds that comprise our language. These sounds are referred to as phonemes, with graphemes being the letter combinations that represent these sounds. As children begin to read and write, they learn to associate speech sounds with corresponding letters (phonology). Unfortunately, this can be a complicated process, as the English language does not reflect a purely phonetic system. That is, there is no one-to-one direct correspondence between letters and sounds. Instead, the 26 letters of the alphabet are used to represent the 44 speech sounds. The term *phonics* is used to describe these phoneme-grapheme correspondences and related spelling rules. While the study of phonics is an important component of learning to decode words, effective instruction requires teachers to do much more. Teachers must be sensitive to students' developmental progress as well as to regional and cultural differences. Consider, for example, variations in how the words *tomato*, *potato*, and *aunt* may be pronounced by individuals in Newfoundland, Quebec, and Alberta. Readers are referred to Chapter 4, Word Learning, for a detailed discussion of the role of phonological awareness in beginning reading, phonics programs, and evidence-based practices related to promoting students' decoding and word attack skills.

The **syntactic system** refers to the structural organization of English. While the terms *syntax* and *grammar* are sometimes used interchangeably, the latter is used here to refer to the formal analysis of parts of speech and the generally accepted rules of writing. Specifically, the syntactic system determines the necessary placements and combinations of words in order to convey intended meanings. Morphemes are the smallest meaningful units of language. They may be free-standing (individual words) or bound (markers that change the meaning of words, such as the plural form *-s* or the tense marker *-ed*). As students progress through the elementary grades, they develop their understanding and ability to work with affixes (root words, prefixes, and suffixes). They also learn to comprehend and generate different types of sentences, including questions, statements, and commands. Their understanding of sentence complexity and punctuation develops and they are able to generate increasingly complex sentence structures (simple, compound, and complex) as well as apply punctuation effectively. Students' syntactic understandings enhance their comprehension of text. Even when they are unable to decode words accurately, they are likely aware of the words' position and role in the sentence. For instance, acknowledging that the word *aerodrome* is a noun maintains the essence of the meaning of the following sentence: "We drove to the aerodrome to wave goodbye to our visitors."

Such understandings sometimes allow students to make meaningful substitutions when reading text. In this case, the word *airport* could be substituted. Students' developing understanding of syntax is discussed in Chapter 2, Listening, Speaking, and Beyond, and instructional recommendations related to the teaching of written grammar are described in Chapter 8, Teaching the Writing Tools: Spelling, Grammar, Mechanics, and Handwriting.

The **semantic system** is based on meaning, with vocabulary being its foundation. As children begin to speak their vocabulary develops, with most students knowing approximately 5000 words by the time they begin school. As students progress through the grades, it is estimated that they learn between 3000 and 4000 new words a year, or at least 8 new words a day (Alvermann & Phelps, 1998; Stahl & Nagy, 2006). In part, students acquire this reading through their daily interactions with peers, teachers, and families as well as text materials. Classroom discussion and verbal dialogue is an important component of the language arts curriculum, as students' expressive language skills are often an extension of their receptive language skills (consider that students are more likely to use new vocabulary as part of the reading and writing processes after integrating these terms effectively within their speech). Students' comprehension and appreciation of the nuances and meanings of words also becomes more sophisticated and refined with increased interactions with text and verbal exchanges. For instance, students gradually grasp that the words *car*, *automobile*, *auto*, and *vehicle* hold much the same meaning across sentences. Although students acquire the majority of their vocabulary knowledge outside formal instruction, vocabulary instruction—including the study of synonyms, antonyms, homonyms, idioms, metaphors, similes, and wordplay—remains an important component of the language arts classroom. A detailed description of evidence-based vocabulary instructional practices is provided in Chapter 6, Reading Comprehension Strategies for Non-Fiction: Reading in the Content Areas.

The **pragmatic system** refers to the social and cultural aspects of language and reflects the different usages and purposes of language. Language is not static; popular culture and media influence how we communicate, introducing new concepts and terms into our language on a regular basis. Consider the language you use when speaking in a classroom, chatting with friends, or sending an email. The language that individuals use to communicate varies as a function of social, cultural, and ethnic background, as well as geographic region (or what is otherwise referred to as dialect). In this sense, schools can be viewed as contained cultures, where students are expected to acquire and use the rules and conventions of Standard English.

These rules and conventions range from the simple practice of turn taking while speaking to the complex concept of modifying language selection according to the audience at hand. Over time and extended language use, most students come to recognize that the language they use to communicate with friends (in person or online) may not be appropriate when speaking to their teachers or writing formally. Effective communicators possess a repertoire of language registers that allows them to communicate efficiently across a number of social situations. Effective teachers, in turn, are sensitive to students' various dialects and cultural experiences (including popular culture). They recognize their role in providing students with instruction in Standard English while not replacing or denigrating the dialect or vocabulary of the students' home or culture. A discussion of the importance of oral language and classroom discussions is provided in Chapter 2, Listening, Speaking, and Beyond, while Chapter 7, Writing: Exploring the Reading and Writing Connection, outlines various conventions and formats involved in the writing process. Chapter 10, Redefining Literacy: Integrating the New Literacies and a Critical Response to Popular Culture in Your Classroom, provides a critical review of the role of the "new literacies," or what is also referred to as *multiliteracies*, in the classroom as well as evidence-based pedagogy associated with critical literacy instruction.

REFLECTIVE ACTIVITY 3

Reflect on a time when you observed a student learning a new reading- or writing-related skill or activity (e.g., decoding text, printing letters, writing in cursive, completing a research paper, preparing or delivering a formal speech) or reflect on your own learning experiences as a student. Which factors appeared to assist with the learning process and which factors appeared to hinder it? Carefully consider what you know about effective learning and instruction as well as student development. Share your thoughts with another student and categorize your responses under one of the following headers:

- Classroom Environment (e.g., materials, resources, instructional posters and guides, seating arrangement, teacher's desk)

- Teacher Instruction (e.g., initial instruction, additional assistance, peer helpers)
- Students' Cognitive Development (e.g., familiarity with process, effort required to complete task, emotional response to task)

Discuss how students' cognitive development influences the nature of effective instruction and classroom environment, and vice versa. Which variables remain constant and which change across the grades?

In this chapter we provide an overview of students' development according to cognitive constructivist theory as well as an overview of complementary instructional methodologies. We encourage you to revise and redefine your list as you read the remainder of this chapter.

HOW STUDENTS LEARN

Constructivist orientations to learning emphasize that students learn best when they are actively engaged in the learning process—that is, when they are actively participating in making meaning of new information and connecting it to previous experiences. Cognitive constructivist approaches provide insights about how students interact with the environment and use information processing skills to construct knowledge. Social constructivist approaches extend this thinking, emphasizing the important role of others in the construction of knowledge and strategic processes. The emphasis moves from the processing of information by individuals to the construction of knowledge through social interactions and collaborative experiences. It is also recognized that students' cultural and home experiences and expectations influence their orientations toward learning and literacy.

Understanding how students learn influences how we teach all subjects, including the language arts. Similarly, understanding students' growth as learners is important in terms of providing appropriate instruction across the primary, junior, and intermediate grades. We provide specific information with respect to the development of oral language, reading, writing, and spelling skills throughout this text. In this chapter, however, we present several learning models that provide a foundation for language arts instruction and we outline associated instructional implications.

EXPLORING STUDENTS' COGNITIVE DEVELOPMENT

Jean Piaget (1896–1980)

Our current view of literacy is that it is a developmental process in which learning begins much earlier than when students enter school. This view emphasizes the close connection between cognitive development and language learning. Jean Piaget developed a theory of cognitive development that asserted that thought comes before language and that language is a way of representing thought. Children learn and develop their language skills by forming and testing hypotheses, experimenting with sounds and words, and exploring the relationships between the two. Through the process of actively constructing their world, children develop schemata or segments of information that relate to a concept, knowledge base, or event. Children come to acquire and adopt their schemata through the process of assimilation and accommodation. For example, they come to understand that reading involves the exchange of meaningful ideas and requires more than just the successful decoding of words.

Assimilation is the simpler of these two processes and involves the integration of new information into existing schemata. For example, a student who lives in a rural area visits a city and takes a ride on the subway. This new experience creates a new schema related to ways to travel quickly underground in the city. Accommodation is a more difficult and complex process and requires students to modify existing schemata. For instance, a student may believe that, similar to birds, butterflies are hatched from eggs. When the student discovers that butterflies begin life as caterpillars that spin cocoons and then emerge from the cocoons, the existing schema about butterflies needs to be modified.

The process by which these two concepts operate is called equilibration. When students encounter new information, their existing equilibrium is affected negatively and disequilibrium occurs. To return to a state of equilibrium, children engage in the process of either assimilation or accommodation. This process also results in the acquisition of new vocabulary, concepts, and higher levels of understanding.

Piaget divided cognitive development into four sequential stages: sensorimotor, preoperational, concrete operational, and formal operational. Each stage is age dependent and represents a distinctive way of thinking. A brief description of each stage, including some of its defining characteristics, follows.

The Sensorimotor Stage (0–2 Years) During the sensorimotor stage, children learn about objects and begin to form ideas about their world, predominately through physical manipulation (e.g., toys, clothes, furniture). For example, infants learn that touching mobile crib toys in specific ways results in specific noises or motions. Piaget believed that the manipulation of a wide variety of concrete objects is an important element of the development of intelligence, with object permanence being one of the most important accomplishments at this stage. This concept involves understanding that objects and events continue to exist even when they cannot be seen, heard, or touched.

The Preoperational Stage (2–7 Years) The preoperational stage is divided further into two stages. The first one is the preconceptual stage (2–4 years). Here children begin to engage in symbolic thought by representing ideas and occurrences using words and eventually sentences. They also begin to use drawings and dramatic play to represent ideas and events. For instance, young children may use scribbles to represent people, objects, places, and events such as driving to the grocery store. Their drawings become more structured, realistic, and neat as they progress through the primary grades.

The second stage is referred to as the intuitive stage (4–7 years). Here children begin to develop concepts. However, they usually do so from a limited, egocentric perspective. Egocentrism is the inability to distinguish one's personal perspective from those held by others. Children at this stage are also likely to demonstrate animism or the belief that inanimate objects possess lifelike qualities and capabilities. For example, a young child may believe that a teddy bear can feel pain when it falls to the ground. Language accomplishments include the ability to demonstrate syntactic and grammatical awareness during speech. Rather than saying, "No want to go to bed," a child may say, "I don't want to go to bed."

The Concrete Operational Stage (7–11 Years) This stage is marked by students' increased use of intuitive thinking across most concrete learning situations. Students demonstrate the ability to classify objects into various subsets and consider their interrelationships (classifying), order objects along a defined quantitative dimension (striation), and combine relations logically to derive valid conclusions (transitivity). Linguistically, students acquire such linguistic skills as adding prefixes and suffixes to words to alter their meanings and generating complex sentences. For instance, children move beyond stating what they "like" to expressing a specific "dislike" for other objects.

The Formal Operational Stage (11–15 Years) During this time, students develop the ability to reason about ideas that do not fall into their direct experiences. For instance, even if they have never experienced falling off a bike, they are able to understand and imagine how it must feel to do so. They are able to think in more abstract, idealistic, and logical ways.

Implication for Educators Piaget believed that children construct their own learning through interactions with the environment and by transforming, organizing, and reorganizing previous knowledge. Although aspects of Piaget's theory have been challenged, including the synchrony of the proposed developmental stages (Bjorklund, 2000; Case, 2000; Morra, Gobbo, Marini, & Sheese, 2008) and the need to consider the powerful influence of culture and education (Gauvain & Perez, 2007; Greenfield, 2000), his work continues to remind educators about their responsibility to encourage students to explore the world around them and provide them with relevant learning experiences.

Lev Vygotsky (1896–1934)

A contemporary of Piaget, Lev Vygotsky also believed that children actively construct their knowledge and stressed the importance of language and social interactions for learning. Vygotsky's ideas were not introduced to North American educators until the 1960s but have received increasing attention since then (Bodrova & Leong, 2007; Daniels, 2007). According to Vygotsky, children's cognitive skills are mediated by words, language, and discourse; have their origins in social relations; and are embedded in the learners' socio-cultural environment. Vygotsky stressed the importance of verbal discourse as the vehicle for facilitating and transforming mental activity (Tappan, 1998), suggesting that learning can be advanced through interaction with others in co-operative activities (Gredler, 2008). He argued that even young children use language to plan activities and solve problems and that inner speech (sometimes referred to as private speech) is especially important to the learning process (John-Steiner, 2007; Wertsch, 2007). Specifically, Vygotsky believed that proficient learners use inner speech to regulate and guide their learning. Before students can rely on their inner speech, however, they must gain extensive experience using verbal language. For most children, the transition from external to internal speech takes place between the ages of 3 and 7 years and involves talking to oneself. Over time, the self-talk becomes automatic and children can act without verbalizing. Vygotsky's zone of proximal development and scaffolding reflect his belief that verbal communication is essential for effective instruction (John-Steiner, 2007; Tappan, 1998).

The **zone of proximal development** reflects the range of tasks that are too difficult for students to master alone but that can be learned with guidance and assistance from adults or more skilled peers. The lower limit is the cognitive level achieved by the student when working independently. The upper limit is the level of achievement possible with the assistance of a more skilled instructor (Gredler, 2008). The one-on-one instruction provided by many Canadian teachers using reading intervention programs such as Reading Recovery (Clay & Cazden, 1990) is one application of this concept. Over time, students participating in these sessions can improve their reading substantially, demonstrating grade-level or close-to-grade-level performance.

Scaffolding reflects the changing level of support provided to learners across the instructional sessions. When the learning task is new, the level of support provided is typically high, with the instructor usually providing direct or explicit instruction. As the learners' competence increases, less guidance is provided and students are encouraged to work independently whenever possible (Daniels, 2007; DeVries, 2000). We provide an overview below of some of the instructional methodologies that reflect this continuum.

Implication for Educators Vygotsky's theory reflects a social constructivist approach to learning that focuses on the importance of language, social contexts, and culture. Effective teachers are those who hold skilled discourses with students and who facilitate interactions with more skilled peers. Learning occurs in interactive communication sessions with others—a reality that has huge implications for how language arts instruction is carried out in classrooms today.

Information Processing Theory

Behaviourism and its associative models of learning (e.g., classical and operant conditioning) dominated much of our thinking about how students learn until the 1950s and 1960s. At that time, many cognitive psychologists began to acknowledge that they could not explain children's learning without referring to mental processes such as memory and thinking. The information processing approach emphasized that students manipulate, monitor, and strategize about information. Students are viewed as active information processors rather than passive recipients of information. Especially relevant for educators, there was recognition that children's capacity for processing information in cognitively sophisticated ways develops with age and instructional experiences (Munakata, 2006; Terry, 2006).

Three critical elements underlie the information processing approach (Siegler, 2007): thinking, change mechanisms, and self-regulation. Thinking involves the processes of perceiving, encoding, representing, and storing information. Information processing theorists believe that with appropriate training students can demonstrate flexible thinking, being able to adapt and adjust their cognitive approaches in response to changes in task, environment, and goals.

Change mechanisms (encoding, strategy construction, automaticity, and generalization) are responsible for alterations in students' thinking and cognitive processing. Encoding involves transforming information into memory, with learning being enhanced to the extent to which students engage in relevant cognitive processes or learning strategies. However, students' use of strategies is complicated, with their initial efforts requiring them to devote substantial time and effort to their execution. Only with repeated practice are students able to carry out and fully benefit from the use of these strategies. At this point, strategy use is referred to as being automatic. In general, information processing becomes

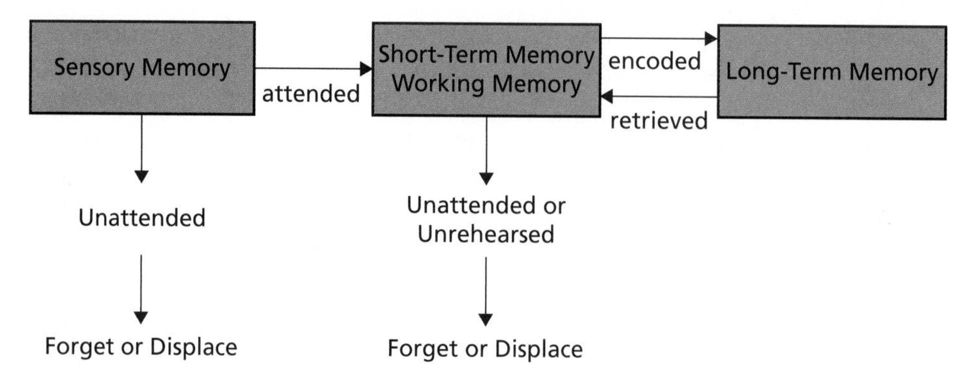

Figure 1.1 Three-Stage Model of Memory

increasingly automatic with age (due in part to underlying changes in working memory capacity and prior knowledge) and relevant instructional experiences.

Developing an effective repertoire of strategies is a critical aspect of becoming an effective learner (Pressley & Harris, 2006). Equally important, students need to understand when and where to use individual strategies and apply them appropriately to new learning tasks. This understanding is an important element of self-regulation and demonstrates metacognitive awareness (Flavell, 2004).

While a complete description of the interplay between memory and learning is beyond the scope of this chapter, how information is initially encoded, retained, and retrieved from memory greatly influences the learning experience. Atkinson and Shiffrin (1968) proposed the original model of memory that involved the processing of information across three stages: sensory memory, short-term memory, and long-term memory. Figure 1.1 provides a representation of these components.

Sensory memory holds about 4 or 5 units of information in its original sensory form, whether it be visual (iconic), auditory (echoic), olfactory, or other. In general, these memories are very brief (lasting about 250 milliseconds) and are lost quickly from memory unless they are somehow rehearsed or given attention. With attention, information from sensory memory is transferred to short-term (or working) memory.

Predominately auditory in nature, short-term or working memory is also limited in capacity, with most adults holding about 7 (plus or minus 2) clusters of information. As in sensory memory, items are retained in short-term memory for only brief intervals of time (about 30 seconds) unless directly attended to or rehearsed. In contrast, long-term memory is virtually limitless in its ability to retain information, with distinctions being made across memory types. Specifically, declarative memory includes semantic information (e.g., general knowledge of the provinces and associated capitals, the multiplication table) and "when and where" information about episodic experiences (e.g., first love, sixteenth birthday, family holiday). Especially relevant to language arts teachers, long-term memory also holds procedural memories, which include skills, strategies, and cognitive processes. Although information processed in long-term memory is stored indefinitely, students may experience difficulty retrieving this information depending on how the information was processed and the frequency of its retrieval.

The Importance of Higher-Level Rehearsal

According to Atkinson and Shiffrin (1968), only information that is attended to (rehearsed or processed cognitively) is transferred from sensory memory to short-term memory (otherwise known as working memory) and then to long-term memory. Unattended information, in contrast, lasts only a few seconds before being dropped from either sensory or short-term memory. Rehearsal is the primary mechanism for retaining information and securing it in storage. The specific nature of rehearsal, however, can be quite varied. In their levels of processing theory, Craik and Lockhart (1972) demonstrated that students' retention of items was minimal following shallow rehearsal, or rehearsal that involved the processing of sensory or physical attributes (e.g., shape of letters, type of print). In contrast, students' retention was maximized when they processed information deeply at a semantic level (e.g., concept attributes).

Although there is evidence that students develop some lower-level repetition strategies such as simple rehearsal and chunking (organizing into units) with maturation, they usually require direct instruction on other forms of higher-level repetition. Providing students with instructions to engage in sophisticated cognitive processes such as elaboration (e.g., considering connections between to-be-learned items and previous experiences) and visualization are recognized as effective methods for improving their retention of information. However, students often do not engage in such elaborate forms of processing information unless they are directly instructed to do so. In part, this reflects the substantial cognitive effort required to engage in these processes until they are practised to the point of automaticity.

A New Look at Working Memory

Critics of the information processing model argue that it is too simplistic and does not acknowledge the ways in which long-term memories can influence the encoding of new information in short-term or working memory. Working memory thus became the preferred term, as it represents an active, constructive process. More elaborate models of working memory reflect a mental area in which information (forwarded from sensory memory or retrieved from long-term memory) is manipulated to engage in higher-order thinking processes such as comprehending written and oral language and problem solving.

Most recent models of working memory include a central executive, phonological loop, visuospatial sketchpad, and episodic buffer (see Figure 1.2; Baddeley, 2000, 2006, 2007). The phonological loop stores speech-based information and the visuospatial sketchpad stores visual and spatial information. Both units work independently, with rehearsal being the mechanism through which items are retained. The episodic buffer is a third storage system intended to link information across the other stores and form integrated units of visual, spatial, and verbal information. The episodic buffer is also assumed to have strong links to long-term memory. The central executive integrates information from the phonological loop, visuospatial sketchpad, episodic buffer, and long-term memory. Using information retained in long-term memory, the central executive makes decisions with respect to which information will be attended to and what processes or strategies will be used to process it. Once processed, information is forwarded to long-term memory for storage. Like their predecessors, the phonological loop, visuospatial sketchpad, episodic buffer, and central executive all have limited capacity.

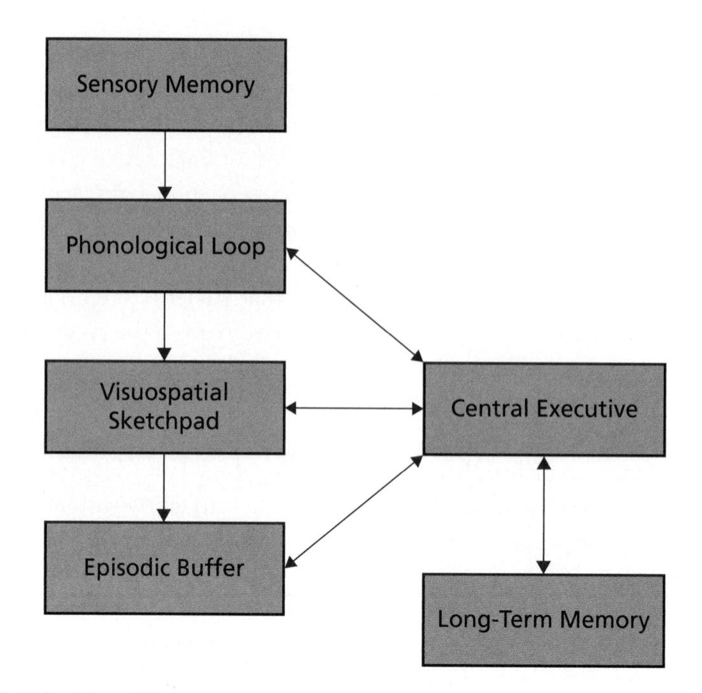

Figure 1.2 Working Memory

Implications for Educators Information processing theory as described here exemplifies the cognitive constructivist approach. Consistent with the developmental theories of Piaget and Vykotsky, teachers can be viewed as cognitive guides and students as learners who are actively engaged in meaning-making (Mayer, 2008). Information processing theory provides teachers with many critical insights about students' cognitive processes as well as how to provide them with effective instruction. For instance, teachers are reminded that students can attend to only a limited amount of information at any point in time and that there are substantial increases in the capacity of students' working memory from 8 to 24 years of age (Swanson, 1999). There are also limits on how quickly students can process information. Students with better working memory tend to demonstrate greater reading comprehension and problem-solving skills than their less advanced peers (e.g., Andersson & Lyxell, 2007).

Providing students with instruction in the use of effective processing strategies can enhance their retention and learning of information. However, deep or elaborative forms of rehearsal require the exertion of substantial cognitive effort until practised to the point of automaticity. Providing students with instruction in new processing skills and new content can be especially taxing. Working memory can be impaired by negative affect or emotions, including anxiety.

These considerations are especially important in the primary grades, when students' working memory is not fully developed and they are learning many new process skills, including those associated with reading and writing. Through scaffolding and providing environmental supports, teachers must balance instruction in the use of evidence-based processing skills and strategies with the introduction of new content. A more detailed discussion of how this can be accomplished is provided throughout the remainder of this chapter.

STRATEGY USE IN THE LANGUAGE ARTS

Language acquisition

WHEN STUDENTS ENGAGE IN ELABORATE COGNITIVE PROCESSING, THEY ARE ENGAGED IN strategic behaviours. Strategy use is intentional and often effortful, especially when first being applied. Over the past 30 years, researchers have identified a number of strategies that improve students' learning (National Reading Panel, 2000). Strategies that have been substantiated as improving student learning through empirical study are referred to as *evidence-based*. Some of these strategies are general and can be transferred across a variety of learning contexts. Others are specific to the task at hand. We recommend that teachers focus on the former whenever possible and have listed some of the most commonly used strategies for decoding, comprehending, and writing in Table 1.1.

Most students do not adopt the use of evidence-based strategies spontaneously. Instead, they require instruction from their teachers. With repeated use, practice, and guided conversations, students come to recognize the parameters associated with specific strategies (i.e., "when" and "where" information). They develop strategy repertoires and are able to use strategies flexibly (monitoring, evaluating, and revising strategy use as needed). They also come to attribute their successful learning experiences to strategy use. When students use evidence-based strategies, their work is usually of high quality and they tend to be confident of their ability to complete new tasks. We discuss effective instructional techniques that promote the use of evidence-based strategies next.

Explicit Strategy Instruction

Explicit strategy instruction is critical to effective reading and writing instruction (Israel & Duffy, 2009; Kamil, Pearson, Moje, & Afferbach, 2011; Pressley, 2006). Good readers routinely use evidence-based strategies. They also know when and where to use these

Table 1.1 Examples of Common General Decoding, Reading Comprehension, and Writing Strategies

Decoding	Integrated picture mnemonic for letter-sound learning: View or create drawing that contains target letter within body of picture
	Visual sight words: Create visual image to reinforce recognition and spelling of target words
	Reading by analogy: Use key letter patterns to decode unfamiliar words
Reading Comprehension	Predicting and activating prior knowledge: Activate relevant prior knowledge or form predictions about target information
	Connecting: Make relevant connections between events within text, text and prior experiences, and text and world
	Summarization: Paraphrase information or follow a prescribed sequence of activities (delete trivial and redundant information, substitute superordinate terms for lists, etc.) to deduce primary message
	Skimming: Rapid viewing of text to identify general gist or meaning
	Scanning: Rapid reading of text to locate predefined target information
	Question-answering: Develop or use question stems to produce and respond to higher-level thinking questions
	Visual imagery: Create mental images or quick sketches while reading
	Story grammar: Identify and process elements of narrative text
	Text structure: Identify and process nature of expository text
	Semantic mapping: Document relations between text concepts and ideas through the use of graphic organizers and other tools
Writing	Sentence prompts: Use open-ended sentence prompts to begin writing process
	Graphic organizers: Complete visual guides that facilitate the generation and organization of ideas and concepts
	Editing checklists and questioning: Identify key components of narrative and expository text in composition; Monitor use and accuracy of writing mechanics
	Mnemonics: Use acronyms to prompt students about various aspects of the writing process (e.g., POWER: plan, organizer, write, edit, revise; PENS: pick a formula, explore words, note words, search for subject and verb; COPS: capitalized the first word and proper names, overall appearance, commas and end punctuation, spelled words correctly; TREE: topic sentence, reasons, examine reasons, ending)

Adapted from Woloshyn, Elliott, and Kaucho (2001).

strategies, a metacognitive skill that results from monitoring and analyzing the learning situation carefully.

There is substantial evidence that students acquire effective reading and writing strategies best when they are provided with explicit, or what is sometimes referred to as direct, instruction (Duffy, 2009; Pressley, 2007; Pressley & McCormick, 2007). Explicit

1. State process and content objectives
2. State why strategy is helpful
3. State when and where to use strategy
4. Share personal learning experience
5. Model strategy (Think Aloud)
6. Provide evidence of strategy effectiveness
7. Provide opportunities for practice
8. Provide prompts and reminders to use strategy across tasks and curriculum

Figure 1.3 Eight Steps of Explicit Strategy Instruction

strategy instruction is an ongoing process that requires teachers to model, guide, and prompt students' use of evidence-based reading and writing strategies. As part of the modelling process, teachers need to verbalize the steps in the strategy, as well as the parameters associated with its use, repeatedly. They often share relevant personal learning experiences related to using the reading strategy. They then provide students with opportunities to practise using the strategy, guiding their attempts until they can carry out the strategy independently. Throughout these lessons, teachers help students "discover" that the strategic approach to reading is superior to a non-strategic one, in part by encouraging them to compare the quality of their learning before and after using the strategy. Even after students have demonstrated a level of mastery using a strategy, teachers need to prompt them to use it across the curriculum (Woloshyn et al., 2001). Figure 1.3 provides an overview of the eight components of explicit strategy instruction.

Teacher Voice 1.1

Learners (students and teachers) must know what, how, when, where and, most importantly, *why* a strategy, concept, skill, or application should be used. Explicit instruction requires that such instructional goals as knowing how and why to use a skill or strategy are clear and attainable. Explicit instruction is paramount for all to realize the learning goals that will be measured.

Dan Trainor, M.Ed.

Elementary teacher and principal

Process and Content Objectives

In general, most teachers are proficient at providing students with information about the content goals, objectives, and outcomes associated with instructional lessons and units. They readily provide students with specific information about the expected results or end products of their learning, often providing them with partial or complete work exemplars. Explicit instruction also requires teachers to engage students in a discussion about parallel process goals. An important part of this discussion involves identifying and labelling underlying strategic processes. For instance, when discussing the writing process, the acronym POWER represents the steps Plan, Organize, Write, Edit, and Revise (Elbow, 1998). Alternatively, the label "All Purpose Question Prompts" refers to higher-order thinking question stems that can be applied across expository text (Al-Fartousi & Woloshyn, 2009; King, 1995; King & Rosenshine, 1993).

When students are engaged in such discussions, they are more likely to recognize the importance of extending cognitive effort when using strategies. They are also more likely to carry them forward when completing related tasks. When such discussions do not occur, students likely will be tempted to complete each step as quickly and effortlessly as possible so that they may move on to the next task, akin to crossing items off a "to-do" list.

Modelling, Contextualizing, and Sharing

Modelling is central to explicit instruction. Teachers who provide explicit instruction use Think Aloud frequently to model the use of reading and writing strategies, understanding that students need multiple demonstrations of strategy use over extended intervals. They also understand that students may experience "cognitive overload" and be overwhelmed if instructed to learn a new process skill or strategy at the same time as learning new materials. Therefore, they often present new strategies in the context of familiar materials, introducing new content only after students have acquired some proficiency in the use of the target strategy (see Sample Lesson 1.1)

SAMPLE LESSON 1.1

Providing an Explicit Lesson: Using Familiar Content to Prepare Students to Use Brainstorming and Venn Diagrams

Step 1: State content and lesson objectives

Today we are going to use a brainstorming strategy with a Venn diagram in order to compare and contrast two events. We are going to practise using the strategy with some fun materials. After we have practised, we are going to use some strategies to compare and contrast the primary characters in *The Very Last First Time* by Jan Andrews and *Chin Chiang and the Dragon's Dance* by Ian Wallace (see Chapter 9, The Role of Children's Literature).

Step 2: State why the strategy is helpful

Brainstorming is a very important strategy, especially when writing, as it helps us consider all possible responses and options. By considering all possible options, we are more likely to formulate a well-thought-out composition. If we do not brainstorm, we may be tempted to use the first idea or response that we can think of and may miss selecting a better option. Our writing is better after we have brainstormed all possible options.

Step 3: State when and where to use the strategy

We can use brainstorming whenever we need to write a report or project. Brainstorming is most helpful at the beginning of the writing process—that is, when we are planning and organizing our ideas. We can also use brainstorming when problem solving or when we need to develop an action plan. When writing, brainstorming helps us "consider all possible options" and make good writing choices.

Step 4: Share personal learning experience

I can remember completing a few essays and projects in school when I did not brainstorm before writing. I didn't want to take the extra time to think through all possible topics for writing. I just wanted to finish the assignment. Unfortunately, I often found that I ran out of ideas quickly and that my writing was disorganized. I wished I had selected another topic and planned my writing better. Over time, I began to brainstorm ideas for writing. Although it took some time to generate all possible ideas, I was able to make better choices about what to include in my work. It also helped me think about how I wanted to organize my ideas. My writing was definitely better when I used the brainstorming strategy.

Steps 5 and 6: Model strategy using Think Aloud, and Guide student practice

Now, let's practise using the brainstorming strategy and Venn diagram with some fun materials.

I want to share two of my favourite nursery rhymes: "Humpty Dumpty" and "There Was an Old Woman Who Lived in a Shoe." They both have characters that are in trouble and I need to write a compare-and-contrast report.

Let's read the nursery rhymes aloud together and brainstorm all of the problems and challenges that face these characters. They can be physical, social, or emotional. We will record all of the challenges we brainstormed using a Venn diagram. I can then pick and choose the points I will include in my write-up.

Before we begin, does everyone remember the brainstorming rules? There are two: (1) All responses are included, and (2) Everyone participates.

Okay, I'm going to start brainstorming now. What do I know about Humpty Dumpty? Well, when I think about his physical characteristics, I know his body is a shell and that he is broken. That's two points. I know that he lived on a wall. That's three points. Can anyone add some other ideas here?

- Record student responses.
- Prompt students to consider physical, social, and emotional aspects (e.g., he is alone, his future is bleak, the "community" or "social system" is unable to assist).

Now let's consider the Old Woman. What challenges does she face? Let's brainstorm some ideas and include them in the right circle of the Venn diagram. My thoughts are that she lives in a shoe, she definitely is not alone, she is elderly, and she cannot support her family. What other ideas can we add here?

- Record student responses.
- Prompt students to consider physical, social, and emotional aspects (e.g., her future is bleak, her house is crowded, her life is chaotic, the "community" or "social system" is not assisting).

Okay, now that we have brainstormed as many ideas as possible, we need to consider which of these points are unique to each character and common to both stories. The points that are shared need to be moved into the middle circle of the Venn diagram (see Figure 1.4). For instance, I can see that both Humpty Dumpty and the Old Woman do not have bright futures and that the "social system" is not helping them at this moment. I am going to move these points into the space where the two circles overlap. What are the other shared characteristics?

- Record student responses.

Now I am ready to begin organizing my writing. I am going to review all of the ideas that we brainstormed and make decisions about the ones I want to include in my writing. I am going to start with an opening paragraph and then use one paragraph to describe how Humpty Dumpty is unique and another paragraph to describe how the Old Woman is unique. I will include a paragraph that describes how they are the same. That seems like a good writing plan.

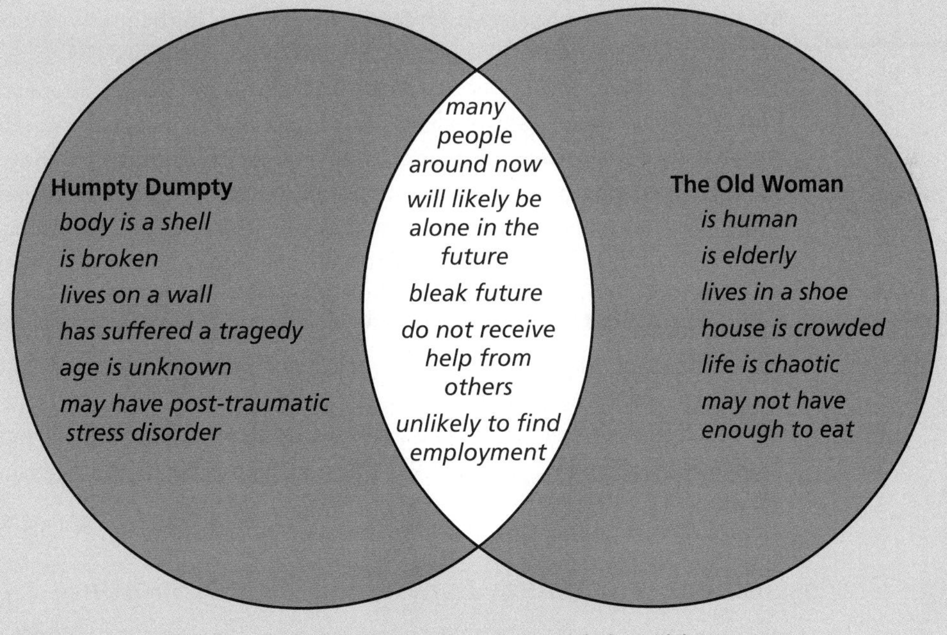

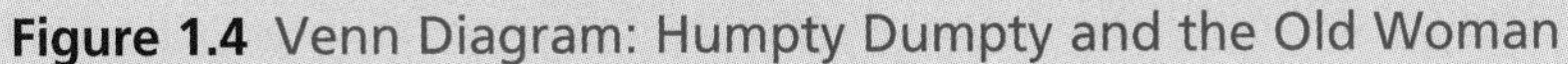
Figure 1.4 Venn Diagram: Humpty Dumpty and the Old Woman

Effective teachers also understand the importance of developing students' metacognitive thinking. Consider that many students may not realize that using strategies increases their learning unless directly told so. Without this appreciation, they may attribute their learning outcomes (whether positive or not so positive) to other attributes such as ability (e.g., "I'm smart," "I'm not smart"), environment (e.g., "The teacher likes me," "The teacher does not like me"), effort (e.g., "I worked hard," "I did not work hard"), or luck (e.g., "The test was easy," "The test was unfair").

Similarly, students may not understand the context or learning parameters in which individual strategies work best and may become frustrated if they use them inappropriately. For instance, asking "why" questions while reading (e.g., Why does this make sense? Why does the author hold this position? Why is this important?) is an effective comprehension strategy when learners possess some relevant prior knowledge about the topic at hand. However, asking such questions will do little to promote learning when students possess limited or no background knowledge. Consider a situation in which a student attempts to use a question-answering strategy while reading about the settlement of an unfamiliar location (e.g., Champlain's exploration of the St. Lawrence River in Lower Canada). Without some appropriate background information, the student is unable to respond meaningfully to the "why" questions and is frustrated by the reading experience.

> Okay, so I have to read this section about Champlain. It tells me that he explored the St. Lawrence River. So why would he do that? I don't know . . . it wasn't discussed in the chapter. He just stopped there! Maybe he was tired of traveling? This isn't a really good reason, but I have no idea why he settled there. Asking why questions isn't working. (Woloshyn et al., 2001)

The student's learning experiences would be much better if he used another processing strategy, such as imagery (envisioning the explorers in their heavy fur coats and boots hunting and fishing in the Northern woods and lakes), that relied less on prior knowledge. Effective teachers provide students with "why, when, and where" information associated with individual strategies so students become aware of parameters associated with their optimal use and consequently are better able to apply them independently.

Effective language arts teachers also share stories of their own learning experiences with their students, emphasizing the importance of using effective reading and writing strategies. Students are often surprised to learn that their teachers also must put considerable effort into reading and writing activities and that the quality of their teachers' work is also dependent on their use of effective strategic processes. For many students, these stories appear to make teachers less "perfect" and more like "students" and provide continued reassurance about the importance of strategy use. We recommend that teachers share such stories when introducing strategies, as they may help develop rapport and trust in the classroom and encourage risk taking and open dialogue about reading and writing processes.

Guiding, Practising, Convincing, and Prompting

After modelling, teachers need to provide students with continued practice and support using these strategies, gradually having students assume responsibility for their use

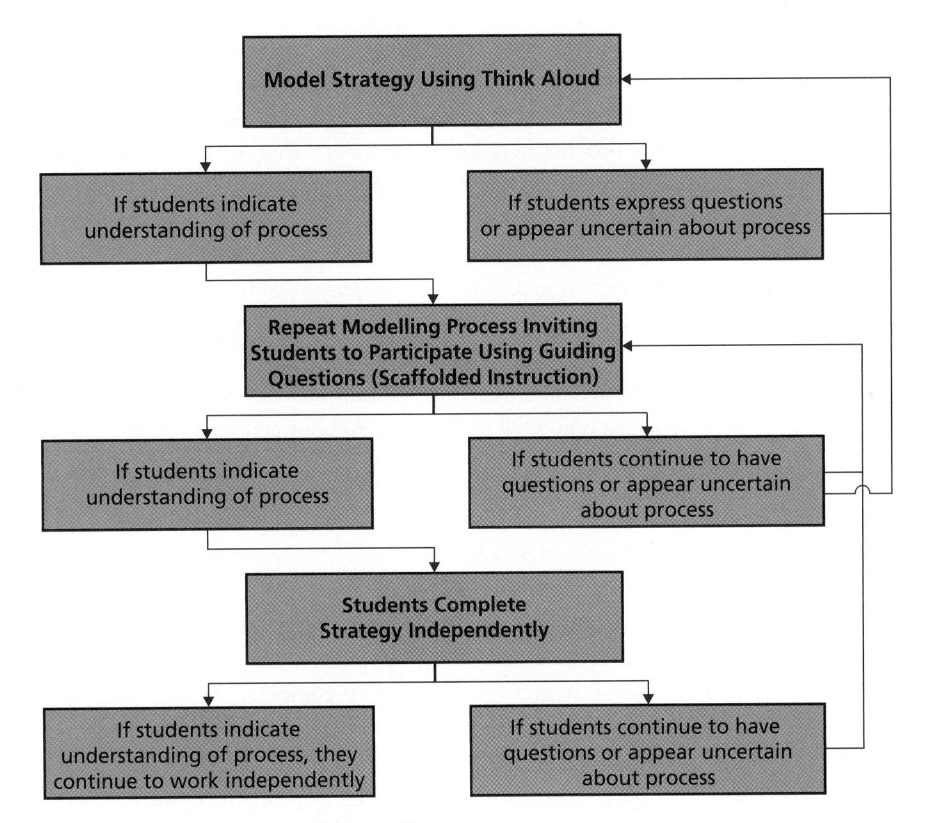

Figure 1.5 Explicit Instruction Cycle

(see Figure 1.5). This gradual method of release is called *guided instruction*. Guided instruction is consistent with social constructivist models of learning, in which learners "construct" knowledge based on interactions with others. In the classroom, guided instruction is usually provided by the teacher in the format of prompting and questioning. Other times, it can be provided by skilled peers.

> What is a good strategy to use when . . . ?
> What do I need to know or do to start using this strategy?
> How can I check whether this strategy has been helpful?

Modelling and guiding instruction are interactive processes, with teachers continually monitoring students' responses and adjusting their instruction accordingly (reducing prompts when students respond appropriately; reverting to modelling and guided practice when students express uncertainty or erroneous responses). Over time and with extended practice, students internalize these dialogues and use them to guide their independent reading and writing activities.

Effective teachers also encourage their students to be reflective of the learning process, establishing conditions that encourage students to value the use of evidence-based reading and writing strategies. In other words, they establish situations that "convince" students that the cognitive effort they spend using strategies is warranted in terms of increased learning. Such situations may be as simple as having students compare the quality of their work before and after strategy use or as sophisticated as having them tally feedback from classmates and parents.

Finally, these teachers also help students appreciate that with increased practice strategies become familiar or automatic, and seemingly effortless to use. Similarly, they prompt and cue students to transfer strategy use across various reading and writing tasks. These prompts are specific in nature and clearly associate a strategic process with a content objective (e.g., Don't forget to make and record your predictions before reading your chapter this evening, Using a Venn diagram may be a good tool for summarizing the similarities and differences between the two main characters). These teachers understand that students are unlikely to use relevant strategies across new tasks spontaneously, even when these tasks are similar to those completed in the past. Anchor charts in the classroom also serve as reminders about strategy use.

Caution Learning how to use evidence-based strategies effectively takes time and motivation on the part of both teachers and students. Initially, students require substantial time and extensive guidance and support to learn how to execute strategies. Once they have demonstrated proficiency in the use of one strategy, they can be introduced to another strategy so that, over time, they develop a strategy repertoire. With practice, students will learn to execute strategies faster and more competently. Teachers typically need in-service and ongoing mentoring to become proficient strategy instructors (Duffy, 2009; Israel & Duffy, 2009; Woloshyn, Elliott, & Riordon, 1998). They need to devote personal time to learning how to provide explicit instruction and class time for modelling and guided instruction. We believe, however, that the benefits associated with providing students with such instruction will outweigh any initial reservations about time and effort spent teaching explicitly.

Developing an Instructional Repertoire

Explicit instruction is one of many instructional methods used by effective language arts teachers. These teachers recognize that they need to vary their instructional approach in response to students' learning needs. Explicit instruction is best when introducing students to strategies and learning processes. As they develop proficiency, teachers will want to incorporate other inquiry and student-centred approaches in their instruction, thus facilitating students' independent strategy use and learning.

For these sessions to be successful, teachers need to establish an environment in which discussion can flourish and students' voices and responses are respected. In part, teachers accomplish this by providing pre-discussion instruction in relevant reading, listening, and responding strategies. They also spend time teaching students the communication skills necessary for collaborative work, including how to listen, take turns, and provide constructive and respectful feedback.

Co-operative Learning

Co-operative learning occurs when students work in small groups to help each other learn. More than three decades of research support the use of co-operative learning as an instructional venue for improving students' academic and social performance (Johnson, Johnson, & Stanne, 2000). However, co-operative learning involves more than simply placing students into groups (Kagan, 2001). Students must possess critical skills before they can collaborate effectively. These skills include the following:

1. **Positive interdependence** requires that the success of individual students be dependent on the success of their group. Co-operative learning activities often require students to acquire and present specific information to others in their group, with the understanding that students learn more effectively when they are responsible for teaching concepts to others. Teachers can facilitate this process by ensuring that students receive appropriate pre-instruction in the use of relevant learning strategies.
2. **Positive face-to-face interactions** require students to develop a sense of sharing, understanding, and accumulated group knowledge. Positive peer interactions and participation in decision making enhances most students' motivation to learn. To promote these skills and affects, teachers typically have students engage in team-building activities. Usually, teachers have students engage in these activities at the beginning of the year and then provide them with continued opportunities to practise these skills.
3. **Interpersonal and small-group skills** require students to use effective communication techniques, including conflict resolution strategies and decision-making processes. To facilitate such communication, teachers often assign specific roles (e.g., recorder, questioner, encourager, summarizer, reflector) to students, with these roles being rotated across all group members over the course of a unit or extended activity. Again, teachers must take care to provide students with initial instruction in the nature of these roles before having students assume them in the context of a co-operative learning activity.
4. **Individual accountability** requires students to demonstrate their independent learning. Without some measure of accountability, students may either contribute little or allow others to complete the work. Therefore, it is critical for teachers to assess the knowledge of individual students as well as the group product.
5. **Critical reflection** requires students to engage in reflective dialogue about their academic and social experiences while in group. These reflections include their abilities to communicate and interact effectively with others and to achieve their academic goals. Again, teachers need to provide students with specific instruction about how to engage in this type of reflection prior to participation in co-operative groups. Many students also benefit from the use of formatted assessment tools (e.g., Likert scales, checklists) and question prompts (e.g., Did every student offer suggestions? Were all suggestions valued? Were differences in opinion resolved respectfully?).

Unlike other small-group activities, co-operative learning is a carefully coordinated, teacher-directed activity. For it to work successfully, teachers must provide students with advance instruction in each of the elements of co-operative learning as well as ample opportunities to practise these skills. Ideally, such instruction and practice should occur in the context of familiar materials and "easy" tasks (e.g., developing a group mascot and motto, debating the merits of popular music, participating in team-building activities). Teachers also need to provide pre-instruction in all relevant strategies that students will need to complete the learning task successfully. Finally, teachers will want to control group membership, assigning students to heterogeneous or mixed-ability groups. When forming these groupings, teachers will need to consider gender, ethnicity, and socio-economic status. Teachers often have students work in pairs and triads prior to assigning them to co-operative groups consisting of four to six students. We suggest reviewing the works of such educational researchers as Johnson and Johnson (2009), including their co-operative learning website at www.co-operation.org; Kagan (1994); Gillies (2007); and Sharan (2010) for additional information on how to prepare students to work collaboratively.

Once students have acquired these prerequisite skills they are ready to engage in social constructivist learning activities. A literature circle is one such instructional activity commonly used in the language arts. We describe the nature of literature circles next.

Instructional conversation

Literature Circles

Sometimes referred to as book clubs or learning clubs, literature circles can help students become better readers (Casey, 2008/2009; Certo, Moxley, Reffitt, & Miller, 2010; Whittingham & Huffman, 2009). Literature circles are founded on the beliefs that reading is transactional and that readers construct their comprehension actively by bringing meaning to the text as well as by taking meaning from it (Campbell Hill, Johnson, & Schlick Noe, 1995). Literature circles also are an excellent tool for extending guided reading. Extended readings, including novels and sometimes non-fiction chapters, are used most often in literature circles, increasing students' opportunities to gain and refine independent reading skills.

Literature circles integrate listening and speaking with reading and writing, but the focus is on listening to others and contributing to the oral discussion. They tend to be fluid and flexible in nature, although students are often assigned roles with associated duties (especially when they first begin to engage in reading discussions). Unlike simple reading groups, literature circles reflect places where students are free to think, share, and participate in critical inquiry (see Chapter 10, Redefining Literacy: Integrating the New Literacies and a Critical Response to Popular Culture in Your Classroom, for an extensive discussion of critical literacy and how to instruct students to response critically to text). Most importantly, literature circles provide a forum that enables students to explore and extend their understandings and interpretations of shared text in a relaxed manner with peers, thereby promoting reading enjoyment and motivation.

Rosenblatt's reader response theory (1978) reminds us that there are two approaches for responding to literature: aesthetic (reading for pleasure) and efferent (reading for information and knowledge acquisition). Rosenblatt also warns us that many teachers present students with questions that tend to hurry them toward a predetermined meaning rather than encouraging them to explore multiple interpretations. When carried out effectively, literature circles enable students to expand their initial understandings from an aesthetic point of view and share their critiques and insights from an efferent point of view. Throughout this process, students are required to listen carefully to their peers, to think deeply, and to negotiate understandings that extend beyond those any one member might generate independently. In other words, discussing a shared text with others is an effective pedagogical tool, especially when dialogue is dynamic and rich (Raphael, George, Weber, & Nies, 2009).

In the primary grades students usually meet once a week, whereas in the junior and intermediate grades teachers can set the number of pages or chapters to be read by the next session, with students meeting two to three times per week. As part of their discussion, students are usually called on to share a personal response to the reading, identify a favourite passage, ask questions, or discuss any aspect of the text that they find especially meaningful or thought provoking. While teachers report groups of four to eight students as ideal (Brabham & Villaume, 2000), other variations are possible. Once groups have been formed, a reading schedule is typically devised. During time spent reading, students have the opportunity to improve their reading skills and practise previously taught reading strategies. Students then meet to review the text, respond to teacher- and student-generated questions, and share their perspectives and impressions.

Student Voice 1.1

> We talk about what the story was about. We make connections, like text-to-self and text-to-world, which involves making connections to yourself, other books, and stuff. We all have our own opinions to share with each other. If there's something we don't understand, we can all talk about it. There really is no wrong answer when talking in the group. Reading is a lot more fun if you relate to the book.
>
> Brittany B.
> Grade 7 student

Successful literature circles also require students to assume ownership and be accountable for their discussions, with many teachers providing students with specific duties and responsibilities. Table 1.2 lists some of these possible roles; teachers are encouraged to select those roles that they believe match the text best. Teachers also need to devise a rotation schedule so that all students assume responsibility for each of the selected roles at one point while reading the text. Again, the students' ability to complete these roles is dependent on teacher modelling, with effective teachers providing students with opportunities to practise each of the selected roles in advance.

Teacher Voice 1.2

> A few years ago I was teaching Grade 5. I noticed that the students did not "buy into" their assigned roles (summarizer, illustrator, clarifier, recorder) while working in literature circles; no one was staying on task. About the same time, our literacy teacher visited our classroom, modelling different reading strategies (visualization, summarization) and leaving us with a set of posters. We extended those strategies into our literature circles. Working in groups, the students used the posters to create a revised title for each "role" and a corresponding definition. The class then voted as a whole to select final names and definitions for each of the pre-selected roles. They picked silly names like "Cool Connectors" and "Hot Pink Inferencers." I no longer needed to "police" students; I could hear that they were on task and completing their roles. It is important that students understand that they are accountable for the quality of their discussions. They need to take responsibility and ownership over their conversations if they are to be meaningful.
>
> Liz McAnanama
> Junior and intermediate teacher

To provide teachers with assessment data, as well as to promote subsequent reading and discussion, teachers often have groups share their readings and interpretations with their classmates. Such sharing sessions may include having students provide a verbal

Table 1.2	Common Literature Circle Roles and Associated Responsibilities for Reading Narrative Text
Discussion director	Develop a list of questions for the text. Focus on central or main ideas and concepts versus details. Questions may focus on the nature and interconnectedness of the characters and events or may be based on personal responses, feelings, and concerns. Questions can also centre on the author's writing purpose.
Summarizer, reporter, director	Generate a brief summary of the assigned reading. Summary should include main events and ideas. Begin the session by reading the summary aloud. Alternatively, present a dramatic version of the summary (e.g., assuming the role of a media reporter or directing others to participate in some form of an enactment).
Clarifier, word wizard, vocabulary enhancer	Track important words and concepts used in the assigned reading (those that are repeated frequently, used in unusual ways, or provide important insights). Define (using text or dictionary) unfamiliar terms and concepts. Guide the group in a discussion about their meaning and importance.
Connector, reflector	Generate connections between the assigned reading, self, and world. Consider how text events and characters' responses relate to the daily experiences of self and others. Consider how story relates to other books or works by the same author. Consider why the author has chosen to share this story, as well as his or her lens or perspective. Guide the group in a discussion exploring these issues.
Illustrator, artist	Create a drawing or some form of visual related to the reading (e.g., sketch, cartoon, diagram, flow chart, stick figure, picture, logo). Images can represent story events, settings, or characters. Alternatively, images can provide text-to-self or text-to-world connections. Guide discussion around the image.
Investigator, literary luminator	Select critical sections of the text to read aloud to the group. Important sections may include particularly meaningful, powerful, funny, or puzzling events that warrant discussion or ongoing monitoring. Guide group in discussing the meaning and relevance of the text selections.
Predictor	Generate ongoing predictions based on assigned readings. Monitor, elaborate, or eliminate previous predictions based on new information. Record revised predictions and bring to the group for discussion.
Travel tracer, sequel planner	Monitor whereabouts of the main characters and provide defining characteristics of the settings. Lead a discussion about the importance of setting in terms of story events. Keep a detailed description of each setting over the course of the text. Consider recording details using action maps, diagrams, or some other visual format.

Adapted from Daniels (1994, 2002) and Daniels and Steineke (2004).

Note: Teachers are encouraged to adjust these roles for use with non-fiction materials.

summary or create posters, blogs, videos, or other print-based or multimedia materials. Assessment should also include some form of anecdotal observational notes completed during the literature circle sessions. It is important that students participate in their own assessment through the use of reflective comments, self-evaluation, and goal setting. Teacher-led group evaluation and debriefing can also be useful in helping students improve their conversational skills and interactions.

Caution Literature circles provide students with extended opportunities to read widely from interesting, diverse, age-appropriate texts (while all members of the circle must be reading the same core book, smaller groups within a class can read separate works connected by theme, author, or genre). Text selection, not reading ability, is thus the criterion that determines membership in a literature circle. Good sources for Canadian children's literature for younger readers can be found at www.ucalgary.ca/~dKbrown and for older students can be found at www.readingrants.org. Teachers are challenged to ensure that all students have access to the content of these texts, including those who may struggle with the reading process or for whom English is a subsequent language. The use of Read Aloud, audio recordings, listening centres, and buddy readings may be especially effective (Raphael et al., 2009).

CREATING A BALANCED LANGUAGE ARTS PROGRAM

THINK BACK TO HOW YOU WERE TAUGHT LANGUAGE ARTS AS A STUDENT. TRADITIONALLY, language arts instruction consisted of listening, speaking, reading, and writing, with greater emphasis on the latter two components. In part, this instructional emphasis was the outcome of foundational research documenting that students' learning performances were positively correlated across the four elements (Loban, 1976). Today, language arts instruction includes the elements of viewing and visually representing, acknowledging the importance of visual literacy. We briefly discuss each component below, indicating where additional information regarding student development and instructional techniques can be found in this text.

Listening

Most students' first contact with language is through listening. Listening is a critical element of effective communication. Effective listening is an active process that requires students to be focused and engaged. Unfortunately, listening is often a neglected element of language arts instruction. Students need to learn how to listen carefully and purposefully (consider how you listen differently when acquiring information, problem solving, or enjoying a narrative). Teachers also need to be aware that what students "hear" will be influenced by their prior knowledge and experiences and that they will sometimes need to provide students with prerequisite knowledge as well as skills. Effective listening may also include the processing and comprehending of non-verbal messages and communication formats (body posture, tone of voice, facial expressions). Effective listening strategies and instructional approaches are discussed in Chapter 2, Listening, Speaking, and Beyond.

Speaking

The majority of students enter school capable of speaking, with talk representing another critical element of effective communication and learning. Indeed, early research suggested that oral language was a powerful indicator of students' overall academic success. Effective learning is just as dependent on teachers' abilities to speak to students as it is on students' abilities to interact verbally with each other. Like reading, speech can be used for a variety of efferent and aesthetic purposes. Many students prefer speaking to reading, writing, or visually representing. To work co-operatively and engage in socially constructed learning, students need to be able to resolve discrepancies effectively and provide constructive feedback. See Chapter 2, Listening, Speaking, and Beyond, for further teaching suggestions related to developing students' speaking abilities.

Reading

Reading is an active, strategic process dependent, in part, on students' prior knowledge, lived experiences, interests, and motivation. There are many reasons to read, ranging from information gathering (efferent) to reading for pleasure (aesthetic), with some individuals holding stronger beliefs about the importance of one versus the other. We encourage teachers to reflect on their reading beliefs, habits, and orientations, as they are likely to convey these orientations to their students (either consciously or unconsciously). Effective reading requires proficiency in decoding as well as comprehension. Accordingly, balanced instruction includes instruction in phonics, decoding, word learning, spelling, comprehension, and other related skills (see Chapter 4, Word Learning, for a detailed discussion of effective instructional approaches related to decoding and word learning and Chapter 5, Comprehension of Narrative Text, for instruction related to comprehension). Effective language arts teachers are those who encourage students to read diverse texts as well as develop their abilities to derive meaning from the texts and engage in meaningful interactions with others. Effective language arts teachers also recognize the multiple types of reading and provide students with opportunities to engage in each type routinely. We provide a brief overview of each reading type below, indicating where additional information can be found in this text.

Read Aloud programs involve the teacher or other proficient reader reading text aloud to students. In general, students of all ages and grades enjoy participating in Read Aloud, which contributes to developing comprehension skills through listening. While Read Aloud is a readily embraced practice by teachers in the primary grades, it unfortunately is infrequently used or not used at all by many teachers in the junior and intermediate grades. See Chapter 5, Comprehension of Narrative Text, for a detailed discussion of how to select high-quality texts for Read Aloud sessions, as well as techniques to engage and monitor students in the reading process.

Buddy reading occurs when two students or a student-adult pair read (or reread) a text aloud together. Usually the pair reads in turn but sometimes they read in unison. While this activity is generally enjoyable and collaborative, it also serves to help struggling readers attain fluency. In this case, a stronger reader is usually paired with a weaker one (often across grades). The older student practices oral reading skills and serves as a role model for the younger student. In other instances, students read a section together that neither could read as effectively alone. By collaborating, they can decode unfamiliar words and discuss comprehension and interpretation challenges. This technique is a valuable method of providing additional practice for beginning readers. It is also an effective method for working with students with special needs or with those who are learning English. Chapter 4, Word Learning, provides specific information about how to establish a buddy reading program in the classroom.

Shared reading is often conducted with beginning readers using big books or other large-print materials to enable them to participate successfully in a reading experience. Initially, the exercise begins with the teacher reading aloud and the students following the print. This is followed by a rereading during which students join in. The reading can be repeated until students are able to read the selection independently. The teacher (or student helper) points to the words as the class reads, to highlight the direction of the print as well as letters, words, and sentences. Shared reading can also be accomplished when students have individual copies of the same book. Again, students follow along as the teacher reads aloud to prepare them to read the selection independently later. Variations include choral reading, during which everyone reads in unison, or having small groups read assigned sections. Teachers can also use this technique with older students by reading the first few chapters of a longer text that the students will continue reading independently. Such reading facilitates students' comprehension of text by introducing key vocabulary and establishing text structure. The overall value of shared reading is that it moves students toward fluency and enables them to feel success as readers. Chapter 4, Word Learning, and Chapter 5, Comprehension of Narrative Text, provide additional information about this reading type.

Guided reading is a teacher-directed reading experience that uses material that is slightly above the level at which students can read comfortably and independently (i.e., their instructional level). This process is highly prescriptive, with teachers scaffolding reading skills and strategies to build students' independent reading. Substantial research supports the use of guided reading as a way to enhance students' reading levels (Clay, 2001; Cunningham, Hall, & Sigmon, 2004; Fountas & Pinnell, 1996). This reading type is described in detail with an accompanying sample lesson in Chapter 5, Comprehension of Narrative Text.

Independent reading is an essential component of a reading program. When students read independently, they tend to read silently at their own pace, often with materials they have selected. Independent readers sense that they are "real" readers, inspiring a love of reading and lifelong learning. Several studies have demonstrated that the amount of in-class time spent on independent reading is significantly related to reading scores (Adams, 1990; Anderson, Hiebert, Scott, & Wilkinson, 1985). Many teachers choose to use programs such as USSR (Uninterrupted Sustained Silent Reading), SSR (Sustained Silent Reading), ScSR (Scaffolded Silent Reading), and DEAR (Drop Everything and Read) for 15 or 20 minutes each day to ensure that their students have opportunities for independent reading. Key to the success of these programs are consistency, student accountability, teacher participation, and the availability of levelled, high-interest books. Additional information about how to establish this reading type in the classroom can be found in Chapter 4, Word Learning, and Chapter 5, Comprehension of Narrative Text.

Writing

Like reading, writing is an active and strategic process that individuals complete for a variety of purposes, ranging from informal notes to formal reports. Writing also requires individuals to consider their audience, adjusting style, tone, and content accordingly. The audience and purpose also help determine the extent to which students will need to follow the elements of the writing process, including planning and pre-writing, translating and drafting, reviewing and revising, and publishing. Writing mechanics are also important considerations for student writing, with effective teachers providing instruction in spelling, grammar, punctuation, and handwriting. With continued writing practice and support, students can develop a better sense of self as author. See Chapter 7, Writing: Exploring the Reading and Writing Connection, for a detailed description of the writing process and Chapter 8, Teaching the Writing Tools: Spelling, Grammar, Mechanics, and Handwriting, for instructional suggestions related to writing mechanics.

Viewing

The process of viewing includes comprehending various multimedia formats, including television, movies, DVDs, dramatic productions, photographs, illustrations, diagrams, symbols, and hypertext. As with print-based materials, students need instruction in how to comprehend visual representations. This instruction should be strategy-based, with many effective reading comprehension strategies also being effective viewing ones. The critical processing of these visual materials is a key element in comprehension, with instruction including consideration of marketing techniques, world perspectives, gender, privilege, and status. Students also need to develop their oral language, vocabulary, and writing skills to discuss, share, and form commentary on what they view. An extensive discussion of critical literacy and multiliteracies is provided in Chapter 10, Redefining Literacy: Integrating the New Literacies and a Critical Response to Popular Culture in Your Classroom.

Visually Representing

When students create meaning through video, film, photography, dramatic performance, pictures, illustrations, posters, symbols, or hypertext, they are engaged in visually representing. Akin to writing, visually representing is a creative and strategic process in which students need to consider the audience and purpose of their work and engage in problem solving. Students need to be able to anticipate difficulties and address those that arise throughout the creation process. Many students enjoy participating in this alternative format of communication. Valuing these products academically may enhance students' confidence and sense of self as learner and may be especially important for students experiencing learning difficulties or for whom English is a subsequent language. Teaching strategies and techniques for engaging students in visually representing is provided in Chapter 10, Redefining Literacy: Integrating the New Literacies and a Critical Response to Popular Culture in Your Classroom.

Despite being presented as separate elements in the language arts curriculum and resource documents, these six components are interconnected and interactive and are used reciprocally. Therefore, balanced language arts programming requires that listening, speaking, reading, writing, viewing, and visually representing be taught simultaneously and in an amalgamated manner across the elementary grades. Balanced instruction also involves using a repertoire of instructional strategies and approaches, including explicit instruction of evidence-based strategies, guided reading, and literature circles. Effective language arts teachers know the learning circumstances that complement each instructional approach (e.g., using explicit instruction when first teaching a strategy or process, using literature circles to reinforce students' independent reading skills and promote quality discussion).

SUGGESTIONS FOR PROFESSIONAL DEVELOPMENT

1. Spend some time observing or speaking with a teacher about his or her instructional techniques. Reflect on the number of different instructional methodologies used throughout the day. Consider how the selected methodologies complement students' developmental and skill level and how they might change over time.

2. Take a quiet moment for yourself to accomplish this guided imagery task. Shut your eyes and think of one of your former elementary, secondary, or post-secondary teachers. When you have thought of one, follow these steps:
   - Picture that teacher in your mind's eye. Try to remember his or her appearance and facial expressions and the classroom environment.
   - Now place yourself in the picture with this teacher. What are you wearing? Where are you? How are you interacting? How are you both feeling?
   - Open your eyes and think about this teacher again. Do you remember what this teacher taught you? Do you remember how this teacher treated you? Which is a more dominant memory: what you were taught or how you were treated?
   - Does this experience reveal any passion about the kind of teacher you want to be? Try to articulate why this teacher remains in your memory.
3. Begin a file (hard copy or electronic) and record high-quality children's literature that you already know, that you see students reading in school, or that are referenced in your classes. Note the general theme and plot of each as well as the general reading level for future reference. Simultaneously start a file where you record evidence-based reading, writing, and learning strategies; techniques; or other classroom practices that you could use or adapt in future practice.
4. Observe or speak with a teacher in each of the primary, junior, and intermediate grades. Review their programming with respect to the six components of language arts.
   - How much instructional time is devoted to listening, speaking, reading, writing, viewing, and visually representing?
   - What are students' responses to instruction in each area? Which content area seems most familiar? Most interesting? Most effortful?
   - How does the amount of instruction vary across the primary, junior, and intermediate grades?
   - How is instruction in each area integrated across the curriculum?

   If possible, share your observations with each teacher, seeking additional input and clarification.

MyEducationLab

MyEducationLab is an interactive, virtual learning tool that will help improve your understanding of the concepts taught in this textbook and in your course. Through this engaging resource, you will have access to simulations of real classroom experiences, exercises that will help you improve your knowledge of key concepts, and additional resources that will help you in your teaching career. Use this online tool with your textbook to help you succeed in your studies and beyond!

Chapter 2
Listening, Speaking, and Beyond

Learning Objectives

In this chapter you will discover

- How family literacy influences students' early reading and writing experiences.
- How to determine school readiness.
- How to accommodate for gender differences in young children.
- How to create a literate kindergarten environment.
- How to conduct conversations in the classroom.
- How to integrate drama in the language arts curriculum.
- How to implement activities that combine listening and speaking.
- How to conduct a Readers' Theatre.

BRENT CROSS: RURAL EDUCATOR, PRINCIPAL, AND KINDERGARTEN TEACHER

Brent Cross prides himself on being a flexible, strong educator with the ability to wear many hats. He is a rural educator by choice and has taught in a number of small communities in British Columbia. His current responsibilities include being principal of a small school (60 students) as well as the music teacher (he trained as a high school music specialist) and kindergarten teacher. Brent has developed clear pedagogical principles that direct his teaching. He believes that every teacher should possess a dynamic "tool box" of techniques and strategies that can be adapted to any teaching situation. He believes that no single approach is superior. Instead, Brent continually adds to his tool box so he can have a broader range of instructional tools. He also believes that it is imperative to have a solid understanding of the developmental nature of literacy and numeracy. Playfulness is an important theme in Brent's approach to education. He enjoys playing with words and numbers in ways that enable his students to remain engaged while learning.

Brent explains that teaching in rural communities requires the ability to teach at any level, as school organization varies depending on student enrolment and distribution across the grades. Last year, he assumed the kindergarten job for the first time and found that he "loved" this challenging position.

Recognizing the importance of oral language development, Brent begins each day with circle activities that involve a great amount of talk. He has a greeting discussion, creates the calendar for the day, and reads a book to his class. He is vigilant in ensuring that the discussion varies each morning, as he does not want students to develop the habit of repeating the same conversations or allowing one or two students to dominate discussions.

Reading a book aloud is also an important morning activity. Brent ensures that he asks questions that enable students to make connections to their personal experiences, to other stories, and to the classroom word wall. He also asks them to form predictions and complete an associated activity. For instance, when the text was about bugs, Brent took the students on a bug hunt. When the leaves began to change colour, he read a story about trees and had the students observe particular trees. Other times, Brent reads a "behavioural" story or a story that connects to a social skill. For instance, he read a story about how to sit in a circle periodically throughout the year. He also held discussions about the schoolwide "word of the month" (e.g., *courtesy*) and its corresponding behaviours.

After circle activities, students work on their journals, where they print the letters of the alphabet. When everyone has achieved this goal, they move on to creating words and sentences. They reproduce the words and sentences and draw corresponding pictures. Brent encourages the students to play with letters, paper, and pencils.

Under Brent's direction, the kindergarten to grade 5 students come together for music, with the kindergarten students contributing by playing rhythm instruments. Brent likes to train students in leadership skills so that he becomes "obsolete." One year, his choir was invited to play for the province's lieutenant-governor at the same time he was invited to speak to a graduating class from another community. Not wanting to disappoint either group, Brent trained both the major band and the jazz band to respond to designated student leaders. He was proud when both groups received accolades for their performances.

After lunch, students engage in some form of independent reading. Sometimes, Brent allows students to select a book and "read" it themselves; other times, he reads a book aloud or students from the older grades read one-on-one with the kindergarten students. Many of his students are "on the cusp" of becoming independent readers and he believes that these structured activities are critical to their development.

> I think metacognition is a vital part of learning, so at the end of the day I always asked students, "What was your favourite part of the day?", "What did you learn?", "What might you have done differently?" and prompted them to provide in-depth answers.

Learning to read is one of the most important activities of childhood. For those who develop this skill easily, the enthusiasm of becoming a successful reader may be a distant memory. For those who struggle to acquire this skill, however, the memory can be painful.

REFLECTIVE ACTIVITY 1

Take a moment to reflect on the following:

- Who taught you to read?
- Describe the process that was used to help you learn to read.
- Who read aloud to you?
- When did you become aware that you could read?
- How did you feel while you were learning to read?
- How did you feel when you were finally able to read?
- Who did you tell that you could read?

If you are having trouble remembering your own processes, ask your parents about them.

Children begin developing literacy skills well before they enter formal schooling. For most children, the first three years of life are rich in literacy experiences that contribute to their "big picture" of communication, as well as to the value of traditional and non-traditional print materials (Gunning, 2005). This period of early language exploration and experimentation is called *emergent literacy*. The term is descriptive, with the word *emergent* indicating a belief that the impetus for development comes from within the child and occurs gradually and over time as a result of interactions in the home and in the community. These early years are critical in that they form the foundation for subsequent literacy learning (Bredekamp, 2002; Justice, 2003).

FAMILY LITERACY AND EARLY READING

THE TERM *FAMILY LITERACY* IS USED WIDELY TO REFER TO THE WAYS IN WHICH FAMILIES accomplish daily tasks and activities or develop programs that facilitate the literacy development of their members. It is well established that nuclear families, extended families, and communities play critical roles in children's literacy development, with children having greater opportunities to learn when their parents actively promote and discuss literacy activities (Tamis-LeMonda, Bornstein, & Baumwell, 2001). Supporting family literacy is an ongoing focus across Canada, with each province and territory providing some form of programming or initiative that encourages and supports family literacy. For instance, in British Columbia, Families in Motion is a community-based, multicultural family literacy program for adults and their 3- to 4-year-old children. Come Read with Me is a family literacy project in Saskatchewan that helps parents recognize the important and influential role they assume as their children's first literacy teachers. In Newfoundland, a literacy program called PRINTS (Parents' Roles Interacting with Teacher Support) is designed to provide parents with the tools they need to create a home environment that fosters literacy development. In Quebec, Learning with My Child is a literacy program that focuses on parental involvement in their children's reading.

Young children look to their parents as role models with respect to literacy-based activities and attitudes, with some researchers suggesting that the home environment is more influential than the school environment in shaping students' attitudes toward literacy (Kassow, 2006; Zuckerman, 2009). When we ask teacher candidates to reflect on how they first learned to read, almost all remember being read to by parents or caregivers. Reading, in these instances, was often associated with a nurturing environment (e.g., cuddling, sitting on a knee, bedtime routine) and recalled as an enjoyable experience. Fewer recall interactions with their teachers. Take a moment to consider your earliest reading memories again.

However, literacy and literacy-related activities do not exist without conscious persistence. When families become economically, socially, or emotionally distraught, literacy practices in the home can suffer (Dickinson & Tabors, 2001; Thomas, 1998). The experience of children who come from homes where literacy is not valued or emphasized especially concerns educators. Often, parents in these homes experience reading difficulties or disabilities themselves (Gunning, 2000; Jalongo, 2000). While this phenomenon is positively correlated with low socio-economic status households, this relationship is not absolute and teachers must avoid making generalizations or forming stereotypes. There is considerable variability in the frequency and quality of home literacy experiences across all social statuses (Thomas, 1998), with most differences reflecting parents' attitudes toward reading, interest in reading, and expectations for their children's literacy success. The frequency and manner of parental interactions with children in literacy activities such as reading aloud or helping with homework are very influential (Beals, 2001).

Teacher Voice 2.1

As a mother of two emergent readers and an elementary school teacher, I have very strong beliefs about the importance of the family and students' early reading experiences. I started reading to both of my children when they were just babies. Each night we continue to read, with me reading to them and them reading to me. As a teacher, I know how important this is for their reading development. As a mom, I value the quality time we spend together making reading fun!

Lori Moukperian
Elementary teacher

School Readiness

Upon entering school, children are generally expected to gain new skills that enable them to learn to read and write. These skills include learning what constitutes a word and learning how to recognize and talk about discrete sounds (Berko Gleason & Ratner, 2009). Children are ready to learn that the alphabet letters represent sounds of the language and can begin to talk about these connections. They also need to recognize themselves as members of a larger social group than has previously been the case for many of them.

There are a number of biological and environmental factors that affect students' language development. Children do not learn language in a social vacuum. According to Noam Chomsky (1955), the world-famous linguist, all individuals are "hard wired" to learn language. Consider that the majority of children across the world, regardless of their cultural and linguistic background, acquire language at about the same age and in about the same order (Hoff, 2006). However, the *rate* of language acquisition varies in ways that cannot be explained by biological factors alone (Hoff, 2006). There is sufficient variation in the rate of language development to suggest that environment is also an important factor (Tamis-LeMonda et al., 2001). Young children need to be encouraged to speak in a variety of contexts and should be praised for their efforts. Children benefit greatly when their parents and other adults ask them questions and engage them in ongoing conversations.

Somewhat disconcertingly, children's vocabulary development is positively related to their parents' socio-economic status (Willms, 2003). Statistically, it has been shown that children from low-income families receive only half as much language experience in their early years as children from middle- and high-income families (Evans, 2004; Goldenberg, 2004; Neuman & Celano, 2001). However, this is not an assumption that teachers should make about any child, as there are many exceptions and myriad other family and community factors related to language development. For instance, the number of siblings, parental reading habits, family cohesiveness, and social support all play a role in the rate and extent of language development. Family members who read regularly to children and ask them questions about what has been read are providing them with an advantage when they enter school (Wasik & Hendrickson, 2004), just as students who do not possess strong vocabularies tend to be at risk for reading difficulties and other learning challenges (Biemiller, 2007).

Children are neither exclusively biological language users nor exclusively social constructors of language (Berko Gleason & Ratner, 2009). Rather, it is the interaction of these two components that contributes to language development. Most children have observed adults around them reading newspapers, magazines, and books and have seen adults writing items such as lists, letters, and notes. Many children have been read to regularly by an adult. They also may have observed the letters on their favourite cereal box or the letters that form the name of their favourite restaurant. Other children may be able to write their own names and understand that letters make the same sounds in any word. Obviously, some children do not have these experiences, so it follows that the stage of literacy awareness and development can differ widely. What the child learns at home and in the community should be the foundation for literacy learning in the classroom, as it makes sense to continue the natural growth of language in the same way it was developed in the preschool years. A skilled teacher can recognize various levels of literacy development and link new school experiences with previous learning and awareness.

Daycare Centres and Early Childhood Education

Many Canadian children (although not all) are enrolled in daycare or early childhood education programs prior to beginning kindergarten. Many of these programs are of high quality and contribute to students' positive success in school and even in later life (Barnett, 1995; Bredekamp, 2002). This kind of high-quality programming can be especially important for children considered to be at risk (e.g., those from low-income families, abusive families, and families that spend little time interacting with their children).

Developmental Gender Differences

It is generally accepted that girls "outpace" or demonstrate advanced language development relative to boys in the preschool years. It is well recognized that many girls develop complex grammatical skills as much as a year earlier than boys (Guerian, 2006, 2010; Kindlon & Thompson, 1999; Millard, 1997). Boys are less likely to express their emotions and frequently do not use emotional vocabulary to describe how they are feeling (Kindlon & Thompson, 1999). These differences are innate in brain functioning. For instance, females have stronger functioning in memory and sensory intake while males have greater functioning in spatial tasks and abstract reasoning (Guerian, 2010). Girls tend to have better verbal communication skills and rely heavily on verbal communication whereas boys tend to rely heavily on nonverbal communication. Boys and girls also show distinct psychosocial differences and therefore tend to play with their own gender groups. In our present school culture, these differences have huge ramifications. There are some classroom practices and activities that have been identified to ensure academic success for boys and girls. They include the following:

Boys	Girls
Promote fine motor skills through activities such as bead work	Play ball games or other movement games that promote the development of gross motor skills
Encourage the use of blocks and manipulatives for experimentation	Incorporate a water and sand table to conduct experiments
Keep verbal instructions concise and clear	Set up teams and working groups in which girls take leadership roles
Encourage the expression of feelings such as sad, happy, angry	Use manipulatives when teaching math
Personalize desk, coat hook, and cubbyhole to promote identity with the environment	Use puzzles to aid perceptual learning
Take advantage of high energy for daily classroom activities and cleanup	Praise frequently but genuinely
Bring in male visitors from the community or upper classrooms to provide male role models	Promote high energy and leadership

Specific activities that will encourage both boys and girls to learn include:

- One-on-one lessons
- Group work
- Use of hands-on activities in most lessons
- Direct instruction
- Plenty of free play

KINDERGARTEN

THE TERM *KINDERGARTEN*, WHICH MEANS "CHILDREN'S GARDEN" IN GERMAN, WAS created by Friedrich Fröbel, who opened the first kindergarten in Germany in 1840. The success of this approach to early learning resulted in the term *kindergarten* spreading through Europe and to the rest of the world. Kindergarten programs originally were designed to help young children transition from the home environment to formal education (i.e., grade 1). Today, it is a generic term for the first year of compulsory education.

In Canada, all provinces and territories have kindergarten programs that are designed to provide children with a strong academic foundation. In western Canada and in Newfoundland and Labrador, students enter grade 1 after completing one year of kindergarten. Nova Scotia also has a one-year kindergarten program called grade primary.

In Ontario, students complete two years of kindergarten (junior kindergarten and senior kindergarten), with some students participating in half-day programs, others in full-day programs, and still others in every-other-day programs. Currently, there is a graduated movement toward full-day kindergarten in Ontario. In Quebec, the junior kindergarten program is referred to as *prématernelle*. While participation in *prématernelle* is not mandatory, participation in *maternelle* (senior kindergarten) is.

Kindergarten Curriculum

Kindergarten curriculum guides across Canada share many features. For instance, all documents hold that the kindergarten program provides students with a foundation for subsequent learning. For example, "The Kindergarten program is designed to help children build on their prior knowledge and experiences, form concepts, acquire foundational skills, and form positive attitudes to learning as they begin to develop their goals for life-long learning" (Ontario Ministry of Education, 2006a, p. 5). The importance of oral language and listening skills are also emphasized.

> The children are able to express and explain themselves so as to be understood by other children and adults. They are able to listen to questions or instructions and to respond appropriately. They react positively to activities involving their language skills, specifically in the areas of reading and writing. They have been introduced to the various forms and functions of language and they adapt them to different communication situations. (Quebec Ministère de l'Éducation, 2000, p. 61)

In 2008, Manitoba released a support document for kindergarten teachers and speech-language pathologists titled *Listening and Speaking: First Steps into Literacy* (Manitoba Education, Citizenship and Youth, 2008). The stated purpose of this document is to "help Kindergarten teachers and speech-pathologists enhance the oral language of all Kindergarten children within the playful literacy learning work and talk of the Kindergarten classroom" (p. 1). The document reiterates that oral language development is key to success as students begin the literacy process.

In Newfoundland and Labrador, kindergarten is described as "Early Beginnings." The goals of the province's kindergarten programs include developing students' critical thinking as fostered through inquiry, representation and reflection, questioning, and making connections.

To summarize, kindergarten programs focus on developing children's abilities to communicate and interact appropriately with others. They nurture students' confidence in their ability to learn and their sense of self as lifelong learner.

Student Voice 2.1

In kindergarten, I liked playing inside and outside. Inside, I really liked the blocks centre and the crafts centre. I really liked it when the teacher read Robert Munsch books and my favourite is *Put Me in a Book!* It's about a girl who goes into a book and her nose popped out. It was really funny. After reading, we practised learning our words with our little cards with every little word like *in, out, come*. We practised learning those words and I brought them home and my mother and father helped me too. I have tons of friends and I am really excited to go to grade 1.

Julia
Age 6

Creating a Literary Kindergarten Environment

> It is a traditional insight that teaching is not like filling a cup with water; but more like enabling a flower to grow in its own way; but it will not grow and flourish without proper care. Language development, like all human development, will be heavily determined by the nature of the environment, and may be severely limited unless the environment is appropriate. A stimulating environment is required to enable natural curiosity, intelligence, and creativity to develop, and to enable our biological capacities to unfold. (Chomsky, 1987)

The kindergarten environment is one of the most important school environments. Kindergarten teachers are charged with creating an interesting, dynamic, language-rich environment in which print is readily found and active reading, speaking, listening, and writing activities are explicitly valued (Gunning, 2005). Students must have access to a variety of resources and materials that inspire discovery and discussion. The classroom walls should be covered with posters, signs, and student work that maintain student interest, with materials changing frequently. Everyday objects such as doors, clocks, and writing materials should be labelled. Students' names should be displayed prominently on coat hangers, cubbyholes, and workboxes. Teachers should refer regularly to calendars, weather charts, daily messages, birthday lists, helper charts, and routines.

Students should be provided with multiple opportunities to read and write for genuine reasons. They should be encouraged to share personal connections to stories, writing achievements, and oral stories. Students should be provided with the opportunity to make choices about the activities they wish to complete and how they wish to complete them. See Table 2.1 for specific examples of how to create a literary environment.

Students also should be provided access to play and learning centres that contain reading, writing, social studies, science, blocks, and other manipulative materials. Activities at these centres should be play-based, motivational, and unthreatening. Students need to be introduced to each centre and its contents prior to using it, with routines associated with its use clearly established. Such routines include rules about the maximum number of students able to access a centre at any one time as well as the removal and return of materials.

Table 2.1 Creating a Literary Environment in the Kindergarten Classroom

- Read stories aloud.
- Ask children to retell stories.
- Engage children in dramatic play that involves listening, speaking, and, where applicable, reading and writing.
- Explain new vocabulary that occurs in books read aloud.
- Hold daily conversations during which new vocabulary is introduced in context.
- Promote reading activities through the use of print materials and audiobooks for listening comprehension.
- Record corresponding notes while providing verbal information.
- Display student work, pictures, and other aids to learning and change these regularly.
- Create daily calendars, weather charts, daily messages and events, and birthday lists.
- Establish a number of play centres and designate one centre for reading and one centre for writing activities.
- Tell students that the classroom is a learning community and that you are learning too; then demonstrate personal learning.

Finally, children need time to explore and experiment in the kindergarten environment, especially in the context of interacting with print and other literary materials. Teachers who demonstrate a love of reading and writing can positively influence the attitudes of young children (Graves, Juel, & Graves, 2006; Gunning, 2005). This can be especially important in the context of today's rushed family life.

Creating a classroom as a literary community contributes to a desire to become a literate member of the community and encourages students to accept responsibility for maintaining the routines and values of that community (Tompkins, 2004). Students who feel comfortable in their learning communities are more inclined to take risks with respect to their own learning, pushing the boundaries of their learning experiences.

Teachers in these communities assume the role of literacy coach and model. They do not assume control of all decisions; rather, they express openness to students' ideas and choices. Strong rapport between teachers and students forms the foundation of this community, with students readily expressing their opinions and beliefs. When teachers present themselves as learners and demonstrate delight in their personal learning as well as their students' learning, a true community of learning is established.

Caution Literary environments like the ones described above do not just "happen." Teachers need to make conscious efforts to establish routines and rapport with their students during the first few weeks of the school year. Unfortunately, many beginning teachers fail to realize the importance of establishing these routines, expectations, and patterns of interaction early in the school year, and as a result struggle for much of the remainder of the year. Nothing can be assumed and everything must be demonstrated, practised, and reinforced firmly from the first day onward. By the end of the first month, students should know what is valued in the classroom community and what is expected of them. Although it is creative to have spontaneous breaks from routine, these must be understood by the students to be unusual events. The security that students feel in a predictable, comfortable environment contributes to their overall feeling of belonging and establishes a focus on learning.

Designing Literacy Play Centres

The Reading Centre The reading centre should include bookshelves filled with interesting fiction and non-fiction books. These books need to be rotated frequently, with new books introduced regularly (e.g., at show and tell, during circle time, through announcements). Texts that are read aloud should be featured prominently, with multiple copies available to students. Students can also lend a favourite book from home for a short period so their friends can read it, although it must be stressed that these books do not leave the centre. Some reading areas include a carpeted area for students to gather or pieces of carpet, pillows, stuffed animals, and beanbag chairs that students can use while reading—all features that make the area enticing and comfortable for young children.

The Writing Centre The writing centre should contain upper and lower case samples of the alphabet, with an emphasis on the latter. Simple words can be displayed as well. Materials should be presented at students' eye level so they can refer to them readily. The centre should be stocked with an ample supply of writing instruments (e.g., large and small pencils, crayons, markers) and various sizes of paper. The paper should be unlined so students do not focus unduly on spacing. Other items can include chalkboards, whiteboards, magnetic letters, and a computer with an easy-to-use word processing program. Glue and paste, safety scissors, staplers, and stickers are good additions. A picture dictionary is also a valuable resource; students should be encouraged to contribute their own dictionaries or dictionary items throughout the year. As in the reading centre, the materials available at any one time should not reflect the full complement. Rather, teachers should rotate, add, and take away items according to students' literacy development and interests and the academic program. It is important for teachers to remember that the emphasis at this centre is on expression and exploration rather than on conventional spelling or handwriting (Gunning, 2005).

The Listening Centre In the listening centre, students should have access to audio recordings (e.g., CD-ROMs, books on tape) of favourite books and texts that have been read aloud by their teachers, as well as a selection of new materials. As in the reading centre, multiple copies of audiobooks should be available, with students encouraged to form small groups while listening and responding to materials. It is important that teachers prepare and guide students when listening to new materials by using such instructional techniques as a "walk through" (i.e., showing students the front cover, title, and illustrations in a text while asking them to make predictions). Students should be encouraged to read along while listening to recordings of their favourite stories. This activity can be extended by having students record their own readings.

The Drama Centre In the drama centre, children have an opportunity to be creative and practise "make-believe." This kind of play is intense, with oral language assuming a dominant role. Materials in this centre can be varied and include props such as dress-up clothes and common household and workplace items. As in other centres, materials need to be rotated on a regular basis, with teachers introducing and modelling new items.

Connecting with Parents

Many parents are or want to be a part of their children's literary lives. Furthermore, most schools work diligently to build and maintain strong relationships with parents. Effective teachers communicate with parents frequently, providing them with details about their children's progress. Many teachers prepare a monthly newsletter outlining upcoming events and reviewing relevant curriculum areas. Calling or writing to parents to share "good news" with them regarding their children's progress is also very important. Teachers need to remember that some parents are anxious about their children's success and often there is a great deal of pressure on a child to begin to read. Many parents, therefore, will seek advice from their children's teachers with respect to how they can contribute to their children's literary success. Remember to assure parents that their role is an important one. Table 2.2 lists some suggestions that teachers can provide to parents who wish to promote reading at home.

Table 2.2 Promoting Reading at Home: Suggestions for Parents

- Be a reader yourself so you can model the pleasure of reading.
- Get into the habit of taking your children to the library. Let them have their own library cards and make their own selections. Check a book out yourself.
- Schedule about 30 minutes a day for reading. Reading is a skill that needs practice, so encourage your children to read for fun every day.
- Read aloud to your children. Schedule at least 10 minutes each day at a time that is convenient for you and your children (dinner, after school, bedtime). Read only books that you also enjoy.
- Read aloud to your older children. Children are never too old to enjoy being read to.
- Talk to your children about what is read.
- Give books as gifts and design a special place where your children can have their own library.
- If you are not a good reader, you can still encourage your children by letting them read to you. Talk to them about what is read.
- Use reading as a privilege. For instance, let children stay up for 15 extra minutes if they are reading in bed.

Hint Teachers meeting with parents at the beginning of the school year or on registration day may wish to read *Leo the Late Bloomer* by Robert Kraus as a way to establish the belief that each child's development is unique.

BEYOND KINDERGARTEN: DEVELOPING STUDENTS' LISTENING AND ORAL LANGUAGE SKILLS

THE DEVELOPMENT OF LISTENING AND ORAL LANGUAGE SKILLS PLAYS A CRITICAL role in the literacy process. Speaking and listening are essential life skills that need to be included in all language programs throughout the elementary years, as they form the core of communication throughout life. Much language learning has already been accomplished by the time children enter formal education, with young students demonstrating various degrees of communication expertise (Berko Gleason, 2009).

While language acquisition is normally universal and is largely a maturational process, environmental factors contribute to and enhance its development (Hoff, 2009). While environments vary widely, they provide students with two critical insights for successful language acquisition. First, they demonstrate that language is used to communicate with others. Second, they provide children with samples of speech that suggest the connection between sound and meaning, encouraging them to discover the relationship between the two (Hoff, 2006).

By the time children are 3 years old, they usually are speaking in sentences and have a vocabulary of about 1000 words. By the time they enter kindergarten, this base has increased to about 5000 words (Gunning, 2005), with most students also having developed a basic syntactic system. By age 5, most children have essentially mastered the phonology of their language (Hoff, 2006). This early development is highly dependent on the quality and quantity of the talk to which they are exposed. It is imperative, therefore, that parents and teachers talk to children (Hart & Risley, 1995; Risley, 2003). Unfortunately, as increasing emphasis is placed on beginning reading and writing skills throughout the primary grades, some teachers relegate only minor roles to oral language and listening skills. Instead, it is important for teachers to create a variety of activities that enable learners to interact using these important modes of language.

Teachers must understand the relationships between the various components of communication that they teach in their language programs. According to the social constructivist view (see Chapter 1, Discovering Yourself and Your Students as Language Learners), children learn language because they are biologically prepared to do so (Chomsky, 1975). Language is essentially a social behaviour and research supports the idea that language development is the result of a biological predisposition coupled with a language acquisition drive that requires interaction with speakers (Hoff, 2009; Parr & Campbell, 2007; Vygotsky, 1978). It is important to remember that the acquisition of reading and writing skills is similar to the development of oral language and listening skills in young children (Bomer, 2006; Parr & Campbell, 2007). For instance, the syntactic system (i.e., the structures of language used in talk) is similar to the structures that students encounter when they begin to read and write. Students' initial experiences with these structures occur in oral language development. Successful literacy programs should build on and extend students' before-school literacy experiences and learning. It is incumbent on teachers to provide the learning conditions that support students' acquisition of reading and writing skills as readily as those that support their development of oral language and listening skills. A teacher's own early experiences with oral language and self-expression may provide additional understanding and are worthy of reflection.

REFLECTIVE ACTIVITY 2

- Do you remember your early attempts at communication?
- Why do you remember this process?
- How old were you when you developed your first words and associated them with some meaning?
- What do you remember about your first days at school? How did you feel?
- Do you remember what you said the first time you stood up to talk to your class?

These memories can help teachers develop empathy for their students as they move through the developmental stages of literacy. They also may help teachers to remember the emotional impact of these important learning stages. These memories may serve to underscore the following important common elements between learning to talk and learning to read and write:

- Children are highly motivated to learn to communicate for authentic purposes that enrich their lives.
- Children are surrounded by speech and are presented with many role models, including adults, other children, and the media.
- Children's attempts to communicate orally are supported through their interactions with adults and peers.
- Children learn to speak by identifying and recognizing patterns in language.
- Children make sense of their experiences through storytelling.

Hearing versus Listening

It has been estimated that we spend as much time listening as we spend on all other communication skills combined (Booth & Swartz, 2004). Research on listening in classrooms reveals that children spend a great deal of their in-school time listening and that teachers are largely unaware of how much time they spend talking to their students (Parr & Campbell, 2007; Stewig & Nordberg, 1994). While teachers typically demand that their students "listen carefully," they seldom spend any time teaching them how to do so (Tompkins, Bright, Pollard, & Winsor, 2011). Of course, few teachers themselves have ever received training in listening. Rather, there is an assumption that effective listening develops naturally. It is important to recognize that listening and hearing are not the same processes.

Hearing Hearing refers to the physical reception of sound waves through the ears and is a necessary first step in the listening process. It is not infrequent for a teacher to be the first person to suspect that a student is experiencing some form of hearing loss or impairment based on daily interactions. It has been estimated that 5 to 10 percent of children in mainstream classrooms experience mild to moderate hearing impairment (Santrock, Woloshyn, Levy-Gallagher, Di Petta, & Marini, 2010). While these students ultimately may cope quite well in the classroom, they are likely to experience some initial delays in language development and vocabulary acquisition. In addition, primary grade students are prone to ear infections, which can temporarily alter their hearing. Effective teachers are vigilant observers and consider the following factors when assessing students' hearing abilities:

- Difficulty making phonetic distinctions (the ends of words, low-pitched consonants)
- Unusual voice characteristics (pitch, articulation)
- The use of gestures to communicate
- Appearing withdrawn from others
- Failing to participate in verbal activities
- Responding slowly to instructions and following the behaviour of peers
- Seldom responding to questions or sharing experiences

Effective teachers are also cautious about sharing their concerns with students' parents, recognizing that any one of these behaviours, or a combination of them, can represent "normal" behaviour for many students or be driven by other factors. For instance, general inattention or extreme shyness can result in some of these behaviours. Students whose first language is not English and for whom English is not spoken in the home may also demonstrate these behaviours. In other words, teachers need to be careful about reaching conclusions too quickly.

Listening Listening refers to the process that integrates the physical act of hearing with cognitive and affective behaviours so that students:

- Receive oral messages
- Attend to these messages
- Assign meaning to these messages
- Respond appropriately to these messages

Receiving and Attending

In the primary grades, teachers can direct students' attention to the importance of listening by asking simple questions such as "Why should we listen?" and "When should we listen best?" The ideas that follow can be summarized and displayed in chart form to emphasize their importance. Teachers can introduce the idea of listening by having students stop all activity and focus on the sounds they hear around them. It is especially interesting for students to identify all of the sounds they must ignore if they are to attend to those who are speaking directly to them.

In the older grades, the topic of listening can be integrated into health or science units through exploration of the physiological characteristics of hearing or noise pollution. Students can be introduced to the concept of onomatopoeia, or the imitation of sounds in words such as *hiss*, *buzz*, and *clip clop*.

Students of all ages will benefit from discussion of non-verbal messages, including eye contact, body position, and facial expressions. Students need to recognize that these behaviours, as well as tone and pitch, provide important clues to the underlying messages contained in words.

Understanding and Responding

When students in a classroom listen to a message or participate in a discussion, they bring a variety of background skills to the task (Bredekamp, 2002). They listen with their heads, hearts, and ears, calling on their prior knowledge, language, and vocabulary skills, cognitive abilities, and creativity to derive meaning from spoken words (Stewig & Nordberg, 1994). Similar to effective readers, effective listeners form metal images, make predictions, form questions, and consider their collective experiences when forming meaning from verbal dialogues.

Other aspects that contribute to students' understanding and responsiveness to verbal messages include their beliefs about the "worthiness" of the messages. Most individuals can relate to the experience of "tuning out" when they have judged the topic of little interest or when they have been distracted by a personal problem or event. Past emotional experiences are the conduit for new information and when new information puts past experiences into dissonance, new ideas are frequently discounted in favour of holding tenaciously to old ones. Eventually, individuals stop listening. It is also important to have an internal commitment to the task or topic under discussion in order to disregard minor distractions and focus on the listener at hand. If distracting noises from other students or some other part of the environment are too great, understanding and responding may not happen—even if listening appears to be occurring.

Listening: Developing Students' Listening Skills through Read Aloud

A basic principle related to listening at any grade level is to provide a clear expectation and purpose for listening. One relatively simple way that teachers can provide students with a purpose is by posing questions before and during the daily Read Aloud. This basic strategy applies to any time the teacher uses video, television, or movies for educational purposes. In these cases, a number of questions can be developed. As the students hear the answers, the visual can be stopped and discussed and a new listening task can be established for subsequent material. In each case, students have a specific purpose for listening and learning can be enhanced. It is imperative that teachers provide the essential prior knowledge for such activities as—no matter how purposeful the questions—if students cannot connect the new material to previous knowledge, they will eventually stop listening.

Another technique involves providing students with "listening clues" while reading, while giving instructions, or during direct instruction by including phrases such as *this is important* and *I'm only going to say this once*. These clues become a listening routine that is effective only if the teacher is consistent and does not repeat instructions. A student who has listened to the teacher can repeat the instructions if someone has failed to listen the first time.

Be explicit about the importance of listening with your students and provide them with regular feedback. Have students assess their own growth as listeners. Model being a good listener yourself. Respond to your students when they speak in class in a way that models active critical listening.

Read Aloud as an Enjoyable Listening Activity

Reading aloud to students of all ages is one of the pleasures of the profession, with unabashed enjoyment being the ultimate objective. Reading aloud requires that listeners use the same set of cognitive processes that is used in reading. Furthermore, activities that strengthen students' listening capabilities improve their reading comprehension (Morrow & Gambrell, 2001; Stewig & Nordberg, 1994; Vacca et al., 2006). By guiding students to reflect carefully while listening, teachers are promoting the development of reading comprehension skills (Zbaracki, Opitz, & Ford, 2006). The following are examples of teacher prompts that will encourage students to think about what they are hearing while listening to either non-fiction or fiction materials, thus deepening their comprehension.

Examples of Listening Prompts for Non-Fiction

- Listening for the main idea
- Listening for details
- Listening for specific information
- Listening for discrepancies between the author's beliefs and students' beliefs

Examples of Listening Prompts for Fiction

- Listening for inferences related to the relationships between characters
- Identifying emotions, including those of the characters' and the author's mood
- Listening for the author's opinions and orientations
- Listening for sequence
- Listening for context clues to identify the setting and characters

The listening process is easier if the material is engaging, exciting, and presented at an appropriate level of difficulty. Effective teachers possess a repertoire of materials that have broad appeal and select Read Aloud materials that generally are about two years above the independent reading level of their students. Effective teachers are also conscious of providing students with multiple experiences and a variety of materials, including fiction, non-fiction, poetry, myths and legends, classics, mystery, and adventure. Repeated readings are strongly related to comprehension and Read Aloud materials should be made available to students who wish to reread them independently. In some instances, teachers may wish to provide students with either hard or electronic copies of Read Aloud materials so they can follow along. Struggling readers and students for whom English is a subsequent language especially benefit from the provision of print copies of Read Aloud materials.

Read Aloud Choices Make a Difference

Most reading experts stress the importance of creating a balance between teacher-selected reading materials

For my partner, Richard, and my daughters, Hillary and Dawn.

–Anne Elliott

For those who encouraged, inspired, and taught me best:
Bob, Raymond, Rebecca, Helen, and Nick.

–Vera Woloshyn

and student-selected ones, recognizing that students benefit from the opportunity to make selections based on their interests. With respect to Read Aloud programming, teachers need to be responsive to students' suggestions for novels and other reading materials. To facilitate this process, many teachers provide students with a limited number of selected materials (e.g., 3 to 4 novels) and ask them to choose from among these offerings.

It cannot be assumed that students will make appropriate selections. Therefore, teachers must be able to identify students' interests and reading levels and have a personal knowledge of literature that can be used as the basis for Read Aloud activities. Additionally, teachers need to consider the importance of exposing students to a variety of text to avoid the constant and exclusive selection of a favoured author, series, or genre. While this can be a challenging process for some beginning teachers, especially those who have not read children's literature since childhood, they can develop these skills and reading repertoires over a number of years. Many teachers enjoy the process of revisiting old favourites as well as discovering new texts.

What Is a Good Book? This is a question that has been pondered by generations of teachers, with no simple answer or "one list serves all" criteria. The answer shifts from generation to generation as the nature of children's literature and the nature of childhood changes substantially over time (Buckingham, 2001; Facer, Furlong, Furlong, & Sutherland, 2004; Gee, 2003). Consider the relatively recent prevalence of digital text and the increasing popularity of graphic novels and multi-modal genres (Peterson & Swartz, 2008). On the other hand, there are texts that have withstood the test of time, such as fairy tales, *Charlotte's Web*, *The Secret Garden*, and many fables, tall tales, myths, and legends that have become beloved cultural icons.

When we talk about "good" Read Aloud materials, whether they are narrative or non-fiction texts, there is an implicit association with reading pleasure. In this context, a pleasurable reading experience involves a text that compels the reader to continue reading. For instance, in the context of picture books this involves captivating illustrations coupled with engaging text. While thousands of texts are published each year, many are not of high quality and teachers must wade through this large number of offerings to make quality choices. In an age of digital distraction, the books that students encounter in the classroom are an important part of their literacy development (Peterson & Swartz, 2008). This reality places an additional onus on teachers when they are selecting books to share with their students.

If there is one unequivocal truism about selecting a "good" book, it is that the adult reader must enjoy the text. No matter how "worthy" or acclaimed a book may be, if the adult reader does not respond favourably to it, it is a poor choice for use in the classroom. Students will recognize the teacher's lack of enthusiasm and invariably their enjoyment of the text will be minimized.

When a book is well selected and well read there are many benefits to students. It is important to remember that both fiction and non-fiction should be read aloud and that there are benefits associated with each (see Tables 2.3 and 2.4). Remember that many students prefer non-fiction to fiction.

Finally, and perhaps most importantly, a good book that is well chosen and well read, either fiction or non-fiction, provides listeners with a pleasurable and entertaining reading experience.

Table 2.3 Benefits of Listening to Good Fiction

A good book provides students with an understanding of the universality of the human condition, helping students relate to the story and understand more about themselves and their society.

The Hello, Goodbye Window by Norton Juster and Chris Raschka provides the reader with a "bird's-eye" view of the everyday world through the kitchen window of a grandparent's house. It also celebrates the love between children and grandparents.

Franklin books by Canadian author Paulette Bourgeois and illustrator Brenda Clark. The first book in the series, *Franklin in the Dark*, describes the experiences of a turtle that is afraid of the dark. Teachers can use the text to help students understand the universality of fear. Other titles in this series provide similar illustrations of the human condition.

Not a Nickel to Spare: The Great Depression Diary of Sally Cohen by Canadian author Perry Nodelman. In this powerful story, the primary character experiences anti-Semitism against the backdrop of the Great Depression. This book requires a sensitive teacher to provide critical background and facilitate discussion that enables students to understand both recent history and current societal issues.

Ghost Train by Canadian author Paul Yee (Governor General's Literary Award, 1996). A Chinese-Canadian girl retraces her father's experiences helping to build the Trans-Canada Railroad. Her pain and her search for meaning offer insights and understanding about this period in Canadian history.

Other recommended titles: *Girl on the Other Side* by Deborah Kerbel; *Rules* by Cynthia Lord (Newbery Honor, 2007); *The Crazy Man* by Canadian author Pamela Porter (Governor General's Literary Award, 2005); *The Book Thief* by Markus Zusak (Commonwealth Writers' Prize for Best Book, 2006).

A good book can help students understand and connect with cultural diversity that is a prevalent part of the Canadian mosaic.

The Breadwinner, *Parvana's Journey*, and *Mud City* by award-winning Canadian author Deborah Ellis feature a young girl struggling to survive in war-torn Afghanistan. Effective teachers can guide students to identify similarities and differences between their culture and the Afghan culture as portrayed in these texts.

Brothers of Hope: The Story of the Lost Boys of Sudan by Mary Williams and illustrated by R. Gregory Christie is a powerful story of courage and the power of the human spirit. Although it is a picture book, the content of this text is well suited for older students.

Shadow in Hawthorn Bay by award-winning Canadian author Janet Lunn describes the difficult journey that 15-year-old Mary Urquhart makes when travelling from Scotland to North America. The author provides the reader with a description of life in Upper Canada in 1815.

Other recommended titles: *A Bottle in the Gaza Sea* by Valerie Zenatti; *The River Between Us* by Richard Peck; *The Boy in the Striped Pajamas* by John Boyne; *A Small Tall Tale from the Far Far North* by award-winning author and illustrator Peter Sis.

A good book portrays human motives, allowing students to identify with or react to a fictional character.

Scaredy Squirrel at Night by Melanie Watt. Scaredy Squirrel has been having bad dreams about vampires so he is afraid to go to sleep. He comes up with a plan to avoid sleeping. Students will readily identify with the fear of bad dreams and be able to commiserate with Scaredy Squirrel.

Some of the Kinder Planets by award-winning Canadian author Tim Wynne-Jones provides the reader with a series of short stories about ordinary teenagers who find themselves in extraordinary situations.

Sharla by Canadian author Budge Wilson. Sharla has just moved to a new town and is angry with everyone. When she starts to work as a photographer, things turn around until her life is threatened and she needs to face a new reality.

Other recommended titles: *Heartbeat* by Sharon Creech; *Locomotion* by Jacqueline Woodson; *Stargirl* by Jerry Spinelli; *The Thrilling Life of Pauline de Lammermoor* and *The Saver* by Canadian author Edeet Ravel.

A good book provides students with vicarious experiences that move them beyond the present time and space.

A Screaming Kind of Day by award-winning Canadian author Rachna Gilmore (Governor General's Literary Award, 1999). A deaf girl has a bad day.

A Prairie as Wide as the Sea: The Immigrant Diary of Ivy Weatherall by Canadian author Sarah Ellis. Eleven-year-old Ivy accompanies her family to the Prairies with high hopes and determination to make a new life in Canada. The family's problems soon become almost insurmountable and Ivy's parents wish to return to England. Ivy however, falls in love with the Prairies in all their grandeur.

Who is Frances Rain? by Canadian author Margaret Buffie. Lizzie's summer vacation with her grandmother is interrupted when her family decides to accompany her. To escape them, Lizzie explores an island close by and finds a pair of old glasses. When she puts them on, she is surprised to see a woman and girl from the past. While trying to find out who they are, Lizzie gains insights into her own family situation.

Other recommended titles: *Greener Grass: The Famine Years* by award-winning Canadian author Caroline Pignat; *Good Masters! Sweet Ladies!: Voices from a Medieval Village* by Laura Amy Schlitz (Newbery Medal, 2008); *The Root Cellar* by Janet Lunn (Canadian Library Association, Book of the Year for Children Award, 1982).

A good book reveals societal tensions and promotes discussion of issues associated with tolerance and fairness.

Duck! Rabbit! by Amy Krouse Rosenthal and Tom Lichtenheld encourages readers to enter a debate about whether the front cover illustrates a duck or a rabbit. The text can be used to encourage students to recognize that individuals view the world in unique and distinct ways.

Underground to Canada by Canadian author Barbara Smucker. This story of the Underground Railroad, which terminated in Canada, can lead to discussions of justice and tolerance.

Esperanza Rising by Pam Munoz Ryan. When Esperanza and her mom are forced to leave their home and work in a Mexican farm labour camp, they must learn a new way of life that lacks the luxuries of their previous one.

Other recommended titles: *One More Border: The True Story of One Family's Escape from War-Torn Europe* by Canadian author William Kaplan; *If the World Were a Village: A Book about the World's People* by Canadian author David Smith; *The Other Side* by Jacqueline Woodson.

A good book extends students' vocabulary and introduces them to new concepts and ideas.

The Tale of Despereaux: Being the Story of a Mouse, a Princess, Some Soup, and a Spool of Thread by Kate DiCamillo (Newbery Medal, 2004). The author describes the adventures of Despereaux, a mouse, who is on a mission to save a human princess. The author assumes the voice of the narrator periodically to introduce the reader to unfamiliar terms and vocabulary.

Amelia Bedelia is a character found in a series of books by Peggy Parish. Amelia Bedelia takes a series of figures of speech and acts on them literally, to comic effect.

Miss Alaineus: A Vocabulary Disaster by Debra Frasier describes the misadventures of a grade 5 student who misinterprets a vocabulary assignment as a result of a cold, to the amusement of her classmates.

Other recommended titles: A Series of Unfortunate Events series by Lemony Snickett; *Airborn* by award-winning Canadian author Kenneth Oppel; *The Boy from the Sun* by Duncan Weller (Governor General's Literary Award, 2007); *The Boy Who Loved Words* by Roni Schotter.

Table 2.4 Benefits of Listening to Good Non-Fiction

A good book provides students with answers and responses to issues and items that they wish to learn about. Over time, students discover that books are valid sources to find answers to their questions. These experiences may contribute to students becoming lifelong learners.

Borealis: A Polar Bear Cub's First Year by Canadian author Rebecca Grambo describes a polar bear cub's first adventures through pictures and words.

The Magic School Bus books by Canadian authors Joanna Cole and Bruce Degen combine science with fictional stories.

Deep in the Jungle and other texts by Mary Atkinson are part of the Snapshots Science series. Texts integrate literacy, science, and math concepts.

Just the Facts: Inventions & Discoveries by Dee Phillips, Brian Alchorn, and Catharine Chambers. Students learn about different inventions that changed the world, geological discoveries, and amazing medical breakthroughs.

Other recommended titles: *Deserts Are Not Deserted* by Avelyn Davidson; *Water Wonders* by Canadian author Frieda Wishinsky; *The Boy Who Invented TV: The Story of Philo Farnsworth* by Kathleen Krull.

A good book can generate interest and excitement that encourages students to explore their world.

Ibis: A True Whale Story by Canadian author John Himmelman. Based on the true story of the first successful whale-entanglement release, readers relive two dangerous rescue attempts to release a humpback whale from a fishing net.

Bobbie Rosenfeld: The Olympian Who Could Do Everything by Anne Dublin represents the life of Franny "Bobbie" Rosenfeld, a great Canadian athlete who competed in multiple Olympic sports.

Beyond the Dance: A Ballerina's Life by Chan Hon Goh and Cary Fagan. This autobiography provides a first-hand account of the physical and emotional challenges faced by a young woman who strives to become a ballerina while adjusting to a new life in Canada.

Other recommended titles: *A Canoe Trip* by Canadian author Bobbie Kalman; *Born to Write: The Remarkable Lives of Six Famous Authors* by Canadian author Charis Cotter.

A good book contains illustrations that can clarify concepts and ideas.

A Second Is a Hiccup: A Child's Book of Time by award-winning Canadian author Hazel Hutchins and illustrator Kady MacDonald Denton uses rhyme and illustration to mark the passage of seconds, minutes, hours, and years.

Fire! The Renewal of a Forest by Canadian author Celia Godkin presents the cycle of forest fires in both pictures and words.

A Thousand Years of Pirates written and illustrated by award-winning Canadian author William Gilkerson documents the history and times of pirates, including such notorious individuals as Blackbeard and Grace O'Malley. Pirates' lives at sea are described as they steal and pillage the riches of others.

Other recommended titles: *A Brave Soldier* and *Four Pictures by Emily Carr* by Canadian author Nicolas Debon; *Mission Control, This is Apollo: The Story of the First Voyages to the Moon* by Andrew Chaikin; *Redwoods* by Jason Chin.

A good book extends students' vocabulary, presenting them with new terminology and concepts.

The Cloud Book by Tomie de Paola. Readers are provided with scientific facts about clouds, legends, and steps for identifying clouds.

In Your Face: The Culture of Beauty and You by Canadian author Shari Graydon. Readers are introduced to popular advertising techniques specially designed to target young consumers and are encouraged to critique messages associated with body image, happiness, and success.

Weird Weather: Everything You Didn't Want to Know About Climate Change but Probably Should Find Out by Kate Evans. Using a comic book format, readers are presented with information on climate change as well as suggestions about how individuals can promote positive change.

Other recommended titles: *Hurricanes!*, *The Moon Book* , and other texts by Canadian author Gail Gibbons; *As Long as There Are Whales* by Canadian author Evelyne Daigle; *Accidental Discoveries: From Laughing Gas to Dynamite* by Canadian author Larry Verstraete.

A good book helps students understand the importance of well-organized and well-categorized information.

Big Trucks, Big Wheels by Petrina Gentile, Bobbie Kalman, and Marc Crabtree. This book shows children's favourite trucks, including fire trucks and eighteen-wheelers.

Follow That Map! A First Book of Mapping Skills by Canadian author Scot Ritchie presents primary grade readers with information on the basic elements of maps, including keys, legends, symbols, and directions. Readers are provided with an overview of the different types of maps and their uses.

Transformed: How Everyday Things are Made by Canadian author Bill Slavin. Readers learn how to make a variety of objects, including guitars, cat litter, cheese, paper, toothpaste, and wire. Along with pictures and information on how they are made, the authors have included historical information about the objects.

Other recommended titles: *How Many Baby Pandas?* by Sandra Markle; *I Found a Dead Bird: The Kids' Guide to the Cycle of Life & Death* by Canadian author Jan Thornhill; *The Frog Scientist* by Pamela S. Turner.

A good book broadens students' views of the world.

An Elephant in the Backyard by Richard Sobol. Readers learn about an endangered species and the culture of an Asian country by reading about a 4-year-old domesticated Asian elephant that lives in Ban Tha Klang, Thailand.

Hana's Suitcase by Canadian author Karen Levine describes how Hana Brady's family had their previously happy life turned upside down by the Nazis.

One Hen: How One Small Loan Made a Big Difference by Canadian author Katie Smith Milway. Readers learn about a boy and his life in Africa and about how his village learned to collaborate to help each other.

Let's Eat! What Children Eat around the World by Beatrice Hollyer details the lives of five children from around the world, including their homes, families, lifestyles, traditions, and typical foods.

Other recommended titles: *Adventures on the Ancient Silk Road* by Canadian authors Priscilla Galloway and Dawn Hunter; *Children of War: Voices of Iraqi Refugees* by award-winning Canadian author Deborah Ellis.

It is particularly vital that teachers provide a listening program (Read Aloud) when considering that few students identify independent reading as a favoured activity (Elliott, Bosacki, Woloshyn, & Richards, 2002). Listening, therefore, is a vital foundational component not only of learning to speak but also of becoming literate and enjoying independent reading.

Oral Language

Many adults have difficulty expressing themselves articulately and, as a result, public speaking is an underdeveloped skill for many people as well as a source of great angst. Reading experts across Canada emphasize the importance of oral language in the literacy process. There is a strong emphasis on helping students to develop the oral communication skills they need to understand and interact with others, to express themselves fluently and with confidence, and to interpret and respond to media communications (including using media venues to communicate personal beliefs, knowledge, and ideas). Teachers need to provide students with many opportunities to engage in talk and interactive dialogue throughout the day. Oral language skills need to be developed in every grade. In the early grades, this requires establishing consistent routines and explicit instruction in listening, question answering and responding, and the conventions of acceptable discussion. In junior and intermediate grades, oral language should be a daily activity during which students learn to critique each other's ideas, present material in a persuasive and informative manner, and express themselves orally with confidence and purpose in a variety of contexts.

Stages of Oral Language Development Most young children acquire oral language in a predictable sequence, although there can be considerable variations among individuals (Reutzel & Cooter, 2004). Generally, the initial stages of language development occur during the first three months of life, when babies become familiar with adult faces and spoken language and begin to make babbling sounds. First words usually appear between 10 and 13 months, and by 18 to 24 months babies are usually able to string two words together. By this time, they have begun to grasp the importance of language as a tool for communication.

Development of Phonology and Morphology During their second year, children generally know about 50 words and are able to combine two or three words to form brief statements (e.g., "Daddy go," "dog good," "me do it"). They usually are also able to demonstrate sensitivity to the sounds of spoken words (Berko Gleason & Ratner, 2009). For instance, they recognize rhyming words, words in simple poetry, and silly words and can identify syllables in phrases.

About this time, children demonstrate an awareness of morphological rules (i.e., the patterns of language that tell how sounds are combined). For example, "Today I sing this song but yesterday I sang another song. I am a singer." Children also begin to use plurals and possessive forms of nouns and place appropriate endings on verbs (e.g., "That toy is his and this one is mine. We have lots of toys." I was running when I fell." "I jumped off the porch."). Children at this stage often overgeneralize these patterns, saying things such as "he goed" and "she comed," with many of these irregularities persisting for some time. Adults are advised to neither overreact to these generalities nor adopt them in "baby talk." Eventually and quite naturally, children adopt the irregular patterns that are so common in English.

Syntax The awareness of syntactical patterns, which refers to the language patterns of combining words in phrases and sentences, typically occurs naturally for young users of the English language. As children gain more experience with language, they begin to expand their initial single noun and verb statements (Tager-Flusberg, 2008). They come to demonstrate syntactic understandings (e.g., adjectives always precede nouns). They extend their use of tense, correcting their overuse of present tense to include the proper use of past and future tenses. At the same time, their sentences become longer. Again, interactions with fluent adult speakers are critical here.

Semantics and Pragmatics As children mature, they expand their vocabulary to include using sentences to express experiences and convey meaning. By age 6, most children possess a speaking vocabulary of between 8000 and 14 000 words, underscoring the ongoing language learning curve from birth to the beginning of grade 1. By the time they start formal schooling, children have developed some level of communicative competence and are able to apply that competence appropriately in various social contexts. For instance, they understand the different communication competencies required for face-to-face, telephone, and internet-based discussions. Similarly, they are able to differentiate the nature of "appropriate" conversations when speaking with parents, teachers, friends, and siblings.

Oral Language and Listening Skills in the Curriculum

In Canada, all provinces and territories have emphasized the development of oral language and listening skills in their language arts curriculum, accentuating the importance of providing students with opportunities to engage in a variety of oral activities (see Table 2.5 for a brief description of some of these provincial documents).

Table 2.5 Emphasis on Oral Activities across the Provinces and Territories

In **British Columbia**, students engage in oral activities to develop their speaking, listening, and thinking abilities. Learning expectations indicate that students will use speaking and listening when engaged in exploratory and imaginative play to express themselves, ask for assistance, exchange ideas, and experiment with new ideas or materials. Additional expectations include engaging in speaking and listening activities to share ideas about pictures, stories, informational text, and experiences.

Manitoba has created a support document for kindergarten teachers and speech-language pathologists called *Listening and Speaking: First Steps into Literacy.* The document iterates that "oral language development is the key to the success of early literacy learners. Listening and speaking support the development of children's thinking and reasoning, and their reading, writing, viewing, and representing skills" (p. 6).

Ontario's curriculum document states that "oral communication skills are fundamental to the development of literacy and essential for thinking and learning" (Ontario Ministry of Education, 2006b, p. 9). It references three overall expectations related to listening and speaking.

Students will:

1. Listen in order to understand and respond appropriately in a variety of situations for a variety of purposes;
2. use speaking skills and strategies appropriately to communicate with different audiences for a variety of purposes;
3. reflect on and identify their strengths as listeners and speakers, areas for improvement and the strategies they found most helpful in oral communication situations. (Ontario Ministry of Education, 2006a, p. 14)

In the **Quebec** curriculum, kindergarten students are expected to communicate using the resources of language. This includes showing an interest in communication, starting and maintaining a conversation, and adhering to the subject of the conversation. Students are also expected to pay attention to the message and to express their understanding of information received.

In **Newfoundland and Labrador**'s curriculum document titled *Early Beginnings! A Kindergarten Curriculum Guide*, the importance of oral language and listening are stressed, with a focus placed on encouraging students' dialogues with peers and adults. The document supports the central role of oral language in literacy acquisition, stating that oral language is a means of making sense of experiences and new learning.

Common suggestions for oral activities include the following:

- Discussions about personal interests and hobbies
- Discussions of current affairs at the school, municipal, provincial, federal, and international levels
- Discussions related to school work, which may include opportunities to:
  - Brainstorm
  - Discuss strategies for problem solving
  - Debate issues
  - Present and defend ideas
  - Critique the ideas of others

Educators have identified four categories of talk that should be included in language arts programming: conversations, aesthetic talk, efferent talk, and drama activities. Each of these categories is reviewed below.

Conversations Conversations, or connected discourse, occur daily in all human environments. It is through conversation that we learn much about our environment, build and maintain relationships, and share our ideas and experiences. Students' ability to sustain conversation develops dramatically between grades 2 and 5, with more modest progress continuing to grade 12 (Hoff, 2006).

There are documented differences in the conversations of males and females. Boys tend to play in large groups that include males of different social statuses and ages. While hierarchical patterns emerge, there is little exclusion and the social hierarchy is in flux. Males often use dialogue to assert dominance and gain attention (Guerian, 2006, 2010; Kindlon & Thompson, 1999). Girls, on the other hand, tend to play in smaller, homogeneous groups in terms of age and social status. Compared to males, females' play and conversations are more co-operative and non-competitive. While boys jockey for position in their groups, girls tend to compete for membership in exclusive groups (Hoff, 2006). Additionally, males tend to converse showing much less emotion than females (Guerian, 2006; Kindlon & Thompson, 1999). Teachers who understand these general conversational patterns are better able to establish classrooms conversations that foster a climate of trust and caring and encourage all students to participate. It is through such conversations that students, in part, develop empathy, understanding, and respect for the opinions and values of others.

Two "rules" that govern "good" conversation are turn taking and co-operation. Taking turns is an important skill if ideas are to be shared and respected between and among people during a conversation. Those who tend to dominate either by not allowing others the space to talk or by denying one member the time to speak do not possess good conversational skills. Being co-operative includes attending to quality (i.e., providing informative contributions, providing neither too much nor too little information, speaking the truth and avoiding what may be false or lack evidence), being relevant and avoiding redundancy, and presenting in an appropriate (i.e., clear and respectful) manner.

Conversations That Contribute to Learning It is well recognized that student learning is enhanced when children are provided with the opportunity to relate new information they are learning to their previous ideas and experiences. Therefore, it is important that students use their own words as they interpret and make sense of new ideas (Pressley et al., 1992; Wittrock & Alesandrini, 1990). Small-group conversations are especially beneficial, as they maximize students' opportunities to contribute. They provide opportunities to be spontaneous, ask questions, seek a variety of opinions, and engage in reflective thinking (Gunning, 2005). Moving from small-group to large-group discussions allows for the generation of new ideas and additional clarifications that can extend and deepen ideas. There are three basic kinds of conversations that teachers can use on a regular basis: informal conversations, formal conversations, and grand conversations.

Teachers need to encourage informal conversations in their classrooms from the earliest grades onward. For example, a teacher can draw a few students together during seat work or free activity to observe an object, reflect on an idea, or brainstorm a solution to a problem. Through these informal conversations, teachers can provide students with valuable opportunities to acquire skills associated with small-group discussions. In addition, students' perceptions of self and self-esteem can be strengthened as they interact positively with their peers. Such conversations reinforce dialogue as a problem-solving and coping strategy and reinforce the use of discussion instead of withdrawal or anger. Informal discussions encourage language learning, as they challenge students to express their thoughts and ideas clearly. Teachers often assume the role of facilitator during these conversations, allowing students to talk among themselves. Dynamic play centres in the early primary grades can motivate small-group conversations and problem-solving activities. This means that play centres must contain interesting props and must be changed or modified regularly to maintain ongoing enthusiasm and interest. While this kind of informal discussion occurs frequently in the primary grades, teachers need to be reminded to continue to engage students in these activities in the later grades (Parr & Campbell, 2007).

Formal conversations are those that are planned by teachers as programmed learning situations. Once teachers have structured these conversations and explained student responsibility, the small-group discussions are conducted by students with little teacher input. Typically, they are about 20 minutes long and build on students' existing skills. Over time, formal conversations should become a regular component of the language arts curriculum. Table 2.6 outlines the steps associated with facilitating formal conversations in the classroom.

Grand conversations are conversations held by the entire class. What makes these conversations different from other classroom talk is that a student leads them. The conversations are characterized by authenticity and spontaneity rather than by teacher-directed questions. The teacher can either choose to act as a passive observer and not participate or can elect to participate as an equal and interested member of the community. In these whole-group conversations, students are free to debate, critique, and build on each other's ideas and they learn that meaning-making comes from within and about sharing ideas in a social context. In such a democratic environment, community building is a natural outcome.

These conversations are often used in response to literature and students are free to express their ideas without the imposition and domination of teacher questions. In this format, students frequently make connections between their own life experiences and the literature they have been reading. Another positive aspect of this dialogue is that there is no "correct" answer and students share ideas while expanding their views of the literature in a social context. Research indicates that while students generally explore theme, story events, and characters, they are less likely to discuss the author's structure, motivation, and use of figurative language (Martinez & Roser, 1995). As an active

Table 2.6 How to Structure a Formal Conversation

1. **Select a topic.** The topic can be selected by the teacher or negotiated by the class by asking for suggestions and then reaching consensus on a preferred topic. In either case, the topic should be current in order to engage students, generate sufficient depth, and encourage students to express a variety of opinions and ideas. Examples: Do the Olympics benefit the host city economically? Is the gun registry in Canada an effective way to prevent crime? Are school uniforms a good idea? Does violence in the media cause people to commit violent crimes in real life? What can an individual, a family, a country, and a community do to help prevent global warming? What advantages and disadvantages are there to having homework assigned regularly?
2. **Activate relevant prior knowledge.** Some teachers require students to record their initial thoughts, beliefs, responses, and position on the topic in question. Regardless of whether teachers require students to record their thoughts, it is important to provide them with sufficient "think time" prior to engaging in a formal conversation.
3. **Form small groups.** Groups consisting of four to six students are considered to be most appropriate for formal conversation, as they allow for a variety of thoughts and perspectives while providing students with sufficient time to express their ideas. Groups can be formed by teachers based on their knowledge of students or students can be permitted to choose their own groups. It is wise to vary this process over the course of the school year.
4. **Establish and reinforce rules and procedures.** Effective teachers spend considerable time preparing students to engage in formal conversations. An important component of this preparation involves establishing and reinforcing the rules and procedures associated with successful discussions, including:
   - Attend to each student's ideas
   - Avoid dominance by one student
   - Practise turn taking and avoid interrupting others
   - Respect all ideas
   - Ask questions for clarification
   - Address disagreements without anger
   - Use humour whenever possible while resolving disagreements
   - Extend and building on presented ideas when relevant

   Depending on students' prior experiences, teachers will vary the amount of time they spend establishing and reviewing these protocols. When working with young or experienced students, teachers are advised to focus explicitly on one or two of these skills at any time before introducing subsequent ones.
5. **Provide sufficient discussion time.** During the discussion period, teachers are encouraged to move from group to group to monitor the conversations and provide assistance as needed. The activity, however, should be mostly student-centred. Teachers' observational notes recorded during this time can be useful for subsequent assessment and evaluation.
6. **Wrap up and debriefing.** Students may or may not arrive at a consensus by the end of the allotted discussion time. It is important for teachers to validate the discussion process over the need for agreement or consensus. Teachers are encouraged to hold debriefing sessions to gather feedback from individual groups. The debriefing should focus on two questions:

   What conclusion was reached and what ideas were raised related to the topic under discussion?

   Did students follow the rules and routines associated with effective discussions?

participant, teachers can intervene occasionally to ask open-ended questions to spark further discussion or critical thinking.

Table 2.7 provides teachers with a set of criteria for assessing the quality of student participation in classroom conversation.

Table 2.7 Criteria for Assessing Students' Participation in a Conversation

- Contributes thoughtfully to the conversation
- Contributes respectfully
- Shares ideas
- Maintains eye contact with peers when talking
- Builds on and extends the ideas of others
- Asks questions when appropriate
- Includes others in the conversation
- Avoids group conflict
- Addresses conflict appropriately
- Establishes an overall conclusion if available
- Demonstrates leadership ability

Aesthetic Talk Aesthetic talk includes readers' ideas and emotions associated with their literary experiences. It also includes interpreting what has been read or heard in literature. This kind of talk is very common in classrooms as students are called on to discuss texts that they read independently or respond to a teacher-led Read Aloud. Generally, aesthetic conversations involve having students share their opinions, reactions, and interpretations with specific reference to the text in question. This sharing experience tends to enhance and extend their comprehension of reading materials (Tompkins, Bright, Pollard, & Winsor, 2008).

While teachers will want to take advantage of the opportunity to model and share their responses to text (e.g., building on the ideas of others, asking questions for clarification, relating text to personal experiences), their presence is not mandatory. That is, students can engage in aesthetic discussions independently. Comfort with "thinking aloud" is one foundational skill that contributes to the overall success of an aesthetic conversation. Students need to feel free from rebuke or ridicule when they share their ideas, with the onus on teachers to establish a positive classroom environment. Teachers can use a variety of instructional formats and techniques to encourage aesthetic conversations in the classroom, including literature circles, reader response, grand conversations, and drama activities such as Readers' Theatre. Table 2.8 provides a set of instructional steps associated with facilitating aesthetic conversations in the classroom.

Efferent Talk Students need to use efferent talk when they want to inform or persuade their listeners. In the primary grades, efferent talk can take the form of show and tell (also called show and share) and interviews. In the junior and intermediate grades, efferent talk may include the sharing of reports, formal speeches, and debates. In all of these activities, teachers need to model appropriate thought processes and routines, emphasizing the importance of organization and illustrating the use of visual and other presentation aids as appropriate.

Efferent talk is an important skill set that students need to add to their repertoire to achieve future success in school and success later in life in the workplace. Efferent talk

Table 2.8 Teaching Steps for an Aesthetic Discussion

1. Read aloud an excerpt, short story, or novel to the class (ideally, a complete story).
2. Provide sufficient time for students to provide written responses.
3. Place students in groups to share their responses and impressions, encouraging them to relate the story to their own experiences.
4. Encourage students to provide critiques of the story.

   Note: Remember that short stories can have a big impact on students in the junior and intermediate grades. Examples include:

   Ghost Train by Paul Yee
   Favorite Greek Myths by Mary Pope Osborne
   In Flanders Fields: The Story of the Poem by John McCrae by Linda Granfield
   Hana's Suitcase by Karen Levine
   Some of the Kinder Planets (select a story; e.g., "The Night of the Pomegranate") by Tim Wynne-Jones
   Very Last First Time by Jan Andrews

is often formed around world issues and concepts such as politics, war, the environment, immigration, individual rights, and multicultural issues.

In this context, students try to clarify their own thinking about how these more abstract concepts are related to each other. Information to help them establish their ideas is available via the internet, television, radio, newspapers, informational books, films, and videos. Since students generally are just beginning to formulate their ideas in new and abstract ways, they may be influenced strongly by their parents' beliefs. When students explore a topic of interest, experiment with their own beliefs, and consider the beliefs of others, they are learning social skills related to problem solving and consensus seeking. While the content of these conversations is important, acquiring these social skills is equally as significant for their future learning.

When planning a lesson that encourages efferent talk, teachers need to prepare questions that direct the lesson and encourage critical thinking. They also need to provide students with ample time to consider the questions and inform them that they may "change their minds" if persuaded by the ideas of others. Finally, students need to be encouraged to ask questions and seek relevant information as part of these discussions. Small-group discussions can be especially effective for ensuring that ideas and concepts are well explored. Small-group discussions followed by larger dialogues such as grand conversations often provide students with a deeper level of conceptualization. Sometimes it is appropriate to have students generate questions and complete initial research on a topic before they assume any conceptual positions.

Drama Activities Improving students' oral communication is a shared goal of drama and language arts educators. For both school-aged children and adults, oral communication is rooted in the spoken word. By assuming roles in various drama activities, children experiment with spoken vocabulary appropriate for a range of characters (Booth, 2005). Vocabulary, however, is only one aspect of oral communication, and speech involves elements beyond words themselves. In conveying and interpreting ideas, *how* words are spoken is just as important as *what* words are spoken.

Volume and tempo, pitch and inflection, calmness or agitation of tone: these factors combine with words to communicate emotion, intention, and meaning. When speakers are seen as well as heard, communication is enhanced visually through posture, gestures, and facial expression. Drama activities allow children to participate in and reflect on all aspects of oral communication.

In daily life, speaking usually takes the form of conversation among two or more people. Oral communication is thus primarily a social or shared activity. The "art of conversation" includes the ability to follow certain customs, rules, and traditions of society. Skilful conversationalists listen as well as speak; they contribute ideas, elicit others' opinions, and respond appropriately in ways that move the conversation along. Like conversation, drama activities are a form of social interaction in which students participate orally and build on the ideas of others. Most frequently, drama activities employ the theatrical convention of fictional conversation or dialogue. Whether students are creating their own scenarios or using a script provided by the teacher, conversing through drama activities builds valuable oral skills of social communication (Cornett & Smithrim, 2001).

Drama activities can be embedded in language arts lessons readily. For younger students, five minutes or so is sufficient time for any single activity. With practice, older students can work "in role" for longer durations. It is usually not necessary or advisable for students to "perform" their drama work for the class, eliminating concerns and fears associated with presenting a polished product to an audience. Sometimes teachers will assume a role alongside students. In such instances, it is important for teachers to provide the class with clear "transitional" signals with respect to going "into role" and "out of role" (e.g., When I sit in this chair, I will become the mayor of the town. When I leave the chair, I will become myself again). At the end of each drama activity, the class should reflect on their experiences through teacher-led discussion. See Tables 2.9, 2.10, and 2.11 for suggestions on readily implementable classroom drama activities, remembering that numerous topics taken from stories or novel study are possible within each framework.

Table 2.9 Drama Activities, Primary and Junior Grades

- When reading a story aloud to younger children, the teacher should model appropriate volume, inflection, and tone, especially when speaking lines of dialogue. On a second reading, the teacher may read dialogue with inappropriate vocal qualities and ask the class to comment on the reading. This will initiate a conversation about vocal elements of speech. The students may "instruct" the teacher on reading with effective volume, tempo, pitch, and intonation. The teacher may then ask the students to demonstrate an appropriate posture to accompany various lines of dialogue. Post-activity class discussion should focus on the relationship among characters, printed words, vocal qualities, and physical communication.
- After reading a story, the teacher may ask students to identify emotions portrayed by different characters. Students individually select one of these emotions, without telling anyone what the emotion is. Using their bodies but no words, students create an appropriate posture and facial expression to depict their selected emotion. Classmates use visual cues to identify the emotions portrayed. (To reduce time requirements and possible embarrassment, three or four students may volunteer to demonstrate at the same time.) As a whole class, students

(Continued)

Table 2.9 Drama Activities, Primary and Junior Grades *(continued)*

resume their emotion's posture and facial expression and imagine an event at school that could provoke the same response. The teacher "taps into" the students in turn by touching each one on the shoulder. When touched, the student tells what school event would make someone feel the emotion depicted. Post-activity discussion should focus on the fact that characters in a story experience and communicate the same emotions as students themselves.

- The teacher may ask students to imagine what happened to a character in the story either just before or just after the story occurred. In pairs, students spontaneously dramatize a short conversation between the character and any other character to depict their imagined event. Post-activity discussion should focus on the content of these conversations and the process of creating imaginary conversations (e.g., What characters were involved in your conversation? What was your conversation about? How did it begin? How did it end? How did you and your partner go about creating the conversation? What problems did you meet? How did you solve them? How did you use your voices and bodies to help communicate the meaning of your words?).
- The teacher posts a sentence (e.g., I'm going to tell the teacher) in a highly visible location. Pre-activity discussion identifies information provided by the statement without any vocal or physical clues. Students then speak the sentence aloud based on different circumstances, adding appropriate vocal and physical qualities (e.g., You have just been hit by the school bully. Your friend has slipped on a patch of ice and hurt herself badly. You and your partner have just completed a very difficult math problem. You have found what looks like a medicine bottle on the playground. You have just seen someone steal money in the gymnasium change room). Post-activity discussion should focus on the fact that words can express different forms of emotion and intention depending on circumstances, vocal qualities, and physical clues.
- At a particularly exciting moment of a story or novel, the teacher pretends to be a main character and sits in the "hot seat." Students pretend to be other characters in the story or newspaper reporters, police, etc. In role, students pose questions to the teacher, who responds in role as the character. "Hot seat" questions elicit information about the character's thoughts, plans, and feelings leading up to the exciting story event. (In older grades, students may become "hot seat" characters after the teacher has modelled the activity.)
- "Voices in the head" is a technique that can be used to examine the thoughts of any character from any story. At a point in the plot when a character is faced with a difficult decision, students imagine one or two statements or questions that could be running through the character's mind. Students shut their eyes and think of one statement or question. The teacher quietly walks about the room, tapping students on the shoulder. When tapped, each student says his or her statement or question. When all statements or questions have been vocalized, class discussion should focus on the kinds of ideas the voices have expressed.
- As a variation of "voices in the head," students may create two-line chants that express a character's state of mind, problems, or fears. (Dominant features of a chant are rhyme, rhythm, and repetition. A two-line chant should rhyme, have a distinct rhythm, and be repeated to create a four-line finished product.) When practising their chants, students should be encouraged to include appropriate vocal elements (e.g., volume, tempo, intonation).
- For well-known stories or fairy tales, students can imagine incidents that occur outside the main storyline. *Sleeping Beauty*, for example, begins with a feast to celebrate the birth of a royal baby. Students may work in role as groups of servants organizing the event. One group plans the menu; one group chooses a design for the invitations; one group draws clothing for the king and queen; one group creates the banquet hall floor plan; one group organizes the stables for guests' horses. After making their decisions, the groups report back to the class, with the teacher in role as chief servant.
- Two additional activities, simulation framework and interview framework, are suitable for students in grades 6 to 8. Numerous topics, taken from stories or novel study, may be used with each framework. The examples in Tables 2.10 and 2.11 use topics taken from contemporary issues of interest (polar bears and careers).

Table 2.10 Drama Simulation: Polar Bear as Endangered Species, Intermediate Grades

Step 1 Identify a problem and goal to be addressed in the simulation. Example: The polar bear population is decreasing and the species is in danger of extinction. Our goal in the simulation is to offer suggestions that will reduce its death rate.

Step 2 Have students generate a list of five or six people or groups that are connected to the problem. These people become the characters involved in the simulation. Example: licensed hunters, research scientists, zookeepers, ecotourism guides, Inuit, and oil company executives.

Step 3 Divide the class evenly into groups. Assign each group the perspective or role of one of the character groups identified in Step 2.

Step 4 Identify an imaginary meeting location for the characters to discuss the problem. As a class, determine the visual aspects of this setting. Identifying concrete elements of the setting helps set the tone of the meeting and builds belief in the simulation. Example: The polar bear meeting takes place in a formal conference room of Environment Canada in Ottawa. Participants are seated at a large wooden table with plush leather chairs and brass nameplates made especially for the meeting. The room has large windows with thick red drapery.

Step 5 Discuss the appropriate posture, tone of voice, choice of words, and rules of etiquette that characters should display in the imaginary setting. Example: You have been invited to Ottawa at the expense of the federal government to discuss the problem of polar bears. Your meeting room is formal and equipped very expensively. How should the characters sit? How should they speak? How should they behave toward each other?

Step 6 Explain to the class that you, the teacher, will be playing a character in the simulation. Your role will be moderator of the discussion. The simulation will begin when you give the signal that you are now "in role" as your character. Example: I will be playing the role of Assistant Deputy Minister of the Environment. The signal for us to begin the simulation will be when I leave the room and re-enter to welcome you all to the meeting.

Step 7 Begin the simulation by entering in role and welcoming the class to the meeting. Stress the characters' expertise and the seriousness of the issue. Example: Good morning everyone, and welcome to our meeting here in Ottawa. As you know, we have come together to discuss the important issue of polar bears. You were all selected to be part of today's discussion because of your reputation, interest, and knowledge of the situation. Thank you on behalf of the Government of Canada for taking time in your busy schedules to help us solve this very serious problem.

Step 8 Explain that students assuming the roles of each type of stakeholder (e.g., licensed hunters, research scientists, zookeepers, ecotourism guides, Inuit, oil company executives) will meet as a committee. (That is, there is one committee of licensed hunters, another of research scientists, etc.) Each committee will prepare an opening statement explaining the importance of the problem to their specific group. Each group selects a spokesperson to present their statement orally. Example: I would like to begin our meeting today by inviting members in each group to take a few minutes together to create an opening statement for the meeting. In your opening statement, please tell us about your current interactions with polar bears and explain their importance in your lives. Please select one spokesperson who will read your statement aloud to the entire group.

Step 9 After hearing all opening statements, give the groups time to prepare two questions for each of the other groups.

Step 10 In role, allow students to pose and answer questions. Any member of a group may respond. During this process, no one else is allowed to interrupt or pose a secondary question. After offering an answer, the selected group poses another question to a different group. The session continues in this format. Moderate and coordinate the flow of questions and solicit clarification or further explanation as needed.

Step 11 When the questioning process is completed, instruct students to form new groups. The task of the new groups is to develop suggestions that would be reasonable and beneficial to all stakeholders. Groups present their suggestions orally. Record the suggestions on chart paper and thank students for their participation in the meeting.

Step 12 Out of role, have students discuss the suggestions offered by the groups as well as the simulation process (e.g., Are the suggestions logical and plausible? How well was each group listened to? How did the groups reach their decisions?). Other follow-up activities may include having the class compose letters to the government or a local newspaper voicing their concerns and offering their suggestions.

Table 2.11 Interview Framework for Careers, Intermediate Grades

Step 1: Character Selection

Have students select a career in which they believe they would be successful and respected. Have students retain their real names throughout the exercise. Do not allow students to assume the role of an existing or historical person. Example: Students may wish to become politicians but they may not portray themselves as Prime Minister Stephen Harper.

Step 2: Question Preparation

Have the class generate a list of open-ended questions they could use when interviewing any professional. Example: What made you decide to go into this line of work? What training or education did you complete? What qualities make you successful in your job? Have each student select six or seven questions from the class list to ask a successful career person.

Working in teacher-assigned pairs, students decide who will be the "professional" and who will be the "reporter." Provide general information to help establish the context. Example: The successful career person is well known in the community. The local newspaper has invited her to be the subject of a neighbourhood success story. Both the professional and the reporter know that the interview is an important moment for them and their families, and they want to make a good impression.

Then, provide additional information specific to each role. Example: The reporter is new to the job and has never conducted a live interview before. Today he will fill in for an absent senior colleague. He receives the interview questions minutes before the interview begins. He knows nothing about the person he is interviewing. This interview is very important to the reporter. It will define his career at the newspaper.

Step 3: The Interview

All interviews occur at the same time. They begin with the professional sitting at a desk or table and the reporter entering the room and introducing himself or herself. The professional then responds in one sentence by informing the reporter about his or her career title. Example: The reporter shakes the professional's hand and states, "Good morning, my name is Stephen and I'm here from *Mississauga News* to talk to you about your work." The professional responds by saying, "Thank you very much for your interest in my career as a pilot."

Using the questions selected earlier, the reporter interviews the professional for approximately three minutes. Both students stay in role the entire time. The professionaluses his or her imagination when answering the questions.

Step 4: Role Reversal

Reassign students to new roles as either professionals or reporters (professionals assume the role of reporters and vice versa). Working in newly assigned pairs, reporters and professionals follow the same procedures outlined in the first interview.

Step 5: The Brief Biography

Assign students to groups of three. In turn, students use the information generated in their interviews to tell each other about themselves as successful career people. This is not an additional interview session. Rather, it is an opportunity for students to create brief biographies of their roles while others listen attentively.

Step 6: The Moment of Recognition

Divide the class into groups consisting of approximately four students each. In turn, students within each group create a "frozen picture" (tableau) of the moment when the professionals realized they wanted to pursue their chosen careers. Other members of the group assume the role of "relevant others" who are involved in the professionals' career paths. Example: A successful baker might have decided to follow this career path after learning a family recipe from his or her grandmother. The baker's tableau might depict himself or herself serving family members the baked good. Group members in the tableau would depict the baker's family enjoying the delicious food.

Students take turns creating their tableaux. They describe their "moment of recognition" to their group members, assign tableau characters, and determine the placement, facial expressions, and gestures of characters in the tableau.

Step 7: Class Reflection

Students discuss the interview, tableau, and biography activities as a whole class.

Discussion should focus on the following questions:

1. As reporters, what techniques and strategies did you use to ensure a successful interview?
2. As professionals, how did you respond to the interview answers? What strategies did you use when answering?
3. What factors contributed to the "believability" of your roles? (Consider factors beyond the content of the interview answers, including tone of voice, facial expression, and body language.)
4. How did it feel to portray someone who was successful in a career that you would like to pursue?
5. What aspects of your role as a professional did you choose to highlight in your brief biography?
6. What did you learn about the career of your choice by participating in these activities?

Teacher Voice 2.2

Before moving to the university setting where I instruct pre-service teacher candidates in drama pedagogy, I taught drama in four different Ontario school boards. Although based in the secondary system, I consulted regularly in elementary drama classrooms and also devised a unique theatre program for young audiences that drew more than 3000 elementary students per year. In numerous elementary classrooms I have witnessed the power of drama to enhance cross-curricular skills of literacy, co-operative learning, and perspective taking.

Dr. Debra McLaughlin
Professor

BRINGING LISTENING AND SPEAKING TOGETHER

Choral reading

Show and Tell

This enjoyable activity is a daily routine in many kindergarten and primary grade classrooms. Show and tell, or show and share, requires students to integrate speaking and listening and serves many educative and social goals. As children bring objects from home and share them with the class, the speaker is provided with a forum that enables him or her to forge connections between school and home. At the same time, the other students participate in a listening activity.

When done well, show and tell provides an important vehicle for language development. When done poorly, however, the activity can result in inattention and minimal learning. Some of the pitfalls associated with show and tell include excessive repetition, lack of teacher participation (e.g., attending to menial class activities such as collecting money or forms), and unstructured or unsustainable listening environments. The latter is particularly challenging, as many students are poor presenters and require listeners to exert considerable effort to make meaning of the presentation. Teachers can facilitate this process greatly by expressing interest, asking questions, and prompting faltering presenters. Readers are encouraged to review the critical show and tell routines and procedures listed in Table 2.12.

Assessing Show and Tell Presentations There are a few options available for teachers when assessing students' show and tell performances. For instance, teachers can use a simple observational checklist with room for comments (see Table 2.13). When working with older students, teachers can gain additional information by having

Table 2.12 Show and Tell Routines and Procedures

Presenters
- Need to bring something interesting to talk about
- Need to plan presentation content before speaking
- Can bring only one item at a time
- Should not bring the same item twice
- Should stand at the front of the class
- Need to project voice so that everyone can hear easily
- Should look at the class while speaking
- Should pass the item around so that listeners can view it

Listeners
- Should show interest by paying attention and focusing on the presenter
- Should prepare questions
- Need to provide positive feedback to the presenter

Teachers
- Should show interest and focus on the presentation only
- Should stand to the side
- Should prompt the presenter when necessary
- Should ask questions
- Should remind students of the routines and expectations
- Should not dominate the discussion

Table 2.13 Show and Tell Observational Checklist

- Interesting presentation
- Coherence of presentation
- Voice projection
- Eye contact
- Body language
- Appropriate length
- Vocabulary used

students participate in a debriefing session during which they reflect on their presentation strengths and areas of need. (Such follow-up activities may be intimidating for young students and negatively affect their presentations.) Since each student will have several opportunities to present over a term, teachers can use the collected data to demonstrate growth in oral language and presentation skills.

Public Speaking

Public speaking is the learned art of making a prepared speech in front of an attentive audience. Through practice, students can develop confidence in their abilities to speak clearly and effectively while communicating their ideas to an audience. Usually, students select the topic and the purpose of their presentations, which can range from description, persuasion, information sharing, entertainment, and shared experiences. Public speaking allows for the integration of reading and writing and the development of oral communication skills. Unfortunately, many people of all ages dread public speaking (Santrock & Halonen, 1999; SchoolNet News Network, 2001), making it especially important to provide students with early positive experiences. Table 2.14 provides guidelines for helping students prepare for public speaking presentations.

Student Voice 2.2

> In grade 6, I gave a speech about the Stanley Cup. The kids in the class found it interesting because I told them facts that they didn't know like the history of the Cup and the old names of the hockey teams. I was a little nervous speaking in front of the class at first, but that didn't last long. I would like to do another speech this year—I think I would talk about baseball, basketball, or rock and roll.
>
> Zach
> Grade 7 student

Debates

Debates are basically structured discussions. They are an old tradition extending to the ancient Greek philosophers. Today, they are viewed as an effective format for generating excitement about an issue, especially when groups hold opposing views.

When debates are held in the classroom, learning occurs across all communication areas, including listening, speaking, reading, and writing. Participating in a debate can facilitate students' public speaking skills, critical thinking skills, research skills, and collaborative skills (www.csdf-fcde.ca/english/resources/NLSDU_Teachers_Guide_to_Debate.pdf). Students become engaged in "structured controversy" during which more than one side of an issue is discussed and they are required to back their arguments with research and reason (www.saskdebate.com). Debates also encourage analytical thinking and the ability to distinguish fact from opinion as well as the ability to identify biases. Through these activities, young people begin to examine moral and social issues in a way that encourages exploration of competing views and contributes to more informed development of ideas and world views. The role of the teacher is to ensure that the classroom provides a respectful, ethical, and collaborative context in which these processes can unfold.

Typically, debates consist of two teams, one of which supports a proposed resolution (the affirmative) while the other team (the negative) opposes it. Beyond familiarizing students with these terms, teachers should emphasize the importance of debate in almost every workplace (students initially may identify these skills as relevant to politicians and lawyers only). Debate topics typically emerge from current events, novel study, or school activities and tend to be more meaningful if they are generated by students rather than chosen by teachers. Unlike the process of public speaking, students must be prepared to react to contentions made by their peers, making it impossible to prepare exact speeches. Rather, students must prepare discussion points and be prepared to defend their views. Debates vary in their formality, ranging from informal discussions to highly structured ones. Teachers are advised to hold informal debates in the middle and junior grades, when students have few relevant experiences, and move toward formal debates in the intermediate grades.

Table 2.14 Preparing Students for Public Presentations

Planning As a class, discuss the purpose for the speech at hand, the intended audience, and the process that students need to follow, from selecting a topic to delivering it publicly. A general discussion of the nature and types of speeches as well as factors that contribute to making a speech interesting is also appropriate.

Have students brainstorm possible topics for speeches in a large group and then form small groups for further personal decision making. Teachers should encourage students to use graphic organizers to support their planning. Over a defined interval, students need to declare the topics they have selected.

Writing When all speech topics have been selected and declared, group them by category. Categories can include but are not limited to:

a) Direct experience

b) Topics of interest

c) Research topics

Regroup topics according to whether the intention is to persuade, inform, or entertain.

Reiterate the importance of the audience. Students need to recognize that there may be more than one type of audience that must be considered (e.g., peers, parents, judges, school board officials).

Introduce the three main parts of the speech and provide critical questions that students can use to determine the "goodness" of these elements.

1. *Introduction*: Does the introduction establish the topic of the speech and gain audience interest?
2. *Body:* Are points logically organized and not redundant? Has the interest of the listener been maintained by starting each section with a strong point and ending it with an even stronger one?
3. *Conclusion:* Does the conclusion reflect the original purpose as stated in the introduction? Does it serve to summarize and reinforce the overall message?

Have students consider the following questions and prompts according to the topic and speech type:

1. *Persuasive speeches:* Do the main ideas of the speech contribute directly to the primary reason for choosing the topic? Does the speech represent the speaker's beliefs about the topic at hand?
2. *Informative speeches:* Has the topic been reviewed in a comprehensive manner. Have who, what, where, when, why, and how questions been addressed?
3. *Entertaining speeches*: Will the experiences, stories, and information presented here amuse the audience? Will it sustain the audience's attention for an extended interval?

Presenting Show students how to prepare cue cards to support the presentation of their speeches. Tell them that it is not necessary to memorize speeches "word-for-word." Rather, they should be rehearsed well enough that they can maintain some eye contact with the audience. Discuss the importance of posture, voice projection, and speed of delivery. Have students practise their speeches both in class and at home.

Note: Presenting a speech is an easier exercise for some students than others, with some students experiencing excessive stress and anxiety as a result of this process. In such cases, it is important that teachers provide students with appropriate counselling and coping strategies.

Informal Debates In informal debates, teachers help students clarify a topic for discussion. Students are then provided with time to formulate and record their thoughts, either affirming or negating the resolution. The teacher asks those who wish to speak in support of the resolution to stand on one side of the classroom and those who wish to speak against it to stand on the other side of the room. If students are uncertain about which side they wish to support, they remain in their seats.

A lectern from which speakers address the class is set up at the front of the room. A student from the supporting side of the debate is asked to make the first statement. Then the opposing side counters with an alternative statement. Students take turns, speaking for or against the issue. Throughout the debate, students can physically reposition themselves to reflect a change in orientation, including any students who were undecided and had remained seated. Eventually, one side of the room will be more crowded than the other and the teacher can declare an outcome. Alternatively, a panel of students can be selected to determine when a conclusion has been reached.

Caution As there is little preparation for this type of impromptu debate, students must be reminded to refrain from repeating or paraphrasing the arguments made by their peers. Instead, they can demonstrate their agreement by moving to the area that the speaker represents.

Formal Debates Before students engage in a formal debate, it is wise to provide some type of demonstration, perhaps by reading a recorded debate or watching a video.

Formal debates usually consist of two teams, with two to four people on each team. The amount of preparation time is determined by the debate topic. The two most common types of topics are policy debates (e.g., Should students be required to wear uniforms?) and value debates (e.g., Are we living in the best time ever?). While students require substantial time to research their topics for policy debates, less time is required to prepare for value debates, which are generally philosophical in nature.

Formal debates follow a structured procedure. A chairperson is designated to introduce the participants and to call on them in turn, a timekeeper is designated to monitor each speaker, and a judge (or a group of judges) can be assigned to determine the winning team. While many scheduling variations are possible, the following is one example involving teams consisting of two affirmative and two negative presenters.

Speaker	Time
First affirmative	2 minutes
First negative	2 minutes
Second affirmative	2 minutes
Second negative	2 minutes
Break for further preparation	2 minutes
Affirmative summary and rebuttal	2 minutes
Negative summary and rebuttal	2 minutes

Evaluation Presentation style, research, and delivery should all be factors when deliberating the winning debate team. Specific students can be appointed as "judges" (either by their teachers or classmates) or all students can be provided with a ballot. After a class has become expert at debating, an outside judge such as a school administrator can be invited to determine the outcome. As with all skills, the debating process is a learned one that requires repeated practice over the course of the school year.

Readers' Theatre

Contextual analysis and story dramatization

Readers' Theatre involves the dramatic reading of a script by a group of students. Scripts can be read directly from a book or can be adapted from a text. Common text

Table 2.15 How to Produce a Readers' Theatre

Step 1: Select a Script

Teachers either can choose the script or have students provide input with respect to potential readings. If students are writing the script, teachers need to provide them with adequate preparation time in the classroom (minimizing the need to complete this work as homework).

Step 2: Rehearsal

Teachers will need to provide students with classroom time for rehearsal. Students should consider their use of voice and pitch as well as their gestures and facial expressions as part of this time. They should be encouraged to be familiar with the script by reading it several times, but should avoid over-rehearsing.

Step 3: Production

Students typically sit or stand in a row in front the classroom and read their lines in turn. At times, students may wish to orchestrate the entrance and exit of special characters. If sitting, readers may wish to stand when speaking their lines or take a step forward if they are standing. The entire production is carried by the strength of the interpretive reading. Only in the most exceptional circumstances can students use a significant prop.

sources include fairy tales, fables, novel sections, short stories, and historical documents. Examples include a dialogue from the Chicken Little story, *The Sky Is Falling*, or the trial of Louis Riel. Alternatively, students can create their own scripts.

Working in small groups of four to six students, group members are assigned the roles of specific characters. They are charged with reading in an interpretive manner using the exact words contained in the text. There is also a narrator who reads the non-speaking parts that set the stage and explain the characters' actions. Depending on the length of the production, more than one student may assume this narrator role.

This kind of drama activity is unique in that the narrator and characters sit or stand in close proximity, with the interpretational and the emotional elements being expressed through voices, facial expressions, or gestures. There are few physical actions or movements associated with the dramatic presentation and there are no costumes or props. Students do not memorize their parts but rather "read" from the script. (Note: effective readings require that students be familiar with the text prior to presentation.) As a result, students require minimum time to prepare to participate in Readers' Theatre. Table 2.15 describes the steps that should be followed to produce a Readers' Theatre.

Caution Teachers need to select dialogue-intensive text when considering materials for Readers' Theatre, remembering that all other sections will be read by the narrator.

SUGGESTIONS FOR PROFESSIONAL DEVELOPMENT

1. Develop a list of family and early literacy programs in your community. What type of programming is available? Consider volunteering at a literacy centre.
2. Volunteer in a kindergarten classroom. Lead circle time if possible. Make careful observations about the use of routines, oral language, literacy materials, students'

social patterns, and play. Consider the differences between boys' and girls' language and play patterns.

3. Read about Jean Piaget's four stages of cognitive development (http://thebrain.mcgill.ca/flash/i/i_09/i_09_p/i_09_p_dev/i_09_p_dev.html). Piaget (1959) developed a theory of cognitive development in which he asserted that thought comes before language and that language is a way of representing thought. Children learn and develop their language skills by forming and testing hypotheses, experimenting with sounds and words, and exploring the relationships between the two. Consider the implications of Piaget's theory with respect to how we conduct language learning in classrooms today and the belief that *Silence is NOT golden!*
4. Select a contemporary topic of general interest to students (e.g., protecting the environment, the role of media in young people's lives, the importance of volunteerism). Facilitate a grand conversation with a group of students in a primary grade (e.g., grade 2) and in a junior grade (e.g., grade 4). Does the quality of the conversation differ across the grades? Do students in each grade present unique arguments? Do they present shared viewpoints? How much facilitation is required to engage students in conversation and what techniques can teachers use to encourage all students to participate in the discussion?

CHILDREN'S LITERATURE REFERENCES

Andrews, J. (2003). *Very last first time*. Toronto, ON: Groundwood Books.

Burnett, F. H. (2010). *The secret garden*. New York, NY: Candlewick.

Granfield, L. (1995). *In Flanders Fields: The story of the poem by John McCrae*. Toronto, ON: Lester Publishing.

Kraus, R. (1984). *Leo the late bloomer*. New York, NY: HarperCollins.

Levine, K. (2002). *Hana's suitcase*. Toronto, ON: Second Story Press.

Osborne, M. P. (1989). *Favorite Greek myths*. New York, NY: Scholastic Inc.

Pearson, K. (1989). *The sky is falling*. Markham, ON: Viking Kestral.

White, E. B. (2004). *Charlotte's web*. New York, NY: HarperCollins.

Wynne-Jones, T. (2000). *Some of the kinder planets: Stories*. Toronto, ON: Groundwood Books.

Yee, P. (1996). *Ghost train*. Toronto, ON: Groundwood Books.

MyEducationLab

MyEducationLab is an interactive, virtual learning tool that will help improve your understanding of the concepts taught in this textbook and in your course. Through this engaging resource, you will have access to simulations of real classroom experiences, exercises that will help you improve your knowledge of key concepts, and additional resources that will help you in your teaching career. Use this online tool with your textbook to help you succeed in your studies and beyond!

Chapter 3
Assessing and Evaluating Your Students as Language Users

Learning Objectives

In this chapter you will discover

- How to recognize and distinguish the various purposes of assessment.
- How to reconceptualize the role of assessment in student learning.
- How to administer and interpret standardized assessments across the language arts.
- How to identify controversies associated with the use of high-stakes assessment.
- How to complete general assessment techniques for determining students' beginning reading skills and abilities.
- How to complete miscue analyses, running records, and informal reading inventories.
- How to implement a response to intervention model when working with students who have reading and writing difficulties.
- How to develop and implement classroom-based assessments for students' reading comprehension.

TODD ROBINSON: BALANCING CURRICULUM, ASSESSMENT, AND EVALUATION IN A GRADES 6 AND 7 SPLIT CLASS

Todd Robinson is in his eleventh year of teaching and has spent most of those years with the junior grades. Todd emphasizes that he is grateful for his job when so many beginning teachers are looking for permanency. He also indicates that he enjoys teaching preadolescent students. "I like being with these kids while they grow up and that is no small thing. I think that the life lessons that I become a part of are very important, often eclipsing the actual curriculum." Todd acknowledges that the job has changed dramatically over the years and believes that it involves much more than imparting curriculum knowledge, developing associated skills, and helping students obtain information. He believes that much of his daily in-class time involves helping students develop as individuals and understand themselves as learners.

Todd finds teaching a grades 6 and 7 split class challenging given the age and maturity differences among his students. He also finds managing the curriculum across the two grades to be "tricky." When asked about his language arts program, Todd replied, "My expectations are a little different for the two groups but I try to focus on the big picture: what these students are going to need for their future work in terms of writing, speaking, reading, and becoming good listeners." Todd uses technology to support his students' learning and finds them to be "technologically savvy." He expresses concerns, however, that sites such as Wikipedia help create a false impression that finding comprehensive material is easy. He considers it a challenge to keep students from using these sites to "slap scads of material together into a report" without bringing a critical lens to the information or synthesizing it. He therefore tries to encourage them to become critical consumers of the content and quality of what they find on the internet.

Assessment and evaluation in a split-grade class also represent a challenge for Todd. Although the criteria may remain the same for a particular task, he establishes different expectations for each grade. He talks about this issue with his students so they understand that, as they mature, expectations become higher. However, Todd qualifies this by saying he is also adamant about meeting students at their current levels: "The grade number on the door is not as important as where the student is and moving him or her forward."

Each student keeps a comprehensive portfolio that is sent home at the end of each month. Todd decides which artifacts will be included, with representative samples from all tasks. Recently, his students completed a science unit exploring different types of aircraft. Before beginning the unit, the class discussed the learning expectations they wanted to achieve and the criteria they would use to evaluate the project. Todd used these criteria when grading the assignment. The independent study, along with a copy of the expectations and the students' grades, were sent home as part of an end-of-the-month portfolio.

Culminating tasks are important components of Todd's language arts program. Ideally, these tasks are integrated in nature, tapping into several skill sets and requiring problem solving. Todd also believes that students should be provided with choice when responding. Backward design is used when developing these activities, starting with establishing the information and skills that students are expected to acquire and then working backwards to determine appropriate tasks to ensure that these expectations are met.

Finally, Todd is a firm believer in the value of Read Aloud programs. He read the first two books of a trilogy in class and was gratified when about two-thirds of his students took the initiative to read the third book independently. When reading aloud, Todd takes advantage of teachable moments and believes that these oral language and critical thinking discussions are among the most productive components of his language arts program, with students engaging in intense conversations about who they are, what they believe, and various life issues. Aware that his students do not have the experience of living in a diverse society, he read aloud *Elijah of Buxton* by Christopher Paul Curtis, a story that reflects his own historical and cultural background.

Todd also believes in the benefits of working collaboratively with his colleagues. His division holds regular meetings about learning and teaching pathways. At these meetings, teachers also identify areas of common concern. Once a concern is identified, they establish goals that are communicated to parents through newsletters. Currently, the teachers in the junior and intermediate divisions are working on understanding "point of view" (as part of critical thinking). To help establish these foci, teachers consult the results of various standardized tests. They then ask themselves what can be done to help students move forward in mastering this particular skill. Extensive records are kept, starting with a pretest to establish beginning points (measured in percentages). Once targeted instruction has been provided, students complete a post-test to determine "if we have closed the gap a bit." Throughout the intervention, teachers keep observational records so they have data that substantiate changes throughout the learning process. Todd notes the powerful learning gains that can be achieved when teachers work collaboratively.

REFLECTIVE ACTIVITY

Reflect on a time in your schooling when you had a positive experience with evaluation. Consider a test on which you did well, a presentation that was well received, a report card of which you were proud, or a project that received high praise.

- Identify why this is a positive memory.
- What aspects do you remember?
- Who did you tell and what was their reaction?

Now think back to a time when you had a negative experience with evaluation. Remember the circumstances and factors that contributed to the negative experience.

- How did you feel about yourself?
- Who did you tell and what was their reaction?
- Compare the two experiences and discuss the differences with a peer.

Now reflect on a time (if you can) when you received a poor evaluation and did not feel negative. What contributed to this experience? Alternatively, think about a time when you received a good evaluation but did not feel positive about the experience. What contributed to these feelings?

- Compare these two experiences and share your thoughts with a peer.
- What (if any) overall conclusions can you draw based on these past memories?

Accountability became a watchword for educators in the 1990s (Earl, 2003) as it became evident that we were moving toward a globalized economy. Concerns were being expressed in countries around the world about the quality of education its citizens were receiving and whether graduates would be able to compete in the world economy. Equity issues were also raised about the status of disadvantaged youth and whether they were being further disadvantaged by less-than-optimum schooling that denied them opportunities to reach their full potential. Pressure began to be asserted on school boards to provide the public with information about the curriculum and how students compared with their peers across Canada and around the world. This caused an increased interest in standardized testing and statistical information about schools and school systems both locally and nationally.

The Organisation for Economic Co-operation and Development (OECD) conducts research in 65 countries that make up 90 percent of the world's economies through the Programme for International Student Assessment (PISA). These standardized tests are administered to 15-year-olds in the areas of math, science, and reading. The tests require students to draw on their prior knowledge, analytical and problem-solving skills, and communication skills. It is believed that a high ranking on PISA correlates to economic success, making the test an indicator of whether school systems are preparing students adequately for the emerging global economy. Testing is conducted every three years, with the most recent results (2009) indicating that all Canadian provinces performed at or above the OECD average in all three subject areas.

On a national level, teachers throughout Canada are required to administer a number of provincial standardized tests to students each spring. These tests are frequently used to make comparisons across students, classes, schools, and boards of education, with results often reported in the press.

While individual teachers can feel undue pressure if their students perform poorly, with resulting pressure being placed on students, the purpose of using standardized tests is to improve the quality of education (Hart & Teeter, 2001). Teachers and schools can use the results most effectively for instructional planning and monitoring students' learning progress. In these contexts, results can be especially useful in determining students' relative areas of learning strengths and needs. Regardless of how educators feel about large-scale standardized tests and their subsequent comparisons and conclusions, it is important for teachers to be well versed in all assessment and evaluation procedures, as they are a reality in today's teaching profession.

In this chapter, we provide an overview of the general purposes of assessment. Detailed information about the administration and interpretation of standardized tests across the language arts is provided, including discussion of the controversy related to the use of high-stakes assessments. We then shift focus to the assessment of early reading skills, including the use of miscue analysis, running records, and informal reading inventories. We provide this focus as a strong foundation, since reading skills are associated with academic success (Jackson & Coltheart, 2001). The implementation of response to intervention models is also discussed with regards to students who demonstrate reading difficulties. We end the chapter with a discussion of teacher-created, classroom-based reading comprehension assessments, acknowledging that these assessments are used most frequently by teachers. Information regarding standardized and teacher-created assessments for listening, speaking, writing, viewing, and visually representing is provided throughout the remaining chapters in this book.

Administering a formal reading inventory

PURPOSE OF ASSESSMENT

Assessment and evaluation are two interconnected processes. Assessment is the process of collecting, synthesizing, and interpreting information. It involves decision making regarding student progress and instructional planning. Evaluation is the process of interpreting collected data and assigning an associated value or mark. Such values can be numerical, alphabetical, or categorical. Collectively, assessment provides teachers with the means to understand, document, and enhance student learning through the development and implementation of relevant instruction (Brookhart, 2004; Popham, 2008; Valencia, 2011).

Assessment can vary in its format and purpose and is often conceptualized as diagnostic, formative, or summative. While, historically, assessment has been largely summative in nature, there is increasing emphasis on formative assessment processes in the classroom (Earl, 2003; Popham, 2008).

Diagnostic Assessment

Diagnostic assessment is typically completed prior to instruction, with the intention of analyzing students' learning needs and guiding instructional planning. These assessments may be delivered to either groups of students or individuals. For instance, teachers in the primary grades often complete running records with their students at the beginning of the school year to gather insights about their reading levels. Alternatively, teachers may request that individual students who they believe are experiencing reading or writing difficulties complete more extensive assessments to determine appropriate instructional accommodations or modifications. These assessments are often administered by resource teachers or other professionals in the school (e.g., psychometrist, speech-language pathologist) and may require specialized knowledge for their interpretation (see Interpreting Standardized Assessments below; McKenna & Dougherty Stahl, 2009; Popham, 2008; Richek, Caldwell, Holt Jennings, & Lerner 2005). Teachers ultimately have an important role in implementing any recommendations resulting from these assessments as part of classroom instruction and are encouraged to review these instruments critically with respect to evaluating their fit with classroom curriculum.

Formative Assessment

Formative assessment is completed throughout an instructional unit with the intention of providing feedback to students about their learning and performance (e.g., what facts, concepts, and skills are being acquired successfully; what facts, concepts, and skills require additional attention and focus). For instance, teachers may have students submit draft copies of their writing as part of the writing process, providing them with guiding feedback with respect to the content and form of the composition. Similarly, teachers may engage students in structured discussions throughout a novel study to monitor their understanding of the story elements and their ability to analyze content critically. To be most effective, this feedback must be specific to individual students and responsive to their learning strengths and needs. As a result, teachers will need to differentiate instruction (William, 2010).

Equally important, formative assessment provides information to teachers with respect to their instructional success and subsequent planning (e.g., where to focus additional instructional emphasis, concepts that require reteaching, and which students require additional support and instruction; Black & Wiliam, 2009; Popham, 2008). For example, upon reviewing students' writing drafts, teachers may decide to revisit the use of descriptive language or quotations when representing dialogue. Alternatively, after reading several chapters of a novel, they may instruct students to complete open-minded portraits or double-entry journals (see Chapter 5, Comprehension of Narrative Text) to encourage them to consider the complexities of the main characters.

Performance-Based Assessment Performance-based assessment is a type of formative assessment that focuses on student achievement and the process of learning. It is considered to be in alignment with standards-based education and outcomes-based education. Performance-based assessments involve providing students with a well-defined task in which they are required to respond by producing, creating, or performing in an authentic manner (Afferbach, 2007; Popham, 2008). Examples of performance-based tasks include creating a painting, researching a report, and preparing a presentation, exhibition, or performance of any kind (e.g., dance, music, athletics, public reading). A more extensive discussion of using performance-based assessment is provided at the end of this chapter.

Interim Assessment Interim assessment is situated between formative and summative assessment. In general, it mirrors summative or diagnostic assessment and is administered to individual students periodically throughout the school year (usually three to five times). Interim assessments provide teachers with instructional feedback, predictions, and evaluations (Valencia, 2011). For instance, students' performance can provide teachers with insights about subsequent instruction. Interim assessments can also be used as screening tools to identify students who may be experiencing reading and writing difficulties. For instance, teachers working with beginning readers may wish to assess students' phonological awareness and word attack skills throughout the primary grades. Older students may benefit from periodic assessments of reading fluency and comprehension. Finally, interim assessments can provide indicators of how students will perform on summative measures, including high-stakes assessments (Valencia, 2011). In the latter case, teachers must evaluate fit between assessments (especially if commercially produced) and curriculum as well as correlates with other measures of performance.

Summative Assessment

Typically, summative assessment is administered at the end of an instructional unit and is used to determine students' learning and performance for related information and skills (Popham, 2008; Valencia, 2011). For example, teachers may have students complete a unit test or culminating project to determine their understanding of the characters and events represented in novels such as *Hatchet* by Gary Paulsen or *The Giver* by Lois Lowry. Students may be asked to make multi-modal presentations or perform research tasks. Experts believe that this is the most frequently used form of assessment, with teachers and students alike being most familiar with it. Within the past decade, there has been greater use of high-stakes standardized tests as summative assessments. We discuss the controversy around these instruments in the Standardized Assessments section below.

Reconceptualizing Assessment

Recently, there has been in shift in the language and underlying thinking used to identify the purposes and functions of assessment (Earl, 2003; Manitoba Education, Citizenship and Youth, 2006; Popham, 2008). Assessment is now viewed as a key component of learning for both teachers and students, who are viewed as learning partners. Assessment provides an indication of what students understand and a blueprint for deciding what to do next.

Teacher Voice 3.1

Exemplary teachers for decades have known that teaching is "data-driven." Educators are now formally engaged in assessment "as learning." This professional practice means we must integrate baseline assessment with daily observation, anecdotal evidence, and moderated marking with colleagues as we allow student work to drive instruction.

Dan Trainor, M.Ed.
Elementary teacher and principal

Assessment for Learning Assessment for learningis most readily equated with assessment that is summative in nature and often associated with the development of common instructional goals as well as uniform instruction and assessment. It occurs after instruction and is used to verify what students know and which standards they have achieved. It is also used to determine students' placements relative to their peers. Assessment for learning has been broken into three components.

> Assessment **for** Learning is formative assessment that occurs during instruction to inform the next stage of the learning.
>
> Assessment **as** Learning is assessment that occurs when students monitor their own learning and use feedback from their self monitoring to make adjustments, adaptations, or changes in what they understand. Students are involved in the construction and analyses of assessment materials. This process is believed to support students' metacognitive development and problem-solving skills and occurs during instruction. In order to engage in such reflection, students must also possess a clear understanding about the standards and criteria associated with individual tasks and activities.
>
> Assessment **of** Learning is a summative assessment designed to certify the learning and to report to parents and students about their progress. (Earl, 2006)

In this model, the priority is to facilitate and enhance student learning and it involves consideration of students' areas of strength and need. As part of this process, teachers are challenged to review the effectiveness of their instructional practices routinely and adjust their instruction accordingly (see the Differentiated Instruction section in Chapter 11, Working with Students with Diverse Learning Needs). Students often are privy to the results of this assessment so they can regulate and adjust their learning processes accordingly. Assessment as learning involves having students reflect on the products of their learning as well as on their learning processes.

Performance-Based Accountability Performance-based accountability (PBA) encourages changes in schools that will enhance student learning and success (Ben Jaafar & Earl, 2008). The move toward PBA policies has fostered changes that encourage and enhance students' successful learning. Five identifiable dimensions comprise the PBA framework (Ben Jaafar & Earl, 2008). These five dimensions are testing structures, standards setting, consequential use of data, reporting, and professional involvement (Armstrong, 2002).

1. **Testing structures.** Testing structures describes the scope, prevalence, and timing of the tests. Therefore, the subjects, the grades, the timing, and the release of results provide the shape of the testing system.
2. **Standards setting.** Content standards are usually established to relate to the learning outcomes in curriculum documents. This alignment will serve to frame the interpretation of results (Hamilton & Koretz, 2002).
3. **Consequential use of data.** Student performance is measured by provincial tests and then value judgments are used to translate the results into something that holds meaning. For instance, either achievement levels or ranking of students can be done. Awards or grade promotion can be consequences, as can public reporting of results to attract students or funding (Hess, 2002).

4. **Reporting.** The intended audience is determined and then reporting is conducted based on performance standards and the testing structure. Performance levels of specific groups of students can be reported.
5. **Professional involvement.** This dimension refers to the level of involvement of the educators, which is essential if change is to occur (Hargraves, Earl, Moore, & Manning, 2001). This dimension is included in all models of PBA but the degree and type of involvement may differ. This is the critical factor in determining how educators make meaning from the results and use that meaning to improve school practices.

STANDARDIZED ASSESSMENTS

Standardized tests are commercially prepared instruments that measure students' performances across uniform conditions. They involve the use of established "standard" procedures for administration, scoring, and reporting (McMillan, 2008). While teacher-created tests tend to focus on information and skill sets that are associated with specific instructional units, standardized tests focus on information and skill sets that are common across classrooms. They also are designed to demonstrate reliability and validity; that is, they produce consistent and reproducible measures of student performance (reliability) as well as a measure for a predefined concept or skill (validity). Information pertaining to the reliability and validity of an instrument is presented in the accompanying technical or instructors' manual, but the onus is on test providers to review this information in consideration of the unique needs of their students.

Most commercially available reading and writing assessments can be categorized along the following dimensions: group versus individual tests, norm-referenced versus criterion-referenced, and screening versus diagnostic (McKenna & Dougherty Stahl, 2009). Table 3.1 provides an overview of the primary characteristics of each dimension and Table 3.2 lists examples of standardized instruments that can be used by teachers and other education professionals to assess students' learning across the language arts.

Administering Standardized Assessments

Throughout their careers, most language arts teachers will experience situations in which they recommend individual students, who they have identified as experiencing reading or writing challenges, for extended assessment and possible identification for additional specialized instruction. As part of this process, teachers may have the opportunity to work with other education professionals, including school psychometrists; speech-language pathologists; individuals who test and measure mental and psychological ability, efficiency, potential, and functioning; and psychologists. Teachers may elect to administer some form of standardized tests to groups or individual students (in the latter case, often as a prerequisite for referral for an extended assessment). In either case, teachers can play an important role in administering standardized tests and preparing students to complete these tests. Table 3.3 outlines some guidelines for this process.

Table 3.1 Characteristics of Standardized Tests

Group versus individual	Group tests can be administered to students in small-group or classroom settings. Group tests usually require students to interpret and respond to test items independently. Test givers may sometimes read aloud a formatted set of instructions. Group tests are time efficient. Group tests may be administered to individual students, but individual tests cannot be administered to groups of students. Individual tests are administered to one student at a time and usually require students to provide verbal responses. Administration of individual tests is dependent on students' responses, often providing opportunities for metacognitive prompting and observation. Individual test findings are generally considered to be more reliable, accurate, and informative than those associated with group tests.
Norm-referenced versus criterion-referenced	Norm-referenced tests allow test givers to compare individual students' performances to those of a group of similar children who completed the assessment previously. Test givers are responsible for reviewing information about test norms when determining whether the test instrument is an appropriate "fit" for students. Criterion-referenced tests allow test givers to compare individual students' performances to pre-established benchmarks or expectations. Many standards-based accountability tests (e.g., EQAO) are criterion-referenced. Norm-referenced tests are generally more common than criterion-referenced tests and provide greater insights about student performance.
Screening versus diagnostic	Screening tests provide a broad estimate of students' overall achievement level and often provide insights about areas that require more refined assessment. Diagnostic tests provide specific and detailed information about students' strengths and areas of need. These tests are especially useful for instructional planning. Diagnostic tests are one of several data sources, including classroom observation, used to assess students' performance and determine instructional focus.

Table 3.2 Examples of Standardized Instruments Used to Assess Students' Abilities across the Language Arts

Skill	Standardized Assessment
Word knowledge	*Expressive Vocabulary Test*, 2nd edition (EVT-2) *Receptive One-Word Picture Vocabulary Test*, 4th edition (ROWPVT-4) *Peabody Picture Vocabulary Test*, 4th edition (PPVT-4) *Listening Comprehension (LC) Scale* *Oral Expression (OE) Scale*
Phonological awareness	*The Test of Awareness of Language Systems* (TALS) *The Phonological Awareness Test*, 2nd edition (PAT-2) *Comprehensive Test of Phonological Processing* (CTOPP) *Phonological Awareness Literacy Screening* *Lindamood Auditory Conceptualization Test* (LAC-3)
Verbal language	*Test of Language Development: Primary*, 4th edition (TLD-4) *Test of Language Development: Intermediate*, 4th edition (TLD-4) *Test of Adolescent and Adult Language*, 4th edition (TOAL-4)
Memory	*Test of Memory and Learning*, 2nd edition (TOMAL-2) *Learning Efficiency Test*, 2nd edition (LET-II) *Children's Memory Scale* (CMS)
Word attack and decoding	*Test of Word Reading Efficiency* (TOWRE) *Graded Word Reading Test* (GWRT) *Single Word Reading Test*, 16th edition (SWRT-16) *Slosson Oral Reading Test*, revised 12th edition (SORT R3)
Reading (oral)	*Gray Oral Reading Tests*, 4th edition (GORT-4) *DIBELS Oral Reading Fluency* *Test of Oral Reading and Comprehension Skills*, 4th edition (TORCS-4)
Reading comprehension (silent)	*Gates-MacGinitie Reading Test*, 4th edition (GMRT-4) *Stanford Diagnostic Reading Test*, 4th edition *Test of Reading Comprehension*, 4th edition (TORC-4)
Listening comprehension	*The Listening Comprehension Test – 2* (LCT-2) *The Listening Test*
Writing and spelling	*Diagnostic Screening Test: Spelling*, 3rd edition (DSTS-3) *Test of Early Written Language*, 2nd edition (TEWL-2) *Test of Written Language*, 4th edition (TOWL-4) *Written Language Assessment* (WLA) *Test of Written Spelling*, 4th edition (TWS-4) *Test of Grammatical Skills*
Comprehensive reading and writing assessment batteries	*Canadian Achievement Test*, 4th edition (CAT-4) *Canadian Test of Basic Skills* (CTBS) *Stanford Achievement Test*, 10th edition (Stanford 10) *Woodcock Diagnostic Reading Battery*, 3rd edition (WJIII DRB) *Analysis of Reading Difficulty*, 3rd edition (DAR)

Table 3.3 Guidelines for Administering Standardized Tests

- Be familiar with guidelines and instructions for test administration. Carefully review information contained in the examiner's booklet.
- Prepare the classroom or designate a suitable space for testing. Ensure proper lighting, seating, etc.
- Seek advice from others who have administered previous assessments. Be familiar with schoolwide policies and protocols.
- Be familiar with guidelines and protocols associated with providing students with accommodations and modifications.
- Provide students with practice in processing verbal and written instructions.
- Provide students with opportunities to complete example tests when available.
- Ensure that students are familiar with the format of test items (e.g., multiple-choice, true/false, short answer), the criteria associated with successful responses, and any restrictions associated with test completion (e.g., time limits).
- Provide students with general test-taking strategies and skills (e.g., relaxation exercises, time management, skipping difficult items, checking responses).
- Provide students with general information about the purpose of the assessment, its scoring protocol, and its intended use whenever possible.
- Be familiar with reporting methods associated with assessment findings as they relate to students, parents, and other relevant stakeholders (e.g., media, resource teachers, counsellors, speech-language pathologists).

Interpreting Standardized Assessments

Regardless of whether teachers are directly involved in the administration of standardized assessments, they often are privy to the results of this testing, with the expectation that they will provide appropriate and responsive instruction. To accomplish this task, teachers need to understand whether students completed test items with relative ease and accuracy or with difficulty. They also must be able to judge how students performed relative to their peers, with reference to the normal distribution (or what is sometimes referred to as the "bell curve") being especially useful. In a normal distribution, the majority of scores cluster around the mean and relatively fewer scores fall farther away from it. Many natural phenomena, including height, weight, and intelligence, tend to follow the normal curve. Similarly, normative scores obtained for assessments that are reliable and valid demonstrate a normal distribution (McKenna & Dougherty Stahl, 2009; Richek et al., 2005). Figure 3.1 provides an illustration of the normal distribution curve and its defining characteristics, including mean and standard deviation. Briefly, the mean represents the average of a group of scores and the standard deviation represents how much those scores vary from the mean on average.

When scores fall along the normal distribution, norm-based performance indicators are usually used for interpretation. Most test-makers provide multiple forms of norm-based data, including percentile rank scores, stanine scores, *z*-scores, grade-equivalent scores, and age-equivalent scores (McKenna & Dougherty Stahl, 2009; Richek et al., 2005).

Raw Scores Raw scores represent the number of correct responses students achieve on a defined set of test items. Raw scores are difficult to interpret and have little comparative

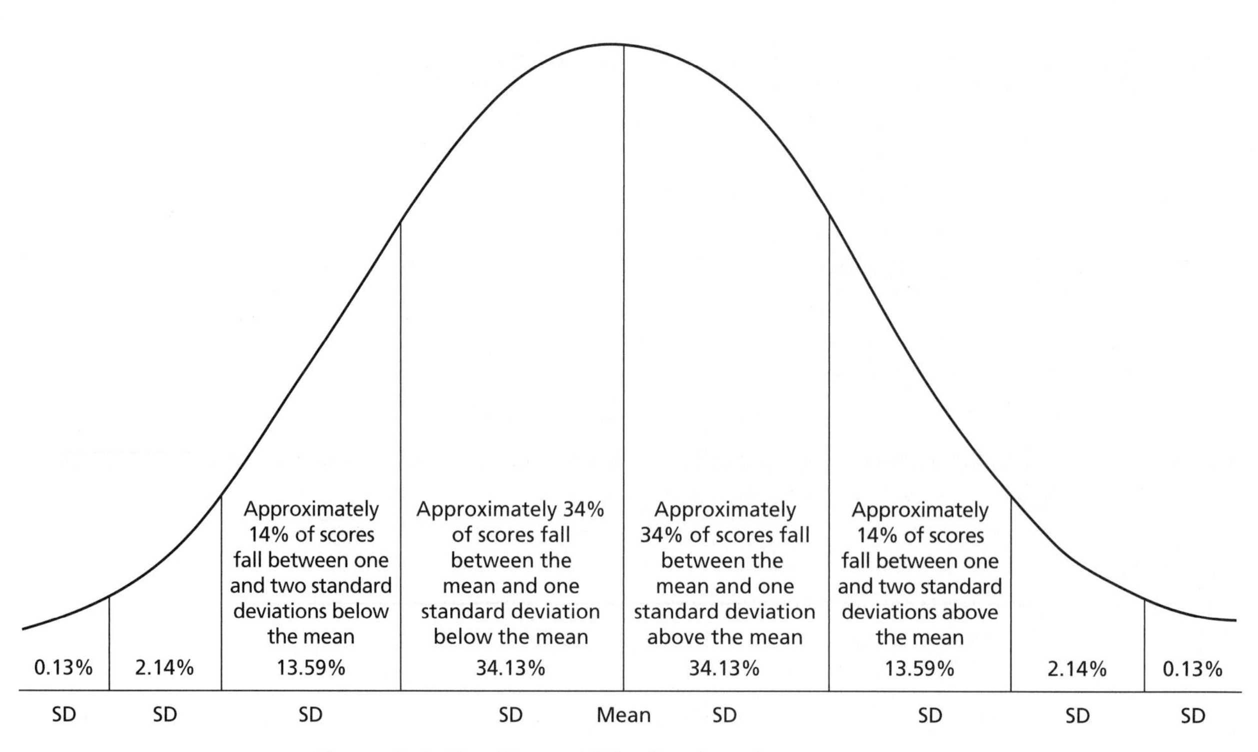

Figure 3.1 The Normal Distribution Curve

value across individuals, subtests, or subject areas. Accordingly, they need to be transformed into some form of standard score, and test-makers provide a number of conversion tables to accomplish this.

Standard Scores Standard scores are expressed in terms of their deviation from the mean and involve calculations of standard deviation. Percentile rank scores, stanine scores, and *z*-scores are examples of standard scores. Unlike raw scores, standard scores provide the opportunity to compare students' performance across time, subtests, and tests (McKenna & Dougherty Stahl, 2009; Richek et al., 2005).

Percentile rank scores represent the percentage of a defined distribution (group of students) that is situated either at or below the score in question. Percentile rank scores range from 1 to 99, with 50 representing the middle score and denoting the average performance. For instance, a student who achieves a percentile rank score of 75 on a reading instrument is performing as well as or better than 75 percent (or less well than 25 percent) of the students who comprise the test norm.

Generally, students who perform within the 23rd to 76th percentile are considered to be demonstrating average performance relative to students who comprise the test norm (with students demonstrating low-average performance needing additional support and resources). Students below the 23rd percentile are considered to be scoring below average and would benefit from direct intervention and programming. Percentile scores do not refer to the percentage of test items answered correctly, nor can they be averaged across subscales (McKenna & Dougherty Stahl, 2009; Richek et al., 2005).

Stanine scores represent students' performances on a nine-point scale, where scores ranging from 1 to 3 are considered to be below average, scores ranging from 4 to 6 are considered to be average, and scores ranging from 7 to 9 are considered to be above average. Some test-makers have further refined stanine scores so that a score of 4 is considered borderline and a score of 5 is considered average. Again, students who demonstrate below-average or borderline performance scores should be provided with focused instruction and programming.

Stanine scores are less precise than percentiles and cannot be compared across subject areas (i.e., students' stanine scores in reading cannot be compared to those in science or mathematics). However, it is possible to gain insights by comparing students' stanine scores across time or across subtests within a subject area (i.e., comparing reading comprehension and listening comprehension), with the general rule being that differences of two points or more reflect authentic performance differences versus differences due to measurement error (McKenna & Dougherty Stahl, 2009; Richek et al., 2005).

Standard deviation and ***z*-scores** represent students' performances in terms of their proximity to the mean. The z-score reflects the number of standard deviations a student performs above or below the mean (see the calculation that follows).

$$\text{z-Score} = \frac{\text{X (Raw score)} - \overline{\text{X}}\text{ (Mean)}}{\text{Standard deviation}}$$

Grade-Equivalent Scores

Grade-equivalent scores represent students' performances in terms of grade and month in school (using a 10-month scale). For instance, a grade-equivalent listening comprehension score of 6.4 represents the typical performance of a defined sample of grade 6 students in late December or early January. These scores are most meaningful in instruments that contain large item sets arranged in order of difficulty, where younger students tend to be provided with easier items and older students with more difficult ones (McKenna & Dougherty Stahl, 2009; Richek et al., 2005).

While grade-equivalent scores can provide valuable information related to student progress over time, they also have been misused and misinterpreted. For instance, if a grade 4 student earns a grade-equivalent score of 6.5, it means that the student's score is about the same as the typical score of grade 6 students tested in late January or February *with the same materials*. A grade-equivalent score of 6.5 does not imply that the student has the reading skills ordinarily acquired by the middle of grade 6, as is often erroneously assumed. Grade-equivalent scores also should never be used for grade placement. In this context, organizations such as the International Reading Association (McKenna & Dougherty Stahl, 2009) have discouraged the use of these scores, advocating instead for the use of other scores, including percentile rank and stanine scores.

Age-Equivalent Scores

Age-equivalent scoresrepresent students' performance in terms of relative standing in reference to the entire norm group. For example, if an individual, regardless of age, obtains an age-equivalent score of 12-3, his or her performance was the same as that of the average 12-year, 3-month-old individual in the specified norm. Age-equivalent scores are best thought of as ranks that represent relative standing.

The relationship between some of these norm-based scores and the normal distribution curve is illustrated in Figure 3.2.

Putting It Together: Next Steps

For some, making meaning from information contained in standardized assessments may seem to be a daunting and overwhelming task. Fortunately, psychologists, psychometrists,

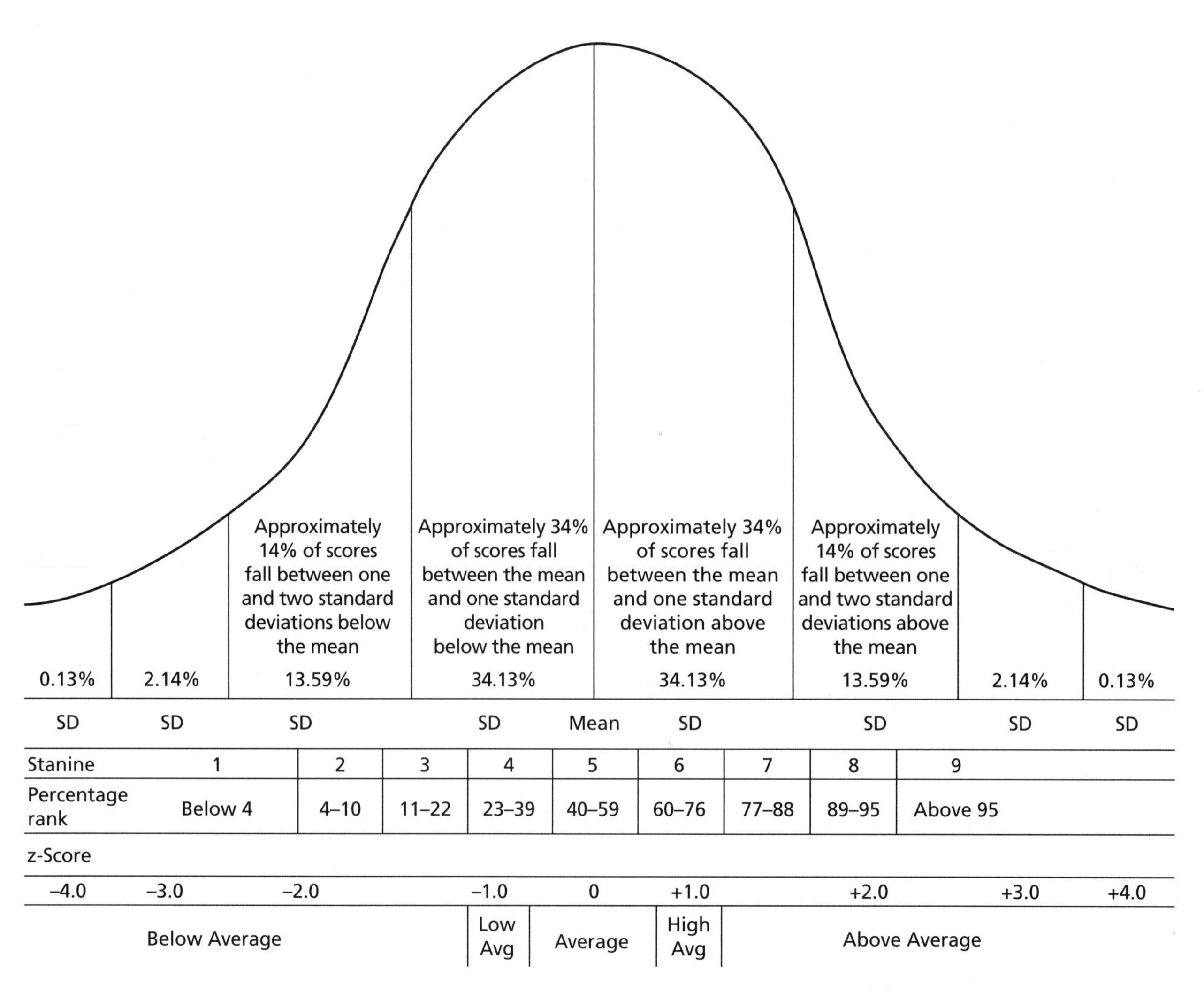

Figure 3.2 Relationship between the Normal Distribution Curve and Common Standard Scores

speech-language therapists, resource teachers, and other school specialists who complete these assessments often provide a profile of students' learning strengths and areas of need as well as program recommendations. These recommendations may include the development of individual educational plans (IEPs) including accommodations and modifications. In such circumstances, teachers still play a vital role in programming for students.

As those who work most closely with students, teachers are often required to select the recommendations that are most likely to succeed in terms of students' personality and learning orientations, the learning context, and the classroom. Teachers often are best able to identify how recommendations can be implemented successfully in the classroom. Additional discussion of working with students with reading and writing exceptionalities is provided in Chapter 11, Working with Students with Diverse Learning Needs, as well as throughout the text. We encourage teachers working with these students to consult others in the field and the many professional resources available through such organizations as the Council for Exceptional Children (www.cec.sped.org), the International Reading Association (www.reading.org), and the National Council of Teachers of English (www.ncte.org).

Caution While the findings associated with these assessments may provide important insights into the underlying nature of student performance and confirm areas of learning strength and need, they should never be used as the sole basis for programming decisions (e.g., remedial, supplemental, gifted). To this end, we encourage teachers to review these instruments critically with respect to evaluating their fit with classroom curriculum. We also remind teachers that multiple sources of student performance data, including classroom data, need to be considered in addition to consultations with students and their parents.

High-Stakes Assessment

The term *high-stakes testing* is often used when the results of standardized assessments have implications for students' promotion, graduation, or scholarship (Agrey, 2004). In Canada, all provinces and territories require students to complete some form of standardized assessment, with the majority of these tests containing a reading and writing component. In many cases, the development and scoring of these assessments is overseen by a third-party testing agency. For instance, in Ontario, the Education Quality and Accountability Office (EQAO) regulates the administration of standardized reading and writing tests for all students in grades 3 and 6. Students in Prince Edward Island also complete standardized reading and writing tests in grades 3 and 6. Those in British Columbia complete standardized tests in reading comprehension and writing in grades 4 and 7, while students in Manitoba complete similar tests in grades 3 and 8. Many provinces also require students to complete some form of reading-based assessment in secondary school (e.g., the Ontario Secondary School Literacy Test at the end of the grade 10). Interested readers are encouraged to review individual Department of Education websites to locate additional information about specific requirements in each province or territory.

The use of high-stakes assessment is controversial. While advocates argue that the tests provide valuable information regarding students' learning and hold schools accountable for student performance (Ben Jaafar & Earl, 2008), the use of these tests is opposed by many educational researchers, practitioners, and professional organizations, including the Canadian Psychological Association, the Canadian Association of School Psychologists (Simner, 2000), and the Canadian Teachers' Federation (2009). Critics argue that the use of these instruments may encourage teachers to direct classroom time to test preparation rather than to regular programming. Teachers and students may express undue stress and anxiety prior to and during the test, which can affect performance scores negatively. The reporting of high-stakes assessment has also been criticized in that it does not disclose all relevant data needed for interpretation and thus encourages invalid comparisons between schools.

Student Voice 3.1

Writing the test was stressful. The test lasted for three days. We had lots of breaks and lots of snacks. The test doesn't count for our report card, but we still spent time doing practice booklets in class. I'm glad it's over!

Zain
Grade 3 student

Student Voice 3.2

I haven't written the provincial test yet but we have been writing practice tests in class. I don't really know what the test is used for, but my teacher said it would not be part of our report card. My teacher also said we should practise because the test gets harder every year. I'm a little nervous about writing it.

Kyle
Grade 6 student

Regardless of these debates and concerns, it appears that students will continue to complete high-stakes assessment for the foreseeable future. Accordingly, language arts teachers have an important role in preparing students to complete these and other standardized tests. Teachers are reminded to review the general guidelines in Table 3.3 to prepare themselves and their students for these tests.

ASSESSING BEGINNING READING

Observation is a key component in assessing students' language skills and abilities. Teacher observation complements more formal and objective assessments, providing a better picture of each child's language skills (Martin, 2010). Examples of observational assessments include documenting patterns of behaviour when students are reading, writing, completing a word game, or reading aloud. Observation is integral to daily oral language, listening, and question-answering during group reading. Observation, however, can be time consuming and subjective if only one lens is used. For this reason, this method needs to be combined with other data assessment tools. Techniques in which observation plays a role include anecdotal notes, conferences, checklists, miscue analyses, running records, and informal reading inventories.

Anecdotal Notes

Anecdotal notes should accompany teacher observation so they become systematic rather than sporadic and include all students (Mariotti & Homan, 2005). Anecdotal notes can be made daily, focusing on two or three students each day, with additional notes for any unusual or significant observation related to other students. Each note should be accompanied by the date and time. These notes reveal patterns of language behaviour that can indicate strengths and weaknesses and reveal where additional assessment is needed. Several organizational schemes are possible; teachers simply need to select one and be consistent.

Conferences

Scheduled conferencesor student-teacher interviews normally take 10 or 15 minutes per student, but the information gained is very useful. Other conferences are impromptu based on problem solving and can also reveal useful information. The teacher's role is primarily that of listener (Tompkins, Bright, Pollard, & Winsor, 2011). If conferences are organized and scheduled carefully, each student should participate in an individual conference each month. During the conference, students should be encouraged to reflect on their strengths and accomplishments and establish personal goals. Having young children read aloud from a book they are reading in class can also provide insightful feedback.

Checklists

Checklists are useful for tracking student progress in the use of skills and strategies in a variety of contexts. They can record the presence or absence of particular skills, competencies, achievements, or stages of development (Martin, 2010). The items, wording, and sequence of these lists indicate the teacher's beliefs about what is important. Teachers can create focused checklists for specific learning tasks or broader ones to check for skill acquisition. Ready-made checklists are also available. This form of assessment is versatile, as students can create checklists for a task as a group and then use them for self-assessment. Checklists often point directly and concisely to areas that need improvement as well as to areas of strength.

Miscue Analyses

Miscue analyses are one of the most widely used assessment procedures to help determine students' instructional needs. The process involves analyzing students' reading errors to determine which reading cues and reading strategies are being used and which require instruction. Kenneth Goodman, a forefather of this approach, believed that the graphophonic, syntactic, and semantic cuing systems (see Chapter 1, Discovering Yourself and Your Students as Language Learners) were central to the decoding of text. Analyzing students' oral reading errors could provide insights into whether they were attending to the letters and sounds of words, to their meanings, or to both.

Indeed, the use of the term *miscue* versus *error* marks the idea that some errors are semantically appropriate substitutions (*car* for *auto*, *plane* for *jet*). Other types of errors monitored during miscue analysis include substitutions, mispronunciations, and omissions (McKenna & Dougherty Stahl, 2009). Miscue analysis is usually completed when students demonstrate difficulty reading fluently and with comprehension and involves working with students individually. The process involves four steps, as outlined below.

Step 1: Prepare Copies of Text

The teacher needs to prepare two copies of the text: one for the student and the other for him- or herself. Materials usually consist of one or more short passages that represent a level at which the student is likely to experience success reading but also encounter some difficulties (i.e., instructional level).

Step 2: Have Student Read Text Aloud

Instruct the student that he or she is to read aloud without any help and will be asked to retell the story at the end. (Although not part of the miscue analysis per se, this instruction ensures that the student will access all available decoding and comprehension strategies.) While the student is reading, the teacher records the session on the separate copy. The teacher records all errors, using some form of coding schema.

Many teachers elect to use an audio recorder to assist in this process (which allows the teacher to listen to the reading again for subsequent review). Audio recordings may be especially helpful when first completing miscue analyses or when working with students who demonstrate substantial difficulty reading aloud. Teachers are encouraged to make observation notes related to students' use of punctuation, prosody, and hesitations while reading. Table 3.4 provides a list of common miscues demonstrated by students when reading aloud. Table 3.5 lists specific examples of student miscues.

Table 3.4 Common Student Miscues during Read Aloud

Omission	Student skips or misses word
Insertion	Student inserts extra word
Substitution	Student replaces word in text with semantically similar one (e.g., *car* for *auto*, *plane* for *jet*)
Reversal	Student reverses order of two or more words in text
Repetition	Student repeats word (or phrase) in text more than once
Self-correction	Student provides correct word after making one or more errors
Teacher-provided word	Teacher provides target word following student mispronunciation or prolonged interval without providing response

Table 3.5 Sample of Student Miscues

Text	Student Miscue	Teacher Record
Then he saw his mother.	**Omission:** . . . he saw his mother.	(Then) he saw his mother.
The forest had a big lake.	**Insertion:** In the forest had a big lake.	(In) ^ the forest had a big lake.
She worked with them.	**Substitution:** She worked with him.	them She worked with him.
Where can I go Father?	**Reversal:** Where I can go Father?	Where can I go Father?
The girl went to the movies.	**Repetition:** The the girl went to the movies.	R The the girl went to the movies.
He saw his father.	**Self-correction:** He was he saw his father.	was He saw his father.
He flew in a helicopter.	**Nonsense substitution:** He flew in a hillicoppy.	hillycoppy He flew in a helicopter.
The dog ran down the street and into her house.	**Incorrect phrasing:** The dog ran down the street and into her house.	The dog ran down the/street and into/her house.
"Help, Mother!" she said.	**Punctuation ignored:** Help Mother she said	"Help[,] Mother[!]" she said.

Text	Student Response	Graphically Similar	Syntactically (Functionally) Similar	Semantically Similar
aided	added	√		
shy	she	√		
travelled	traveller	√	√	√
union	onion	√		
conditions	continents	√	√	
concerned	cornered	√	√	
possibly	probably	√	√	√

Figure 3.3 Examples of Student Miscue Analysis

Step 3: Have Student Recall Text and Respond to Questions
Have the student recall the text after reading, providing him or her with relevant question prompts as necessary. Record whether the student is able to recall details as well as story elements and main ideas and identify any inferences. Teachers will want to monitor whether students are able to generate text-to-text and text-to-world extensions. This information provides teachers with important insights as to whether decoding difficulties are affecting reading comprehension. This component is helpful, as some students will struggle with individual words and phrasing but gain the meaning of the selection. Alternatively, some students may appear to be fluent readers, but the attention they afford to word identification may preclude reading for meaning or comprehension.

Step 4: Review Decoding Errors
One challenge associated with reviewing students' errors is to identify patterns across and within text (see Figure 3.3). Another challenge is to provide meaningful recommendations for instruction. For instance, students whose errors are dominated by substitution of meaning are of relatively minor concern since these errors do not prevent students from gaining meaning from text. These students are likely to benefit from metacognitive prompts while reading. Students whose errors consist of substitutions based on the beginning or ending letters of words are of more concern. These students require greater instruction in word attack processes and are likely to benefit from instruction in reading by analogy and other relevant strategies.

Running Records

Running record

Running records are used to help determine appropriate reading materials for students and monitor their reading progress (Ontario Ministry of Education, 2003). They are used most often with beginning readers, starting with simple materials and advancing to more difficult ones (Clay, 1987; Ross, 2004). They require slightly less preparation than miscue analyses in that teachers are not required to score a second copy of the text (although they can opt to use one). Rather, teachers check off words read correctly, keeping track

of errors only. They also provide teachers with the option of using authentic texts and materials that are readily available in the classroom. The process involves four steps, as outlined below.

Step 1: Select Text

The teacher needs to select a short book (it is usually best if a complete narrative is contained in the reading passage) or passage, approximately 100 words in length (acceptable range is between 100 and 200 words). Experts such as Marie Clay (1987, 1993) recommend that the selected text be one that the student can read with about 90 to 95 percent accuracy. The selected text may be either narrative or expository, with the teacher encouraged to consider the student's interests and reading habits. The teacher should also be conscious of illustrations and visuals contained in the reading passage, as these may provide the student with decoding cues and contain additional information beyond that found in the text.

There is some controversy about whether the book selected should be a familiar one or a new reading experience. Those who advocate for a new text believe that a more accurate assessment of students' skills can be determined if they are unfamiliar with the text. Regardless of the text selected, teachers would be wise to gain some familiarity with the text beforehand, especially if they do not have access to a second copy while students are reading.

Step 2: Have Student Read Text Aloud

The teacher provides a check mark or some other symbol for each word that the student reads correctly. The teacher also records any student errors or miscues by noting the provided response as well as the text item. Recording student attempts is especially important for subsequent analysis exploring the nature of errors. Errors include substitutions, omissions, insertions, and teacher-provided responses. If the student loses his or her place while reading the text, the teacher redirects the student to the proper position and this response is considered a single error. Self-corrections and repetitions are recorded and monitored but are not counted as errors. Each time the same word is read incorrectly in the text, an error score is recorded; an exception is made for the mispronunciation of proper names, which are only counted once (single error).

After the student reads a benchmark book and the running record is completed, he or she completes an oral retelling of the story. The student is asked to close the book and retell the story in as much detail as possible. If the student demonstrates difficulties retelling specific parts or details of the story, the teacher can use prompts such as "Tell me more about (character X)" or "What happened after . . . ?" The student's retelling is analyzed for information about:

- Main idea and supporting detail
- Sequence of events
- Characters
- Setting
- Plot
- Problem and solution
- Response to text-specific vocabulary and language

Step 3: Calculate Performance Score

The accuracy score represents the total number of words read correctly divided by the total number of words contained in the passage. This score is multiplied by 100 to obtain the percentage. In general, scores of 90 percent or better are considered to indicate good progress. Students who present error rates higher than one per nine words of text (1:9) are likely demonstrating frustration with the text selection.

$$\frac{\text{Total number of words read correctly}}{\text{Total number of words (excluding title)}} \times 100$$

Teachers also may be interested in analyzing students' self-corrections, as this number can provide some insights with respect to self-regulation and self-monitoring processes. The self-correction score represents the number of self-corrections divided by the total number of errors multiplied by 100.

$$\frac{\text{Total number of self-corrections}}{\text{Total number of errors + Self-corrections}} \times 100$$

Step 4: Review Errors

In addition to monitoring the number of errors committed by the student while reading, the teacher should analyze the errors with respect to their semantic, syntactic, and visual similarity to the text being read.

- Is the error similar in meaning to text?
- Does the error hold the same syntactic position as text (e.g., verb, adjective)?

- Is the error graphically similar to the text?
- Does the error begin with the same letter(s) as the text?
- Does the error have the same middle letter(s) as the text?
- Does the error end with the same letter(s) as the text?

The teacher should also monitor the student's behaviours (e.g., finger-tracking of text, attention to punctuation, overall reading prosody) while reading. Collectively, this information can provide the teacher with insights with respect to how the student decodes text. This process should be completed several times throughout the school year, with the teacher being especially attentive to changes in error patterns and self-corrections. According to research, literacy achievement is positively affected in schools where teachers use running records for ongoing assessment (Ross, 2004).

Informal Reading Inventories

Informal reading inventories (IRIs) can help teachers determine the reading level of individual students so that critical decisions can be made about selecting appropriate materials for instruction. Determining students' current reading levels is one of the most frequent and foundational tasks of language arts teachers. If students are provided with materials above their instructional level, they will be frustrated and growth in reading skills will be minimal. They are also likely to develop negative attitudes about reading. If students are provided with reading materials that are well below their instructional level, they will be bored or unchallenged and will lose interest, with little growth occurring. To avoid both of these scenarios, teachers need to find the instructional level of each student so that each one is comfortably located within the *zone of proximal development* (Vygotsky, 1978). Teachers should be familiar with the characteristics of each of the following levels:

The **independent level**, or what is sometimes referred to as the free-reading level, represents the level of text at which students can read without any teacher assistance and is most appropriate for independent reading activities.

The **instructional level** represents the text level at which students require teacher assistance to gain meaning from the text. The text contains many unknown words or concepts or student background knowledge is insufficient. This is the optimal level for direct instruction and guided reading.

The **frustration level** represents the lowest level of text at which students are likely to experience frustration with the reading experience, even with teacher support. Attempts to instruct at this level are generally disheartening and futile for students and teachers alike. However, students may enjoy listening to texts at this level (Read Aloud or shared reading), as their listening comprehension level is usually higher than their reading comprehension level.

IRIs provide teachers with a published set of assessment materials usually consisting of graded word lists, graded reading passages and corresponding comprehension questions (miscue analysis), and graded passages that can be read aloud to students with accompanying comprehension questions (listening comprehension). These materials are typically presented in increasing order of difficulty (usually beginning at the pre-primary level and advancing to the secondary school level; McKenna & Dougherty Stahl, 2009). Some IRIs provide metacognitive prompts and require students to complete Think Aloud protocols while reading. Many IRIs contain other reading assessments, including letter identification, phonological awareness, phonics, and reading interest and reading orientation questionnaires that can be completed at any time.

Similar to running records and miscue analyses, IRIs are completed with students on an individual basis. Analyses of students' performances can assist teachers in gathering substantial information about students' reading levels, including areas of strength and instructional need. These analyses can also provide insights about appropriate reading materials for individual students, with some reading researchers and educators viewing them as foundational to classroom reading assessment (Walpole & McKenna, 2006). We agree that completing IRIs with students can be an essential component of an effective language arts program, but caution teachers to consider these results for consistency with daily classroom behaviours (Provost & Lambert, 2010). Similarly, teachers need to follow up and advocate for additional assessment when findings suggest that students are experiencing substantial difficulties (i.e., two grade levels or more below current placement). Table 3.6 lists examples of IRIs.

The process of completing an IRI involves three steps, as outlined below.

Step 1: Complete Graded Word List

Graded word lists provide teachers with a measure of the students' abilities to recognize words in isolation and are used to estimate students' reading levels as well as to determine entry levels for the graded reading passages. The student is instructed to read aloud

Table 3.6 Examples of Informal Reading Inventories
Analytical Reading Inventory: Comprehensive Standards-Based Assessment for All Students Including Gifted and Remedial, 9th edition (2010) by Mary Lynn J. Woods and Alden J. Moe (Allyn & Bacon)
Bader Reading & Language Inventory, 6th edition (2009) by Lois A. Bader and Daniel L. Pearce (Allyn & Bacon)
Basic Reading Inventory: Pre-Primer through Grade 12 & Early Literacy Assessments, 10th edition (2008) by Jerry L. Johns (Kendall/Hunt Publishing Company)
Classroom Reading Inventory, 10th edition (2011) by Warren Wheelock, Connie Campbell, and Nicholas Silvaroli (McGraw-Hill Companies)
Comprehensive Reading Inventory: Measuring Reading Development in Regular and Special Education Classrooms, 5th edition (2007) by Robert B. Cooter, E. Sutton Flynt, and Kathleen Spencer Cooter (Prentice Hall)
Critical Reading Inventory: Assessing Students Reading and Thinking & Readers Passages, 2nd edition (2008) by Mary D. Applegate, Kathleen B. Quinn, and Anthony J. Applegate (Allyn & Bacon)
Ekwall/Shanker Reading Inventory, 5th edition (2009) by James L. Shanker and Ward Cockrum (Allyn & Bacon)
Informal Reading Inventory: Preprimer to Twelfth Grade, 8th edition (2011) by Betty Roe and Paul C. Burns (Wadsworth Publishing Company)
Qualitative Reading Inventory, 5th edition (2010) by Lauren Leslie and JoAnne Schudt Caldwell (Allyn & Bacon)

sets of unformatted target words. The teacher uses separate scoring sheets to record the student's responses for accuracy, stopping once he or she reaches the frustration level. The teacher may find it helpful to review the nature of the student's errors, triangulating these data with those gained from the subsequent miscue analysis (Step 2). If the student demonstrates significantly lower-than-expected performance scores, the teacher should consider confirming his or her knowledge of letter names and sounds and, if necessary, sounds segments (i.e., phonological awareness).

Step 2: Complete Graded Reading Passages

Using the results of the graded word list as a guide for an entry point, the student reads the graded passages aloud. Although normal protocols recommend that students begin reading text at their instructional level, we recommend that teachers have reluctant readers or those experiencing reading difficulties start with passages below the indicated instructional level to build confidence and comfort with the materials and procedure.

The student is provided with unmarked copies of each text and instructed to read aloud. The teacher uses accompanying scoring sheets to complete a miscue analysis. Once the student has completed the Read Aloud, he or she is asked a series of comprehension questions. Both the miscue analysis and the comprehension responses are used to determine whether the text is at the student's independent, instructional, or frustration reading level. In general, reading levels are calculated using the following criteria:

Independent level: Students recognize 99 percent of the words correctly and demonstrate a comprehension level between 90 and 100 percent.

Instructional level: Students recognize 95 to 98 percent of the words correctly and demonstrate a comprehension level of around 75 to 80 percent or higher.

Frustration level: Students recognize less than 90 percent of the words and demonstrate a comprehension level of less than 70 percent.

If the text is deemed to be at the student's independent or instructional reading level, the process is continued until a frustration score is reached. If the first passage read results in a frustration score, the process is continued with easier texts until instructional and independent levels have been determined. Most instruments also provide passages for students to read silently, with reading levels reflecting reading time and comprehension accuracy.

There is some debate about the inclusion of self-corrections and repetitions as miscues (the former may reflect metacognitive monitoring and the latter attempts to gain meaning while reading), with instruments varying in their scoring of these errors. Teachers need to pay careful attention to the specific scoring criteria associated with each IRI. They should also note the number of admissible instances when they can provide students with words from the passage should they pause for prolonged intervals while reading.

Caution: There is considerable variability across IRIs with respect to the types of text passages (i.e., narrative, expository, mixed) and the nature of reading comprehension questions used (Nilsson, 2008). Teachers also need to consider the potential positive influence of students' prior knowledge and interests when answering reading comprehension questions, as many published inventories contain information relevant to American history, geography, and political and current events. Indeed, we know of no IRI designed specifically for use with Canadian elementary students (the *Canadian Adult Reading Assessment* provides a valid tool for adults). We encourage teachers to review several IRIs before selecting one for use in their classrooms.

Step 3: Complete Measure of Listening Comprehension
After the student has reached his or her frustration level while reading aloud, the teacher should continue to assess for listening comprehension. Measuring the student's listening comprehension involves the teacher reading passages aloud to the student and asking him or her associated reading comprehension questions. Listening comprehension is the maximum level at which the student is able to answer 75 percent of corresponding comprehension questions accurately. Assessing the student's listening comprehension can provide insights into his or her reading abilities, and is especially helpful in discerning whether reading difficulties are predominately based on decoding (i.e., large discrepancy between reading instructional level and listening comprehension level).

Caution: It is important to remember that there are no advantages to granting students higher scores than they achieved. Inappropriately placed students spend more time accomplishing reading tasks, with their achievement levels dropping and their attitudes about reading suffering (Gunning, 2005).

Using Levelled Texts as Assessment Tools

Test developers have combined the use of authentic texts (associated with running records) with the structure of IRIs. As part of these assessments, students are provided with levelled texts that are often presented in the format of a book. Multiple texts, including expository and narrative materials, are provided at each level, with teachers encouraged to complete running records several times throughout the school year.

Teachers are provided with print copies for completing running records and miscue analyses (i.e., meaning and semantic, syntactic, visual and graphophonic). After students read text aloud, they are asked to recall it, with teachers providing guiding questions as necessary. Students are also asked to describe their thinking while reading to gather information related to use of strategic processes. Students' comprehension responses are used to gather insights into their reading processes and understanding of print materials, with students' miscue analyses used to deduce a reading level (see Chapter 12, Creating Your Language Arts Classroom: How Do You Begin? for detailed information on using levelled texts in the classroom).

In Canada, the *Development Reading Assessment* (Canadian edition, 2003), *Benchmark Assessment System* (2010) and *PM Benchmark Reading and Assessment* (2003) are commonly used instruments in the primary grades. Assessments such as CASI (2007)—which stands for Comprehension, Attitude, Strategies, Interests—are often used in the junior and intermediate grades. These assessments focus on reading comprehension (assessing students' comprehension, attitude, strategies, and interests) and can be administered to groups of students. For the most part, these assessment kits are stand-alone units in that they do not provide remedial or instructional complements (i.e., levelled text for independent or guided reading, instructional and independent learning activities). However, there are some noteworthy exceptions, including *Leveled Literacy Intervention (K–2)* (Fountas & Pinnell, 2009), which provides teachers with levelled readers and associated intervention lessons.

Caution Teachers must be careful to distinguish between using levelled texts as described here (i.e., for assessment purposes and usually as part of commercial kits) and using them as part of independent or shared reading in the classroom. Having students read levelled text designed for assessment purposes as part of their daily reading invalidates these texts as assessment tools. We acknowledge the importance of using levelled texts as part of students' daily reading and strongly encourage teachers to develop levelled reading centres in their classrooms. To this end, we provide specific information about how to use levelled texts as part of students' independent reading programs in Chapter 12, Creating Your Language Arts Classroom: How Do You Begin?

Response to Intervention

Across Canada, teachers and paraprofessionals are increasingly using response to intervention (RTI), or what is also referred to as response to instruction, as a method for improving all students' learning, as well as identifying those at risk for reading and other learning difficulties (Fuchs & Fuchs, 2006; Fuchs, Fuchs, & Vaughn, 2008). Basically, RTI requires classroom teachers to monitor students' responses to the provision of evidence-based instruction and intervention. RTI is considered to be a proactive, preventative approach in which decision making is informed by student data. It requires collaboration among classroom teachers, resource teachers, administrators, and other school professionals.

RTI involves a multi-tiered decision-making process in which student responses to instruction are evaluated and monitored carefully.

Tier 1: Students receive evidence-based instruction in the context of general classroom instruction. Students who do not demonstrate adequate progress or learning in this context are provided with Tier 2 instruction.

Tier 2: Involves more intensive, targeted small-group or one-on-one instruction. Students who demonstrate learning gains return to Tier 1 instruction with the gradual release of additional supports. Students who still do not demonstrate adequate learning gains are referred for Tier 3 instruction.

Tier 3: Involves intensive instruction usually provided by a reading specialist or special educator (Swanson & Vaughn, 2011). Once students demonstrate progress they return to either Tier 1 or Tier 2 instruction (or some combination of the two).

In some schools, RTI has been proposed as an alternative to IQ testing, with the belief that using this approach will expedite access to services for students with learning exceptionalities and reduce overall costs associated with special education. RTI focuses on students' strengths, successes, and learning achievements rather than on their "deficits" or weaknesses (Kavale, Holdnack, & Mostert, 2005) and requires teachers to provide differentiated and intensified reading and writing instruction to struggling readers (Swanson & Vaughn, 2011).

Advocates argue that the process requires educators to make selective decisions regarding programming options for students with learning difficulties and to monitor their responses to such instruction carefully. This process of observation and adaptation increases the likelihood of successful programming unfolding in the regular classroom and decreases the need for out-of-classroom programming. Ultimately, students who do not respond positively to a series of evidence-based intervention strategies will be identified formally and provided with a modified program of study (Fuchs & Fuchs, 2006).

When using RTI in classrooms, teachers are required to follow a three-step process that involves providing at-risk screening, monitoring students' responsiveness to targeted instruction, and developing or adopting the instructional program in accordance with collected data (Fuchs & Fuchs, 2006; Kavale et al., 2005).

Screening The RTI model requires teachers to participate in universal screening in which every student in designated grades participates in a brief, age-appropriate reading assessment (e.g., phonological awareness tests, graded word lists) to identify those at risk for reading and writing failure. Using corroborating classroom-based data, students who do not respond to effective instructional practices and who are at risk for reading and writing difficulties are identified. Early screening is especially critical (i.e., kindergarten and grade 1), as early intervention is believed to improve students' long-term academic performance and circumvent Tier 3 instruction.

Monitoring Although all effective language arts teachers aspire to provide students with the most effective instruction possible as part of their regular programming, some students will fail to demonstrate adequate learning and growth (according to predetermined cut-off points, usually representing the lowest 20 percent of the class; Swanson & Vaughn, 2011). In these cases, students may require adaptations to regular instruction or alternative instructional procedures. For example, teachers may provide more explicit instruction to small groups of students or have them participate in a supplemental program such as Reading Recovery or Book Buddies (see Chapter 11, Working with Students with Diverse Learning Needs).

This instruction is often provided in collaboration with resource teachers, paraprofessionals, trained peers, and other school staff. When developing this instruction, it is critical that teachers establish clear learning goals based on students' learning needs. Some needs may reflect foundational skills such as letter naming or word reading. Others may be more complex, including vocabulary and comprehension. The nature of the learning need will influence the time required for intervention (Swanson & Vaughn, 2011), with data related to students' progress toward mastery of specific skills or general measures (e.g., reading fluency) being collected, reviewed, and monitored routinely by all those working with them.

To truly gauge the effects of intervention, teachers must provide adequate time for students to participate in such programming. In general, students should participate for 20 to 40 minutes a day across 10 to 30 weeks (Fuchs, Fuchs, & Vaughn, 2008). Teachers also need to plan their intervention programs carefully, making sure to implement evidence-based practices versus popular or "trendy" practices that do not enjoy research support. This may be somewhat challenging, as it requires teachers to possess an understanding of the elements of evidence-based practices and be willing to question recommendations and practices advocated by consultants and school boards (Grierson, Gallagher, & Woloshyn, 2007). Finally, teachers need to ensure that they record the results of these sessions diligently and methodically.

Instructional Programming After 50 to 100 sessions of interventions, students demonstrate one of three outcomes: (1) adequate progress toward goals, (2) limited progress toward goals, or (3) inadequate progress toward goals (Fuchs, Fuchs, & Vaughn, 2008). Fortunately, researchers have documented that the majority of students demonstrate adequate growth and are able to return to regular classroom instruction with the gradual release of interventions (McMaster, Fuchs, Fuchs, & Compton, 2005). Those who show limited or no progress (about 10 percent) will likely benefit from continued interventions or segregated programming.

ASSESSING READING COMPREHENSION

THERE ARE A VARIETY OF CLASSROOM-BASED METHODS AND TOOLS THAT TEACHERS can use to assess students' understanding of text. Many of these techniques and tools are integral to the instructional process (Brookhart, 2003; Wixson & Carlisle, 2005). In other words, many of the same methods and tools used to promote students' reading comprehension can also be used in assessment and evaluation (Wiggins & McTighe, 2005). For example, teachers can monitor students' comprehension of story events by asking questions during the reading of text. They can observe students' affective responses to text and evaluate whether students can relate characters' experiences to their own. Similarly, they can listen as students discuss other probable story outcomes and resolutions.

Teachers need to be conscious of the type of comprehension being assessed. The RAND Reading Study Group (2002) identified three levels or types of comprehension: knowledge, application, and engagement. Briefly, knowledge includes successful understanding of text structure, integration of prior knowledge with text information, and critical evaluation of its content. Application involves the extension of acquired knowledge into new situations and tasks, and engagement refers to the readers' involvement with the text. For the most part, teachers are skilled at assessing and evaluating students' knowledge of text. Unfortunately, there is relatively little focus directed at the levels of integration, evaluation, application, and engagement (National Research Council, 2001; Paris & Stahl, 2005). One challenge for teachers is to develop and implement a balanced approach for assessing students' comprehension of text.

Below, we review four common classroom-based informal assessment practices for the comprehension of text: question-answering, recall and retelling, Think Aloud and questionnaires, and authentic and performance-based assessment activities.

Question-Answering

Questioning represents the primary tool through which teachers assess students' understanding of text. This questioning may occur in either oral or written format. An overview of the four primary question types or categories (literal, inferential, critical, and creative) and how teachers may use question prompts to promote students' comprehension of narrative text is provided in Chapter 5, Comprehension of Narrative Text.

Bloom's revised cognitive taxonomy of learning defines six levels of increasingly complex question types (see Figure 3.4; Anderson & Krathwohl, 2001). A distinction can be made among the categories with respect to the level of thinking required from students, with a general distinction being made between lower-level and higher-level

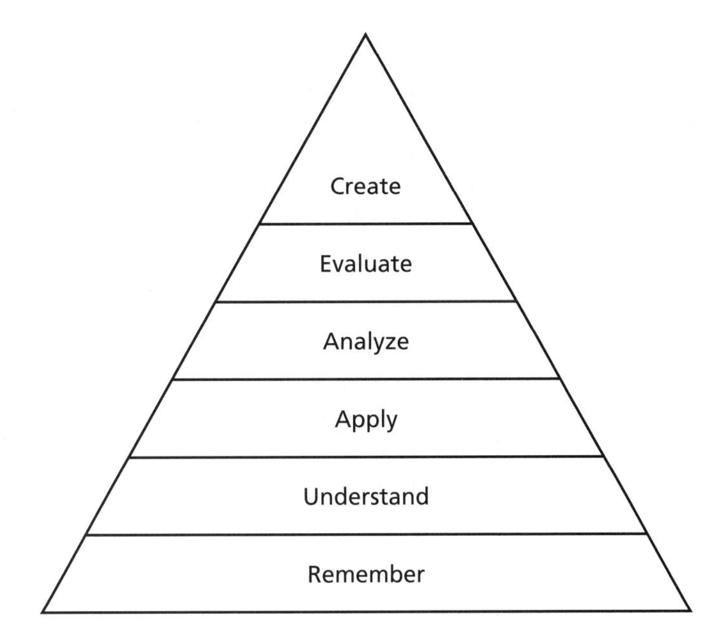

Figure 3.4 Bloom's Cognitive Taxonomy

questions. While lower-level questions (remember, understand) require students to retrieve information contained in text, higher-level questions require students to demonstrate divergent thought, engage in problem solving, and extend their thinking beyond print (apply, analyze, evaluate, create). Teachers are encouraged to consider this taxonomy when formulating instructional goals and when developing a rich repertoire of questions that can be used to assess students' differing understandings of text.

Teachers need to be conscious of their use of higher-level and lower-level questions, being careful to include both as part of their before, during, and after reading assessment activities (Afferbach, 2007). Initially, teachers may want to include a substantial number of lower-level questions to build student confidence and confirm their basic understanding. Greater numbers of higher-level questions can then be introduced as students demonstrate foundational knowledge of the text. Teachers also need to consider how frequently they will use planned questions, especially while reading aloud. In general, teachers must include sufficient numbers of questions before and during reading to accurately assess students' understanding of materials but not so many that they disrupt students' processing of text. By pre-reading text materials, teachers can plan out the thoughtful inclusion of relevant questions at "transition points" or "natural breaks" within the text.

Effective teachers will want to interject questions spontaneously throughout their lessons based on their observations of students' responses to text. Students' reading abilities and prior experiences and the level of text difficulty are factors that influence the appropriate use of questions. We encourage teachers to provide students with opportunities to "look back" at text when answering questions, acknowledging that without such explicit direction many students would not do so or believe that looking back was analogous to "cheating."

Finally, teachers need to consider the use of publisher-produced questions found in many commercial reading programs and instructional guides. While these questions can provide critical starting points for assessing students' comprehension of text, teachers need to evaluate these materials carefully for their overall quality and balance (i.e., proportion of lower-level versus higher-level questions) as well as the specific needs and learning preferences of their students. Teachers are encouraged to review and adopt commercial materials in ways that provide students with meaningful and relevant reading instruction and assessment.

Recall and Retellings

Having students retell stories and text information is one of the most widely used and readily implemented assessment instruments, with this procedure becoming increasingly common in many published IRIs (Leslie & Caldwell, 2006). Teachers can begin the retelling procedure by providing the following directions: "Tell me the story in your own words," or "Tell me what information was contained in this passage." Teachers may call on students to retell text as part of teacher-student conferences or small-group discussions. These conferences should be uninterrupted and focused, usually lasting about 10 to 15 minutes. Alternatively, students may be directed to provide written retellings as part of reading responses and journal activities. Younger students can be provided with wordless picture books and directed to provide an oral retelling of the text (Paris & Paris, 2003). The quality of students' retelling is largely based on their inclusion of story elements, informational units, sequential and coherent presentation of events, and reference to text-to-self and text-to-world extensions (Caldwell & Leslie, 2005).

There are, however, several substantive limitations associated with the interpretation and evaluation of student data gathered through story recall and retellings. Scoring students' open-ended retellings can be time consuming and care must be taken to match students' responses to a predefined text structure or grading rubric. Scoring can become especially complicated when analysis moves beyond the students' literal retelling of story elements to include inferences, connections to personal events, and the inclusion of irrelevant or erroneous information (Romero, Paris, & Brem, 2005; Sudweeks, Glissmeyer, Morrison, Wilcox, & Tanner, 2004).

Students' verbal abilities also need to be considered when evaluating retellings. Since the linguistic production demands associated with retelling are high, there is some concern that retellings may not reflect the true extent of students' comprehension. For example, young students tend to omit information about characters' motives and feelings as part of their retellings (Dougherty Stahl, 2009). Completeness of retellings is also a concern when working with English language learners, shy or verbally reserved students, or those who have limited vocabularies or expressive language difficulties (Leslie & Caldwell, 2009; Paris & Stahl, 2005).

Providing students with question prompts, or what is otherwise referred to as cued recall, either after or during the retelling process is one technique that may dissipate some of these concerns. Providing students with recall prompts reduces the cognitive requirements associated with retaining story elements and organizing them for retelling. It also provides students with insights about the type of information their teachers deem to be important and can help them in structuring their retellings.

We recommend that teachers include cued recall processes (prompts and guiding questions) as part of their retelling protocols, as cued recall and retellings are likely to elicit different aspects of student comprehension. Examples of common retelling and cued recall prompts include the following:

Narrative Text

- Tell me the story in your own words.
- What happened next?
- Can you tell me more?
- Why did that happen?
- Why is that important?
- Why did he or she do that?
- How did he or she change?
- What is the importance of that event?

Expository Text

- Tell me everything you remember about the text.
- Can you tell me more about that?
- What else do you remember?
- If you were going to tell a friend about this book in just a few words, what would you say?
- What is the most important thing you learned from reading this text?
- How do you feel about this text?
- Would you tell a friend to read this text? Why or why not?

Think Aloud and Questionnaires

Having students articulate their thought processes while reading text passages aloud is becoming an increasingly common assessment tool that can provide teachers with valuable insights about students' use of strategic processes while reading (Leslie & Caldwell, 2009). Teachers must be sensitive to the frequency with which they prompt students to use Think Aloud and the placement of these prompts throughout the text (too frequent prompting may deter students' processing of text). One advocated approach is to have students use Think Aloud after each paragraph (Leslie & Caldwell, 2006).

Think Alouds are used as part of the retelling and cued recall process, and the quality of Think Aloud comments reflect a variety of factors, including the nature of instruction, text coherence, and reading purpose (Leslie & Caldwell, 2009). Although the scoring criteria for analyzing students' Think Aloud may be quite varied, quality responses are generally considered to include evidence of paraphrasing, making inferences, monitoring, and predicting (Leslie & Caldwell, 2006; Trabasso & Magliano, 1996). From this perspective, teachers can analyze students' Think Aloud responses to assess their use of reading strategies.

Teachers also may wish to explore quantitative self-report questionnaires designed to assess students' use of strategic processes. While only a few such scales are available for commercial use, measures such as the *Strategy Inventories Index of Reading Awareness* (Jacobs & Paris, 1987), *Metacognitive Strategy Index* (Schmitt, 1990), and *Major Point of View for Readers* scale (Keene & Zimmerman, 1997) can be used to monitor growth in students' metacognitive awareness. The first two questionnaire instruments consist of multiple-choice items that can be administered in large-group settings. The latter requires students to use Think Aloud while reading a passage and requires teachers to interview students subsequently about their use of such strategy processes as questioning, predicting, and imaging (Dougherty Stahl, 2009).

Authentic and Performance-Based Assessment

Performance-based assessments are open-ended tasks that require students to apply their knowledge and skills to create a product or solve a problem (Gronlund, 2006; National Research Council, 2001; Taylor & Nolen, 2008). Assessment tasks completed in a real-life context are called authentic assessments. Authentic assessments are associated with increased student motivation, as they tend to maximize student choice and have "real-world" application (McMillan, 2008). Alternatives to book reports (see Table 3.7), theatrical presentations, Readers' Theatre, author studies, and student publishing may be used as the basis of authentic assessment. Authentic assessments provide teachers with critical formative feedback on their instruction as well as on students' reading performance. They require substantial time to complete, are accumulative in nature, and require careful planning on the part of teachers. The use of performance-based assessment allows teachers to honour the complexities of the reading process, learning, and instruction (Afferbach, 2007; Stiggins, 2008).

Student Voice 3.3

We don't really like book reports where you have to hand in a written report. One good way to do a book report is to create a board game. You get to design your own board and your own rules. Other people become interested in the book when they need to answer your questions.

Bradley and Malcolm
Grade 8 students

Consider a junior grade class that has just finished reading *The Pied Piper of Hamelin.* They decide to transform their classroom into a medieval village complete with drawbridge and ramparts. Each student selects one citizen from the village (e.g., baker, mayor, teacher, shoemaker, judge) who will be included in a re-enactment of the story. As part of the dramatization that is written and organized by the students, a guest is invited to play the role of the Pied Piper and to receive the petitions of the townspeople to return their children. Assessment is based on students' written and oral presentations.

In a longer unit involving the reading of the novel *Hatchet*, intermediate grade students develop survival guides for remote geographical locations such as rainforests and deserts. Expanding on journal entries and reading activities completed while reading the novel, students work in small groups to research the terrain, climate, flora and fauna, and natural resources of their chosen location. They then transform this information into an illustrated survival guide.

To use performance-based assessment effectively, students must be provided with clear expectations for the final product. This information is shared with students through the use of rubrics and exemplars. Rubric development requires teachers to complete an analysis of the process-related strategies and skills needed to complete the task successfully. Teachers should be able to provide responses to the following

Table 3.7 Alternatives to Book Reports

- Have students write a letter to the author. Check the internet, as some authors have websites that encourage dialogue between themselves and their readers.
- Have students prepare a one-minute radio advertisement persuading others to buy and read this book. Listen to similar advertisements and have students create a timed dialogue that can be shared. Students who are listening can choose the two books they would like to "purchase" and read.
- Have students pretend that they are interviewing a character from the story. Students write interviews in a question-and-answer format. Interviews can be dramatized and then edited as a result of the process.
- Have students choose a favourite passage from the book and describe what is appealing about the passage. Encourage students to choose something pivotal and important to the book.
- Ask students to create a top 10 list (e.g., The Top 10 Things I Learned from This Book). These lists can comprise facts in general, aspects of the story, or new understandings.
- Direct students to create a test based on the book. These tests should include matching, multiple-choice, true/false, short essay, and essay questions. Several "tests" can be combined and given to the class.
- Pair students who are reading the same book and instruct them to email each other to share their ideas and reactions to the story. Students should establish at least four points in the book when they will stop and email each other questions, thoughts, connections, and predictions so far.
- Have students write a character sketch for someone in the story. This could be a central character or an intriguing minor character. The sketch should describe appearance and personality traits but also include favourite colour, horoscope sign, favourite sports, TV shows, etc.
- Have students design a new cover for the book. The cover includes an illustration, an original summary of the book, information about the author and illustrator, and information about other books by the author.
- Ask students to write the story from another point of view. This can be either the entire story or a critical section.
- Help students convert the book into a puppet show and present the story or an exciting scene from it. Puppets can be simple (stick, finger, or paper bag puppets).
- Show students how to make a mobile from items related to the story. Discuss symbols and representations.

questions: What are you asking students to do? Why are you asking them to complete this task? How do students demonstrate their achievement of learning goals with observable products or performance (Afferbach, 2007)? Equally important, teachers must articulate these expectations with students and often with their parents, providing them with examples of exemplary performance. These expectations and guidelines need to be reviewed frequently throughout the assessment process and students should be encouraged to develop self-assessment practices (see Chapter 7, Writing: Exploring the Reading and Writing Connection).

Portfolios and self-assessment

Portfolios as Assessment

A portfolio is a representative sample of a student's work that enables teachers to keep records, add items, evaluate performances, make plans to meet needs, and review progress in terms of knowing and doing (Martin, 2010). It ties learning and assessment together in a concrete manner that demonstrates progress, learning styles, and accomplishments. Portfolios support instructional approaches that emphasize the student's role in constructing understanding and the teacher's role in promoting understanding. Many educators believe that performance assessment in portfolios is better suited for measuring the attainment of twenty-first-century skills and knowledge than are the more traditional assignments and tests (Palm, 2008). A comprehensive portfolio provides a holistic picture of a student's daily progress and provides a solid set of data for assessment. It can include initial drafts and the final product of assignments as well as self-assessments. Portfolios can also be used to support collaborative learning by offering an opportunity for students to share and comment on each other's work. All portfolios involve students in their own education so that they take charge of their personal collection of work, reflect on what makes some work better than other work, and use this information to make improvements in future work.

The steps in the portfolio development process are as follows:

Collection: Students should be encouraged to review all of their work carefully, as not all pieces are included.

Selection: Students can include works in progress, best works, and collaborative tasks. Selections can be determined by students, by teachers, or be negotiated by both.

Reflection: Students are required to participate in some form of self-assessment.

Projection: Students are required to look ahead and set new goals based on their current portfolios (Danielson & Abrulyn, 1997).

Assessment portfolios depend on teachers assigning tasks that allow students to demonstrate an understanding of a topic in a real-world, authentic context in which specific knowledge and skills are applied. Portfolio criteria can be developed collaboratively and applied equitably. Examples of tasks include the following:

- Design and construct a model
- Write a letter to an agency, a newspaper, a member of Parliament, etc.
- Perform a science experiment
- Create a survey, conduct it with a sample of people, and write a report on the findings
- Interview three experts in (choose subject area) and write a report about associated findings
- Critique and summarize a predefined reading
- Create a dramatization of a novel, historical event, or advertisement
- Self-reflection

Establishing Criteria for Assessment of the Portfolio Without criteria, assessment of the portfolio cannot be consistent and fair. Individual portfolio pieces can be assessed using many of the tools discussed previously (checklists, rubrics) and simultaneously provide a stimulus for dialogue between teacher and student. It is important to remember that the criteria used in assessing the portfolio should align with the instructional objectives given by the teacher at the start of the assignment (Airasian, Engemann, & Gallagher, 2007). There is no question that assessing portfolios takes time, as individual pieces, student reflections, and summaries need to be assessed to provide a summative score for the portfolio. To complete their portfolios well, students should be provided with assessment criteria beforehand. Criteria can include the following:

- Comparing drafts with final products
- Spelling, grammatical, and mechanical errors
- Appropriate and accurate use of research data
- Emergence of main ideas
- Consistency and clarity throughout
- Evidence of self-reflection and growth
- Documenting established objectives
- Evidence of peer evaluation

Finally, students should reflect on the accomplishments of their portfolio and have input into areas they need to work on. While it is important for students to understand their own growth, it is equally important to report that growth to others. During conferences, students should be encouraged to convey such insights to their teachers. This information is then recorded in the portfolio. Students frequently share the portfolio with their families. When meeting with parents, portfolios enable teachers to provide a clear and concrete overview of student progress.

SUGGESTIONS FOR PROFESSIONAL DEVELOPMENT

1. According to Damian Cooper, "Assessment must be good for students. That means it must promote learning, and be fair, equitable, and sensitive to individual needs" (www.damiancooperassessment.com). Discuss this statement and make reference to in-class practices that would meet these goals. Ask a teacher how he or she meets these goals.
2. Body language and physical demeanour can tell you a lot about whether a student likes reading. Students who dislike reading are frequently poor readers (although they may be simply disinterested in the reading material). Hone your observation skills by sitting at the back of a classroom during any kind of silent reading time.
   - Observe a small group of students and record their behaviours. Reflect on the amount of time spent "doing nothing" or "hunting for the page" versus reading, thinking, writing, etc.
   - On the basis of your observations, speculate about whether the students are good, average, or poor readers. Ask the teacher to check the accuracy of your observations and conclusions.
3. Listen to a primary student read aloud. Using a copy of the text, conduct a running record of the student's reading. Consider the patterns that emerge in terms of strengths and weaknesses and take your results to the teacher to discuss their accuracy.

4. Ask to review several student portfolios.
   - How are differences in students' achievement levels and personalities reflected in the portfolios? Speculate about what specific reading and writing goals students may have generated as part of their portfolios.
   - Discuss your observations with the teacher.

CHILDREN'S LITERATURE REFERENCES

Curtis, C. P. (2007). *Elijah of Buxton*. Markham, ON: Scholastic.

Lowry, L. (2002). *The giver*. New York, NY: Laurel Leaf.

Paulson, G. (2006). *Hatchet*. New York, NY: Simon and Schuster Children's Publishing.

Chapter 4
Word Learning

Learning Objectives

In this chapter you will discover

- How to develop students' phonological and phonemic awareness.
- How to assess phonological and phonemic awareness skills.
- How to teach phonics.
- How to create an interest in word learning.
- How to teach sight words.
- How to help students develop skills for identifying unfamiliar words.
- How to assess students' reading fluency.
- How to work with students who are experiencing fluency difficulties.

MARILEE LAMOND: PRIMARY SPECIALIST

For more than 25 years, Marilee Lamond focused her career on being a primary specialist. Spending most of her time in grade 1, her passion is teaching young students how to read. Marilee's classroom actions are guided by the belief that setting high standards brings out the best in her students. "You accept students where they are in their learning. You build up their skills from there, providing a lot of praise and celebrations for their accomplishments."

One successful technique that Marilee uses with early readers is to select simple reading materials so that students experience immediate success. These successes then become the building blocks for subsequent accomplishments.

Beginnings are very important. On the first day of school, Marilee asks her students about their hopes for the upcoming year. "Most say that they want to learn to read. Some come and confide in me that they can't read." She reassures all of them that they will learn to read and that they will be able to read to their parents by the winter break. She then implements a number of carefully planned lessons and activities that will enable her students to meet this goal.

She begins by working holistically with the class. On the first day, students complete a shared story describing their new classroom. Marilee then begins the first of many word learning activities by pointing to each word while reading and rereading the shared story. As soon as students are able to read each word contained in the story, she explains to them that they are already reading!

In the first term, students work with Marilee to create a new story daily, using familiar events, nursery rhymes, and poems as starting points. While reading and rereading the story, she points to each word and then provides a phonics lesson focusing on initial consonants and moving to final and middle consonants. She consistently asks her students, "What makes sense here?" For instance, "Jack and Jill went up the . . . What makes sense here?" This regular prompt allows students to look at the picture, the surrounding words, and the title to determine the missing word. In this manner, Marilee provides her students with a number of word identification strategies that they can use whenever they are reading.

Follow-up activities include matching or circling words, reading words from the story in isolation, and reordering the story after Marilee has cut it into its component words. She selects stories that reflect and support student learning in sciences and social studies and provides for the integration of reading and writing activities. In this way, Marilee is able to achieve many learning objectives simultaneously while providing a motivational context for literacy activities.

Marilee is adamant about the importance of developing students' word identification skills at this level: "Word learning is the key to everything you do in grade 1." She regularly provides students with instruction in sight words and uses other familiar words as the basis for the study of critical letter patterns and letter-sound relations. She cautions that while most students usually know individual letter names and their corresponding sounds from the kindergarten program, it is critical for primary teachers to provide this instruction if students do not have this knowledge.

Marilee also has students complete many theme-related books in which they record new words. They take these books home and read to their parents. As the school year progresses, she begins research activities that require students to review information sheets she has developed containing facts about such topics as the seasons or polar bears. Students work in pairs to highlight the parts of the text they believe are important. They are then directed to share their summaries with each other and make their own books. These booklets and folders contain a list of objectives and assessment criteria so that parents can understand what their child is learning and how well he or she is achieving.

Marilee believes that, at this level, assessment is best completed on a one-on-one basis. She listens to students read and keeps extensive notes about the strategies and skills that each student uses to identify words. For instance, she wants to know whether students are "sounding out unknown words or using context clues." This type of information provides her with critical information about how to shape her instruction.

Now retired, Marilee is sharing her knowledge about the craft of teaching with beginning teachers. She admits that there are times when she misses the challenges and the joys of teaching students to read: "Some days when I enter a classroom to assess beginning teachers, I really miss being there myself."

REFLECTIVE ACTIVITY

Most young children love to hear stories read aloud, which prompts them to anticipate being able to read independently. The Harry Potter book series, and the media frenzy associated with each book's release, is an excellent example of how a good text can inspire young students to read independently. Imagine a young child who has just received a new Harry Potter book and who, with great anticipation, is sitting down to read the first page. Further imagine that the following words are encountered almost immediately:

Inhabitants

Gossip

Scarce

Drawing room

Century

Depending on their experiences with language, any of these words could negatively affect comprehension of the first part of the story. For instance, *inhabitants* is not frequently encountered in stories for very young children and Canadian children may not know the term *drawing room*.

1. What would children be most likely to feel upon encountering unknown words on the first page of a book?
2. What would be the likely outcome of this reading experience?
3. What strategies would you use if you were to encounter a similar situation in your own reading?

Student Voice 4.1

I really like my mom, or anyone really, reading to me but I also like reading by myself in my head.

Zoya
Grade 3 student

Guided reading

THE IMPORTANCE OF WORD KNOWLEDGE

STUDENTS FREQUENTLY ENCOUNTER NEW WORDS, WHETHER AS PART OF THEIR conversations with others, during independent reading, or in interactions with print and the media. As reading and writing activities depend strongly on word knowledge, a good vocabulary and strong word attack skills are essential components of literacy. Successful reading and writing depend on being able to identify and spell words, especially high-frequency words, efficiently (Allington & Cunningham, 2001; Burns, Griffin, & Snow, 1999; Johnson, 2001). If readers spend a disproportionate amount of time trying to decode individual words, they will not be able to focus on the overall message contained in the text. When this occurs, motivation to continue reading frequently falters as well (Fountas & Pinnell, 1996; Guthrie & Cox, 2001; Hiebert & Raphael, 1998).

There are four types of vocabulary: listening vocabulary, speaking vocabulary, reading vocabulary, and writing vocabulary (presented in descending order according to size). Listening vocabulary, which is the largest type, consists of words and phrases that are understood when heard. Speaking vocabulary consists of words and phrases that are used when speaking, while reading vocabulary consists of words and phrases that can be identified and understood during reading. The smallest type, writing vocabulary, is made up of words and phrases that are available to individuals when writing. Effective teachers provide a literacy-rich environment in which learning across all four vocabulary groups is nurtured. While there is considerable overlap across these types of vocabulary, students can demonstrate inconsistent growth across the categories. Students may be familiar with the use of a term or concept as part of their speaking and listening vocabularies but be unable to use the same term or phrase as part of their written vocabulary.

In this way, many words are neither absolutely known nor totally unfamiliar. According to the National Early Literacy Panel (2008), there are three basic levels of vocabulary learning:

1. **Unknown:** The word and its meaning are totally unfamiliar.
2. **Acquainted:** The word is somewhat familiar in terms of its basic meaning.
3. **Established:** The word is very familiar and can be recognized readily and used correctly.

Each of these levels, in turn, can be applied across the four types of vocabulary.

The gradual and erratic nature of word learning underlines the importance of talk, Read Aloud, and collaborative tasks in the classroom, as well as reading and writing activities that allow for vocabulary development across all four categories. The question remains: How can teachers implement literacy programs that enable students to learn new vocabulary?

Alphabet Principles

Did You Know . . . ?

The English language has one of the largest and most complex vocabularies in the world.

Words can be spelled phonetically about 50 percent of the time.

Twenty-six letters of the alphabet represent 44 phonemes.

Five hundred spellings represent 44 phonemes.

Three hundred different letter combinations represent 17 vowel sounds.

(Graham & Miller, 1979)

STAGES OF READING DEVELOPMENT

THINK ABOUT THE SKILLS YOU EMPLOY AS AN ADULT READER. NOW REMEMBER yourself as a beginning reader. Consider the changes that you have undergone in your reading abilities and thinking processes. While there is universal agreement that reading is a sophisticated process that requires years to develop, Jeanne Chall (1983) was among the first researchers to document how students progress in their reading development. She identified that students progress through a continuum of six reading stages, each of which is described briefly below.

Stage 0: Pre-Reading Stage (birth to age 6)

This stage represents the greatest interval of time, with most learning occurring in the home environment. This stage also corresponds with increased control of other aspects of language, including syntax and vocabulary. During this time, children discover and acquire insights about letters, words, and books. For example, they begin to understand and identify the sounds at the beginnings and endings of words. Many children also demonstrate some internal knowledge of reading (e.g., holding a book in the proper direction, distinguishing words from pictures) and are able to retell favourite stories from memory. Effective teachers, however, recognize that students enter school with mixed abilities (e.g., some students can recognize individual words such as their name or road signs and are able to approximate print, while others cannot) and adjust their instruction accordingly. This adjustment to individual differences is imperative, as many of these early skills are essential to later reading development and success.

Stage 1: Initial Reading or Decoding Stage (grades 1 and 2; ages 6 and 7)

One of the central features of this stage is students' ability to associate arbitrary letters with corresponding parts of spoken words. During this stage, students develop a sense of the alphabetic principle and are able to apply sound-spelling relationships. They understand that spoken words are made up of a finite number of sounds. At end of this stage, students demonstrate increased insights about the spelling system. Stage 1 reading is identified as representing several phases. In the first phase, students' reading tends to be characterized by word substitution errors, representing their limited knowledge of words and the world, and may be qualitatively similar to students in the pre-reading stage. In the second phase, students' reading is characterized by an increase in "non-responses" or response failures. When they are made, decoding errors tend to be graphically similar to text. In the third phase, students return to making semantically similar errors, which are a function of their increased knowledge of reading and the world.

Stage 2: Confirmation, Fluency, and Ungluing from Print (grades 2 and 3; ages 7 and 8)

During this stage, students need to bring prior knowledge to their reading and consolidate the skills acquired during stage 1. Students in this stage continue to relate print to speech. It is essential that students are provided with the opportunity to read many familiar books (familiar content and familiar structure), as reading familiar text allows them to focus on the printed word, strengthening their word attack and decoding skills and thus building reading fluency. Providing students with multiple opportunities for reading practice also helps them develop reading fluency. Effective teachers are vigilant about gaps that may appear among students at this stage and are aware of external factors that may contribute to such discrepancies (e.g., differences in socio-economic background, English as a subsequent language).

Stage 3: Reading for Learning the New Stage: A First Step (grades 4 to 8 or 9; ages 9 to 13 or 14)

Students in this stage begin to relate print to ideas. Reading becomes another way of "knowing." Indeed, by the end of stage 3, reading may represent students' dominant way of knowing (with previous methods of knowing predominately involving observation and listening). However, since students' word and world knowledge are still developing, it is recommended that they be presented with materials that are relatively clear in focus and provide one perspective or viewpoint (versus multiple perspectives). Students also need to acquire skills with respect to "how" to learn from text (e.g., skimming, scanning), especially as greater emphasis is placed on reading in the content areas and as texts become longer with more abstract ideas and more complex language structures. Chall has suggested dividing this stage into two phases: the first representing students in grades 4 to 6 and the second representing students in grades 7 to 9, with this latter stage resembling adult reading (stage 4). As students move between the two phases, they increase their ability to analyze text and to respond critically.

Stage 4: Multiple Viewpoints Stage (secondary school; ages 14 to 18)

In this stage, students can process materials that provide multiple perspectives or viewpoints. Texts are characterized by increased length and depth (relative to text read in earlier stages). Students continue to acquire complex concepts and new points of view, with instruction focused on providing them with evidence-based reading and learning strategies and skills.

Stage 5: Construction and Reconstruction Stage (post-secondary school; ages 18 and older)

In this stage, readers make judgments about what to read (as well as what not to read) and how to read materials (i.e., reading approach). They are able to construct new knowledge at an abstract and complex level. Ideally, they demonstrate metacognitive awareness for text materials, the reading process, and themselves. Effective instruction at this stage is individualized to provide students with specific skills that complement their reading needs.

In sum, each of the stages described here contains specific skills and conditions that are subsumed in the sequential stages (although students sometimes can demonstrate advancement without all criteria). Teachers interact most directly with students in stages 1 to 5. Students in stage 1 develop a sense of the alphabetic principle and use sound-spelling relationships. In stage 2, students develop their decoding skills and reading fluency and begin to apply strategies that assist them to derive meaning from text. In stage 3, students encounter a wide variety of texts and reading contexts. They must further develop their vocabularies and adopt evidence-based strategic processes. In stages 4 and 5, students are expected to analyze text critically and consider multiple viewpoints. By stage 5, reading resembles a constructive process in which readers connect new information to their previous knowledge to construct and refine their existing understandings of concepts while engaging in critical analysis and synthesis of materials. With maturity, readers can demonstrate different stages for different reading purposes (e.g., stage 5 for university course reading, stage 3 while reading for pleasure). Effective teachers recognize the reading needs of individual students and provide them with the knowledge and skills that allow them to move on to the next stage while promoting their enthusiasm to be readers and writers.

Teaching vocabulary

BEGINNING WORD LEARNING

Phonological Awareness and Phonemic Awareness

Understanding that the English language consists of units of sound and being able to make connections between letters and sounds is critical to the reading process (Snow, Burns, & Griffin, 1998). Phonological awareness is a broader concept (encompassing phonemic awareness) that involves understanding that the English language consists of units of sound that vary in size (Caldwell & Leslie, 2009; Goswami, 2000). Significant attention has been placed on students' development of phonological awareness at the syllable, onset and rime, and phoneme levels. In general, students who possess phonological awareness recognize that words represent sound units and are composed of distinct sound parts (i.e., syllables), morphemes (i.e., the smallest linguistic unit in a word that can carry meaning), and individual sounds (i.e., phonemes). Among these three components, students who struggle with the reading process most often demonstrate difficulties with phonemic awareness (Caldwell & Leslie, 2009; Ehri & Nunes, 2002; Lonigan, Shanahan, & Cunningham, 2008).

Students who demonstrate phonemic awareness are able to recognize and manipulate units of sounds in words. For instance, they are able to match words by sounds, recognize rhymes, and generate words with the same beginning, middle, and end sounds. They are also able to blend sounds to form new words, segment words into discrete sounds, and identify and substitute sounds in words (i.e., engage in wordplay). Some students find these tasks to be challenging, in part because these units of sound are devoid of meaning and most students are inclined to consider the semantic (meaning) versus linguistic properties of words.

Student Voice 4.2

If you don't know how to read a word you should break it up and read one half and then the other half. You should look for anything that you know in the little parts of the word and then stick the parts together like glue. That is how you can read the real word—like putting the *blue* with the *berry* when reading the book *Dear Mr. Blueberry*.

Abby
Grade 3 student

Development of Phonological Awareness

For most children, phonological awareness begins through their early oral interactions with their family members (Duursmal, Augustyn, & Zuckerman, 2008; Haney & Hill, 2004; Snow et al., 1998). Children who have experienced rich language activities in the home appear to be receptive to playing with the sounds of language. These experiences are often spontaneous and may include such enjoyable activities as singing, chanting rhymes, rehearsing tongue twisters, playing word games, and listening to children's rap music. For instance, one author recalls reading Dennis Lee's *Alligator Pie* to a kindergarten class and helping them make up new verses to the title poem by adding alligator pizza and alligator cake with appropriate rhymes, accompanied by much laughter and clapping. Other experiences can include the shared reading of storybooks, especially predictable and rhyming texts.

The other author recalls reading *Rainy Day Magic* by award-winning Canadian author Marie-Louise Gay to her young children as a before-nap activity (the book describes the make-believe adventure of two young girls who are confined to the house on a rainy day). With very little practice, her children could recite all of the words in the text and quickly developed actions to accompany the rhyming lyrics. They enjoyed chanting alliterations such as "A slippery slide/On a snake's scaly gown" and then creating their own, such as "A terrible tumble/On a tiger's toothy crown" and "A hilly hike/On a hippo's huge backside." They also substituted rhyming words on their favourite pages, extending the characters' adventures.

Teachers are wise to encourage parents of young students to continue such rich language-building activities in the home.

Phonemic Awareness and Early Reading Phonemic awareness is one of the best predictors of early reading success (Cunningham, 2007; Dickinson, McCabe, Anastasopoulos, Peisner-Feinberg, & Poe, 2003). Young students who exhibit phonemic awareness demonstrate higher reading achievement in the primary grades than their peers who do not demonstrate such awareness (Ball & Blachman, 1991; Juel, 1988; Stanovich, 1988). Equally important, however, is that participation in high-quality early literacy activities promotes students' phonemic awareness (Chapman & Tunmer, 2003; Hill & Nichols, 2006). That is, students' phonemic awareness can improve as a function of participating in literacy-rich activities, which, in turn, better prepares them for beginning reading activities. Students who demonstrate phonological awareness, especially at the phonemic level, are well positioned to begin reading. Unfortunately, not all children enter the classroom with sound phonological awareness, with students who experience chronic ear infections, central auditory processing deficits, speech and language delays or impairments, or low socio-economic status being potentially at risk.

More positively, there is substantial evidence that teachers can provide students with instruction that promotes their phonological and phonemic awareness, with such instruction being especially important for at-risk readers (National Reading Panel, 2000). Ideally, this instruction is a central component in preschool and kindergarten programming, although older students who struggle with the reading process may benefit from such instruction (Ehri & Nunes, 2002). Similar to home experiences, the majority of this instruction should be playful and engaging.

Teacher Voice 4.1

Unlocking the alphabetic code is critical for young children to develop print literacy. This is a complex process that can be made enjoyable through the use of multi-sensory activities. In my experience, programs that include kinesthetic and musical cues for each letter sound foster increased learning by actively engaging children. Use of such programs, together with abundant opportunity to apply their knowledge of sound-symbol correspondence through encoding and decoding print, can bring learning to life and support the literacy growth of young children. This sets the stage for their continued academic success as literacy learners in all grades and subject areas.

Arlene Grierson, Ph.D.
Literacy and language professor and *Jolly Jingles* author
Former literacy consultant and elementary school teacher

Teaching Phonemic Awareness in the Classroom In general, teachers are encouraged to focus instruction on segmenting and blending activities in favour of other phonological awareness activities, as these skills are related most directly to reading and spelling processes. Teachers are also encouraged to include many rhyming activities as part of their classroom instruction, since rhyming is a skill that is not fully developed until the end of kindergarten for most students (Caldwell & Leslie, 2009). Finally, teachers are encouraged to include instruction that requires students to use letters while manipulating phonemes (a more effective format than oral activities only; Ehri & Nunes, 2002). See Table 4.1 for some instructional ideas related to developing students' phonemic awareness. Readers are also encouraged to explore suggestions provided by reading specialists such as Yopp and Yopp (2002) and Manyak (2008).

Table 4.1 Teaching Suggestions for Promoting Phonemic Awareness

Alliteration

- Who knows a word that begins with a . . . ? Who knows a word that ends with . . . ? Who knows a word that has the middle sound . . . ? (Pictures can be used as clues.)
- Play "I spy with my little eye."
- Read books with alliteration or letter patterns. Popular titles include:
  - *Six Sleepy Sheep* by Jeffie Ross Gordon
  - *Alligator Arrived with Apples: A Potluck Alphabet Feast* by Crescent Dragonwagon
  - *Four Famished Foxes and Fosdyke* by Pamela Duncan Edwards
  - *Princess Prunella and the Purple Peanut* by Margaret Atwood
  - *Rude Ramsay and the Roaring Radishes* by Margaret Atwood
  - *Busy Buzzing Bumblebees and Other Tongue Twisters* by Alvin Schwartz

Sorting Tasks

- Have students complete picture sorts (sort by beginning, middle, and end letters) to discover the underlying relationships among the sounds of words. Increase complexity by position of sort as well as by the number of items.
- Replace pictures with objects and words to discover the underlying sounds and patterns among words. Have students participate in a scavenger hunt for items that represent the sound of a target letter or object (Yopp & Yopp, 2000).

Example: Provide students with a three- or four-letter word and read the word aloud. For each letter in the word, show students a corresponding letter card and place it face down in a pocket chart, following the tune of "Are You Sleeping Brother John?"

Beginning, middle, end; beginning, middle end
Where is the sound?
Where is the sound?
Where is the *fff* in *fan*?
Where is the *fff* in *fan*?
Let's find out.
Let's find out.

Have students identify the position of the sound (beginning, middle, end) in the word, by selecting one of the letter cards from the pocket chart. Provide feedback as required and continue with the other phonemes in the word.

(Source: Bear, Donald R.; Invernizzi, Marcia; Templeton, Shane; Johnston, Francine, *Words Their Way*, 3rd Edition, © 2004. Adapted by permission of Pearson Education, Inc., Upper Saddle River, NJ.)

Blending and Segmenting

- Provide students with a series of isolated sounds and ask them to put together a "mystery item." (Provide semantic cues if necessary: My favourite pet is a */d/o/g/;* When it is cold outside it is important to wear our winter */m/i/tt/e/n/s/*; I spy something that is round. I spy a */b/a/ll/.*)
- Have students identify the series of sounds that comprise a target word.
- Modify common games to focus on blending and segmenting (e.g., require students to sound out each sound of target words while taking steps forward as part of the game Mother May I?) (Yopp & Yopp, 2002).

Examples:

Blending Chant

Have students follow the tune from a well-known children's song while completing blending or segmenting activities. For example, follow the tune of "If You're Happy and You Know It, Clap Your Hands":

> If you think you know this word, shout it out!
> If you think you know this word, shout it out!
> If you think you know this word,
> Then tell me what you've heard,
> If you think you know this word, shout it out!

After singing, the teacher says a segmented word such as /k/ /a/ /t/ and students provide the blended word *cat*. (Source: Yopp, 1992).

Segmentation Cheer

> Listen to my cheer.
> Then shout the sounds you hear.
> *Sun! Sun! Sun!*
> Let's take apart the word *sun*.
> Give me the beginning sound. (*/s/*)
> Give me the middle sound. (*/u/*)
> Give me the ending sound. (*/n/*)
> That's right!
> */s/u/n/*—Sun! Sun! Sun!

(Source: http://www.readingrockets.org/strategies/blending_games)

Rhyming Tasks

- Provide students with several words and ask them to identify which items rhyme (or do not rhyme).
- Have students substitute rhyming words while reading favourite nursery rhymes and songs.
- Read poetry books such as *Monster Motel* by Douglas Florian, in which fictitious creatures such as Littly Shy Shegs and Slimy Slatches are described through alliteration and rhyme.
- Include rhyming books as part of daily Read Aloud and in classroom libraries. Popular titles include:
  - *Bears in Pairs* by Niki Yektai and Diane deGroat
  - *Chicka Chicka Boom Boom* by Bill Martin, Jr.
  - *Clap Your Hands* by Lorinda Bryan Cauley
  - *Five Little Monkeys Sitting in a Tree* by Eileen Christelow
  - *Goodnight Moon* by Margaret Wise Brown
  - *Green Eggs and Ham* by Dr. Seuss
  - *Hop on Pop* by Dr. Seuss
  - *Jiggle Wiggle Prance* by Sally Noll
  - *Pigs Aplenty, Pigs Galore!* by David McPhail

(Continued)

Table 4.1 Teaching Suggestions for Promoting Phonemic Awareness *(continued)*

- *Ten Little Crocodiles* by Colin West
- *Whose Mouse Are You?* by Robert Kraus

- Many songs also make use of rhymes, such as "The Ants Go Marching," "Down by the Bay," "Row, Row, Row Your Boat," "Three Blind Mice," "Humpty Dumpty," and "The Farmer in the Dell." Have students sing these songs several times, altering various verses by substituting different rhymes.

Counting Tasks and Elkonin Boxes (Say-It-Move-It)

- Have students count aloud while moving poker chips (tap/clap/jump) for each sound they hear in a target word (see Figures 4.1a and 4.1b). Provide students with increasingly complex words. (Note that the kinesthetic activity provides an easy method of assessment for teachers.)

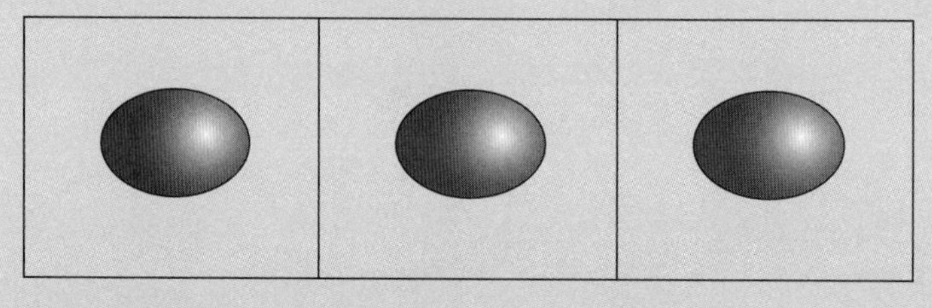

Figure 4.1a Elkonin Box for "Moon"

Three boxes are required to represent the word *moon*, which is segmented into three phonemes: */m/oo/n/*

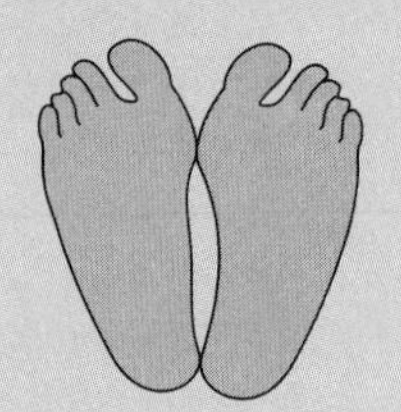

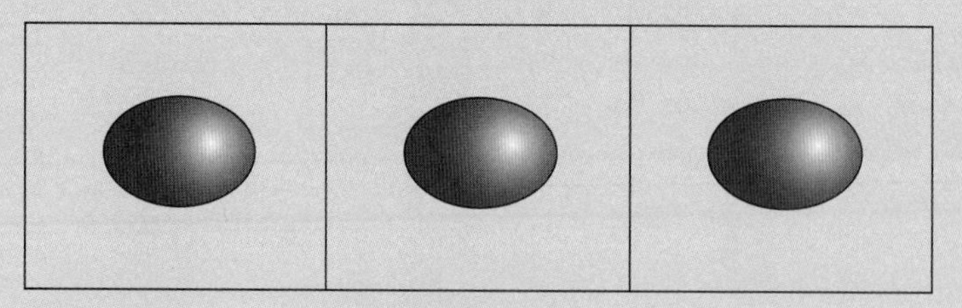

Figure 4.1b Elkonin Box for "Feet"

Three boxes are required to represent the word *feet*, which is segmented into three phonemes: */f/ee/t/*

- Progress to providing students with several letter cards and asking them to move corresponding letter sounds into the box (Blachmann, 2000).
- For suggestions about how to select appropriate items for Elkonin boxes and teach students to "hear" sounds in words, see McCarthy (2008) and Gunning (2005).

Word Building and Wordplay

- When students are able to complete Elkonin box tasks successfully, they are usually ready to begin word building activities with letters (Stahl, 2002).
- Teachers provide a set of letters and students form words in progressive difficulty (two-letter, three-letter, four-letter, etc.).
- Wordplay is often involved, with students being provided with hints and clues to manipulate individual letters to form new words.
- Read students books that feature wordplay. For instance, *Runny Babbit: A Billy Sook* by Shel Silverstein contains a collection of poems that play on spoonerisms (i.e., mixed-up first letters of two words).

Examples:

Using the letters *a*, *e*, *e*, *u*, *l*, *p*, *r*, and *s*, make the word *sure*.

(Hint: I am *sure* that you will win the talent show.)

Remove the *e* and add an additional letter to indicate a type of speech that is difficult to understand.

(Hint: It is important that you do not *slur* your words.)

Add another letter to indicate a noisy sound.

(Hint: It is impolite to *slurp* your soup.)

(Adapted from Rasinski, 2001.)

What's in My Head?

My word begins like *cover.*

My word rhymes with *star.*

My word has three letters.

Someday when I am older I will drive a ______. (car)

My word has five letters.

My word begins with the sound that I hear at the beginning of *swim.*

My word rhymes with *feet.*

Chocolate is very ______. (sweet)

(Source: Benchmark School, 1998.)

Direct and Explicit Instruction

When explicit instruction is required, it should be age appropriate and relatively brief, averaging about 10 to 15 minutes per day and never exceeding 30 minutes. The small-group format is most effective and allows for targeted instruction based on student interest and need. Finally, this instruction session should be holistic, connecting to a meaningful unit (e.g., book study, Read Aloud, thematic unit). Teachers must also remember that

Table 4.2 Resources for Helping Students Develop Phonological Awareness

Earobics Step 1 and Step 2 (2000) by Jan Wasowicz, Cognitive Concepts, Inc.
Launch into Reading Success (2000) by Lorna Bennett & Pamela Ottley, Pro-Ed.
Oo-pples and boo-noo-noos: Songs and activities for Phonemic Awareness 2nd Edition (2003) by Halie Kay Yopp & Ruth Helen Yopp, Harcourt Brace School Publishers.
"Phonemic Awareness: Moving from Oral Language to Beginning Links with Print" in *Learning about Print in Preschool* (2009) by Dorthy Strickland & Judith Schickedanz, International Reading Association.
Road to the Code: A Phonological Awareness Program for Young Children (2000) by Benita Blachman, Eileen Ball, Rochella Black and Darlene Tangel, Baltimore: Brookes.
Sounds Abound (1993) by Hugh Catts & Tina Vartiainen, LinguiSystems.
The Phonological Awareness Handbook for Kindergarten and Primary Teachers (1998) by Lita Ericson & Moria Fraser Juliebö, International Reading Association.

such instruction is insufficient to promote good reading; rather, it is only one component of a larger literacy program. Teachers are encouraged to adapt commercially available products such as *Launch into Reading Success (Book 2)* (2011) by Lorna Bennett and Pamela Ottley, *Phonological Awareness Training for Reading* (1994) by Joseph Torgesen and Brian Bryant, and *Sound Start: Teaching Phonological Awareness in the Classroom* (1997) by Orna Lenchner and Blanche Podhajski when delivering structured lessons. Table 4.2 provides a list of resources for helping students develop phonological awareness.

Older Students

In general, relatively little attention has been focused on the effects of phonological awareness training in older students, including those with identified reading challenges (for some exceptions, see Felton & Miller, 2001; Vellutino & Scanlon, 1987; Williams, 1980). More positively, the studies completed with older students suggest that they too may benefit from phonological awareness training. Teachers are reminded about the importance of using age-appropriate materials when working with older students and are encouraged to review such resources as *Earobics 1 for Adolescents and Adults* (software program with home versions available) and *Phonological Awareness Training for High Schools (PATHS)*.

Student Voice 4.3

When you don't know a word in the book you can skip over it and look for picture clues and other clues. Or you could look for little letter patterns and try and sound out each section. You can also ask your teacher.

Zach
Grade 7 student

Caution: Second Language Learners

Teachers need to be especially sensitive when working with students whose first language is not English. In general, these students automatically will process unfamiliar items in the context of their first language. Difficulties can than arise when these language systems differ from the phoneme categorization system used for English, with this being especially true for older students who have learned to read using logographic (versus alphabetical) writing scripts. As a result, many of these students will not be able to identify differences in phonemes or produce corresponding sound units. For instance, many Asian speakers do not differentiate between the phonemes */l/* and */r/* (Ehri & Nunes, 2002).

ASSESSING PHONOLOGICAL AND PHONEMIC AWARENESS SKILLS IN PREPARATION FOR BEGINNING TO READ

Teachers who are interested in assessing students' phonological and phonemic awareness skills can select from a variety of commercial products and standardized instruments (see Table 4.3). Most instruments can be administered within 10 to 15 minutes. Observation is also an important assessment tool and teachers are encouraged to observe students in a systematic fashion as part of their daily programming. As with instruction in all areas of the language arts, effective assessment is related to effective instruction, and many of the assessment ideas provided here overlap with instruction content. Some assessment suggestions follow.

Same–Different Rhyming

- Provide students with examples of words that rhyme and explain that when two words rhyme, they share the same end sound (e.g., *frog* and *bog*, *ring* and *sing*).
- Provide students with examples of non-rhyming words and explain that when words do not rhyme, their end sounds differ (e.g., *brick* and *bang*, *chain* and *chair*).
- Extend this exercise to include rhyme production by having students provide rhymes in response to target words (e.g., can you tell me a word that rhymes with *cat*, *sun*, *pump*, *train*?).
- Teachers are encouraged to use rhyming words from available resources (e.g., Yopp, 1995a; 20-item rhyming test) or make their own word lists (minimum of 15 items).
- See *Qualitative Reading Inventory*, 5th edition (Leslie & Caldwell, 2010) for guidelines for producing word lists.

Isolating Sounds

- Provide students with a series of objects, pictures, or words and ask them to identify the beginning sounds of words.
- Provide students with progressively more difficult tasks, moving from beginning sounds to those at the end and then in the middle of words. (Note: Middle sounds are the most difficult.) Example: Ask students if they can identify the sound that is at the beginning of the following words: *summer*, *sun*, *sign*, *seal*. Then ask them to identify the sound at the end of the following words: *bent*, *went*, *hint*, *want*. Finally, ask them to identify the sound in the middle of the following words: *coat*, *vote*, *boat*.

Table 4.3 Resources for Assessing Phonological Awareness

Comprehensive Test of Phonological Processing (CTOPP; Wagner, Torgesen, & Rashotte, 1999)

- Measures students' phonological awareness, phonological memory, and rapid naming across various subtests, including blending words and non-words, segmenting words and non-words, phoneme reversal, memory for digits, and rapid colour, digit, letter, and object naming
- Two versions available (5 to 6 years and 5 to 24 years)
- Administered to individual students
- Requires approximately 30 minutes to administer

The Phonological Awareness Test 2 (PAT2; Robertson & Salter, 2007)

- Measures students' phonemic awareness across five skills: segmentation, isolation, deletion, substitution, and blending
- Measures students' sensitivity to rhyme, knowledge of graphemes, and decoding, with an optional spelling test
- Assesses students' abilities from the second semester of kindergarten to grade 2
- Administered to individual students
- Requires approximately 40 minutes to administer

The Test of Awareness of Language Segments (TALS; Sawyer, 1987)

- Measures segmentation abilities in order of sequential difficulty (i.e., sentences into words; words into syllables; words into sounds)
- Administered to individual students
- Students' success at each level determines number of items to be administered

Rosner Test of Auditory Analysis (Rosner, 1975)

- Measures students' abilities to delete phonemes from words
- Recommended for students in kindergarten to grade 2 and for older students experiencing reading difficulties
- Administered to individual students
- Requires approximately 5 to 10 minutes to administer

Yopp-Singer Test of Phonemic Segmentation (Yopp, 1995b)

- Consists of 22 words that represent combinations of two and three sounds
- Measures English-speaking kindergarten students' ability to separately articulate sounds of spoken words (e.g., *dog* → *d/o/g; rice* → *r/i/ce*)
- Administered to individual students
- Requires 5 to 10 minutes to administer
- Predicts reading and spelling performance in grades 2 to 6

Segmenting Sounds

- Provide students with a series of target words or nonsense items and have them repeat them back one sound at a time. Example: Say the word *late* one sound at a time. Response: /l/ā/t/. Example: Say *trōst* one sound at a time. Response: /t/r/ō/s/t/. Example: Say *flim* one sound at a time. Response: /f/l/i/m/. Note that the use of nonsense items controls for students' vocabulary and provides a true measure of their segmenting skills (versus word recognition).
- Present words in order of progressive difficulty. Words with two phonemes are usually easier to segment than those with three phonemes or more. Consonant-vowel blends (e.g., /b-o/ in *boat*) are easier to segment than consonant clusters (e.g., /s-t/ in *stamp*, /m-p/ in *lamp*; Ehri & Nunes, 2002).

Blending Sounds

- Provide students with a series of target sounds and ask them to repeat the item as a whole word or nonsense item. Example: What do the sounds /b/ō/n/ say? Response: *bone*. Example: What do the sounds /s/t/ă/m/p/ say? Response: *stamp*. Example: What do the sounds /sh/ĭ/b/ say? Response: *shib*. Again, the use of nonsense items controls for students' vocabulary and provides a true measure of their blending skills (word recognition) and their letter-sound relationship abilities.
- Present sound segments in order of progressive difficulty. Items containing stop constants are usually more difficult to blend (*p, b, t, d, k, g, ch, j*) than items containing continuant constants (*m, n, f, v, x, z, th, sh, l, r*). (Note that it is difficult to pronounce *p* or *b* without adding an *uh* sound; Ehri & Nunes, 2002.)

CREATING AN INTEREST IN WORDS

SOME EDUCATORS HAVE INDICATED THAT FREQUENTLY THERE IS INSUFFICIENT classroom focus on word learning (Biemiller & Boote, 2006), suggesting the need for more robust vocabulary instruction throughout the grades. An awareness and interest in words can be stimulated by focusing on the meaning of new words and their power to enhance communication. This kind of instruction includes directly teaching new words and following up with thought-provoking and pleasurable interactive games and activities (Beck, McKeown, & Kucan, 2002). By modelling a playfulness with words, a sense of fun and enjoyment can be created that will encourage students to take pride in their expanding vocabularies. Encouraging students to add a verse to Shel Silverstein's humorous poetry in *A Light in the Attic* or *Where the Sidewalk Ends* creates playfulness using rhythm and rhyme. The poetry of Dennis Lee, Toronto's poet laureate, in *Alligator Pie*, *Garbage Delight*, or *Bubblegum Delicious* has delighted many students, and the poems easily lend themselves to the creation of additional verses. Lee and Silverstein provide excellent examples of how to play with language.

Possessing a repertoire of vocabulary games is an asset for teachers as they continue to help students expand their vocabularies. For instance:

- *Mystery Word*: This game involves selecting a new word (perhaps from an upcoming curriculum unit) and placing the first letter on the board under the words *Mystery*

Word. Each day or more frequently, add another letter until someone can identify the word. When the word is identified, spend a few minutes talking about its meaning and practising using it in a sentence. This can be an ongoing class activity that takes very little instructional time but helps expand students' repertoire of words.

- *Vocabulary Jeopardy*: In this game, the teacher selects a category and makes a series of statements that must be answered with a question. For example, in the category *Plant Life*, the teacher states, "The chemical process where plants turn chemicals and nutrients into food." Response: "What is photosynthesis?"
- A teacher can place a word, such as *angry*, on the board. Students can brainstorm as many words as possible that identify a similar emotion (annoyed, frustrated, ticked off, disgruntled, peeved, wrathful, put out, perturbed, etc.).
- Many other games can be found on the internet at www.reggie.net/teaching/vocab.htm and at www.ehow/how_2069516_teach_vocabulary.html.

Games are more successful learning vehicles than spelling bees or directing students to try to locate unknown words in a dictionary.

Indirect Instruction

In a rich literacy environment, children learn most of their vocabulary indirectly through a variety of social interactions (Cooter & Reutzel, 2004; Gunning, 2005) as well as through a regular Read Aloud program. Teachers can build on this social learning by providing experiences, both actual and vicarious, about which children can talk and read. The follow-up discussion after a literacy experience is extremely important for learning new vocabulary, as teachers can intentionally introduce new words and repeat them naturally throughout the discussion. These new words need to be related to background knowledge by asking students to respond to the unknown word using a personal judgment or observation. For instance, if the word is *fluke*, ask students to identify something good that has happened to them that they consider a fluke. The value of these discussions is that children are exposed to advanced vocabulary and, when given the opportunity to participate in these discussions, children will learn from each other. The more discussions in which students participate, the more words they have the potential to learn!

With this in mind, a teacher is constantly trying to create experiences that will enable language development. For instance, a simple walking trip to a local park or even within the schoolyard can be organized to observe the signs of winter or spring. New words introduced into the conversation may include *shrivelled*, *withered*, *coarse*, and *cycle*. Alternatively, the reading of a book such as *Big Sarah's Little Boots* by Paulette Bourgeois can spark discussions about outgrowing clothes in a new season, passing old clothes to younger siblings, and shopping for new clothes. New words may include *struggle*, *favourite*, *acceptance*, and *sibling*. Indirect instruction in this manner can be extremely effective, largely because it is presented in a motivational, familiar context. When an unfamiliar word is encountered while reading aloud, the teacher should stop and define the word and, after the story is completed, ensure that the word is used in the following discussion. While word learning in these scenarios reflects indirect instruction for students, it is a very conscious and direct activity on the teacher's part.

Direct Instruction

Direct instruction can help students learn difficult words such as those that are conceptually based and not part of their everyday language experience. When teachers provide direct instruction for new words that students are about to read independently or hear in a Read Aloud, better comprehension occurs. Direct instruction includes teaching students to use word-learning strategies that they can apply independently. For instance, before reading a book that is an autobiography, the teacher may introduce the words *autobiography* and *biography* and show how both the meaning and the composition of the words are related. Beware of presenting new words only as definitions, as they will not be retained by students. Instead, words should be presented in sentences that illustrate the meaning and then students should be encouraged to generate sentences containing the new words. The discussion can include asking the class whether the generated sentences provide accurate use of the new words. Learning new vocabulary in this way is enhanced not only by trying to generate a sentence but also by assessing the accuracy of sentences posed by peers.

Principles of Effective Vocabulary Instruction

1. Words are best learned naturally in meaningful texts in which the structure of the word is connected to the meaning.
2. Teachers should provide both a definition of a new word and a context for the word during direct instruction. The best method is a simple circular instructional model. Present the word in context so that the meaning is evident. Discuss the meaning in the context. Remove the word from the context and write it by itself so it is seen as a single entity. Discuss its structure in terms of sounds, silent letters, syllables, or double letters and ensure correct pronunciation. Finally, put the word back in context by having students provide sentences that contain the word and demonstrate its meaning. These sentences can be written on a board or chart. The last step is to add the word to the classroom's word wall so it can be included in any games or activities.
3. Vocabulary should be taught in depth as well as in breadth. By depth, we mean that new vocabulary needs to connect with students' existing knowledge. By breadth, we mean spending the time to learn new words to expand the repertoire of words that are understood by students. There are three levels of processing necessary for this to occur in vocabulary learning (Linan-Thompson & Vaughn, 2007; Stahl, 1986). First, students learn simple associations by using their existing word knowledge to learn new words by recognizing synonyms and using word associations. For instance, they may know the word *pants* but not *pantaloons*, or they may know the word *query* but not *querulous*. Second, students need to be able to expand simple associations by fitting new words into sentences, by finding antonyms, or by being able to classify the new words with similar words. For instance, they may be familiar with the word *follow* but not with *precede*, or they may be familiar with *split* but not with *adhere* or *cleave*. Finally, the student needs to be able to define the new words in his or her own words, complete blanks in sentences with the new words, or connect the new words to personal experiences.
4. When a new word represents a concept, it is best presented in a framework that shows the connections to other concepts and words that make up a network. It also should

be related to students' prior knowledge. For instance, if the new word is *government*, it could be taught in association with words such as *prime minister*, *voting*, *laws*, *Canada*, *local representatives*, *municipal*, and *federal*.

5. Students need multiple exposures to new vocabulary to improve word knowledge and comprehension when reading. By placing new words on the word wall and playing games using these words, students are more likely to incorporate a new word into their speaking, reading, and writing vocabularies. In older grades, it is helpful if the teacher uses the word in discussions both at the time of learning and subsequently.

Beyond sight words, which are frequently present in text, there are two kinds of words that students encounter in print. These are words that they know but may not instantly recognize and new words that they have never heard or seen previously. Students need help in both areas. They need word attack skills to identify words when they already know the meaning. They also need to expand their personal repertoire of familiar words.

DECODING AND PHONICS

Studying spelling words

No aspect of reading has been the subject of more debate than phonics and its role in the beginning-to-read process. Phonics was the central component of *The Great Debate* led by Jeanne Chall (1996), which reverberated from the 1960s to the millennium in educational circles. During this time, proponents of phonics instruction were accused of neglecting comprehension skills and those who adhered to a "whole language" comprehension–based approach were accused of not providing beginning readers with the necessary skills to "sound out" unknown words using phonics. This very public debate between phonics and whole language was based on a false dichotomy between the role of decoding (phonics) and whole language (focusing on comprehension), as reading instruction is not complete without both components. Students need both the ability to decode and the ability to comprehend messages in text if they are to become fluent readers. More recently, the issue has been resolved by the philosophy of creating a balanced reading program that includes phonics instruction as part of the reading process. The "Great Debate" has been clearly resolved; phonics skills are absolutely necessary for every reader at every stage of development (Gunning, 2005). Effective teachers understand the reading process and know how to embed phonics instruction into a balanced reading program (Gordon & Donnon, 2003).

Phonics refers to teaching beginning readers how to connect the sounds of spoken English with letters or groups of letters and how to blend the sounds of letters together to produce approximate pronunciations of unknown words.

Generally, the emphasis in phonics instruction is on spelling patterns and not individual letters, because there is no absolute one-to-one correspondence between phonemes and graphemes in English. Sounds are spelled in different ways. For instance, some sounds (especially vowel sounds) vary according to where they are found in the word. There are approximately 44 speech sounds in English but, since English is not a purely phonetic language, there are only 26 letters. There are many ways to combine the 26 letters to make the 44 sounds. Many letters stand for more than one sound (e.g., *c* in *cat* and *cent*). Many sounds are represented by more than one letter (e.g., *f* in *father* and *ph* in *telephone*; *sh* in *ship* but also *sh* in *mishap*). Despite the discrepancies, children learn to pronounce these 44 sounds when they begin to talk.

When the English tongue we speak
Why is break not rhymed with freak?
Will you tell me why it's true
We say sew but likewise few?
And the maker of the verse.
Cannot rhyme his horse with worse?
Beard is not the same as heard
Cord is different from word.
Cow is cow but low is low
Shoe is never rhymed with foe.
Think of hose, dose and lose
And think of goose and yet of choose
Think of comb, tomb and bomb,
Doll and roll or home and some.
Since pay is rhymed with say
Why not paid with said I pray?
Think of bold, food and good.
Mould is not pronounced like could.
Wherefore done, but gone and lone
Is there any reason known?
To sum up all, it seems to me
Sounds and letters don't agree.

(Written by Lord Cromer. Published in *The Spectator*, August 9, 1902.)

Phonic Elements

Before attempting to teach phonics, it is essential that teachers know the basic elements of phonics that make up most of the patterns and generalization patterns. Teachers must be alert to the knowledge that their students already possess and where lessons need to be taught and reinforced.

Consonants Most consonants represent a single sound consistently, although there are a few exceptions. C, for instance, does not represent a single sound. When followed by *a*, *o*, or *u*, it is pronounced as /*k*/ as in *cow*, *can*, and *cut*. When *c* is followed by *e*, *i*, or *y*, it is pronounced /*s*/ as in *cent*, *city*, and *cycle*. G also represents two sounds, as illustrated by the word *garbage*. Generally g is pronounced /*g*/ as in *glass*, *go*, *get*, and *gap*, but when followed by *e*, *i*, or *y*, it is usually pronounced /*j*/ as in *gem*, *giant*, and *gypsy*.

There are two kinds of consonant combinations:

- **Blends.** Blends occur when two or three consonants combine so that their individual sounds are blended together, such as in *skill*, *shell*, *flap*, *spring*, *belt*, and *green*.
- **Digraphs.** A digraph occurs when two letters are combined to produce a single sound that is not represented by either letter. The five most common digraphs are:
  - *ch* such as in *church*, *each*, and *chill*
  - *sh* such as in *should*, *show*, *trash*, and *marsh*
  - *th* such as in *south*, *thin*, and *think*
  - *wh* such as in *when*, *whale*, and *white*
  - *gh* (less common) such as in *laugh*, *enough*, and *ghost*

Vowels Five letters make up the vowel system *a*, *e*, *i*, *o*, and *u*, with *w* and *y* becoming vowels when they are used in the middle and at the end of syllables and words. Vowels are much less consistent than consonants, as they represent several sounds. The most common sounds are:

- **Short vowels** are /*a*/ as in *mat*, /*e*/ as in *met*, /*i*/ as in *mill*, /*o*/ as in *box*, and /*u*/ as in *put*.
- **Long vowels** are the same as their letter names, illustrated by *cake*, *meet*, *like*, *boat*, and *rule*. Long vowel sounds are generally spelled with two vowels, which makes them digraphs (e.g., *sail*, *beat*, *spoil*, *boat*) except when the long vowel is at the end of a one-syllable word or a syllable, as illustrated by *be*, *go*, and *trial*.
- **When** *y* **is a vowel at the end of a word,** it is pronounced as long *e* (e.g., *baby*, *happy*, *silly*) or long *i* if the words are one syllable (e.g. *by*, *cry*, *try*).
- **Vowel diphthongs** are speech sounds produced by blending a vowel with a glided sound. Two vowel combinations that are consistently diphthongs are *oi* and *oy*. Examples are *boil* and *boy*.
- **When the letter** *r* **and** *w* **follow one or more vowels,** the pronunciation is influenced and thus changed somewhat, as illustrated by *car*, *far*, *are*, *hear*, *bear*, *first*, *pure*, *cow*, *window*, *power*, and *how*.

Phonic Generalizations and Patterns

While English does not have a direct one-to-one correspondence between letters and sounds, some additional generalizations or patterns are possible to identify:

- Q is followed by *u* and is pronounced as /*kw*/ such as in *quick*, *queer*, *queen*, and *quilt*.
- The CVC pattern refers to instances when a one-syllable word has only one vowel that comes between two consonants; the vowel is usually short (e.g., *bat*, *cap*, *sat*, *land*).

- When there are two vowels in a one-syllable word and one of them is an *e* at the end of the word, the first vowel is long and the final *e* is silent (sight words *have* and *come* are exceptions) (e.g., *cake*, *home*, *sale*). This is referred to as the CVCe pattern.
- When a vowel follows a consonant in a one-syllable word, the vowel is long (e.g., *go*, *be*, *me*). This is referred to as the CV pattern.
- When *gh* follows *i*, the *i* is long and the *gh* is silent (e.g., *night*, *fight*,*sight light*).
- In words beginning with *kn* or *wr*, the first letter is not pronounced (e.g., *knee*, *knock*, *write*, *wrinkle*).

Teaching Phonics

There are a variety of methods and techniques that can help students learn the relationships between sounds and letters and the generalizations and patterns in our language. The analytic and synthetic methods, discussed below, are the two main approaches (Gunning, 2005). The following principles of phonics instruction are germane to all methods.

1. We learn by seeking patterns and making generalizations. It was this pattern-seeking tendency rather than being told a series of rules for spoken language that helped us learn to speak and pronounce words correctly. Therefore, reading teachers should help students see language patterns, not deliver a set of phonic rules. Children can pronounce words—even nonsense words—but cannot tell you why they pronounced them as they did. Let students discover their own patterns and form their own generalizations from them (Tierney & Readence, 2005). It is up to the teacher to provide lessons where these generalizations are emphasized in ways that are obvious to students.
2. Phonics combines auditory and visual modes. A phonic association is formed when students can identify the sound and associate that sound with a letter or a group of letters. Reading programs that focus in part on teaching letter-sound relationships from the beginning of the literacy experience tend to be more effective than those that do not. Each phonic lesson must have an auditory and a visual component.

   Graphemes (visual) + Phonemes (auditory) = Phonic association

3. Isolated phonics lessons are effective only if students experience immediate application with connected text (Adams, 1990). A good children's book can be a helpful resource for providing practice with phonics in context. Alphabet books can be particularly helpful with initial consonants. For instance, *M is for Maple* by Michael Ulmer and *ABC of Canada* by Kim Bellefontaine and Per-Henrik Gürth have a distinctly Canadian focus.
4. Explicit phonics instruction is usually completed by grade 3. If students continue to require phonics instruction in the junior grades, it is usually conducted in a remedial setting or one-to-one with the teacher.
5. Well-organized phonics instruction starts with a flexible but thoroughly planned scope and sequence. As a general rule, it is advisable to start with initial consonants, as their sounds are more consistent. The consonants should not be presented in order;

rather, those that are easiest to say and that occur with the highest frequency should be presented first (e.g., /*s*/, /*m*/ and /*r*/). After about 10 initial consonants, vowels can be introduced so that some words can be formed from the letter-sound correspondences students have learned (e.g., short *a* is usually introduced first, although long *e* and long *o* are also easy to hear at the end of a word).

6. Overall, the phonic tasks include:
   - Identifying sounds of consonants in initial and final positions
   - Blending consonants
   - Identifying special consonant digraphs (e.g., *th*, *ch*, *wh*)
   - Distinguishing short and long vowel sounds
   - Distinguishing double vowels
   - Distinguishing vowel digraphs
   - Distinguishing vowel diphthongs
   - Identifying vowels followed by *r*
   - Identifying the effect of a final *e*
   - Discerning the sounds of *y*

   (Adapted from Heilman, Blair, & Rupley, 2001)

Caution Too much emphasis on phonics instruction in isolation from connected reading can cause the learner to think that identifying words through sound connections is reading. A characteristic of poor readers is that they can "call all the words" correctly but do not understand what they have read. In such cases, the reader will focus on word identification rather than on comprehending the overall message in the text (Heilman et al., 2001).

Methods of Direct Instruction

Analytic Teaching Method

This method has an auditory emphasis and starts and ends in a reading context. It refers to words that are already known to help students to identify a particular phonic element. This direct instruction lesson can be taught **inductively**, where the teacher provides a number of known target words in context and guides the students to make the phonic generalization. Alternatively, it can be taught **deductively**, where the students are told the pattern and must provide additional examples to verify the pattern for themselves. These methods work well for any phonic pattern (e.g., final consonants, short vowels, vowel diphthongs).

Lesson Steps for the Inductive Approach

1. Select a series of known words that all illustrate a phonic pattern. For example, *th*—*that, think, this, bath, Mother, Martha, another, thirty*.
2. Put the words in sentences and underline the targeted words.

   Mother told *Martha* *that* she *thought* it was time for her to take her *bath*.

   Martha said *that* she wanted to watch TV.

   Mother replied *that* she could watch for *another* *thirty* minutes.

3. The teacher reads the sentences aloud and asks the students to identify what sounds and looks alike in the underlined words, soliciting the pattern of sound and letter for *th*.
4. The teacher asks the students to help place all of the targeted words in a column.

   Mother
   Martha
   that
   thought
   bath
   another
   thirty
5. The teacher then writes *th* separately and everyone utters the sound.
6. The teacher asks for more words that contain *th* and writes them on the board in a column.
7. Together, the students and the teacher put the new *th* words in sentences and those sentences are read aloud.

Lesson Steps for the Deductive Approach

1. The teacher selects at least three words with the same pattern that are in the students' listening and speaking vocabularies and lists them on the board (e.g., *dog, done, danger*).
2. The teacher reads the words aloud and tells the students that they all start with the letter *d* and utters the sound /*d*/ in isolation.
3. Students practise the sound in isolation and then identify other words with the /*d*/ sound.
4. The teacher writes the words in a column on the board.
5. The teacher solicits a sentence for each word and writes it on the board.
6. Students may write the letter *d* and choose a word that contains the sound /*d*/ and write it in their notebooks.

Synthetic Teaching Method While the analytic method focuses on whole words, the synthetic method focuses on letter sounds first. In both methods, a student must be able to divide the unknown word into syllables or structural elements and attempt to pronounce the smaller units and then blend the units together (Heilman et al., 2001). The purpose of a synthetic lesson is to increase vocabulary through the use of consonant substitution and to help students employ the strategy of blending letter sounds with word elements (Tierney & Readence, 2005). Word families often become the basic method in the synthetic approach. Word families are word elements that contain both vowels and consonants with which an initial consonant can be blended. For instance, a word family can be *ake*, with which can be synthetically blended *c*, *m*, *b*, and, *l* to form *cake*, *make*, *bake*, and *lake*. These word families are based around patterns that students can take advantage of when they try to identify unknown words as they learn to read.

When applying the synthetic method, the known sounds can be in any position in the word and can be either vowels or consonants. For instance:

Substitution of Initial Consonant

- at
- pat
- sat
- fat
- mat
- cat

In this example, new words are generated by using the same word family as the model word and changing the beginning consonant sound.

Substitution of Consonants at the Beginning and End of Vowel (short *a*)

- a
- sad
- bat
- lap
- mad
- van

This example is slightly more challenging because the vowel remains constant and a new word must be formed by added a consonant at the beginning and the end.

Caution Some prior knowledge of language is essential to use word families effectively.

1. Students require a small personal bank of known words.
2. Students should be able to hear rhyme and recognize that words that look alike at the end probably rhyme. This may require the use of auditory discrimination activities to help students distinguish between rhyming and non-rhyming words.
3. Students must have knowledge of individual consonant sounds.

The synthetic method does not necessarily ensure immediate success for all students. Without a great deal of practice, students may not automatically search for a known pattern when they encounter an unknown word in context. Using word families extensively in isolation without prompting them in actual reading may be a problem. Students will need to be shown explicitly the relevance and application of word families to reading text selections and be provided with extensive practice activities (see Figure 4.2 for an example).

Teaching Phonograms or Word-Building Patterns

It is helpful to introduce students to basic rimes and onsets that appear frequently in language and form word families (e.g., *p* [onset] + *ine* [rime] = *pine*; word family = *line, mine, shine, dine, spine*). Students should be directed to look at how a word starts (initial consonants) and how it ends. This activity also helps students see the patterns that are inherent to language and understand how learning one word can lead to learning many words (e.g., *cake, make, bake, sake, lake, shake, flake*). The pattern is reinforced when these phonograms are presented vertically and students generate several words after the pattern has been established. They can see the **onset** as an initial consonant sound and

Step 1

1. Create five cards with known words for each student (e.g., *bell, cat, jump, log, sit*).
2. Write a word on the board and have students check their cards for a word family match.
3. Demonstrate how the words are the same and how they are different.
4. The process continues with the teacher adding more word cards to each student's collection until there are 16 cards in total.
5. The act of searching through a small group of cards for a match helps students become independent at matching words on their own in text.

Step 2

6. Print a word on the board and ask students to find a word family match without consulting their cards. Students are now relying on their memory and their total thinking process to provide a match.
7. The final stage of this process occurs when students are reading and they encounter difficult words. The teacher prompts them to think of a word family match that ends like the unknown word as an aid in identifying it.

This sample exercise indicates how teachers can scaffold learning by gradually helping students gain independence through practice and support.

Figure 4.2 A Sample Practice Activity

the **rime** in terms of VC (vowel, consonant; *e;*g., *at*), VCC (vowel, consonant, consonant; e.g., *ink*), or VCe (vowel, consonant, followed by silent*e*; e.g., *ake*). Figure 4.3 illustrates a method for teaching phonograms.

Students can build words using their understanding of onsets and rimes in a number of ways:

1. Building words by adding onsets to rimes.
   - Read a story that contains *it* words.
   - At the conclusion, write *it* on the board and ask the students to generate onsets that make specific *it* words, such as *sit*. Key question is: What is the same and what is different?

p	at	s	ack	l	ike
s	at	fl	ack	b	ike
f	at	p	ack	m	ike
c	at	l	ack	p	ike
m	at	b	ack	sp	ike
b	at	h	ack	h	ike
h	at	bl	ack	d	ike
r	at	j	ack		

Figure 4.3 Teaching Phonograms

2. Building words by adding rimes to onsets.
   - Present an onset (e.g., *p*) and have the students supply the rime. They can be prompted by asking what needs to be added to *et* to make the word *pet* or *met*.
3. With the class, prepare a model word chart on which each word that serves as a model can be drawn. For instance, for *ake* a cake could be used and for *in* a pin would serve. The chart may take a few days to complete but it can then be posted to provide a model for language patterns that will help students use more words in their writing.
4. Students can make an illustrated booklet that depicts one word family of their choice.
   - The booklets can be shared in pairs.
   - They can be collected and redistributed so students can read a new word family.
   - They can be taken home to share with parents.

During reading activities and teacher-led story writing, word family patterns can be reinforced.

WORD RECOGNITION

High-Frequency Words and Sight Words

Studies about words in print indicate that 109 words account for more than 50 percent of all words in student textbooks and only 500 words account for 90 percent of the words in such texts (Adams, 1990). High-frequency words, or sight words, are those words that appear frequently in most texts and account for the majority of written words. High-frequency words are commonly used words that are often referred to as the "glue" of our language (Hiebert & Raphael, 1998). For example, in the previous sentence alone there are five such words: *are*, *to*, *as*, *the*, *of*. These glue words are primarily prepositions, conjunctions, pronouns, and articles that form the structures of sentences and whose meaning is hard to define in isolation. As young children begin to access print, an automatic and instantaneous recognition of these words is important so they can focus more fully on the verbs, nouns, adjectives, and adverbs that convey the majority of the message of the sentences (Hirsch, 2003). To garner meaning from what they read and to become engaged with the message, students cannot spend cognitive time puzzling over frequently encountered words.

High-frequency words are often referred to as Dolch words, named after E.W. Dolch who, in 1948, compiled a list of the 220 most commonly used words from a survey of young children's readers he conducted (see a sample Dolch chart in Figure 4.4). According to Dolch, these words must be recognized instantaneously if young readers are to achieve fluency. Dolch organized these words in a list according to the order of frequency with which they are encountered rather than degree of difficulty. The original list did not include nouns, although Dolch subsequently compiled another list of 95 high-frequency nouns. Many of these words cannot be sounded out using regular letter-sound

a	all	after	always	about
Dolch nouns				
apple	baby	back	ball	bear

Figure 4.4 A Dolch Chart

relationships, although they make up a large number of the words found in books written for beginning readers. There have been many adaptations of Dolch's original list, but all are substantially the same. Many school boards have divided the list into segments or groups so the words can be easily taught over the first three years of school.

Sight words are somewhat ambiguous and abstract in isolation, so young children need their teacher's guidance as they learn to recognize these words instantly and automatically. It is well established that young children learn these words best through direct, hands-on experience. While many have mastered them by the end of grade 1, others will not do so until the end of grade 3.

Sight words need to be taught through repetition. Since repetition is the key to sight word acquisition, teachers need to know a number of approaches, games, and activities that foster viewing the words and identifying them accurately and automatically. Most children require assistance in developing their visual memory for words and although some children may require only a few repetitions, others may require multiple practice sessions. Whatever is required must be provided or reading success will be elusive. Automaticity and accuracy has been achieved when no cognitive energy is required to identify the words (Gunning, 2005). Indicators that automaticity has been achieved include the following:

- Students can read orally with reasonably good expression.
- Students can read silently with good comprehension.
- Students can easily discuss what they have read.

Success in this activity provides students with access to up to 75 percent of what is printed in almost any piece of children's literature (www.k12reader.com/sight-word-teaching-strategies).

Teaching Sight Words

Teaching Sight Words Using Practice Cards

Initially, a teacher can put 10 sight words at a time on practice cards. About each week, another 10 words can be added. As a building process, each card can be copied and distributed to each child in the class. Following the teacher's lead, students point to the words in turn and repeat them after the teacher. After some confidence has been gained with this activity, further practice can be achieved in a variety of ways. Children can work in groups or pairs and try to identify all of the words when they are presented randomly by their peers. As the list grows, the cards can be mixed up and practised in simple games. At a slightly higher and more competitive level, students can be encouraged to increase fluency with the words by using a timed activity, in which each student tries to read the words from the cards as quickly and clearly as possible. The teacher can time them and provide an error beep each time an incorrect response is made. The student who can get through the words the fastest with the least number of errors is the winner. Alternatively, it is less stressful and maybe more constructive to have students compete against themselves. They can be timed on their first attempt and then given two or three opportunities to try again and to improve their time.

It is often constructive to encourage students to take their cards home to practise either alone or with parents. The more time a student spends one on one with an adult, the greater the chances of integrating the words into long-term memory. Many schools solicit the services of volunteers to provide this one-on-one practice with beginning readers or those who have not yet mastered enough sight words to read fluently. If students are struggling, it is helpful to provide them with easier texts or prompt them to read the same text several times.

Teaching Sight Words Using Context When children see words used in natural ways rather than in isolation, they often find them easier to remember because they see the significance of the word and its role in the language. Therefore, literature-based instruction that focuses on sight words is another effective way to reinforce students' learning of these words. This points to the important role for levelled texts that are likely to feature age-appropriate sight words. Teachers and parents can also present sight words in short sentences or, alternatively, help students write their own short sentences incorporating sight words. Many teachers find it helpful to make a morning chart on which students relate the daily events of the class; this chart can then be used to reinforce sight words that emerge from the students' own language.

Teaching Sight Words Using Word Walls Word walls are systematically organized collections of new, frequently encountered words that students need to learn so they can use them when reading and writing. The presence of a word on the word wall identifies it as a key word, which in primary grades serves to reinforce learning frequently used words and in older grades identifies words that are needed for current units of study (Gunning, 2005; Tompkins, Bright, Pollard, & Winsor, 2011). The alphabet provides the organizer and words are placed in rows under each letter of the alphabet. Words should be printed clearly and reasonably large in black marker for easy viewing. When a new word is added, the teacher discusses meaning and spelling irregularities and students collectively decide where it belongs alphabetically on the word wall. It is often a good idea to use different background colours to help students distinguish between words that are similar or to help them recognize regular patterns in words. The primary purposes of word walls are:

- To help students learn new words that they can then use independently
- To teach new words by examining patterns and principles associated with word learning
- To bridge the gap between learning new words to a level of automaticity and students being able to use these words in their reading and writing
- To identify key words that are necessary for current novel study as well as social studies and science topics

How to Build a Word Wall A word wall is a dynamic learning resource with words gradually being added and removed. A good rule of thumb is to add about five words per week and remove words when the students are able to recognize and use those words automatically. When adding words to the word wall, it is important that the teacher be selective by including words that students are likely to see frequently in their reading and want to use in their writing. Word walls need to be accessible for every student from their usual position in the classroom. Students should be so familiar with the words included on the word wall that they can easily locate the words they need with a glance when working independently. It is important that, once words are placed on the word wall, students understand that they are expected to use them and to spell them correctly in all daily work.

Placing a word wall in the classroom, however, is only a first step in the learning of new words. Teachers must also possess a repertoire of strategies for using the words on a daily basis. Practice is critical and a variety of techniques to make practice both purposeful and fun is vital.

Practice Activities That Promote Learning Sight Words

I Spy The teacher or another student thinks of a word on the word wall and starts by providing up to five clues. For example:

It is one of the words on the word wall.

It has five letters.

It begins with the same letter as *cat*.

It rhymes with *same*.

It is one of the words in this sentence: Marla and I came home from school together.

Students then guess the word either orally or by writing it.

Bingo Bingo cards are made using all of the words on the word wall. It is useful practice to have students make the cards by choosing the words that will be on their cards. These cards then become a class set for playing bingo. Each child has one card. The teacher draws words from a container and students must check their cards to see if the word is present. For each successive game, students exchange cards. Prizes can include doing favourite classroom tasks or gaining privileges.

Word Sorts Students can be directed to sort the words on the word wall using a variety of criteria—for instance, finding all four letter words, all words ending in silent *e*, words that rhyme, or words containing blends (*ch*, *sh*, *st*, etc). The game can be started by the teacher saying, "There should be 12" or "Who can find the most?"

Rhyming Words This game is useful because it serves to illustrate language patterns. For instance, the teacher can direct students to use *make* from the word wall to list other words that rhyme, such as *lake*, *bake*, *sake*, *rake*, *cake*, and *fake*. The pattern becomes more evident for young students if they are placed in a column:

make

lake

bake

sake

rake

cake

fake

Students generally respond favourably to seeing who can find the most rhyming words.

Individual Word Books for Young Students

An individual word book is a student's collection of known words, usually consisting of high-frequency words (Gunning, 2005). The book (some teachers use large rings, punching a hole in a word card to add new words) should represent all of the words a student can recognize automatically and can use in written language. As students learn new words to a level of automaticity, they are added to their books. Some classrooms also have a collective word book or keep a record of new words on a word wall. In these cases, new words are added to the word wall; when the students recognize each word automatically, it can be recorded in their individual word books. To ensure that these words are recognized automatically, it is a good idea to work with the books for a few minutes each day. This can be done in pairs and the assignment can be to quiz each other; to sort words into action words, colour words, and animal words; or to create sentences with the words in their books.

The individual word book allows for individual differences in the rate of word acquisition, enabling students who want to learn particular words to do so. For instance, one author remembers a student's need to learn the words *hospital*, *ambulance*, *heart attack*, and *doctor* after a beloved grandparent was hospitalized. Many students take great pride in their word book and take it home to demonstrate their prowess for parents. Some teachers start with a small word box; when several words have been accumulated in the box, the individual word book is created by placing all words in alphabetical order. Once about 100 words have been accumulated, most word books become too cumbersome to handle with ease. At this point, most students will have developed decoding skills to the extent that the word books have lost their usefulness as a learning tool (Graves, Juel, & Graves, 2001).

Skills to Help Students Identify Less Frequently Encountered Words

It is critical to remember that the goal of teaching vocabulary is ultimately to promote independent word learning skills. Teaching vocabulary even very diligently will result in the addition of about 400 words during a school year (Beck et al., 2002; Beck, McKeown, & Omanson, 1987). However, students have to learn thousands of words a year, so it is imperative that teachers couple specific word learning instruction with morphemic analysis, prefixes and suffixes, context clues, and dictionary skills.

Morphemic Analysis

A morpheme is the smallest unit of meaning in language, such as *will*, *dog*, and *be*. Parts of words that change the meanings of the word are also morphemes, such as *s*, *ed*, and *ing*. *Will* is a **free morpheme** because it conveys meaning as it stands alone. *S* and *ed* are also morphemes but are called **bound morphemes** because they convey meaning only when attached to a free morpheme. Root words are free morphemes to which bounded morphemes can be added. When root words have an addition to the front, the addition is called a *prefix*. When the addition is at the back, it is called a *suffix*. Morphemic analysis is the ability to determine a word's meaning through examination of its root and any prefixes and suffixes. An ability to recognize roots, common prefixes, and common suffixes is a great asset in word recognition at any reading level. For instance, the word *will* can take many forms, such as *willing*, *willed*, *unwilling*, *willingly*, and *unwillingly*. A student faced with the word *unwillingly* can feel uncertain and overwhelmed by its length and shape. However, when the word is broken down into its root and suffix, most students can identify it.

At a higher reading level, the rootword *crypt* means "hidden" and can take many forms in words such as *cryptogram*, *cryptology*, and *cryptic*. Another example is the root word *script*, which means "write" and can be found in such words as *manuscript*, *scribe*, *proscribe*, and *scripture*. The key to this skill is to help students look for roots and familiar prefixes and suffixes as a way to unlock unfamiliar words.

A repertoire of root words and an understanding of their ability to stand alone with meaning is essential prior knowledge before teaching specific lessons on prefixes and suffixes.

Teaching Prefixes

Prefixes are generally easier to grasp than suffixes because they tend to have concrete, constant meanings and consistent spellings. Common prefixes are *pre*, *anti*, *re*, *con*, *in*, *de*, *dis*, *un*, and *al* (as in *always*).

Prefix Lesson

1. Construct the meaning of the prefix. Put the following words on the board: *redo*, *review*, *recycle*, *recommend*, *refresh*, *reuse*, and *restore*. Discuss the meaning of each word; ask students to identify the prefix (what is the same for each word?) and to generate sentences orally to illustrate the meaning of these words. Together, discuss the meaning of *re* as a prefix, noting how it changes the meaning of the root word. Using Think Aloud, model how to use the knowledge of the prefix to determine meaning. Finally, divide each word into syllables.
2. Provide guided practice.
   - Students can write the *re* words in a series of sentences.
   - Provide them with the word *prepay* and ask them to generate other words that use the *pre* prefix. When they are done, ask them to share their lists and identify the meaning of the prefix *pre*.
3. Have students read a section of text—fiction or non-fiction—and locate the words with prefixes. Discuss their findings together.

Teaching Suffixes

There are two kinds of suffixes: derivational and inflectional.

Derivational suffixes change the part of speech of a word or the grammatical function of the word. For example:

- *ful*: *joyful* means "full of joy"
- *less*: *fearless* means "without fear"
- *y*: *dirty* means "having dirt"

Inflectional suffixes are the grammatical adaptations of words according to tense and their place and purpose in the sentence. For instance, *s*, *ed*, and *ing* are essential beginning-to-read components of word learning. They are followed shortly by the need to know *er*, *est*, and *ly*. Most students are already using these suffixes easily in their oral language when they enter school (Gunning, 2005). Suffixes are taught in the same manner as outlined above for prefixes.

While individual introductory lessons (or in later grades, review lessons) on root words, prefixes, and suffixes are essential, it is playfulness and practice that are key to helping students develop the habit of looking for roots, prefixes, and suffixes when identifying words. The most important aspects of learning this skill are appropriate prompts by the teacher and repeated practice in context. For instance, the teacher can write the word *rain* in a class story and ask students to generate as many words as possible using it. Responses would include *rainy*, *rained*, *raining*, and *rains*. The morning message, a class story, or the introduction of spelling words are all regular useful vehicles for providing contextualized practice.

Context Cues Context cues help students identify unknown words by constructing their understanding of what they are reading in terms of what seems to make sense (Tompkins et al, 2011). Instruction in this skill should permeate reading from its inception (Gunning, 2005). More specifically, context cues require that students draw on prior knowledge during reading while simultaneously considering syntax (grammar and word order) and semantics (meaning of the surrounding words). To this end, students can be taught three distinct questions to ask themselves when they encounter an unfamiliar word in text. These questions are based on the student's familiarity with spoken language.

1. What do I already know that will help me figure out the meaning of this word?
2. What do the surrounding words in the sentence suggest the meaning might be?
3. When I look at the sentences before this word and when I look at the sentences after this word, what do they tell me that will help me identify this word?

While many students may learn to use context clues intuitively, others require explicit instruction and regular prompts to do so. The following is an example of a passage where context may help with word recognition and it exemplifies how teachers can help students develop the skill of using context. Assume that a student is reading the following passage aloud and stops at the word *vehicle* because it is unfamiliar.

> Automobiles played a strong role in our family life in the small town where I grew up. My father owned a grocery store in the 1950s but decided to become a General Motors dealer on the side to make some extra money. To get a dealership started he had to buy two cars, a blue sedan and a sporty red sports car. He had no actual showroom so he parked both **vehicles** in front of the grocery store.

Here are two distinct ways to help the student determine the meaning of *vehicle*.

1. The teacher could conduct a Think Aloud process and model the following:

   Well I don't know this word but I am going to read the sentence again and when I come to the word I will say "hmmm." I see the word *parked* and the father has parked cars on the street. The word must be referring to cars or automobiles so it must mean the same as car but it starts with *v*—oh—*vehicle*.

2. Ask questions to direct the students to use the context cues.

   Read the sentence again and say "hmmm" for the unknown word.
   What is being discussed in the surrounding sentences?

What did the father park on the street?

What is the first letter, first syllable?

What is another word that means car and automobile?

Students will need much guided practice to become independent users of context cues. Generally, it is advisable to do several examples co-operatively and then let students work independently to suggest meanings of targeted words in a variety of passages taken from both non-fiction and fiction sources. During practice, they can either write or explain orally the process they used to determine the meaning of the target word.

Dictionary Skills It is evident that using the dictionary is an important skill associated with word learning. In helping students to develop effective dictionary skills, teachers are providing the means for self-teaching and improvement in spelling (Beech, 2004). Although students do not use a real dictionary in grades 1 and 2, preparation for dictionary use begins there. They create their own word books and eventually place the words in alphabetical order, simulating a dictionary. There are some simple pictorial dictionaries available for beginning readers. However, research supports the delayed use of a dictionary until students know hundreds or even thousands of words (May & Rizarrdi, 2002). By grade 3, the average student possesses a sufficient repertoire of words and is ready to learn the effective use of a dictionary, both in print and electronic form. Generally, in grade 3, students start with a junior dictionary in print form.

Unfortunately, in today's busy classroom dictionary skills are often neglected, although it is clear that there is value in possessing the ability to locate a word in the dictionary to determine its meaning and to be able to pronounce it and spell it (Heilman et al., 2001). As preparation for dictionary learning, students need to see teachers modelling the value of consulting a dictionary in print and online when all other forms of word identification have been inconclusive (Tompkins et al., 2011). There are three valuable learning objectives for dictionary instruction:

1. Being able to find a specific word
2. Determining how to pronounce it
3. Selecting the correct meaning for the context in which it is used

Caution Research does not support learning the definitions of new words from a dictionary. When students have been asked to locate the meaning of new words in a dictionary and write a sentence, the results have verged on disastrous in terms of accurate word learning (Scott & Nagy, 1997).

While it is not difficult to demonstrate the use of guide words to locate a known word in the dictionary, it is more problematic to locate an unfamiliar word. This is where students require more guidance, as they need to hypothesize the possible spellings of the word and check the most probable ones. The following steps can be identified and practiced, with either a print or an online dictionary:

1. Check for root words and words that may be related (e.g., *decision/indecisive*, *publisher/publication*, *teach/teacher*, *destruct/indestructible*).
2. Pronounce the word and listen to all of the sounds.

3. Create a list of potential spellings.
4. Use the dictionary to check alternatives, starting with the most likely one.

PUTTING IT ALL TOGETHER: READING FLUENCY

HAVE A STUDENT READ A PASSAGE ALOUD.

- Does she read in a fluid fashion, grouping words and phrases in meaningful units that preserve the meaning and syntax of the text, or does she read in a word-by-word fashion, ignoring syntax and meaning?
- Does he read with varied volume and expression, maintaining a conversational pace throughout the reading, or does he use a monotone voice?
- Is she able to decode the majority of words in the text and retain its meaning or does she demonstrate poor word accuracy?
- Is he able to retell and retain the meaning of the passage or does he express confusion and uncertainty about its content?

When determining the answers to these and other questions, teachers are assessing students' reading fluency.

Despite being acknowledged as an area of difficulty for poor readers, reading fluency was a skill largely ignored by educators and reading teachers. At best, fluency was noted as the process of "reading with expression." Today, fluency is acknowledged as an essential component of the language arts curriculum, with some experts suggesting that that up to 25 percent of instructional reading time be devoted to fluency instruction (Johns & Berglund, 2010). This increased attention has followed, in part, from the publication of such influential reports as *Preventing Reading Difficulties in Young Children* (Snow et al., 1998) and the report of the National Reading Panel (2000).

Definition of Reading Fluency

Early definitions of fluency focused on the speed and accuracy of reading text. However, these definitions were deemed lacking when it was discovered that some students are able to process and decode text efficiently without deriving comprehension (Samuels, 2002, 2006).

More recent definitions of fluency include the ability to read orally with speed, accuracy, and proper expression, or what is otherwise referred to as prosody (National Reading Panel, 2000). Prosody includes voice quality, tone, emphasis, phrasing, pausing, and attention to punctuation (Johns & Berglund, 2010). Difficulties associated with understanding the specific effects of prosody on comprehension, as well as understanding how to assess it, have resulted in considerable debate about the inclusion of this criterion (Samuels, 2002, 2006), although most educators agree on the contribution of prosody to the reading process, especially when listening to students read aloud. See Table 4.4 for examples of fluency assessment tools that include prosody.

Today, fluency is defined as the ability to decode words automatically and effortlessly so that materials are comprehended (Samuels, 2006). Inherent in this definition is the understanding that, as word recognition becomes more automatic or effortless, greater cognitive attention can be devoted to the comprehension of materials and deriving

Table 4.4 Examples of Fluency Assessment Tools That Include Prosody
Four-Point Fluency Rubric (2007) by Johns, Berglund, and L'Allier
Four-Point Fluency Rubric for Oral Reading (2010) by Johns and Berglund
Multidimensional Fluency Rubric (1991) by Zutell and Rasinski
Oral Reading Fluency Scale (1995) by National Assessment of Educational Progress

meaning from text. Indeed, students' word recognition skills may be so automatic that they do it unconsciously.

Teachers need to be cognizant of the differences associated with silent reading versus reading aloud. In silent reading, fluency can be defined as the extraction of maximum meaning at maximum speed. When reading aloud, however, the process is more demanding, as readers must be conscious of the needs of the audience and alter their pace accordingly (Samuels, 2002).

To reiterate, fluency is the bridge between identifying words and constructing meaning (Johns & Berglund, 2010; Rasinski, 2009), with fluent readers being able to maintain their performance over long periods of time, retain skills after long periods with no practice, and generalize their skills across text. The question arises as to whether teachers can promote students' fluency by encouraging them to monitor their processing of text and by adopting strategic processes that allow them to maximum comprehension when reading across various texts (otherwise known as deep fluency; Samuels, 2002, 2006).

Identifying Students Who Require Support with Reading Fluency

Time spent reading is one of the characteristics that differentiates better readers from poorer ones. It has been estimated that proficient readers read up to 10 times as many words annually as their peers who struggle with the reading process (Samuels, 2002). With continued experiences and practice reading, this gap increases across the grades. This phenomenon is referred to as the Matthew effect (Stanovich, 1986) and describes the situation where good readers become increasingly stronger and poor readers become increasingly weaker.

Samuels (2002) provides specific criteria for teachers to consider when selecting students for reading fluency intervention:

- Listening comprehension is better than reading comprehension
- Slow rate of oral reading comprehension (less than 60 words per minute)
- More than one recognition error for every 10 words
- Poor oral reading expression

Developing Reading Fluency

Teachers can engage in several behaviours and instructional routines that help students develop reading fluency. Many of these behaviours are consistent with effective language arts programming discussed elsewhere in this text, including:

- Reading aloud regularly
- Providing students with access to a range of reading materials (reading levels and topics)
- Providing students with strategic instruction intended to promote their understanding of text
- Demonstrating personal commitment and motivation for reading

Collectively, these behaviours reinforce the value of reading and encourage students to become self-directed, independent readers.

Teachers can also provide systematic reading experiences that facilitate students' reading fluency. Such activities include providing students with sustained independent reading time and having students participate in high-quality, shared, and performance reading activities. At times, however, teachers will need to provide students with targeted fluency instruction. We discuss these reading activities next, as well as some common targeted approaches and the characteristics of students who are most likely to benefit from such interventions.

Sustained Independent Reading Students should be encouraged to consider the analogy to sports when discussing the importance of sustained reading. Just as professional athletes practise on a daily basis, good readers acquire and refine their skills through regular practice and engaging with level-appropriate reading materials. Independent reading sessions provide students with the opportunity to transfer and apply the strategies and skills presented by their teachers and make them automatic. That is, sustained reading intervals assist students in transferring their oral reading practices when reading silently. Sustained silent reading (SSR) can also help students discover and defend their reading interests.

Although many reading experts are cautious in their recommendation of SSR programs (Allington, 2006; Krashen, 2002, 2006; National Reading Panel, 2000; Shanahan, 2006; Stahl, 2004), or what are sometimes referred to as DEAR programs (Drop Everything and Read), they are a common classroom practice. In part, caution about the use of SSR reflects the degree to which these programs vary in terms of their structure, materials, and support. Criticisms include the lack of meaningful student-teacher interactions, teacher monitoring and feedback, teacher guidance for material selection, student accountability, and on-task behaviour. Unfortunately, in some SSR programs, students read materials without any guidance from their teachers. They read materials of their choosing without any regard to reading level (difficulty) and are rarely required to discuss content (Reutzel, Jones, Fawson, & Smith, 2008).

We, like others, recommend that teachers assume active and supportive roles in students' sustained reading activities. In such supported programs, sometimes referred to as scaffolded silent reading, or ScSR (Reutzel et al., 2008), teachers guide students in their text selections, providing them with a range of genres and levelled materials (with students being required to read across genres). Ideally, students are expected to read for about 20 minutes each day, selecting text at their independent reading level (i.e., 95 percent or more accuracy with 90 percent or better comprehension). As part of such programs, teachers explicitly teach evidence-based reading strategies and monitor students' reading progress. Teacher-student conferences provide an excellent opportunity for teachers to monitor students' sustained reading activities, and teachers are encouraged to have students complete a running record and answer comprehension questions during these conferences.

Choral Reading Choral reading is a valuable technique to encourage the development of fluency and expression in reading, as it integrates reading with listening and speaking (Tierney & Readence, 2005). During a choral reading lesson, many oral reading skills can be emphasized and practiced, including reading with expression, interpreting punctuation, phrasing, varying speed, and voice projection.

Poems and text with repeated parts lend themselves especially well to choral reading. There are many possible variations to the approach, although it always involves two or more people reading together. For example, when reading in unison, the entire group reads aloud together. In echo reading, the teacher reads a few words and the students repeat them immediately, imitating the teacher's expression and phrasing. In refrain reading, the leader reads the majority of the text while the others follow along, reading the refrain aloud in unison. In shared reading, teachers and students share in reading sections of the text aloud. Similarly, two or more groups alternate reading sections of the text aloud in antiphonal reading. Variations are limited only by the teacher's imagination and creativity (Gunning, 2005; Palumbo & Willcutt, 2006).

Choral reading is a positive and non-threatening way for poor readers and readers for whom English is a subsequent language to practise being readers (Heilman et al., 2001). Once students are familiar with the text, they can be encouraged to practise reading creatively with expressiveness. See Table 4.5 for examples of shared reading and performance reading activities in the classroom.

Teachers are cautioned to remember that even the best-structured shared reading experiences and SSR and ScSR reading programs *alone* may be insufficient with respect to promoting student reading. Rather, some students will require direct guided instruction and intervention to become successful, fluent readers.

Repeated Readings Repeated readings are perhaps one of the best known and most widely used methods for promoting students' reading fluency. Developed more than three decades ago (Samuels, 1979), the original technique required students to read and reread short meaningful passages (about 50 to 100 words in length) until fluency was reached (with fluency defined as obtaining a reading speed of 85 words per minute).

Table 4.5 Examples of Shared Reading and Performance Reading Activities in the Classroom

- Partner reading
- Buddy reading
- Recorded readings
- Talking books
- Readers' Theatre
- Radio reading
- Performance poetry

For other suggestions, see Johns and Berglund (2010).

Teacher Voice 4.2

I assess students' reading to determine how I can help them become better readers. Although many of the students with whom I work are able to identify words using decoding and other strategies, it takes some of them a disproportionate amount of time and they are falling short on fluency measures. When the fluency falls short, I find that students often don't understand and remember passages or things that they've read, sometimes missing the bigger meanings in chapters and books. My problem is to determine how to improve the automaticity of their word identifications so that fluency scores improve.

I have experimented with letting students record their voices using tape recorders and have had students record their voice on the computer. Students can then listen to themselves and self-monitor progress. I've used audiobooks (online, CD, tape). Students are able to listen to the story and see the book at the same time. The recorded story can be used for the student to practise reading along at an appropriate pace or rate.

I have found that using repeated readings helps improve scores as well. First, we read word by word together and they use their finger to point to each word. We repeat the same reading as many times as necessary until they are ready to read the section without their finger. I then ask them to read stressing flow and expression. They can see their own progress and the improvement in fluency scores supports this method. I have also used Reader's Theatre to provide opportunities for students to read aloud and perform in the classroom. Reader's Theatre allows students to take on the roles of characters to help them read with expression. As they practise for their performance, they are reading and rereading lines, which helps improve their fluency.

Lisa Muldoon
Literacy improvement project teacher, K–8

Students were encouraged to begin with "easy" passages, reading them aloud to adults who recorded decoding errors and reading speed. When fluency was achieved, students progressed to more difficult passages. While demonstrated to facilitate reading fluency in young students, including those with cognitive impairments, the approach eventually came to be considered too labour intensive for use in the classroom.

Samuels and his colleagues revised and adapted this approach for easy implementation in the classroom (Samuels, 2002). In the revised model, the role of the teacher is reduced, with students assisting and monitoring each other's reading performances. Table 4.6 provides an overview of the revised method.

Paired Reading Paired reading, or what is sometimes referred to as duolog reading, is another format of repeated reading that maximizes the roles of peers and other readers (e.g., older students, classroom volunteers, parents). Briefly, the process requires proficient readers to guide and monitor the reading efforts of struggling readers, gently correcting errors and reading with their partners. As part of this process, struggling readers are able to signal to their coach or tutor when they want to read independently or when they require additional assistance. Paired reading has been demonstrated to improve students' reading accuracy and comprehension across a variety of grades and reading levels, with students who struggle with reading benefiting the most from these interactions (for comprehensive reviews, see National Reading Panel, 2000; Topping, 2006a, 2006b).

Caution Although paired reading is intended to be a highly structured reading experience, this term is sometimes misused as a catch-all phrase for any paired reading activity.

Table 4.6 Simplified Method of Repeated Readings

1. Teacher reads a passage aloud while students follow the text independently.
2. Readers use commonly found passages, usually those found in basal readers or library books.
3. Students are assigned to work in mixed-ability pairs.
4. Students take turns reading the passage aloud, assuming the roles of "teacher" and "student," where "students" read the passage aloud while "teachers" monitor for accuracy.
5. The passage is read four times, with students assuming each role twice.

We encourage teachers to carefully review the steps associated with paired reading, as outlined in Table 4.7 and Figure 4.5, before implementing this approach in their classrooms.

Audio Recordings and Computer-Based Fluency Programs Today, audio recordings of many popular and classic texts are readily available. Teachers may be tempted to provide struggling readers with audio copies of these texts with instructions to read along silently. However, *without adequate instructional support* this may become a frustrating experience, as the reading rate associated with many commercial products is well beyond that of struggling readers or the reading voice may be heavily accented or demonstrate a strong dialect. One alternative is to have students and their peers and reading coaches create personal audio recordings of selected materials.

Table 4.7 Implementing Paired Reading in the Classroom

1. Form student-tutor reading pairs (best if student pairs differ only slightly in reading ability). Pairs should meet 3 times per week for 10-minute sessions over a minimum of 6 weeks (or 5 times per week for 5-minute sessions).
2. Have pairs select reading materials. Materials should be of high interest to the student and slightly above his or her independent reading levels. The tutor must be able to read materials independently. Encourage the student and tutor to use the five-finger method (or other relevant criteria) when selecting materials.
3. The pair discusses the reading selection prior to reading aloud. The pair continues to discuss the text during and after reading the passage aloud.
4. The pair reads aloud together, with the tutor adjusting his or her pace to the student's pace. If the student makes a mistake, the tutor corrects any errors and the pair resumes reading together.
5. The student signals the tutor when he or she will read independently. The tutor monitors the student's reading and is ready to assist as necessary. If the student makes an error or pauses or struggles to decode a word for longer than 4 or 5 seconds, the tutor corrects or provides a response.
6. The pair reads together again until the student indicates that he or she is ready to read independently. Initially, pairs complete most reading simultaneously. Over time, students assume the lead in reading text independently for the majority of the session.

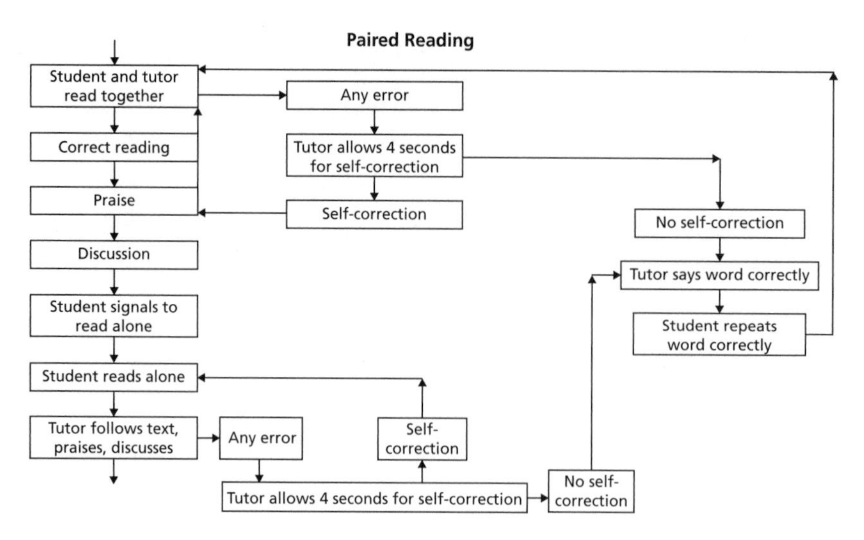

Figure 4.5 Flow of Paired Reading

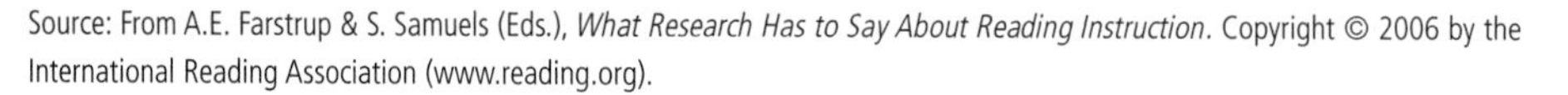

Source: From A.E. Farstrup & S. Samuels (Eds.), *What Research Has to Say About Reading Instruction*. Copyright © 2006 by the International Reading Association (www.reading.org).

Teachers may wish to explore commercially available software programs when developing and implementing repeated reading programs in their classrooms. Programs such as *Fluent Reader* (Renaissance Learning, 2004) can be used to monitor students' reading fluency over a variety of texts and to form decisions about when to provide students with more advanced reading materials. In general, students find the use of such technology motivating and appreciate the immediate feedback such programs provide. However, as with audio recordings, these programs require careful oversight by teachers to include a strong emphasis on reading comprehension.

Older Students There is little debate that the rate at which students can decode unfamiliar words accurately is a substantial factor in their reading success. Indeed, students' ability to identify single words is the greatest contributing factor for reading fluency (Samuels, 2002, 2006). Unfortunately, the number of low-frequency (uncommon) words that students encounter increases dramatically after grade 3, making it difficult for older, struggling students to demonstrate the same level of reading fluency as their peers. In other words, while these older students are likely to respond well to concentrated fluency programming, they are unlikely to demonstrate the same reading fluency as their peers who read proficiently.

Assessing Students' Oral and Silent Reading Fluency

Oral Reading Fluency Norms One fairly simple and popular method for identifying students' oral reading fluency is to determine the number of words they can read correctly per minute (WCPM). This measure reflects two of the primary features of fluency: rate and accuracy. Research has determined that students' oral reading rates provide a good predictor of reading comprehension and can be used to assist in monitoring students' reading progress and identifying students who may

Table 4.8 Oral Reading Fluency Target Norms

Grade	Fall (WCPM)	Winter (WCPM)	Spring (WCPM)
1		10–30	30–60
2	30–60	50–80	70–100
3	50–90	70–100	80–110
4	70–110	80–120	100–140
5	80–120	100–140	110–150
6	100–140	110–150	120–160
7	110–150	120–160	130–170
8	120–160	130–170	140–180

Source: Rasinski (2004).

benefit from fluency intervention (Johns & Berglund, 2010). Table 4.8 presents normative reading rates for students by grade level and season and Table 4.9 outlines how to calculate students' oral reading rates. Teachers should interpret these findings cautiously, as most norms are U.S.-based and include data from a variety of learners, including those with reading challenges and exceptionalities and those for whom English is not a first language.

Silent Reading Fluency Norms Less information is available with respect to assessing students' silent reading fluency norms. As a general rule, students demonstrate faster reading speeds when reading silently than when reading aloud (with speeds increasing up to one and a half times). Also, after grade 8, students usually demonstrate minimal gains with respect to silent reading rates. Table 4.10 provides some general normative guidelines for students' silent reading rates. Again, teachers are encouraged to interpret such information cautiously, keeping in mind individual differences between students, especially those for whom English is a subsequent language or who experience reading difficulties.

Caution It is important that teachers consider students' comprehension of text when evaluating students' oral or silent reading rates.

Table 4.9 Calculating Students' Oral Reading Rates

1. Select an unfamiliar passage at the student's grade level (about 250 words). Use the readability formula to confirm reading level, if necessary.
2. Have the student read aloud for one minute (audio record the session). Emphasize that the student should read text in a "normal" manner and rate.
3. Record reading errors. Errors include mispronunciations, substitutions, reversals, omissions, and words provided by the teacher.
4. Subtract the total number of errors from the total number of words read to obtain the words correct per minute (WCPM) score.
5. Compare the student's score against the grade norms.
6. Repeat the process with another text to increase validity of the assessment. Use the average score obtained by the student across the reading sessions.

Table 4.10 Silent Reading Target Rates (With Comprehension)

Grade	Silent (WCPM)
1	<81
2	82–108
3	109–130
4	131–147
5	148–161
6	162–174
7	175–185
8	186–197

Source: Johns and Berglund (2010).

SUGGESTIONS FOR PROFESSIONAL DEVELOPMENT

1. Explore some commercially available phonics programs. How are these programs structured? What type of exercises and activities do they require children to complete? Is this programming consistent with the evidence-based practices outlined in this chapter?
2. Visit a local library or school library. Review picture and chapter books designed for early readers that feature the alphabet or letter patterns or that emphasize rhyme. What features of these texts promote word learning? How can teachers use such authentic literature as part of their language arts program? Begin a personal resource list.

   Take additional time to review children's dictionaries, encyclopedias, thesauruses, and other resource texts. How are these resources structured? Are visual and print formats used to enhance student learning? How can teachers and students create similar resources in the classroom? Add exemplary texts to your resource list.
3. Observe primary grade students who demonstrate varied reading abilities. How do students respond to unfamiliar words? What strategies and techniques do they use to decode these words? How do students deduce word meanings?

   Spend time reading with students in a junior or intermediate grade. How do these students respond to unfamiliar words? What strategies and techniques do they use to decode these words? How do students deduce their meanings? Reflect on whether the approaches used by older students differ from those used by their younger peers.
4. Volunteer to help a struggling reader improve his or her reading fluency. Use paired reading or another appropriate approach described in this chapter. What is the student's response to this reading approach? Monitor changes in the student's reading fluency over time.

CHILDREN'S LITERATURE REFERENCES

Atwood, M. (2003). *Rude Ramsay and the roaring radishes*. New York, NY: Bloomsbury USA Children's Books. 🍁

Atwood, M., & Kovalski, M. (2002). *Princess Prunella and the purple peanut*. Toronto, ON: Key Porter Books. 🍁

Bellefontaine, K., & Gürth, P.-H. (2006). *ABC of Canada*. Toronto, ON: Kids Can Press. ✤

Bourgeois, P. (1987). *Big Sarah's little boots*. Toronto, ON: Kids Can Press. ✤

Brown, M. W. (1947). *Goodnight moon*. New York, NY: HarperCollins.

Cauley, L. B. (1992). *Clap your hands*. London, UK: Putnam Juvenile.

Christelow, E. (1991). *Five little monkeys sitting in a tree*. Orlando, FL: Sandpiper Publishing.

Dragonwagon, C., & Aruego, A. (1992). *Alligator arrived with apples: A potluck alphabet feast*. New York, NY: First Aladdin Paperbacks.

Edwards, P. D. (1997). *Four famished foxes and Fosdyke*. New York, NY: Katherine Tegen Books.

Florian, D. (1996). *Monster motel*. Orlando, FL: Sandpiper Publishing.

Gay, M. L. (1989). *Rainy day magic*. Newton Abbot, Devon, UK: David and Charles Publishing.

Gordon, J. R. (1993). *Six sleepy sheep*. Toronto, ON: Puffin. ✤

Kraus, R. (1970). *Whose mouse are you?* New York, NY: Simon & Schuster Children's Publishing.

Lee, D. (1974). *Alligator pie*. Toronto, ON: Key Porter Books. ✤

Lee, D. (2005). *Bubblegum delicious*. Toronto, ON: Key Porter Books. ✤

Martin, B., Jr. (1989). *Chicka chicka boom boom*. Bel Air, CA: Beach Lane Books.

McPhail, D. (1996). *Pigs aplenty, pigs galore!* Toronto, ON: Puffin. ✤

Noll, S. (1993). *Jiggle wiggle prance*. Toronto, ON: Puffin. ✤

Schwartz, A. (1992). *Busy buzzing bumblebees and other tongue twisters*. New York, NY: HarperCollins Children's Books.

Seuss, Dr. (1960). *Green eggs and ham*. Toronto, ON: Random House Books for Young Readers.

Seuss, Dr. (1963). *Hop on pop*. Toronto, ON: Random House Books for Young Readers.

Silverstein, S. (1981). *The light in the attic*. New York, NY: HarperCollins Publishers.

Silverstein, S. (2002). *Where the sidewalk ends*. New York, NY: HarperCollins Children's Publishers.

Silverstein, S. (2005). *Runny babbit: A billy sook*. New York, NY: HarperCollins Children's Publishers.

Ulmer, M. (2001). *M is for Maple*. Bolton, ON: Sleeping Bear. ✤

West, C. (1988). *Ten little crocodiles*. Somerville, MA: Candlewick Publishers.

Yektai, N., & deGroat, D. (1987). *Bears in pairs*. New York, NY: Aladdin Publishing.

MyEducationLab

MyEducationLab is an interactive, virtual learning tool that will help improve your understanding of the concepts taught in this textbook and in your course. Through this engaging resource, you will have access to simulations of real classroom experiences, exercises that will help you improve your knowledge of key concepts, and additional resources that will help you in your teaching career. Use this online tool with your textbook to help you succeed in your studies and beyond!

Chapter 5
Comprehension of Narrative Text

Learning Objectives

In this chapter you will discover

- How to implement Read Aloud programs.
- How to select appropriate resources for your reading programs.
- How to teach story structure elements to improve students' comprehension.
- How to structure questions that encourage students to think about and comprehend what they read.
- How to incorporate comprehension strategies when reading narrative text.
- How to conduct effective guided reading lessons.

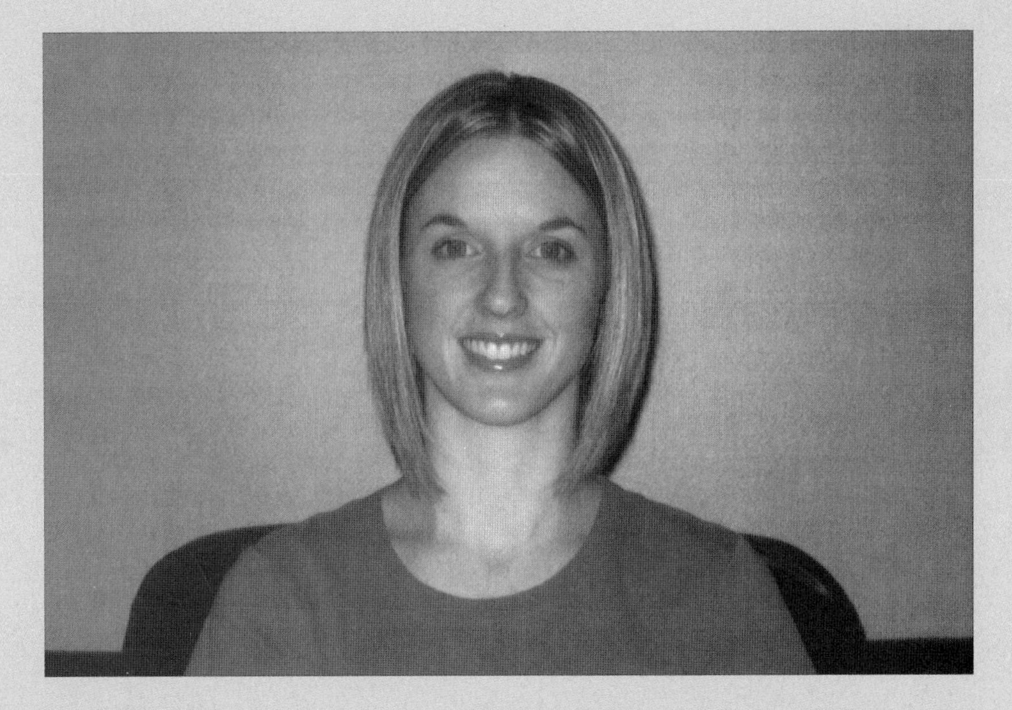

KAREN EVANGELISTA: GRADES 3 AND 4 TEACHER AND LITERACY COACH

Eight years ago, Karen Evangelista began her teaching career as a long-term appointment and simultaneously began working on her Reading Specialist certificate. Currently, she is teaching a grades 3 and 4 split class. Karen believes that programs that allow students to identify their personal strengths need to be developed and that teachers should strive to differentiate instruction as much as possible to meet students' needs. In her classroom, balanced literacy activities coupled with explicit strategy instruction often focus on the literacy basics. "I am working very hard to create activities that are fun and engaging and that motivate them to learn."

Karen teaches a variety of mini-lessons, often to small groups of students, that focus on numerous examples of the strategy they are mastering. This month, they have been focusing on higher-order questioning skills such as critical thinking. Karen has been teaching her students to ask open-ended questions so that they can have purposeful talk.

> I can ask, "So who are these characters in the story and what might they have done otherwise?" Then they have to infer, which is not boring for them because there is more than one answer. They know that they have to provide support from the text to explain why they are giving that answer.

Recently, Karen was appointed as the literacy coach for the entire school. Her role is to provide literacy leadership and to build a strong collaborative team among the primary and junior teachers as they strive to improve standardized test results in literacy. She co-plans and models reading strategy lessons for her colleagues. They meet to determine the big ideas they will focus on and the strategies that will accompany this instruction.

Karen has recently started a new program in her classroom called The Daily Five, based on a book of the same name by sisters Gail Boushey and Joan Moser (2006). A number of teachers on her staff are also "on board." The Daily Five involves a series of balanced literacy tasks that students complete daily while the teacher meets with small groups or confers with individuals. The five areas are (1) read to self, (2) listen to reading, (3) read to someone, (4) word work, and (5) work on writing. Initially, students need to review expectations daily, but eventually they know precisely what to do without Karen needing to remind them. Her class also follows a very strict routine. Students know that Karen must not be interrupted when she is working with a group or conferencing. This program fits well with Karen's strong belief in differentiated instruction and provides students with a sense of ownership over their own learning.

In Karen's classroom, students have a two-week period in which to complete a reading alone assignment that involves retell, relate, and reflect, which they record in their workbooks. They also must make a connection to something else they have read and write a summary of the reading. Karen then holds individual conferences with students and also collects their workbooks. The program works well for Karen, as the students need to become more responsible: "They are proud of their independent work. They also have choice, which motivates them." This program cuts down on paper-and-pencil marking but creates purposeful, meaningful activities that meet key expectations. As Karen says, "It is a win-win!"

Karen's experiences as literacy coach have helped her grow as a teacher. For Karen, the success of her students is the most important goal.

> I have one student whom I also had last year. His mother does not speak English and there is no father in the home. When the student first arrived, his sentence structure was very weak—the vocabulary just was not there. Now, after a year and a half, he is achieving at a Level 3. He works hard, accepts constructive criticism, and is anxious to improve. It is amazing to me how he has progressed. With all the talk we do in class and the explicit strategy instruction, I can see how he has really benefited. I think of him as a real success story!

REFLECTIVE ACTIVITY

Read the following text aloud and then answer the questions below.

Borandic is an murient blof with many scribs; it stits from borite, an olk which braks like karances. Karances glarker the exbarp by glarking the borite and starping it in stanker-glarped borbs. The tarances starp a slarp. This slarp is goped through several other borunses finally frasting a stagety, sprinchant stankle. Borandum is a stargurt, spinking borandic and corigen. The borandic is narcerated from the borite by means of storacity.

QUESTIONS

1. What is borandic?
2. From what does borandic stit?
3. How does karances glarker the exbarb?

4. Through what is the slarp goped?
5. What is borandum?
6. How is borandic narcerated from the borite?

You probably were able to answer most of these questions. Although you were able to read the section phonetically and answer the questions found directly in the text, you may have questioned how much true comprehension was occurring. You likely used your knowledge of letter-sound relationships and your knowledge of surface structure to formulate responses. You used rote auditory recall to conduct literal processing of the text in order to answer the questions correctly. We use this example to emphasize that decoding and answering questions alone is not necessarily an effective way of encouraging comprehension or assessing whether students are able to gain meaning from text. You do not want to teach in a way that allows students to appear to be comprehending when, in fact, no such activity is happening!

NARRATIVE TEXT

If students are to become proficient readers, they need to acquire skills to comprehend text. Thus, comprehension instruction is a central focus of reading programs. Comprehension instruction includes efforts that teach students how to derive meaning from text (Durkin, 1978; Pressley, 2000). To accomplish this task, teachers need to understand the reading process as well as possess a repertoire of instructional strategies that promote comprehension. Effective reading teachers do not teach students to comprehend per se; rather, they provide students with comprehension skills and strategies that enable them to access the meaning of text independently.

Comprehension of narrative text differs from reading for content or information. Narrative text is familiar to most people, as we tend to make sense of our lives by telling stories, with this pattern generally developing in early childhood. Therefore, many students may already have acquired a sense of story by listening and sharing their own stories prior to beginning formal reading instruction. If they are familiar with the shape of story, comprehending narrative text may be a more natural transition into literacy than comprehending informational text (McTavish, 2008).

Although most teachers acknowledge the importance of comprehension, they do not tend to teach comprehension strategies explicitly to their students. As part of the foundational American study conducted in 1978, Dolores Durkin documented that teachers in grade 4 classrooms spent less than 1 percent of their time teaching students reading comprehension strategies. Rather, the majority of the time was devoted to questioning students to assess whether comprehension had occurred. Class structure typically consisted of teachers assigning reading and then asking questions either orally or in written form. The answers to the questions were judged to be either right or wrong and no further instruction occurred, even when the answers were incorrect. Instead, when an incorrect response was provided as part of taking up questions orally, teachers usually moved to another student who could provide a correct answer. Although this study galvanized educators to improve the quality of comprehension instruction over the next several decades, subsequent studies have found that this pattern still exists in many classrooms today (Collins-Black, Gambrell, & Pressley, 2003). In this chapter, we will describe various genres of narrative text and provide an overview of effective comprehension strategies for the classroom. We begin, however, with a discussion of reading motivation, as students' willingness to read is a critical factor in any reading program (Miller & Faircloth, 2009).

Reading Motivation

Teachers can influence students' motivation to read—or the depth, focus, and persistence of their reading behaviour—through the way they present and interact with text (Bandura, 1977, 1989; Edwards & Turner, 2009; Kanfer, Ackerman, Murtha, Dugdale, & Nelson, 1994; Wharton-McDonald & Swiger, 2009). Students' motivation depends in part on their expectations for success and their valuing of the text and the activity (Pintrich & Schunk, 2002). The issue of motivation has often been neglected or ignored in favour of metacognitive skill development (Miller & Faircloth, 2009).

Recent research supports the dynamic role of motivation as central to successful comprehension (Miller & Faircloth, 2009; Peterson & Swartz, 2008). It can be argued that it is motivation that determines students' level of engagement in a task and thus their willingness to employ comprehension strategies. Any teacher who has seen a student become engaged in a text related to a favourite hockey player or pop singer will understand the importance of engagement, especially when the text is written at a level beyond the student's reading ability. The real challenge is to engage students in text that is motivational so that they *want* to comprehend what is happening. Choice of reading material, then, becomes an important component of any reading comprehension program. Teachers must develop a repertoire of texts and stories that will engage students in a variety of reading situations. In other words, it is not sufficient to know "how" to teach students to comprehend text; effective reading teachers also need to know "what" text and materials to select.

The Harry Potter phenomenon is a good example of how text can engage students, and it belies the idea that students will not elect to read in an age of media enticement. Initially, many students read the Harry Potter books by J.K. Rowling purely and simply because they were engaging. This engagement undoubtedly led some students toward a love of reading. As time passed, it became culturally necessary to know the Harry Potter stories. Harry quickly became a movie hero and his image appeared on websites, lunch boxes, school binders, and many other sources of popular media.

The Twilight series by Stephenie Meyer (*Twilight, New Moon, Eclipse*, and *Breaking Dawn*) validates that the Harry Potter phenomenon is not unique. This vampire-based fantasy and romance series has became a popular culture trend among young readers, with the books also being released as movies. For some young readers, an experience with popular media may motivate them to read a book. Certainly, the commercial success of this series indicates that much reading is occurring! Since the first book appeared in 2005, more than 70 million copies have been sold around the world in 38 different languages.

While it is not easy to find the right book for the right student, it is evident that we can glean some ideas from the kinds of books that have appealed to and motivated millions of young readers to read.

Student Voice 5.1

We listened to stories in class this year. We listened to *Charlie Bone* and *Star Wars*. My favourite was *Charlie Bone*. I really liked the storyline—it was mysterious. Listening to a story is relaxing and everyone pays attention. It is something different and a nice break from reading by yourself.

Nick
Grade 5 student

Read Aloud Programs

Grand conversations

Some teachers mistakenly believe that Read Aloud programs are for non-readers or early readers only, with such programs often disappearing from the crowded middle and upper grade curriculums. In reality, having students of all ages and grades relax while listening to a good book means that they are spending time in solid skill development (Golden, Meiners, & Lewis, 1992). Read Aloud programs can play an important role in developing and extending students' independent reading abilities. Consider the following benefits associated with Read Aloud programs:

1. **Increased vocabulary.** It is well substantiated that possessing a strong knowledge of vocabulary is positively related to reading comprehension (Baumann, 2009; Baumann & Kame'enui, 2004). One way that students learn new words is by hearing them spoken in a meaningful context.
2. **Increased understanding of sentence structure.** Often students speak in simple structures, with adults responding in the same way. The language of a story is often rich and varied. Familiarizing students with the various structures found in stories can improve their comprehension of text when reading independently.
3. **Increased understanding of standard forms of English.** Many students use forms of non-standard English, mostly as a result of language they acquire outside of school. The correction of these non-standard patterns can cause substantial stress and a sense of inadequacy among students. Instead, teachers are encouraged to provide students with a model of Standard English that they, in turn, are expected to use in their classroom discussions and interactions. Research supports this method of standardizing language rather than constant correction (Wells, 2007). Becoming more familiar with Standard English patterns also helps students comprehend text more readily.
4. **Springboard for creative activities, dramatizations, and discussions.** When stories or parts of stories are retold or discussed, comprehension deepens. These activities can provide a way to discuss difficult issues such as illness and death or bullying.
5. **Variety of textual formats.** Teachers should ensure that Read Aloud choices reveal the variety of writing formats available in literature. Through these experiences, students can develop a sense of the differences and variations in written language.
6. **Motivation to refine reading skills.** Listening to an accomplished reader can draw students into the delights of reading higher-level books and encourage them to develop their independent reading skills further.

7. **Enriched general knowledge.** Students can broaden their horizons of general knowledge by listening to an adult read. The acquisition of schemata outside their personal experiences helps students comprehend and imagine beyond the events of their own world.
8. **Developed sense of story.** Part of the human experience is to make sense of the world and our experiences in it by telling stories. The ability to read and comprehend narrative text rests in part on confirming predictions about what will happen next. In listening to stories, students learn about the shape of stories, including conflict resolution. Learning to expect basic story elements helps students comprehend when they are reading independently.
9. **Enhanced writing.** Writing, a skill that develops concurrently with comprehension, can be improved by listening to new vocabulary and by learning story structures.
10. **Pleasure.** Most importantly, reading aloud adds genuine pleasure to the day. When this experience is well crafted, it becomes a special part of the school day and one that is anticipated with relish. An additional benefit is the desire to replicate the experience through reading independently.

Student Voice 5.2

Sometimes my teacher reads really nice novels, for example, *Pippi Longstocking*. She stops to show the pictures.

Anastasia
Grade 2 student

Teachers' Text Selections

The choices that teachers make with respect to their Read Aloud programs are critical. Text selection may be especially challenging for a number of reasons. Students' reading interests grow and change as they develop greater reading ability (Peterson & Swartz, 2008). One student's favourite book may be uninteresting to another, making it difficult for teachers to select books for Read Aloud and instructional purposes that will appeal to a majority of students. What follows are some ideas that can help with text selection.

Some books have stood the test of time well. These texts can be termed *classics* because they meet the criteria of having timeless storylines and themes as well as having characters who have appeal beyond the immediacy of popular culture. These books have engaged at least two generations of readers and are passed on from one generation to the next. Good examples are such books as *The Lion, the Witch and the Wardrobe* by C.S. Lewis, *Charlotte's Web* by E.B. White, *Winnie-the-Pooh* by A.A. Milne, and *A Wrinkle in Time* by Madeleine L'Engle. These books can be challenging for many young readers, so they may require introduction by an adult.

Generally speaking, students' listening levels are about two years above their independent reading levels. This suggests that teachers should select material for their Read Aloud program that is at a level higher than the average independent reading level of the class. Another influence on choice of material is the engagement level of the text. Texts that are complex and have both genders represented are likely to engage many students.

Students' listening comprehension will be improved if students are provided with relevant prior knowledge before Read Aloud.

Teacher Voice 5.1

> My first goal would be to have the children enjoy the book and see that reading is a pleasurable experience. The selection should stimulate the imagination, keep their attention, and foster enthusiasm. Just as adults enjoy an exciting plot, character development, and resolution to the problem, so do children. The enjoyment for me is always the positive response from the class.
>
> Marilee Court-Lamond
> Grades 1 and 2 teacher

If a teacher makes a selection for a Read Aloud program and, after a chapter or two, it is evident that the students are not enjoying the story, an alternate text should be selected. The original text should be made available to any student who was engaged in the story. Teachers need to have a backup selection in case of such an eventuality.

Teachers can begin a Read Aloud by selecting two or three texts, discussing the background of each, and allowing the students to choose which one they collectively want to read. Teachers should never read a book to a class without having read it themselves beforehand. Prior reading ensures that teachers are adequately prepared for text content and have deemed the book appropriate for students. For example, a book such as Katherine Patterson's *The Bridge to Terabithia*, which contains the death of a central character, would not be appropriate for a class in which a student has experienced a recent death among family or friends.

Beginning teachers may find it useful to consult lists of award-winning books. Currently, there is excellent writing being done in the area of children's literature, with some educators suggesting that the best popular writing in Canada today is appearing in the areas of children's and young adult literature. Tables 5.1 and 5.2 provide an overview of some prestigious Canadian literature awards, both national and regional.

Table 5.1 National Awards for Canadian Children's and Young Adult Literature
Amelia Frances Howard-Gibbon Illustrator's Award
Canadian Library Association, Book of the Year for Children
CLA Young Adult Canadian Book Award
Elizabeth Mrazik-Cleaver Canadian Picture Book Award
Geoffrey Bilson Award for Historical Fiction for Young People
Governor General's Literary Award, Children's Literature
Information Book Award
IODE Violet Downey Book Award
Mr. Christie's Book Award
Ruth and Sylvia Schwartz Children's Book Award
Vicky Metcalf Short Story Award

Table 5.2 Regional Awards for Canadian Children's and Young Adult Literature

Sheila A. Egoff Children's Literature Prize	Best children's book by a British Columbia author.
R.Ross Annett Award for Children's Literature	Best children's book by an Alberta author. Chosen by the Writers Guild of Alberta.
Manitoba Young Readers' Choice Awards	Established by the Manitoba School Library Association. Selected by students in grades 4 through 8 in Manitoba.
The Silver Birch Award	Established by the Ontario Library Association. Selected by students in grades 3 through 6 in Ontario.
Ann Connor Brimer Award	Best children's book by a resident of the Atlantic provinces.

> For a story to truly hold a child's attention, it must entertain him and arouse his curiosity. But to enrich his life, it must stimulate his imagination; help him to develop his intellect and to clarify his emotions; be attuned to his anxieties and aspirations; give full recognition to his difficulties, while at the same time suggesting solutions to the problems which perturb him. (Bettelheim, 1977, p. 5)

EXPLORING CHILDREN'S LITERATURE

THE TEXTS THAT STUDENTS ENCOUNTER IN THEIR LIVES BOTH WITHIN AND OUTSIDE of school are cultural in nature and contribute strongly to the way they build their identities, beliefs, values, and world views (Luke, 2000). Through these encounters, students seek to interpret the world and to determine their place in it (Anstey & Bull, 2006; Hobbs, 2006). It is the teacher's responsibility to understand the impact on students' lives that the books to be shared over the course of the school year will have. Teachers must guard against choosing only their own childhood favourites or selecting too heavily from their favourite genres. Students need to be given a variety of genres when books are presented for sharing or studying in the classroom. It is important that the books chosen cut across all genres and formats. Reading programs should also include opportunities for students to make independent choices, allowing them time to indulge in a favourite series or genre. In the following sections, we provide brief descriptions of the most popular formats of traditional text, including picture books, chapter books, graphic novels, and poetry. We also review specific genres and provide examples from the plethora of possibilities that teachers and students can explore.

Books for Early Readers

Picture Books Since 1658, students have delighted in picture books, which characteristically represent an integration of story and image. Picture books can take many forms. For instance, wordless picture books communicate meaning solely through images and the imagination. One example is *Flotsam* by David Wiesner. This story describes a boy who spends time at the beach looking at flotsam. He finds a camera complete with film that astonishes him. In the end, he decides to return the camera to the sea for someone else to discover. There is a sense of connectedness around the world in the universality of wonder and discovery. Other picture books have only a few words and communication is mostly through the images. One example is *Night Cars* by Teddy Jam and Eric Beddows, in which the everyday world is seen through the eyes of a young child and memories of childhood resonate throughout.

Picture books can also provide emerging readers with the opportunity to practise being readers by acquiring meaning from text. Predictable texts are highly structured, using rhythm and rhyme to help young students predict what will happen next and motivate them to read further. Good examples of predictable texts are *The Owl and the Pussycat* by Edward Lear, *The Wonderful Pigs of Jillian Jiggs* by Phoebe Gilman, and *Alexander and the Terrible, Horrible, No Good, Very Bad Day* by Judith Viorst.

Teachers can find much to teach students in the junior and intermediate grades about text and image by choosing picture books such as *Ghost Train* by Paul Yee and *When Jessie Came Across the Sea* by Amy Hest. Many excellent picture book titles can be found in listings of the winners of the Governor General's Literary Award, Children's Literature—Illustration (Table 5.3) and the Caldecott Medal (Table 5.4). For readers of all levels, picture books can serve to provide aesthetic enjoyment and to enhance overall comprehension.

Chapter Books Chapter books provide an important bridge between picture books and novels and thus are an important tool in primary grade classrooms. Once students have demonstrated a mastery of picture books and predictable texts, and once they have gained an initial understanding of story structure, they usually are ready to engage in chapter book reading. Like picture books, most chapter books contain illustrations and graphics that enhance the readability of text. Like novels, chapter books present an extended reading experience and provide readers with rich characters and plots. While chapter books exist in a variety of genres—including adventure, fantasy, and historical fiction— they are considerably shorter than traditional novels. With chapters often being limited to only a few pages, beginning readers find themselves motivated to continue with the reading process over multiple sittings.

Jon Scieszka's humorous The Time Warp Trio (titles include *Knights of the Kitchen Table, Tut, Tut,* and *See You Later, Gladiator*) is a popular chapter book series featuring the adventures of three young boys who, through the powers of a magic book, travel back and forth in time. Young readers are likely to be captivated by the adventures of Junie B. Jones (titles include *Junie B. Jones and the Stupid Smelly Bus, Junie B. Jones and Some Sneaky Peeky Spying*), a kindergarten student who brings a unique perspective to daily events.

Many factors contribute to the readability or reading level of chapter books, including students' familiarity with plot and characters, text structure, and vocabulary. Levelled series are available from many publishers, with most spanning the grades 1 to 4 levels. Reading chapter books may be especially empowering for beginning readers and motivating for older students who struggle with the reading process. Primary grade teachers are encouraged to incorporate the use of chapter books as part of their daily Read Aloud programs and to encourage their students to select chapter books for independent reading. Chapter books present an important and powerful tool in promoting a lifelong love of reading.

Table 5.3 Governor General's Literary Award, Children's Literature—Illustration, 2000–2010

2010	Jon Klassen, *Cat's Night Out* by Caroline Stutsen.Toronto: Simon & Schuster. Daniel Sylvestre, *Rose: derrière le rideau de la folie* by Élise Turcotte. Montreal: Les éditions de la courte échelle.
2009	Jirina Marton, *Bella's Tree* by Janet Russell. Toronto: Groundwood Books. Janice Nadeau, *Harvey* by Hervé Bouchard. Montreal: Éditions de la Pastèque.
2008	Stephane Jorisch, The *Owl and the Pussycat* by Edward Lear. Toronto: Kids Can Press. Janice Nadeau, *Ma meilleure amie* by Gilles Tibo. Montreal: Les Éditions Québec Amérique.
2007	Geoff Hocking, *The Boy from the Sun* by Duncan Weller. Vancouver: Simply Read Books. *Geneviève Côté, La petite rapporteuse de mots* by Danielle Simard. Montreal: Éditions Les 400 coups.
2006	Jan Thornhill, *Ancient Thunder* by Leo Yerxa, Toronto: Groundwood Books. Rogé, *Le gros monstre qui aimait trop lire* by Lili Chartrand. Saint-Lambert, QC: Dominique et compagnie.
2005	Ron Gonsalves, *Imagine a Day* by Sarah. L. Thomson.New York: Atheneum Books for Young Readers. Isabelle Arsenault, *Le coeur de monsieur Gauguin* by Marie-Danielle Croteau. Montreal: Éditions Les 400 coups
2004	Stéphane Jorisch, *Jabberwocky* by Lewis Carroll. Toronto: Kids Can Press. Janice Nadeau, *Nul poisson où aller* by Marie-Francine Hébert. Montreal: Éditions Les 400 coups.
2003	Allen Sapp, The *Song Within My Heart* by Dave Bouchard. Vancouver: Raincoast Books. Virginie Egger, *Recette d'éléphant à la sauce vieux pneu* by Carol Tremblay. Montreal: Éditions Les 400 coups.
2002	Wallace Edwards, *Alphabeasts* by Wallace Edwards. Toronto: Kids Can Press. Luc Melanson, *Le grand voyage de Monsieur* by Gilles Tibo. Saint-Lambert, QC: Dominique et compagnie.
2001	Mireille Levert, *An Island in the Soup* by Mireille Levert. Toronto: Groundwood Books/Douglas & McIntyre. Bruce Roberts, *Fidèles éléphants* by Yukio Tsuchiya. Montreal: Éditions Les 400 coups.
2000	Marie-Louise Gay, *Yuck, a Love Story* by Don Gillmor. Toronto: Stoddart Kids. Anne Villeneuve, *L'Écharpe rouge* by Anne Villeneuve. Montreal: Éditions Les 400 coups.

Table 5.4 The Caldecott Medal, 2000–2010

2010	*The Lion & the Mouse* by Jerry Pinkney. Little, Brown and Company Books for Young Readers
2009	*The House in the Night* by Susan Marie Swanson. Houghton Mifflin Company.
2008	*The Invention of Hugo Cabret* by Brian Selznick. Scholastic Press.
2007	*Flotsam* by David Wiesner. Clarion.
2006	*The Hello, Goodbye Window* by Norton Juster. Michael di Capua Books/ Hyperion Books for Children.
2005	*Kitten's First Full Moon* by Kevin Henkes. Greenwillow Books/ HarperCollins Publishers.
2004	*The Man Who Walked Between the Towers* by Mordicai Gerstein. Roaring Brook Press/Millbrook Press.
2003	*My Friend Rabbit* by Eric Rohmann. Roaring Brook Press/Millbrook Press.
2002	*The Three Pigs* by David Wiesner. Clarion/Houghton Mifflin.
2001	*So You Want to Be President?* by Judith St. George.Philomel.
2000	*Joseph Had a Little Overcoat* by Simms Taback. Viking.

Exploring Literary Genres

Graphic Novels

The graphic novel is an outgrowth of the more famous comic book, but with a lengthier and more complex storyline. The story is presented through a combination of visual and textual elements, with strong interaction between the two. The graphic novel can present stories in a variety of genres. Graphic novels also appeal to young readers who are transitioning from picture books to novels. Chapter books and novels that have a substantial number of illustrations can be called graphic novels. For instance, the immensely popular Captain Underpants series appears in graphic novel format. Many older novels such as *The Hobbit* and *Frankenstein* are being released as graphic novels that may appeal to older readers. The plays of William Shakespeare have been reproduced as graphic novels that combine the traditional story with the language and images of popular culture (e.g., *No Fear Shakespeare*: *Romeo and Juliet*). These renditions are controversial among traditionalists but serve to make the classical stories available to students mired in popular culture and unfamiliar and impatient with Elizabethan English. The genre is particularly suited to fantasy and adventure genres where character development may be less important than the plot line.

Poetry

Poetry uses distilled language or even simple language to capture the essence of an idea, experience, or concept. It encompasses emotional, visual, and physiological dimensions and its vision is unlimited. Often poetry has a rhyme, a cadence, or a rhythm that appeals to the ear—especially the young ear. The majority of poetry for young students emerged from oral traditions, with these poems being especially useful in helping beginning readers access print, as they can easily predict what is coming next. This feature is part of the lasting appeal of nursery rhymes, Dr. Seuss books, and books by Shel Silverstein. Another perennial favourite children's poet is Dennis Lee, with his clever combination of rhythm and rhyme in nonsense poems such as *Alligator Pie* and *Willoughby*

Guys Read: An After-School Reading Program for Boys

We had been doing a lot of thinking about how boys read, what materials are available to them in the classroom and library, and how technology could be incorporated with reading. We developed a boys-only, after-school program focused on graphic novels. The program also included a nutrition and fitness component. The boys would select a novel and read it for about 20 minutes (they were so fascinated with the materials you could hear a pin drop). Then we completed a "mini-lesson" using some form of technology, such as a SMART Board, and a lot of hands-on activities. Sometimes we would invite males from the community, such as a local basketball player or politician, to be guest readers. The role modelling helped sustain the boys' motivation and demonstrated that all types of people read. The sessions finished with a nutritious snack (bananas, granola bar, juice) and a physical activity. It was an awesome program!

Todd Bright
Principal, Forestview Public School

Wallaby Woo. Students respond readily to these poems, as they can chant along with the words and create new verses by using the names of classmates.

Unfortunately, many students' enjoyment of poetry does not survive the middle grades, which may suggest that teachers have not maintained the early interest or focus on this genre. How can teachers address this issue? Studies show that students prefer humorous themes rather than serious ones, narrative poems, poems about animals, and poems about familiar experiences. They also respond favourably to poetry that has strong rhythm, rhyme, and sound. Teachers should make selections that maintain students' enjoyment for poetry rather than overanalyzing structures and figures of speech. Jean Little's poem "After English Class" provides an excellent reminder that having students overanalyze text can detract from reading enjoyment.

After English Class

I used to like "Stopping by Woods on a Snowy Evening."
I liked the coming darkness,
The jingle of harness bells, breaking—and adding to—the stillness,
The gentle drift of snow. . .

But today, the teacher told us what everything stood for.
The woods, the horse, the miles to go, the sleep—
They all have hidden meanings.

It's grown so complicated now that,
Next time I drive by,
I don't think I'll bother to stop.

Material from *Hey World Here I Am!* written by Jean Little.

Fairy Tales Reading about fantasy worlds can assist students' understanding of the real world (Warner, 1994). This orientation may, in part, explain the persistent appeal of fairy tales for young students. Fairy tales are retellings of ancient stories that were told and retold to humanize bestial and barbaric forces through metaphor (Zipes, 1991). They tend to be among the earliest stories shared with children by adults. The pervasiveness of fairy tales has been illustrated by the same story, such as *Cinderella* or *Little Red Riding Hood*, often being shared across many cultures. Thus, these stories are an important part of the early reading experience. Fairy tales are narrated from a third-person perspective, although different characters' points of view can be reflected. For example, *Cinderella* can be told from the perspective of the stepsisters, the stepmother, or the prince.

As a genre, all fairy tales follow the same structure, although they differ in their details. The characters are clear and usually quite one-dimensional, with the hero or heroine quickly evident. The plot and problem are also easily identified, as is the resolution. Fairy tales tend to start with "Once upon a time" and end with "They lived happily ever after." Several efforts are usually required to solve the central problem, with a resolution typically attained on the third attempt. The ending emphasizes the triumph of good over evil and thus is usually very satisfying to the reader. This strict adherence to a familiar pattern assists students in comprehending the text and making predictions.

Folk Literature This is a broad category that includes folk tales, fables, myths, and tall tales and that appears in all Canadian curricula. There is generally no identifiable author, as this literature has emerged over time from oral traditions. Although there are many variations, the general shape of the story in folk literature remains the same. These tales often reveal the values of a culture, either past or present, and unite individuals across time (Frye, 1991; Yolan, 1981). Some of these tales and myths have a mystical function that expresses the wonder of the universe. Every culture, for instance, has a creation myth that establishes the beginning of time. Other stories explain natural phenomena and human nature. Good examples are *The Loon's Necklace* and *The Enchanted Caribou* by Elizabeth Cleaver. Greek mythology contains an excellent collection of ancient stories that provide insight into the human psyche. For instance, "The Golden Touch" (the story of King Midas) found in *Favourite Greek Myths* carries the same message today as it did in ancient times. Teachers are encouraged to choose some of these stories to share with their class over the year.

Classics Some teachers may wonder if the classics or the old stories should be used with students. The answer is yes! Classics are stories that have stood the test of time because of their universal themes and the enjoyment that successive generations have derived from reading them. For instance, Mary in *The Secret Garden* makes friends and develops a love of the garden that allows her to transform herself from a miserable, self-centred, demanding individual into a happy, loving person.

Unfortunately, some of the older classics contain language and ideas that are unfamiliar and unappealing to students (see the first page of *Robinson Crusoe*). Books such as *Charlotte's Web*, *The Secret Garden*, *Anne of Green Gables*, *The Wonderful Wizard of Oz*, *The Adventures of Tom Sawyer*, and *The Wind in the Willows* are examples of recent classics with more familiar language.

Historical Fiction Historical fiction is set in the past, with characters and events that could have existed at that time. The stories are generally very plausible and may include references to, and interactions with, real historical characters. The "realness" of this genre allows students to experience past events vicariously. While students read and enjoy the story, they are expanding their knowledge of the world and becoming interested in such subjects as social studies and history. Students are empowered to recognize the very real consequences for people experiencing past events rather than viewing them merely as abstract constructs. Exploring this genre assists students in understanding that their lives have been affected by those before them and that they, in turn, can affect the lives of future generations. Historical fiction can also assist students to appreciate the universality of human needs across history. In some cases, it helps them learn about their own cultural heritage or about the heritage of classmates and friends.

It is imperative that teachers choose books that represent the time and the culture accurately while presenting the story in a thought-provoking and universally understood manner. Characters must act within the traditions and norms of their times. Good examples of books that have received acclaim and have served teachers well as novel studies or Read Aloud selections include *Sarah, Plain and Tall* by Patricia MacLachlan, *Underground to Canada* by Barbara Smucker, and *The Sky is Falling, Looking at the Moon*, and *The Lights Go on Again* by award-winning Canadian author Kit Pearson. Other titles include *Daniel's Story* by Carol Matas and the Dear Canada series, which includes *Footsteps in the Snow: The Red River Diary of Isobel Scott* by Carol Matas and *A Prairie as Wide as the Sea: The Immigrant Diary of Ivy Weatherall* by Sarah Ellis.

Adventure This genre is a perennial favourite among students and can often be used to "hook" reluctant readers. Typically, such stories have a fast-paced plot that rivets the reader through anticipation and curiosity. The plot's action may be more important than character development, as a clearly defined goal dominates the story. Often adventure stories are like journeys in which the characters learn more about themselves as a result of surviving the adventure or achieving the goal. In Canada, adventure stories are often presented as survival in nature, such as Farley Mowat's *Two Against the North* and *The Curse of the Viking Grave*. The Northern Adventure series by James Houston provides another example of adventure stories set against the harsh Northern beauty of Canada. The popular book *Hatchet* by Gary Paulsen also follows this survival formula in a satisfying and riveting way.

Mystery This is another popular genre that teachers have used to entice students and enhance their motivation for reading. Mystery stories are formulaic in nature. They are generally action oriented, with the author creating an atmosphere of suspense throughout the text. The plot is engaging and characters usually are clearly defined either as protagonists or antagonists. Plots typically are one-dimensional with a clearly defined problem that must be solved. Sometimes the author invites readers to participate in solving the mystery by providing clues, messages, and directions throughout the text. For instance, in *Chasing Vermeer* by Blue Balliett readers can find hidden messages within the chapter illustrations and decipher a pentomino code to solve the stolen art mystery (similar challenges can be found in sequels *The Wright 3* and *The Calder Game*). Other examples of popular mysteries are books by Eric Wilson such as the Tom and Liz Austen mysteries (titles include *Terror in Winnipeg* and *The Ghost of Lunenburg Manor*). Another classic mystery story is *The Westing Game* by Ellen Raskin.

Fantasy Fantasy stories are set in places that reside only in the imagination. They are usually about people and creatures who do not exist and who interact in ways that are impossible. These are the qualities that make these stories so appealing to students' creative minds. This genre provides a way for students to understand their own world by exploring a new world transformed by imagination (Temple, Martinez, Yokota, & Naylor, 1998). For some readers, fantasy touches their deepest feelings and speaks to the best and most hopeful parts of humanity.

There are two kinds of fantasy: high fantasy and low fantasy. In high fantasy, an entire world quite separate from the real world, complete with its own cultures and protocols, is created. One popular and enduring example of high fantasy is J.R.R. Tolkein's Lord of the Rings series. C.S. Lewis's Narnia series and Philip Pullman's trilogy His Dark Materials are other popular examples.

In low fantasy, magical elements are embedded in the real world and boundaries are maintained between the two worlds. The personification of animals who live like humans but retain some of their animal characteristics is a common feature in fantasy stories for young readers. For example, in the much beloved *The Velveteen Rabbit*, stuffed animals and toys come to life with memorable outcomes. Another example of low fantasy involves "time slip" stories in which characters travel back in time to experience a previous culture and learn lessons that help them solve problems in their real lives. *The Root Cellar* by Janet Lunn and *A Handful of Time* by Kit Pearson are good Canadian examples of time slip novels.

Science Fiction This genre is based on what might happen in the future if existing laws of physics and scientific principles differed or developed in unanticipated ways. Unlike fantasy, science fiction holds some degree of plausibility. Scientific concepts generally are woven into the story to lend an aura of plausibility, usually in relation to future life. The imagination holds a dominant part in this genre, even in the context of everyday life. Consider that flight would have been a creative, imaginative idea 150 years ago, as storied in a series by Canadian author Monica Hughes (*The Keeper of the Isis Light*, *The Guardian of Isis*, and *The Isis Pedlar*).

Much of science fiction involves the discovery and application of new scientific discoveries, principles, and technologies and it frequently encompasses time travel or travel to distant worlds and planets. Examples include *Spacer and Rat* by Margaret Bechard, *Among the Hidden* by Margaret Peterson Haddix, and *The Dark Side of Nowhere* by Neal Shusterman. Science fiction texts often contain aliens and other non-human life forms that threaten the survival of humankind, as in H.G. Wells's *The War of the Worlds* and John Wyndham's *The Day of the Triffids*. The existence of parallel worlds and the struggle to understand and preserve humanity are also common themes in science fiction. Nancy Farmer's *The House of the Scorpion* chronicles the struggles of a young male clone whose body parts are to be harvested.

Problem Novels

As the antithesis to classic stories, problem novels were first identified in the early 1960s when stories for students began to focus on social and family conflicts. Writers began to present stories about formerly taboo topics such as alcoholism, premarital relations, homosexuality, divorce, and death. Typically, the protagonist experiences difficulties with self, society, or another person. In a well-written problem novel, the character and the conflict are both well developed and interrelated and the story provides insights into the ways individuals think and behave in a challenging situation (Peterson & Swartz, 2008). A good example is Jean Little's novel *Mama's Going to Buy You a Mockingbird*, about a boy whose father is dying of cancer and who finds comfort in a new friendship and the positive memories of his father. Judy Blume has written a number of entertaining stories, such as *Are You There God? It's Me, Margaret*, about a young girl's coming of age, and *Deenie*, about a young girl facing her parents' divorce. Other examples are *Kira-Kira* by Cynthia Kadohata and *Feather Boy* by Nicky Singer.

Teachers should avoid selecting novels in which the characters are stereotypical, the problem is so overwhelming that it affects the credibility of the story, or the problem is solved in a simplistic and sentimental manner lacking either reality or justice. Sometimes parents are presented as ineffectual or even as an alienating presence. The notion that parents cause and contribute to problems but rarely offer a loving solution can be disturbing to readers.

Some educators believe that portraying the realities of life honestly and openly may help students develop a deeper understanding of relationships, challenges, and themselves as well as of their potential to confront difficult issues in their lives. Readers may discover that their problems are not unique. While most teachers acknowledge that students require intensive and varied supports while experiencing crisis, they also believe that reading related stories can help students appreciate and understand such events.

Young Adult Literature

Young adult literature is a relatively recently recognized publishing category that encompasses a wide variety of text types (e.g., short stories, novels, graphic novels, poetry) and genres, including adventure, romance, fantasy, biography, and autobiography. These texts are intended for readers aged 12 years and older and are often mature in nature, addressing real-world challenges such as family dysfunction and divorce, abuse, death, sexuality, and one's identity. Adolescents and young adults constitute the primary characters in young adult literature, with authors using language conventions that are readily understood and relevant to youth.

An early example of such a text is S.E. Hinton's *The Outsiders*, published in 1967. More recent titles review controversial topics such as war and violence (*The Breadwinner* by Deborah Ellis, *Tasting the Sky: A Palestinian Childhood* by Ibtisam Barakat), alcohol and drug abuse (*Looking for Alaska by* John Green, *Boy A* by Jonathan Trigell), ethnicity and identity (*The House on Mango Street* by Sandra Cisneros, *The Skin I'm In* by Sharon Flake, *Red Glass* by Laura Resau), and sexuality, homosexuality, and teen pregnancy (*Forever* by Judy Blume, *Stained* by Joanne Hichens, *Vintage: A Ghost Story* by Steve Berman).

Teachers often use young adult literature as part of independent and shared reading activities to motivate and capture the interest of students in junior and intermediate grades, especially reluctant and struggling readers. Teachers are also encouraged to pair young adult literature with classics and other genres to promote students' understanding and interest in the latter. For instance, readers may connect more readily to such classics as *The Adventures of Tom Sawyer* (Mark Twain) after reading about the adventures of the Watson family as narrated by Kenny, who describes the family's travels from Michigan to Alabama in *The Watsons Go to Birmingham—1963* (Christopher Paul Curtis). Similarly, parallels may be drawn between *Lord of the Flies* (William Golding) and the abuse of societal status and girl culture as described in *The Clique* (Lisi Harrison).

Teachers are cautioned to use care when selecting young adult literature, as many texts contain graphic descriptions, explicit language, and profanity and portray high-risk or violent behaviours. However, such concerns are often balanced with increased student attention, enhanced motivation for reading, and the belief that such texts provide students with coping strategies when they confront difficult social situations and real-life challenges.

Table 5.5 provides selected examples of the genres of children's literature discussed above.

Table 5.5 Selected Examples of Children's Literature

Chapter Books to Novels

Bellingham, B. (2005). *Lilly's special gift*. Halifax, NS: Formac Publishing. 🍁

Berenstain, S. (2005). *The Berenstain bears go back to school*. New York, NY: HarperCollins.

Bradford, K. (2005). *Ghost wolf*. Victoria, BC: Orca Books. 🍁

Campbell Gaetz, D. (2006). *Sea dog*. Victoria, BC: Orca Books. 🍁

Kerrin, J.S. (2005). *Martin Bridge: Ready for takeoff!* Toronto, ON: Kids Can Press. 🍁

Kimpton, D. (2004). *Princess Ellie to the rescue*. London, UK: Usborne Publishers Ltd.

Lobel A. (1970). *Frog and toad are friends*. New York, NY: HarperCollins.

McDonald, M. (2009). *The sisters club*. Sommerville, MA: Candlewick Press.

Parish, P. (1985). *Amelia Bedelia goes camping*. New York, NY: HarperCollins.

Park, B. (1992). *Junie B. Jones and the stupid smelly bus*. Toronto, ON: Random House.

Scieszka, J. (1991). *Knights of the kitchen table*. Toronto, ON: Penguin.

Poetry

Booth, D. (Ed.). (1989). *Til all the stars have fallen: Canadian poems for children*. Toronto, ON: Kids Can Press. 🍁

Booth, D. (Ed.). (1990). *Voices on the wind: Poems for all seasons*. Toronto, ON: Kids Can Press. 🍁

Bouchard, D. (1994). *Voices from the wild: An animal sensagoria*. Vancouver, BC: Raincoast. 🍁

Downie, M. A. & Robertson, B. (Eds.). (1987). *The new wind has wings: Poems from Canada*. Toronto, ON: Oxford University Press. 🍁

Engle, M. (2008). *The surrender tree: Poems of Cuba's struggle for freedom*. New York, NY: Henry Holt and Company.

George, D. (1974). *My heart soars*. Saanichton, BC: Hancock House. 🍁

Hughes, L. (1996). *The dream keeper and other poems*. New York, NY: Random House.

(Continued)

Table 5.5 Selected Examples of Children's Literature *(continued)*

Poetry *(continued)*

Lee, D. (1974). *Alligator pie.* Toronto, ON: Key Porter Books. 🍁

Lee, D. (2006). *Garbage delight*. Toronto, ON: Key Porter Kids. 🍁

Loughead, D. (1998). *All I need and other poems for kids*. Etobicoke, ON: Moonstruck Press. 🍁

Silverstein, S. (1981). *A light in the attic.* Toronto, ON: Fitzhenry & Whiteside.

Stevens, R. (2002). *I did not eat the goldfish and other poems*. New York, NY: Macmillan Children's Books.

Wakan, N. (1993). *Haiku: One breath poetry*. Vancouver, BC: Pacific Rim Publishers. 🍁

Classics

(Found in a variety of publication forms but timeless and worth sharing)

Barrie, J. M. (1904). *Peter Pan.*

Burnett, F. H. (1911). *The secret garden.*

Baum, L. F. (1900). *The wonderful Wizard of Oz.*

Caxton, W. (1484). *Aesop's fables.*

Grahame, K. (1908). *The wind in the willows.*

Kipling, R. (1894). *The jungle book.*

Lindgren, A. (1950). *Pippi Longstocking*.

Mitchell, W. O. (1947). *Who has seen the wind.* 🍁

Montgomery L. M. (1908). *Anne of Green Gables.* 🍁

Richler, M. (1978). *Jacob Two-Two meets the Hooded Fang.* 🍁

Spyri, J. (1884). *Heidi.*

Stevenson, R. L. (1883). *Treasure island.*

White, E. B. (1952). *Charlotte's web.*

Williams, M. (1922). *The velveteen rabbit.*

Historical Fiction

Anderson, L. H. (2008). *Chains*. New York, NY: Simon & Schuster.

Brink, C. R. (1936). *Caddie Woodlawn*. New York, NY: Simon & Schuster.

Bruchac, J. (2002). *The winter people*. New York, NY: Penguin.

Curtis, C. P. (2007). *Elijah of Buxton*. New York, NY: Scholastic.

Edmonds, W. D. (1989). *The matchlock gun.* Kirkwood, NY: Putnam.

Hale, S. (2007). *Book of a thousand days*. London, UK: Bloomsbury.

Lasky, K. (1986). *Thenight journey*. New York, NY: Penguin.

Lunn, J. (1981). *The root cellar*. Toronto, ON: Random House of Canada. 🍁

MacLachlan, P. (1985). *Sarah, plain and tall*. New York, NY: HarperCollins.

Matas, C. (1993). *Daniel's story.* Markham, ON: Scholastic Canada. 🍁

Pearson, K. (1993). The guests of war trilogy. Toronto, ON: Penguin Canada. 🍁

Peck, R. (2003). *The river between us*. New York, NY: Penguin.

Scanlan, L. (2005). *The horse's shadow*. Toronto, ON: Penguin Canada. 🍁

Selznick, B. (2007). *The invention of Hugo Cabret*. New York, NY: Scholastic.

Wilder, L. I. (1935). *Little house on the prairie*. New York, NY: HarperCollins.

Yolen, J. (2004). *Prince across the water*. New York, NY: Penguin.

Adventure

Cooper, S. (1973). *The dark is rising*. New York, NY: Simon & Schuster.

George, J. C. (1991). *My side of the mountain*. New York, NY: Penguin.

Houston, J. (1988). *Whiteout*. Toronto, ON: Key Porter Books.

Kehret, P. (2004). *Abduction*. New York, NY: Penguin.

Konigsburg, E. (1995). *From the mixed-up files of Mrs. Basil E. Frankweiler*. New York, NY: Simon & Schuster.

Norriss, A. (2004). *Aquila*. New York, NY: Puffin Books.

Oppel, K. (2007). *Darkwing*. New York, NY: HarperCollins.

Oppel. K. (2009). *Starclimber*. New York, NY: HarperCollins.

Paulsen, G. (1999). *Brian's return*. New York, NY: Random House Children's Books.

Paulsen, G. (2010). *Woods runner*. New York, NY: Random House Children's Books.

Smith. R. (2007). *Peak*. Orlando, FL: Harcourt Books.

Sutherland, R. (1990). *Suddenly a spy*. Toronto, NY: Scholastic Canada.

Weston, R. P. (2008). *Zorgamazoo*. New York, NY: Penguin.

Mystery

Adler, D. A. (1991). *Cam Jansen: The mystery of the stolen diamonds.* New York, NY: Penguin.

Broach, E. (2008). *Masterpiece*. New York, NY: Henry Holt & Company.

Brooks, M. (2007). *Mistik Lake*. Toronto, ON: Groundwood.

Dowd, S. (2007). *The London Eye mystery*. New York, NY: Random House.

Ferguson, A. (2006). *The Christopher killer*. New York, NY: Penguin.

Hamilton, V. (1996). *The house of Dies Drear*. New York, NY: Simon & Schuster.

Heneghan, J. (1995). *The mystery of the gold ring*. Toronto, ON: Scholastic Canada.

Howe, D. (1979). HHH d*Bunnicula: A rabbit-tale of mystery*. New York, NY: Simon & Schuster.

Peacock, S. (2000). *The mystery of Ireland's eye*. Toronto, ON: Puffin Canada.

Stewart, T. L. (2007). *The mysterious Benedict Society*. New York, NY: Hachette Book Group.

Wilson, E. (2002). *The Emily Carr mystery*. Toronto, ON: HarperCollins.

Wilson, E. (2007). *Red River ransom*. Toronto, ON: HarperCollins.

Fantasy

Babbitt, N. (1975). *Tuck everlasting*. New York, NY: Farrar, Straus and Giroux.

Baird, A. (2001). *The witches of Wilowmere*. Toronto: Penguin.

Beam, M. (2007). *Earth to Nathan Blue*. Toronto, ON: Puffin Canada.

Boston, L. M. (1955). *The children of Green Knowe*. Orlando, FL: Harcourt Books.

Clare, C. (2007). *City of bones*. New York, NY: Simon & Schuster.

de Lint, C. (2004). *The blue girl*. New York, NY: Penguin.

Horrocks, A. (2000). *Topher*. Toronto, ON: Stoddart Kids.

(Continued)

Table 5.5 Selected Examples of Children's Literature *(continued)*

Fantasy *(continued)*

Juster, N. (1961). *The phantom tollbooth*. New York, NY: Random House.

Lewis, C. S. (1998). The chronicles of Narnia series. New York, NY: HarperCollins.

Marr, M. (2007). *Wicked lovely*. New York, NY: HarperCollins.

Mull, B. (2007). *The candy shop war*. Salt Lake City, UT: Shadow Mountain Publishing.

Skelton, M (2006). *Endymion spring*. Toronto, ON: Puffin Canada. 🍁

General Fiction

Beam, M. (2009). *Last December*. Toronto, ON: Penguin Canada. 🍁

Cummings, P. (2004). *Red kayak*. New York, NY: Penguin.

Deans, S. (2001). *Racing the past*. New York, NY: Henry Holt and Company.

Ellis, D. (1997). *The breadwinner*. Toronto, ON: Groundwood. 🍁

Ellis, D. (2000). *Looking for X*. Toronto, ON: Groundwood. 🍁

Griffin, A. (2005). *Where I want to be*. New York, NY: Penguin.

Ibbitson, J. (2008). *The landing*. Toronto, ON: Kids Can Press. 🍁

Johnston, J. (1994). *Adam and Eve and Pinch-Me*. Toronto, ON: Stoddart. 🍁

Madden, K. (2005). *Gentle's holler*. New York, NY: Penguin.

Murray, J. (2003). *Bottled up*. New York, NY: Penguin.

Nelson, B. (2004). *Rock star superstar*. New York, NY: Penguin.

Pearson, K. (1997). *Awake and dreaming*. Toronto, ON: Puffin Canada. 🍁

Woodson, J. (1994). *I hadn't meant to tell you this*. New York, NY: Bantam Doubleday Dell.

Wynne-Jones, T. (1996). *The maestro*. New York, NY: Orchard Books. 🍁

Yee, P. (1996) *Ghost train*. Toronto, ON: Groundwood. 🍁

Young Adult

Barnes, J. (2009). *Tales of the madman underground.* New York, NY: Viking Children's Books.

Bray, L. (2009). *Going bovine.* New York, NY: Delacorte Press

Farmer, N. (2002). *The house of the scorpion.* Cambridge, MA: Atheneum Books.

Green, J. (2005). *Looking for Alaska*. New York, NY: Dutton Juvenile.

Hrdlitschka, S. (2008). *Sister wife*. Victoria, BC: Orca Books. 🍁

Lawrence, I. (2006). *Gemini summer*. New York, NY: Delacorte Press. 🍁

Myers, W. D. (1999). *Monster*. New York, NY: HarperCollins.

Pignat, C. (2008). *Greener grass: The famine years*. Markham, ON: Red Deer Press. 🍁

Rapp, A. (2009). *Punkzilla.* Cambridge, MA: Candlewick Press.

Selvadurai, S. (2005). *Swimming in the monsoon sea.* Toronto, ON: Tundra. 🍁

Stevenson, R. (2008). *A thousand shades of blue*. Victoria, BC: Orca Books. 🍁

Wieler, D. (1990). *Bad boy*. Toronto, ON: Groundwood 🍁

Wynne-Jones, T. (2010). *The Uninvited*. Cambridge, MA: Candlewick Press. 🍁

Yancey, R. (2009). *The monstrumologist*. New York, NY: Simon & Schuster Books for Young Readers.

Yang, G. L. (2007). *American born Chinese.* New York, NY: McMillan First Second Books. 🍁

Zusak, M. (2006). *The book thief.* Mississauga, ON: Knopf Books for Young Readers.

Stories and Story Structure

Stories play a critical role in how students make sense of the world and define their roles in it. In this sense, they are basic to students' narrative reading experiences. Stories share a common and sometimes complex structure. Collectively, these structures are often referred to as *story schema, story structure*, or *story grammar*. Typically, students develop a conceptual understanding of the beginning, middle, and end in the primary grades (Applebee, 1978; Golden, Meiners, & Lewis, 1992). Most students also understand that some form of a "problem" is introduced in the beginning of the story and resolved by the end. However, these initial understandings do not absolve teachers from providing instruction about story structure. As students become competent at problem identification and the identification of basic story elements, it is important to provide them with a more detailed and sophisticated consideration of story elements. At the same time, more complex stories should be introduced in which authors extend and manipulate these elements and their interplay to present complex characters, diverse settings, and layered plots.

Research has demonstrated that all students benefit from instruction in story structure, with their understanding and retention of story information increasing following this instruction (Duke & Pearson, 2002). Providing students with systematic instruction about story elements also enhances their oral storytelling abilities and written compositions (Golden 1984; Golden, Meiners, & Lewis, 1992). Less-skilled and struggling readers typically demonstrate an underdeveloped knowledge of story structure and are especially likely to benefit from direct instruction (Gersten, Fuchs, Williams, & Baker, 2001).

Teachers therefore need to provide *all* students with instruction in story structure elements and how they interact to form a story. In general, providing students with multiple and regular experiences with authentic stories is an effective method of promoting their understanding of story structure. However, such authentic experiences need to be supplemented with systematic instruction (Pressley, 2006).

In the following sections, we review each of the elements of story structure and provide suggestions for instruction. Almost all stories contain the elements of characters, setting, point of view, plot or problem, and theme.

Characters Characters are often the most important elements of a story, as readers connect readily to well-developed, engaging, and interesting characters. Characters are persons, personas, or entities that are critical to the story, with distinctions being made between the main and secondary roles. Characters may be entirely fictional or based on real or historical people. Characters may take many forms, including human, supernatural, mythical, divine, and animal.

Main characters are those that have been fully developed and are often difficult to identify as either exclusively good or bad. Therefore, they behave in complex and sometimes unpredictable manners. Authors provide sufficient detail about the characters' physical, mental, and emotional attributes so that they often can seem "real" to the reader. Main characters often need to be considered from multiple perspectives, including the physical, mental, and emotional. Teachers can encourage students to consider multiple perspectives by using simple charts, such as the one in Figure 5.1 (Rozelle, 2005).

Main characters frequently change significantly throughout the course of the story, usually because they gain new understandings, values, beliefs, or world views. In many young adult stories, characters often undergo major changes or transformations through which they lose

Physical	Mental	Emotional
Inuit girl	Curious	Joyful
Age about 12	Becoming independent	Brave
Black hair	Resourceful	Excited
(*Very Last First Time* by Jan Andrews)		

Figure 5.1 Character Chart for Eva Padlyat

Physical	Mental	Emotional
Initially		
Sickly	Self-centred	Unhappy
Pale	Demanding	Angry
Frail	Uncaring of others	Impatient
At the End		
Healthy	Caring of others	Happy
Strong	Friendly	Excited
Energetic	Connected to the Earth	Appreciative
(*The Secret Garden* by Frances Hodgson Burnett)		

Figure 5.2 Character Chart Illustrating Change over Time: Mary Lennox

some of their innocence and become more mature. For instance, Mary Lennox in *The Secret Garden* is sickly and pathetic at the beginning of the novel but she grows and changes through her interaction with nature and other characters until she is strong and vital (see Figure 5.2). Other well-known examples of characters that mature across time include Harry, Ron, and Hermione in the Harry Potter series and Bilbo Baggins in *The Hobbit*. Students can be asked to complete open-minded portraits (see Figure 5.3), which involves drawing an illustration of the character's head and inserting words to indicate his or her characteristics, or to complete a cube (see Figure 5.4), which involves generating questions about characters and taking turns responding to "rolls of the die."

In contrast, secondary or supporting characters typically lack such complexities and usually present only one or two defining traits throughout the course of the story. These characters are sometimes described as flat or static, although they may contribute to the growth of the main character and play a pivotal role in the story. Sometimes, these characters capture the hearts and minds of readers. An example is Gollum in The Lord of the Rings series, who can be singularly defined by his obsession with the recovery of the ring. The characters in *The Wonderful Wizard of Oz* are relatively flat as well, with each being defined by only the one wish they desire from Oz.

Setting Setting includes the time, the location, and the circumstances in which the story is told. The setting is important because it provides the backdrop for the story and may influence the way the story unfolds. Setting also can be extended to include

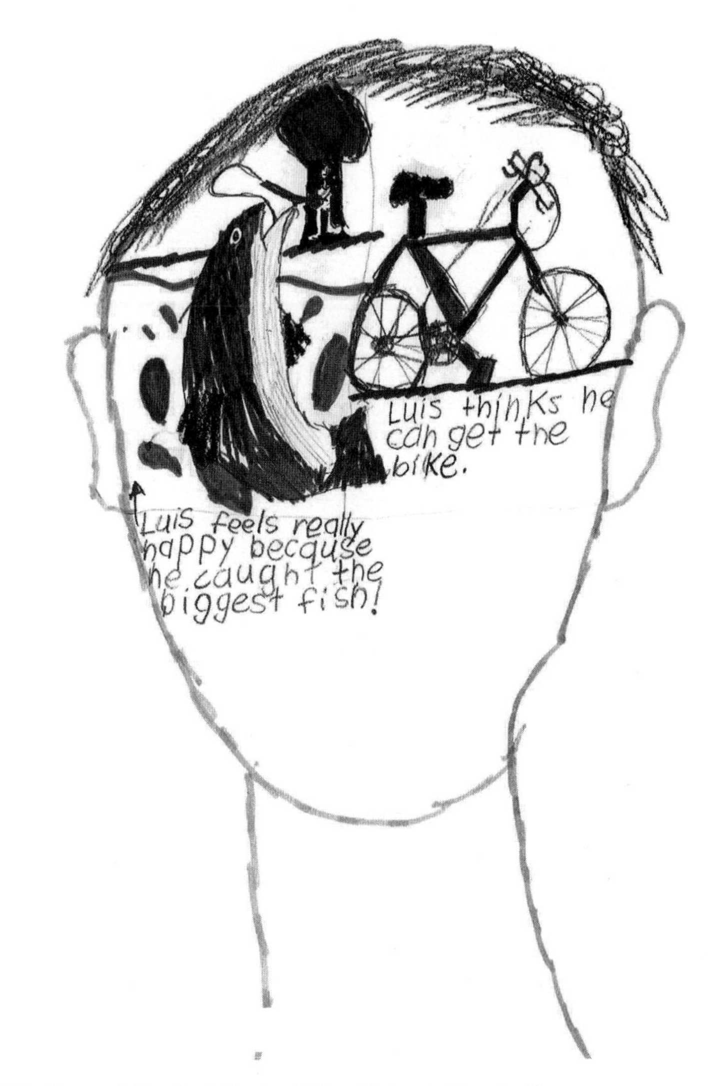

Figure 5.3 Open-Minded Portrait by Shane, Grade 5

societal orientations and dispositions. The setting helps to establish the mood of a story and includes culture, historical time frame, geography, location, and time. Stories can be set in the present, past, and future and usually include some passage of time. This passage of time can vary from a few hours to years and be non-linear in nature.

The setting can be especially important for young readers if the text is set in the past. It may be difficult for students to make the appropriate inferences based on past circumstances and attitudes that are no longer prevalent today. In *The Sky is Falling* by Kit Pearson, it may be difficult for students to understand Norah's "suffocating fear" of being torpedoed during her trip to Canada from Britain at the beginning of World War II without prior discussion. Students also may not understand how gas masks provided children with a sense of security during that time. In another example, students may not appreciate such texts as *Duncan's Way* by Ian Wallace if they live outside of Newfoundland and do not realize the economic realities associated with the decline

Create a Cube Print one of the following phrases (or variation) on each side of the cube:

What did the character look like?

What did the character think or believe?

What emotions did the character feel?

Why would you like or dislike having this character as a friend?

Who do you know who is like the character?

How is the character realistic? unrealistic?

As a class, determine a character that will be the focus of the cube activity or generate a list of potential characters for discussion. Students toss the cube like a dice and answer the question that appears on the "top" of the cube.

This activity can be completed by small groups or by individuals as part of an oral or written activity.

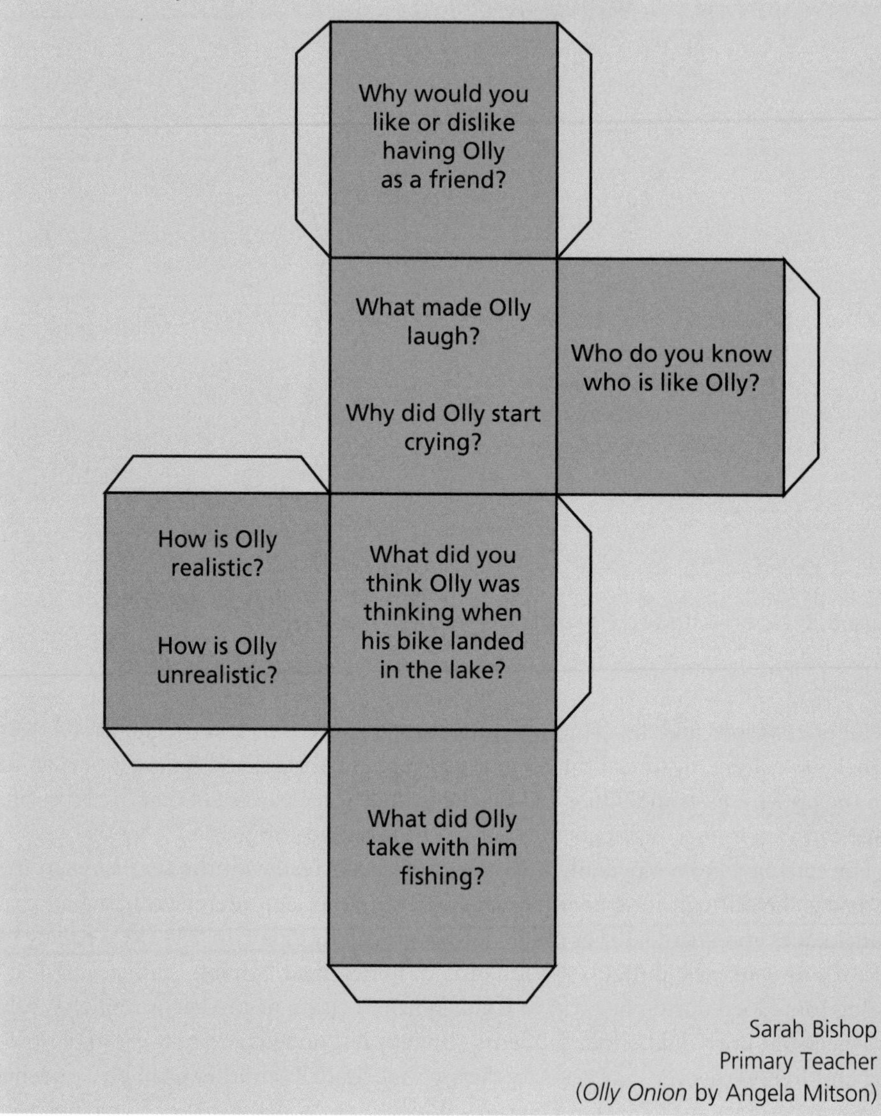

Sarah Bishop
Primary Teacher
(*Olly Onion* by Angela Mitson)

Figure 5.4 Create a Cube

Table 5.6 Teaching Strategies for Developing Students' Understanding of Setting

Puppet plays. By adapting a story to a puppet play, students must make decisions about appropriate backdrops.

Visualization and drawing. Instruct students to draw a cover for a response journal that must include a setting found in the story. This activity requires students to reflect on the setting and become more aware of its significance to the story.

Provide relevant background knowledge. Use pictures, videos, and other forms of media to begin a discussion about setting. Providing students with background information is especially important when the setting is in the past. Although this activity can be time consuming, it is time well spent in terms of preparing students to comprehend the text.

Family research. Consider providing students with a "take home" activity that requires them to ask their parents or grandparents (or relevant others) about a story setting in the past.

of the fishing industry. See Table 5.6 for suggested teaching strategies for developing students' understanding of setting.

Point of View Point of view, or what is sometimes called viewpoint, refers to the lens through which the story is told. Viewpoint is a critical story element and influences the way in which readers experience, understand, interpret, and relate to characters, events, and themes. The narrator is the character through whose eyes the story unfolds and through which the story is experienced. When the first-person viewpoint is used, the story is told through the eyes of one character. The words *I* and *we* are used frequently with first-person viewpoints and the reader gains a sense of familiarity with that character's feelings, thoughts, and behaviours.

The omniscient narrator is a reliable narrator from outside the story who provides the reader with information about characters' thoughts and actions. In some cases, the narrator reveals information that the characters do not possess or understand about themselves. In other cases, the story is told through the thoughts, experiences, and actions of one character (e.g., Harry Potter). Some popular third-person narrators include Lemony Snicket in the series called A Series of Unfortunate Events, James E. Robinson in *The Flower of Grass*, and Philip Pullman in the trilogy His Dark Materials.

When the narration of a story alternates between first and third person, multiple viewpoints or multiple person narratives are being used. In these stories, authors move back and forth between an omniscient third-person narrator to a more personal first-person narrator. Multiple viewpoints also allow readers to experience different characters' views and can be used to describe separate events that occur simultaneously but in different locations.

Teachers often encourage students to explore multiple perspectives when reading, with many picture books and short stories providing alternative orientations to traditional texts. These texts provide teachers with easily managed and time-efficient materials to initiate discussions about culture, gender, beliefs, and values. A good example is *The True Story of the Three Little Pigs* by Jon Scieszka, which provides the wolf's viewpoint of a classic fairy tale. Other examples include *The Frog Prince Continued* by Jon Scieszka, *The Paper Bag Princess* by Robert Munsch, and *Prince Cinders* by Babette Cole. These alternative tales delight students and can be used to encourage them to retell or rewrite stories from the perspective of the "other." See Table 5.7 for additional teaching strategies for developing point of view and multiple perspectives.

Plot Plot is arguably the most important story component because it describes the primary sequence of events. The plot describes the characters' action plans and goals as well as the obstacles and problems they must overcome to achieve them. For readers to respond favourably to narratives, the plot must demonstrate a plausible sequence of events. In its most basic form, plot consists of a beginning (introduction), middle (development), and end (resolution). The reader is introduced to the critical event, or what is otherwise referred to as the problem, at the beginning of the story. The body of the story is then dominated by the decisions and actions adopted by characters as they attempt to obtain their goals, overcome challenges, and resolve their difficulties. Characters typically experience multiple hardships and conflicts prior to plot resolution, with the highest point of tension being referred to as the climax of the story. Characters can experience conflicts with other characters, nature, society, and themselves. Typically, stories end when the character achieves the defined objective or when the problem is resolved. Sometimes the plot can be sustained over a series of books, with each book contributing to a larger overarching plot. Harry Potter, Anne of Green Gables, and The Breadwinner Trilogy are good examples of how sequels can be developed within the same plot structure, with each

Table 5.7 Teaching Strategies for Developing Point of View and Multiple Perspectives

Make a cube. Print the name of one character on each side of the cube. As an oral activity, ask a question related to the story and toss the cube to a student. The student catches the cube and answers the question from the perspective of the identified character. Repeat the same question until all characters' perspectives have been identified.

or

Print the terms *Past*, *Present*, and *Future* on each side of the cube. Follow the same procedure as above, forming responses on the basis of time.

Double-entry journals. Provide students with a few direct quotations from a story and ask them to copy the quotations on the left half of their papers or response journals. Students respond from the perspective of two or three characters on the right side. Older students can select their own quotations.

Alternative endings. Students can generate alternative endings to text in a variety of ways, including changing the ending of a familiar story to reflect the perspective of a different character.

or

Read only part of a story to students and have them write, enact, or illustrate the ending. Read the real ending once they have completed their versions. Oral sharing of such activities encourages students to understand that multiple perspectives can be found in a story.

Table 5.8 Teaching Strategies for Developing Students Understanding of Plot

Provide students with a series of questions or prompts.

a) What is the problem or conflict in this story?
b) How do characters attempt to solve the problem or conflict?
c) Locate the point in the story when the problem is about to be solved.
d) What is the solution to the problem or conflict?

Create a plot line.

Have students identify the problem or conflict type.

a) Is there conflict between characters and nature, such as in survival stories?
b) Is there conflict between or among characters?
c) Is there an internal conflict that a character must identify and solve to grow as a person?
d) Is there conflict between characters and society or societal expectations?

text illustrating the importance of hope and the power of resilience. See Table 5.8 for teaching strategies to develop students' understanding of plot.

Theme Theme is a broad idea, message, or lesson conveyed in the text. This message is usually about life, society, or humanity and is typically multidimensional. Themes cannot be easily summarized in a single word or phrase. Many times, themes explore seemingly timeless and universal ideas such as understanding of self and others, resolving conflict (good versus evil), and empowerment. These themes appear to be prevalent across time and cultures. While themes can be expressed explicitly in the text (friendship in *Charlotte's Web*, acceptance of self in *The Skin I'm In*, overcoming fear in *The Sky Is Falling*), at other times they need to be deduced and are presented in an implicit manner. When themes are implied, readers are required to process the text at an abstract level. It is not surprising, then, that individuals often interpret text themes differently and sometimes in ways that are inconsistent with the author's intentions. Table 5.9 provides teaching strategies for developing students' understanding of theme.

Table 5.9 Teaching Strategies for Developing Students' Understanding of Theme

Locating and Understanding the Theme

a) If the theme is stated explicitly in the text, have students locate it.
b) If the theme is implicit, have students examine characters' actions, internal monologues, and external dialogues.
c) Have students examine the author's narrative for clues (i.e., third-person point of view).
d) Provide critical questions (e.g., Why did the author write this story?) that direct students to consider the overall message.
e) Examine and discuss the title (e.g., Why do you think the author chose this title? What do you think might be a better choice for the title?)

COMPREHENSION STRATEGIES

TEACHERS NEED TO POSSESS A REPERTOIRE OF SPECIFIC STRATEGIES AND TEACHING techniques used to help students comprehend text. While initially this may appear to be a daunting mandate, decades of empirical research support the use of a defined number of reading comprehension strategies and instructional approaches (McGuinness, 2004; National Reading Panel, 2000; RAND Reading Study Group, 2002). In the following sections we provide an overview of these instructional approaches and comprehension strategies. Specifically, we identify each strategy, explore its importance to the reading process, and provide examples of how it might be used in the classroom. These suggestions are far from exhaustive and teachers need to remember that the same strategy can be used across multiple grades and instructional contexts and in response to varied student needs. This is the "craft" or creative component of being an effective reading teacher.

Using Predictable Text

Young students need to understand that reading involves more than decoding words; rather, they are looking for a message. Predictable texts refer to those stories that are based on a repeated pattern. Predictable texts may use repeated phrases or rhythm and rhyme that allow the reader to anticipate readily what will happen next. Furthermore, students are able to confirm their hypotheses in a natural and non-threatening manner. This process builds self-confidence and helps create a positive attitude toward reading. Creative teachers can use such texts interactively with students and create an atmosphere of enjoyment. For example, in *Alexander and the Terrible, Horrible, No Good, Very Bad Day* by Judith Viorst there is a sequence of words similar to a chorus that is repeated throughout the story and renders it highly predictable. *Green Eggs and Ham* by Dr. Seuss (as well as most other books by this author) relies strongly on rhythm and rhyme to create predictability. Teachers can introduce students to the structure of predictable text by reading pattern books and providing language experience lessons as part of their instructional programming (see Table 5.10).

Table 5.10 Reading Pattern Books

Day 1

1. Say the title and show any pictures. Ask students to predict what the story will be about.
2. Read a few pages and ask, "What will happen next? Why?" Accept multiple responses.
3. Continue reading. If there are repeated phrases, encourage students to chime in.

Day 2

4. Reread the story, pointing to the words as you read. Have students choral read the repeated or predictable parts.
5. Read a section of the text, leaving out a word. Have students predict what the next word will be.
6. Have individual students "read" predictable, repeated, or rhyming sections of the text.

Language Experience Lessons

In this approach, teachers guide small groups of students in the creation of a text. Student authorship makes this text predicable. It is imperative that this approach be built on a shared experience that can be as simple as a walk to a local store or a discussion about a classroom pet or as elaborate as a class trip to a circus. By reading and writing about a shared experience, students are able to readily "make meaning" of text. Language experience lessons are usually carried out with groups of six or eight students and follow the general procedure outlined below.

1. The teacher leads an extensive oral discussion about the shared experience, allowing each student to contribute his or her ideas.
2. Each student is asked to contribute one idea about the experience.
3. The teacher records each idea as a sentence and writes the student's name beside his or her ideas. The teacher reads each word aloud while writing so that all students can watch the words being formed. Students approve of their sentences, editing them if necessary.
4. After all students have contributed ideas, the teacher reads the entire set of sentences aloud while pointing to each word.
5. The teacher leads a discussion about possible titles for the work and negotiates the selection of a final title. Through this process, students identify the main idea of the text.
6. Subsequent activities vary according to student abilities. Some students may be able to read the entire section, while others may only be able to recognize their names and read their personal contributions.

Teaching Story Structure

While it is important that teachers take time to review and explore each of the elements of story structure, students will also need to identify these elements as a collective to grasp the "big picture" of a story. To facilitate students' understanding of story structure, teachers are encouraged to incorporate direct instruction about it as part of their reading lessons. Instruction in story structure will require several lessons at a minimum. These lessons can be incorporated as part of students' before, during, and after reading activities and experiences. Direct instruction consists of teacher modelling, guided practice, and independent practice (see Sample Lesson 5.1). Instruction involving the use of graphic organizers and question-answering forms the basis of this teaching.

Graphic Organizers

Even very young students can come to understand that every story contains a problem or plot. Using the "problem" as the focus of discussion, students can then be directed to identify the beginning, middle, and end of a story. Over time, they will recognize that the problem is usually identified in the beginning of the story and the solution or resolution is at the end. The following steps can be followed to bring all elements of story structure into focus for young students.

1. Provide students with multiple opportunities to identify the problem using simple pictures and stories. It is important to select pictures and stories that have no subplots or alternative interpretations that may confuse students. A fairy tale such as

SAMPLE LESSON 5.1

Teaching Story Structure in the Primary Grades

Text *Amos's Sweater* by Janet Lunn and Kim LaFave

Objectives

Students should be able to identify the beginning, middle, and end of the story. They should also be able to identify the problem and discuss how the ending solved the problem.

Introduction

Ask students to listen to the story and to identify the problem.
Read the story out loud.
Solicit students' responses about the problem and identify the correct response.
Brainstorm solutions for the problem (i.e., how it might be solved).

Lesson Steps

1. Review the problem as identified during reading.
2. How was the problem solved?
3. Draw a line on the board to identify the beginning, middle, and end of the story.
4. Have students identify the events that fall into each section of the story.
5. How do you know the story has ended? (i.e., When was the problem solved?)

Recapitulation

Reread the story and ask students to confirm reworded information.

Application of New Learning

Select another story and identify the story elements. A good choice would be *Big Sarah's Little Boots* by Paulette Bourgeois.

Ask students to create a problem and write a story that solves it. Have students use a separate page for each element:

1. The Problem
2. The Beginning
3. The Middle (attempts to solve the problem)
4. The End (problem solution)

Assessment of Independent Learning

Students will independently complete a chart identifying the problem and beginning, middle, and end of the story for *Big Sarah's Little Boots.*

The Princess and the Pea would be a good choice, as would a picture of a hippo stuck in a bathtub. Students should identify the problem and agree as a group on its nature. It is generally helpful to record the problem at the end of the discussion.

2. Ask students to consider alternative endings that solve the problems represented in familiar stories. This activity can be either completed verbally or integrated into a writing assignment. An important element, however, is the public sharing of alternative endings.
3. Identify the problem and other elements using unfamiliar stories. Stories such as *Amos's Sweater* by Janet Lunn can be used to identify story elements that can also be used as a template in helping students write their own narratives.

> *Amos's Sweater* is the story of old Amos, a sheep, who felt cold after Aunt Hatty cut his wool and knit a sweater to keep Uncle Amos warm. Amos tried repeatedly to get his sweater back until finally kind Aunt Hatty returned it to him. The resolution finds Amos happily in the pasture with the other sheep—wearing his sweater.

Problem: ______________________________

Beginning		Middle		End
____________	+	____________	+	____________

Figure 5.5 Simple Graphic Organizer for Story Structure

Teachers can complete this simple but important lesson by reading the story to the students and asking them to identify the problem. After the problem is firmly established, the students can identify the beginning, middle, and end of the story using a timeline of words or pictures. Teachers can then introduce and model the completion of a graphic organizer to record the story elements (see Figure 5.5). Students can then use pictures or words to complete these graphic organizers independently.

In a similar fashion, teachers can model the use of more advanced graphic organizers with older students who are beyond the beginning-to-read stage (see Figure 5.6). Again, teachers need to emphasize how the various elements of a story work together to create the whole.

Question-Answering Providing students with questions related to story elements is another effective strategy for improving their understanding of text and overall story structure (Israel & Duffy, 2009; Pressley, 2006; Short & Ryan, 1984). Providing students with generic question stems is especially effective, as students are more likely to transfer and generalize the use of these questions when reading independently. Sometimes referred to as "content-free" questions, many of these open-ended questions can take the form of queries intended for the author (Beck, McKeown, Hamilton, & Kucan, 1997; Caldwell & Leslie, 2005). Students engaged in questioning the author are likely to contemplate prompts such as the following: What is the author trying to saying? What does the author mean? What is the author's message? Does this connect to what we read before? Table 5.11 contains an extended list of generic and content-free question stems.

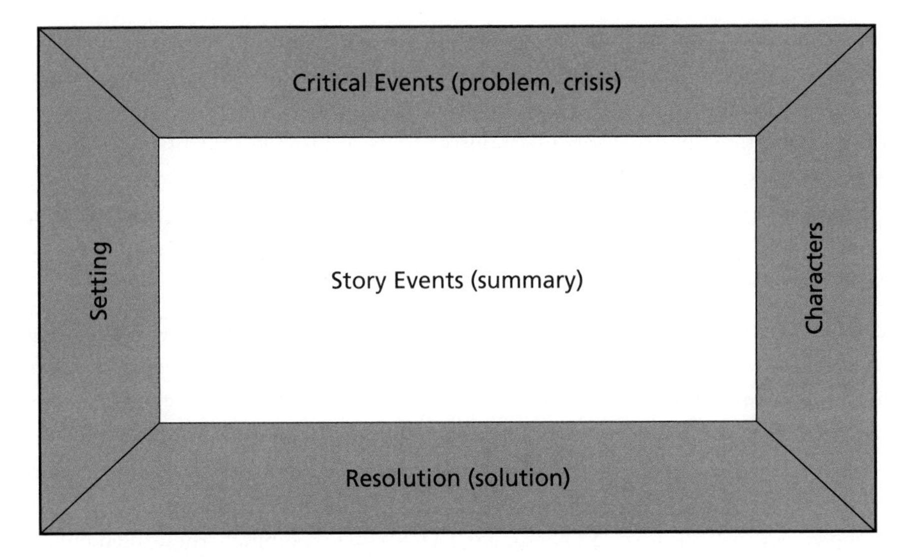

Figure 5.6 Advanced Graphic Organizer for Story Structure

Table 5.11 Question Prompts for Understanding Story Structure

Characters	Who is the main character? Why do I think so?
	Who are other important characters? Why are they important?
Setting	When did the story take place?
	Where did the story take place?
	How is the setting important to the story?
Events	What do I predict will happen next? Why do I think this?
	Is this story true to life? Why or why not?
Critical event (plot or problem)	What problems did the main character face?
	What does the character need? How is the character trying to solve his or her problem?
	Is the character in trouble? Why?
	What does the character feel about the problem?
Solution or resolution	How did the story end?
	How did the main character solve the problem? Do I agree or disagree with what the character did? Why?
	How did the character feel at the end?
	Is there anything I don't understand?
	What would I do to solve the problem?
	What surprised me about this story?
Theme	What is the author trying to say? What is the author talking about? What is the author's message?
	Does this connect to what I have read before? Does this connect to what the author has told us before?
	If I was going to write to the author, what would I say?

Adapted from Caldwell and Leslie (2005); Pressley and Woloshyn (1995).

Teachers must take great care to model the use of question-answering strategies prior to having students use them independently. As part of their modelling, teachers need to ask questions in the context of a meaningful text and provide appropriate responses. It is equally important that teachers use multiple texts to provide students with numerous examples of question-answering. They can then scaffold instruction, providing supportive whole-class and small-group opportunities for students to generate and respond to story questions. Only when students demonstrate proficiency using questions in these structured sessions should they be directed to use them independently.

Predictive Story Frames Effective reading teachers are those who demonstrate responsiveness to students' needs and the ability to manipulate resources and materials in meaningful manners (Almasi, 2003). For instance, the advanced graphic organizer presented in Figure 5.6 can be adapted to engage students in question-answering about story elements before (i.e., predictions about future events), during (confirmation of previous predictions and subsequent predictions), and after (summarization) reading (Foregrave, 2003; Woloshyn & Foregrave, 2003). We combined these elements into one graphic organizer called a predictive story frame (see Figure 5.7). Grade 4 students

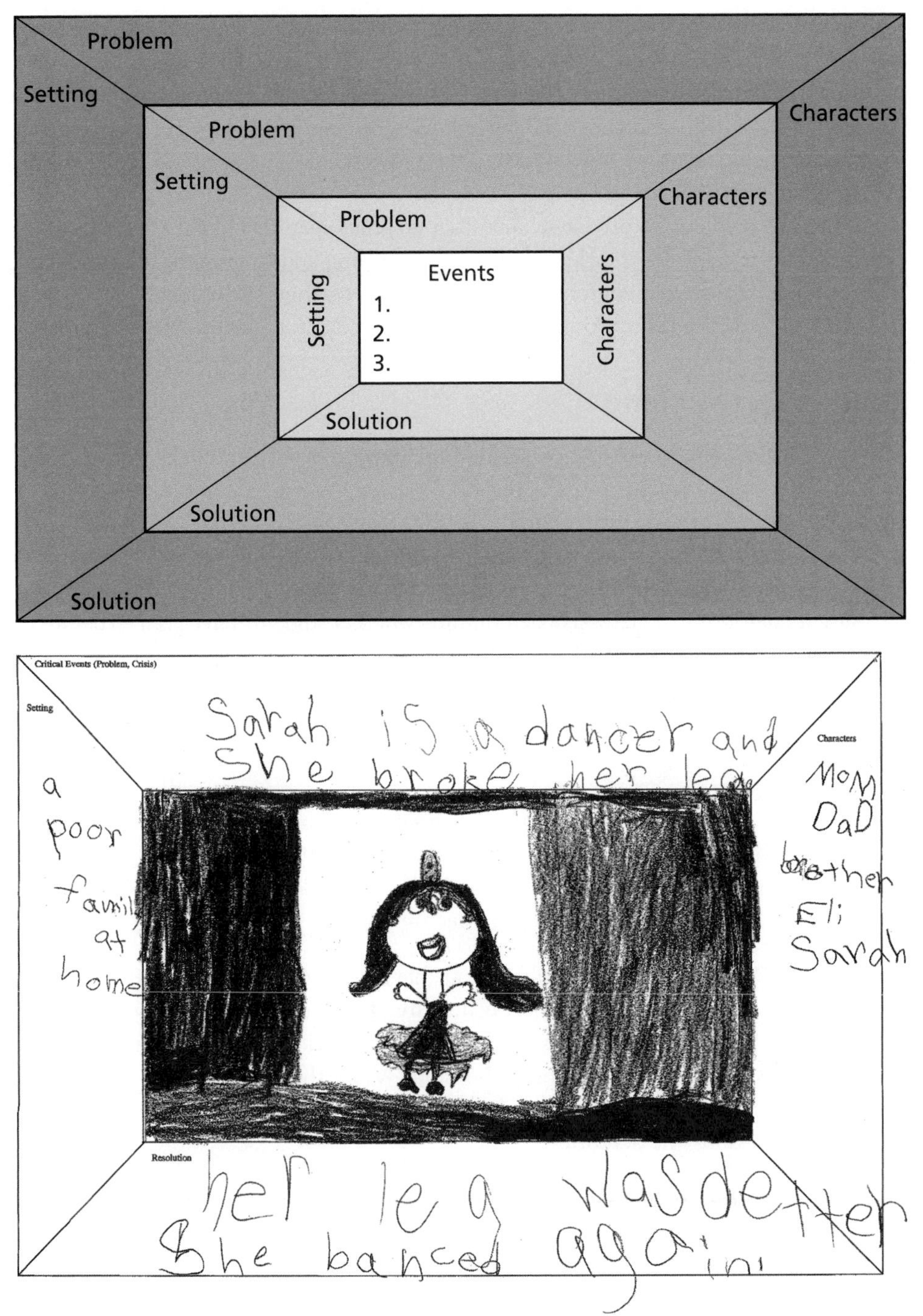

Figure 5.7 Predictive Story Frame

who used the predictive story frame, including those considered below-average readers, answered comprehension questions better than or as well as students who used a more traditional story map. In addition, they recalled more correct information about story elements than their peers and generated fewer erroneous responses when questioned about the text. Students reported enjoying using the predictive story frame and found that it helped them remember the story.

Using the predictive story frame and other graphic organizers like it encourages students to activate relevant prior knowledge before reading and to monitor their thoughts while reading. The predictive story frame also provides teachers and students with a summary tool and a method of tracking their responses to text throughout the reading process.

Teacher Questioning

"Let us . . . make a study of the art of question-asking, one of the central disciplines in the Language education" (Postman, 1979, p. 140). Questions are central to the exploration of story structure, with the quality of these questions contributing to students' overall comprehension. Good questions encourage students to think about the events in the text, the author's purpose, and their related experiences. Unfortunately, many teachers limit the use of their questions to a method of determining whether students have grasped details of sequential events, instead using them as a means of encouraging students to be thoughtful about the meaning embedded in the text.

Teachers also need to educate themselves not only on how to ask good questions but also on how to encourage students to provide thoughtful responses. This includes providing enough time for students to think prior to accepting a response (usually about five to seven seconds). Teachers also need to train themselves to really listen to responses so they can ask the kinds of follow-up questions that encourage further thinking and whole-class discourse. Finally, teachers need to present themselves as learners through questioning rather than as experts who acknowledge correct responses.

Literal Questions

Literal-level questions have answers that are located directly in the text and represent the lowest level of inquiry. They represent the majority (about 75 percent) of all questions asked by teachers. These questions require minimal thought and do little to deepen students' comprehension. While they have a place in teachers' questioning repertoires, they should not be overused. The following are some examples of literal-level questions and activities.

Questions that require students to recall significant details.
These are directly embedded in the text and astute students can easily identify correct responses from the pages. Examples: What colour was the wagon? How old was the main character?

Questions that help students follow a sequence of events or ideas.
Examples: Tell me the story again. What happened first? What happened next?

Questions that help students identify cause and effect.
Using familiar stories—even fairy tales—can establish the relationship between cause and effect. Examples: Why was the Pied Piper angry at the people of Hamelin? What did the Pied Piper do as a result of his anger?

Questions that help students translate text into mental images.
Teachers can ask students to close their eyes and picture a setting, a character, or an event in the story. After a pause, students can be asked to describe what they visualized. After a story, students can be asked to draw their idea of some aspect of the story. Alternatively, students can be assigned a section of the story to draw and the results can be organized chronologically into a class book. Examples: Close your eyes and create a mental picture of the main character, setting, or conflict. Draw a picture of the main character, the setting, or your favourite part of the story.

Inferential Questions Students' ability to think about the inferences in the story or the aspects of the story that are beyond the written page improves with practice. All students, no matter how young, can respond to inferential questions. Questions that require students to determine the main idea are especially important for a number of reasons. If students are to be aware of the author's message or reason for writing, they need to be able to identify the main idea. Identifying the main idea is also an important skill related to summarizing and outlining. Examples of inferential questions follow.

Questions that require students to form predictions.
These types of questions provide students with a purpose for reading. Based on available knowledge, at various stages throughout the story students make predictions about what will happen next and then continue reading to see if their predications were correct.

- They can discuss the title to make a prediction about what the story will be about.
- They can read a section, predict the next events, and then continue reading to prove or discover.
- They can stop partway through a story, write an ending, and then read the ending of the story and compare.
- They can orally suggest alternate endings.

Questions that require students to read between the lines.
Example: Read the following sentence. "The little girl stood at the streetcar stop holding her ears and stamping her feet." Where do you think the story takes place and why? What time of year is it and why?

What do we know about a character as a result of:

- What he or she says?
- What she or he does?
- What others say?
- What the author says?

Questions that require students to recognize main ideas.
Examples: What is the author trying to tell you? What is this really about? What would be a better title?

Critical Questions While inferential questions probe the intention of the author, critical questions reflect readers' responses to the author's intentions. Critical questions require students to apply judgments to what they are reading. Teachers often neglect to include critical thinking questions as part of their instructional repertoires. The following are some ways to promote critical thinking in students.

Questions that require students to distinguish between realism and fantasy. Even very young students can be asked to determine whether a story is fact or fantasy. This is harder than it might appear, as many stories are factual except for one fanciful component around which the story may be developed. Examples: What parts of this story could really happen? What parts of the story are make-believe?

Questions that require students to distinguish fact and author bias. Examples: Review a newspaper article and recount events. Review editorial comments or letters to the editor and identify various opinions. Evaluate advertisements with respect to surface features and underlying messages. What are the facts in this text? What does the author believe about these facts? Why do you think the author wrote this story? What point of view did the author reveal by writing this story in this way?

Questions that require students to provide a personal evaluation. Examples: Did the characters act as you expected? Explain. Is the story plausible based on your experience?

Creative Questions When asking creative questions, teachers often use the story as a springboard for further discussion or activities based on the topics or themes raised in the story. Creative questions and activities are limited only by the imagination of the teacher and the students together. Dramatic or artistic responses can be nicely integrated into content area programming. Students can complete additional research about topics raised in the story, during discussion of the story as a whole class or small group, or independently. Activities such as Readers' Theatre or research or art projects are appropriate.

Figure 5.8 provides an example of how teachers can incorporate the four kinds of questions as part of their story questioning protocols when reading text passages.

Using Questions Effectively Read the excerpt from *Cemetery Path* by Leonard Ross in Figure 5.9 and consider the accompanying questions. Which teacher do you believe elicited the higher quality of discussion and insight about the story?

Ms. Barnes asks many questions covering many aspects of the story. She elicits one answer for each question and acknowledges that the response is correct. While Ms. Trigger asks only two questions, she accepts several responses for each question. For instance, several students thought that Ivan would complete the challenge successfully and overcome his fear. Several others thought he might try to trick the Lieutenant and place the sabre in the cemetery early the next morning. Still others thought Ivan would decide to go around the cemetery as he always did.

In response to Ms. Trigger's thought-provoking questions, students decided that Ivan had been bullied by the Lieutenant and his men and were outraged. Some students blamed the whole episode on drinking and bad judgment. Some said that

The war was the most exciting thing that had ever happened in Norah's ten years, and this summer was the best part of it. Other summers were a pleasant, mild blur of building sandcastles on the beach near Granddad's house in Camber. But one day at the end of last August, Norah had found herself filling sandbags instead of playing.

Now there was a bright edge to everything; even the weather was exaggerated. The coldest winter in a hundred years was followed by a short spring and an early summer. As the war news grew worse and the grown-ups huddled anxiously around the wireless, day after day dawned hot and clear. At night, the sky's inky blackness was pinpointed with strangely brilliant stars, the only lights in Britain besides the search lights that were not blacked out.

Every evening this week the news announcer had given out the "scores" of the battle in the sky as if it were a football match. Norah could hardly remember what life had been like before this war. How could anyone bear to be sent away from it? Tom was right—they were lucky that their parents were so sensible.

But then she felt afraid again, because she wasn't at all sure that her parents would remain sensible.

Literal Questions

Close your eyes and picture yourself at a beach as Norah had been for many summers. What do you see?

What factors have caused Norah to feel anxious?

How old was Norah?

Inferential Questions

Why was Norah filling sandbags rather than making sandcastles as she had done in previous summers?

Why was Norah afraid that her parents would not remain sensible?

Critical Questions

Do you think students should be called upon to help build defences for a war?

Do you think a battle in war should be compared to a football game?

Creative Questions

Conduct a research project about the students who were sent away from London during the war and who came to Canada.

Describe a time when you went away from your family and felt homesick.

Figure 5.8 Using Literal, Inferential, Critical, and Creative Questions

the Lieutenant bore the greatest responsibility because he was a leader. A small but determined group of students stated that Ivan's death was the result of greed over the five gold rubles. One student thought that Ivan wanted to salvage his self-esteem and accepted the dare.

Ivan was a timid little man—so timid that the villagers called him "Pigeon" or mocked him with the title "Ivan the Terrible". Every night Ivan stopped in at the saloon which was on the edge of the village cemetery. Ivan never crossed the cemetery to get to his lonely shack on the other side. The path through the cemetery would save him many minutes, but he never had taken it—not even in the full light of the moon.

Late one winter's night, when bitter wind and snow beat against the saloon, the customers took up the familiar mockery.

Ivan's sickly protest only fed their taunts, and they jeered cruelly when the young Cossack Lieutenant flung his horrid challenge at their quarry.

"You are a pigeon, Ivan. You'll walk all around the cemetery in this cold—but you dare not cross the cemetery."

Ivan murmured, "The cemetery is nothing to cross, Lieutenant. It is nothing but earth, like all the other earth."

The Lieutenant cried, "A challenge then! Cross the cemetery tonight, Ivan, and I'll give you five rubles—five gold rubles!"

Perhaps it was the vodka. Perhaps it was the temptation of the five gold rubles. No one ever knew why Ivan, moistening his lips, said suddenly, "Yes, Lieutenant, I'll cross the cemetery!"

The saloon echoed with their disbelief. The Lieutenant winked to the man and unbuckled his sabre.

"Here Ivan. When you get to the centre of the cemetery, in front of the biggest tomb, stick the sabre into the ground. In the morning we shall go there. If the sabre is in the ground—five gold rubles to you!"

Ivan took the sabre. The men drank a toast: "To Ivan the Terrible." They roared with laughter.

The wind howled around Ivan as he closed the door of the saloon behind him. The cold was knife sharp. He buttoned his long coat and crossed the dirt road. He could hear the Lieutenant's voice, louder than the rest, yelling after him, "Five rubles, pigeon! If you live!"

Ivan pushed the cemetery gate open. He walked fast. Earth, just earth . . . like any other earth. But the darkness was a massive dread. Five gold rubles . . . the wind was cruel, and the sabre was like ice in his hands. Ivan shivered under the long, thick coat and broke into a limping run.

He recognized the large tomb. He must have sobbed—that was drowned in the wind. And he kneeled, cold and terrified, and drove the sabre into the hard ground. With his fist, he beat it down to the hilt. It was done. The cemetery . . . the challenge . . . five gold rubles.

Ivan started to rise from his knees. But he could not move. Something held him. Something gripped him in an unyielding and implacable hold. Ivan tugged and lurched and pulled—gasping in his panic, shaken by monstrous fear. But something held Ivan. He cried out in terror, and then made senseless gurgling noises.

They found Ivan the next morning on the ground in front of the tomb that was in the centre of the cemetery. His face was not that of a frozen man's but of a man killed by some nameless horror. And the Lieutenant's sabre was in the ground where Ivan had pounded it—through the dragging folds of his long coat.

From Cemetery Path by Leonard Ross.

Teacher 1: Ms. Barnes

Why would Ivan not cross the cemetery?

Describe the weather.

What was Ivan going to gain by crossing the cemetery?

What were the men drinking that night?

How was Ivan dressed that night?

How do you know Ivan was full of fear in the cemetery?

Teacher 2: Ms. Trigger

(Right after the sentence *Ivan shivered under the long, thick coat and broke into a limping run*): What do you think is going to happen to Ivan?

(At the end): What caused Ivan's death?

Figure 5.9 Questioning the Classroom: A Comparison of Two Approaches

The quality of dialogue that follows from a story is largely dependent on the kinds of questions that teachers elect to use. When questions focus on in-text details, exchanges are generally quite perfunctory. Higher-level thinking questions tend to lead to a lively discussion and an exchange of ideas that ultimately extend students' comprehension of the text. In this case, the use of one prediction question and one inferential question sparked a grand conversation about several aspects of human nature.

Importance of Student-Generated Questions

Guided reading

While teachers generally assume the role of generating questions, it is important for them to remember that having students generate questions independently is a vital part of becoming a skilled reader. When students generate and respond to their own and their peers' questions, it has been shown that comprehension is improved (Palinscar, 1986; Palinscar & Klenk, 1991). Students are more likely to generate questions when teachers model and guide them in the use of open-ended questions (i.e., inferential, critical, and creative questions) and use content-free question prompts (see Table 5.11).

Students learn to ask their own questions best when they have an explicit model and when they are prompted to do so. Teachers can model a series of questions that can be asked before reading, during reading, and after reading a text. The teacher can gradually scaffold these questions to students, especially during a guided reading lesson. Examples of appropriate questions follow.

Before Reading
What will be the topic of this story?
What do I know about this topic?
What do I want to learn about this topic?

During Reading
What have I learned so far?
What do I think will happen next?

After Reading
Did I gain the information I expected?
Is there anything else I wanted to know?

Questions for the Author
Why did you write this story?
What message were you intending to provide?
What beliefs do you have about . . . ?
Why did you choose to tell the story from the perspective you did?

Students can then be asked the following critical opinions:

Do you agree with the beliefs of the author?
Do you think the characters acted in a realistic manner?
Whose voice was missing in this story?
What might that voice have said about this story?

Self-Questioning That Prompts Students to Make Connections

It is well known that good readers draw on their prior knowledge to make the connections that enable them to comprehend text effectively. Poor readers often do not make these connections. All students have some prior knowledge, experiences, opinions, and emotions that they can draw on to make connections to the text they are reading. Teachers can help students make connections by providing them with explicit questions that will encourage them to pause to make these connections. Keene and Zimmerman (1997) identified three simple connections that improved comprehension when applied to text. These connections help readers understand how characters feel and why they act in certain ways. The connections also help the reader form a clearer image of what is being read. Determining these connections keeps the reader focused and engaged in an active way. Identifying such connections also helps the reader remember what has been read (Tovani, 2000). These relatively simple connections are text-to-self, text-to-text, and text-to-world.

Text-to-self connections are generally very personal ones that only the reader can make by connecting past experiences in life to the material being read. An example of a text-to-self connection might be: "This character feels the way I do when I get into trouble" or "This setting reminds me of when I went to summer camp."

Text-to-text connections can be made when readers are reminded of other things they have read on the same topic, in the same series, or by the same author. These connections across texts provide insight because readers are thinking of how the story connects to another familiar text. An example of a text-to-text connection might be: "This character has the same problem as the character in a story I read last year" or "I remember these characters from the previous book in this series I read."

Text-to-world connections are bigger connections that a reader brings to the text based on a personal world view. These ideas often go beyond personal experiences and may reflect beliefs and values learned from various places, including home and mass media. Teachers often conduct conversations around these issues when teaching science, social studies, or literature. An example of a text-to-world connection might be: "I saw a movie about this topic and it had some of the same ideas," "I read another book about a character that was also new to the country," or "I don't believe that the main character is treating his friends fairly."

To teach this strategy, teachers should spend time modelling how to make these various connections for students. Connecting statements can be modelled initially and charts can be made to provide ongoing prompts for students when they are reading. Some examples follow.

Text-to-Self

What does this remind me of in my life?
How is this different from my life?
How does this relate to my life?
What were my feelings when I read this?

Text-to-Text

What does this remind me of in another book I've read?
How is this text different from other books that I have read?
Where have I read something like this before?

Text-to-World

What does this remind me of in the real world?
How is this different from things that happen in the real world?
How did that part relate to the world around me?

When teachers perceive that students lack the necessary prior knowledge to make connections, merely providing the questions will not bridge the gap. Rather, it may be necessary to build the necessary background knowledge prior to reading the text. A note of caution regarding this strategy: If students make connections that dominate their thinking, the task can distract them from the meaning of the text. Therefore, throughout instruction students need to be challenged to explain how their connections are contributing to their comprehension of the text (Harvey & Goudvis, 2000).

Other Comprehension Strategies

Think Aloud

Think Aloud is an instructional strategy in which students are encouraged to verbalize their thoughts or to think "out loud" while reading. When used efficiently, the Think Aloud procedure encourages students to use relevant reading comprehension strategies, form predictions, and engage in higher-level thinking while processing text (Caldwell & Leslie, 2009; Israel & Duffy, 2009). Before students are able to use Think Aloud independently, teachers must model the Think Aloud process while students follow the text silently. By assigning designated "STOP" sites (after every two or three statements, at the end of each paragraph, at critical transition points), teachers demonstrate how proficient readers connect new information with prior knowledge, ask questions, summarize and paraphrase, seek clarity, and actively make meaning of text. After students become comfortable with the Think Aloud process, they can take over the modelling process (see Table 5.12). Think Aloud can be incorporated into students' silent

Table 5.12 Using Think Aloud

1. Students and teacher have the same print copy of an unfamiliar story or text.
2. The teacher reads aloud while the students follow silently.
3. At regular intervals the teacher stops reading and looks at the students while thinking aloud about what has been read. During this time, the teacher reflects on his or her prior knowledge, makes personal connections, asks questions, expresses surprise, and predicts what will come next.
4. The teacher resumes reading.
5. The teacher repeats the reflection process throughout the text.
6. At the end of the selection, the teacher explains explicitly to the class that he or she was trying to make personal sense of the text and form predictions. He or she explains that this is what people do when they read but that it is normally done silently.
7. On another day, the teacher repeats the process but then asks a student to read aloud and demonstrate his or her thinking process.
8. This process is practised repeatedly over time, with students assuming greater and greater responsibility for reading passages aloud.

or shared reading activities and is an integral part of guided reading and other instructional approaches presented throughout this book.

In the following examples, two teachers demonstrate the use of Think Aloud. The text being read appears as regular print and their Think Aloud reflections are in italics.

> Someone had set a trap in the field, the metal kind that bites an animal until the animal is forced to chew off its own leg.
>
> *STOP: I have seen traps like this in movies and nature shows. They are very big and made of strong steel. I think they can break an animal's leg instantly.*
>
> The teeth dug through Sam's skin, making a circle of red on his thin ankle. For some reason his face was red, as if someone were squeezing his neck. He looked at me pleadingly. "Help me," he said. For a second I thought his foot was cut off.
>
> *STOP: I wonder whether Katie will be strong enough to remove the trap. She is only a young girl. Perhaps she will run back to the house for help. She must be feeling very scared and alone.*
>
> (Text from *Kira-Kira* by Cynthia Kadohata)

> Being on the lam was a whole lot of fun . . . for about five minutes.
>
> *STOP: I don't understand what this means. I have no idea about what it means to "be on the lam." I wonder if it is a place?*
>
> Every time my heart beat I could feel the blood pushing hot and hard on the inside of my sting spots and the bite of my hand.
>
> *STOP: I wonder what or who has bitten Bud. Maybe the evening bugs.*
>
> But I couldn't let that slow me down, I had to get out of this neighbourhood as quick as I could.
>
> *STOP: Bud is running away. He must be very scared.*
>
> It was a lot later than I'd ever been up before and I was kind of scared of the cops catching me.
>
> *STOP: I don't think that I could be as brave as Bud to run away, especially at night There probably were not many street lights and I remember how dark the night seemed when we were camping up north in the summer. You could barely see your hand in front of your face without using a flashlight.*
>
> I had to be real careful, even if it was the middle of the night, even if I was crouching down, sneaking along the street like Pretty Boy Floyd.
>
> *STOP: I remember that name from a gangster movie. Bud must feel like a criminal sneaking around and trying to avoid being caught by an adult. I guess "being on the lam" means you are trying to run away and not get caught.*
>
> (Text from *Bud, Not Buddy* by Christopher Paul Curtis)

Visual Imagery Several decades of research support the use of visual imagery as an effective reading comprehension strategy and as a foundational element of many reading comprehension instructional techniques and procedures, including guided reading and reciprocal instruction (Israel & Duffy, 2009; National Reading Panel, 2000). Visual imagery, or what is otherwise referred to as *mental imagery* or *imagining*, involves the process of creating visual representations of text while reading. These representations may include descriptions of story elements such as characters and settings or the unfolding of story events. Images are highly individualized and idiosyncratic since they exist in the mind of the reader. In other words, these images are "cognitive" in nature, with some reading researchers drawing an analogy between using visual imagery and watching a "mental" movie while reading (Hibbing & Rankin-Erickson, 2003). When readers generate visual images while reading, they are likely to experience an aesthetic or affective response as well (Sadoski & Paivio, 2004), reporting that they "lived the text" or "brought the text to life."

Readers are more likely to produce images for text passages that represent concrete (versus abstract) items and events and for familiar content (Sadoski & Paivio, 2004). While creating visual images is a relatively easy mental activity, most readers do not engage in this activity spontaneously. More positively, providing students with instruction to use visual imagery requires only brief training and teacher scaffolding (Gambrell & Koskinen, 2002; Sadoski & Paivio, 2001) and can be especially beneficial for students who struggle with the reading process.

Providing students with instructions to use visual imagery can be as simple as directing them to "make a picture in your mind" and giving examples of quick sketches or partial pictures (see Figure 5.10). Having students produce quick sketches while listening to text provides teachers with a method for monitoring their overall comprehension of text.

Teachers are encouraged to incorporate Think Aloud as part of their quick draws. As part of the Think Aloud, teachers can underscore the comprehension advantages associated with using visual imagery and discuss their affective responses to text (e.g., "Reading this section made me laugh, as it reminded me of my dog's crazy behaviour"; "I could feel the heat of the sun on David's back as he struggled to climb the mountain"). Once students have an opportunity to practise this approach, they should be encouraged to share their images and quick sketches as part of whole-group and small-group discussions. Such sharing can lead to enriched discussions of text materials and reinforce the simplicity of using this reading comprehension strategy.

PUTTING IT ALL TOGETHER: GUIDED READING

During reading

As is the case with teaching story structure, it is important that teachers adopt a holistic approach to teaching the reading comprehension strategies discussed in this chapter. Such an integrated approach to instruction is especially important considering that effective readers possess a repertoire of comprehension strategies that they use interchangeably while processing text (Pressley, 2006). The guided reading lesson provides teachers with one such instructional tool (Cunningham, Hall, & Cunningham, 2000). While Sample Lesson 5.2 provides a generic template for using guided reading, teachers need to recognize that the emphasis and direction of any one lesson depend greatly on the text content and students' reading abilities.

The selection of materials for the guided reading lesson is critical. According to Vygotsky (1978, 1986), students learn effectively only in their "zone of proximal

My favorite part of the book was when Roderick and Greg had to rake leaves for thier Grandmother. She said she would give them a cup of hot chocolate for every bag of leaves. Roderick had an evil plan to only fill the bags part of the way full, and made Greg do all of the work.

From: Diary of a Wimpy Kid #2
Roderick Rules

Author: Jeff Kinney

Figure 5.10 Example of a Partial Sketch by Mason, Grade 5

development." This means that teachers need to select materials that are slightly above students' independent reading level. Teachers can use several methods, including reading inventories, observation, and formal assessment of reading and writing competencies, to ensure that an appropriate level is selected. Sample Lesson 5.3 provides an example of a guided reading lesson for junior grades.

Factors to Consider When Implementing Guided Reading

Grouping by Ability It is unlikely that all students in a class are at the same level, making it necessary that they will be periodically grouped for specific instruction. It is important to understand and remember that it is unwise to leave students in the same group for an extended interval, as their self-esteem can be affected negatively. Effective teachers group and regroup students according to a variety of criteria, including ability, interests, and peer relations. It is well known that motivation plays a role in students' comprehension of materials. Teachers who place lower-level readers with higher-level peers in challenging reading situations (thus creating a mixed-ability group) have found that the former rise to the occasion and that their zone of proximal development is stretched (Vygotsky, 1986).

Grade Level While guided reading is an especially effective teaching approach in the primary grades, it is also very effective for instruction through the junior grades. This is especially true when teachers consider the large variation in students' reading skills within any one grade level. In the junior grades, there will be students who have not yet reached a level of fluency sufficient to enable them to read independently. In a few cases, teachers may find the guided reading lesson useful in the intermediate

SAMPLE LESSON 5.2

Guided Reading

Planning

The teacher reads the story and determines the main idea and which focus would be appropriate. Often there are several options, and teachers in the primary grades in particular should decide which theme will be emphasized.

Setting A group of chairs, or students and teacher gather around a table.

Characters Teacher and ideally five to eight students.

Introduction

The teacher presents the story using all information available prior to reading. This may include:

a) Title

b) Pictures

c) Abstract or blurb that gives insight into what the story is about

d) Vocabulary that may be unfamiliar can be introduced at this time, either explicitly or with teacher modelling the use of the new words in the discussion

e) Discussion of background knowledge necessary to comprehend the text (schema theory)

Establishing a Purpose for Reading

From these (and maybe other) sources of information, the teacher should conduct a discussion of the topic of the story, the main idea, the characters, and the setting. The question should be: "From all of the information we have been able to gather, what do you think this story will be about?" At this point, several students should provide responses.

Starting to Read

For primary grades, the teacher or a student may choose to read the first page or two aloud to engage students quickly in the story. Conversely, students can be told to read silently to answer a specific question. Always provide starting and stopping points, usually page numbers (e.g., "Read pages 6 and 7 to find the answer and then stop.").

Continuing the Process

When ready to assign another section for silent reading, as a general rule the teacher asks students to predict what they believe will come next. If students comprehend the story to that point, they will be able to make intelligent and logical predictions. Ideally, a few students can make diverse predictions so the teacher can direct them to continue reading to see who is right. The teacher then asks another question and designates the next portion of text to be read. Discussion of the question follows and further questions may be asked. The process repeats until the story is ended.

During the discussion that occurs throughout the story, the teacher asks questions related to the developing theme. The teacher's questions also include ones that enable students to relate their own experiences to the story: Have you ever felt like that? Has anything like this ever happened to you? What are your fears? What would you do in a similar situation?

Conclusion

At the conclusion of the story, the teacher asks a series of questions related to the story as a whole. After ensuring that students comprehend the story at a basic literal level, questions that encourage deeper thinking about the story are asked. This is when inferential and critical questions can be explored in depth related to the story as a whole. Examples of questions related to theme include: Why did the author choose to write this story? What is the author really saying here? What do you think about what the author is saying?

Application of New Learning

After the steps above have been accomplished, an independent assignment can be given that will encourage a deeper understanding of the story. These assignment questions will depend on the story itself. Drama, Readers' Theatre, and response journals are all appropriate assignments.

SAMPLE LESSON 5.3

Guided Reading: Junior Grades

Text *Literacy in Action Grade 4:* The Chinese Violin.

Planning

The teacher should read the story and look closely at the pictures. At this time, it is useful to consult the teacher's guide that accompanies the text. Determine a focus. Examples: How do illustrations affect the way you visualize the story? How do people make meaningful connections with others?

Objectives

Overall Students will be able to use strategies to understand and appreciate a story.

Specific Students will be able to use pictures to add to their understanding of a story.

Students will understand the importance of including others.

Students will understand the universality of needing to connect to others.

Assessment

Observational notes on the group's collaborative skills of (1) taking turns, (2) listening to others' ideas, and (3) completing the task successfully.

Students will be able to identify how they can use pictures to help comprehend the story.

Students will be able to identify three ways in which they can welcome a newcomer to their school.

Introduction

The teacher gathers the students and asks the following question: What hobbies or interests do you have that you can share with other people and your family? The teacher asks students to close their eyes and imagine themselves doing this activity with their friends or family. A few minutes of silence are provided and then the teacher asks students to share by asking the following question: How do these activities or interests connect you to other people? The teacher should share a personal experience from either childhood or current life.

The teacher passes out the books and asks the students to turn to page 47 and look at the title of the story and the picture. The teacher asks questions about the picture and the title that will provide some schemata for reading the story.

Direction for Reading "Where do you think the story will take place? Read to the end of page 49 to find out." The teacher then takes responses related to the following setting questions.

Discussion Questions

Describe Lin Lin's village.

How do you know she loved her village?

How do you know that Lin Lin found Vancouver strange?

Have any of you ever moved to a new community?

Looking at the picture, can you identify some of the things that are different for Lin Lin in her new home in Vancouver? (leaves on ground, cars, no flowers)

How can you tell from the picture that Lin Lin takes comfort from her father's presence? (hand on her shoulder, smiling)

Direction for Reading "Turn to page 50. Looking at the picture, tell me what you think is making Lin Lin feel better about her new home." The teacher takes responses (at park, near water, hands in air, playing violin comforted her). "Read to the bottom of page 51 and find out if you are right."

Discussion Questions

Why is the violin music important to Lin Lin?

How is Lin Lin feeling now?

Which of Lin Lin's senses is bringing her comfort in the park?

Which of the senses would help you most if you were in Lin Lin's place?

Direction for Reading "Turn to page 52. Look at the picture and think about what it tells you about the relationship between Lin Lin and the teacher. Read to the bottom of page 53 and find out more about this relationship."

Discussion Questions

How do you know that people enjoyed the violin music that Lin Lin's father played?

How was Lin Lin's father feeling about his new home?

How did Lin Lin and her father help each other?

If Lin Lin attended your school, how would you make her feel welcome and connected to you?

Why do you think the author wrote this story? What did she want you to think about?

What else would you like to know about Lin Lin?

Direction for Reading "Turn to page 54 and look at the picture. What do you think is happening now to Lin Lin? Keep reading and find out if you are right."

Discussion Questions

What was the importance of the violin in Lin Lin's new life?

What music do you love listening to? Shut your eyes and pretend you are listening now. Share how you feel.

Application of New Learning

The following are examples of possible application activities:

1. Write about some kind of music that is important to you and explain why it is important.
2. Identify all the ways the pictures help you understand the events in the story.
3. Get in groups of three and brainstorm ways to make newcomers feel welcome in your school and in your classroom. List your best three ideas.

grades, where some students still require assistance in developing their comprehension skills and abilities.

Materials Multiple copies of books or stories are needed so that all group members can read the same material simultaneously. The books or stories need to be at the students' instructional level. That is, reading materials must be challenging for students to read independently but not so challenging that they cannot read without the teacher's help and guidance. As a general guide, in the early grades the story selected should be short enough to be completed during one instructional time frame. In older grades, teachers may conduct such a lesson for the first chapter of a novel to develop students' schemata and interest for reading subsequent chapters independently.

Prior Knowledge There is little doubt that prior knowledge is the single greatest factor influencing student learning. The activation of relevant prior knowledge before reading provides students with a framework or schema for upcoming text and can increase their motivation to read it. Activating relevant prior knowledge also encourages students to make meaningful connections between new information and their previous experiences and can assist them to process unfamiliar vocabulary, make inferences, and synthesize text.

Sometimes, however, students do not possess relevant prior knowledge or they may possess prior knowledge that is inconsistent with information contained in the text. For instance, if the story involves an experience of riding on a subway train and the students live in a community without this form of transit, they may have difficulty understanding what is happening in the story. Alternatively, a story may contain values or beliefs that differ from students' orientations and expectations. In these cases, it is imperative that teachers provide students with relevant prior knowledge to avoid severely limiting students' abilities to comprehend text. Teaching techniques used to provide students with relevant prior knowledge include discussion and use of picture books and other print materials, videos, and other media formats.

Teacher Voice 5.2

In my role as a teacher consultant, I have the opportunity to support teachers in the development and delivery of their literacy programs. One of the greatest challenges I face is convincing teachers about the advantages associated with literacy programs that have been mandated through the school board or Ministry of Education.

Recently I was working with a junior grade teacher who was implementing guided reading. While I was able to provide him with relevant teaching materials and resources throughout the term, I suspected that, initially, he was somewhat doubtful about the value of guided reading.

I was very pleased when that same teacher approached me at the end of term to share his final experiences. He reported that his students' reading skills had improved and that he was ecstatic about their increased levels of reading engagement. He attributed these gains to guided reading and was looking forward to using it again with his incoming class.

When teachers observe students' growth and new learning, they become truly aware of the power of guided reading.

Alison Cooke
Teacher consultant

Avoid Round Robin Reading Round robin reading refers to having students systematically take turns reading aloud, an approach that has been demonstrated to be ineffective since it causes student anxiety and inattention. Poor readers may anticipate and practise their section ahead of time or they may feel so worried about being embarrassed that they are unable to concentrate on the meaning of what is being read (Tompkins, Bright, Pollard, & Winsor, 2005). Instead, teachers are encouraged to engage in alternative reading formats such as choral reading, echo reading, shared reading with overhead, reading with audiotape, or popcorn reading.

Direct instruction

Instructional Routines The success of the guided reading lesson depends, in part, on the use of established routines. Students who are not participating in the guided reading lesson directly must be provided with a clearly defined task to complete during the 20- to 30-minute lesson. They need to understand that the teacher is not available for questions during this period and that they must ask each other for assistance.

It is also imperative that students understand that the guided reading lesson is highly structured. They need to become accustomed to stopping at the end of the designated section and waiting for others to finish (usually for no more than 10 seconds). The lesson will not be successful if students do not stay together or if they read ahead. Students need to understand that they will be provided with reading direction before they proceed to the next section.

SUGGESTIONS FOR PROFESSIONAL DEVELOPMENT

1. Read three children's books that you have never read before. As a language arts teacher, you need a personal repertoire of children's books that you enjoy as well as those that have received some acclaim.
2. Register for an international conference. There are a variety of international reading conferences (e.g., International Reading Association, National Council of Teachers of English, National Reading Council) organized primarily for teachers. There are also local and provincial literacy associations that hold a variety of events and workshops (e.g., Reading for the Love of It). Several provinces have reading associations that are affiliated with the International Reading Association (e.g., Alberta Provincial Council, British Columbia Literacy Council, Manitoba Reading Association, North of 60 Council, Saskatchewan Reading Council, and Ontario Reading Association). These associations also hold a number of yearly activities of interest to language arts teachers. Often school boards will sponsor teachers who commit to sharing their experiences with colleagues.
3. Start a book group for teachers. As a group, decide whether to read children's books, professional books, or popular books. Share these book group experiences with students as a model of the pleasures of reading.
4. Visit Library and Archives Canada (www.collectionscanada.gc.ca/read-up-on-it/index-e.html). Register to receive their yearly report on Canadian children's books (*Read Up on It*) as well as bookmarks for your class.

CHILDREN'S LITERATURE REFERENCES

Andrews, J. (1985). *Very last first time*. Vancouver, BC: Douglas & McIntyre.

Balliett, B. (2005). *Chasing Vermeer*. Toronto, ON: Scholastic Paperbacks.

Balliett, B. (2007). *The Wright 3*. Toronto, ON: Scholastic Paperbacks.

Balliett, B. (2008). *The Calder game*. Toronto, ON Scholastic Press.

Barakat, I. (2007). *Tasting the sky: A Palestinian childhood*. New York, NY: Farrar, Straus and Giroux.

Baum, L. F. (2000). *The Wonderful Wizard of Oz*. New York, NY: HarperCollins.

Bechard, M. (2005). *Spacer and rat*. New York, NY: Roaring Brook Press.

Berman, S. (2007). *Vintage: A ghost story*. Bel Air, CA: Haworth Positronic Press.

Blaisdell, B. (1995). *Favourite Greek myths*. Mineola, NY: Dover Publications

Blume, J. (1970). *Are you there God? It's me, Margaret*. New York, NY: Yearling Books.

Blume, J. (1991). *Deenie*. New York, NY: Laurel Leaf Library.

Blume, J. (2007). *Forever*. Toronto, ON: Simon Spotlight Entertainment.

Bourgeois, P. (1987). *Big Sarah's little boots*. Toronto, ON: Kids Can Press.

Browning, R. (1988). *The Pied Piper of Hamelin*. New York, NY: Frederick Warne and Co.

Burnett, F. H. (1987). *The secret garden*. Newport Beach, CA: Tween.

Child, L. (2006). *The princess and the pea*. New York, NY Hyperion Book CH.

Cisneros, S. (1994). *The house on Mango Street*. Monte Vista, CO: LLC United States.

Cleaver, E. (1987). *The enchanted caribou*. New York, NY: Simon & Schuster.

Cole, B. (1997). *Prince Cinders*. New York, NY: Puffin.

Curtis, C. P. (1997). *The Watsons go to Birmingham—1963*. New York, NY: Yearling.

Curtis, C.P. (2004). Bud,not Buddy. New York, NY: Laurel Leaf.
Defoe, D. (2001). Robinson Crusoe. New York, NY: Modern Library.
Dr. Seuss. (2003). *Green eggs and ham*. New York, NY: Random House.
Ellis, D. (2000). The breadwinner trilogy (*The breadwinner, Parvana's journey, Mud city*). Vancouver, BC: Groundwood Books/Douglas & McIntyre.
Ellis, S. (2001). *A prairie as wide as the sea: The immigrant diary of Ivy Weatherall*. Toronto, ON: Scholastic Canada.
Farmer, N. (2002). *The house of the scorpion*. New York, NY: Atheneum/Richard Jackson Books.
Flake, S. (2000). *The skin I'm in*. New York, NY: Hyperion Book CH.
Gilman, P. (1988). *The wonderful pigs of Jillian Jiggs*.Toronto, ON: North Winds Press.
Golding, W. (2002). *Lord of the flies*. New York, NY: Faber and Faber.
Grahame, K. (1908). *The wind in the willows*. Toronto, ON: Scribner.
Green, J. (2007). *Looking for Alaska*. New York, NY: Speak.
Harrison, L. (2004). *The clique*. New York, NY: Little Brown.
Hest, A. (1997). *When Jessie came across the sea*. Somerville, MA: Candlewick Press.
Hichens, J. (2009). *Stained*. Winchester, UK: Ransom Publishing.
Hinton, S.E. (1967). *The outsiders*. New York, NY: Dell Publishing.
Hughes, M. (1980). *The keeper of the Isis light*. London, UK: Mammoth.
Hughes, M. (1981). *The guardian of Isis*. London, UK: Mammoth.
Hughes, M. (1982). *The Isis pedlar*. London, UK: Mammoth.
Jam, T., & Beddows, E. (1991). *Night cars*. Toronto, ON: Groundwood Books.
Kadohata, C. (2005). *Kira-Kira*. New York, NY: Simon & Schuster.
Lear, E. (2008). *The owl and the pussycat*. London, UK: Usborne Publishing Ltd.
Lee, D. (1974). *Alligator pie*. New York, NY: Macmillan.
Lee, D. (2008). *Willoughby wallaby woo*. Toronto, ON: Key Porter Books.
L'Engle, M. A. (1963). *A wrinkle in time*. New York, NY: Farrar, Straus and Giroux.
Lewis, C. S. (1981). *The lion, the witch and the wardrobe*. New York, NY: Macmillan.
Lewis, C. S. (2001). *Thechronicles of Narnia series*. New York, NY: HarperCollins.
Little, J. (1978). *Stopping by woods on a snowy evening*. New York, NY: Dutton Juvenile.
Little, J. (1984). *Mama's going to buy you a mockingbird*. Toronto, ON: Penguin Canada.
Little, J. (1986). *Hey world, here I am!* Toronto, ON: Kids Can Press.
Lunn, J. (1981). *The root cellar*. Boston, MA: Houghton Mifflin.
Lunn, J. (1988). *Amos's sweater*. Vancouver, BC: Douglas & McIntyre
MacLachlan, P. (1986). *Sarah, plain and tall*. New York, NY: Harper & Row.
Matas, C. (1993). *Daniel's story*. Toronto, ON: Scholastic Canada.
Matas, C. (2002). *Footsteps in the snow: The Red River diary of Isobel Scott*.Toronto, ON: Scholastic Canada.
Meyer, S. (2005). *Twilight*.New York, NY: Little Brown Young Readers.
Meyer, S. (2008). *Breaking dawn*. New York, NY: Little Brown Young Readers.
Meyer, S. (2008). *New moon*. New York, NY: Little Brown Young Readers.
Meyer, S. (2009). *Eclipse*. New York, NY: Little Brown Young Readers.
Milne, A. A. (1992). *Winnie-the-Pooh (Original ed.)*.New York, NY: Puffin.
Mitson, A. (1979). *Olly onion*. Suffolk, UK: Studio Publications.
Montgomery, L. M. (1908). *Anne of Green Gables*. Boston, MA: L.C. Page & Company.
Mowat, F. (1956). *Two against the North*.Toronto, ON: Scholastic Book Services Canada.

Mowat, F. (1987). *The curse of the Viking grave*. Toronto, ON: McClelland & Stewart.

Munsch, R. (1980). *The paper bag princess*. Toronto, ON: Annick Press Ltd.

Park, B. (1992). *Junie B. Jones and the stupid smelly bus*. New York, NY: Random House Books for Young Readers.

Park, B. (1994). *Junie B. Jones and some sneaky peeky spying*. New York, NY: Random House Books for Young Readers.

Patterson, K. (1978). *The bridge to Terabithia*. Springfield, OH: Crowell Publishing Company.

Paulsen, G. (1987). *Hatchet*. Seattle, WA: Bradbury Press.

Pearson, K. (1987). *A handful of time*. New York, NY: Viking Kestrel.

Pearson, K. (1991). *The sky is falling*. Toronto, ON: Puffin Canada.

Pearson, K. (1992). *Looking at the moon*. Toronto, ON: Puffin Canada.

Pearson, K. (1999). *The lights go on again*. New York, NY: Viking Penguin.

Peterson Haddix, M. (2000). *Among the hidden*. New York, NY: Simon & Schuster Children's Publishing.

Pilkey, D. (2002). *The new Captain Underpants collection* (Books 1 to 5). New York, NY: The Blue Sky Press.

Pilkey, D. (2008). *The tra-la-laa-mendous Captain Underpants collection* (Books 5 to 8). New York, NY: The Blue Sky Press.

Pullman, P. (2003). His Dark Materials trilogy (*The golden compass, The subtle knife, The amber spyglass*). New York, NY: Yearling.

Raskin, E. (1978). *The Westing game*. New York, NY: E. P. Dutton

Resau, L. (2007). *Red glass*. New York, NY: Delacorte Books for Young Readers.

Robinson, J. E. (2008). *The flower of grass*. Toronto, ON: Monarch Books of Canada Limited.

Rowling, J. K. (1998). *Harry Potter and the sorcerer's stone*.Toronto, ON: Scholastic Press.

Rowling, J. K. (1999). *Harry Potter and the chamber of secrets*.New York, NY: Arthur A. Levine Books.

Rowling, J. K. (2000). *Harry Potter and the prisoner of Azkaban*. Toronto, ON: Scholastic Paperbacks.

Rowling, J. K. (2001). *Harry Potter and the goblet of fire*. London, UK: Bloomsbury Publishing.

Rowling, J. K. (2004). *Harry Potter and the order of the phoenix*. Toronto, ON: Scholastic Paperbacks.

Rowling, J. K. (2006). *Harry Potter and the half-blood prince*. Toronto, ON: Scholastic Paperbacks.

Rowling, J. K. (2008). *Harry Potter and the deathly hallows*. New York, NY: Arthur A. Levine Books.

Scieszka, J. (1991). *The frog prince continued*. Toronto, ON: Scholastic Inc.

Scieszka, J. (1996). *The time warp trio: Tut Tut*. New York, NY: Viking.

Scieszka, J. (1996). *The true story of three little pigs*. New York, NY: Puffin USA.

Scieszka, J. (2002). *The time warp trio: See you later, gladiator*. New York, NY: Puffin.

Scieszka, J. (2004). *The time warp trio: Knights of the kitchen table*. New York, NY: Puffin.

Shelley, M. (2000). *Frankenstein*. New York, NY: Signet Classics.

Shusterman, N. (1999). *The dark side of nowhere*. New York, NY: T or Books.

Singer, N. (2002). *Feather boy*. New York, NY: Delacorte Books for Young Readers.

Smucker, B. (1977). *Underground to Canada*. Toronto, ON: Clarke, Irwin.

Snicket, L. (2006). *The complete wreck* (*A series of unfortunate events*, Books 1 to 13). New York, NY: HarperCollins.

Tolkien, J. R.R.(1988). The Lord of the Rings series. Chicago, IL: Houghton Mifflin.
Tolkien, J. R.R. (1991). *The Hobbit*. Cambridge, UK: UK General Books.
Toye, W. (1990). *The loon's necklace*. Don Mills, ON: Oxford University Press.
Trigell, J. (2004). *Boy A*. London, UK: Serpent's Tail.
Twain, M. (1876). *The adventures of Tom Sawyer*. New York, NY: Penguin Books.
Viorst, J. (1987). *Alexander and the terrible, horrible, no good, very bad day*. New York, NY: Simon & Schuster Students' Publishing.
Wallace, I. (2000). *Duncan's way*. Toronto, ON: Groundwood Books.
Wells, H. G. (1993). *The war of the worlds*. Bowser, BC: Aerie.
White, E. B. (1952). *Charlotte's web*. San Francisco, CA: Harper & Row.
Wiegle, M. (2008). *No fear Shakespeare: Romeo and Juliet*. Houston, TX: Sparksnotes.
Wiesner, D. (2006). *Flotsam*. New York, NY: Clarion Books.
Williams, M. (1958). *The velveteen rabbit*. New York, NY: Doubleday Books for Young Readers.
Wilson, E. (1980). *Terror in Winnipeg*. Santa Rosa, CA: Stoddart.
Wilson, E. (1983). *The ghost of Lunenburg manor*. New York, NY: HarperCollins.
Wyndham, J. (1951). *The day of the triffids*. New York, NY: Modern Library.
Yee, P. (1996). *Ghost train*. Toronto, ON: Groundwood Books.

MyEducationLab

MyEducationLab is an interactive, virtual learning tool that will help improve your understanding of the concepts taught in this textbook and in your course. Through this engaging resource, you will have access to simulations of real classroom experiences, exercises that will help you improve your knowledge of key concepts, and additional resources that will help you in your teaching career. Use this online tool with your textbook to help you succeed in your studies and beyond!

Chapter 6
Reading Comprehension Strategies for Non-Fiction: Reading in the Content Areas

Learning Objectives

In this chapter you will discover

- How to recognize differences between narrative and expository text structures.
- How to select non-fiction for your classroom.
- How to address the challenges associated with reading expository text.
- How to teach vocabulary associated with content area reading.
- How to provide explicit strategy instructions for reading expository text.
- How to conduct reciprocal teaching instruction.
- How to teach study skills and report writing.

DAVE CHUCHMAN: GRADES 4 AND 5 TEACHER

As you walk into Dave Chuchman's grades 4 and 5 split class, you notice that the walls are dominated by signs of a balanced literacy program. From the word wall, to the buckets of books, to the story structure chart, to the chart that says *Put "said" to Bed* with more than 20 alternative words for writing dialogue, the room resonates with literacy learning that addresses a balance between directed reading, independent reading, writing, and word learning. Comprehension strategies are also prominently posted, including *Cultivate Your Schema* ("These kids know what schema is. I don't have to identify it as prior knowledge."), *Make Connections*, *Picture It, Predict, Determine What Is Important, Infer, Summarize and Evaluate*. There is also a chart about the characteristics of non-fiction text. Dave calls these "anchor charts" and posts them so he can refer to them to reinforce learning. The organization and ambiance of the room reflect Dave's personality. He is focused, determined, hard working, and enthusiastic and "loves teaching because of the kids."

In his eleventh year of teaching, Dave is well known as a dedicated teacher whose literacy program is respected by students, parents, and colleagues alike. He motivates his students to "take a step above what they can do" and he tries to "stretch them so they can grow" by focusing on students' interests when he selects literacy topics and tasks. No matter what his students are reading, he tries to "get them to think critically rather than to pull simple details from the text."

An integrated reading program provides the central component of Dave's reading instruction and he attempts to select units that promote the integration of literacy across the curriculum. "Of course, I am always doing my own thing—bringing my own ideas in and branching out according to the student's interests and the long-range plans I am supposed to cover." Although he uses ability grouping for small-group guided reading, on other occasions he uses whole-group guided reading lessons. Whatever size of group he is leading, he varies the approach, sometimes assigning a specified silent reading section and then discussing or conducting the session as a Read Aloud. Regardless of the skill he is teaching, after each section he stops to lead a discussion that encourages students to think critically and inferentially. Three recent comprehension strategies he has focused on are encouraging students to connect the reading to personal experiences, helping them provide a text synthesis, and encouraging them to make inferences throughout. When teaching these skills, he selects a balance between fiction and non-fiction texts. His current focus is helping students recognize that they hold opinions about what they are reading and encouraging them to express those opinions.

Dave's book bin collection runs the length of one wall, representing an investment in a classroom library that he has built over his career. His books are balanced equally between fiction and non-fiction and provide independent reading choices for daily sustained silent reading (SSR) time. Students can also select books from the school library. Sometimes Dave assigns a culminating activity that everyone must do after independent reading, which he makes motivational by basing it on their interests.

Dave believes that his greatest achievement is that his "kids experience success in my literacy program." He recognizes that his personality is one of his strengths, as he is unfailingly fair, polite, and respectful. "We talk about respect and responsibility almost every day. I also talk about the importance of communication, and if someone has a problem I want to talk to that person." Dave wants the best for and from his students and a classroom board titled *Trying Our Best* featuring students' work captures his goals concisely.

Before reading this chapter, follow the instructions below and complete the presented tasks. These tasks parallel those routinely provided to students as part of classroom activities across the country.

REFLECTIVE ACTIVITY 1

Read the following passage and be prepared to answer the questions provided below.

Contrast between Moral and Aesthetic Values

The relation between aesthetic and moral judgments, between the spheres of the beautiful and the good, is close, but the distinction between them is important. One factor of this distinction is that while aesthetic judgments are mainly positive, that is, perceptions of good, moral judgments are mainly and fundamentally negative, or perceptions of evil. Another factor of the distinction is that whereas, in the perception of beauty, our judgment is necessarily intrinsic and based on the character of the immediate experience, and never consciously on the idea of an eventual utility in the object, judgments about moral worth, on the contrary, are always based, when they are positive, upon the consciousness of benefits probably involved. Both these distinctions need some elucidations.

Hedonistic ethics have always had to struggle against the moral sense of mankind. Earnest minds, that feel the weight and dignity of life, rebel against the assertion that the aim of right conduct is enjoyment. Pleasure usually appears to them as a temptation, and they sometimes go so far as to make avoidance of it as virtue. The truth is that morality is not mainly concerned with the attainment of pleasure; it is rather concerned, in all its deeper and more authoritative maxims, with the prevention of suffering. There is something artificial in the deliberate pursuit of pleasure; there is something absurd in the obligation to enjoy oneself. We feel no duty in that direction; we take to enjoyment naturally enough after the work of life is done, and the spontaneity of our pleasures are what is most essential to them.

George Santayana, *The Last Puritan* (1936)
From *A World of Ideas* by Lee A. Jacobus (1986, pp. 613–614)

Comprehension Questions

1. What was the main idea of the text?
2. What is the relationship between pleasure and morality?
3. How does the author view aesthetic judgments?
4. Do you agree or disagree that moral judgments are perceptions of evil? Explain your response.
5. How is morality connected to the prevention of suffering?

Reflection Questions

1. Could you read this text at your usual speed and comfort level?
2. Was this text difficult to read? Why?

The text in Reflective Activity 1 was written by George Santayana (1863–1952), whose philosophical writings have influenced the world. Most readers, however, struggle with processing this text. Even though they are able to decode each word, the structure of the text makes it difficult to comprehend.

To process the text successfully, readers require prior knowledge of the subject as well as related vocabulary. In this case, context does little to promote meaning of unfamiliar vocabulary. We chose this example to enable you to experience the same kind of frustration and confusion felt by many students when faced with similar texts.

REFLECTIVE ACTIVITY 2

Reflect on the reading comprehension and metacognitive strategies that you used when reading the Santayana text in Reflective Activity 1. Did you change or adjust your reading approach as the text became dense and difficult to comprehend? Did you adopt any of the following strategies?

- Stop and reread
- Adopt a slower reading rate
- Attempt to identity the main idea by removing unnecessary phrases and clauses
- Skim and scan passage to locate a summary of the main idea
- Underline main ideas

Think about where you learned these strategies. Were they taught to you directly or did you learn them on your own?

Alternatively, did you stop reading and move on to the next section of text?

All of these approaches provide insights about how students respond to challenging text.

EXPOSITORY TEXT

Expository texts generally found in content area reading consist of non-fiction materials presented in an organized manner. These materials meet students' needs to acquire new knowledge in a given discipline (Gunning, 2005). Examples of expository text include history, science, geography, biography, and autobiography. There are also a myriad of alphabet and counting books as well as poetry and factual storybooks that fall into this text structure.

As students progress through the grades, there is an increased need to process expository text efficiently. Students read and listen to information texts to learn about themselves, others, and the world around them. Such reading helps them make sense of what they see, hear, and observe in the world. Students also encounter expository text from other sources, including the internet, CD-ROMs, and the media.

REFLECTIVE ACTIVITY 3

The following are two reading passages designated at the grade 4 level. Read each passage carefully and then reflect on each experience.

Passage 1: Mountain Tamers

Amir peered out the window down Fenton Street. Then he turned and asked his mom for the fifth time. "When do you think Grandma will be here?"

Amir would soon be ten. He had asked for just one gift, a Mountain Tamer sled. He had seen it in a store flyer, and his grandma had said she would get it for him. These sleds were purple with red flames along the sides. The kids all knew they were the fastest sleds around.

At last Amir spied his grandma. He quickly put on his jacket and boots and raced out to her car. As he got close, he saw her pulling from the trunk . . . a white-and-pink sled called the Snow Flake! Amir stared in horror.

His grandma gave him a big hug."Happy birthday, Amir!" she said. "Now, I know this is not exactly the sled you wanted. It was sold out. But this is almost the same."

Amir said quietly, "Thank you, Grandma." He hung his head. How could he be seen on a Snow Flake? He had told his friends he was getting a Mountain Tamer.

"But that's not all I got at the store," his grandma went on. "I also got this!" She held up rolls of bright red and orange tape. "I thought we could dress up your sled a bit. You know, make it your own."

Amir helped carry the sled into the garage. He and his grandma got to work.

Source: Jeroski et al. *Literacy in Action, 4B*. Toronto: Pearson Education Canada, 2005 (pp. 72–73). Reprinted with permission by Pearson Canada Inc.

Passage 2: Adaptations

Plants and animals live in many places and have different needs. Their habitat provides them with what they need to live.

Most living things have special features that help them survive in their habitat. These special features are called **adaptations**. Structural adaptations involve an animal's body parts or the parts of plants. Behavioural adaptations involve the way living things act or respond to their surroundings. These kinds of adaptations help plants and animals to meet their needs and to survive.

Structural Adaptations

Structural adaptations can help living things to live in certain conditions. The polar bear lives in one of the coldest habitats in the world. It has many adaptations that help it to survive. The big furry paws of a polar bear act as a snowshoe when the bear is walking on snow. The fur stops the bear from sliding on ice and also keeps the paws warm in the cold.

The hairs of the polar bear's fur are hollow. They act as a tube to allow the warmth of the sun to go right down to the bear's skin and keep it warm in the coldest weather. The white colour of the bear's fur helps it to blend into its habitat, since it is hard to see in the snow and ice. The polar bear also has an excellent sense of smell, which helps when it is hunting seals to eat. Sharp claws and teeth make it easier for the polar bear to catch and eat its prey.

Source: Campbell et al. *Science & Technology 4; Habitats*. Toronto: Pearson Education Canada, 1999 (pp. 21–22). Reprinted with permission by Pearson Canada Inc.

- What do you think are the main differences between the two passages?
- Is one text more easily understood than the other? Which text and why?

The answer to the last question may seem obvious, but it leads to a discussion of the inherent challenges associated with reading expository text.

Nature of Expository Text

Expository texts differ from narrative texts at several levels. In general, expository text is abstract in nature and requires readers to understand complex relations and concepts, acknowledge cause and effect, and identify solutions to problems (Gunning, 2005). In addition, expository texts often present a number of new ideas and contain technical vocabulary (Singer & Donlan, 1989). A further conundrum for students is that the "learning to read" process is most often accomplished with narrative text while the "reading to learn" process is accomplished with expository text. Many teachers are frustrated by the apparent inability of their students to transfer the comprehension skills they have acquired while reading narrative text to the processing of expository text. They fail to consider that the shift from "learning to read" to "reading to learn" involves a different set of skills and strategic processes. See Table 6.1 for the challenges associated with expository text.

It is essential that reading teachers broaden their view of how to teach the reading process to include skill sets associated with the processing of expository text and that they include information texts as part of their language arts programs. Effective comprehension of either narrative or expository text requires students to:

- Retain important information
- Understand the author's intended message
- Interpret the main idea and related implications
- Understand topics deeply
- Apply the message in meaningful, critical, and creative ways

This high level of understanding is increasingly important as expectations for attaining and using knowledge gained in school soar (Schlechty, 2009). Teachers also must recognize that these higher-level thinking skills require substantial time and effort for students to acquire and thus cannot be rushed. Teachers may be tempted to allow students to "figure it out on their own" in response to increased curriculum demands and standardized testing. Such temptation must be avoided.

Fortunately, many modern expository texts are written in a manner that assists students' transition from the "learning to read" to "reading to learn" process. For instance, *The Story of Canada* by Christopher Moore and Janet Lunn presents an illustrated history of Canada in an interesting and engaging manner. Foundational concepts are explained thoroughly in simple terms and real-life examples are used throughout. *Laura Secord: A Story of Courage* by Janet Lunn is written in the same engaging manner, with Maxwell Newhouse's accompanying native folk art illustrations facilitating an understanding of the historical era. Similarly, David Suzuki has authored a number of books for children about the natural world, including *Looking at Insects* and *Looking at Plants*. Suzuki's use of simple language, photographs, and illustrations provides students with an enjoyable reading experience as they transition to the "reading to learn" realm.

Non-Fiction in the Classroom

Student Motivation Learning from text is an active process that requires conscious and deliberate activity. Even the most able students will not learn if they do not

Table 6.1 Challenges Associated with Expository Text

- Contains unfamiliar vocabulary that is often specialized and technical in nature
- New vocabulary is not repeated to reinforce learning
- Requires subject-specific prior knowledge
- Text can involve more symbolism and more abstract conceptualization
- Increased use of subordinate clauses, resulting in complex sentence structure
- Terse writing style without explanatory elaboration
- Requires inferences about unfamiliar concepts
- Unfamiliar concepts need to be retained and related to other concepts
- Information is often presented in graphs and charts
- Reader disinterest in the topic
- Requires perseverance and cognitive effort to process

pay attention and exert some effort while reading (Csikszentmihalyi, 1997; Gonzalez-DeHass, Willems, & Doan Holbein, 2005; Stipek, 1998). Teachers play an important role in establishing a positive learning environment where motivation and perseverance for learning are encouraged.

Most students confront content area reading tasks confident in their abilities. They base this confidence largely on their experiences reading narrative text. Unexpected difficulties in processing expository text can play havoc with a student's confidence as reader and minimize reading motivation, with this being especially true for students who struggle with the reading process (Alderman, 1999; Cox, 2000; Shaywitz, 2003; Stanovich, 2004).

Attribution theorists explain this issue with the belief that individuals are motivated to understand themselves and the world around them to gain a cognitive mastery of their environment (Kelly, 1967; Weiner, 1992; Woolfolk, 2009). Successful students know that they need to put forth substantial effort and use effective processing strategies to become efficient readers. They do not buy into the rhetoric of being "smart" or "naturally able" readers. These attributes are sometimes unintentionally reinforced by parents and teachers during the "learning to read" process. When students adopt these latter attributes, they are likely to perceive any difficulties associated with the processing of expository text with a lack of ability (i.e., being "stupid" or "dumb") or with a biased learning environment (e.g., teacher "hates" me or is "unfair") rather than attribute difficulties to failure to use relevant processing skills, which can be acquired. These negative perceptions can lead to lack of effort and further lack of reading success. Teachers must work to avoid such downward spirals by providing students with successive, systematic skill instruction related to the processing of expository text.

The Early Grades It is critical to provide students with opportunities to explore non-fiction texts in the primary grades. Teachers' Read Aloud choices should include non-fiction materials that correspond with students' interests. Teachers can also take advantage of these Read Aloud sessions to model relevant processing strategies and highlight central features of expository text:

Teacher Narrative: Evan's Story

One January, I left my inner-city teaching assignment to move to a new school board in a middle-income suburban area, where I assumed teaching a grade 5 classroom. Shortly after arriving, I assigned "projects" to the students as part of the social studies program. Students were to complete the projects individually and appeared to be thrilled with the opportunity to complete the task in a less structured manner. During the class, I introduced the topic, shared resources, discussed format, and provided assistance to students as required. I established a due date two weeks later.

On the due date, one of my most conscientious and serious students, Evan, asked if he could bring his final product to my home that evening (I happened to live in the neighbourhood). Somewhat surprised, I agreed. That evening, a car arrived at my house and Evan turned over his project with his father looking on from behind the wheel of the car.

The next day I looked at Evan's project, which appeared to have been painstakingly completed. To my chagrin, he had neatly copied the materials verbatim from his resources. I knew that Evan had done his best to complete the project and that he was proud of his work. He simply did not have the skills to cope with processing expository text. Subsequent examination of other projects revealed much of the same behaviour. I realized that I had made a huge assumption about the skill level of the students. I had done the class a disservice by asking them to complete a task without providing them with the necessary skills. Shortly thereafter, we embarked on a series of explicit lessons about how to locate, comprehend, and summarize content area material. I have never forgotten Evan and the lesson he taught me.

- Text does not need to be read in its entirety; parts can be read independently.
- Text does not need to be read in a linear fashion. Readers can begin at the front, back, or middle of the text.
- There are many gateways for entering non-fiction text, including the table of contents, index, and headings.
- Diagrams and illustrations contain information.

Student Voice 6.1

I like books that give me information because it is fun to learn about different things. I like animal information books, my rock book, and my body book.

Melanie
Grade 1 student

Boys and Reading During the 1990s, there was substantial focus on gender differences in learning. Of primary concern was girls' lower achievement in mathematics and the sciences. More recently and of equal concern is the persistent gap between boys' and girls' reading performance. According to the most recent results of the Program for International Students Assessment (PISA, 2001), girls have demonstrated higher reading scores than boys consistently over the last decade at a global level. Similar conclusions were reached by the Progress in International Reading Literacy Study (PIRLS, 2001),

Table 6.2 Helping Boys Access Content Area Reading

- Ensure that boys have adequate non-fiction titles from which to choose in the classroom.
- Ensure that non-print resources, such as CD-ROMs, are readily available.
- Ensure that texts with visuals are available.
- Use humour wherever possible.
- Match non-fiction materials to boys' interests, activities, and hobbies.
- Introduce boys to well-known and accomplished males (i.e., athletes, actors, community members) who enjoy reading.
- Refer boys to gender-specific websites such as www.guysread.com and www.bigguybooks.com.

which assessed the reading abilities of students from 34 countries. Shockingly, girls in all 34 countries outperformed boys. Although 88 percent of 13-year-olds performed at or above the expected levels of reading proficiency in the 2009 Pan-Canadian Assessment Program (PCVA-13), girls routinely outperformed boys. The results issued by the Ontario Education Quality and Accountability Office (EQAO) over the past few years similarly reveal that girls in grades 3 and 6 outperform boys in those grades in reading.

There is also growing evidence of gender differences in reading ability, preferences, and attitudes (Gambell & Hunter, 2000). Boys require more time to acquire reading skills, read less often than girls, and value the activity less, identifying it as a feminine activity (Gurian, 2001). It can be particularly stultifying for boys to sit in kindergarten to grade 6 classrooms where teachers place great emphasis on reading, writing, and verbal ability (Kindlon & Thompson, 2000; Thompson & Barker, 2008).

Of particular relevance to this chapter, boys are more likely to choose expository text than girls when provided with a reading choice (see Table 6.2 for methods of helping boys access content area reading). Boys also tend to be better at information retrieval and are more likely to read for utilitarian purposes (Smith & Wilhelm, 2002). Boys' selection of reading materials can be diverse and may include instructional manuals, magazines, comics, and newspapers—materials that contain factual content but are not valued or used at school (Moloney, 2002). Boys' preferences also include science fiction, fantasy, hobby, craft, and special interest books.

Teachers' Selections

When selecting books for children, many adults focus on fictional stories and other formats of narrative text, assuming that these genres are more appealing or superior to non-fiction. Teachers must remember, however, that most individuals will read more informational text than narrative text as part of their daily lives. Non-fiction materials can provide students with meaningful information in attractive and engaging ways (Galda & Cullinan, 2002). While essential to students' learning success (Morrow & Gambell, 2001), creating a varied reading program that is well balanced between fiction and non-fiction is not an easy task, especially for beginning teachers, as a sound working knowledge of quality children's books is developed over time.

The booming non-fiction market in Canada and across the globe provides teachers with a wide variety of choices for their classrooms. Expository texts vary in format and can include picture books (including alphabet and counting); history; science; geography; biography; autobiography; activity, craft, and how-to books; poetry; and factual narratives (i.e., information presented through story). The texts listed in Table 6.3 provide evidence of the variety of rich resources available.

Table 6.3 Examples of Expository Texts

Alphabet Books

Grassby, D. (2000). *A seaside alphabet.* Toronto, ON: Tundra Books. 🍁

Kalman, B. (1999). *Canada from A to Z.* New York, NY: Crabtree Publishing Co. 🍁

Martin, B. Jr. & Archambault, J. (2000). *Chicka chicka boom boom.* New York, NY: Beach Lane Books.

McLimans, D. (2006). *Gone wild.* New York, NY: Walker Books for Young Readers.

Ulmer, M. (2001). *M is for Maple: A Canadian alphabet.* Chelsea, MI: Sleeping Bear Press.

Counting Books

Base, G. (2006). *Uno's garden.* New York, NY: Abrams Books for Young Readers.

Martin, B. Jr. & Sampson, M. (2000). *Chicka chicka 1, 2, 3.* New York, NY: Beach Lane Books.

Pachter, C. (2009). *Canada counts: A Charles Pachter counting book.* Toronto, ON: Cormorant Books Inc. 🍁

Taylor. C. (2005). *Out on the prairie: A Canadian counting book.* Markham, ON: Scholastic Books. 🍁

Poems or Songs

Davidge, B. (1994). *The mummer's song.* London, ON:Orchard Books. 🍁

Hesse, K. (1997). *Out of the dust.* Markham, ON: Scholastic Press.

Macy, S. (Ed.). (2001). *Girls got game: Sports stories and poems.* New York, NY: Henry Holt & Co.

Prelutsky, J. (2007). *Me I am!* Deadham, MA: Melanie Kroupa Books.

Activity, Craft, and How-to Books

Gordon, L. (2010). *The super duper art & craft activity book.* San Francisco, CA: Chronicle Books.

Link, M. (2009). *100+ no-sew fabric crafts for kids.* Concord, CA: C&T Publishing.

Ross, K. (2001). *Crafts from your favorite children's stories.* Brookfield, CT: Millbrook Press.

History

Bailey, L. (2002). *Adventures in ancient Greece.* Toronto, ON: Kids Can Press. 🍁

Cox, P. R. (2002). *Who were the Romans?* London, ON: Usborne Publishing Limited. 🍁

Granfield, L. (1997). *In Flanders Fields: The story of the poemby John McCrea.* Markham, ON: Fitzhenry & Whiteside. 🍁

Jackson, E. (2003). *Turn of the century.* Bellaire, CA: San Val Publishing.

Long, W. (1995). *Celebrating excellence: Canadian women athletes.* Vancouver, BC: Polestar. 🍁

Moore, C., & Lunn, J. (2000). *The story of Canada.* Toronto, ON: Key Porter Books.

Science

Daigle, E. (2004). *As long as there are whales.* Toronto, ON: Tundra.

Domm, K. (2005). *Atlantic puffin: Little brother of the North.* Halifax, NS: Nimbus Publishing.

Farrell, J. (2005). *Invisible allies: Microbes that shape our lives.* New York, NY: Farrar, Straus & Giroux.

Jenkins, S. (2006). *Move!* Orlando, FL: Houghton Mifflin.

Patent, D. (2009). *When the wolves returned: Returning nature's balance in Yellowstone.* New York, NY: Walker Books for Young Readers.

Pulley Sayre, A. (2005). *Stars beneath your bed: The surprising story of dust.* New York, NY: Greenwillow Books.

Suzuki, D., & Ellis, S. (2005). *Salmon forest*. Toronto, ON: Greystone Books.

Geography

Beattie, O., & Geiger, J. (1993). *Buried in ice.* Markham ON: Scholastic.

Beeler, S. B. (2001). *Throw your tooth on the roof: Tooth traditions from around the world.* New York, NY: Houghton Mifflin.

Gibbons, G. (2009). *Hurricanes!* New York, NY: Holiday House.

Kerley, B. (2005). *A cool drink of water.* Des Moines, IA: National Geographic.

Kerley, B. (2009). *One world, one day.* Des Moines, IA: National Geographic.

Biography

Ebbitt Cutler, M. (2005). *Breaking free: The story of William Kurelek.* Toronto, ON: Tundra Books.

Levine, K. (2002). *Hana's suitcase* Toronto, ON: Second Story Press.

Lunn, J. (2002). *Laura Secord: A story of courage.* Toronto, ON: Tundra Books.

Reich, S. (1999). *Clara Schumann: Piano virtuoso.* New York, NY: Clarion Books.

Reich, S. (2008). *Painting the wild frontier: The art and adventures of George Catlin.* New York, NY: Clarion Books.

Stone, T. L. (2007). *Amelia Earhart*. New York, NY: DK Children.

Autobiography

Little, J. (1989). *Little by Little: A memoir*. New York, NY: Puffin Books.

Little, J. (1991). *Stars come out within.* New York, NY: Viking Juvenile.

Wheeler, K. (2006). *Amazing kids.* Greensboro, NC: Carson Dellosa Publishing Co.

Winter, J. (2002). *Emily Dickinson's letters to the world.* New York, NY: Farrar, Straus & Giroux.

Factual Narratives

Greenwood, B. (1998). *The last safe house: A story of the Underground Railroad.* Toronto, ON: Kids Can Press.

Greenwood, B. (1998). *A pioneer story: The daily life of a Canadian pioneer family in 1840.* Toronto, ON: Kids Can Press.

Greenwood, B. (1999). *A pioneer Thanksgiving: A story of harvest celebrations in 1841*. Toronto, ON: Kids Can Press.

Greenwood, B. (2003). *A pioneer Christmas: Celebrating in the backwoods in 1841*. Toronto, ON: Kids Can Press.

Greenwood, B. (2007). *Factory girl.* Toronto, ON: Kids Can Press.

Propelled by the information age, informational texts have taken an increasingly important role in students' reading lives. Authors are employing rich writing styles that infuse subject-area discussions with passion and a sense of awe and wonder. More recently, a number of awards have been established to support non-fiction writing, including the *Norma Fleck Award for Canadian Children's Non-fiction Literature*, the *Red Cedar Award* (British Columbia's Young Readers' Choice Award for non-fiction), and *The Toronto Book Award* (presented by Toronto City Council for the best fiction and non-fiction texts). Teachers are encouraged to review these titles when selecting non-fiction materials for their classrooms.

Caution In the rapidly changing world of information, teachers need to revisit and revise their non-fiction selections frequently. Novels and other formats of narrative text are likely to have a longer shelf life than informational text, whose data may become outdated quickly.

Sensitivity to Diversity When Using Expository Text Teachers must be cognizant of the different backgrounds and perspectives of world events held by students of various ethnic and religious backgrounds in their classrooms (Merali, 2008). In many of Canada's larger cities, at least 50 percent of students do not speak English at home. Many classrooms also have students with First Nations heritage. This reality requires teachers to acquaint themselves with their students' backgrounds so they can discuss varying world views and select practices that model sensitivity and tolerance. The choice of materials and topics and methods of lesson delivery should all be considered (Al-Fartousi & Woloshyn, 2009). Teachers who are truly comfortable with Canada's global mosaic are sensitive to the kinds of questions and language they use and explicitly discuss anti-discrimination issues as appropriate. This awareness is even more important in homogeneous classrooms where students may be less likely to be aware of the diversity that is the cornerstone of Canadian society.

Teacher Voice 6.1

It is important that teachers consider students' cultural background and experiences when selecting text materials. This is especially true when using expository materials.

It is also important for teachers to consider whether the reading skill being taught is recognized or practised in the community. For instance, in some cultures it may be inappropriate to question information contained in print. In these cases, it is especially important that teachers select neutral materials and be patient and encouraging of students' efforts.

May Al-Fartousi
Primary and junior teacher and Ph.D. candidate

Hypertext and Media Today we read from many texts, not just books, especially when we are looking for information. When students need information, they are likely to consult the internet and CD-ROMs as readily as they access a book. These texts differ from traditional print in their non-linear structure. Students can click from link to link, view charts and illustrations, and listen to audio presentations. Readers are constantly making decisions about what materials to read and watch and the order in which they will do so (Karchmer, 2001). Thus, the connections and understandings that students form about a topic may depend on the choices they make in terms of reading materials and reading order.

Hypertext presents students with several advantages over traditional print. They can access information in a variety of formats and combinations, including audio (e.g., speech, music), print, and visual (e.g., illustrations, photographs, videos). Students may choose to linger at one link or scan it quickly. Research supports the idea that hypertext and media can address different learning styles more effectively than any single modality of instruction and that it can be especially beneficial in remedial programming (Ayersman, 1996; Reed, Ayersman, & Kraus, 1997). When students work within and create hypertext and media, they need to develop and employ a number of self-directed learning skills related to the finding and interpretation of information and the articulation and communication of ideas, as well as word processing and other computer-related skills (Brusilovsky & Maybury, 2002).

The unique characteristics of hypertext place an additional onus on teachers with respect to instructing students on how to locate and process expository information effectively (Pragnell, Roselli, & Rossano, 2006). Some instructional strategies with respect to using hypertext in the classroom are listed in Table 6.4.

Expository Text Structures

Just as narrative text shares common features such as characters, setting, plot, events, and theme, expository texts also share common features and organizational elements. In general, informational text is presented in one of five formats: descriptive, sequential or list, compare and contrast, cause and effect, and problem and solution. Effective readers can recognize text format and use its associated features to derive meaning from text. We provide a brief description of each text type below before describing specific instructional approaches associated with the processing of expository text.

Descriptive Descriptive texts provide readers with in-depth and detailed information about the features and characters of a specific topic or focus. Typically, descriptive text includes the presentation of multiple examples. While authors often try to provide readers with an image or mental representation of the topic, they also may attempt to relate information through the other senses: smell, touch, hearing, and taste. Examples of descriptive texts include *My Five Senses* by Aliki, *Mysteries of Water Monsters* by Kathryn Walker, *First to Fly* by Canadian author Peter Busby, and *Ice Age Mammoth* by Canadian author Barbara Hehner.

Table 6.4 Teaching Strategies for Using Hypertext in the Classroom

- Provide students with print materials and internet sites
- Clearly identify reading objectives
- Provide students with questions that will assist them in deriving meaning from text
- Have students respond to questions while reading
- Thoroughly discuss students' responses, including sources used
- Encourage students to use hypertext to prepare reports

Sequential or List Sequential or list texts provide readers with a series of items or events that is presented in numerical, hierarchical, or chronological order and that ends in a culminating occurrence or happening. Events can be separated by years, days, hours, or minutes. For example, the Canadian text *A Day at the Sugar Bush* by Megan Faulkner and Wally Randall describes the process of tapping tree sap to make maple syrup and maple sugar. Sequential texts are also referred to as "process" texts, in that they provide readers with a set of directions for completing or performing a defined task (e.g., following a recipe, conducting an experiment, assembling an object, using a word processor). *The Furry News: How to Make a Newspaper* by Loreen Leedy is a good example of such a "how-to" book.

Compare and Contrast Compare and contrast texts provide readers with an overview of the similarities and differences between two or more items, topics, or concepts. Typically, these texts involve a comparison of two independent topics or instances of a single category (e.g., mammals versus invertebrates, Canada versus China, fascism versus democracy, liberal versus conservative). *A Whale Is Not a Fish and Other Animal Mix-Ups* by Melvin Berger, *Butterflies and Moths* by James P. Rowan, and *Crickets and Grasshoppers* by Ann Squire are good examples of such texts.

After reading and analyzing this type of text, students may be called on to determine which of the items, topics, or concepts is "best" or "superior." Other times, readers may be provided with an opportunity to analyze the same topic through multiple lenses or perspectives. A good example is comparing two books or comparing the book and the movie (e.g., Mr. *Popper's Penguins* and *The March of the Penguins*; any John Huston book and a documentary on the northern tundra; the book and the movie of *Hana's Suitcase*).

Cause and Effect Cause and effect texts provide readers with an explanation of how one or more items or events produce resulting effects. Sometimes each event is sufficient to produce the end result, while at other times a set or series of events interact to produce a unique outcome. Readers are usually provided with an overview of each causal factor and then a description of the associated outcome. Sometimes, the order or timing of events is critical, resulting in a "causal chain," such as in the texts *Earthquakes* by Neil Morris and *Storms* by Seymour Simon. Other times, the sequential order of events is irrelevant.

Problem and Solution Problem and solution texts identify a problem or a series of related problems. The author then proceeds to provide readers with one or more potential solutions, sometimes identifying one solution as favourable or superior. Readers are often challenged to consider consequences associated with each potential solution. Examples of such texts include *How to Save the Planet* by Barbara Taylor, *Global Warming* by Laurence P. Pringle, and *Dealing with Bullying* by Marianne Johnston. This text structure is used frequently in advertisements and other types of persuasive text. One popular variation of this text structure is question and answer books, including such titles as *The New Kid's Question and Answer Book: Questions Kids Ask About Nature, Science and the Environment* by Owl Magazine, *Why?: The Best Ever Question and Answer Book About Nature, Science, and the World Around You* by Catherine Ripley, and *How Come? Planet Earth* authored by Kathy Wollard and illustrated by Debra Solomon.

PREPARING STUDENTS TO READ EXPOSITORY TEXT

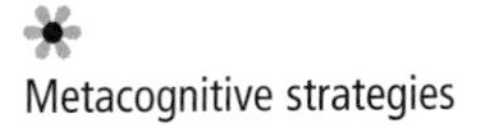

Since students are not required to read expository text or non-fiction materials in sequential order, it is critical that teachers instruct them in how to locate information in the text. To this end, they must provide students with relevant instruction in the use of the table of contents, index, appendices, glossary, titles, and headers. Students also require direct instruction (i.e., teacher modelling and Think Aloud) with respect to reading graphic material. Teachers need to provide students with guided instruction and multiple opportunities for repeated practice through hands-on activities, with co-operative learning being an especially effective form of instruction here. Finally, teachers need to provide students with relevant skills for online data collection, especially with respect to verifying the authenticity of information and data sources. Many times, these lessons are integrated with subject area instruction such as mathematics and science.

There are a number of specific strategies and activities that teachers can employ to help students achieve success when reading expository text. Generally, these strategies can be distinguished as those that focus on vocabulary instruction and those that focus on reading comprehension. Often, strategies associated with effective instruction in one domain are also relevant in the other.

Vocabulary Instruction

It has been estimated that students learn between 3000 and 4000 new words each year or at least eight new words per day (Alvermann & Phelps, 1998; Stahl & Nagy, 2006). While explicit vocabulary instruction is important for specific content and concepts that are being studied, obviously students are not learning all of these words through direct instruction in the classroom (Blachowicz & Fisher, 2010; Cunningham, 2005). Teachers need to establish a classroom environment where incidental word learning occurs through planned exposures and activities such as opportunities for wide reading, talk, and first-hand and vicarious experiences (e.g., Read Aloud). For new vocabulary to become part of students' permanent semantic repertoires, it needs to be accessible at the listening, speaking, reading, and writing levels (Reutzel & Cooter, 2004), so talk is a vital initial component of all vocabulary acquisition. However, content area vocabulary, a critical factor in learning success, benefits from direct instruction. Therefore, a classroom needs to establish a strong balance between informal and formal vocabulary learning. According to Michael Graves (2006), classroom programs need to include the following elements:

- Rich, varied language experiences, especially those gained through plenty of opportunities to read widely.
- Teaching of individual words in a rich, deep, and extended manner
- Teaching word learning strategies such as using context and using known word parts to discover meanings of unknown words
- Fostering word consciousness, which includes a cognitive and attitudinal stance, by creating an awareness of and interest in acquiring new words

The connection between word knowledge and comprehension of content area text is well established (Blachowicz & Fisher, 2000). Pre-teaching pertinent vocabulary in the content areas has shown significant increases in comprehension of texts that

include the previously taught vocabulary (Amaral, Garrison, & Klentschy, 2002). In general, direct vocabulary instruction involves the reinforcement and development of relationships between words and concepts (Graves & Slater, 1996). Consider the four distinct vocabulary relationships in Figure 6.1, reflecting a grade 6 unit on magnetism and electricity. Presenting words so that the relationship among them is clear results in increased word learning, as opposed to having students memorize words or look them up in a dictionary (Bravo & Cervetti, 2009). For instance, in social studies, words such as *culture*, *tradition*, *custom*, and *community* often appear together in text in relationship to each other and benefit from being taught together.

Teachers need to ensure that students are provided with relevant vocabulary and concept instruction if full comprehension of a content area unit (e.g., science, social studies, history, geography) is to occur. In many cases, students' knowledge of pertinent information will vary, with some students possessing complete understanding and others having partial or inaccurate understanding of words and associated concepts. It is imperative that these discrepancies be resolved prior to the unit if comprehension and learning are to be maximized. Of course, teachers also need to make some decisions about what vocabulary and related concepts need to be taught in advance of the unit of study. These decisions should be made based in part on students' abilities and interests as well as on

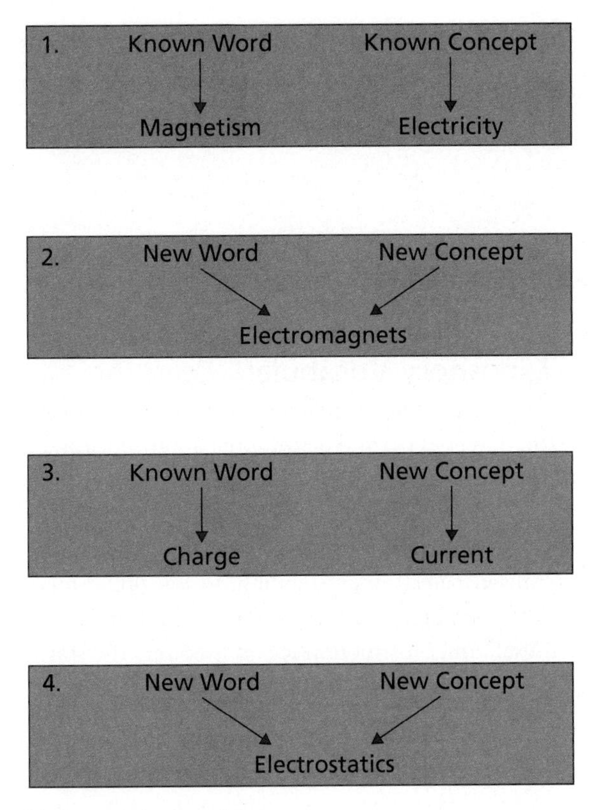

Figure 6.1 Vocabulary Relationships

curriculum expectations. Time spent pre-teaching critical vocabulary is time well spent, reducing the time needed for reteaching and review.

Guidelines for Word Selection The selection of words for direct instruction is critical. Teachers should select words that are frequently used in the discipline, necessary for understanding the topic, and preferably connected to each other conceptually (Bravo & Cervetti, 2009). For instance, select words that:

- Are of high utility in the subject area
- Are necessary for understanding the concepts inherent to the subject
- Are connected to each other and represent concepts

Table 6.5 lists criteria for selecting vocabulary for direct instruction.

Teacher Voice 6.2

Vocabulary is one of the biggest challenges in science education. Most students experience difficulties with the language of science—not just those who are learning English or have learning exceptionalities. Unfortunately, I still see many teachers asking students to write out word definitions. This is a hard task, as students cannot paraphrase easily. Teachers need to tell students overtly about techniques that can help them acquire and understand new vocabulary. That is why vocabulary strategies are really important.

Elizabeth Gebhardt, M.Ed.
Science teacher and curriculum lead writer

Table 6.5 Criteria for Selecting Vocabulary for Direct Instruction

- Relation to key concepts
- Relative importance
- Students' ability and background
- Potential to enhance independent learning

Source: Adapted from Alvermann and Phelps (1998).

Strategies for Expository Vocabulary Learning There are a number of strategies for teaching content area vocabulary effectively that are strongly supported by research. "Rich" instruction goes beyond definitional approaches and gets students thinking and actively using and making connections with new words and concepts (Beck, McKeown, & Kucan, 2002). See Table 6.6 for suggestions for effective vocabulary instruction. It must be remembered that, initially, students will have a range of understandings, from none at all, to vague, partial understanding, to full understanding. Also, learning new vocabulary requires many opportunities to use the words in talk, in print, and in writing over time. The initial direct instruction lesson is merely the starting point.

Semantic Maps Sometimes referred to as semantic webs, semantic maps are visual representations of new words or concepts and a recommended method for teaching words thematically. Target vocabulary is placed in the centre with related words arranged in clusters radiating outward. When developing semantic maps, teachers are encouraged to solicit student input and to conclude their lessons with whole-class discussion about the central idea or concept. This method helps students construct a personal knowledge base as a network of information, which ensures a deeper understanding of important concepts in the content areas. Figure 6.2 provides an example of a simple semantic map used for the study of condensation.

Possible Sentences This strategy was created by Moore and Moore (1992) and is easy to use, as it requires little teacher preparation. This has become a popular approach since it has been shown that students who participated in possible sentence instruction made greater growth in vocabulary acquisition than those who participated in semantic mapping activities (Stahl & Kapinus, 1991). In possible sentences, the teacher chooses words that represent key concepts and uses them to generate sentences. Students discuss the

Table 6.6 Suggestions for Effective Vocabulary Instruction

- Establish what students already know and build on that.
- Provide students with multiple examples of new terms and concepts.
- Integrate oral language as part of the learning process. Include plenty of discussion in which teachers model the new vocabulary and students are required to use it to respond to questions or share ideas.
- Employ a variety of hands-on and co-operative learning activities that require students to discuss and explain new vocabulary to others as well as use it as part of their written responses.

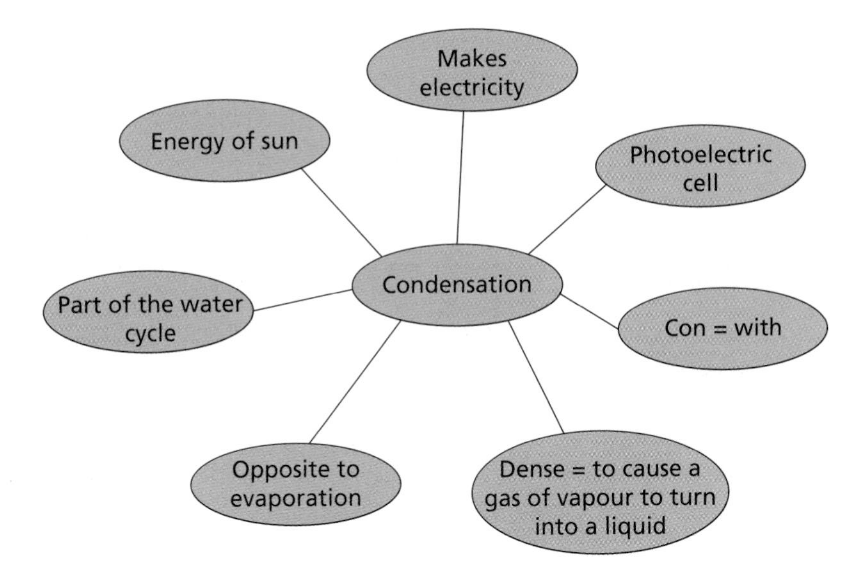

Figure 6.2 Semantic Map of Condensation

sentences and determine if they are true or not based on their existing collective knowledge. If the sentences are incorrect, they discuss how to modify them to make them true. (See Table 6.7 for teaching strategies for possible sentences.) Essentially, the technique requires students to create meaningful statements with unfamiliar vocabulary and is an

Table 6.7 Teaching Strategies for Possible Sentences

1. Teacher lists six to eight new words on the board and pronounces them aloud. For instance, *compound, thorax, vibrate, cicada, pheromones, antennae,* and *survive.*
2. Teacher records associated key words known by students. For instance, *many, shake, insect, feelers,* and *stay alive.*
3. Students make sentences using at least two words from the list. This can be completed orally as a whole group, in small groups, or as an individual activity. For instance, "I saw an insect vibrate his antennae." "Cicadas have antennae that help them stay alive." "Many insects vibrate their pheromones to survive."
4. Teacher assigns the reading of a content area section and identifies the target words. For instance, the teacher assigns a section in a science text about how insects see and sense the world around them.
5. Students determine whether their sentences are "possible" or if they make sense given their contextual understanding of the word in the text. In our example, students together determine that the first two sentences are possible whereas the last sentence does not make sense. They now know that the word *pheromones* refers to the special chemicals that insects produce so they can locate other insects.
6. Finally, at the end of the exercise, the teacher asks for new sentences using at least two of the words in the list. This reinforces the new vocabulary and can be done orally. For instance, "Insects have antennae on their heads that are used for smelling the pheromones produced by other insects." "Cicadas have pieces of skin on their thoraxes that they can vibrate to make a singing noise." "Insects have compound eyes and use the many eyes to help them survive."

effective tool for encouraging them to become actively involved in writing, reading, and discussing key concepts and vocabulary. One of the strengths of this approach is that the technique involves interactions among students that encourage active processing of new information. The technique also involves "playing" with words, which encourages learning.

Matching Activities and Puzzles Matching is a simple method of reinforcing learning of new vocabulary, requiring students to match words with their meanings. Teachers are forewarned that this activity serves only to reinforce new learning and that matching words to their definitions does not guarantee that students will comprehend the underlying concepts, especially abstract ones.

These kinds of reinforcement activities can also be presented as crossword puzzles or other mind games, which can increase student motivation. These activities can be developed readily and made by teachers using formats provided on such websites as www.supercrosswordcreator.com.

Reading Comprehension Strategies

Graphic organizers

Graphic Organizers

Graphic organizers, otherwise known as semantic maps or idea maps, are one of the most basic and readily accessible instructional tools available to teachers and students for processing information text. See Figure 6.3a for an example of a Venn diagram completed by a grade 2 student. Graphic organizers provide readers with a visual structure or framework for organizing and summarizing large amounts of information. They also help readers identify key concepts and ideas and the nature of their interconnectedness. Graphic organizers are often presented at the beginning of a unit of study, with teachers subsequently referring to them throughout the unit. They also serve as review instruments at the end of the unit. Figure 6.3b provides an example of a descriptive graphic organizer for the Confederation of Canada.

In general, students' retention and overall comprehension of text passages increases following the completion of text-relevant graphic organizers (Alvermann & Phelps, 2001; National Reading Panel, 2000). While reproducible graphic organizers are readily available through print resources (e.g., *Tools for Thought: Graphic Organizers for Your Classroom* by Jim Burke, *The Teacher's Big Book of Graphic Organizers: 100 Reproducible Organizers that Help Kids with Reading, Writing, and the Content Areas* by Katherine S. McKnight), software packages (*Inspiration*, *Kidspiration*), and the internet (e.g., www.teacherprintables.net/free-printable-organizers.html, www.teach-nology.com/worksheets/graphic/, http://freeology.com/graphicorgs/, www2.scholastic.com), including the Canadian website www.thecanadianteacher.com/lessonsearch.htm, the challenge remains to increase student understanding of these tools and corresponding text structures. That is, teachers need to inform students about the features of specific graphic organizers in relation to text structures. Providing students with this type of metacogntive information is critical in promoting independent use and generalization of these reading tools. See Figure 6.4 for examples of graphic organizers that correspond to each of the five expository text structures identified earlier in this chapter.

Question-Answering and Question Generation

Providing students with opportunities to form and respond to questions while reading encourages them to activate prior knowledge, explore and deconstruct unfamiliar parts of text, and identify

Figure 6.3a Venn Diagram by Griffin, Grade 2

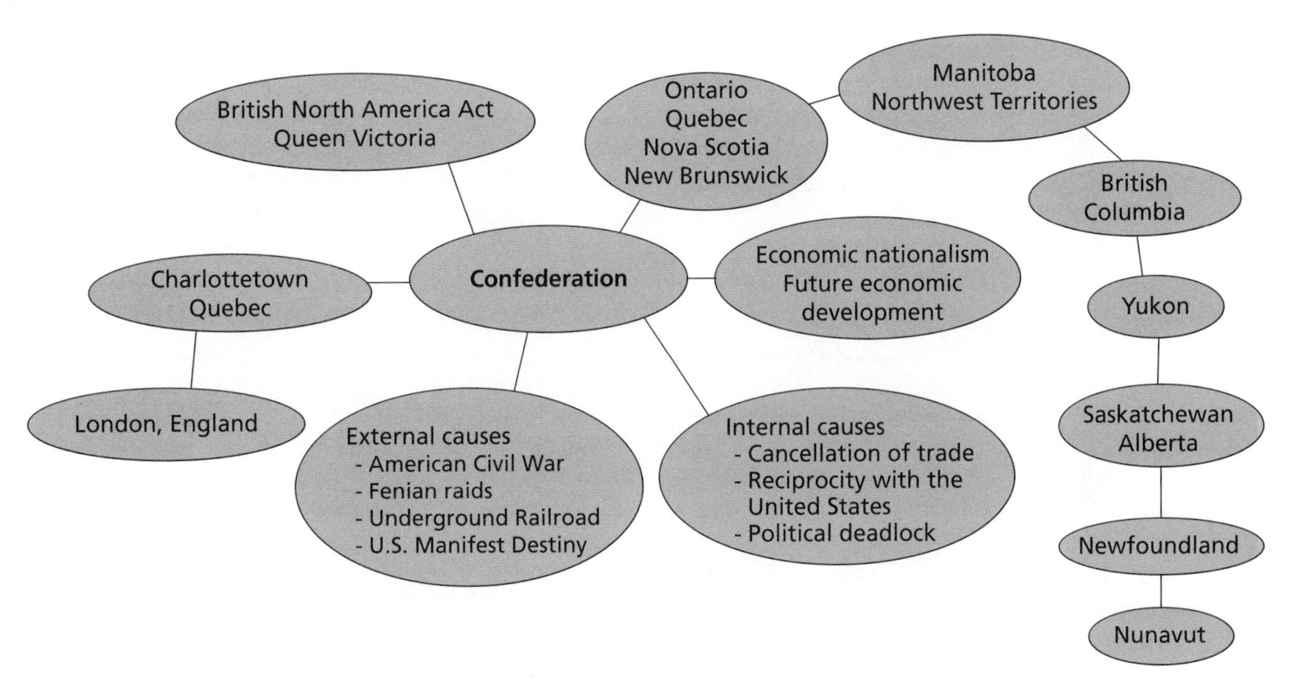

Figure 6.3b Graphic Organizer for Confederation of Canada

information that needs to be reread or requires further investigation (Israel & Duffy, 2009; National Reading Panel, 2000). Done well, questioning increases students' ability to understand and remember new information. Typically, questions are posed by teachers to students and used to generate class discussions or complete text-related assignments.

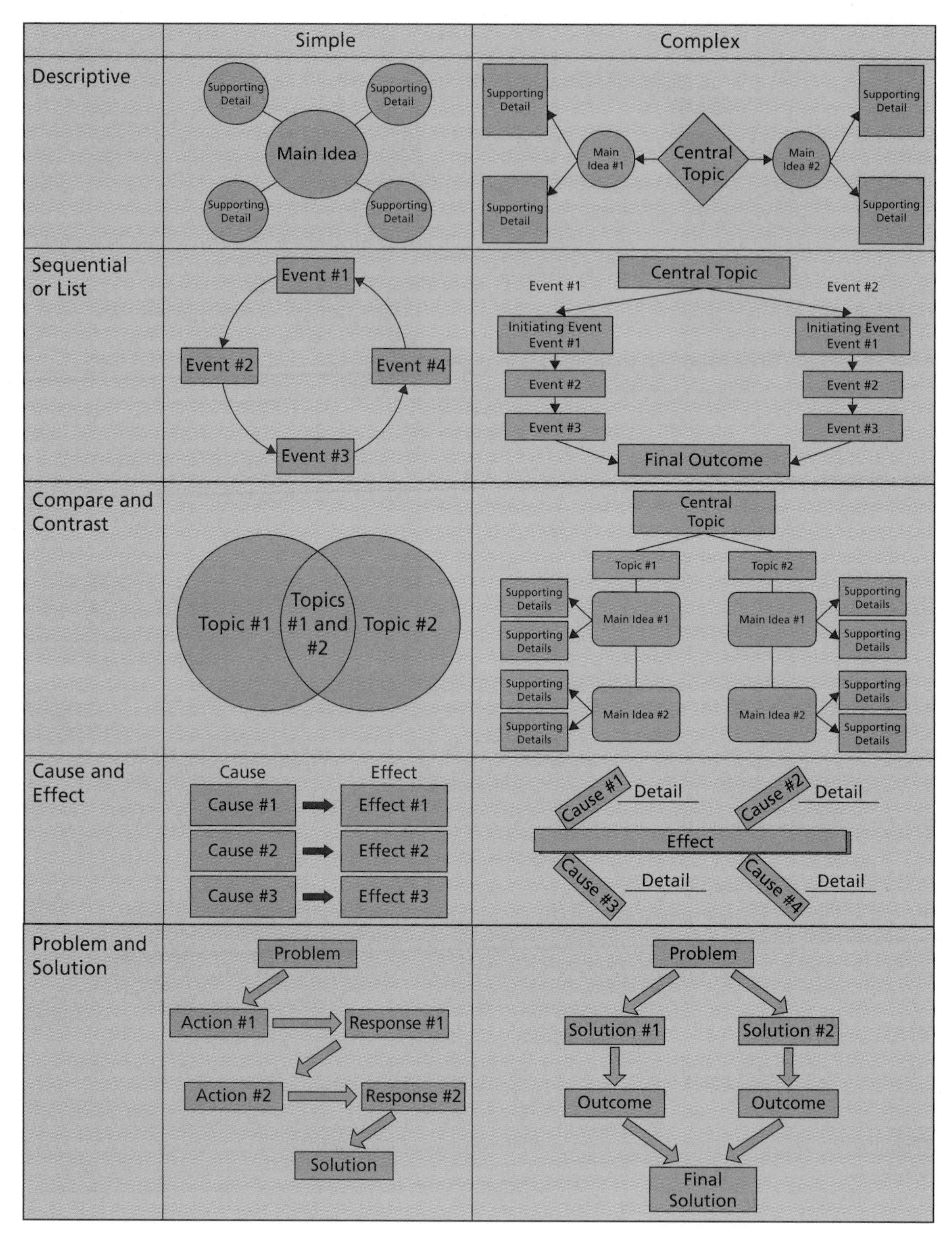

Figure 6.4 Graphic Organizers for Expository Text Structures

Students, however, benefit from explicit instruction and guidance in developing and answering questions (Harvey & Goudris, 2007). Before, during, and after reading, questioning can be especially effective when students are taught how to identify the nature of the question (e.g., inferential, literal, critical thinking) and its associated response.

Generic Question Stems Having students use generic question stems is one technique demonstrated to enhance their comprehension of expository text (Hacker, 2004). In seminal work, King and her colleagues (1990, 1991, 1992; cited in King, 1995) demonstrated that having readers generate and respond to text using generic question stems (see Figure 6.5) improved their understanding of text. Central to this instruction was the differentiation of "memory" questions (i.e., those that require the repetition of text concepts) and "thinking" questions (i.e., those that require the exploration and extension of text through explaining, justifying, and analyzing), with instructional emphasis on the latter.

Encouraging students to use higher-level question stems promotes the development of their analytical, inferring, evaluating, and compare-and-contrast skills and induces critical thinking in the questioner as well as the responder. Providing readers with open-ended question stems can also enhance their metacognitive development, encouraging them to monitor their thinking, assume greater control over their thought processes,

1. Who _______ did _______?
2. When did _______ happen?
3. Where did _______ occur?
4. How would you use _______ to _______?
5. How are _______ and _______ similar?
6. Which _______ do you think is best and why?
7. What conclusions can you draw about _______?
8. How is _______ related to _______ that we studied earlier?
9. Do you agree or disagree with this statement: _______?
10. What is a new example of _______?
11. Compare _______ and _______ with regard to _______.
12. What do you think causes _______? Why?
13. What are the strengths and weaknesses of _______?
14. What is the significance of _______?
15. What evidence is there to support your answer?
16. What is the main idea of _______?
17. Explain why _______. Explain how _______.
18. What is the difference between _______ and _______?
19. What do you think would happen if _______?
20. How does _______ affect _______?

Source: Adapted from King (1995).

Figure 6.5 Generic Question Stems

and respond to text in a sophisticated manner. Question stems can be transferred readily across the content areas and work well across a variety of instructional venues, including individual application, small-group work, and whole-class discussions (Chen & Bradshaw, 2007; Kramarski & Gutman, 2006).

Imagery The written word can provoke images that connect with the senses. For instance, students provided with the word *hamburger* may conjure mental images of the meal's smell and taste. However, not all students generate mental images when attempting to comprehend text. In this context, the old saying *a picture is worth a thousand words* has merit for teachers supporting students to comprehend expository text. Teachers can help students understand that generating visual images can aid in comprehension and are usually idiosyncratic in nature. Teachers can then provide explicit demonstrations about how to create "mind pictures." Consider the imagery-related teaching scenarios presented in Table 6.8.

Table 6.8 Teaching Scenarios Using Imagery in the Classroom

1. Discuss the role of imagery in reading and ask students to examine their ownprocesses for constructing visual aids to help them comprehend. Provide an example by using simple sentences such as "Suddenly the boy fell off his bicycle." Ask students to close their eyes and visualize the scene. Model the Think Aloud process by verbalizing what you see, hear, and feel in your mind. Let students share their images with the class. Finally, hold a discussion that compares the imagery or mind pictures they just created with images provided in television and movies.
2. Select a section from an expository text and read it aloud to the class. Ask the students to visualize the passage and make drawings of their mental images.

   Many explorers dreamed of finding a passage over the top of North America between the Atlantic and the Pacific oceans. Irish naval officer Robert McClure and his crew sailed the ship Investigator *into the passage in 1850. They were trapped by ice for two winters before abandoning ship and they finally sledded out the other end in 1853—the first people to travel through the Northwest Passage.* (Wyatt, 2001, p. 11).

   Ask students to describe their drawings and share their interpretations as either part of small-group or large-group discussions. Prompt students to describe the sounds and feelings associated with their drawings. It is useful for teachers to demonstrate a personal drawing as well. This process needs to be repeated frequently so students will develop the habit of forming mental images while reading.
3. Encourage students to draw their mental images while researching. For instance, student comprehension of Viking sailing ability will be enhanced if they draw an image of a Viking ship on its way to Newfoundland and Labrador.
4. Provide relevant prior knowledge via pictures or video when assigning unfamiliar content area reading. For instance, if students are reading about the search for the Northwest Passage, their ability to form mental images while reading will likely be enhanced if they have been provided with pictures of the Arctic tundra.
5. The use of creative drama helps to build images. Events and ideas from the past can come to life if dramatized in a well-structured class. Students can be divided into groups and provided with an event to enact. As part of the dramatization, they would need to complete independent research, direct their dramatizations, and then consult with the teacher for accuracy. When sharing with the class, a theatre-in-the-round setting can be adapted, followed by discussion.
6. Writing tasks that encourage students to form mental images can be assigned. For instance, students could be asked to describe the feelings of Christopher Columbus's men as they first saw North America or to write a letter home from a sailor who had been "pressed into service" in the War of 1812.

Finding the Main Idea The ability to summarize text or synthesize central concepts and ideas is a critical element of efficient reading. To produce a valid summary, readers must be able to recognize and avoid unnecessary details, as well as form generalizations and connections across meaningful units. In reality, many teachers direct students to identify the main idea of a text without providing any instructional support. While some students are able to derive the gist of a text without such support, others struggle with this process and provide verbatim or close-to-verbatim reiterations of text. More positively, students' abilities to identify main ideas can be greatly enhanced following direction from their teachers.

In general, instruction in finding the main ideas requires students to delete irrelevant details, identify repeated information, recognize interrelated ideas, and create hierarchical categories. Consider the following six-step process used by early reading researchers Brown and Day (1983) when assisting middle grade students to find the main idea contained in paragraphs:

1. Delete trivial information.
2. Delete redundant information.
3. Substitute superordinate terms for list of items.
4. Integrate a series of events with a superordinate action term.
5. Select a topic sentence.
6. Invent a topic sentence if there is none.

Table 6.9 provides an example of how these steps can be applied to a passage related to Chinese New Year.

Table 6.9 Finding the Main Idea: Chinese New Year

Passage

The eve of the New Year is perhaps the most exciting part of the event, as anticipation creeps in. Here, traditions and rituals are very carefully observed in everything from food to clothing. Dinner is usually a feast of seafood and dumplings, signifying different good wishes. Delicacies include prawns, for liveliness and happiness, dried oysters (or ho xi), for all things good, raw fish salad or yu sheng to bring good luck and prosperity, Fai-hai (Angel Hair), an edible hair-like seaweed to bring prosperity, and dumplings boiled in water (Jiaozi) signifying a long-lost good wish for a family. It's usual to wear something red as this colour is meant to ward off evil spirits—but black and white are out, as these are associated with mourning. After dinner, the family sit up for the night playing cards, board games or watching TV programs dedicated to the occasion. At midnight, the sky is lit up by fireworks.

(Source: http://livingstonchineseculture.org/?page_id=23)

Step 1: Delete trivial information

~~**The eve of the**~~ New Year ~~**is**~~ perhaps ~~**the**~~ most exciting part ~~**of the**~~ event, ~~**as**~~ anticipation creeps ~~**in. Here**~~, traditions ~~**and**~~ rituals ~~**are**~~ very carefully observed ~~**in**~~ everything ~~**from**~~ food ~~**to**~~ clothing. Dinner ~~**is**~~ usually ~~**a**~~ feast ~~**of**~~ seafood ~~**and**~~ dumplings, signifying different good wishes. Delicacies include prawns, ~~**for**~~ liveliness ~~**and**~~ happiness, dried oysters (or ho xi), ~~**for all**~~ things good, raw fish salad ~~**or**~~ yu sheng ~~**to**~~ bring good luck and prosperity, Fai-hai (Angel Hair), ~~**an**~~ edible hair-like seaweed ~~**to**~~ bring prosperity, and dumplings boiled ~~**in**~~ water (Jiaozi) signifying ~~**a**~~ long-lost good wish ~~**for a**~~ family. ~~**It's**~~ usual ~~**to**~~ wear something red ~~**as this**~~ colour ~~**is**~~ meant ~~**to**~~ ward off evil spirits—but black and white ~~**are**~~

(continued)

Table 6.9 Finding the Main Idea: Chinese New Year *(continued)*

out, **as these are** associated with mourning. After dinner, **the** family sit up **for the** night playing cards, board games or watching TV programs dedicated **to the** occasion. **At** midnight, **the** sky **is** lit up **by** fireworks.

Step 2: Delete redundant information

The eve of the New Year **is** ~~perhaps~~ **the** ~~most exciting part of the event,~~ **as** ~~anticipation creeps~~ **in. Here,** traditions **and** rituals **are** ~~very carefully~~ observed **in** ~~everything~~ **from** food **to** clothing. Dinner **is** usually **a** feast **of** seafood **and** dumplings, signifying different good wishes. Delicacies include prawns, **for** liveliness **and** happiness, dried oysters ~~(or ho xi),~~ **for all** ~~things good,~~ raw fish salad **or** ~~yu sheng~~ **to** bring ~~good~~ luck and prosperity, ~~Fai-hai (Angel Hair),~~ **an** ~~edible~~ hair-like seaweed **to** bring prosperity, and dumplings boiled **in** water ~~(Jiaozi) signifying a long-lost good wish~~ **for a** ~~family.~~ **It's** usual **to** wear something red **as this** colour **is** meant **to** ward off evil spirits—but black and white **are** out, **as these are** associated with mourning. After dinner, **the** family sit up **for the** night playing cards, board games or watching TV programs ~~dedicated to the occasion.~~ **At** midnight, **the** sky **is** lit up **by** fireworks.

Step 3: Substitute related terms with a general label

The eve of the New Year **is** ~~perhaps~~ **the** ~~most exciting part~~ **of the** ~~event~~, **as** ~~anticipation creeps~~ **in. Here,** traditions **and** ~~rituals~~ **are** ~~very carefully~~ observed **in** ~~everything~~ **from** food **to** clothing. *FOOD* [Dinner **is** usually **a** feast **of** seafood **and** dumplings,] FORTUNE [signifying different good wishes.] Delicacies include FOOD [prawns], **for** FORTUNE [liveliness **and** happiness], FOOD [dried oysters ~~(or ho xi),~~ **for all** ~~things good~~, raw fish salad] **or** ~~yu sheng~~ **to** bring ~~good~~ FORTUNE [luck and prosperity,] ~~Fai-hai (Angel Hair),~~ **an** ~~edible~~ FOOD [hair-like seaweed] **to** FORTUNE [bring prosperity,] and FOOD [dumplings boiled **in** water] ~~(Jiaozi) signifying~~ **a** ~~long-lost good wish~~ **for a** ~~family~~. **It's** usual **to** COLOUR [wear something red] **as this** colour **is** meant **to** FORTUNE [ward off evil spirits]—but COLOUR [black and white] **are** out, **as these are** associated with mourning. ~~After~~ FOOD [dinner], **the** family sit up **for the** ENTERTAINMENT [night playing cards, board games or watching TV programs ~~dedicated~~ **to the** ~~occasion~~. **At** midnight, **the** sky **is** lit up **by** fireworks.]

Step 4: Substitute related actions with a general categorical label

The eve of the New Year **is** ~~perhaps~~ **the** ~~most exciting part~~ **of the** ~~event~~, **as** ~~anticipation creeps~~ **in. Here,** traditions **and** ~~rituals~~ **are** ~~very~~ carefully observed = FOOD, COLOUR, ENTERTAINMENT **in** ~~everything~~ **from** food **to** clothing. *FOOD* [Dinner **is** usually **a** feast **of** seafood **and** dumplings,] FORTUNE [signifying different good wishes.] Delicacies include FOOD [prawns], **for** FORTUNE [liveliness **and** happiness], FOOD [dried oysters ~~(or ho xi),~~ **for all** ~~things good,~~ raw fish salad] **or** ~~yu sheng~~ **to** bring ~~good~~ FORTUNE [luck and prosperity,] ~~Fai-hai (Angel Hair),~~ **an** ~~edible~~ FOOD [hair-like seaweed] **to** FORTUNE [bring prosperity,] and FOOD [dumplings boiled **in** water] ~~(Jiaozi) signifying~~ **a** ~~long-lost good wish~~ **for a family**. **It's** usual **to** COLOUR [wear something red] **as this** colour **is** meant **to** FORTUNE [ward off evil spirits]—but COLOUR [black and white] **are** out, **as these are** associated with mourning. ~~After~~ FOOD [dinner], **the** family sit up **for the** ENTERTAINMENT [night playing cards, board games or watching TV programs ~~dedicated~~ **to the** ~~occasion~~. **At** midnight, **the** sky **is** lit up **by** fireworks.]

Step 5: Select a topic sentence, and Step 6: Invent a topic sentence if there is none

New Year is observed by traditions of food, colour, and entertainment that are intended to bring good fortune.

As students gain proficiency in identifying the main idea of a paragraph, teachers can extend this summarizing activity across multiple paragraphs. In this way, students can gain proficiency in identifying main ideas associated with longer passages.

Summarizing Once students are able to identify the main ideas contained within a section of text, they are well prepared to generate summaries of longer text passages and use graphic organizers and other instructional tools described throughout this chapter. For instance, students can be guided to create hierarchical summaries consisting of a thesis statement, main ideas, and supporting details. Consider the hierarchical summary created

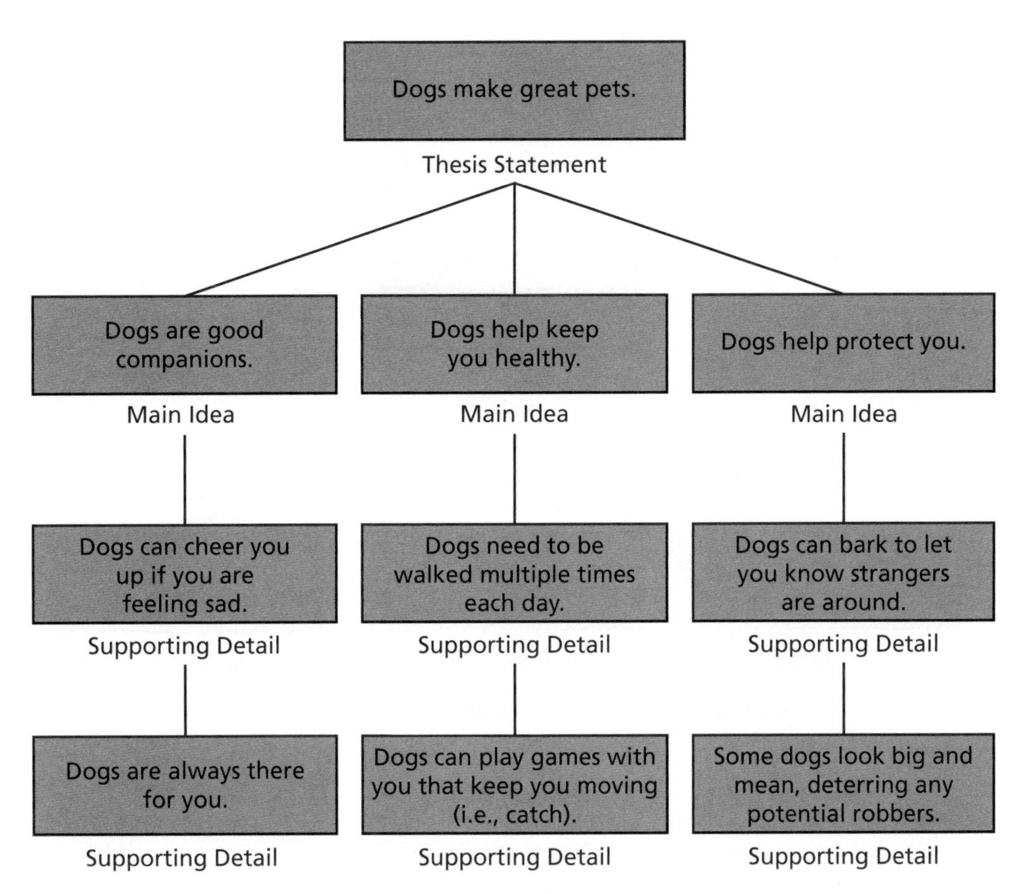

Figure 6.6 Primary Grade Hierarchical Summary: Dogs Make Great Pets

by a grade 3 class elaborating why dogs are preferred pets (Figure 6.6), or the summary created by a grade 5 class after reading *A Pioneer Story* by Barbara Greenwood (Figure 6.7).

Teachers are encouraged to provide students with prompts or questions intended to help them generate meaningful summaries. Such prompts include the following:

- Have I found the overall idea for the paragraph or group of paragraphs?
- Have I found the most important information that explains or discusses the overall idea?
- Have I used any information that is not directly related to or does not explain the overall idea?
- Have I used any information more than once?

Flexible Reading Rates Reading rate refers to the speed at which readers attempt to process text. In general, effective readers adjust their reading rates to accommodate for the purpose of the reading. A slower rate may be likely if it is important to comprehend the material fully. The rate of reading can be faster, however, if the purpose is to determine the gist of the materials, search for a specific piece of information, or determine whether the text will meet the research needs of the project. Recall the passage you were asked to read at the beginning of the chapter (Contrast between Moral and Aesthetic Values).

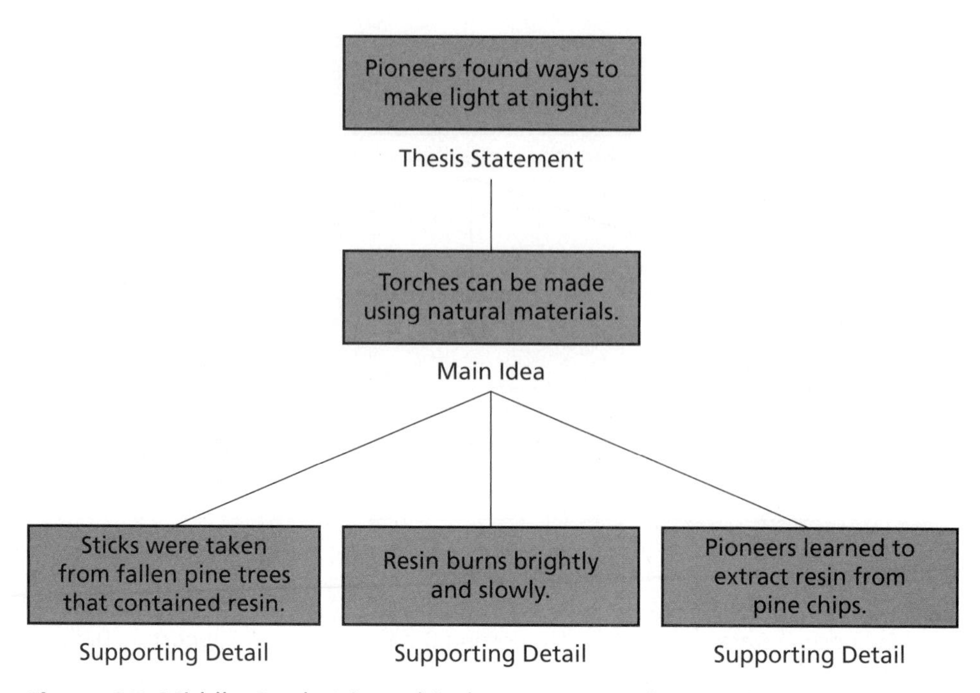

Figure 6.7 Middle Grade Hierarchical Summary: Making Light

There was a good probability that you slowed your reading rate as you attempted to comprehend the complicated text. When students read a science text or a mathematics problem, they often need to process every single word to comprehend the message fully, especially if the content is abstract or contains new vocabulary. Unfortunately, many students rarely adjust their reading rates without explicit instructions to do so.

Teachers may be required to provide students with lessons demonstrating the impact of reading rate to ensure that they employ flexible reading rates as appropriate. In such lessons, teachers should select at least three different passages that differ with respect to density of language, complexity of thought and organization, and use of headers. The teacher then instructs the students to read and answer questions associated with each passage. The teacher should then guide students in reviewing the specific reading rates associated with each text and help them identify the factors associated with text difficulty and reading purpose.

Teachers will need to remind students to adjust their reading rate in response to content area as part of subsequent lessons. While students need to reduce their reading rates consciously when processing complex expository text, there are other times when they will need to accelerate their reading rates, such as when looking for specific pieces of information for the gist of the material. Skimming and scanning are skills associated with such accelerated reading and are described next.

Skimming When students read content area material quickly for the purpose of gathering the main idea and general impressions about the text, they are skimming. Skimming involves the intense previewing of reading materials. When skimming, students are not required to "read" every word. Instead, they attempt to orient themselves to the organization and general focus of the material. For instance, when attempting to determine

Table 6.10 Teaching Strategies for Skimming

1. Select a section of expository text that has well-defined organizational and typographical aids as guideposts (e.g., titles, headers, diagrams, maps). Talk to students about the need to skim material online or in a book to determine if it will suit their needs.
2. Provide students with a copy of the reading passage. Tell them that they are to focus on attaining the "gist" of the material versus gathering details. Tell them that they should be able to survey the material and identify what they will learn from reading it. For instance, if students are studying the voyages of Captain Cook, they should be able to tell if all three voyages are discussed in the resource, if Cook's accomplishments on each voyage are described, and how and where he died.
3. Time students' skimming of the text and ask them to turn over the text when the majority of the class appears to have completed the activity. Have students identify the introduction and the author's main point. Read all headings and subheadings. Pay attention to italicized or highlighted print.
4. Provide additional questions related to the general content of the passage, but also prompt a discussion about skimming, stressing that it is a quick survey of the materials rather than word-for-word reading. Repeat with subsequent selections to provide students with practice, beginning with familiar texts and topics.

whether material contained in the text can be used for the completion of a research project, students should review the introductory statements, headings, subheadings, and the conclusion. As with other strategies and skills, teachers need to teach skimming explicitly and students' performance will improve with practice. See Table 6.10 for some teaching strategies for skimming text.

Scanning Scanning refers to the ability to move the eyes rapidly over a section of text to locate a specific piece of information. This skill is used frequently when trying to locate a date or information contained in texts and lists such as telephone books, dictionaries, or indices. Once again, students must be instructed to adjust their reading rate to the purpose of the reading activity. This skill is taught best through increasingly challenging practice. Teachers may find social studies and related text especially useful here. See Table 6.11 for some teaching strategies for scanning text.

Lookbacks Briefly, the lookback process involves reviewing text to find or verify content. Many struggling readers seldom practise this technique. In fact, they may consider lookbacks to be an admission of poor reading or even to be cheating (Caldwell & Leslie, 2005). Students need to be reassured that all good readers practise lookbacks.

Developing Students' Self-Regulation and Metacognition Metacogniton or comprehension monitoring refers to being able to recognize what is known and what is unknown in the context of a learning task. In addition, proficient readers are able to describe what reading methods and strategies they use to derive meaning from text. Poor readers, on the other hand, seem to be unaware of such strategic processes and usually are unable to describe their thinking during reading (Reutzel & Cooter, 2004). In the early 1980s, Brown (1982) developed a four-step model for

Table 6.11 Teaching Strategies for Scanning

1. Provide students with a page number and ask them to find a piece of information that is easy to locate (i.e., information that is italicized, bolded, or highlighted) so they know precisely what they are looking for. Have students raise a hand when they have located the information. Repeat the exercise several times until most students raise a hand promptly. Example: What were the names of Columbus's ships? Answer found in italics in the text: *La Niña*, *La Pinta*, and *La Santa Maria*.
2. Provide students with a carefully crafted question that replicates the wording used in the text. Have students scan the text to answer the question. Provide students with multiple examples and opportunities for practice. Example of question: Who had the honour of being the first white man to see the Pacific from the New World? Text that answers question: "To Balboa went the honour of being the first white man to see the Pacific from the New World."
3. Repeat the process using questions with text-independent wording (i.e., questions that do not mirror the wording of the text). Although many students find this step challenging, possessing a sound understanding of the purpose of scanning can facilitate this process. Example of question: Describe a Viking ship. Text that answers question: "People living on England's coast a thousand years ago would run in terror at the sight of a 'dragon ship.' The dragon ship had an oaken bow that sliced the waters as its long oars dipped and its square sail spread in the wind. This was the war ship of the Vikings." Here, students are required to extrapolate the answer that is embedded in the text. An answer might be: "The ship was made of oak, and had long oars and a square sail."

teaching students metacognitive processes. Reading educators have enhanced this model subsequently to include an emphasis on capitalizing on students' strengths as well as developing areas of need.

1. Determine the nature of the material to be learned. Is the text narrative or expository?
2. Consider the essential task involved. Identify what is being sought in the text.
3. Consider personal learning strengths and areas of need (e.g., strong visual memory, extensive prior knowledge, good problem-solving skills).
4. Select and employ appropriate learning strategies to achieve the reading goal and be able to discuss the reasons for selecting the strategy.

Questioning Repertoires

As a teacher you want to fully engage your students by establishing a purpose for content area reading. If teachers successfully set the stage for such reading, students will be able to refine their purpose and become self-directed, self-motivated problem solvers. Providing students with strategies and resources for the systematic processing of information text is a critical component of establishing such a learning environment. As with narrative text, students process information text best if they activate relevant prior knowledge, ask higher-level thinking questions, and monitor their reading for understanding. Self-knowledge and self-monitoring, also known as metacogniton, are

Table 6.12 Using K-W-L Charts in the Classroom

What I Know (K): Have students brainstorm about a defined topic. Record students' collective thoughts using chart paper or the blackboard. Keep this information for subsequent review. Alternatively, have students record their prior knowledge independently. Have students share ideas as a whole class.

What I Want to Learn (W): Ask students what they would like to learn or clarify about the topic. (If students do not possess prior knowledge about the topic, substitute "Want to Learn" with "Need to Learn" and provide them with learning expectations.) Complete this activity as a whole class, in small groups, or as individual activity. Students should be taught to categorize and group information they wish to acquire.

Teacher reads the text aloud or students read the text independently.

What I Learned (L): Have students record their new learning, qualifying responses that relate to their "Want to Learn" or "Need to Learn" questions (step 2).

the keys to successful independent reading. K-W-L, SQ4R, and ReQuest are three well-established instructional approaches that have been used by many teachers to enhance students' processing of expository text.

K-W-L Many teachers use K-W-L charts, making them one of the most popular expository reading tools in the classroom. They are simple to use, build on students' prior knowledge, establish a purpose for reading, and are applicable across the curriculum (Ogle, 1986; see Table 6.12). The **K** represents what students **Know** (What do I already know about this topic?), the **W** represents **What** students wish to learn (What would I like to learn about this topic?), and the **L** represents new **Learning** (What did I learn?).

K-W-L is especially effective for encouraging students to share their ideas, beliefs, and experiences. It readily lends itself to teacher-directed activities as well as to co-operative and independent learning and can be used across the primary to intermediate grades. In fact, K-W-L charts are virtually limitless in their application. Figure 6.8 provides an example of a K-W-L chart developed by grade 2 students as part of a research project on cats. The teacher assisted the students in assembling the chart following a series of classroom discussions and guided reading sessions.

SQ4R Survey, Question, Read, Recite, Review, and Reflect is another common reading approach that has been used widely as a teacher-directed activity to promote independent reading (Robinson, 1962). The method provides students with a systematic approach for processing text and consists of the following steps:

1. **Survey (or preview).** Students read the title, introduction and headings and review illustrations while skimming the text to ascertain a general idea of its content.
2. **Question.** Students formulate questions that they believe will be answered in the text.
3. **Read.** Students read the text section, seeking responses to the posed questions.
4. **Recite.** Students share responses to questions as part of paired or independent reading.

What do I already **Know** about cats?	**What** would I like to learn about cats?	What did I **Learn** about cats?
They are soft. They come in many colours. There are big cats and little cats. Sometimes they fight. They purr when they are sleeping. We read a lot of stories about cats. They say "meow" when they are hungry. They have sharp nails that can scratch the furniture. They like to lick themselves.	Why do cats' eyes shine in the dark? How are lions and tigers different from cats that are pets? How long do cats live? Why do cats fight? Why do cats sleep so much? Do all cats say "meow"?	Cats like to hunt at night so their eyes have a lens and a mirror that bounce light back and act like reflectors so they can see better. There are many cats that cannot be pets because they are big and wild. These cats are lions, tigers, leopards, jaguars, and snow leopards. There are also smaller wild cats such as the puma, the lynx, and the bobcat. They are all much bigger than cats that are pets. Pet cats live between 14 and 20 years but some live longer. Wild cats live between 10 and 20 years. Male cats fight over females. Female cats fight to protect their babies. Cats sleep most of the day but are active in the morning and in the evening. They are used to being up at night. All cats say "meow" to communicate.

Figure 6.8 Primary Grade K-W-L Chart for Cats

5. **Review.** Students re-examine the selection to affirm what they have learned, rereading it as necessary.
6. **Reflect.** Students make notes in a journal or share findings with others to solidify and clarify learning.

For students to gain a level of automaticity, teachers need to model each step frequently through a series of mini-lessons and then provide numerous opportunities for guided practice. It is only after substantial practice that students can be expected to use this process independently.

ReQuest This instructional approach was created as a means of increasing students' understanding of text through reciprocal questioning (Lenski, Wham, & Johns, 1999; Manzo, 1969). As part of this approach, teachers must model how to ask "good" (i.e., higher-level thinking) questions related to the content of the text. Overall, this approach provides teachers with maximum flexibility, as it can be used with individuals, small groups, and whole classes. As with all strategy-based approaches, teachers begin by directing and modelling, gradually releasing control to students. The following steps provide a framework for the ReQuest instructional approach:

1. **Students generate questions.** Teacher and students read a section of expository text silently. They close their books and the teacher asks the students to pose questions related to what they have read. The teacher then responds to the questions as fully as possible based on the information provided in the text.
2. **Teacher generates questions.** Expanding on questions presented by the students, the teacher presents additional questions that raise new issues and ideas. Teacher-generated questions should help students focus on the main ideas of the text.
3. **Continued reading.** Teachers and students continue to read text silently and present additional questions.The teacher directs the nature of questions so that students recognize the relationship between information presented across text sections.
4. **Predict and set purpose for additional reading.** Teachers guide students in formulating questions that direct the remainder of the reading (e.g., What additional causal factors might be introduced next?). It is critical that teachers guide students to generate questions that can be answered by continued reading.
5. **Complete reading text.** Students complete reading the text independently.
6. **Respond and discuss.** Questioning and discussion continues after completion of the reading, with the teacher asking literal-level questions throughout this process that require students to activate their prior knowledge and provide opinions and interpretations.

Verifying Information and Comparing Sources Reading non-fiction critically is a crucial skill for effective learning. Students should not be placated into believing that everything found in print is true. They need to be encouraged to ask questions, compare sources, and evaluate what they find. Teachers can present the following questions and considerations to help students read information critically:

- How does this compare with my personal observations and experiences?
- What are the author's qualifications?
- Is the information presented as fact or opinion?
- Is the material current?
- How does the information presented compare with other books or online resources?
- Does the information presented answer the questions that prompted the search (i.e., satisfy the purpose for reading)?

PUTTING IT ALL TOGETHER: RECIPROCAL TEACHING

Comprehension instruction is most effective when instruction is "text focused" and "interactive" in nature (Applebee, Langer, Nystrand, & Gamoran, 2003; National Reading Panel, 2000; Pressley, 2006). That is, it is most effective when students exchange ideas freely among themselves and with their teachers, working collaboratively to derive and construct meaning from text. There is general acceptance that groups often derive meanings and interpretations that are beyond those produced from individual efforts. When students work collaboratively to process text, their combined efforts result in unique interpretations that no one member of the group would likely have produced independently.

Teachers must provide students with a repertoire of effective comprehension strategies as well as the knowledge and skills necessary to coordinate their use. While researchers have documented the benefits of teaching students to use and regulate individual comprehension strategies (Israel & Duffy, 2009), providing students with instruction in a combination of before-, during-, and after-reading strategies is preferable. Consider that, when processing authentic text, skilled readers rarely use comprehension strategies in a sequential or predetermined order (Reutzel, Smith, & Fawson, 2005). Rather, effective readers intentionally select and combine strategies from their existing repertoires, monitoring and adjusting their use as necessary.

Reading research supports the use of several interactive comprehension instructional approaches, including but not limited to reciprocal teaching (Palincsar & Brown, 1983), Peer-Assisted Learning Strategies (PALS; Fuchs, Fuchs, & Burish 2000), collaborative strategic reading (CSR; Klingner & Vaughn, 1999), and Concept-Oriented Reading Instruction (CORI; Guthrie & Ozgungor, 2002). Collectively, these instructional approaches emphasize the social-constructive nature of reading and the role of discussion for meaning-making. We argue that, despite being initially time consuming and requiring high levels of teacher knowledge, preparation, and engagement (Hacker & Tenent, 2002; Wharton-McDonald & Swiger, 2009), their implementation is well warranted in light of the resulting student reading gains.

More than three decades of research support the use of reciprocal teaching as an effective reading methodology for narrative and expository text. Benefits have been documented for elementary grade students, including those with learning exceptionalities (Al-Hilawani, 2003; Lederer, 2000), secondary school students (Alfassi, 2004), and those learning English as a subsequent language (Fung, Wilkinson, & Moore, 2002).

Reciprocal teaching relies on informed discussions between teachers and students (Palincsar, 1986, 2003; Palincsar & Brown, 1983). (See Figure 6.9 for a reciprocal teaching lesson plan.) These discussions are supported by the use of four reading comprehension strategies: (1) predicting, (2) questioning, (3) clarifying, and (4) summarizing. Collectively, these strategies have been referred to as the "Fabulous Four" (Oczkus, 2003; see Figure 6.10). Others have extended the model to include a fifth component: critical analysis (Ash, 2002).

Predicting is an ongoing process that requires readers to form "best guesses" about text content based on their prior knowledge and clues gathered from previewing the text (e.g., titles, headers, tables, diagrams, and illustrations). Predictions often take the form of "I" questions, such as *I think*, *I bet*, *I wonder if*, *I imagine*, and *I suppose*, with teachers directing students to reflect on their predictions throughout the reading process.

Questioning involves forming and responding to higher-level thinking questions. Working with partners or by themselves, students take turns assuming the role of "teacher" and presenting their peers with questions related to the main idea of the text. Prior to independent work, teachers provide students with modelled instruction and guidance in generating questions based on the prompts *who*, *what*, *where*, *when*, *why*, *how*, and *what if*.

While many students can identify unfamiliar terms and phrases in the text, they experience greater difficulty identifying larger sections of text that require clarification. In part, these difficulties often reflect students' abilities to decode words without grasping the central idea or larger meaning of the text. Clarifying involves using "fix-up" strategies

Unit Study: Heat in the Environment

Materials: *Investigating Science & Technology 7* by Pearson Education Canada.

Objective: Students will be able to use the strategies of predicting, questioning, clarifying, and summarizing while processing text related to temperature and thermometers. Students should demonstrate an understanding of text and provide a summary of the reading.

Assessment: Students will complete a semantic web summarizing the main ideas associated with the reading about temperature and thermometers. Students will be able to identify unfamiliar vocabulary and concepts and provide a definition of these terms.

Predicting

Ask students about how to make predictions. What clues from the textbook can they use to form predictions? Ask students to explain how making predictions prepares them for the reading task.

1. Have student groups create and record their predictions for the text. Remind them to review captions and illustrations.
2. Have groups share their predictions with each other. Construct a Venn diagram documenting students' common and unique predictions.
3. Have students read the text while confirming (or repudiating) their predictions.
4. Monitor students' predictions, providing assistance as necessary.
5. Have students reflect on how creating predictions can help them while reading.

Questioning

Explain to students that making and answering questions about the text will help them understand it. Ask students about the types of questions they can generate. Ask students to share experiences where they have formulated questions to "test" their understanding of information contained in the text.

1. Provide students with the following question prompts: *who*, *what*, *where*, *when*, *why*, *how*, and *what if*. Have students work with a partner to compose questions for each prompt.
2. Have students review text and record answers to their questions.
3. Have student pairs share questions and responses.
4. Ask students to share ideas about how to create good questions.
5. Monitor student groups, providing assistance as necessary.

Clarifying

Explain to the students that clarifying unfamiliar concepts and words in the text is critical to helping them understand the text. Ask students to review how they can deduce the meaning of unknown words and concepts.

1. Have students work in pairs to record any unfamiliar words and ideas.
2. Have student pairs exchange lists of unfamiliar words and ideas to create a master list for the classroom. Provide students with the following sentence starters:

   I didn't understand the part where . . .

   This (sentence, paragraph, page, chapter) is not clear . . .

   This doesn't make sense . . .

   I can't figure out . . .

(continued)

Figure 6.9 Reciprocal Teaching Lesson Plan

3. Review unfamiliar terms as a whole class and have students provide definitions whenever possible.
4. Have students work in pairs to review the text for any remaining items and concepts.
5. Have students share and discuss any remaining definitions, providing clarification as needed. Provide definitions for any remaining terms.
6. Have students reflect on the process of clarifying unknown words and concepts. What strategies and techniques did they use when clarifying? Were they better able to understand the text once they had clarified unknown items?

Summarizing

Explain to students that creating summaries of text will help them remember information in the text better and will provide them with a valuable study tool. Also explain that it is often easier to create summaries for smaller sections of text versus whole chapters. Remind students that it important to record only the most important points from the text. Ask students how they can make decisions about what information to include in their summaries; that is, how do they differentiate between important and less important ideas?

1. Place students in groups of four.
2. Provide students with the following sentence starters:

   The most important ideas in this text are . . .

   This part was about . . .

   The first time students summarize they should use these prompts to summarize:

   First. . . , Next . . . , Then . . .
3. Using the first few paragraphs of the text, model the steps for completing the graphic organizer and generating a summary.
4. Provide students with a blank organizer and assign a single page of text to each group. Monitor students' work as they complete this task, providing students with guiding questions and prompts to have them record the most relevant ideas contained in the text.
5. Review each group's completed summary as a class. Discuss whether the most important ideas have been recorded and revise the summaries as needed.
6. Combine the summaries to create a master summary for the text.
7. Have students reflect on the process of creating a summary and determining the most important ideas contained in the text. Were they able to differentiate between main ideas and supporting details?

Source: Developed by Chelsey Smith, primary and junior teacher and M.Ed. candidate.

Figure 6.9 Reciprocal Teaching Lesson Plan *(continued)*

such as word attack strategies, rereading, activating prior knowledge, and asking a friend to illuminate the meaning of unfamiliar words, concepts, and phrases.

Summarizing requires students to paraphrase the most important ideas contained in the text. Teachers provide mini-lessons intended to prevent students from providing word-by-word retellings and use relevant prompts such as *The most important idea is* and *This part was about.*

Typically, each strategy is introduced as part of whole-class instruction, with teachers scaffolding instruction as part of small-group instruction. Over time, students are encouraged to use the strategies independently as part of literature circles and other inquiry-based activities.

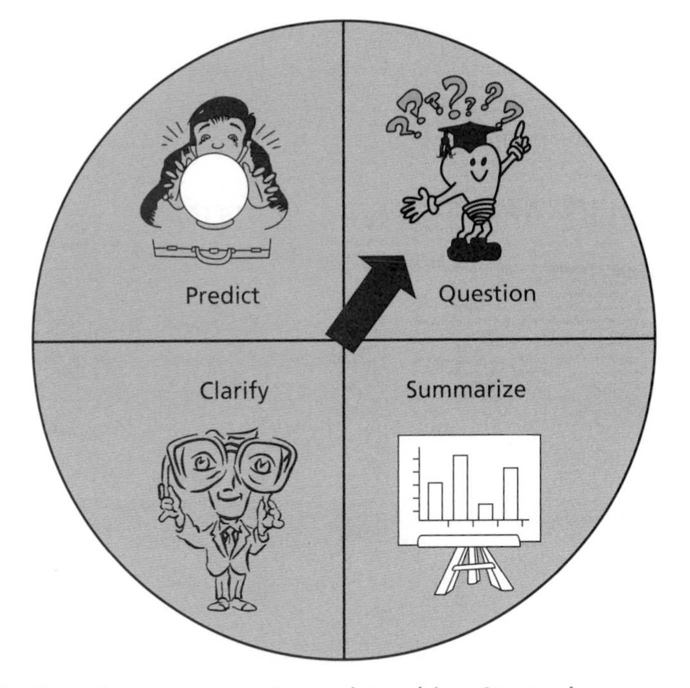

Figure 6.10 "Fabulous Four" Reciprocal Teaching Strategies

Source: Adapted from Oczkus (2003).

During whole-class instruction, the teacher uses Think Aloud to model the use of all four strategies as a collective. As part of this process, teachers call on students to verify the accuracy of the teacher's thinking processes and make alternative suggestions with respect to strategy use (e.g., teacher provides a summary of the paragraph and students respond as to whether summary is accurate and succinct, teacher asks questions about paragraph and students evaluate quality of questions and provide responses). The teacher also provides metacognitive information about "when" and "why" to use each strategy.

The use of labels and prompts is especially helpful when identifying strategic processes for students in the primary grades. For example, when working with primary grade students, reading researcher Lori Oczkus (2003) recommends presenting each strategy through characters. For instance, Madam the Predictor wears beads and long gloves and works with a crystal ball to make predictions about text content. Quincy the Questioner assumes the persona of a game-show host and uses a microphone to quiz contestants about text content. Clara the Clarifier wears a feather boa and large glasses while searching for context cues about the meaning of unknown words and phrases, while Sammy the Super Summarizer possesses a cowboy hat and lasso to "round in" main ideas. To develop students' metacognitive development, teachers end the lesson by having students reflect on their success in using each strategy and how particular strategies enhanced their understanding of the text

Students' acquisition of the "Fabulous Four" is further strengthened during small-group instruction when teachers work with flexible groupings (e.g., mixed ability, strategy need, students' choice) of four to six students to process levelled text. During these sessions, students share their thinking processes while using the strategies and gradually assume the role of "teacher," providing their peers with feedback. Students also assume responsibility for reflection, sharing, and prompting each other to associate comprehension gains with strategy use. Students continue to practise using these strategies during literacy circles and other structured group-based reading practices. See Table 6.13 for additional instructional repertoires.

STUDY SKILLS AND REPORT WRITING

Study Strategies

PALS: A reading strategy for grades 2 to 6

Students need to possess a repertoire of effective study skills to be successful learners. Unfortunately, teachers often assume that students have developed good study skills. While some students manage to acquire such skills independently, the majority benefit from explicit instruction in this area, especially with respect to processing and retaining

Table 6.13 Other Instructional Repertoires

Peer-Assisted Learning Strategies (PALS)

Overview

- Whole-class tutoring program designed to supplement regular language arts programming
- Effective for primary through secondary school students, including English-language learners, low-ability learners, and students with learning disabilities
- Teacher models reading comprehension strategies and provides guided practice
- Teacher places students in pairs, partnering higher-level readers with lower-level ones
- Students select reading materials that correspond to the instructional level of the less-able reader

Steps

1. **Partner Reading with Recall**

   More-skilled peer reads text aloud for about 10 minutes, modelling relevant word recognition, decoding, and reading comprehension strategies

   Less-skilled reader then rereads the same passage aloud and provides a retelling of the passage

2. **Paragraph Shrinking**

   Students record the main idea of each paragraph in 10 words or less

3. **Prediction Relay**

   Students create and check predictions for each half-page of text

   Students repeat steps for the remainder of the text

   Teacher reviews process with whole class

Collaborative Strategy Reading (CSR)

Overview

- Expands on the procedures of reciprocal teaching and co-operative learning
- Effective for all students
- Teacher models reading comprehension strategies and provides guided practice through co-operative learning activities
- Students are assigned to mixed-ability groups and assume specific roles (e.g., leader, clunk expert, gist announcer, recorder, timekeeper)
- Students rotate through each role

Steps

1. **Preview**

   Students activate relevant prior knowledge (brainstorm) and generate predictions

2. **Monitor for Understanding**

   Students identify "clinks and clunks" while reading

   Clink = information that is understood

   Clunk = information that is not understood and requires using a "fix-up" strategy (e.g., rereading, word analysis, context clues)

3. **Identify Main Ideas**

   Students ask critical questions such as *Who/what is this about*? *What is most important about the who/what*?

4. **Summarize**

   Students represent new learning using graphic organizers and other representation

   Students complete CSR learning logs, engage in whole-class discussion, and participate in reteaching or extension activities

   Teacher circulates to monitor student groups, reteaching and guiding as necessary

   Teacher reviews process with whole class

Concept-Oriented Reading Instruction (CORI)

Overview

- Emphasis on comprehension strategies and student motivation through inquiry-based learning
- Suitable for whole-class instruction, small-group instruction, paired reading, and independent reading*
- Effective for upper primary and middle grade students
- Teacher provides direct instruction, guided practice, and independent use
- Teacher articulates knowledge goals to students and provides them with real-world experiences
- Reading comprehension strategies include: (a) activating prior knowledge, (b) questioning, (c) searching, (d) summarizing, and (e) representing information graphically

Steps

1. **Observe and Personalize**

   Students activate prior knowledge to help establish inquiry-based goals for unit

   Students formulate questions based on their observations and interests

2. **Search and Retrieve**

   Students research topics using texts and media resources

   Teachers provide explicit instruction in use of relevant strategies

3. **Comprehend and Integrate**

   Students use strategies to process new information

   Students use graphic organizers to share new learning and create summaries

   Students relate new learning to topics and questions of personal interest

4. **Communicate**

   Students communicate new learning (e.g., chapter book, storybook, information book, persuasive essay, multimedia presentation)

*Students gain autonomy through material selection

Source: Adapted from Israel and Duffy (2009).

information from expository materials. Students who possess such skills can apply them to optimize their reading time and maximize their learning. Building strong study strategies, habits, and attitudes is time well spent in the classroom, as resulting gains can influence students' future academic successes. Teachers can acknowledge the importance of these processes by providing academic credit for their identification and use (e.g., giving credit on a test describing study strategies, providing credit for first drafts or study notes). In the following section, study guides, learning logs, mnemonics, and note taking will be described.

Study Guides Teacher-generated study guides can be used to help students identify the most important information contained in the texts. They can also be used to provide students with the criteria for culminating tests or tasks. Students are less likely to second-guess their teachers with respect to critical content. The use of study guides can help reduce students' text anxiety (Alvermann & Phelps, 1998; Tierney & Readence, 2005). Teachers should follow the steps outlined below when developing study guides:

1. Select a text, internet site, or other information source.
2. Provide students with an objective or reason for reading.
3. Identify key concepts, clarify language, and provide relevant background knowledge.
4. Develop a set of questions for students to complete while reading the text.
5. Provide students with a copy of the questions, allowing space for them to record their notes as they read. If appropriate, provide space for students to record new learning. Teachers should also provide space for students to record any questions as a result of reading the text.
6. Discuss responses in either large or small groups, with teachers clarifying and elaborating information as discussed.

At the completion of this process, students should have developed a set of extensive notes that can be used for future reference or when preparing for a test.

Student Voice 6.2

Studying helps you do well on tests. When I study, I copy down the main titles and important information. Then I will reread the information and write it again. Sometimes I use a study sheet from the teacher or make up my own questions. I expect that I will have a lot more studying to do when I am in high school.

Josh
Grade 8 student

Caution There are several limitations associated with study guides. First, the construction of effective study guides is time consuming and effortful, with teachers encouraged to work collaboratively in the development. Furthermore, study guides are teacher-directed and students do not make decisions about the focus or importance of text concepts. Over time, study guides should be less teacher-directed and prescriptive and increasingly open-ended (Tierney & Readence, 2005). An interim step is to have students complete open-ended study guides, with teachers providing content emphasis as necessary.

Learning Logs Learning logs are a simple way to help students form connections between their feelings or emotional responses and content learning. Teachers who use learning logs believe that students learn more by writing about personal reactions and thinking processes than by recording new content only. Generally, learning logs are completed at the end of a class, week, or unit. They provide students with a resource for recording research findings as they explore new topics. As part of this journal, they record new information acquired from books, articles, and other sources. Over time, the log can be used to help students solidify and organize new learning. Mathematics teachers have found it helpful for students to integrate learning logs into the math class, as they can articulate their thoughts about new math concepts. It is helpful to see that math is not just about numbers and rigid answers but also a process and a dialogue. Sometimes teachers encourage students to draw a line at the bottom of the journal and then use the space underneath to record reflections, questions, and related ideas. While learning logs are not used for evaluation, they can help teachers assess students' learning experiences (Barchers, 1994). Teachers also can use students' learning logs as the basis for student-teacher conferences.

Mnemonics A mnemonic device is a learning aid that can help students remember a critical fact or series of facts. Basically, mnemonics help students create associations between easy-to-remember or already-known constructs and to-be-learned information. While the association is often illogical or arbitrary, the process of using mnemonics facilitates retention of the concept. In general, mnemonics are either verbal or visual in nature.

Verbal Mnemonics Acronyms are one common and popular type of verbal mnemonic. For instance, the ordered colours of the rainbow (red, orange, yellow, green, blue, indigo, and violet) can be remembered by using the first letters of each colour to create the name *Roy G. Biv*. This acronym is short and relatively easy to remember and serves as a clue to recalling the ordered colours of a rainbow. Another popular acronym mnemonic is HOMES, used to help students remember the five Great Lakes (Huron, Ontario, Michigan, Erie, and Superior). Another widely used example of a verbal mnemonic is the following poem:

> Thirty days has September, April, June, and November
> All the rest have thirty-one
> Except February . . .

Visual Mnemonics Visual mnemonics are another approach used to remember important facts. Visual mnemonics work by associating an image or a character whose name sounds like the item that must be memorized. One example of a visual mnemonic is that a Bactrian camel's back is shared like a B (two humps) and a dromedary camel's back is shaped like a D (one hump). Another example is the phases of the moon, or DOC, where D stands for the waxing moon, O is the full moon, and C stands for the waning moon: *Dog comes in (the room) and Cat goes out.*

Note Taking When completed effectively, note taking assists students to organize lesson content and provides them with a means for reviewing content information. Unfortunately, note-taking skills are not associated with any subject area per se, with some teachers seemingly assuming that students will acquire this important skill independently. This assumption is faulty and there are many benefits of providing students with direct instruction in note taking. Having students complete notes increases their involvement in class, reinforces their learning, and provides a method for reviewing critical information quickly. Learning to take good notes is particularly relevant for students in the junior and intermediate grades who are preparing for secondary school (Manzo, Manzo, & Thomas, 2009). In its simplest form, note taking consists of three steps:

1. Recording
2. Organizing
3. Studying

Recording Recording notes are completed throughout a lesson. Eventually students may develop their own style and variation on recording their notes but it is important initially for teachers to suggest and guide students at each stage of the note-taking process. One approach is to have students leave an eight-centimetre margin on each page for comments and questions. Some experts suggest that students should write on only one side of the paper and should number each page carefully (Tierney & Readence, 2005).

Organizing Organizingnotes is most effective when time is provided immediately after class. It is the organization of the notes that makes them useful as an aid to learning and for study purposes. Organizational skills include:

1. Using headings
2. Grouping subtopics under headings
3. Use of abbreviations
4. Producing a written summary

When organizing, students should be directed to label various notes in the margin. By labelling, students are grouping ideas and identifying important content. At this time students can add any information they have missed. These additions can also be placed in the margins. If there is insufficient space, students can use the blank back of the page.

Studying Studying should be modelled by teachers prior to a test or task. As part of this process, teachers need to identify the nature of the evaluation process (e.g., short answer, matching, fill-in-the-blank). By providing class time for studying, teachers reinforce the importance of this activity and the utility of maintaining good notes.

Debriefing after the test or task also provides students with the opportunity to discuss how they applied their learning. In addition, they should be encouraged to reflect on their study processes and strategies and evaluate which worked well for them. Finally, students should develop a plan for studying in the future, identifying specific strategies and processes that they will use again. This debriefing process is especially helpful in reinforcing the value of using reading strategies and study skills.

Report Writing

It is important to teach students across the grades how to write effective reports, both as part of a group and individually. Reports are written on content area topics that vary according to curriculum expectations, but generally reports revolve around big topics and big ideas. Each student or group of students may report on an aspect or part of a topic. These components are then compiled and become a large class report. The report-writing process includes collecting data through interviews, books, and the internet. Even young students should be encouraged to transform their reports into multimedia presentations. Basically, students either collaboratively or individually learn where to search for answers to questions about a topic (one created by either the group or the teacher) and write a report to share what they have learned with others. Even though there are myriad ways to structure these sessions, teachers need to model and scaffold report-writing skills in the same manner as other reading skills.

Collaborative Reports The following six steps will help students work together in a structured manner to produce a collaborative report.

1. **Select a topic.** After the teacher has introduced the general topic (e.g., Confederation, Egyptian studies, Middle Ages), students work in pairs or small co-operative learning groups (four to six students) to determine which parts or specific aspects of the topic they will research and report on (e.g., culture, social hierarchies, religion, habitats). It is important that students assume ownership of their choices to enhance their motivation to complete the inquiry process.
2. **Brainstorm research questions.** Teachers have students work in pairs or small groups to develop questions they would like to answer during their research project. Many teachers will want to review students' research questions to ensure that they are comprehensive and relevant to the research process. Teachers may also use this as an opportunity to review resources that students plan to consult.
3. **Gather and organize information.** This is the stage of collaborative work when students will need to determine who will do what. Here, the questions prepared earlier are paramount, as the information students are researching should be quite specific. The questions can serve as task and data organizers as well. This stage takes time and the teacher may want to have the group choose a leader to direct the negotiation. Inevitably, some tasks are either easier or perceived to be more "fun" than others and the teacher should be prepared to help with the negotiation of tasks if necessary.

   Students conduct their research using books and textbooks, videos, films, the internet (i.e., Wikipedia), CD-ROMs, field trips, interviews, or observations. Many teachers set a minimum prerequisite of three sources. Students need to be reminded that "copying" directly from a source is plagiarism and therefore "wrong."
4. **Draft report.** Using the writing process as a guide, students write a rough draft of their report. At this time, they need to make decisions about how to display their data. Proofreading and correcting the mechanics of their reports are also important components of the drafting process. Considerable class time will be required to accomplish this step and teachers need to conference either formally or informally with each group.
5. **Compile.** After each group has completed its draft, the teacher collects the reports and merges them into one document. The references for each question should be identified. A whole-class Read Aloud can identify redundancies and inconsistencies in the document before the final version is compiled.
6. **Publish.** Each student should receive a copy of the final report. A copy can be bound and placed in the classroom and school library, if appropriate.

Individual Reports Preparing an individual report is similar to preparing a collaborative report, with two distinct differences. First, students should choose their own topic-related questions, with these questions being somewhat narrower in scope than those established by a group. Second, the work should be the complete responsibility of the individual student.

SELF-EVALUATION AND PEER EVALUATION

Self-evaluation encourages the practice of reviewing personal work and being reflective about it. Teachers need to guide students to ask themselves questions such as "What do I like best about my work?" or "What would I change if I could only change one thing?" as they complete the unit. These informal self-evaluations can be done orally as part of teacher-student conferences or be written reflections. Alternatively, checklists can be provided and used for self-evaluation, peer evaluation, and teacher evaluation. These checklists can be completed separately or on the same sheet of paper; the discrepancies between all assessors can aid the reflective process and help students strive to improve in identified areas (see Figure 6.11).

Peer evaluation encourages students to work together, thus making the classroom less teacher-directed and moving students toward becoming independent learners. Social skills play a large role in peer interactions and are developed through this process. It is important to remember that, like any other skill, evaluation of one's peers is developmental and requires structure and monitoring. Students need models of how to offer

Before Reading	**Yes**	**Sometimes**	**I Forgot**
1. I read the title and the introductory paragraph.			
2. I read all headings and the final summary.			
3. I looked at all maps, charts, graphs, and photos.			
4. I predicted what the text would be about.			
5. I identified questions that I thought the text would answer.			
During Reading	**Yes**	**Sometimes**	**I Forgot**
1. I read to answer my questions.			
2. After each section, I stopped to see if my questions had been answered.			
3. I formed pictures in my mind as I read.			
4. I reread any parts I did not understand immediately.			
5. I used the surrounding words and pictures to help me understand any new vocabulary.			
6. I used the headings, maps, and charts to help me understand the text.			
After Reading	**Yes**	**Sometimes**	**I Forgot**
1. I went back to see what was the most important information in the text.			
2. I thought about whether all of my questions had been answered.			
3. I thought about what I still wanted to know about the topic.			

Figure 6.11 Self-Evaluation Strategy Checklist for Expository Text

supportive comments and gentle suggestions for improvement. Teacher-led demonstrations, modelling, and dramatizations are effective methods of initiating discussions about how to be an effective peer evaluator. Foundational principles need to be discussed and agreed on as part of these sessions, including the following:

- Everyone's ideas are valued.
- Students are expected to listen to each other respectfully.
- Comments and suggestions need to be relevant to the topic at hand.
- Some positive statements must be made.
- Suggestions for improvement must be offered.
- Everyone is expected to consider and respond to the suggestions and comments provided by peers (although these do not need to be incorporated into the final product per se).

One method of assisting students to become good peer evaluators is to prepare a focused response sheet. Throughout this process, the teacher needs to remain observant and vigilant, albeit in the background. At times, it may be necessary to join peer sessions to gently guide and direct the discussion so it remains focused, positive, and helpful. The final component is a teacher-led debriefing about how well the peer evaluation process functioned.

SUGGESTIONS FOR PROFESSIONAL DEVELOPMENT

1. Explore a historical event or topic from multiple perspectives. For instance, include a Middle Eastern perspective as part a traditional unit exploring medieval times or a First Nations perspective on the Truth and Reconciliation Commission of Canada. Alternatively, explore other events such as the internment of Japanese Canadians in British Columbia during World War II or the 1992 constitutional referendum from the perspectives of Japanese Canadians, Québécois, First Nations, and other Canadians. Provide students with varied texts when exploring each topic, highlighting the importance of the author's perspective.
2. Start a study club, study group, or homework support club for students. Provide students with strategic instruction while completing assignments and projects or preparing for tests. Have students explore websites on study guides and strategies such as www.studygs.net, www.how-to-study.com, and www.educationatlas.com/study-skills.html.
3. Bring a copy of the local newspaper to class and have students explore articles of interest. Many local newspapers provide schools with reduced fees for classroom subscriptions. You can also explore magazine subscriptions and online websites designed for young readers, including those studying abroad (for an excellent listing of many free or subsidized online resources, see www.shambles.net/pages/students/OLmags).
4. Explore online and multimedia educational resources such as Historica (www.historica), designed to promote the teaching and learning of Canadian history and heritage; Cool Science (www.hhmi.org/coolscience), which is written for students and

emphasizes science around the home; and the Canadian website Let's Talk Science (www.letstalkscience.ca). Acquire and develop a collection of non-print expository resources that can be incorporated into your daily lessons.

CHILDREN'S LITERATURE REFERENCES

Aliki.(1989). *My five senses*. New York, NY: Collins.

Berger, M. (1995). *A whale is not a fish and other animal mix-ups*. Toronto, ON: Scholastic.

Busby, P. (2003). *First to fly*. New York, NY: Crown Books for Young Readers.

Faulkner, M., & Randall, W. (2004). *A day at the sugar bush*. Toronto, ON: Scholastic Canada.

Greenwood, B. (1998). *A pioneer story: The daily life of a Canadian pioneer family in 1840*. Toronto, ON: Kids Can Press.

Hehner, B. (2001). *Ice Age mammoth*. Toronto, ON: Scholastic Canada.

Johnston, M. (1996). *Dealing with bullying*. New York, NY: The Rosen Publishing Group.

Leedy, L. (1991). *The furry news: How to make a newspaper*. New York, NY: Holiday House.

Levine, K. (2002). *Hana's suitcase*. Toronto, ON: Second Story Press.

Lunn, J. (2001). *Laura Secord: A story of courage*. Toronto, ON: Tundra Books.

Moore, C., & Lunn, J. (1995). *The story of Canada*. Toronto, ON: Key Porter Books.

Morris, N. (1998). *Earthquakes*. St. Catharines, ON: Crabtree Publishing.

Owl Magazine. (1993). *The new kid's question and answer book: Questions kids ask about nature, science and the environment*. Toronto, ON: Maple Leaf Press.

Pringle, L. P. (2003). *Global warming*. San Francisco, CA: Chronicle Books.

Ripley, C. (2004). *Why?: The best ever question and answer book about nature, science and the world around you*. Toronto, ON: Maple Tree Press.

Rowan. J. P. (1983). *Butterflies and moths*. Toronto, ON: Scholastic Canada.

Simon, S. (1992). *Storms*. New York, NY: HarperCollins.

Squire A. (2004). *Crickets and grasshoppers*. Toronto, ON: Scholastic Canada.

Suzuki, D. (1986). *Looking at insects*. Toronto, ON: Stoddart Publishing Company Limited.

Suzuki, D. (1985). *Looking at plants*. Toronto, ON: Stoddart Publishing Company Limited.

Taylor, B. (2001). *How to save the planet*. New York, NY: Oxford University Press.

Walker, K. (2009). *Mysteries of water monsters*. St. Catharines, ON: Crabtree Publishing Company.

Wollard, K., & Solomon, D. (1999). *How come? Planet Earth*. New York, NY: Workman Publishing.

MyEducationLab

MyEducationLab is an interactive, virtual learning tool that will help improve your understanding of the concepts taught in this textbook and in your course. Through this engaging resource, you will have access to simulations of real classroom experiences, exercises that will help you improve your knowledge of key concepts, and additional resources that will help you in your teaching career. Use this online tool with your textbook to help you succeed in your studies and beyond!

Chapter 7

Writing: Exploring the Reading and Writing Connection

Learning Objectives

In this chapter you will discover

- How reading and writing are connected.
- How to implement the writing process.
- How to implement a variety of writing formats in the classroom.
- How to use technology to enhance student writing.
- How to assess students' writing.
- How to conduct a teacher-student writing conference.
- How to establish a writers' workshop.
- How to create a community of writers.

LINDA OUT: COMMITTED READING AND WRITING EDUCATOR

Linda Out teaches a grades 3 and 4 split class with 24 students in a small school in British Columbia. Located in a rural community, Linda's school has kindergarten to grade 6 with about 80 students divided among four classrooms. As someone who has taught in small communities for her entire career, she is familiar with the juggling required to teach split grades. Linda believes that the best way to address the breadth of curriculum expectations is to adopt an integrated curriculum and to be flexible. For instance, she regularly integrates her social studies program with her literacy program and makes connections between her science and math programs.

Linda is particularly proud of her students' achievements in reading and writing. She is eager to ensure that her students enjoy reading and are able to respond appropriately to text in oral and written formats. When she became concerned that students were not staying on task during silent reading, which was scheduled immediately after lunch, she began reading *Tuck Everlasting* aloud. Students then engaged in a form of reading response that required them to create postcards, retelling and summarizing the story from a first-person rather than third-person perspective.

Linda's philosophy includes being honest with students, helping them raise the bar for their performance, and providing them with choices so they can be creative. Many of her activities have an open-ended aspect that enables students to feel empowered. This approach accommodates different ability and skill levels.

The writing program in Linda's class is well designed and extensive. She always starts a writing task by conducting a brainstorming session and then working with students to set criteria for the writing task. For instance, when students wrote creation myths, they brainstormed story elements. When they wrote about the future, they brainstormed about innovative transportation and communication systems.

Linda then places the students in pairs and has them complete a "walk and talk" exercise (ideally outdoors) during which students listen to each other, share their writing ideas, and report to her on their partner's ideas. "I believe that when you explain your ideas to someone, you maximize your thinking." Students then return to the classroom to complete a graphic organizer for their writing. "I think the initial steps are important. It provides that processing time where ideas start to gel." A great deal of the thinking is accomplished before these students ever begin to write.

It is not until the next day that the students begin writing. The revising and editing processes take place throughout the remainder of the week. Linda reads each student's writing draft using a colour-coding system for her edits. Students know that parts marked in green are "good to go," yellow indicates an area that needs revision, and red indicates that grammar, spelling, and cohesion need to be corrected. Linda also believes in the value of peer editing, but cautions that students must be taught *how* to edit for this process to be effective. "You can't assume that just because two students are together that they can edit, unless they have had practice. At this level, students really need feedback from me if they are going to improve their writing." Linda believes that her efforts to provide feedback raise the bar for her students' writing ability. She notes that her students are generally very proud of the final version of their writing.

REFLECTIVE ACTIVITY

Ask a middle grade student (10 to 14 years old) to write a short composition or essay on a topic of his choice. Do not provide any parameters with respect to completion time, length, or format. Ask him to "think aloud" as he completes the activity, observing his actions carefully and reflecting on the following questions:

- Does he establish a writing goal (e.g., to persuade, to describe)?
- Does he consider the intended audience?
- Does he brainstorm and reflect on his lived experiences and world knowledge? Does he access additional sources for relevant information?
- Does he plan or organize the presentation of information?
- Does he appear to "dump" or "knowledge tell" thoughts and ideas as quickly as possible?
- Does he spend considerable time and energy revising spelling, grammar, and punctuation?
- Does he produce more than one draft? If so, what is the nature of any changes in the composition?
- Reflect on your own approach to writing. In what ways are the student's efforts similar to your own? In what ways are they different?

Now compare your observations with those of writing researchers who have documented students' natural compositions:

- Students typically do not establish a purpose for their writing. They rarely consider the purpose for their compositions or their intended audience.
- Students typically do not generate sufficient content for their writing. They rarely activate relevant prior knowledge or seek additional content information irrespective of its availability or accessibility.
- Students typically rush to record as much information as possible when writing, giving little consideration to its coherence or flow.
- Students typically present poor sentence construction and spelling. Their handwriting and keyboarding skills are often weak.
- Students typically do not complete drafts of their writing, with their first products often being their final compositions.

Research reveals that very few students engage in any pre-writing, planning, brainstorming, rereading, or editing activities (Scardamalia, 1981), with this being especially true for younger students and students with learning exceptionalities (Troia, 2006). More positively, there is substantial evidence suggesting that, with relatively modest prompting, students can be redirected to be goal-oriented and strategic in their writing, focusing their efforts on content and meaning (Bradley, 2001; Burns, 2001; Jones, 2003; McCutchen, 2006; Perez, 2001; Pritchard & Honeycutt, 2006; Rowe, 2008). These results reinforce the importance of teaching students of all ages and abilities about strategies associated with the writing process (De La Paz & Graham, 2002; MacArthur, Graham, & Harris, 2004; Perry & Drummond, 2002).

THE NATURE OF WRITING AND WRITING INSTRUCTION

Interactive writing

IN CONTRAST TO READING, WRITING IS A HIGHLY PERSONAL AND CREATIVE ACTIVITY that often serves to shape thinking and learning (Stewig & Nordberg, 1994). Through writing, students discover connections, raise questions, and describe processes, which in turn serve to deepen their understanding of a topic. Although sometimes appearing in curriculum guides and program plans as separate subjects, writing and reading are related processes and learning in one area supports learning in the other. These processes employ many of the same skills and strategies so that students can apply what they have learned in one area to another area.

With the dynamic role of technology in today's society, the functions and forms of written expression are changing. Writing can be a form of social communication, have a functional purpose (e.g., a grocery list or directions, an attempt to persuade), or be an expression of inner thought. Writing plays an important function in people's work and personal lives and thus takes a central place in the literacy curriculum.

In Canada, there is general unanimity across the provinces in terms of expectations for classroom instruction of writing. (See Table 7.1 for characteristics of effective writing teachers.) In Quebec, a student should be "comfortable expressing his or her views, ideas and needs to others" (English Language Arts, www.mels.gouv.qc.ca/REFORME/publications/Prog_form_primaire_a.htm). In Nova Scotia, "learning to write is a process

Table 7.1 Characteristics of Effective Writing Teachers

- They create a classroom rich in print.
- They recognize that students learn best in environments that are engaging and positive and encourage students to play with language.
- They observe and monitor students' writing regularly, responding to individual student needs as required.
- They possess a repertoire of effective instructional techniques and strategies. They plan direct instruction to accommodate student needs and identify "teachable moments" as part of whole-class, small-group, or individual instruction.
- They encourage students to notice and explore language patterns in oral and print forms.
- They praise student success in a genuine manner.
- They demonstrate a contagious enthusiasm and love of language.

that involves thinking and composing, considering audience and purpose, choosing a form and using the conventions of written language" (https://sapps.ednet.ns.ca/Cart/items.php?CA=1&UID=20090105052535). In Manitoba's Curriculum Framework of Outcomes and Standards, writing is described as part of a balanced program in which writing skills enable "students to explore, shape, and clarify their thoughts and to communicate them to others" (www.edu.gov.mb.ca/k12/cur/ela/docs/frameworks-ktosl.html). In Ontario,

> Writing . . . provides students with powerful opportunities to learn about themselves and their connections to the world. Through writing, students organize their thoughts, remember important information, solve problems, reflect on a widening range of perspectives and learn how to communicate effectively for specific purposes and audiences. . . . Writing also helps students to better understand their own thoughts and feelings and the events of their lives. (The Ontario Curriculum, 2006, p. 12)

The Reading–Writing Connection

It is critical for teachers to understand that the connection between reading and writing is mutually supportive and that learning in reading improves writing and vice versa (Gunning, 2005). Consequently, reading and writing are seldom taught as separate subjects. Rather, they are interdependent components of a balanced language arts program.

One effective method for enhancing the reading-writing connection is to spend time daily reading and writing about authentic events (Allington, 2006; Pressley, Allington, Wharton-McDonald, Block, & Morrow, 2001). In the primary grades, the morning might begin with the teacher collaboratively writing a morning message with the class. In the junior or intermediate grades, the teacher might read an interesting article from the newspaper or the internet and have students respond in their journals, which are subsequently shared with others. Integrated reading and writing activities should connect to students' lives. Just as reading should appear in several forms, from reading aloud to silent independent reading, writing should also take several forms, from private journals to writing for an audience. As with reading, teachers need to appreciate the importance of modelling and participate in writing activities with their students whenever possible.

Gender Differences in Writing

Gender differences in school achievement have received much attention in recent years (Martino & Kehler, 2007; Younger, Warrington. & McLellan, 2005). The contemporary classroom is often a verbal-emotive world, which is less suited to the learning of boys than the learning of girls. Educators have noted repeatedly that school environments, especially in the primary grades, are feminized and that average boys struggle to meet the academic expectations of a curriculum that emphasizes reading, writing, and verbal ability—especially when these activities do not relate well to their abilities or interests (Rowe, 2008). Not surprisingly, many girls are more confident than their male peers with respect to their writing abilities (Pajares & Valiante, 1999).

It is important that teachers are aware of the ways in which boys' and girls' writings differ, with this potentially being especially true for students from marginalized groups or communities (Peterson, 2006). In general, boys prefer to write about adventures and events beyond their immediate experiences. They tend to produce action-based compositions (with or without violence) with main characters who often act alone. Their writings usually contain few female characters, and these characters assume passive roles when they are present (Anderson, 2003; Newkirk, 2000). (See Table 7.2 for suggestions for helping boys to write.) Girls, in contrast, tend to prefer writing about events within their experiences, including interactions with friends and family. Their work is more likely to be social in nature, with characters who work collaboratively (Anderson, 2003).

All students' writing performances can improve as a function of explicit instruction in the use of effective writing processes and strategies as well as opportunities to work collaboratively with others (Hidi, Berndorff, & Ainley, 2002). We describe the nature of such instruction next.

Table 7.2 Helping Boys to Write

1. Establish collaborative writing projects (i.e., ask two or three boys to research a topic that interests them, collect pictures as well as information, and create a presentation for the class).
2. Keep verbal instructions brief.
3. Use male mentors and role models such as fathers, grandfathers, and male teachers or administrators.
4. Make your writing assignments authentic and related to boys' interests; for example, have them assume the identity of a TV broadcaster and write a report for an important sports event, or establish a mystery bag and have students write a murder mystery using all of the items as clues.
5. Incorporate the use of the internet and other technology as part of the writing program.
6. Praise students' successes and improvements.

THE WRITING PROCESS

During the 1960s and 1970s, writing was taught as a process of encoding speech into print, with an emphasis on teaching spelling, grammar, and handwriting. Writing was viewed as a series of separate skill sets, and each skill was taught in an isolated manner. In the 1980s, educators came to view writing as a craft, largely as a result of the work of Donald Graves (1983, 1994, 2003) and others (Atwell, 1998; Calkins, 1994, 2009; Murray, 2001) who viewed writing as a process. Writing was recognized as a complex set of skills that focused on the three cueing systems—graphophonics (command of print code), syntax (grammar), and semantics (meaning making)—plus the physical process of creating print (i.e., printing, writing, word processing) and self-expression. Writing was identified as a generative process. By the 1990s, teachers were systematically and explicitly teaching writing genres, emphasizing the setting, purpose, and culture of the writing activity.

Today, teachers and educational researchers agree that the writing process is a complicated one involving multiple cognitive and metacognitive skill sets. Like reading, writing requires students to construct meaning and develop effective strategies (Boscolo, 2008; Hillocks, 2008; Kellogg, 2000). Most writing instruction is based on the model of writing proposed by Flower and Hayes (1981), which holds that writing reflects the individual's cognitive skills and environment and the act of writing, which consists of three complex processes: planning, translating, and reviewing. Students who follow the writing process and use relevant writing strategies are metacognitively aware. Planning, problem solving, revising, and metacognitive strategies are thought to be especially important in improving students' writing (Graham, 2006; Pritchard & Honeycutt, 2006).

Caution Teachers are cautioned against the notion that writing occurs in a linear manner. Writing does not occur in a strict plan-write-review sequence. Instead, writing is a generative process that is recursive in nature. Effective writers continually review and adjust their writing, revising their plans, generating new content, and rewriting draft versions.

Planning and Pre-Writing

Planning is often the least considered component of the writing process, although it is strongly related to the quality of the composition (Graves, 2003). As part of the planning process, effective writers reflect on their prior knowledge and experiences for concepts and ideas and acquire new information as needed (consulting texts and media resources). Equally important, students need to understand the purposes and styles of writing that best match specific audiences. Sadly, discussions about how to create such "matches" rarely unfold in the classroom. We encourage teachers to incorporate the following prompts and questions as part of their writing instruction:

- Who will read this?
- Why am I writing this (e.g., to entertain my friends, to convince an audience that I am right)?
- What is the best format for my writing (e.g., story, persuasive essay, letter, description)?
- Why did I choose this topic?
- What do I want other people to believe is important?
- Will my reader be convinced by my writing?

Students who do not acknowledge and accommodate the social context of reading and writing often struggle with both.

Many students find it difficult to select a writing topic. Even when assigned a topic for their compositions, they often claim to "have nothing to say." Some students may benefit from an oral discussion about writing intentions and consideration of audience, interest, and significance. Teachers can provide students with a series of questions or prompts that can help them generate writing ideas and extend their discussion of a topic:

- Why is the topic important?
- What are my beliefs or opinions about this topic?
- Can I share something interesting from my life here?
- How might others view this topic? What are their opinions or beliefs?
- How can I convince others that my opinion is correct?
- What questions do I have about this topic?

Teachers can also engage students in a number of planning activities designed to facilitate their ability to generate writing topics. Table 7.3 provides some examples of such activities, many of which can be implemented independent of assigned writing activities.

Table 7.3 Strategies to Help Students Select Writing Topics

Object Description

- Show students an object. Objects can be those commonly found in the classroom or at home (e.g., apple, book, hair band, eraser) or be more eccentric (e.g., birthday party invitation, dog collar, cage).
- Have students observe the object carefully and record their responses to the following sensory prompts:

  What does it look like?

  What does it smell like?

  What does it sound like?

  What does it taste like?

  What does it feel like?

  What does it make me think about?
- Have students speculate in their responses when they are uncertain about the particulars of an object.

Visual Prompts

- Provide students with a visual prompt such as a picture, drawing, or photograph.
- Instruct students to study the visual prompt and encourage them to think broadly.
- Provide critical questions related to story structure:

  Who is the main character? Who else is in the story?

  Where and when does the story take place?

  What do the characters do? How do they feel?

  What happens in the story? Is there a problem? How does the story end?

  What happened before the picture? What is happening in the picture? What happened after the picture?

Sentence Starters

- Provide students with a sentence opener or with a phrase that can be used to begin a sentence:

  I think . . .

  One reason . . .

  Even though . . .

  For example . . .

  The greatest moment . . .

  I wish . . .

  I love . . .

- Have students record as many ideas as possible in response to the prompt, using single words or jotting notes.

Story Extenders

- Provide students with a familiar or unfamiliar story.
- Have students extend the story by recording as many ideas as possible in response to the following prompts:

  Include an additional character.

  Change the behaviour of the main character.

  Provide an alternative ending. What are the implications of each ending for the story?

  Change the setting. Place the story in the past or future.

  Tell the story from the perspective of another character (e.g., the spider in "Little Miss Muffet"; the stepsisters in Cinderella*; Templeton, the rat in* Charlotte's Web*).*

Free Writes

- Provide students with a word or phrase (e.g., supernatural phenomenon, happiness, global warming, freedom).
- Instruct students to record any ideas that occur to them as quickly as possible on a blank sheet of paper.
- Instruct students that they are not to lift their pen or pencil from the paper (or fingers from the keyboard) until instructed to do so and that the objective of the writing activity is to record as many ideas as possible.
- Include a time limit for this writing (5 to 15 minutes is usually sufficient).
- Remind students that there are no correct or incorrect responses and that they should not be concerned about spelling or grammar.

Graphic Organizers

- Provide students with a broad concept or theme related to the activity at hand (e.g., when asked to write a biography, provide students with the prompt: *People that I admire*; when asked to write a description, provide students with the prompt: *My favourite place*; when asked to write a persuasive argument, provide students with the prompt: *If I could change one thing . . .*).
- Have students complete a semantic map or other graphic organizer, including supporting details whenever possible.

Organizing requires students to make decisions with respect to selecting the most relevant information for presentation and the presentation format. These decisions are influenced, in part, by reflecting on the intended audience and the purpose of the writing activity (Flower & Hayes, 1981; Pritchard & Honeycutt, 2006). Students should be encouraged to take time to review carefully the thoughts and concepts generated as part of the brainstorming process and to assess the ideas they wish to bring forward. This may be as simple as highlighting ideas and concepts that students wish to integrate into their writing while crossing out those that will be omitted. Older students should prioritize their ideas and thoughts to present them in a logical and effective manner.

It is especially important that teachers provide explicit instruction with respect to the organization process. Students need to be shown how to outline and organize their writing. They should be encouraged to use graphic organizers and other tools that can help them identify and order clusters of related ideas. Many students are especially motivated when provided with the option of using organizational software programs such as Inspiration 3 or Storybook Weaver Deluxe. Finally, they need to be provided with constructive feedback on their efforts.

Translating and Drafting

Perhaps the task most readily associated with writing is translating, which is also referred to as drafting. Translating requires the transformation of generated and organized materials into acceptable print format (i.e., syntactically and grammatically correct statements). While much of writing instruction in schools involves teaching students how to write sentences and paragraphs properly, writing is a much more sophisticated process in which writers are charged with meaning-making. Teachers are advised to allow students to focus on the content of their writing versus writing mechanics (spelling, grammar, punctuation) during this process. That is, students should be encouraged to write continuously, "pouring out" their ideas for subsequent reflection and revision. Writing at this stage may look messy and incomplete, with students modifying and moving content repeatedly. Labelling or recording such writing as *DRAFT* is an effective method of reminding students, teachers, and parents that *content* versus *mechanics* is the primary focus here. Students may benefit from conferences with their teachers and peers during this process.

Student-Teacher Writing Conferences

Mini-lesson: Adding details

Writing conference

A teacher-directed writing conference can occur at any point in the writing process, and is a focused, effective method to help improve student writing. The conference's main purpose is to affirm that the student has something important and interesting to say (Calkins, 1994; Gunning, 2005). The conference should last between 10 and 15 minutes and students should be provided with advance notice of their turn. By the end of the conference, students should have gained new directions and ideas about how to improve their writing, as well as some praise or encouragement for their current efforts.

The decision about how to help students improve their writing is undeniably challenging, especially when there are a multitude of skills that can be improved. Generally, teachers are encouraged to ignore mechanical errors and focus on the expression of ideas (pervasive grammatical, spelling, and mechanics errors can be addressed as part of whole-class or small-group instruction). Teachers are encouraged to ask questions such as:

- What do you think the next step will be?
- Why did you make that choice or decision?
- Can you explain this part more fully?
- Where do you think you did a really good job?

Teachers' assessment of student responses will help them understand both students' writing strengths and areas for revision and subsequent focus. Teachers are encouraged to maintain a record of each conference, allocating six to eight pages for each student. This practice enables the teacher to recall previous decisions quickly and provides a record of writing growth (Atwell, 1998). Alternatively, students can maintain writing folders that contain their completed pieces, works in progress, and conference notes.

At some point in the year, students are generally ready to hold writing conferences in pairs or triads. Some preparation for these conferences is necessary, with teachers providing a procedural routine, modelling the process, monitoring the process initially, and even creating a feedback sheet. The following process can work effectively:

1. The students listen carefully while the author reads his or her composition.
2. The listeners then repeat what they heard to the author.
3. The listeners can request additional information about the composition as necessary.
4. The listeners make suggestions to the author.
5. The listeners praise the author, citing a favourite part of the writing.
6. Students reverse roles.

Caution Teachers must take great care when establishing writing groups, making sure that students are well versed in how to provide constructive feedback in a respectful manner. Successful student-teacher writing conferences underscore the idea that writing is a process that involves feedback and revision; it is not a time to present a final product for evaluation.

Writers in Electronic Residence (WiER)

Inspired by the desire to enhance the writing skills of students in his secondary school classroom, Trevor Owen founded Writers in Electronic Residence (WiER) in 1988 with the assistance of Gerri Sinclair (a professor at Simon Fraser University) and Lionel Kearns (a Canadian poet).

WiER connects Canadian authors with Canadian students and their teachers through online conferences. Students who participate in the program are provided with the opportunity to receive constructive feedback about their narrative compositions (poems, narratives, or short stories). As part of online forums, published Canadian authors (e.g., Jenni Blackmore, Rukhsana Khan, Richard Van Camp, Sylvia McNicoll, Eric Walters) read, analyze, discuss, and critique students' works, offering positive feedback and suggestions for subsequent revisions. A panel of professional authors is assigned to work with either elementary, intermediate, or senior students over a 12-week interval, forming an "electronic literary salon." Under the direction of a facilitator or moderator, a few salons are then grouped into a conference, so that students receive input from several writers. Their feedback is complemented by that provided by other students from the across the country who serve as virtual peer editors.

Of particular interest, WiER also provides teacher candidates with the opportunity to participate in a "virtual practicum" where they can work alongside professional writers, teachers, and students. As part of the practicum, teacher candidates review and provide feedback to students' compositions. Teacher candidates can also work as WiER interns.

For additional information about WiER, its structure and effectiveness, students' experiences, and related testimonials, visit www.WiER.ca/index.php/home.

Reviewing and Revising

Pow challenge

Reviewing, or what is otherwise referred to as revising, is a major component of successful writing and involves improving the quality of the written document through two processes: editing and proofreading. Of these processes, students tend to be most familiar with the latter, which involves reviewing text for mechanical errors. However, research supports that, with relatively modest prompting, students can be redirected to focus their revisions on content and meaning (McCutchen, 2006; Pritchard & Honeycutt, 2006).

Monitoring one's writing progress is especially important in becoming a good writer (Graham, 2006; Graham & Harris, 2001, 2009). This includes reflecting on whether the content of the document fulfills the identified purpose of the writing activity as well as on the suitability of the document's language and tone. Editing includes writing multiple drafts, receiving feedback from individuals who are knowledgeable about writing (teachers, parents, peers), and learning how to use critical feedback to improve subsequent writing. As mentioned above, student-teacher conferences and student writing groups can be especially effective venues for students to share their writing drafts. Students are then responsible for reflecting on and evaluating the merits of the feedback provided and incorporating it into subsequent drafts.

When writers use standard writing conventions effectively, their work is more readily accessible to readers. However, most teachers agree that an emphasis on spelling, grammar, punctuation, and other writing mechanics does little to improve the quality of students' compositions. Furthermore, when such instruction occurs, it is most effective when provided in the context of authentic writing activities rather than in isolation. Accordingly, we advise teachers to provide students with mechanical feedback only after they have completed an almost final draft of their work (ideally several days after the completion of such drafts). Teachers are encouraged to model this process by demonstrating revisions to their own compositions.

To facilitate the revision process, teachers are encouraged to have their students use editorial "think sheets" and planning guides, which include proofreading and editing checklists (see Figure 7.1). These checklists should be completed by both student authors and peer editors.

Student Voice 7.1

I wrote a letter to Santa Claus telling him that I would like an American Girl doll for Christmas. I did a rough copy first where I wrote all my points down. My teacher and I read it over next and fixed up any spelling mistakes. I then put my letter on fancy paper and sent it to Santa Claus. It is important that the letter has no spelling mistakes so that Santa can read it!

Lauren
Grade 4 student

Publishing

Publishing is an equally important component of the writing process and provides students with an opportunity to share and celebrate their written work. Publishing may occur across several formats, including some form of public reading (author's chair, book buddy, video), public display (classroom books, library, or home), or electronic posting (school website or blog). See Table 7.4 for more suggestions on how to publish student writing, all of which encourage students to take pride in their finished products.

Editing Checklist

Vocabulary

- Sentences begin differently.
- Descriptive and interesting language is used.
- Words are not repeated unnecessarily.

Content and Structure (Coherence and Flow)

- The title is meaningful and fits the writing well.
- The beginning captures the reader's attention.
- The main idea is clearly stated.
- There is a beginning, middle, and end.
- Sentences and paragraphs appear in a logical order.
- Examples and details are described sufficiently.
- Examples and details support the principal arguments.
- Ideas and details are connected with sophisticated transitions.
- The conclusion is clearly stated.

Overall

The purpose of the writing is clear to the reader.

The best part of the composition is: ____________________

The parts that would benefit from more work are: ____________________

One detail that should be added to make the writing clearer is: ________________

One change that would make the writing more interesting is: ____________________

Proofreading Checklist

Capitalization

- Each sentence begins with a capital letter.
- Names of people and places are capitalized.
- Each word in the title is capitalized.

Spelling, Grammar, and Punctuation

- All sentences are complete and contain a noun and a verb.
- All words are spelled correctly.
- Each sentence ends with a period, question mark, or exclamation mark.
- There are no run-on sentences.
- Quotation marks indicate where speech begins and ends.
- Apostrophes are used in contractions and possessives.
- Commas are used to indicate where to pause.
- Verb tenses are correct.
- Verbs and subjects agree.
- Paragraphs are indented.

(continued)

Figure 7.1 Editing and Proofreading Checklists

Common Proofreading Symbols

^	Add	Reading captures the ^ and imagination. (heart)
⊙	Add period	Reading captures the heart and imagination⊙
(!)	Add exclamation mark	Reading captures the heart and imagination(!)
(,)	Add comma	Reading captures the heart(,) and imagination.
#	Add space	Reading captures theheart and imagination. (#)
¶	New paragraph	¶ Reading captures the heart and imagination.
ℓ	Take out	Reading captures the heart mind and imagination.
∼	Change order	Reading captures the imagination and heart.
↵	Add idea	Reading is good for the heart and imagination. (How is this good?)
a̲	Capitalize	reading captures the heart and imagination.
Ⓐ	Use lower case	Reading captures the Heart and imagination.
○sp	Spell correctly	Reading captures the haert and imagination.

Figure 7.1 Editing and Proofreading Checklists (*continued*)

Table 7.4 Publishing Student Writing

- Create a book or big book (share with another classroom).
- Produce a class or school anthology.
- Produce a class or school newspaper.
- Produce a report or PowerPoint presentation.
- Produce a bulletin board, brochure, or poster.
- Post compositions on a classroom website, blog, or other online forum.
- Produce an audio or video recording.
- Host a writers' or poets' café.
- Host a public reading in the community.
- Host an author's chair.
- Host a young writers' group.
- Adopt a pen pal (local, national, international).
- Produce a self-publication for the class library.
- Create and perform a puppet play.
- Perform a Readers' Theatre.
- Participate in writing contests (school, local community, national, international).
- Submit articles to the local newspaper or young adult journal or magazine (e.g., *GirlSpeak*, *Kid-Cast*, *Native Youth Magazine*, *Poet Grow-Op*, *Secret Worlds Magazine*); for additional youth publications, see www.newpages.com/npguides/young_authors_guide.htm.

Technology and the Writing Process

Technology has influenced the ways in which students engage in every aspect of the writing process, including planning and pre-writing, translating and drafting, reviewing and revising, and publishing (National Writing Project & Nagin, 2006). Specifically, technology promotes the recursive nature of writing, allowing students to move freely and frequently between each element (e.g., a student may plan a section of his or her composition, create a small draft, revise or elaborate on the writing plan, edit the first draft based on the revised plan, and continue drafting). Students can gain access to information instantly through the internet, and technology facilitates collaborative writing (e.g., students and teachers can use word processing features such as "track changes" and comment features to provide critical feedback while developing compositions). Students can also incorporate graphics and other software features that support their writing and foster their creativity. Word processing has taken much of the drudgery out of revising work, and spelling and grammar checks can greatly enhance the overall readability of students' compositions and reduce concern and anxiety over the revision process. Finally, technology extends the reach and accessibility of students' writing, providing a potentially unlimited audience.

Students who understand that their writing is "under development" or "in flux" are more likely to experiment and take risks when composing (moving text sections, altering phrases, adding or removing content). Teachers can use technology as a forum to model the writing process as well as a tool to access and monitor students' ongoing compositions. It is therefore imperative that teachers assist students in developing competencies in the use of technologies as part of writing instruction.

TYPES OF WRITING

THROUGHOUT THE SCHOOL DAY, STUDENTS ENGAGE IN MULTIPLE FORMS OF WRITING, ranging from formal to informal. Sometimes this writing will require students to engage in all elements of the writing process, while at other times this will be unnecessary. Similarly, sometimes students will write using the conventional pen-and-paper format, while at other times they will use word processing and other technologies. In this section, we provide a brief overview of some of the most common writing found in the classroom including journal writing, letter writing, and blogging. Readers are reminded to review Chapter 6, Reading Comprehension Strategies for Non-Fiction: Reading in the Content Areas, for additional information on how to prepare students for report writing.

Quick Writes

Quick writes (sometimes called free writing or stream-of-consciousness writing) can be used in a variety of subject areas, facilitating the integration of writing across the curriculum. It is a useful technique for activating students' prior knowledge (schema) about a topic. Briefly, the teacher introduces a topic and asks students to write everything they know about that topic for about 10 to 15 minutes, encouraging them to make personal connections to the topic based on their previous experiences or past readings (Tompkins, 1998).

Students then share their quick writes either in small groups or as a class (about 10 minutes). When small groups are used, designated students share their groups' collective ideas with the whole class. After the whole-class discussion, students are usually

instructed to select key or interesting ideas and write an elaborated piece. Alternatively, the teacher can record key phrases and words on the board. Quick writes are brief yet purposeful. They encourage students to use writing to focus thinking.

Journals

The journal provides a safe forum for self-expression and critical thinking (Gammill, 2006). Journal writing can be started in the early grades, with students drawing pictures and "writing" about them, and continued throughout much of the junior and intermediate grades. Journals vary considerably in format, with teachers encouraged to adopt several formats as part of their language arts programming.

Personal Journals Many individuals keep journals to chronicle and make sense of daily life. The issues that concern them are frequently the substance of such reflections. It is generally accepted that spelling, capitalization, punctuation, and grammar are not the focus of this activity (Tompkins, Bright, Pollard, & Winsor, 2011). Rather, the focus is on students' expression of thoughts and ideas. As a result, personal journals are often disorganized and may contain invented spellings. See Table 7.5 for examples of children's literature featuring diaries or journals.

Teachers who decide to include personal journals as part of their language arts programming will need to consider the following:

- Will the activity be completed on a daily, weekly, or random basis?
- What time of day would work best for silent writing? How much time will I provide for this activity?
- How will I model the importance of this activity?
- Will students' responses be private or will I provide feedback (if the latter, how often)? Will I encourage students to share their journals with peers?

Table 7.5 Examples of Children's Books Featuring Diaries or Journals

Alexie, S. (2007). *The absolutely true diary of a part-time Indian.* New York, NY: Little, Brown Books for Young Readers.

Benton, J. (2007). *Dear dumb diary: Let's pretend this never happened.* Markham,ON: Scholastic.

Cronin, D., & Bliss, H. (2003). *Diary of a worm.* New York, NY: Balzer & Bray.

Cronin, D., & Bliss, H. (2005). *Diary of a spider.* New York, NY: Balzer & Bray.

Cronin, D., & Bliss, H. (2007). *Diary of a fly.* New York, NY: Balzer & Bray.

Cushman, K. (1994). *Catherine, called Birdy.* New York, NY: Clarion.

Frank, A. (1993). *The diary of a young girl.* Jefferson City, MO: Scholastic Professional Books.

Griffith, H. V. (1988). *Journal of a teenage genius.* New York, NY: Troll Communications.

Hale, S. (2007). *Book of a thousand days.* New York, NY: Bloomsbury USA Children's Books.

Juby, S. (2003). *Alice, I think.* New York, NY: HarperTeen.

Kimmel, E. C. (2003). *Lily B. on the brink of cool.* New York, NY: HarperCollins.

Kinney, J. (2007). *Diary of a wimpy kid.* New York, NY: Harry N. Abrams.

Kinney, J. (2008). *Rodrick rules.* New York, NY: Amulet Books.

Kinney, J. (2009). *Dog days.* New York, NY: Amulet Books.

Kinney, J. (2009). *The last straw.* New York, NY: Amulet Books.

Kinney, J. (2010). *The ugly truth.* New York, NY: Amulet Books.

Moriarty, J. (2004). *The year of secret assignments.* New York, NY: Arthur A. Levine Books.

Moss, M. (1996). *Amelia writes again.* New York, NY: Simon & Schuster.

Rennison, L. (1999). *Angus, thongs, and full-frontal snogging.* New York, NY: HarperTeen.

Russell, R. R. (2009). *Dork diaries: Tales from a not-so-fabulous life.* New York, NY: Simon & Schuster.

Russell, R. R. (2010). *Dork diaries: Party time.* New York, NY: Simon & Schuster.

Russell, R. R. (2010). *Dork diaries 2: Tales from a not-so-popular party girl.* New York, NY: Simon & Schuster.

Sheldon, D. (2002). *Planet Janet.* Somerville, MA: Candlewick.

Townsend, S. (1982). *The secret diary of Adrian Mole, aged 13¾.* West Berlin, NJ: Townsend Books.

Zindel, P. (1987). *The amazing and death-defying diary of Eugene Dingman.* London, UK: Starfire Publishing.

- What will I do if a student reveals a disturbing event or thought?
- What will I do if a student or group of students does not participate in this activity?
- Will I provide writing prompts or allow students to write on topics of their choice?

While the answers to these questions can vary and may change over time, it is important to provide students with clear guidelines about routines and associated expectations.

Teacher Voice 7.1

I recall a student in grade 5 who liked to write fast-paced, narrative stories. Every day he wrote and shared his writing with the class. Other students looked forward to hearing the next episode of their classmate's story.

Anne Elliott
Teacher educator

Young Children's Journals Young children can draw in their journals or they can combine drawing and writing (Short & Harste, 1995). Initially, very young children may include scribbles, shapes, numbers, and letters in their "writing." While invented spellings of words seem strange, they represent an initial stage of writing development and contribute to students' growth as writers. Through these journals, children can discover that writing is a forum to express their ideas and experiences.

Student Voice 7.2

> When the teacher calls me over to read the words, I know most of them and she says, "Good work, Daniel." I also know how to write in my journal and I wrote about Thanksgiving and going to Grandma's. I like reading and writing better than using my iPad.
>
> Daniel
> Grade 1 student

Dialogue Journals Dialogue journals involve an ongoing written dialogue between two writers. The dialogue can be between the teacher and a student (admittedly a labour-intensive activity) or between two students (Boling, Castek, Zawillinski, Barton, & Nierlich, 2008). Alternatively, teachers can establish collaborative relations with another class and pair students for journal sharing. Dialogue journals can also be established between students and other adults such as grandparents (Gunning, 2005). Dialogue journals provide practice in reading and writing, especially when teachers or other adults direct their correspondence to the students' reading level.

Dialogue journal responses do not need to be lengthy. Rather, recipients respond as if they were in dialogue with the author. They react to the ideas, ask for more information, and offer advice (Calkins, 1994, 2009). Table 7.6 provides some guidelines for adults participating in dialogue journals with students.

Dialogue journals can be used to address students' behavioural and learning concerns (Levin, Nolan, Kerr, & Elliott, 2011) or when a student is learning English as a subsequent language. These dialogues can provide teachers with insight on the nature of students' learning problems, as well as on the success of intervention efforts, while providing a reassuring support for struggling learners (Bean & Rigoni, 2001).

Reading Response Journals Reading response journals are used when students are reading or listening to a story. The purpose is to encourage students to think deeply

Table 7.6 Dialogue Journal Guidelines for Adults

- Provide authentic praise and encouragement.
- Do not write extensively.
- Do not comment on spelling or grammar. Include the same language spelled and expressed correctly in your responses.
- Ask only one or two questions and encourage students to ask questions as well.
- Provide new information or ideas about the topic that will aid students' understanding.
- Respond promptly.

and thoughtfully about the text. Rather than generate summaries about the text, students are encouraged to express their ideas about it, relate the material to their own experiences, form predictions, and discuss aspects of the text that intrigue them. They can also keep a list of unfamiliar words and concepts and complete a vocabulary study as part of their journal response.

To challenge and extend students' thinking, teachers are encouraged to model responses and monitor those provided by students. Students should be encouraged to share some of their responses to provoke discussion. Teachers can often use students' responses as springboards for discussion about a variety of topics, including human relationships, points of view, and the author's purpose.

Modelling also provides students with the guidelines for effective responses (teachers will need to provide extensive modelling at the beginning of the year, including prompting and cueing as students gain experience in generating responses). As part of the modelling process, teachers can demonstrate such responses as:

- Relating to and analyzing characters
- Evaluating characters' behaviours and interactions with others
- Formulating predictions
- Reflecting on their own affective response to the story
- Suggesting alternative endings
- Asking questions about the story

As part of the assessment of students' growth as writers, teachers are advised to assess the kinds of responses students make without such prompts. These prompts then can be introduced gradually across the course of the story. Table 7.7 provides one example of a reading response activity. Observe that the described activity:

- Provides writing choice
- Represents a student-centred, shared writing activity
- Focuses on the writing of ideas rather than on mechanics, spelling, and grammar
- Presents the teacher as writer
- Establishes the class as a writing community
- Integrates writing, reading, listening, and speaking

Double-Entry Journals Double-entry journals can help students structure their thinking about texts and become more engaged in their reading (Tompkins et al., 2011; Tovani, 2000). When using double-entry journals, students need to divide their pages into two sections. The left side of the page is used to record quotations or concepts that they select from the text. The right side is used to relate the quotations or concepts to other texts or to their everyday experiences. Generally, a teacher needs to set a minimum number of quotations to be selected for this task, with between one and three being optimum. Assigning too many quotations will reduce the amount of thinking and attention spent on each one.

Alternative approaches include asking students to provide a summary of the story on the left side of the page and to write their reflective ideas on the right, or having students form predictions on one side and track their accuracy on the other. Young students can use pictures when completing double-entry journals.

Table 7.7 Reading Response Activity

1. Read three very different text selections aloud. Read the texts slowly and with expression, but with no additional comments either before, during, or after reading. Suggested selections include:
   - *Aesop's Tales*
   - Poetry (e.g., "The Messy Room" or any other poem by Shel Silverstein for junior grade students, "Ozymandias" by Percy Shelly for intermediate grade students)
   - A contemporary selection from a newspaper or magazine
   - A short story or myth (e.g., the Greek myth *The Midas Touch*)
2. Provide students with sufficient time to write a response for the text selection that had greatest appeal to them. Emphasize that students should focus on expressing their thoughts and opinions versus worrying about writing mechanics. Inform students that they will be sharing their response with a few of their peers.
3. Generate your own response to one of the texts (ideally the text selected by the least number of students).
4. Organize students into small groups based on their selected topic. Have students read their responses aloud, with the group asking questions and providing comments after each reading. Help students monitor their time so that each participant has equal opportunity for reading and discussing his or her selection (total time: 20 to 30 minutes). Join one group to share your own response.
5. As a whole class, discuss the following questions:
   - What surprised you when your peers responded to your writing?
   - What new perspective did you derive on your topic?
   - What ideas were clarified or modified?
6. Provide students with a separate session to revise and proofread their response.

Teachers can gain critical insights into students' learning by reviewing journal entries; the left-hand entries indicate the ideas and concepts that students find most important or interesting and the right-hand responses reveal their understanding of them.

Math Journals A journal serves the same function in math class as it does in language arts; it is a learning tool that helps students clarify their thinking and learn new vocabulary and that provides opportunities for reflection and self-evaluation (Kostos & Shin, 2010; Tuttle, 2005). Math journals are especially useful in helping students develop an appreciation of the problem-solving process versus unquestionably following a set of hierarchical rules.

Math journals enable teachers to evaluate students' progress and identify their strengths and learning needs. This kind of insight helps teachers determine whether review or reteaching is necessary for the whole class, a small group, or an individual. Math journals can also be used to communicate with parents.

When starting math journals, teachers must demonstrate patience, as it takes time for students to recognize mathematical thinking processes and communicate them effectively in print. Math journals are most effective when students are learning new concepts, and

Table 7.8 Writing Prompts for Math Journals

- I was right because . . .
- I wish I knew more about . . .
- If I were helping a friend solve this problem, I would . . .
- How did you finally solve this problem?
- What method did you use to solve this problem? Why?
- Was this hard or easy? Why?
- What other strategies could you use to solve this problem?
- What do you like about math? What do you not like about math?
- What would you like to do better next time?
- Where else could you use this type of problem-solving?

Source: Adapted from http://math.about.com/library/weekly/aa123001a.htm.

Table 7.9 Sharing and Reflecting on Students' Journals

- Students work in pairs and share their writing.
- Students work in small groups, with each student sharing one sentence.
- Volunteers share their entries with the class.
- Students mark individual entries for the teacher to read.
- Students select one entry as a focus for a writers' workshop.
- Students review their entries, identifying areas of strength, growth, and need as well as overall interests and themes.

Source: Adapted from Stewig and Nordberg (1994).

experts recommend that teachers allocate about 10 minutes at the end of the math lesson for students to document their learning experiences (Burns, 2007). Table 7.8 lists some prompts that teachers can use when students are completing math journals and Table 7.9 provides suggestions for how students can share and reflect on their journals.

Guided Writing

When teachers model, think aloud, and provide guiding questions, they scaffold or support student learning (Dixon-Krauss, 1996), and guided writing is based on this learning principle. Guided writing involves teaching a specific skill or strategy, such as using an advanced organizer, to the whole class. Using a teacher-led example, the teacher begins the lesson by modelling and thinking aloud. The teacher and class then complete a shared example. When the teacher is convinced that the majority of students have grasped the target skill or strategy, students are placed into small writing groups where they are encouraged to discuss, negotiate, write, and edit together. During this time, teachers monitor, support, and guide students. Students then

Table 7.10 Examples of Guided Writing in the Classroom

- After reading an article on the threatened demise of polar bears, a grade 5 class completes group reports in which they gather additional data and organize their ideas. Students then present their reports. After sharing with the whole class, they grade the quality of their work. Students then write an independent report about the *Titanic*, employing all of the previously practised skills in a new context.
- In a grade 3 class, a teacher models how to write a narrative following a class visit to the local aquarium. Students are then placed in small groups to write about the trip. This is followed by students writing a personal narrative about a trip they have completed or wish to complete.
- A teacher models the importance of the beginning of a story by reading a variety of beginnings to her grade 1 class. Students are placed in groups to negotiate an opening sentence for a specific story. As each group shares its story starter, the teacher records the responses. Students then select one of the story starters to begin their own story.

practise writing independently and teachers continue to provide support through individual conferences and consultations. Using guided writing in the classroom can increase students' writing skills and motivation (Oczkus, 2007). See Table 7.10 for examples of guided writing in the classroom.

Student Voice 7.3

Sometimes when I am writing a story, I have trouble starting. I sometimes also have difficulty putting all of my thoughts into words when journal writing. My favourite thing about writing is being creative.

Madeleine
Grade 5 student

Letters

While much of modern communication consist of emails and text messages, students still benefit from understanding the conventions of letter writing (Tompkins et al, 2011). Although as a society we tend to write few letters, those we do write are usually of great significance (e.g., seeking employment, providing a reference, expressing an opinion) and thus deserve some attention as part of the language arts curriculum.

Most letters fall into one of two categories—friendly or business—with each format following distinct conventions.

Friendly Letters Reading books written in the form of letters (see Table 7.11) or letters to the editor from your local newspaper to students can be motivating for letter-writing activities. Developing a pen pal program is also an effective way to develop students' friendly letter-writing skills. Teachers are encouraged to consider forming pen pal partnerships with other classrooms at the local or international level. As with any other composition, letters should be drafted, revised, and proofread prior to being delivered.

Table 7.11 Examples of Children's Books Featuring Letter Writing

Picture Books

Ada, A. F. (2001). *Yours truly, Goldilocks.* New York, NY: Atheneum.

Ahlberg, J., & Ahlberg, A. (1986). *The jolly postman: Or other people's letters.* New York, NY: Little, Brown Books for Young Readers.

Ahlberg, J., & Ahlberg, A. (1991). *The jolly Christmas postman.* London, UK: Viking UK Juvenile.

Ahlberg, J., & Ahlberg, A. (1995). *The jolly pocket postman.* London, UK: Viking UK Juvenile.

Brown, J. & Nash, S. (2003). *Flat Stanley.* Scarborough, ON: HarperCollins.

Christelow, E. (2006). *Letters from a desperate dog.* New York, NY: Clarion Books.

Cronin, D., & Lewin, B. (2000). *Click, clack, moo: Cows that type.* New York, NY: Atheneum.

Day, L., & Dworkin, D. (2005). *Chain letter. Berkeley,* CA: Heyday Books.

Harrison, J. (2001). *Dear bear. Minneapolis,* MN: Carolrhoda Books.

James, S. (1991). *Dear Mr. Blueberry.* New York, NY: Aladdin Picture Books.

Joyce, S., & Dubosque, D. (1994). *Post card passages.* Columbus, NC: Peel Publishers.

Leedy, L. (2006). *Postcards from Pluto: A tour of the solar system.* New York, NY: Holiday House.

Pak, S. (2001). *Dear Juno.* New York, NY: Viking Juvenile.

Chapter Books and Novels

Cleary, B. (2000). *Dear Mr. Henshaw.* Scarborough, ON: HarperCollins.

Dunn, M. (2002). *Ella Minnow Pea: A novel in letters.* Port Moody, BC: Anchor.

Falvey, D., & Hutt, J. (2009). *Letters to a soldier.* New York, NY: Marshall Cavendish Corp.

Harper, H. (2007). *Letters to a young brother: MANifest your destiny.* New York, NY: Gotham.

Harper, H. (2009). *Letters to a young sister: DeFINE your destiny.* New York, NY: Gotham.

Keats, E. J. (1998, first published 1964). *A letter to Amy.* New York, NY: Viking Juvenile.

Lewis, C. S. (2001). *The screwtape letters.* San Francisco, CA: HarperOne.

Woodruff, E. (1992). *Dear Napoleon, I know you're dead, but . . .* New York, NY: Yearling.

Street
City, Province
Postal Code
Date

Dear ______________________,

____

____

____

____

____

____

Your Friend, Love, Warmest regards, Best regards,

Signature

Figure 7.2 Friendly Letter

Conventions associated with friendly letters are:

1. The writer's complete address is included in the top right corner of the page, followed by the date.
2. The salutation—*Dear* [recipient's name]—is on the left side of page.
3. The first sentence should be indented.
4. The body of the letter includes friendly information.
5. A complimentary closing is included at the bottom right side of the page (*Your friend*, *Love*, *Warmest regards*, *Best regards*), followed by the signature of the writer (handwritten in pen if the letter is typed).

Trent Penpal Community Writing Program

For more than 20 years, students in the Peterborough and Oshawa regions in Ontario have been exchanging letters with pen pals at Trent University. As part of this year-round program, approximately 325 emergent grades 1 and 2 writers are partnered with teacher candidates.

The program is officially launched at the beginning of each school year by the elementary students making a field trip to the local university to meet their pen pals. Pen pals then correspond on a monthly basis, meeting several times throughout the year to celebrate special events, strengthen rapport, and gain a greater sense of community.

The letter-writing sessions provide students with a forum to support and enhance each other's writing efforts, as well as an opportunity for their teachers to provide explicit writing instruction (Berrill & Gall, 1999, 2000).

Program founder Dr. Deborah Berrill explains that the letter-writing experience differs from most classroom writing activities in that students belong to an extended community of writers. Every student, regardless of his or her reading and writing abilities or backgrounds, is expected to be a letter writer. In turn, every student's letter is valued and honoured.

> On the days when the letters arrive, the students congregate on the carpet where they are individually called to the teacher's chair to receive them. Each student's letter is opened and read aloud (by either the teacher or the student). During the reading, time is taken to discuss relevant letter-writing protocol (e.g., mailing and return addresses, figures of speech, vocabulary, punctuation, question-asking and answering). After the reading, all students are encouraged to ask questions or make comments about the letter, often providing the writer with potential responses for subsequent correspondence. Following the reading of the last letter, students return to their seats to begin the process of writing their reply letters.

Business Letters Many students are unfamiliar with the format of the business letter. Students benefit from multiple examples, teacher modelling, and shared letter writing and are likely to be especially motivated by topics that relate to their daily lives (e.g., writing to the principal about a school policy, writing to the local newspaper, or writing to apply for a job). As with the friendly letter, drafting, revising and proofreading should be emphasized as part of the instructional process. Finally, teachers must be careful that students do not interpret attention to form as being of greater importance than content.

That is, students should appreciate the importance of presenting ideas succinctly and concisely when generating business letters.

Conventions associated with business letters include the following:

1. The writer's complete address is included in the top left corner of the page, followed by the date.
2. The recipient's name and complete address appear under that of the writer.
3. The salutation—*Dear* [recipient's formal name]—is on the left side of page.
4. The first sentence is indented.
5. The body of the letter includes concise, well-worded statements.
6. The formal closing is at the bottom right side of the page (*Sincerely*, *Yours truly*, *Yours faithfully*), followed by the signature of the writer, handwritten in pen if the letter is typed.

Integrated Letter-Writing Activity Teachers are encouraged to integrate letter-writing activities into their reading, social studies, or history units. For example, students can assume the identity of a favourite or interesting character and write a friendly letter to another character or historical figure (see Table 7.12). Alternatively, students can retain their identity and write a letter inquiring about or commenting on the characters in the text. Teachers can collect students' letters and circulate them throughout the class, directing students to respond to each other (students may be required to complete

Writer's Street
City, Province
Postal Code
Date

Recipient's Name
Business Name
Street
City, Province
Postal Code

Dear ____________________,

____
____
____
____
____

Sincerely, Yours truly, Yours faithfully,

Signature

Figure 7.3 Business Letter

Table 7.12 Suggested Integrated Letter-Writing Activities

- Write to Eva Padlyat from *Very Last First Time* by Jan Andrews, asking about her life in Ungava Bay.
- Write to Parvana from The Breadwinner Trilogy by Deborah Ellis, asking about her life today in Afghanistan.
- Assume the identity of a common sailor on Samuel de Champlain's voyages to the New World and write a letter to your family describing life on board the ship.
- Assume the identity of John Cabot and write a letter to his financial backer in England describing his first sighting of North America.
- Assume the identity of Harry Potter and write a letter to Hermione discussing how their story has been told around the world.

additional research as part of this response). Such letters can also provide teachers with insights into students' understanding of the text or historical period being studied.

Blogs

Blogs are websites that allow individuals to create personal webpages of text and other multimedia. In their simplest form, they are described as online journals (Huffaker, 2004; Kennedy, 2003). Distinctly different from other websites, blogs provide a place where individuals can post comments and participate in online conversations (Boling et al., 2008). Blogs also are distinct from emails and other forms of online communication in that comments are posted in reverse chronological order (i.e., the most recent post appears first). Only the blog owner controls the blog and creates new topics, thus controlling the cohesiveness of the discussion.

Literacy teachers have used blogs to discuss and receive feedback about classroom events (Ray & Coulter 2008; see Table 7.13). Teachers can also use blogs to foster collaborative writing projects or topic discussions (Richardson, 2005). As part of participating in blogs, students can gain access to diverse points of view (Ellison & Wu, 2008). Blogs also increase the students' sense of belonging to a learning community (Huffaker, 2005). Other learning benefits include the following:

- Students are required to be precise when communicating ideas. They need to "get to the point."
- Submission dates can be used to archive students' development and understanding of concepts.
- Feedback is expected, encouraged, and immediate.
- Images and other multimedia items can be posted, thus providing multiple means of communication (Kajder & Bull, 2003).

Email and Text Messaging

Email and text messaging are increasingly popular and are often the preferred methods of written communication, offering both opportunities and dangers (Livingstone, 2003). According to a 2005 survey (Young Canadians in a Wired World—Phase II;

Table 7.13 Possible Uses of Blogs in the Classroom

- Collaborative discussions: Students can post their ideas and comments in response to a discussion topic or assignment. Teachers can guide discussions and provide higher-level thinking prompts to encourage critical thinking.
- Reflections: Students can share reading responses or other reflections.
- Journals: Students can use blogs as online journals.
- Publishing: Students can publish their writing and receive feedback from peers and others.
- Tutoring: Teachers can post additional instructional materials such as videos, readings, and podcasts. Students can retrieve this information when seeking assistance or enrichment activities.
- Assignments and announcements: Teachers can post homework assignments, student feedback, and announcements.
- Celebrations: Teachers and students can announce award winners, student accomplishments, or other honours and public recognitions, including photographs of class and school events.

www.media-awareness.ca/english/research/YCWW/phaseII/key_findings.cfm), 86 percent of students reported having email accounts. Twenty-eight percent of grade 4 students reported using instant messaging, with this number increasing to 43 percent in grade 5 and to 62 percent in grade 11. These methods of communicating are fraught with the potential for miscommunication, especially as spelling and grammar rules are often ignored in the interest of speed and informality. However, language arts instructors can reduce some of the potential for miscommunications by teaching students basic email and text messaging skills, etiquette, and safety (see Tables 7.14 and 7.15).

Table 7.14 Basic Etiquette (or "Netiquette") for Communicating via the Internet

- Send messages to the correct people. Check that messages are addressed to the intended recipients before sending. Be especially careful when replying to a message that includes multiple recipients.
- Avoid sending or forwarding junk mail.
- Be sensitive that attachments can contain viruses. Whenever possible, incorporate pictures and other attachments into the body of the message.
- Be conscious of tone, which refers to the expression of mood or emotion. Appear friendly and respectful rather than curt or demanding.
- Avoid controversial issues such as religion, race, and gender-related topics, as seemingly private communication can quickly become public. Remember that the written word can be difficult to interpret in the absence of tone of voice and facial and body clues.
- Avoid sending messages when upset. If possible, wait a few days before responding or save a draft response to review later before sending.
- Do not type an entire message in capital letters, as this is often interpreted as shouting.
- Make a good impression by paying attention to spelling and grammar.
- Use paragraphs when formulating longer responses to increase the readability of your message.
- Be polite and use please and thank you. If you have inadvertently sent a hurtful message to the wrong person, or if your message has been misunderstood for any reason, apologize immediately.

Table 7.15 Safety Protocols When Communicating via the Internet

- Be selective about those with whom you communicate. Remind students that individuals may not be who they seem.
- Use caution when talking with strangers. Do not share personal details about yourself or your family and friends.
- Do not share anyone's email address without his or her permission.
- Do not break any laws. If it is against the law in the real world (e.g., slander, bullying), it is against the law in cyberspace.
- Never share your passwords or login information.
- Never agree to meet in person with anyone you have met via the internet.

PUTTING IT ALL TOGETHER: WRITERS' WORKSHOPS

THE TERM *WRITERS' WORKSHOP* REFERS TO A CLASSROOM PRACTICE THAT SIMULATES the kind of atmosphere in which professional authors write. This simulation reinforces to students that they are truly authors and that their compositions are important (Calkins, 1994; Graves, 1994). The workshops are designed to provide students with regular intervals of uninterrupted, focused, and personal writing time during which they can acquire and refine critical writing skills (Tompkins, Bright, Pollard, & Winsor, 2008).

The writers' workshop is composed of four distinct components. First, the teacher provides students with a mini-lesson about a specific writing skill. Second, the students are provided with time for writing. Third, they participate in individual and group conferences. Finally, they share their compositions as a whole class. Sometimes, teachers find it useful to integrate the writers' workshop into other subject areas such as science and social studies, especially when research projects or other writing activities are integral to those units.

Prior to beginning the writers' workshop, teachers may wish to rearrange the classroom so that students are seated in small groups to facilitate sharing. Teachers may also want to ensure that the writing centre is well stocked in terms of paper, writing utensils, dictionaries, Post-it Notes, and staples (as well as computers and word processing software, if available). It is critical that students be familiar with each element of the writing process and be able to differentiate writing tasks that require them to complete all of these elements.

Students will need to create a writing folder in which they store all of their rough work and writing drafts. To help students gain familiarity with the writers' workshop and to establish it as a workable classroom routine, the teacher should guide the class through one complete composition, including publication. Eventually, students will adopt their own pace as they complete various stages of the writing process independently, resulting in a classroom of writers completing diverse activities and writing tasks at any one time.

Teacher Voice 7.2

When my students are writing, I circulate but try not to interrupt those who are engaged. Rather, I focus on those who seem stuck or frustrated. I talk to them about how to make a personal connection to the topic. Some students also seem to need confirmation as they go along, so I read their drafts, focusing on their ideas but also looking for flow and coherence.

Hilary Elliott
Intermediate teacher

Table 7.16 Lesson Plan: The Writers' Workshop

Step 1: Mini-Lesson

The purpose of this lesson is to use explicit instruction and modelling to teach a specific writing skill, technique, or concept to the whole class (Gunning, 2005). The lesson should be brief, lasting between 5 and 10 minutes. The teacher should also model dating each piece of writing so that the practice becomes routine.

Mini-lessons for primary and junior grade students could involve separating a favourite story into beginning, middle, and end; creating a semantic web summarizing the main ideas or plot; or reviewing the use of specific punctuation. Such lessons can be based on teachers' observations of students' needs, such as pervasive errors in previous writing.

At the intermediate level, teachers might model story mapping, note taking for gathering data, or paragraph structure. On occasion, a guest writer may be invited to the class to model a specific writing skill as part of the mini-lesson. A critical factor of this step is that students see their teachers as writers who benefit from creating drafts, using organizers, and revising and editing (Cunningham & Allington, 2006).

Step 2: Sustained Writing Time

This part of the workshop is the most extensive, lasting at least 30 minutes. During writing time, students are encouraged to use the word wall and other resources when concerned about spelling or other writing mechanics. However, the emphasis at this time is on recording their ideas on topics of their choice. Teachers can also use this time to provide individual students with a specific lesson based on their individual needs.

Step 3: Group and Individual Conferences

As part of sustained writing time, teachers will want to host a series of student-teacher conferences. These conferences can be short and informal or longer and more formal, conducted either with individuals or in small groups. At the beginning of the writing process, conferencing often occurs during the first 20 minutes of the writing period as teachers move around the classroom to meet with individual students. Teachers are encouraged to circulate among students to avoid having them form a line to wait for assistance. As part of these conferences, teachers should ask students to describe their writing topic, read a section of their composition, or clarify their next steps. It is important to touch base with each student at least once over the course of a week.

During the revising and editing stages of writing, teachers usually allocate longer intervals to conference with individual students. Students read their entire pieces aloud and teachers provide editorial comments about possibilities for reorganizing, clarifying, and elaborating. Through this teacher-led process, students learn the kinds of responses they can provide to their peers during student-to-student conferences. As students become more familiar with these conferencing processes, small groups of students can meet to receive feedback. When students are ready for independent peer conferences, a true community of writers has been established.

After meeting with their teachers and classmates, students make final decisions about revisions. One possible decision may be not to complete a particular piece of writing. If this decision is made, students then date their work, place it in their writing folder, and begin something new.

Step 4: Sharing and Publishing

The sharing time encompasses the final 10 to 15 minutes of the writers' workshop each day. At this important stage, students can experience the pride of being authors and of having others read and enjoy their writing (Cunningham & Allington, 2006). The class gathers together and some members share either writing in progress or completed pieces. In some classrooms, teachers designate an "author's chair" where students sit to share their writing. After a published piece is read, students applaud and offer compliments to celebrate work well done. Completed compositions may also be displayed or published in some other format for additional viewing.

The writers' workshop is designed to provide students with the opportunity to participate in extended, meaningful, authentic literacy activities. The teacher's primary role is to promote a writing routine and foster a community whose members take pride in their growth as authors.

Table 7.16 provides an overview of a lesson plan for hosting a writers' workshop.

Caution Although the writers' workshop is embedded in a non-judgmental community of learning and sharing, some students remain reluctant writers. To help reluctant writers become engaged, ask them to write about familiar materials, including personal experiences.

WRITING ASSESSMENT

Evaluating and Responding to Students' Writing

How writing is evaluated influences how students will approach future writing tasks and activities. Effective teachers are aware of the distinction between evaluating and responding to students' writing, appreciating that the latter involves providing students with high-quality feedback on their compositions. Responding to students' work also requires teachers to provide them with formative feedback about their pre-writing activities and drafts. Evaluation, on the other hand, involves providing students with summative comments about their final product. Students are much more likely to develop and extend the boundaries of their writing skills when teachers respond to students' work in a formative fashion (Beach & Friedrich, 2006; National Writing Project & Nagin, 2006; Soven, 1999).

Indirect Writing Assessment

When assessing students' writing, teachers can adopt one of two general approaches: indirect or direct. Indirect measures do not require students to produce original writing compositions. Rather, students are asked to recognize writing conventions and skills in formulated materials. In this sense, indirect measures are those that estimate students' probable writing ability (Murphy & Yancey, 2008). Teachers can create their own indirect questions or use published resources.

While indirect measures can provide educators with valuable information with respect to students' current knowledge about writing conventions and skills, it is important that teachers acknowledge the limitations associated with such measures, including the following:

- It provides few insights into students' cognitive and reflective processes while writing (e.g., planning, drafting, editing).
- It can be confounded with students' knowledge and compliance with test-taking protocols (e.g., responding to multiple-choice or fill-in-the-blank questions) and test questions (e.g., what is the question asking?).
- There is an increased emphasis on grammar, punctuation, usage, and other writing mechanics.

Direct Writing Assessment

Direct measures, on the other hand, require students to produce one or more written compositions, which in turn are evaluated by one or more assessors. For instance, students may be asked to submit a single document generated within a defined interval or multiple documents produced over an extended interval (writing portfolios or folders). In general, educators favour direct measures, as they are considered to be authentic and consistent

Table 7.17 Commercially Available Tests of Indirect and Direct Writing

Oral and Written Language Scales (OWLS)

Written Expression Scale (WES)

(5 years to 21 years)

Students respond to oral, written, and pictorial prompts.

Measures students' use of conventions (handwriting, spelling, punctuation), syntactical forms (modifiers, phrases, sentence structures), and ability to communicate meaningfully (relevance, cohesiveness, organization).

PRO-ED (1995)

Test of Early Written Language (TEWL-2)

(4 years to 10 years, 11 months)

Basic writing subscales measure students' spelling, capitalization, punctuation, sentence construction abilities, and metacognitive knowledge.

Students respond to picture prompts and write a narrative text in the contextual writing subscale.

PRO-ED (1996)

Test of Written Expression (TOWE)

(6 years, 6 months to 14 years, 11 months)

First subtest measures students' skills associated with basic writing (e.g., spelling, capitalization, punctuation, word usage).

Students complete a composition after reading or hearing a prepared story starter in second subtest.

PRO-ED (1995)

Test of Written Language, 4th edition (TOWL-4)

(7 years, 6 months to 17 years, 11 months)

Five contrived writing subtests measure students' knowledge of vocabulary, spelling, punctuation, logical sentences, and sentence combining.

Two subtests measure students' spontaneous writing.

PRO-ED (2009)

Woodcock-Johnson III Test of Achievement

(2 years to 90+ years)

Six subtests of contrived writing measure students' spelling abilities, writing fluency, writing samples, editing abilities, spelling of sounds, and use of punctuation and capitalization.

(2001)

Writing Process Test (WPT)

(8 years to 19 years)

Students plan, write, and revise an original composition.

Six development scales measure purpose and focus, audience, vocabulary, style and tone, support and development, and organization and coherence.

Six fluency scales measure sentence structure, sentence variety, grammar and usage, capitalization, punctuation, and spelling.

PRO-ED (2009)

Source: Adapted from Calfee and Wilson (2004).

with the view of writing as an active and ongoing process (Murphy & Yancey, 2008). As with indirect writing measures, teachers can create their own assessments or use published resources. Table 7.17 describes indirect and direct writing subtests found in some commercially available assessment tools.

Teachers need to be aware of other factors beyond students' writing skills that may influence their performance, including the following:

- A limited knowledge of the subject or topic area
- An unfamiliarity with the linguistic and rhetorical patterns presented in writing rubrics, which may be different from those associated with students' primary culture
- Varied interpretation of writing tasks (i.e., tasks interpreted differently among students and their teachers)

These limitations also may affect how individual teachers respond to and evaluate student writing.

WRITING PORTFOLIOS

Recently, many educators have favoured the use of writing portfolios, which allow students' writings to be reviewed over the course of a defined term or school year. As part of this process, students are invited to select materials for inclusion in their portfolios (with an accompanying explanation or reflection). Other times, portfolio submissions reflect activities and projects required by their teachers. The use of writing portfolios has been associated with an increased emphasis on higher-order thinking skills, increased teacher expectations, and greater emphasis on student growth and development (Murphy & Yancey, 2008).

Collecting multiple samples of students' writing over a term or academic year can provide teachers with many insights about students' understanding of the writing process and growth as writers. Students can also benefit by reviewing their compositions over time, especially when guided to reflect on their use of the writing process as well as their writing strengths and needs (i.e., metacognition).

Prior to implementing, responding to, and evaluating writing portfolios in their classrooms, we encourage teachers to deliberate the following factors and considerations.

Completion Time

Assessment procedures must provide students with adequate time to plan, organize, write, and edit their composition. With time, students can produce longer compositions, which in turn provide teachers with greater insights into students' ability to generate well-developed and coherent compositions as well as their strengths in applying writing mechanics and conventions.

Multiple Genres and Content Areas

Students may respond differently to writing activities intended for discrete audiences and purposes. Students' writing abilities may vary across genres (i.e., students may be proficient in producing a narrative but struggle with producing a persuasive article or argument) and content areas.

Writing Prompts

The quality of students' compositions may vary as a function of the directions provided for the writing activity (a writing prompt). Many students respond best when explicit directions instead of open-ended ones are provided.

Holistic, Trait, and Analytical Rubrics and Scoring Protocols

Teachers need to consider the specific nature of the scoring criteria or rubric they will use to evaluate students' work, choosing from three basic scoring approaches: holistic, primary or trait, and analytic. Holistic scores are based on general impressions of the composition as defined by overall quality descriptors (e.g., the student presents a strong persuasive argument; the student's report incorporates five-paragraph essay format). While time efficient for teachers, these global scales are limited in that they distort the complex skills and traits involved in writing and provide little direction for instruction (Murphy & Yancey, 2008).

Trait-based scoring formats, on the other hand, focus on a defined feature associated with a specific writing activity (e.g., voice *or* organization), while analytical scores reflect students' performance across a number of defined features or traits (e.g., organization, voice, *and* coherence). The 6 + 1 Traits of Writing model described below is a common example of such a scale. Alternatively, teachers may elect to use a combination of holistic and analytic criteria. Selecting a scoring method is an important decision, as each method will provide different patterns of results and corresponding insights about students' abilities (Murphy & Yancey, 2008).

Increasingly, educators are calling on students to share responsibility for the assessment of their own and their peers' compositions. In general, having students participate in the creation of grading rubrics and scoring criteria increases their motivation, engagement, and commitment to the writing process. Students are also more likely to be receptive to feedback related to their writing strengths, growth, and areas of need (National Writing Project & Nagin, 2006).

Caution It is critical for teachers to ensure that students possess the appropriate knowledge and skills to provide constructive feedback (Simmons, 2003). Without such skills and training, students may provide only negative and judgmental comments or use praise as a reflection of social relationships (Beach & Friedrich, 2006).

6 + 1 Traits of Writing

The 6 + 1 Traits of Writing is an assessment tool designed by teachers to help assess and score student writing. It is usually applied as a rubric, with many examples available on the internet (e.g., http://educationnorthwest.org, http://effectiveteachingarticles.blogspot.com/, www.youtube.com/watch?v=6QcTWAnxdGM).

The popularity of 6 + 1 Traits of Writing has provided a blueprint that enables teachers to teach writing more effectively. It makes it easier for teachers to prioritize, individualize, and focus writing instruction (Culham, 1995, 2005). It has also provided a common language for discussing, teaching, and evaluating students' writing effectively and consistently. Rather than dictating the writing curriculum, it provides a framework for examining it and ensuring that students write in different genres and for different audiences and purposes. The 6 + 1 Traits of Writing also provide an understandable language for communicating with students and parents about writing progress.

Briefly, the traits are:

Ideas: Ideas are the content of the writing or the heart of the message, which reflects the writers' purpose.

Organization: This element reflects the internal structure, the order of ideas, and the logical and coherent development of the writing.

Voice: Voice reflects the passion, tone, and feelings of the writer, and according to Culham (2005, p. 12) is "the soul of the piece."

Word choice: The words are best when they are rich, varied, and precise while illuminating the ideas for the reader.

Sentence fluency: Sentence fluency is the flow of language and the sound of the words. It appeals to the ear, not just the eye.

Conventions: This element refers to the degree that the author has used grammar, spelling, and the mechanics of language correctly.

Presentation: The presentation refers to the form and layout of the piece and the way in which it is pleasing to the eye.

Teachers need to teach the traits separately, with chunks of time allocated to developing each one. For instance, thinking aloud is a useful technique when demonstrating the various traits, with teachers encouraged to create a writing example while their students observe them. As part of this process, it is important that teachers demonstrate all steps of the writing process and consider all traits while writing. This may take a couple of days and teachers are encouraged to circulate hard copies of their writing to facilitate this process. Alternatively, professional or student samples can be used and analyzed for all traits. Ideally, teachers will want to include several genres as part of these sessions, so that students understand that the traits are found across all writing forms.

Generally, the rubric is built on a five-point scale (see Figure 7.4), where "5" indicates that a student possesses a strong knowledge base and skill level and "1" indicates the absence of this knowledge base and skill level (and thus the need for continued, concentrated instruction in this area).

5 = STRONG	Overall strong control over skills, with many strengths evident.
4 = EFFECTIVE	On balance, the strengths outweigh the weaknesses and only a few revisions are needed.
3 = DEVELOPING	Strengths and need for revision are about the same.
2 = EMERGING	Need for revision outweighs the strengths.
1 = NOT YET	Writer is showing very little control so far.

Figure 7.4 Five-Point Scoring Scale

Prior to using the rubric as an assessment tool, teachers should provide students with a copy of it so they can become familiar with the scoring criteria and associated scale (see Figure 7.5). Teachers may also want students to use the scale to assess their writing. In these cases, students' self-assessment rubrics should be attached to their compositions so that teacher and student assessments can be compared.

Trait	5	4	3	2	1
Ideas	Writing is clear and focused. Holds readers' attention and relevant details enrich central theme.	Writing is somewhat clear and focused. Generally holds readers' attention and most details add to the central theme.	Writer is beginning to define the topic but writing is lacking strong clarity and focus. More relevant details are needed.	Writer is at the very beginning stages of defining the topic. Overall development is weak and readers' attention falters. Few relevant details.	No sense of purpose and central theme is unclear. Details are missing. Does not hold readers' attention.
Organization	Organization enhances central idea. Readers move through text in a compelling manner.	Organization generally enhances central idea. Reading is somewhat compelling.	Organization is strong enough to enable readers to move through text quite easily but reading is generally not compelling.	Some organization is evident. Reading through the text is challenging at times. Readers must persevere, as the text is not very compelling.	Writing lacks a clear sense of direction. Ideas, details, and events lack structure. Readers are not compelled to continue.
Voice	Writer speaks directly to readers and is compelling and engaging. Purpose of the writing and the connection to readers are strong.	Writer generally speaks to readers and is generally compelling and engaging. Purpose and connection to readers are usually strong.	Writer seems sincere but not fully engaged so writing is not compelling or engaging. Purpose and connection to readers are mixed.	Writer may be sincere but the readers feel disconnected and disengaged. The purpose is generally unclear.	Writer seems indifferent to topic. Writing lacks purpose and is not engaging for readers. Readers feel totally disconnected
Word choice	Words convey message in an interesting and natural way. They are powerful and engaging.	Words convey the message and are generally interesting and engaging.	Words are functional but lack engagement and interest. Writer's meaning is evident.	Words are not always functional. Readers' interest and engagement are missing. Meaning is usually clear.	Limited words. Specific meaning is unclear. Little or no interest and engagement for readers.

(continued)

Figure 7.5 The 6 + 1 Traits of Writing

Sentence fluency	Writing has an easy flow, rhythm, and cadence. Sentences have varied structure and provide for expressive reading.	Writing has some flow, rhythm, and cadence. Sentences need more variation in structure to ensure consistent expressive reading.	Text has a steady beat but lacks musical, fluid qualities. Flow, rhythm, and cadence generally lack consistency.	Text is clear but lacks beat and musical, fluid qualities. Flow, rhythm, and cadence not consistent.	Sentences are choppy and awkward. Phrasing is not natural. Flow, rhythm, and cadence are missing.
Conventions	The writer demonstrates a good grasp of standard writing conventions (e.g., punctuation, grammar, spelling). Few errors. Readers are not distracted by errors.	The writer generally demonstrates a grasp of standard conventions (e.g., punctuation, grammar, spelling). Some errors are present (e.g., punctuation, grammar, spelling). Readers are generally not distracted by errors.	Reasonable control over some standard writing conventions (e.g., punctuation, grammar, spelling). Several errors are distracting to readers.	Insufficient evidence of control over standard writing conventions (e.g., punctuation, grammar, spelling). Readers are generally distracted by errors.	Many errors in standard writing conventions (e.g., punctuation, grammar, spelling). Errors distract readers, making text difficult to read.
Presentation (Plus 1: Optional)	The form and presentation of text enhances readers' connections and understanding. Pleasing to the eye.	The form and presentation of text generally enhances readers' connections and understanding. Generally pleasing to the eye.	Message is understandable in this format and readers can make fairly good connections. Somewhat pleasing to the eye.	Message is generally understandable in this format with a few exceptions. Slightly pleasing to the eye.	Message is difficult to understand, with presentation format distracting from meaning. Not pleasing to the eye.

Figure 7.5 The 6 + 1 Traits of Writing *(continued)*

SUGGESTIONS FOR PROFESSIONAL DEVELOPMENT

1. Begin a personal teaching journal. Express your ideas about teaching and learning in the classroom. When working with students, reflect on their responses to writing and reading. Share your writing and reflections with students whenever possible.
2. Join an author's group in your community. Reflect on your writing development and the feedback provided to you by others. Volunteer to assist at or host a writers'

workshop at a local school, sharing your experiences as an author with students. Consult with local publishers with respect to publication possibilities for these young authors.

3. Observe students in the primary grades (grades 1 to 3) as they complete various writing activities. What is the nature of their writing? How would you assess their stage of writing development? What aspects of the writing process do they demonstrate?
4. Explore the lives and works of celebrated Canadian children's authors (some excellent suggestions are Deborah Ellis, Phoebe Gilman, Gordon Korman, Kenneth Oppel, and Eric Wilson). When did these authors produce their first publications? How did they sustain their motivation as authors? How have their interests and writings changed over time? Volunteer to organize a young authors' conference in a local school. Your colleagues can work in pairs to provide a workshop activity that integrates reading, drama, art, etc., and that is motivational for aspiring young writers. If funds permit, invite a local author to participate in the event.

Chapter 8

Teaching the Writing Tools: Spelling, Grammar, Mechanics, and Handwriting

Learning Objectives

In this chapter you will discover

- How to conduct an effective spelling program.
- How to teach spelling strategies using auditory, visual, and kinesthetic methods.
- How to teach the use of prefixes and suffixes.
- How to help students use Standard English.
- How to conduct grammar mini-lessons.
- How to teach grammar in a literary context.
- How to teach the mechanics of writing.

MILICA VELJIC: DEDICATED TO INDIVIDUALIZED INSTRUCTION

After completing a two-year teacher preparation program at the University of Calgary with a focus on children's literacy, Milica is beginning her third year of teaching (and her second year in grade 3). Her love of children's literature ensures that literature is central to her daily programming, with her students completing Read Aloud and independent reading daily. "My love of literature comes out in everything we do. When reading together, I take care to pick books that reflect quality writing and avoid simpler texts that students can read alone."

Milica's school adopts the Reggio Emilia philosophy, an inquiry-based approach to early childhood education that involves creating a child-centred program. Following this philosophy, learning is an inviting process in which students are intrinsically motivated to learn. The teacher's role is that of a facilitator who sets few boundaries and encourages individualized learning.

Milica has a particularly strong spelling program in her class and believes that it is important for students to be able to spell the words they use in their writing activities correctly. She also believes that students need to expand their vocabulary while simultaneously learning the meaning and spelling of new words and that parents can play an important role in supporting students' learning. To this end, Milica provides families with an overview of her spelling program at the beginning of the school year as well as suggestions for helping children learn to spell. These suggestions include using visual cues and repetition and incorporating words as part of authentic writing activities. Finally, she encourages parents to establish a regular study schedule with their children.

Recognizing the individual differences that exist among her students' abilities, interests, and skills, she requires that her students create their own spelling lists as well as study predefined words. The individualized word lists can be taken from students' daily journals or from the daily challenge words that reflect key vocabulary about topics being studied (e.g., the word *quartz* from a unit on rocks and minerals). Daily readings provide another source of potential spelling words.

The number of words studied each week varies by student, with each child usually selecting between 5 and 10 items. When students need assistance in choosing their words, Milica reminds them that they can select items from the books they are reading or from their journal writings. She also encourages them to choose words that they are would like to incorporate into their daily vocabulary. She guides students to select a modest number of items to optimize the likelihood of their learning success. "I am comfortable with whatever number they choose, provided that they can experience success learning them."

Students record the new words in their agendas at the beginning of each week, reviewing and studying them throughout the week. At the end of the week, the students dictate their individualized lists to each other in pairs. Milica places students with similar abilities together for this activity. Items that are spelled incorrectly are carried forward to the next list. Students also maintain a *Words Words Words* book in which they record these challenging words alphabetically. Apart from monitoring students' weekly progress, Milica also administers a standardized spelling test three times per year.

To ensure that her students also develop their grammar when writing, Milica watches for patterns of difficulty and provides students with individualized instruction as part of her regular teacher-student conferences. Milica admits that individualizing her instruction to meet her students' learning needs is very labour intensive. However, she believes that maintaining a child-centred focus is well worth her efforts.

REFLECTIVE ACTIVITY 1

Reflect on the last academic or formal paper you wrote.

- Did you struggle to recall the correct spelling of any words while writing?
- If yes, how did this challenge affect your writing process?
- What strategies, techniques, and tools did you use to resolve your spelling challenge?

Reflect on your spelling experiences as a young student.

- Do the strategies and approaches you use now differ from those of your youth?
- Discuss your responses.

SPELLING

CORRECT SPELLING IS OFTEN ASSOCIATED WITH EDUCATIONAL SUCCESS AND ATTAINMENT while poor spelling is often associated with illiteracy and academic struggles (Blachowicz, Fisher, & Ogle, 2006; Bradley & Bryant, 1999; McQuirter Scott & Siamon, 2005). Fortunately, the ability to spell well is within the grasp of most students. Fifty words account for almost 50 percent of words used by elementary students, 1000 words account for 86 percent, 2000 words account for 92 percent, and 3000 words account for 95 percent (Thomas, 1979), with only about 300 words accounting for the majority (86 percent) of students' most frequent spelling errors. A spelling vocabulary of only 3000 words is sufficient for fluent and proficient communication for both children and adults (Graham, 1983; Woloshyn & Pressley, 1995), with the use of technology making mastery of these items especially achievable.

Spelling Development

Emergent writers

Even before they are able to write, most young children understand that writing carries meaning. They begin to recognize signs and symbols that hold consistent meaning in their environment. For instance, they observe that cars always stop at *STOP* signs. They observe that when adults read their favourite books, they follow a sequence of letters presented on the page. They recognize that writing is a method for recording ideas, thoughts, opinions, feelings, and stories.

Children's initial writing attempts often consist of scribbles interspersed with familiar letters and symbols. While they usually can "read" or share the meaning of their "writing" with adults, these retellings are often inconsistent and vary over time. Just as in the case of oral language and reading, these early attempts hold great significance, with most students passing through identifiable stages of spelling development (Bear Invernizzi, Templeton, & Johnston, 2003; Gentry & Gillet, 1992; McQuirter Scott & Siamon, 2004; Reutzel & Cooter, 2005).

Developmental Spelling Stages In the scribbling and drawing stage, children experiment with making symbols and other marks such as shapes, circles, dots, and lines (Gentry, 2004). As they progress through this stage, their scribbles begin to look more and more like adult cursive writing. Gradually they learn that print writing is different from drawing, although both are forms of written expression.

In the prephonemic stage, or what is otherwise referred to as emergent spelling or precommunicative spelling, children identify and use real letters (usually in capital form) to represent meaning. However, these letters almost never represent their phonemic sounds. Instead, the letters are used as placeholders and can represent a syllable, word, or entire thought. Adults can deduce the meaning of each letter representation by asking young writers to read aloud their compositions. This form of spelling is common in preschool and junior kindergarten (Gentry, 2010).

The next stage is called the semiphonetic stage or early phonemic stage. At this stage, children begin to use letters (mostly capitals and consonants) to represent words. However, students now demonstrate an understanding that letters represent a consistent sound (Invernizzi & Hayes, 2004). One of the first words that young children recognize is their name, with students frequently transferring these letters into their writing. At this stage, students often represent the initial sound in a word (e.g., M for mom). Over time, students expand their spelling to include the first and last sounds of a word, using two or more letters

Figure 8.1 Student Writing Sample 1 by Gwenn, Grade 1

to represent a word. For instance, *fmr* may be used to represent the word *farmer* and *hkn* may represent the word *chicken*. Other times, students will represent one or two phonemes in a word and finish with a random series of letters (e.g., *night* as *NtXtS*). Typically, prephonetic spellers are in kindergarten or grade 1, know their letters, and are beginning to read and spell. Transition from this stage to the next one may be quick and abrupt, with many grade 1 students transitioning across these stages within a matter of weeks or months.

In the letter-naming stage, or what is otherwise referred to as phonetic spelling, students begin to use one or two consonants and a vowel to represent words (Reutzel & Cooter, 2004). Usually late in grade 1 or in grade 2, these students understand that writing progresses from left to right and represent their writings accordingly. They tend to adopt a sequential sounding-out strategy, representing individually articulated sounds with letters that share acoustic similarities. For instance, *because* may be presented as *becuz*, *feet* as *fet*, and *table* as *tabl*.

In the transitional stage, students' writing efforts consist of a mix of phonemic and conventional or morpheme (meaning-based) spelling patterns (Graves, 1994, 2003). Overall, these students have abandoned the belief that each sound needs to be represented by one letter. (See Figures 8.1 and 8.2 for examples.) While simple vowels and consonants often are represented correctly, complex and irregular patterns are not (e.g., *wotched* for *watch*). Students are able to print many high-frequency words and their knowledge of the phonetic system enables others to understand their print messages readily. However, students often overgeneralize word patterns in the same way they overgeneralize grammatical

I like dogs beecus they
lic me and chas me.
Sumtims they bite me
and sumtims they
fech.

Figure 8.2 Student Writing Sample 2 by Brynlee, Grade 1

patterns when learning to speak. For instance, the silent *e* is frequently omitted (especially in low-frequency words) and double consonants are ignored. Consider the following two statements written by grade 2 students:

> Wednesday was my resitl. I playd first. We had cookies and purch. The kids had their pister takeing.
>
> July 18th is a weddin and I am a floer girl. My Mom is the made of oner.

The final stage is called the conventional stage. While this stage may suggest a high level of proficiency, few students or adults spell everything correctly. Students also vary considerably with respect to the types of strategies and word knowledge they possess. Difficulties in this stage may be exacerbated by English-language spelling exceptions and idiosyncrasies where the pattern of pronunciation and the pattern of spelling are inconsistent. Examples of such idiosyncrasies include the following:

- *shepherd* and *telephone* (*ph* is pronounced differently)
- *bishop* and *mishap* (*sh* is pronounced differently)
- *polish* (to shine something) and *Polish* (from Poland)
- *week* and *weak*
- *to*, *two*, and *too*
- *they're*, *there*, and *their*
- *desert* (to abandon), *desert* (a dry region), and *dessert* (the last course at dinner)

More positively, the systematic study of letter patterns, spelling rules, and word structure enables students to write most unknown or unfamiliar words with a high degree of accuracy and certainty (Templeton & Morris, 1999).

Teacher Voice 8.1

Spelling growth enhances more than just the conventions of written language. As students learn about the patterns of sound, structure, and meaning in English, they can apply this knowledge to vocabulary and reading tasks. The interconnections of spelling, reading, and vocabulary are powerful factors in literacy development.

Ruth McQuirter Scott, Ed.D.
Professor

Capitalization and punctuation

Assessing Students' Spelling Development

Teachers may be interested in assessing students' developmental spelling stage, especially when working with students in the early primary grades or those demonstrating spelling difficulties. The *Developmental Spelling Test* developed by Richard Gentry (1982, 1985) is one readily available and administered instrument (available at http://gse.uci.edu/docs/DEVELOPMENTAL_SPELLING.pdf). Briefly, this instrument provides educators with a scoring guide that correlates students' spelling responses to the developmental spelling stages described above (e.g., *mtr* for *monster* = semiphonetic spelling; *bumpped* for *bumped* = transitional spelling). Teachers may be interested in exploring developmental spelling assessments and resources developed by other educational researchers such as Karen Ganske (1999, 2000).

Most students are aware of the importance of conventional spelling when they begin school, often asking teachers, parents, and others about the correct spelling of individual words. The question then arises as to how teachers should best guide students in their spelling efforts. In part, the instructional approaches adopted by teachers should reflect students' development understanding of words. In general, teachers are encouraged to begin instruction in conventional spelling by the middle of grade 1, as most students will possess strong phonological awareness and incorporate consonants and vowels in their invented spellings (Templeton & Morris, 1999).

Caution While it is important for teachers to recognize and understand the developmental spelling stages, they must also appreciate that students should not be rushed or hastened through them and that there will be considerable variation across students in any one classroom. Students often show progress in one area and regression in another. These uneven progressions can be attributed to the cognitive overload that results from trying to master a new skill (Berko Gleason & Ratner, 2009). Teachers are reminded that students learn best when they are provided with gentle guidance and enthusiastic support for their efforts.

Students' Perceptions of Spelling Ability

Despite the evidence of systematic development of spelling abilities across the grades, many students do not perceive themselves to be proficient spellers. Indeed, students' perceptions of their spelling abilities tend to decline across the grades, with many reporting negative emotions when discussing spelling instruction (Stipek & MacIver, 1989; Woloshyn & Pressley, 1995). Furthermore, many students who presented themselves as seemingly proficient spellers in the primary grades demonstrate spelling difficulties throughout the junior and intermediate grades (Powell & Aram, 2008).

When asked to explain how they spell unfamiliar and challenging words, the majority of poor spellers report relying on phoneme-grapheme relations and "sounding words out" letter by letter. In contrast, proficient spellers report using visualization (i.e., trying to visualize how words and units look) and letter patterns (i.e., substituting an unknown word part with the spelling pattern of a similar-sounding word) and analyzing word meanings (morphology). In addition, some students report using relevant spelling rules as a supplement to these strategies (e.g., Dahl et al., 2004; Woloshyn & Pressley, 1995).

Status of Spelling Instruction

Recall the type of spelling instruction you received as a student. For many adults, spelling instruction began with a pretest of 10 to 15 teacher-selected spelling items on Monday, completion of word sort and other activities throughout the week, and a spelling post-test on Friday. The era of students completing spelling dictation as a class, with many students getting half or more of the words wrong, is over. Today, many teachers allow students to choose at least some of their spelling items, with the number of items varying among students.

There is no one best method for teaching spelling. Instead, teachers need to be cognizant and responsive to students' varied spelling needs and abilities and provide them with corresponding instruction. Furthermore, teachers need to provide students with a repertoire of effective spelling strategies and resources that mirror those used by proficient spellers. This instruction is especially effective when accompanied by metacognitive discussion about *what*, *when*, and *where* to use each strategy. Many times, instruction in one process (e.g., spelling by analogy) will be conditional on another defined skill set (e.g., acquisition of letter patterns), requiring instruction in several spelling strategies (e.g., imagery and rhyming).

Student Voice 8.1

Spelling is important. Every Friday we have a spelling test. My mom and dad help me study my words. They say the word and I write it down. If I get it wrong, I need to copy it again. We have learned some big words this year like *windmill*, *backpack*, and *classroom*, as well as small words like *wet*, *if*, and *it*.

Hayden
Grade 2 student

How to Select Spelling Words

Without direct instruction, students are unlikely to develop an awareness and understanding of sound and meaning patterns in words while reading text independently. Spelling lists can be an effective tool in such instruction. The question arises, however, as to how these lists are best structured.

In many Canadian classrooms, students review lists of target spelling items as a weekly activity. For students in the primary grades, these lists may consist of 10 or fewer items reflecting critical sight words and letter patterns. Students in the junior and intermediate grades should be assigned longer lists (approximately 10 to 12 and 20 words, respectively) consisting of frequently misspelled items and items that lend themselves to morphological analysis. Ideally, the spellings of these words are unfamiliar to most students in the classroom, as the use of unknown word lists is superior to the study of mixed known and unknown lists (e.g., Graham & Miller, 1979). Students can also supplement and individualize their spelling lists by adding unfamiliar items that they encounter as part of their daily writing (Templeton & Morris, 1999).

Caution Teachers should avoid relying on student-selected spelling items exclusively, as the emphasis will switch from the study of transferrable letter patterns to individual items.

Focus on Spelling Patterns Educational researchers agree that spelling patterns (including morphemic and meaning-based units) should be the primary focus of spelling instruction, as they can be generalized across many words. Teachers are encouraged to provide younger students with instruction about common letter patterns (e.g., Gaskins, 2005). Older students should study polysyllabic and spelling-meaning relationships (Cunningham, 2000; Ganske, 2008; Powell & Aram, 2008).

Focus on Sight Words Sight words are high-frequency words that are recognized automatically by effective readers and writers. Primary grade teachers are encouraged to include such words on students' spelling lists. Junior and intermediate grade teachers can include hard-to-spell words as well as critical vocabulary items from across the content areas. Teachers are encouraged to consult print resources (e.g., *Month-by-Month Phonics for Upper Grades* by Cunningham and Hall [1998]; *Mindful of Words: Spelling and Vocabulary Explorations 4–8* by Ganske [2008]) and online resources (e.g., http://oxforddictionaries.com/page/spellingcommonmisp/common-misspellings; www.yourdictionary.com/library/misspelled.html) for lists of commonly misspelled words.

Use Developmentally Appropriate Lists Spelling lists need to correspond to students' immediate spelling needs and spelling development. For example, teaching phonetic spellers about polysyllabic words would be developmentally inappropriate. Rather, these students are likely to benefit from instruction in blends, diagraphs, and short-vowel sounds.

Many contemporary spelling series are designed to correspond to students' developmental abilities. We encourage teachers to review Canadian resources and series such as *The Spelling Teacher's Book of Lists* by Jo Phenix (2003), *The Canadian Spelling Series* by Ruth Scott, Sharon Siamon, and Ves Thomas (1999), and *Spell Well* by Lillian Butovsky and Tamara Moscoe (1985). When reviewing these materials, teachers should carefully consider whether the spelling patterns, sight words, and word features reflect the learning needs of their students.

Spelling Rules

There is some debate among educators about the value of providing students with instruction in spelling rules. Opponents often cite the large number of irregularities and exceptions that exist in the English language (Horn, 1969; Templeton & Morris, 1999). An alternative perspective, however, advocates providing students with instruction in those rules that apply to a large number of words and have only a few exceptions (Graham & Miller, 1979; Thomas, 1979). Equally important is providing students with the opportunity to analyze and apply these rules as part of their authentic writing activities. Table 8.1 lists some common transferrable spelling rules and generalizations.

Table 8.1 Transferrable Spelling Rules

1. Rules governing the addition of suffixes and inflected endings:
   a. When a word ends in *e*, the *e* is usually dropped when a syllable beginning with a vowel is added.

skate	skating
bake	baking
race	racing

   b. When a word ends in *e*, the *e* is usually kept when a syllable beginning with a vowel is added.

skate	skater
bake	baker
race	raced

   c. When a root word ends in *y* and is preceded by a consonant, the *y* is changed to *i* when suffixes and endings are added, unless they begin with an *i*.

try	tries	try	trying
reply	replies	reply	replying
spy	spies	spy	spying

   d. When a noun ends in *y* and is preceded by a consonant, the plural is formed by changing the *y* to *i* and adding *es*.

canary	canaries
cavity	cavities
lady	ladies

(Continued)

Table 8.1 Transferrable Spelling Rules *(continued)*

e. When a root word ends in *y* and is preceded by a vowel, the root word is not changed when a suffix or ending is added.

buy	buying
stay	stayed
spray	sprays

f. Words that end with a consonant and are preceded by a single vowel usually require that the consonant be doubled before adding an ending.

fan	fanning
run	runner
stop	stopped

2. Rules governing the use of apostrophes:
   a. Add an apostrophe and *s* to show possession after a single noun (the boy's mittens; the girl's book).
   b. Add an apostrophe alone to show possession after a plural noun ending in *s* (the girls' boots; the boys' books).
   c. Add an apostrophe and *s* to show possession after plural nouns not ending in *s* (the children's hats; the women's book).
   d. Add an apostrophe to show the omission of a letter or letters in a contraction (isn't; I'll; can't; it's; can't).
3. Rules governing the letter *s* and plurals:
   a. Add *es* to form plurals or to change the tense of verbs ending with hissing sounds (*x*, *s*, *sh*, *ch*).

fox	foxes
gas	gases
class	classes
watch	watches
smash	smashes

   b. Change *f* to *v* and add *es* when pluralizing words ending in a single *f*.

leaf	leaves
calf	calves
wife	wives

4. Most abbreviations end with a period.

   Ont.

   Nov.
5. The letter *q* is always followed by *u* in common English words (queen; quote; quiet; quit).
6. No English words end in *v* (glove; cave).
7. The letter *i* usually comes before *e* except after *c* (deceive; receipt).

Source: Adapted from Woloshyn and Pressley (1995).

Spelling Mnemonics

Developed by the early Greeks, mnemonics are memory strategies or "tricks" that help individuals remember critical information. In the context of spelling, students may find mnemonics helpful when learning challenging words, especially those with irregular spelling patterns. Mnemonics can be visual (drawing the silent *t* in *witch* as a witch's hat), semantic (remembering the *pal* in *principal*), or auditory (pronouncing the second *e* as a long vowel sound instead of as a short vowel sound in the word *repetition*). Mnemonics are usually idiosyncratic to individual learners and students should be encouraged to develop their own in response to their unique spelling needs and challenges (McQuirter Scott & Siamon, 2004).

Auditory Strategies

Having students repeat the letters in words is one of the most readily implemented strategies for word learning. Essentially, the strategy requires teachers to guide students in speaking or chanting the spelling of target words. This instruction is often supplemented with kinesthetic reinforcements such as clapping or tapping individual letters or word syllables (e.g., clap each syllable in the following words: *Jan-u-ar-y*, *trans-por-ta-tion*, *e-du-ca-tion*). Other approaches include exaggerating hard-to-hear or silent letters (e.g., February, solemn, pneumonia, mnemonic) and listening for rhyming patterns (e.g., which of the following rhyme?: *frog*, *log*, *frat*, and *blog*; McQuirter Scott & Siamon, 2004). Whenever possible, teachers are encouraged to include discussion about word morphology or meaning as part of such activities (Powell & Aram, 2008).

Auditory, Visual, and Kinesthetic Strategies

Look, Say, and Write is one well-known strategy for learning the spelling of individual words (Graham & Miller, 1979; McQuirter Scott & Siamon, 2004; Templeton & Morris, 1999). This approach involves students studying each letter of the target word, recreating a visual or kinesthetic representation of the word, checking the accuracy of the spelling, and then using the word in print. Having students write words in sand, rice, or in large print on whiteboards or chalkboards with their eyes closed are common methods used to reinforce students' kinesthetic and visual learning of words, as is using letter blocks and other manipulatives.

Spelling words are often "boxed" by outlining the shape of individual letters across many spelling series and word walls, providing students with a visual image of the whole word (see Figure 8.3).

Canadian teacher Kelly Kernaghan and her grade 3 students adopted an innovative procedure that involved using a "magic paint and paintbrush" (Kernaghan & Woloshyn, 1995). Students practised dipping an imaginary paintbrush into an imaginary tin of paint and writing each letter of the spelling word in large print across a blank wall while repeating associated letter sounds. Instruction was then supplemented with discussion of

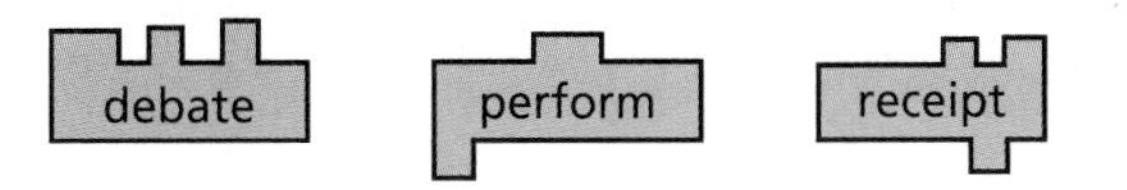

Figure 8.3 Boxed Spelling Words

the benefits of using visual and kinesthetic strategies and extended writing opportunities. Variations of this approach can include having students use a reproduced image of a keyboard to "type" target words.

Irregular, low-frequency, unfamiliar words are best for this type of instruction, with students being encouraged to repeat this process 4 to 5 times for each word. Whenever possible, students should be encouraged to generate and use additional words that share the same spelling or meaning patterns (Templeton & Morris, 1999, 2000).

Spelling by Analogy (Letter Patterns)

Spelling by analogy, or using familiar spelling patterns to spell unfamiliar words, is a well-substantiated approach used by proficient spellers (Englert, Hiebert & Stewart, 1985; Goswami & Bryant, 1990; Westwood, 2005). Similar to its decoding counterpart, reading by analogy, students who use this approach need to appreciate that when two words rhyme or share the same sound, they often share the same spelling ending.

While some proficient readers may adopt this strategy spontaneously, the majority of students will benefit from explicit instruction of this approach. Such instruction involves the following:

- Familiarizing students with the "rhyming rule."
- Providing examples of this rule (e.g., *and* rhymes with *sand*; *cold* rhymes with *bold*; *would* rhymes with *should*).
- Providing students with target words orally and having them identify words that share the same spelling pasterns using word walls, word lists, and authentic text (e.g., identify which words rhyme with *frog*, *swing*, *cow*, *have*).
- Having students use target words in print activities, including fill-in-the-blank exercises and sentence writing. Encourage students to check word walls and other resources when uncertain about spelling and to review their work for accuracy. Minimize the use of external resources and supports over time.
- Providing students with repeated instruction in the use of the spelling by analogy when errors are made, reminding them to generate words that rhyme with the target word and to reflect on their spelling.
    - I need to spell the word *blame*.
    - I hear the syllables *bl/ame* (or I can listen for each of the vowel sounds).
    - I know how to spell *name*, which also uses the *ame* spelling pattern plus the blend *bl*.
    - I need to check my spelling using the dictionary, spell check, or another resource.
    - I need to spell the word *surround*.
    - I hear the syllables *sur/round* (or I can listen for each of the vowel sounds).
    - I know how to spell *round*, which uses the *ound* spelling pattern.
    - I know that *sur* rhymes with *fur*, which uses the *ur* pattern plus *s*.
    - I need to check my spelling using the dictionary, spell check, or another resource.
    - I need to spell the word *conference*.
    - I hear the syllables *con/fer/ence* (or I can listen for each of the vowel sounds).

- I know how to spell *on* and can add the *c*.
- I know that *her* rhymes with *fer*, which uses the *er* spelling pattern plus *f*.
- I need to check my spelling using the dictionary, spell check, or another resource.

It is especially important that students check their derived spellings, as it is possible to select an incorrect spelling pattern. More positively, students' initial spelling efforts are often sufficient to guide them toward the correct spelling of the target word. Consider that, in the example below, spell check provides the following options for the erroneous item: *brine*, *bran*, *brae*, *brain*, and *brand*.

- I need to spell the word *brain*.
- I hear the syllables *br/ain*.
- I know how to spell *plane*, which uses the *ane* spelling pattern plus *br* = *brane*.

- Assessing students on their acquisition of target words as well as rhyming words that share the same spelling pattern.

Caution To use the spelling by analogy approach successfully, students must be able to spell automatically at least one sight word that contains the letter pattern in question. It is possible, however, especially in the primary grades, that students will not possess this knowledge. In these cases, teachers are encouraged to have their students engage in visualization, auditory, and kinesthetic activities that promote the learning of sight words.

Morphology Strategies

Having students study word parts as meaningful units is another common method used to enhance spelling. As students become more aware of words that share the same meaning units (e.g., *definitely* and *definition* → *define*; *publicity* and *publicist* → *public*; *feminine* and *feminist* → *female*; *criticize* and *criticism* → *critic*), their spellings of these items will improve. Morphological awareness contributes positively to students' decoding and spelling abilities (Bear et al., 2003; Carlisle, 2010; Dahl et al., 2004; Williams & Lundstrom, 2007) as well as to their reading comprehension and vocabulary development (e.g., Nagy, Berninger, & Abbott, 2006).

Morphemes are defined as the smallest units of words that contain meaning. They can be free-standing (e.g., *alter*, *aqua*) or bound to words (e.g., *ward* in *forward*, *backward*, *inward*). They can be combined in distinct manners to express specific meaning or grammatical structure. For instance, they can be used to represent tense (e.g., *fix*, *fixes*, *fixed*; *sing*, *singing*, *sang*; *set*, *reset*, *preset*), gender (e.g., *actor*, *actress*; *househusband*, *housewife*), or quantity (e.g., *boy*, *boys*; *prefix*, *prefixes*; *curriculum*, *curricula*; *analysis*, *analyses*). In general, suffixes are morphemes found at the end of words, prefixes are those found at the beginning of words, and base or root words are those that appear in the middle of words.

Prefixes and Suffixes Many spelling and vocabulary texts and resources contain complete lists of the prefixes, suffixes, and root words contained in the English language (as well as those in the Latin and Greek languages). Often these resources are grade-specific (e.g., *Making Words: Hands-On Lessons for Teaching Prefixes, Suffixes, and Roots* and the *Month-by-Month Phonics* series by Cunningham and Hall) and provide students with sequential systematic instruction in the use of prefixes and suffixes. Tables 8.2 and 8.3 list some common prefixes and suffixes.

Table 8.2 Examples of Common Prefixes

Prefix	Meaning	Examples
a, an	not, without	anarchy, anonymous, apathy, atypical
ab	away, down, from, off	abduction, abnormal, absent, absorb, abstract,
ad	to, toward	adhere, advance, adventure
ambi	both	ambidextrous, ambient, ambiguous, ambivalent
anim	alive	animal, animate, animation
counter, contra	against, opposite	contraband, contrary, counteract
eu	good, well	eucalyptus, euphemism, euphoria, euthanasia
ex	out, from	exit, exhale, exhibit, exclude
fore	before, front	forecast, forefather, forehead, foreman, foretell,
il, im, in, ir, un	not, opposing, reverse	illegal, immature, impolite, inappropriate, irregular, unconcerned, unlawful
ortho	straight	orthodontics, orthodox, orthopedic, orthoscopic
meter, metre	measure	kilometre, millimetre, thermometer
micro	small	microfilm, microphone, microscope
mis	wrong, ill	misspell, mistreat, misunderstand
multi	many	multiply, multitude
post	after	posterior, postlude, postpone, postscript
port	carry	portable, porter
pre	before, in front of	predict, prefix, preheat, prelude, pretend, pretext
pro	forward	proceed, proclaim, produce, project, promote, propel
proto	first, earliest	protocol, proton, protoplasm, prototype,
quasi	approximate, resemble	quasi-particle, quasi-scientific
re	back, again	redo, return, revise, revision
trans	across	transcontinental, transport, transportation
ultra	beyond, extremely	ultrafine, ultraquiet, ultrasonic, ultraviolet,
under	beneath, below, too little	undercoat, understand, undertone, undervalue

Table 8.3 Examples of Common Suffixes

Prefix	Meaning	Examples
able, ible	capable of being	curable, drinkable, pourable, readable, washable, flexible, visible
an, ian	belonging to	American, urban, amphibian, Canadian, librarian, musician, politician
ance, ancy	state of, process of	performance, reliance, defiance, acceptance, discrepancy, infancy, pregnancy
ator	one who does	generator, investigator, terminator,
ar, ary, ory	relating to	similar, imaginary, primary, visionary, allegory
dom	condition, office, state	freedom, kingdom, sheikdom, wisdom
ee	one who receives, one who is	appointee, employee, payee, referee, refugee
er, or, eer	one who does	driver, hiker, reader, speaker, writer author, creator, director, auctioneer, pioneer
ful	filled with	beautiful, cheerful, delightful, frightful, wonderful
ify	to make into	clarify, exemplify, pacify, purify, simplify
ification	process of making into	clarification, purification, simplification
ion, sion, tion	state of, condition	billion, bunion, tension, abbreviation, action, exhibition, relaxation
ish	the nature of, resembling, like	bookish, boyish, foolish, selfish
ism	system, quality characteristic	capitalism, conservatism, heroism, optimism, realism
ist	one who performs	cellist, idealist, realist, pharmacist
ize	to make into	capitalize, dramatize, normalize, rationalize, realize
ization	the process of making into	dramatization, normalization, rationalization, realization
less	without, lacking	fearless, harmless, loveless, nameless, worthless
ly	how completed	annually, monthly, quietly, randomly, similarly, weekly
ment	state of being	enjoyment, entertainment, improvement, management

When reviewing these lists, teachers are encouraged to provide students with direct instruction in the meaning of common prefixes (e.g., *in*, *il*, *ir*, *im*, *un*, and *non* mean "not"; *uni* and *mono* mean "one"; *counter*, *de*, *dis*, *un*, *for*, and *un* mean "opposite"). As part of this instruction, teachers need to inform students that the spelling patterns of prefixes remain constant across words.

Similarly, teachers need to explain that the spellings of suffixes remain constant despite variations in their pronunciations. Consider the pronunciation of the following words containing the suffix *ed*: *talked* (sounds like *t*), *rolled* (sounds like *d*), and *waited* (sounds like *id*)(Hauerwas & Walker, 2004). Students can be guided to appreciate that when the use of a suffix changes the spelling of a word, these changes are usually consistent with spelling rules (i.e., change *y* to *i* before adding *ed*; double the final consonant before adding *ing*; drop the final *e* before adding *ed*, *ing*, *able*). Once students have strong foundational knowledge about the nature and role of common prefixes and suffixes, teachers are encouraged to have students analyze complex, polysyllabic words (e.g., *replacement* = prefix *re*, suffix *ment*; *impression* = prefix *im*, suffix *ion*). Teachers working with students in the junior and intermediate grades may find word lists such as *Nifty Thrifty Fifty* to be especially helpful here (Cunningham & Hall, 1998).

It is also important that teachers encourage students to be reflective about their understanding of word spellings and to record their new learning. For example, students can be encouraged to complete a chart like the one presented in Table 8.4 on which they record the syllables, base and root words, prefixes, and suffixes (noting any resulting spelling changes because of the latter) for target items. Students can then share their discovery of new words and spelling patterns with their peers as part of either small-group or whole-class discussion. Such reflection, sharing, and instruction improve students' metacongitive awareness and learning.

Word Sorts

Students often enjoy completing word sorts as a method of solidifying and extending their learning of letter sounds, letter patterns, and unit meanings. Word sorts encourage students to compare and contrast word patterns and generalize their learning to new items. Teachers can either create their own word sort activities or select activities from

Table 8.4 Spelling Reflection Chart

New Word	Syllables	Base and Root Words	Prefixes and Suffixes	New Spellings
renew	re/new	new	re	renewing
impossible	im/pos/sible	possible	im	possibly (drop e and add *ly*)
sufferable	suf/fer/able	suffer	able	insufferable
verify	ver/i/fy	verify	y	verifies (drop *y* and add *ies*)
unbutton	un/but/ton	button	un	unbuttoned
independently	in/de/pen/dent/ly	dependent	in, ly	independence

commercially available products. Just as when selecting spelling series or spelling lists, teachers are cautioned to consider the developmental appropriateness of these materials with respect to their students' spelling needs.

Puzzles and Games

Most students enjoy playing board, card, and electronic games. Traditional spelling games such as Scrabble, UpWords, and Boggle provide students with excellent opportunities to reinforce their spelling skills and extend their learning (many of these games are available online). Teachers may also want to explore spelling-specific software programs such as *Spell It Deluxe*, *Spelling Blaster*, and *Word Maker* or online spelling games (e.g., www.kidsspell.com/spelling-games; www.gamequarium.com/spelling.html; www.gamesgames.com/games/spelling/spelling.html).

We encourage teachers to consider modifying common games such as Sorry, Frustration, and Twister to include spelling items—for instance, by requiring students to spell a word containing a critical letter or to spell a rhyming word after drawing from teacher-created turn cards. See Table 8.5 for examples of spelling games.

Table 8.5 Examples of Spelling Games

Board Games
A B C OY! Game
Alpha Bug Step-n-Spell
Banana Grams
Batter Up Spelling Game
Cadaco Countdown and Spell Up
Clusters
Coodju: Elementary School–Aged Reading and Spelling
Cranium
Endless Games Spill and Spell: The Crossword Cube Classic
Explore & Learn Spelling Bugs
Flippit Word Game
Maxi-Aids Game Spin N Spell
Melissa and Doug Deluxe Wooden See and Spell
Password: Elementary School–Aged Reading and Spelling
See and Spell
See Spot Spell Game
Smart Mouth: Middle School–Age Reading and Spelling
Snap It Up Word Families
Spell Checkers
Spell Down

(Continued)

Table 8.5 Examples of Spelling Games *(continued)*

Board Games *(continued)*
Spell It! Match and Learn
Spelling All Stars Two Game
Spelling Bee Bingo
Spelling Bee Game
Spellominos Word Flash Card Game
Talicor 301 Spelling Beez Learning Game
Trixy and Troy Spell–Link
Word Storm: Middle School–Age Reading and Spelling
Software Games
Disney's Winnie the Pooh: Spelling
Garfield Software/Workbook: It's All About Spelling and Vocabulary
I Love Spelling
Jump Start Spelling
Jump Start Study Helpers Spelling Bee
Learning Center Series Spelling and Grammar
Merriam Webster's SPELL–JAM
Snap! Spelling
Spelling 1-2 Deluxe
Spelling 1st and 2nd Grade
Spelling 2 Pack Software
Spelling Accelerator
Spelling Accelerator, 2nd Edition
Spelling Bee
Spelling Blaster
Spelling Jungle with Yobi the Spelling Wizard
Spelling Made Easy
Super Start! Fun with Vocabulary & Spelling!
Word Whomp Deluxe

Dictionaries

"Looking up" the spelling of unknown words in a traditional dictionary can be an extremely frustrating experience for many students, especially those who are poor spellers. Consider that students need to possess some level of spelling ability and strong dictionary skills before they are able to use a dictionary efficiently. For instance, they need to be able to recognize and use guide words and apply alphabetization skills related to the first three letters (and sometime more) of target words (McQuirter Scott & Siamon, 2004). Nonetheless, using a dictionary is an important component of many word study units. To prepare students to use a dictionary, we encourage teachers to provide them with direct instruction and practice in the skills described above as well as in using such features as the Common Spelling of English sound charts found at the front of most dictionaries (e.g., three ways to spell the *s* sound at the beginning of a word).

Spelling and Rhyming Dictionaries Teachers and students may wish to consult spelling and rhyming dictionaries when confirming the spelling of unknown words. Unlike a regular dictionary, which includes definitions, word origins, and other information (e.g., regular and irregular plural, tense, and adjective formats; synonyms; homophones; related words), these resources list only the target items (see Figure 8.4 for an example). Students may find these resources less cumbersome and easier to use than standard dictionaries.

Correcting Students' Spelling Errors

Correcting students' spelling errors can be a sensitive issue for students and teachers alike. Focusing too much attention on spelling may deter students from taking risks and using sophisticated language and ideas when writing. Consider that most adults prefer to use approximated spellings or "best guesses" when writing rather than interrupt their thoughts, returning to proofread their work later. On the other hand, allowing students to share or publish written documents with spelling errors is concerning, especially to parents. The question arises as to how teachers should best correct students' spelling efforts and encourage them to develop their spelling consciousness so they will reflect on and review their writing spontaneously.

Whenever possible, students should be encouraged to check and correct their own spelling, whether in response to a dictated spelling test or as part of proofreading

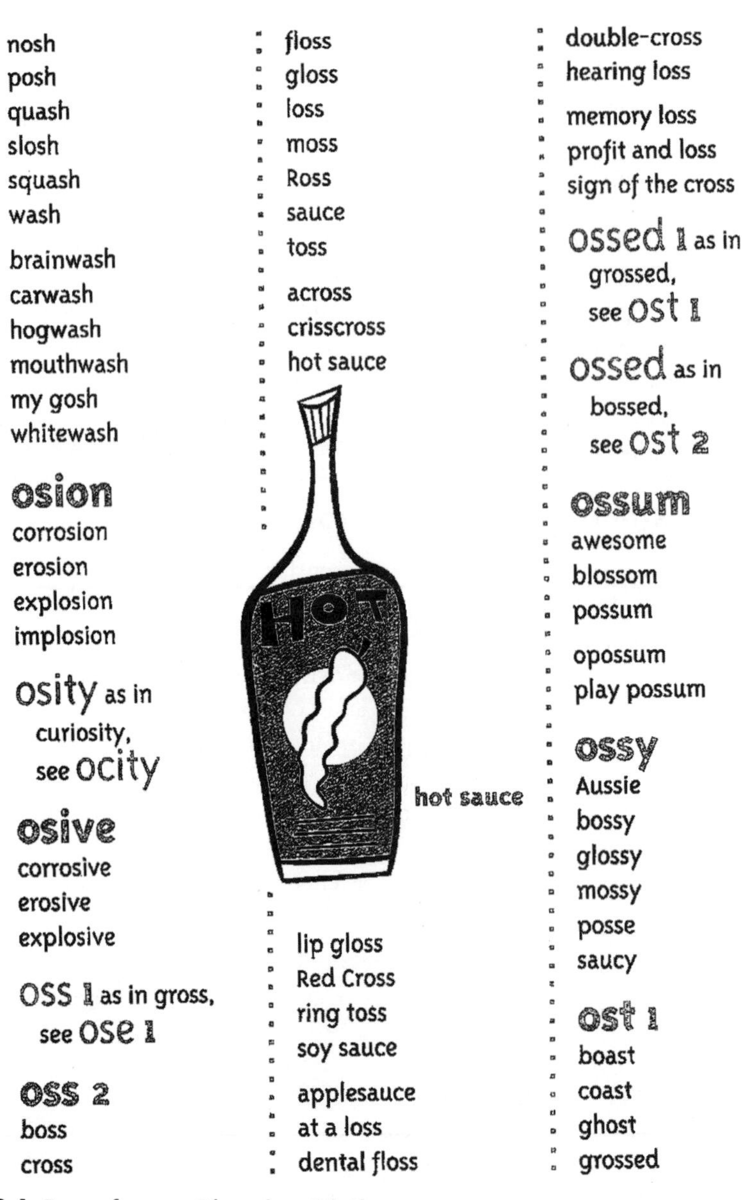

nosh
posh
quash
slosh
squash
wash

brainwash
carwash
hogwash
mouthwash
my gosh
whitewash

osion
corrosion
erosion
explosion
implosion

osity as in curiosity, see **ocity**

osive
corrosive
erosive
explosive

oss 1 as in gross, see **ose 1**

oss 2
boss
cross
floss
gloss
loss
moss
Ross
sauce
toss

across
crisscross
hot sauce

lip gloss
Red Cross
ring toss
soy sauce

applesauce
at a loss
dental floss
double-cross
hearing loss
memory loss
profit and loss
sign of the cross

ossed 1 as in grossed, see **ost 1**

ossed as in bossed, see **ost 2**

ossum
awesome
blossom
possum

opossum
play possum

ossy
Aussie
bossy
glossy
mossy
posse
saucy

ost 1
boast
coast
ghost
grossed

Figure 8.4 Page from a Rhyming Dictionary

their authentic writing. When correcting dictated spelling tests, teachers should provide students with a visual representation of the correct spellings, stating and pointing to each letter in target words (thus allowing students to hear and see the correct spelling).

There is also some value in imitating students' errors in addition to providing them with the conventional spelling (Gerber, 1984, 1986). As part of this approach, teachers reproduce students' incorrect spelling on one side of the page and then provide the correct spelling on the other side. The teacher then highlights any incorrect letters by circling or boxing them, helping students recognize how their spelling effort differed from the conventional one. Students are then required to record the correct spelling and apply it in an authentic writing activity.

Caution Teachers may wish to restrict the number of corrections they provide to students who produce large numbers of spelling errors or who are reluctant writers, limiting their corrections to spelling and vocabulary items. These students should be encouraged to use spelling checks and other technologies when writing.

REFLECTIVE ACTIVITY 2

Take a minute to complete a "quick write" about your experiences learning grammar.

- Who taught you?
- How were you taught?
- How do you feel about grammar now?
- How do you feel about teaching grammar?

Discuss your answers with another person or in a grand conversation with your class.

GRAMMAR

What Is Grammar?

In general, grammar is the way in which the forms of our language are arranged and patterned. The study of grammar considers the forms or structures that are possible in a language. In other words, grammar is a description of the rules that govern how a language's **sentences** are formed.

- The rules that govern the order of words in a sentence are called **syntax**.
- The system that governs the formation of words is called **morphology**.
- Grammar is the study of the **syntax and morphology** of sentences.

The Study of Grammar Three general categories encompass the study of grammar: behavioural, linguistic, and etiquette. First, grammar is a set of formal patterns in which words are used to convey larger meanings, often unconsciously (many adults experience difficulties identifying the grammatical forms they use regularly in their oral and written language). Even young children are able to use complex grammatical forms that they have learned implicitly as part of oral language acquisition. For instance, children gradually adopt correct forms of the negative by imitating the speech patterns of the adults who interact with them. While young children initially may place the words *no* or *not* at the beginning of a statement (e.g., "No go to bed!"), they gradually substitute the words *can't* and *don't* (e.g., "I don't want to go to bed"). They also tend to overgeneralize their language, as in "I no want book" and "I no want to go," before adopting conventional phrasing ("I don't want this book," "I don't want to go") (Tomasello, 1992, 2003).

Second, grammar is included in the field of linguistics, which encompasses the study of the formulation of formal grammatical structures as they relate to meaning. This is the grammar that was traditionally studied in school as a codified set of rules, principles, and definitions that explain how language works. The scientific study of language has provided an appreciation of how language works in the real world with real people.

The third study of grammar refers to the etiquette of its usage. This approach suggests that there are social standards that apply to certain language forms, or to the way we employ our knowledge of the structure of language to communicate with others. In this context, there is no "bad grammar" but rather some forms that are more appropriate than others depending on the situation. For example, reflect on the ways in which people's speech differs when speaking to friends, children, and strangers. Consider also the differences when individuals are speaking in a public forum versus a private setting.

The word *grammar* often invokes a negative attitude among students and teachers alike and grammar remains a controversial area in language arts instruction across the grades (Tompkins, Bright, Pollard, & Winsor, 2011). Nevertheless, curriculum documents across Canada hold teachers responsible for teaching Standard English and language conventions that enable students to present their written work effectively. Unfortunately, isolated grammar lessons do little to promote students' speaking and writing abilities.

Children learn "grammar" intuitively as they learn to speak, and they use grammatical conventions very early in the literacy process. Sometimes children learn non-standard English grammar that, while effective for verbal communication, is inappropriate for writing. Ironically, words and sentence structures must first be available in the students' oral language repertoires before they can be transferred to students' writing.

Historical Approaches to Grammar Instruction Historically, the mission of educators and those who studied grammar was to establish absolute standards for all speakers by codifying and creating rules related to language usage. In reality, these reflected "gentlemen's rules" about what constituted good English. More importantly, this static and didactic approach to language failed to recognize two important attributes: (1) that language structures are created for the purpose of communication, and (2) that language changes over time. For instance, the word *ain't* was added to Merriam Webster's dictionary in 1964 on the basis of its prevalent use and ability to communicate an idea. The word is used frequently in rural dialects, song lyrics, and popular sayings, such as "You ain't seen nothing yet!" In this way, the study of grammar is more descriptive than prescriptive. Grammar is now studied to identify the way it operates today, because new ways of communicating are emerging all the time. It is the most commonly used words, however, that are least likely to change.

Contemporary Approaches to Grammar Instruction The traditional method of teaching grammar by naming and isolating parts of speech and completing worksheet activities is no longer supported by research (Barchers, 1994; Phelps-Gunn & Phelps-Terasaki, 1982). Instead, teachers are encouraged to integrate grammar instruction into their language arts programs so that learning occurs in a meaningful, purposeful, and authentic context (Calkins, 1994; Weaver, 1996). The role of the teacher as a model here is a critical one. Providing students with multiple opportunities to experience quality print-based and media literature is also essential in establishing Standard English grammatical practices.

Some educational stakeholders believe that grammar is neglected in schools (Dean, 2007; Hudson, 2004; Tompkins et al., 2011) and are especially critical about the lack of didactic instruction. Such critics also point to the increasing normative use of informal social language (e.g., text messaging and email) and worry that many students are incapable of using traditional grammar (Budra, 2010). They argue for formal instruction, citing the following advantages:

- Grammar can be used to describe language and how it works.
- Grammatical knowledge of one's native language facilitates the learning of other languages.
- Traditional grammar instruction fosters better writing skills.

Teacher Narrative

When I left my inner-city school setting, I moved to a small city where I taught in a middle-class subdivision. These grade 7 students spoke fairly standard English. In my new school board, it had been decided that grammar would be taught exclusively during the individual conferences conducted as part of the writing process. Being unaware of the board policy, I continued to teach formal grammar as part of the language arts program as I always had done when it was a required component of the curriculum.

One day, a new language consultant came to visit. She "caught" me teaching a formal grammar lesson and took me aside, stating: "We do not teach grammar like that in this board." She informed me that, instead, grammar was taught as part of individual writing conferences with students as they completed real tasks (versus during whole-class activities).

In the following weeks, I did as she recommended. I held 10- to 15-minute conferences with each student regarding his or her writing portfolio. During the conference, I provided each student with individualized mini-lessons about grammatical structures. I noticed, however, that my students continued to make the same errors and felt that the mini-conferences were too brief to truly teach students these lessons.

In an effort to promote students' learning, I started using a 15-minute interval between recess and French to "play with grammar." During this time, I modelled how to change sentences for interest and meaning as well as how to use the parts of speech. We used humorous sentences and the students created complex sentences orally. I purposefully focused on problematic aspects of their writing that I had noticed as part of our conferences and emphasized transferrable patterns. Sometimes I used interesting sentence structures from books we had been reading or from the media. We never used worksheets or fill-in-the-blank activities.

Over the next couple of years, my graduates came back from high school to thank me for "teaching them grammar." Their French and English teachers were pleased that they had a good understanding of the structures and language of grammar. I marvelled at how playing with language for about 15 minutes a day on a regular basis could provide such a solid background.

Research, however, suggests that language acquisition is complex, non-linear, and not very amendable to teacher intervention and control. Instead, learners' understanding of oral and written grammar is established and developed through meaningful communication (Thornbury, 1999). Furthermore, students do not tend to transfer their grammatical knowledge when it is taught in isolation. Instead, the favoured belief is that grammar is learned best when it is integrated into reading and writing instruction, with teachers using the editing and proofreading stages as opportunities for grammatical instruction (Calkins, 1994; Gardner, 2008; Noguchi, 1991; Weaver, 1998). Regardless of these debates, grammar remains a designated part of the elementary curriculum and teachers are accountable for its instruction.

In the Task to Teach to Task approach, the writing or reading task precedes the grammar lesson (Thornbury, 1999). For instance, students may complete a reader's response or a non-fiction writing task prior to grammatical instruction. While students engage in the writing activity, the teacher determines what grammatical knowledge or guidance would assist them in completing the task. Instruction can take the form of an explicit grammar lesson, a mini grammar lesson, or an individual conference. Through the combination of direct instruction and authentic activity, students gradually integrate the new structures into their writing.

Parts of Speech

To understand grammar, students need to understand the words that become the parts of speech represented in a sentence. They also need to know the parts of sentences, types of sentences, and their usage. Fortunately, this is a manageable task since there are only eight parts of speech (some of which have subsections). Teaching these labels to students enables them to discuss grammatical structures easily. Table 8.6 provides a review of each of the eight major parts of speech and corresponding subsections.

Sentences

A sentence is made up of one or more words that express a complete thought. To express a complete thought, a sentence must have a subject and a predicate. The subject is what (or whom) the sentence is about and the predicate tells something about the subject. For instance:

Sarah (subject) *runs* (predicate).

Sarah and her friend (subject) *run on the beach every morning* (predicate).

A simple way to determine the subject is to look for the verb and then ask *who?* or *what?* An exception can be illustrated by the single word "Stop!", which really means "*You* stop!"

Sentence Types

Sentences are classified in one of two manners. First, they can be classified according to the type of message they convey.

- **Declarative sentences** make a statement and end with a period. Example: *They will play basketball.*
- **Interrogative sentences** ask a question and end with a question mark. Example: *Did you score many baskets?*

Table 8.6 Parts of Speech

1. Nouns are words used to identify people, places, activities, ideas, things, and feelings.
   - Proper Nouns: The names of specific people, places, things, or ideas.
   - Common Nouns: Nouns that do not name a specific person, place, or thing.
   - Compound Nouns: Nouns that are made out of two or more words.
2. Pronouns are words used to avoid repeating nouns (e.g., *she*, *it*, *he,they*).
3. Adjectives are words used to modify or describe nouns.
4. Articles are words used to modify the meaning of their partner nouns.
5. Verbs are words used to tell what a noun does, or that it exists.
   - Action Verbs: Words used to tell what somebody or something does, did, or will do.
   - Linking Verbs: Words that do not express action. Rather, they link the subject of the verb with additional information about the subject (e.g., *to be*, *to have*). Examples of linking verbs: *My cats are content to sleep on the couch. Frankenstein is the name of my cat.*
6. Adverbs are words used to modify or describe verbs.
7. Prepositions are words used to introduce a prepositional phrase (e.g., *like*, *in*, *under*, *beside*, *on*). An example of a prepositional phrase: *The cat sleeps on the sofa*. In this example, *on* is a preposition that introduces the prepositional phrase *on the sofa*, which modifies the verb.
8. Conjunctions are words that connect parts of sentences and whole sentences together (e.g., *and*, *but*, *because*, *as*).

Note: Some words can serve several capacities in sentences. Consider the function of the word *paper* in the following sentences:

The child was cutting out *paper* snowflakes. (adjective)

Dad will *paper* the bedroom walls. (verb)

The printer needs more *paper.* (noun)

- **Exclamatory sentences** show strong feeling and end with an exclamation mark. Example: *They are attacking!*
- **Imperative sentences** give a command and end with a period. Example: *Carol, do your work first*. Sometimes the subject of an imperative sentences (*you*) is understood. Example: *Close the fridge door* (*You* close the fridge door).

Second, sentences can be classified according to their structure.

- **Simple sentences** contain only one clause consisting of a subject and a predicate. Subjects and predicates can have modifiers. Examples follow:

  The ice melts.

  The ice melts quickly.

  The ice on the pond melts quickly in the noonday sun.

The snow and ice on the pond melts quickly in the noonday sun. (a simple sentence but with a compound subject)

The ice on the pond warms and melts quickly in the noonday sun. (a simple sentence but with a compound verb).

- **Compound sentences** consist of two or more clauses called independent clauses that are equally important and joined by coordinating conjunctions such as *and*, *but*, and *or*.

  Canada is a beautiful country. (simple sentence)

  Canada is a country with great natural resources. (simple sentence)

  Canada is a beautiful country and it has great natural resources. (compound sentence)

  I tried to speak Japanese. (simple sentence)

  My friend tried to speak English. (simple sentence)

  I tried to speak Japanese and my friend tried to speak English. (compound sentence)

- **Complex sentences** consist of an independent clause joined by one or more dependent clauses. A complex sentence always has a subordinator such as *because*, *since*, *after*, *although*, or *when* or a relative pronoun such as *that*, *who*, or *which*.

  When he handed the teacher his paper (dependent clause), *he forgot the last page.* (independent clause)

  The teacher returned the work (independent clause) *after she marked it.* (dependent clause)

  When the dependent clause comes first, it is followed by a comma.

  Because her father had been transferred, she had to go to a new school.

  When the dependent clause comes at the end, no comma is required.

  Henri and Sally went to the movies after they had finished their homework.

  When the dependent clause comes in the middle of the sentence, no comma is required.

  People who live in glass houses should not throw stones.

- **Compound-complex sentences** consist of two or more independent clauses and one or more subordinate clauses, or what are sometimes referred to as dependent clauses.

  After the party was over (dependent clause), *they all took a taxi home* (independent clause), *but only Jim paid the bill.*

  The dog lived in the backyard (independent clause), *but the cat, who knew he was superior* (independent clause), *lived in the house.* (dependent clause including "but the cat").

Usage

While grammatical writing is considered to be a behaviour, grammatical oral usage is considered to be an etiquette related to "good taste" in grammar. There are two major considerations for teaching grammatical usage. First, it is important to recognize that language standards differ from one social group to the next. Second, it is important to recognize that language standards and forms of expression change over time.

Most adults have multiple "registers" or sets of language forms that they use in particular social contexts. Most also are able to switch between registers according to social circumstances. Most children, on the other hand, have only one register that they have learned from their parents. This register meets most of their daily communication needs.

Teachers are charged with modelling Standard English and increasing the number of registers that students possess. Rather than negating students' current grammatical registers, they should extend their existing repertoires (Hoffman, 2003). One important consideration in this instruction is to avoid "correcting" students' use of non-standard English. Instead, teachers should use these instances as opportunities to model correct form. For instance, if a student says, "I *don't* do that," a teacher could respond with, "Oh, you didn't watch the hockey game on the weekend?" Students should never be made to feel badly about the language they bring from home. Instead, they need to learn alternate ways of communicating. See Table 8.7 for suggestions about how to teach grammar in the classroom.

Teacher Narrative: How to Teach Grammar Effectively

My views about how to teach grammar have vacillated wildly over many years. When I was a young teacher in an inner-city school in Toronto, my grade 4 students, who were not English as a subsequent language students, did not speak Standard English. While my colleagues and I all dutifully and optimistically taught formal grammar lessons, there were no discernable changes in our students' oral language. I remember hearing "ain't" so often (e.g., "I *ain't* got no pencil," "I *ain't* going home") that I decided to address the situation directly. I created a character named "ain't" by placing a figure on a stick. After a lesson on using the terms *am not* and *have not* instead of *ain't*, the students chased "ain't" out of our classroom and stood him up in the hall, telling him firmly that he was not welcome back in our room. "Ain't" was absent from our dialogue for about 10 minutes, but soon re-emerged unscathed and unrepentant! I realized the futility of attempting to change language patterns that were acceptable everywhere in the students' community except in my classroom. I also reflected on my arrogance in assuming that the language my students learned at their kitchen tables was inferior in its communicative value and wondered what message they had received from me about the way their parents and neighbours spoke.

Table 8.7 Suggestions for Teaching Grammar

- Teach grammar in context whenever possible. If instruction occurs in isolation, integrate the grammar lesson into an authentic communicative activity as soon as possible. Provide students with multiple opportunities to communicate using the grammatical structure of focus.
- Teach grammatical forms in association with their meanings. The choices that speakers and writers make when selecting grammatical structures are determined by the meaning they wish to convey.
- Focus on teaching specific grammatical structures that are relevant to students' immediate communication needs. Avoid teaching multiple aspects at once.
- Remember that students require multiple reminders to transfer and generalize the use of grammatical structures across their speech and writing. Grammatical learning is a gradual process.
- Model good grammar and be aware of associated metalanguage (Thornbury, 1999).

Integrating Grammar Instruction with Reading

Students learn about grammar informally through repeated exposure to various structures in their independent reading, guided reading lessons, and Read Aloud programs. Teachers are encouraged to select interesting sentences from these readings and allow students to "play" with underlying structures. Teachers should also model the use of correct terminology for each part of speech. These lessons are often brief and involve minimal writing; several such activities are provided in Sample Lessons 8.1 and 8.2. Teachers and students may also enjoy reading books that reinforce grammatical rules and structures (see Table 8.8 for text suggestions).

SAMPLE LESSON 8.1

Primary and Kindergarten Activities for Integrating Grammar Instruction into Storytime

Step 1

The teacher reads or tells the story of *Three Billy Goats Gruff*. The teacher can adapt the story by adopting different voices for the three goats and the troll, accentuating and elaborating on the troll's questions:

- Who is walking on my bridge?
- Who has been walking on my bridge?
- Why are you walking on my bridge?
- Do you not know this is my bridge and that I do not allow anyone to cross?

Similarly, the teacher accentuates the responses of the three goats:

- It is me, billy goat Gruff.
- I just want to walk over your bridge once today.
- Please allow me to pass.

The teacher completes reading the story aloud and records the new dialogue.

Step 2

The teacher rereads the story after dividing students into two groups: the question group and the answer group. As the three goats attempt to cross the bridge, the teacher points to each word in the recorded text and has one group chant the questions and the other group chant the responses.

Step 3

The teacher repeats the story on a successive day, inviting more students to participate. Students are encouraged to vary the story by asking different questions or having the goats articulate additional reasons for crossing the bridge.

Step 4

Students are directed to draw pictures that they can use to retell the story. Alternatively, students could create a class mural portraying the crossing of each of the three goats. Students collaboratively retell their sections of the story, incorporating questions and statements as modelled earlier.

Note This activity adopts the same approach to text familiarization that children employ when learning their first language, which includes repeated telling and visual and auditory reinforcement. While the teacher does not discuss grammar directly, question marks are incorporated in print and voice is inflected at the end of statements to denote questions. Young students enjoy repeated readings and extend their learning when asked to change the ending, create a puppet play, or retell the story from an alternate point of view.

SAMPLE LESSON 8.2

Primary and Junior Activities for Grammar Instruction when Reading

Activity 1

1. Record the first sentence from the text *Rescue Pup* by Jean Little (2004):
   The puppy was fast asleep.
2. Have students answer the following questions:
   What is the subject? (*the puppy*)
   What is the predicate? (*was fast asleep*)
   How can we make this sentence more interesting and informative? (record students' suggestions)
3. Revise the opening sentence to include adjectives, adverbs, and dependent clauses.
   The small yellow Labrador puppy, who would be known as Rescue Dog, was fast asleep, curled up with his brothers and sisters.
4. Challenge students to create a follow-up sentence using a subject and a predicate, and record it on the board.
   Challenge students to create a more interesting statement by adding adjectives, adverbs, and clauses.
   Repeat this activity.

Activity 2

1. Ask students to write down four adjectives that describe why they enjoyed a book following a Read Aloud. Challenge them to avoid clichés or overused words such as *nice* and *funny*.
2. Have students share their adjectives with a partner and select the best four responses from their shared lists.
   Ask each student group to join another pair and further refine their best four responses.
3. Have students share their lists as a whole class.
4. Discuss the characteristics of adjectives.
   Develop a class list of adjectives that best describes why they liked the story.

Activity 3

1. Ask students to write simple, compound, complex, and compound-complex sentences that describe their favourite part of a book.

Activity 4

1. Copy a compound-complex sentence from a guided reading text. Example: *As he looked, the back door of the truck opened with a loud squeaking and out stepped Todd* (*Some of the Kinder Planets* by Tim Wynne-Jones, 1993, p. 41).
2. Challenge students to reorganize the sentence in ways that maintain its original meaning. Tell students that they are not to include or delete any words.
   The back door of the truck opened with a loud squeaking noise as he looked and out stepped Todd.
   With a loud squeaking noise, the back door of the truck opened and as he looked, out stepped Todd.
   The back door of the truck opened with a loud squeaking noise and out stepped Todd as he looked.
3. Provide students with other examples and challenge them to rearrange the sentence in multiple formats while maintaining its meaning.

Integrating Grammar Instruction with Writing

As students become more familiar with the way sentences are constructed in the books they read, they begin to incorporate these structures into their speech and writing. This transition is more challenging for students who do not speak Standard English at home because these new grammatical structures do not sound right to them. In these instances, the transfer of standard grammatical structures into writing may take longer and teachers must be especially careful not to repudiate students' home languages. Teachers should remind students that written language requires a more formal register than daily conversation (Tompkins et al., 2011).

Table 8.8 Picture Books about Letters, Spelling, Grammar, and Punctuation

Letters and Spelling

Falwell, C. (2006). *Word wizard.* London, UK: Sandpiper.

Turner, P., & Turner, W. (1999). *The war between the vowels and the consonants.* New York, NY: Farrar, Straus and Giroux (BYR).

Walker, S. M., & Luthardt, K. (2008). *The vowel family: A tale of lost letters.* Minneapolis, MN: Carolrhoda Picture Books.

Grammar

Cleary, B. P., & Gable, B. (2006). *I and you and don't forget who: What is a pronoun? (Words are categorical).* Minneapolis, MN: First Avenue Editions.

Cleary, B. P., & Gable, B. (2006). *Slide and slurp, scratch and burp: More about verbs (Words are categorical).* Minneapolis, MN: Millbrook Press.

Cleary, B. P., & Gable, B. (2009). *Quirky, jerky, extra perky: More about adjectives (Words are categorical).* Minneapolis, MN: First Avenue Editions.

Cleary, B. P., & Gable, B. (2010). *But and for, yet and nor: What is a conjunction? (Words are categorical).* Minneapolis, MN: Millbrook Press.

Cleary, B. P., & Prosmitsky, J. (1999). *A mink, a fink, a skating rink: What is a noun? (Words are categorical).* Minneapolis, MN: Lerner Publishing Group.

Cleary, B. P., & Prosmitsky, J. (2001). *Hairy, scary, ordinary: What is an adjective? (Words are categorical).* Minneapolis, MN: Carolrhoda Books.

Cleary, B. P., & Prosmitsky, J. (2001). *To root, to toot, to parachute: What is a verb? (Words are categorical).* Minneapolis, MN: Carolrhoda Books.

Heller, R. (1998). *Behind the mask: A book about prepositions (World of language).* New York, NY: Putnam Juvenile.

Heller, R. (1998). *Many luscious lollipops (World of language).* New York, NY: Putnam Juvenile.

Heller, R. (2000). *Fantastic! wow! and unreal!: A book about interjections and conjunctions (World of language).* New York, NY: Putnam Juvenile.

Maizels, J., & Petty, K. (1996). *The amazing pop-up grammar book.* New York, NY: Dutton Juvenile.

Martin, J. (2004). *Grammar tales: Francine Fribble, proofreading policewoman.* New York, NY: Scholastic Teaching Resources.

Pulver, R., & Rowe Reed, L. (2007). *Nouns and verbs have a field day.* New York, NY: Holiday House.

Punctuation

Berger, S. (2004). *Grammar tales: When comma came to town.* New York, NY: Scholastic Teaching Resources.

Charlesworth, L. (2004). *Grammar tales: The no-good, rotten, run-on sentence.* New York, NY: Scholastic Teaching Resources.

Cleary, B. P., & Lew-Vriethoff, J. (2010). *The punctuation station.* Minneapolis, MN: Millbrook Picture Books.

McCory Martin, J. (2004). *Grammar tales: The mystery of the missing socks.* New York, NY: Scholastic.

Pulver, R., & Rowe Reed, L. (2004). *Punctuation takes a vacation.* New York, NY: Holiday House.

Truss, L., & Timmons, B. (2006). *Eats, shoots & leaves: Why, commas really do make a difference!* Minneapolis, MN: Putnam Juvenile.

Truss, L., & Timmons, B. (2007). *The girl's like spaghetti: Why, you can't manage without apostrophes!* Minneapolis, MN: Putnam Juvenile.

Truss, L., & Timmons, B. (2008). *Twenty-odd ducks: Why, every punctuation mark counts!* Minneapolis, MN: Putnam Juvenile.

Mini-Lessons When teachers read students' writing, error patterns and weaknesses in expression inevitably emerge. These observations can become the focus of whole-class mini-lessons or small-group or individual instruction. Grade-level curriculum expectations can also guide the mini-lessons. Teachers often elect to teach a mini-lesson at the beginning of a writing workshop or other writing activity.

The use of mini-lessons is supported by research if they are conducted in the context of authentic reading and writing activities (versus worksheets and fill-in-the-blank activities) (Atwell, 1998; Calkins, 1994; Dunn & Lindblom, 2003). Mini-lessons are also time efficient (Thornbury, 1999). Playfulness and interaction are good ingredients to include in these lessons for successful learning. When completed, many teachers find it useful to post "anchor charts" to remind students about learned grammatical structures.

There are two approaches for mini-lessons: deductive and inductive.

Deductive Approach A deductive approach is rule driven and time efficient. It begins with the presentation of a rule and is followed by at least two examples of its application. Consider the following scenario.

> A teacher notices that students are not using adjectives in their writing. She starts the lesson by writing the word ADJECTIVE on the board and explaining that adjectives describe or tell something about nouns. They are considered noun modifiers. She then provides examples of adjectives and identifies how they add information about a noun.
>
> 1. The house by the lake is our cottage.
>   The *dilapidated, old, white* house by the lake is our cottage.
> 2. I spent many days there.
>   I spent many *happy, carefree* days there.
> 3. The gardener chose plants suitable for the garden.
>   The *wise, old* gardener chose plants suitable for the garden.
> 4. He caught the ball.
>   He caught the *slippery, slimy soccer* ball.
>
> The teacher comments that, in the second example, the adjectives provide more interesting information about the noun and that a comma separates successive adjectives.
>
> The teacher prints several new sentences on the board and asks students to generate adjectives that describe the nouns. To end the lesson, the teacher directs students to review their writing to locate nouns and decide whether the addition of adjectives would improve these sentences. Alternatively, students could be directed to locate noun-adjective combinations in the texts they are reading.

Inductive Approach The inductive, or discovery, approach involves teachers providing students with examples of grammatical patterns (at least three) and having them infer the underlying rule. Consider the following scenario.

> A teacher notices that students are using only simple sentences in their writing, and wants to introduce compound sentences. The teacher writes the following sentences on the board:
>
> 1. He called. Mary answered.
>   He called and Mary answered.

SAMPLE LESSON 8.3

Sample Mini-Lesson for Teaching Adverbs in Junior Grades

While most junior grade students use adverbs as part of their writing and speech, many are unable to identify and describe the function of these words directly.

Step 1

The teacher writes a noun and verb pairing on the board, chart paper, or an overhead. Students are asked to generate additional pairs.

Children ran.
Dogs barked.
Boys played.

The teacher directs students to consider whether these statements are interesting.

Step 2

The teacher presents students with a series of questions that could help make the sentences more informative and more interesting. The teacher records students' additions and suggestions, making special note of adverbs. For instance, the teacher may provide the following prompts for the statement "Children ran."

- How did they run?
- Where did they run?
- When did they run?
- What do these questions tell us about how the children run?

Step 3

Establish that most adverbs tell about *how*, *where*, and *when* something is done or about the *manner*, *time*, and *place* of an event.

Yesterday, children ran quickly down to the store.

Step 4

Students record three noun-verb simple sentences on cue cards and exchange their cards with a partner. Students add adverbs to their partners' sentences (orally or on the back of the card).

Step 5

Students share their responses and generate additional responses.

2. He asked the students going on the field trip to come to the office.
   They had to pay for the event.
   He asked the students going on the field trip to come to the office and pay for the event.
3. The canoe trip was difficult. They managed to survive it.
   The canoe trip was difficult but they managed to survive it.

Through questioning and prompting, students are asked to identify what is the same in each set of examples. The students are then asked to generate the pattern or rule: two independent clauses can be joined to form a compound sentence when joined by a conjunction.

Students generate compound sentences orally and identify the conjunction. Their responses are recorded so that all students can see as well as hear the grammatical pattern.

Assessing Students' Grammar

Similar to the teaching of grammar, the assessment of grammar is best accomplished in context. Teachers can assign part of a writing rubric for grammatical structures or can develop a checklist of skills that are appropriate for each grade level. They can also list errors found

SAMPLE LESSON 8.4

Sample Mini-Lesson for Teaching Adverbs in Intermediate Grades

Step 1

Ask students to select three sentences from the book they are reading and write them in their notebooks.

Step 2

Have students identify the verbs in their sentences.

Step 3

The teacher puts three columns on the board—*Present, Past, Future*—and explains that these are the times for the action of verbs. Ask students to provide the verbs from their sentences and indicate in which column they belong. (If any verbs are not simple past, present, or future tense, record them in a separate column for subsequent discussion.)

Step 4

Ask students to identify the following patterns:

Differences between present verb endings depending on nouns and pronouns: *I walk, she walks, they walk*

The *ed* pattern to indicate past tense: *I walked, he walked, they walked*

The *shall* and *will* pattern for future tense: *I shall go, she will go, they will go*

The use of irregular verbs:

present: *I go, he goes, they go*
past: *I went, she went, they went*
future: *I shall go, he will go, they will go*

Step 5

Ask students to change each of the three verbs in their original sentences into past, present, and future tense. This can be done orally in pairs or as a written activity.

in students' writing. Collecting and analyzing students' writing samples over time is the best way to observe and document their understanding and use of grammatical structures.

THE MECHANICS OF WRITING

Writers' workshop

THE MECHANICS OF WRITING, OR PUNCTUATION, REFERS TO THE SYMBOLS THAT INDICATE the structure and organization of written language, as well as the intonation and pauses that need to be observed when reading aloud. When used effectively, punctuation provides the writer with control over tone and meaning. Punctuation marks facilitate reading by detonating emphasis and meaning.

Punctuation includes the use of capitals, periods, commas, semicolons, colons, quotation marks, dashes, apostrophes, exclamation marks, and question marks. Students should be provided with instruction on these writing mechanics early, with special attention being paid to these elements as part of proofreading. Students generally become quite adept at editing for punctuation if they are taught the specific uses of each form explicitly. Table 8.9 lists the formats and procedures associated with each punctuation form.

Proofreading

Teachers are encouraged to teach the mechanics of writing by using mini-lessons and then providing students with multiple opportunities to practise their use in the context of their authentic writing. Students will benefit from the placement of anchor charts

Table 8.9 Punctuation Usage

Capitals

- Beginning of a sentence
- Pronoun *I*
- Proper names, places, organizations, and sometimes objects: *Sandra Green, Atlantic Ocean, Doctors Without Borders, The United Nations, Supreme Court*
- Names of religious figures, deities, and holy books
- Days of the week, months of the year, and holidays
- Names of countries, nationalities, and languages: *Canada, Canadian, English, French*
- Major words in the title of a book, song, or article (but not articles and prepositions): *The Sky Is Falling, A Light in the Attic, Some of the Kinder Planets*
- First word of a direct quotation: *The Hindu proverb states, "There is nothing noble in being superior to someone else. The true nobility is in being superior to your previous self."*
- Members of national, social, racial, civic, and athletic groups: *Conservatives, Liberals, New Democrats, First Nations, Toronto Blue Jays, The United Way, The Nature Conservatory of Canada*

Periods

- End of declarative sentences (which are also called statements) and imperative statements (which make demands, express requests, or deny or grant permission):
  The dog was chewing his bone.
  Close the door.
  Please wash your hands.
- Most abbreviations:
  Mr. Ms. Mrs. Dr.
  etc.
  10:00 a.m.
- Electronic file names and internet addresses:
  index.html
  www.brighthub.com

Commas

- After introductory phrases, words, or clauses:
  After a number of preliminary and unsuccessful attempts, he finally solved the problem.
  John, please come here now.
- Between words in a list of at least three parallel words with "and" separating the final word: *The Haitian people have suffered earthquakes, floods, famine, and disease.*
- Around interrupting words, phrases, or clauses:
  That is not the only reason, of course, for his recent success.
  Whatever you do, Sarah, please come home early.

Note: Commas are used to help the reader determine meaning by knowing when to slow down, notice something, or stop. The use of commas has declined over the years. When in doubt about the need to use a comma, the general rule is to leave it out. For instance, the use of a comma before "and" in a string of items is not necessary, although some writers choose to use it.

Semicolons

- When separating closely related independent clauses: *My daughter seldom goes to bed this early; she is afraid she will miss something exciting.*
- When there are too many commas in a list: *There were representatives from Winnipeg, Manitoba; Ottawa, Ontario; Charlottetown, Prince Edward Island; and Vancouver, British Columbia.*

Colons

- Before a list that explains the independent clause: *The committee now consisted of the following people: the mayor, the police chief, the fire chief, and the chair of the town council.*
- Before a statement that explains the meaning of a previous statement: *He visited three cities while visiting Canada: Toronto, Vancouver, and Montreal.*
- In expressions of time: *9:45, 12:00*

Quotation Marks

- When indicating the direct words of a speaker or the exact words from a text:

  "I can't wait to see him play hockey!" exclaimed his mother.
  "Canada is a country whose main exports are hockey players and cold fronts," said Pierre Elliott Trudeau.
  "Our main imports are baseball players and acid rain."
  "Students need to know how to locate the spelling of unknown words in both print and online dictionaries."

Note: The end punctuation for a complete sentence (e.g., period, question mark, exclamation mark) is placed inside the closing quotation mark: *He murmured politely, "Must you really go?"*

When the quotation is broken, the first part of the quotation is followed by a comma: *"I know what I shall do," said Alice. "I will ask them to leave at once."*

When there is a quotation inside a quotation, the inside quotation is surrounded by single quotation marks: *"I am tired of his saying 'Whatever you want' when a decision has to be made," Justin commented in an annoyed voice.*

Dashes

- When interrupting a statement to provide a sudden change of thought, additional comment, or dramatic qualification:

  The speech went on and on and—you guessed it—we missed lunch.
  This was the end of the problem—or so we thought.

- When adding relevant information to the sentence:

  He was so smart—at least he thought he was so smart—that he did not need to learn anything more.

Note: Sentences should represent complete thoughts without the dashes.

Apostrophes

- Precedes the *s* when using a singular noun but follows the s when using a plural noun:

  The dog's water dish needs to be refilled.
  The dogs' water dishes need to be refilled.

- Precedes the *s* with nouns that are always considered to be plural, such as *people* and *children*:

  The children's test results were magnificent.
  The people's rights must be maintained.

Note: Apostrophes are not required when using possessive pronouns: *Friends of hers told us that it's her idea not theirs to refill its water dish.*

(Continued)

Table 8.9 Punctuation Usage *(continued)*

Exclamation Marks

- End of an emphatic declaration, interjection or a command:

  You are no longer to seek political office!
  What on earth are you doing! Stop!
  Hang your coat up!

Questions Marks

- End of a direct question: *Are you coming with us?*

Note: Question marks are not used with indirect questions: *I asked my sister if she was coming.*

Table 8.10 Teaching Activities for the Mechanics of Writing

Activity 1

Select a paragraph from a novel or other text. Rewrite the passage using no punctuation. Negotiate the correct punctuation as a whole-class activity. Repeat the activity over successive days with new paragraphs. Alternatively, select a paragraph and omit only one form of punctuation (e.g., capitals, periods, quotation marks).

Activity 2

Ask students to read a paragraph that has no punctuation. Discuss whether they find the passage easy to comprehend. Provide students with the punctuated paragraph and ask them to read it again. Discuss the difference in their ability to derive meaning from the text.

Activity 3

Use songs, rhymes, and other memory mnemonics for remembering how to use punctuation. See www.songsforteaching.com and www.k-3teacherresources.com/teaching_nursery_rhymes.html for some examples.

Activity 4

Celebrate "Great Mistakes" as opportunities for learning. When students make mistakes, tell them that they have made a "Great Mistake" or "GM," which means that they have an opportunity to learn something. This technique works very well in teacher-student conferences.

or classroom charts that they can refer to while editing and proofreading. Students in the junior grades onward are encouraged to engage in peer editing on a regular basis in addition to reviewing their own work. Table 8.10 provides suggestions for activities that teachers can use when teaching about the mechanics of writing.

Caution Teachers need to remind students of the differences between editing and proofreading their written work, with an emphasis on creating meaningful text.

REFLECTIVE ACTIVITY 3

Write the following sentences using your normal handwriting script.

> *Six very quick zebras jumped high to swat the napping fly.*
> *The quick brown fox jumps over the lazy dog.*

Self-evaluate your writing in terms of your ability to provide a strong model for students who are learning how to write. Consider developing another writing "register" to use with students. Consider the initial instruction you received about how to form letters.

HANDWRITING

HANDWRITING IS A COMMUNICATIVE TOOL FOR WRITERS SIMILAR TO SPELLING, punctuation, and grammar. While some argue that handwriting is an antiquated skill given the prevalence of word processing, the general consensus is that handwriting skills should not be ignored (Tompkins et al., 2011). Consider that there are many occasions when a word processor is not available or handy and the handwritten word is needed. In these cases, it is imperative that the writing be legible so the intended message is relayed. Furthermore, handwriting needs to be an automatic skill so that students can focus on the ideas they wish to express (Connelly, Dockrell, & Barnett, 2005).

Automaticity in handwriting is important for the following reasons:

1. Writing in the early grades is linked to letter and word recognition. Linking handwriting, reading, and spelling can help students gain high-level literacy skills.
2. Handwriting is a basic tool needed for taking notes, taking tests, and completing daily classroom activities.
3. Laboured handwriting may result in a lack of writing and inhibit learning.
4. Laboured handwriting drains students' mental resources needed for higher-level aspects of writing such as expressing content and organizing ideas (Spear-Swerling, 2006).

Choosing the Script

When teaching handwriting, teachers need to select a script. Choices include manuscript (vertical printing), slanted printing (italic printing), or cursive writing. At one time, manuscript was typically taught in grade 1 and cursive writing was introduced at the end of grade 2 or the beginning of grade 3. By grade 4, all students were expected to be proficient in writing in cursive. Starting with manuscript was perceived as ideal since it was similar in format to the print that students were beginning to read. Slanted printing was developed to help students transition to cursive writing. Educational researchers have concluded, however, that these practices fall short of their intended goals and have created difficulties for some children (Graham, Struck, Richardson, & Berninger, 2006; Hackney, 1991). There is no evidence that cursive writing is more easily accessed by students who have first learned slanted or italic printing.

While some young students may possess the eye-hand coordination necessary to adopt cursive writing (and thus bypass manuscript), there is little evidence that students find cursive writing easier. There are, however, distinct advantages associated with having students read and write in the same print (Spear-Swerling, 2006). Learning to print focuses students' attention on the distinctive features and shapes of letters they are learning to recognize in print and strengthens the reading-writing connection.

Prerequisite Writing Skills

Students should demonstrate the following behaviours and skills prior to beginning formal print instruction:

- Ability to use crayons for drawing
- Understanding of words such as *straight*, *under*, *beside*, *wide*, and *round*
- Established hand preference

- Dexterity in fingers and wrist
- Awareness of size, shape, and special relations in art and building activities
- Ability to listen accurately
- Ability to recognize their own name in print
- Desire to write

Practice using paintbrushes, crayons, magic markers, Plasticine, and playdough can help establish some of these prerequisite skills. Teachers also need to be aware of and distinguish between the two identifiable phases related to learning to write: (1) learning to form letters, and (2) practisingto the level of automaticity.

Student Voice 8.2

I already know how to print. I learned from my mom and from my teacher. We filled in dotted lines to make letters. The first word I learned was *the*. My teacher gives us a piece of paper with some words on it. You have to write the words for homework. Some of the kids in my class are still learning how to print.

McKenna
Senior kindergarten student

Facilitating the Transition from Manuscript to Cursive Writing

Most students are ready to begin to make the transition from manuscript to cursive writing by the end of grade 2 or the beginning of grade 3, as they now possess adequate eye-hand coordination. (See Table 8.11 for tips about how to teach both manuscript and cursive writing.) They usually are motivated to begin cursive writing, which is often viewed as a "mature" or "adult" form of writing. Students, especially those who struggle with manuscript (printing), may find the smooth nature of cursive writing welcoming since they do not have to lift their pencil while writing. The following are some instructional suggestions for teaching cursive writing:

1. Start incidentally by recording objects in the environment such as announcements and dates.
2. Place the cursive forms under the manuscript ones, matching individual letters.
3. Start teaching individual letters in lower case. Remember that under strokes are the easiest to produce (e.g., *e*, *l*, *i*).
4. Model how to join letters.
5. Have students practise writing familiar words.
6. Have students keep a writing folder or booklet so they can monitor their progress.
7. Schedule brief lessons frequently, approximately 10 minutes per day.

Left-Handed Students

It is estimated that between 10 and 25 percent of the population is left-handed. Teachers therefore can expect to have a small number of left-handed students in

Table 8.11 Tips for Teaching Students Manuscript or Cursive Writing

- Post a representative alphabet strip in the classroom. Teachers may also find it helpful to provide beginning writers with individual alphabet strips that can be taped to their desks for easy reference.
- Very young students should begin forming letters using unlined paper. They then graduate to large-lined paper to accommodate their level of eye-hand coordination before transiting to smaller-lined sheets.
- When teaching manuscript, inform students that there are only two basic strokes: circles and straight lines. Point out variations of these two forms.
- When teaching cursive writing, inform students that there are three basic formations: under strokes, over strokes, and ovals, with under strokes being the easiest.
- Legibility and a functioning writing speed are the primary goals of manuscript or cursive writing. Students should be free to develop their own style within these confines.
- Learning to write takes time and practice. Brief, regular practice sessions are more effective than irregular or longer lessons.
- Teach students the five key elements related to legibility:
  1. *Shape.* Adopt conventional formations (e.g., *a* and *o* need to be distinguishable, as do *i* and *e*).
  2. *Size.* Adopt print that is neither too big nor too small. Capitals and lower case need to be proportional.
  3. *Space.* Insert spaces of equal distance between words and letters in words.
  4. *Slant.* Right to left is most common, but others are also legible. Students need to be consistent in their orientation.
  5. *Speed.* Sufficient to meet the needs of written language.

their classrooms. Since left-hand preference is determined before school entry, teachers must understand that it is a fixed condition and that learning to write is a more difficult proposition for left-handed children. While the natural hand movement is away from the body, left-handed students must bring their hand toward the centre of their bodies when writing. Writing from left to right also impedes these students' ability to see their writing, as their hand will cover most words. Left-handed students tend to push their pencils rather than pull them. Without direct instruction, left-handed students often develop hooked styles and use a bent wrist in an effort to see their print, developing an uncomfortable and inefficient style of writing. Table 8.12 provides some teaching tips for working with left-handed students.

Students Who Have Difficulty Learning to Write

A few students will have severe enough eye-hand coordination problems that they will have difficulty learning to communicate using writing. Some techniques that teachers have adopted to provide students with additional tactile experiences include:

1. Creating letters from Plasticine.
2. Tracing letters in a sandbox or rice box.
3. Tracing letters using tracing paper and model letters.
4. Connecting numbered dots to form letters.

Table 8.12 Teaching Tips for Working with Left-Handed Students

- Place left-handed students together for instruction.
- Encourage left-handed students to hold the pencil between 3 and 3.5 cm above the tip so their hand obscures less of their view.
- Position the paper to the left of students' midlines and tilt it on an angle so the top right corner of the paper is closer to them than the top left corner (Holder, 2003).
- When beginning to write a line, position students' hands away from their bodies. Have students stop writing when their hand is in front of their body or slightly to the left of their midline (Holder, 2003).
- Ensure that students' wrists are straight and not bent (Holder, 2003).
- Position students' hands below the writing line with a straight wrist (Holder, 2003).

5. Talking through the hand movements associated with forming letters (e.g., "When writing the letter *l*, bring your pencil from the bottom of the line to the top of the line, form a loop to the left, and return to the bottom of the page crossing over your first line. End with drawing a small tail up.").

Evaluation

Very few teachers today formally evaluate students' handwriting. Dated writing samples can be used to document writing development and growth over time. Teachers may wish to consult with physiotherapists and other professionals when they notice students experiencing serious difficulties, or they may wish to provide individual instruction and remediation.

Teacher Narrative

One September, I observed what appeared to be an exemplary grade 4 classroom. The teacher, however, commented on students' lack of pride in their work, messy writing, and poor organizational skills.

I returned to that same class in April. I walked around the room while students were working independently and observed that they were writing clearly and in an organized fashion. I asked the teacher what she had done to facilitate this change.

She told me that she had the students copy a poem or other piece of writing that she found in a book in their best handwriting each Friday during the last 10 minutes of the day. On Monday, she announced the "Writer of the Week" and five "runners up." She recorded each winning student's name on the bulletin board, with an accompanying large star for the writer of the week and five smaller ones for the runners up. Each of the six "winners" had their work posted on the board for the week. She posted each student's work at least once over the course of the term, sometimes on the basis of being "most improved." Over time, students began to demonstrate pride in their work as well as in how they wrote. The legibility of their handwriting improved, as did the organization of their work.

SUGGESTIONS FOR PROFESSIONAL DEVELOPMENT

1. Collect a set of student writing samples (either from students in one grade or from students across several grades). Analyze students' spelling using the *Developmental Spelling Test* (http://gse.uci.edu/docs/DEVELOPMENTAL_SPELLING.pdf) or an equivalent measure. What recommendations would you provide with respect to subsequent spelling instruction based on your analysis?
2. Make a conscious attempt to standardize your handwriting to reflect the traditional forms of letters. Compare your existing handwriting to a standard model. Consider challenges that students might encounter when learning to write.
3. Browse through several dictionaries designed for children, including a picture dictionary, a spelling dictionary, and a rhyming dictionary. List advantages and disadvantages associated with each resource for teachers and for students. Consider beginning a collection of dictionaries and similar resources.
4. Copy three or four statements from a fiction or non-fiction text. Review each statement, identifying the parts of speech. Reflect on your ability to complete this task. Is this activity relatively easy or challenging? Reflect on how your formal knowledge of grammar compares to your ability to speak and write using grammatically correct conventions and forms.

CHILDREN'S LITERATURE REFERENCES

Asbjornsen, P. C. & Moe, J. E. (2001). *The three billy goats gruff*. Boston, MA: Houghton Mifflin Harcourt.

Little, J. (2004). *Rescue pup*. Victoria, BC: Orca Book Publishers.

Wynne-Jones, T. (1993). *Some of the kinder planets*. Toronto, ON: Groundwood Books.

Chapter 9

The Role of Children's Literature

Learning Objectives

In this chapter you will discover

- How children's literature began.
- How Canadian children's literature began.
- How to find books that will appeal to children.
- How to choose literature about diversity.
- How to promote diversity discussions in the classroom.
- How to include Canadian literature in the literacy program.
- How to be an effective storyteller.

KARI-LYNN WINTERS: CANADIAN AUTHOR AND EDUCATOR

Kari-Lynn Winters is a recognized Canadian author and former elementary school teacher. Throughout her career, she has taught in primary and junior grade classrooms. She spent six years in a segregated classroom working with students who were experiencing severe behaviour challenges. As a drama specialist, Kari-Lynn has combined her passion for the fine arts with her passion for Canadian literature. She believes that reading should be an active process in which students become integrally connected and engaged with the text. She is resolute about the importance of using picture books across the grades and in combination with visual and digital literacies, believing that students need to learn how to process pictorial as well as print messages. Kari-Lynn also believes that it is important to include children's literature that relates to students' lives, reflecting their cultural and geographical experiences as well as current issues.

She recalls a recent experience in which she used a picture book that she authored, *When Chickens Fly*, to address issues of discrimination and social justice. Kari-Lynn wrote the text after reading a newspaper article featuring a female athlete who was unable to compete in an Olympic ski jumping competition that was to be held in the province. Her book presents the story of a chicken, Esper, that aspires to compete in the Olympics but is denied the opportunity by virtue of being a chicken.

Prior to reading the text, Kari-Lynn led students in the game Zip, Zap, Zop. Students stood in a circle and took turns calling to each other. At the same time, Kari-Lynn called out criteria that eliminated several students from the game: "If you are wearing a red sweater, you are no longer in the game," "If you are wearing running shoes, you are no longer in the game," and "If you have blue eyes, you are no longer in the game." Students quickly became agitated with these criteria and Kari-Lynn began a discussion about the concepts of "fairness" and "control," reflecting on how the selected criteria contributed to their participation in the game.

As a result of the activity and discussions, students were ready to begin reading *When Chickens Fly*. They were emotionally invested in the story and ready to make predictions, connections, and inferences. About halfway through reading the book (when Esper's request to compete in the Olympics is denied), Kari-Lynn had the students enact the text. Some students were asked to assume the role of members of the Olympic committee while others were asked to provide arguments in support of Esper's participation in the games. Other students engaged in a debate about whether the story represented an instance of discrimination. After she finished reading the text, Kari-Lynn asked the class whether the events portrayed in the book represent current society. "When we went around the circle, most students stated that the book was fictional. Only two students suggested otherwise: one was a Muslim girl; the other was an African-Canadian boy."

Kari-Lynn then shared the newspaper article that had inspired her to write the book. The majority of the students were shocked and outraged that the female athlete was not allowed to participate in the male-dominated sport. When challenged about how they could take action over this issue, the class decided to write letters to their Members of Parliament. Kari-Lynn reflects that this was only one of many possible ways for students to respond to the text, with other possibilities including writing alternative text endings, forming position statements, or producing a Readers' Theatre.

Kari-Lynn spends much of her spare time reading children's and young adult literature, where she finds inspiration for her own writing and teaching. For instance, she created a combined science and drama unit exploring the importance of ladybugs and other garden insects after reading the non-fiction texts *Ladybug Garden* by Celia Godkin, *The Insecto-files* by Helaine Becker, and *Bug Bites* by Diane Swanson. Here, she layered Canadian children's literature with rhythms, tableaux, and soundscapes.

Kari-Lynn believes that students can provide authors with critical insights and often seeks students' feedback on her works in progress. In her "Authors as Mentors" project, online at www.kariwinters.com, Kari-Lynn invites North American students and their teachers to review and provide commentary on her unpublished manuscripts. In this way, students assume the role of editors and co-authors, and Kari-Lynn acknowledges their contributions in the text's dedication.

Kari-Lynn currently holds a faculty position at Brock University in St. Catharines, Ontario. She remains adamant that Canadian literature be featured in Canadian classrooms. She challenges teachers to look for engaging and recent texts to include in their language arts programs versus relying on "classics" or the texts that they read in their youth. She encourages current and future teachers to explore the works of Canadian authors through organizations such as CANSCAIP (Canadian Society of Children's Authors, Illustrators and Performers) and the Canadian Children's Book Centre.

Canadian children's literature is so much more than just entertainment—so much more than just a story before bed. It has the potential to cultivate minds, to inspire dreams, to reflect and notate different cultures, to immerse readers in another world, and to build its readers' self-worth. It speaks to its audience as it instructs, articulates, and clarifies critical ideas. Canadian children's literature engages the mind, the body, and the heart through its rhythmic, illustrated, and storied representations. It guides its readers, while counseling them, challenging them, and supporting them; and at the same time, it offers opportunities for resolution, reflection, and comfort.

REFLECTIVE ACTIVITY 1

Think back to when you were 12 years old or younger. Recall a book that had an impact on you at the time, whether you read the text independently or it was read aloud to you. Record what you remember about the content of the book, the context while reading it, and the impact it had on you.

Locate the book (www.alibris.com is an excellent website to find older texts) and reread it. When you are finished, write your impressions from your adult point of view.

Compare your pre-reading comments with your post-reading comments. Is your child's lens different than your adult one? Do you agree with the following quotation?

> It is interesting to note that a child's favourite books are often consciously the models for, or the most important influence on, his or her later beliefs and ways of living. (Cott, 1981)

CHILDREN'S LITERATURE

THROUGHOUT THIS TEXT, WE HAVE FOCUSED ON *HOW* TO CONDUCT A LANGUAGE arts program and develop students' literacy skills. Equally important, however, is your choice of materials and resources. Selecting high-quality texts and resources can greatly influence students' learning successes. As a professional, you will need to possess a repertoire of quality children's literature, as well as an understanding and appreciation of the role of these resources in language arts. In this chapter, we will mainly feature Canadian children's literature and authors. We are not so myopic as to suggest that teachers exclude some terrific international works; nevertheless, we hope that this chapter will provide you with some insights and considerations regarding the Canadian texts and resources included in your classroom.

Definition of Children's Literature

Children's literature is generally accepted to include all books written for children, excluding works such as comic books, cartoons, graphic novels, non-fiction books, and reference books such as dictionaries and encyclopedias. Children's literature addresses topics of relevance and interest to children through prose, poetry, and fiction (Lynch-Brown & Tomlinson, 1998).

Well-written children's books often appeal to adults as well (consider the Harry Potter series), inspiring publications such as *The New York Times* to create a separate best-seller list of children's books. Alternatively, there are many well-known and well-loved books intended for adults that have been adopted by children (e.g., *Alice's Adventures in Wonderland, Gulliver's Travels, The Adventures of Tom Sawyer*).

Even though some children's books are adult favourites and others are recognized with awards, not all books chosen for students by teachers will be well received. For instance, while the *Secret of the Andes* by Ann Nolan Clark was awarded the Newbery Medal in 1953, it failed to capture the hearts and minds of children. Instead, *Charlotte's Web* (published in the same year and which did not receive a Newbery Medal) became a universal childhood favourite.

Children's Literature and Adult Literature: Similarities and Differences

Children and adults derive similar pleasures from reading literature. We all take pleasure in contemplating characters' feelings and experiences and relating them to our own. We imagine people and places we have never seen (Nodelman & Reimer, 2002). Many children and adults enjoy the "formula" of stories or similarities to stories that they have read and enjoyed before. Many readers prefer a specific genre or a series of novels about the same character. Most children and adults can also appreciate the wonderful illustrations contained in picture books that either carry or enhance print.

Like young children, many adults enjoy reading the same story repeatedly (a close friend of one author admits to reading *Wuthering Heights* every year). On the other hand, students and adults are often delighted to read stories that surprise them and depart from their previous experiences and expectations. Most adults and children also enjoy discussing what they have read with others, as social construction of text contributes to their understanding and appreciation of literature (Galda & Cullinan, 2006).

There also are specific characteristics that can set children's literature apart from adult literature. Consider that adult figures are not central characters in the majority of children's books (Nodelman & Reimer, 2002). Other distinctions often include the following (adapted from Hillman, 1995):

- Description of typical childhood experiences
- Inclusion of children's point of view
- Inclusion of relatively simplistic plots
- Focus on action
- Combination of realism and fantasy
- Inclusion of time travel
- Overall optimism, including a happy and satisfying ending

The Impact of Canadian Children's Literature in the Classroom: Ideology

Teachers should be aware of the impact of the ideology of our culture as portrayed in literary texts for children and the potential that these texts have to influence the ideas that children develop about themselves and others in the world. Often, this ideology is pervasive in toys, games, media, TV shows, and movies, all of which have a powerful effect on children's views of current culture. While these influences are strong, it is likely that a children's book will also have some educational or influential impact (Galda & Cullinan, 2006). Nodelman and Reimer (2002) concur that all books teach something. Many parents and educators also believe that children's books play an important role in integrating new generations of children into the existing society (Bainbridge, Oberg, & Carbonaro, 2005). Many parents, who are the most common purchasers of books to be given as gifts to their children, shop carefully and thoughtfully. Frequently, they share the favourites they remember from their own childhood.

This retelling of stories across generations can serve to maintain a conservative element of society, although the retellings are interpreted in terms of current social conditions as well as the adults' expectations for children's developing attitudes. For instance, consider the way fairy tales have changed over the years, from first being told by the Brothers Grimm and Hans Christian Andersen to frighten and control children to the more recent Disney versions that seek to entertain and delight. This example of extreme difference can be used to identify the multitude of possible interpretations of the same story. In any case, the fairy tale formula always ends with good prevailing over evil and a "happily ever after" prophecy for the future, which for generations has helped reassure children about their world and the way it unfolds.

Some books for children explore morality or social and ethical relationships as well as the history of a society. Some books even offer a blueprint for the future. Parents who wish to shield their children from the possibility of isolation from supportive and loving adults may choose to avoid fairy tales such as *Hansel and Gretel* and *Snow White*, classics such as *Bambi*, and current series such as A Series of Unfortunate Events. Alternatively, if parents view isolation from adults as preparation for independence, they may select *The Secret Garden*, *Swallows and Amazons*, *The Breadwinner*, or the Harry Potter series to highlight the resourcefulness of children when they are independent of adult intervention.

Today, one value shared by most teachers and parents is to ensure that children attain the understanding that Canada and the world abroad are wonderfully diverse. While this appears as a truism, it must be carefully applied in terms of book selection. Books that depict First Nations people in their traditional dress must be tempered with the idea that traditional dress, implements, and housing are part of First Nations history rather than their reality today. Diversity can also be presented superficially (Nodelman & Reimer, 2002), and teachers must guard against stereotyping. An understanding of the universality of the human condition, along with an honouring of cultural differences, is well supported in literature, but it takes a wise teacher to select and interpret text appropriately.

Values are pervasive in children's literature and are bound to have an impact on readers. In a sense, these values are the hidden curriculum, which means that children are absorbing a view of the world over which they have little control. For instance, nonfiction texts about the natural world often communicate angst about the endangered nature of our planet, which has established a preservation mindset in our children that reflects a serious concern of our time. Another positive example of the hidden curriculum is that hope remains a strong element in children's novels, particularly in historical fiction about the Holocaust such as *Daniel's Story* and *Number the Stars*. Some questions persist, however. For example, what values are being presented about gender, consumerism, the environment, multiculturalism, inner and outer beauty, the world as a hopeful place, and the triumph of the underdog?

Readers of all ages have the power to engage in reading experiences that will lead them to examine these ideologies of culture, whether consciously or unconsciously. Teachers can help students discuss and think about the basic messages buried in their action adventure novels and humorous books by empowering them to think critically and thoughtfully about what they have read. Of course, this awareness suggests that teachers need to consider the potential messages contained in the books they choose for classroom use. In a departure from past practices, most schools implicitly permit children to exercise their independence by choosing their own independent reading material. This practice marks our societal and educational belief in the importance of the individual and the right of self-determination.

What Attracts Children to Particular Books?

The topics that appeal to children have remained remarkably consistent over the years (Lehman, 1991; Stoodt-Hill & Amspaugh-Corson, 2008; Wolfson, Manning, & Manning, 1984). Students typically enjoy reading about animals, humorous events, action and high drama, and suspense and mystery. Most students also enjoy works that are optimistic and complete in their plot and that contain an element of surprise. As a general rule, students respond positively to reading works by authors they have enjoyed previously.

Student Voice 9.1

My favourite authors are J.K. Rowling, the author of Harry Potter; Rick Riordan, the author of Percy Jackson; and Jeff Kinney, the author of *Diary of a Wimpy Kid*. I also love Shel Silverstein, especially *The Giving Tree*.

Madeleine
Grade 5 student

THE TEACHER AND CHILDREN'S LITERATURE

Contextual analysis and story dramatization

Exploring literature through Read Aloud

Effective teachers work to create classroom environments where children's literature is valued, shared, discussed, and enjoyed (Stoodt-Hill & Amspaugh-Corson, 2001). To nurture such environments, teachers must possess:

- Knowledge about a wide variety of children's books, genres, and authors
- The ability to identify texts for specific purposes and particular children
- The ability to display enthusiasm for texts and model the essence of being a reader
- The ability to read text aloud in ways that capture students' attention and inspire a love for reading

A Brief Introduction to Some Theories of Children's Literature

There are many different ways to consider children's literature and we will describe some of them briefly to indicate the kind of thinking that is done about children's texts. This overview may provide you with some ideas for further reading. The various theories identified below have the same operating principle: the assumption that literary texts have unity or consistency. This means that all of a text's components support each other to provide a coherent and complete vision of the world.

The Psychoanalytical Perspective A student of classical Freudianism, Bruno Bettelheim was an American child psychologist who spent a large part of his life working with severely emotionally disturbed children and sought to identify archetypal patterns in children's traditional stories. For instance, he identified the concepts of sibling rivalry and Oedipal jealousy in *Cinderella.* He believed that the dark nature of fairy tales—including death, abandonment, and injury—allows children to grapple with their fears in a symbolic manner and that such literary experiences help children grow emotionally. Bettelheim (1976) espoused these beliefs in his book *The Uses of Enchantment.*

Archetypal Theories Carl Jung, a student of Freud, extended his thinking to develop the notion of a collective unconscious (versus the unconscious as a uniquely individual experience). Jung believed that the images associated with the collective unconscious are expressed in dreams and in literature, where universal meanings are attached to archetypal images (Nodelman & Reimer, 2002). Accordingly, children's literature can be analyzed to locate archetypal plots that appear in many stories. Jung also identified the "shadow," or the dark, as a key archetype representing aspects of individuals' personalities. For instance, in Maurice Sendak's *Where the Wild Things Are*, Max's anti-social behaviour (his shadow) is represented as animal-like, and the story describes Max's struggle to manage these tendencies as he becomes a strong, healthy person (Gose, 1988).

Another example of an archetype is the journey of the hero, which was described by Joseph Campbell as a recurring story central to human existence (Campbell, 1949). In this dominant story pattern, children leave home or are called to adventure. After facing and defeating demons and challenges, they return home victorious to provide service to humanity. Campbell argued that this theme springs from the unconscious and demonstrated how this archetypal pattern is found in stories around the world.

Northrop Frye, a world-renowned Canadian literary critic, adhered to Jung's theory, with a particular focus on literary archetypes. According to Frye (1957), an archetype is a symbol that connects one piece of literature to another, helping to unify and integrate literary experiences. Frye believed that literature is the language of the imaginative inner life and serves to connect individuals' inner and outer worlds. This connection calls forth the active and constructive response from readers that originates in the imagination (Frye, 1988). Frye concluded that literary training for children in Western civilization should include analyzing and comparing myths, legends, and fairy tales as well as Bible stories. For instance, by comparing the birth of Perseus to the births of Moses and Oliver Twist, one can conclude that these stories, which emerged in vastly different eras, share the same shape in the telling of the hero's lowly birth and early threat to survival. While Frye developed his theories in the context of world literature, he believed that it was imperative that Canadians study Canadian literature to understand the uniquely Canadian imagination and experience.

Structuralism Claude Lévi-Strauss was a French anthropologist who approached his discipline from the point of view of structural linguistics. Structuralism is the search for the underlying forms of thought in all human activity. Lévi-Strauss believed that it was structures that created meaning, and this transferred to a belief that all cultures are formed from the same basic elements, just as all sentences are formed from the same basic parts of speech. He applied this analysis to literature by determining elements or central ideas and then examining how those elements related to each other (Nodelman & Reimer, 2002). This approach to literature and its basic elements focuses on the unity of stories and how their parts contribute to the structure of the whole. Furthermore, it shows how an individual literary work relates to other works by describing differing relationships among the same basic elements.

Roland Barthes was a French critical theorist who built on the idea that the activities and artifacts of a culture represent its dominant structure. For instance, in Western culture, the colour red causes people to stop and assume danger. Barthes also believed that reading is a social act in which writers share their beliefs with readers. He qualified this, however, by stating that reading for pleasure results in total immersion in a text, which ultimately breaks the confines of culture and culturally associative language. He believed that individuals could rise to new thoughts and avoid conformity in thinking during reading (Allen, 2003).

A BRIEF HISTORY OF CHILDREN'S LITERATURE

It is difficult to identify the exact beginning of children's literature. In the 1600s, children were taught to read with the intention that they study the Bible. This era was strongly influenced by John Locke, the eminent philosopher and physician, who believed that that people are born without any innate ideas and that knowledge is developed through experience. This translated to a commonly held belief that children had a natural and rational appetite for learning and that training, discipline, and reason ensured that the child would develop fully (Mackie, 1976).

In 1658, Bohemian Jan Amos Komenshy published an illustrated informational book for children titled *Orbis Pictus*. This text is considered to be the first picture book published exclusively for children. During the same period, Charles Perrault published the first written copies of fairy tales in France, including *Little Red Riding Hood*, *Sleeping Beauty*, *Puss in Boots*, and *Cinderella*.

In 1744, John Newbery, for whom the children's book award is named, published the first books for children. Although these books tended to adopt a didactic approach to manners and moral behaviour (separate texts were identified for boys and girls), they are considered the foundation of children's literature and the publishing of books specifically geared to children. By the end of the 1700s, chapter books that told short versions of popular stories such as *Tom Thumb* and *Jack the Giant Killer* were sold for a few pennies in England by itinerant peddlers. Battledores, tri-folded pieces of cardboard containing the alphabet, numbers, and some crude reading lessons, also became available. This era was influenced by Jean-Jacques Rousseau, a prominent political philosopher who believed that children were born with an innate sense of right and wrong, that character and morality development were the most important aspects of education, and that all children passed through the same developmental stages.

In the 1800s, the Brothers Grimm recorded German oral stories, including *Snow White*, *Rapunzel*, and *Hansel and Gretel*. By the mid-1800s, Hans Christian Andersen had recorded the oral stories that he heard as a child in Denmark, including *The Little*

Mermaid, *The Emperor's New Clothes*, *The Ugly Duckling*, *The Princess and the Pea*, and *The Snow Queen*. Many adults were displeased with the initial publication of these fairy tales and other imaginative literature, believing that they had the potential to corrupt young minds.

Publication of children's books continued throughout the 1800s, including Lewis Carroll's *Alice's Adventures in Wonderland* (1865), Johanna Spyri's *Heidi* (1880), Carlo Collodi's *The Adventures of Pinocchio* (1883), Robert Louis Stevenson's *Treasure Island* (1883), and Rudyard Kipling's *The Jungle Book* (1894). Many of the stories written for children during this century have been told and retold in succeeding centuries, with many abridged and made into movies.

Early in the twentieth century, American L. Frank Baum published *The Wonderful Wizard of Oz* and British Beatrix Potter published *The Tale of Peter Rabbit* and many other childhood favourites. In Canada, L.M. Montgomery created the Anne of Green Gables series, which has become a national treasure. Other classics, including Kenneth Grahame's *The Wind in the Willows*, J.M. Barrie's *Peter Pan*, and A.A. Milne's *Winnie-the-Pooh*, emerged in this time frame. Dr. Seuss captivated young children with his colourful, imaginative rhyming books, and Roald Dahl produced fantasy novels such as *Charlie and the Chocolate Factory* and *James and the Giant Peach*. And finally, after an unremarkable but prolific period, J.K. Rowling published the first Harry Potter book, sparking a publishing phenomenon and a renaissance in children's reading.

CHILDREN'S LITERATURE IN CANADA

A Brief History

With the noteworthy exception of *Anne of Green Gables*, there was relatively little activity in children's literature in Canada until about 1975, when Canadian literature began to gain some global recognition, largely due to the outdoor adventure and survival stories of such acclaimed authors as Farley Mowat (*Lost in the Barrens*, *Owls in the Family*), James Houston (*River Runners: A Tale of Hardship and Bravery*, *Frozen Fire: A Tale of Courage*), and Roderick Haig-Brown (*Starbuck Valley Winter*, *Saltwater Summer*). In the same tradition, Sheila Burnford published *The Incredible Journey*, which told of the famous outdoor trek of two dogs and a cat. Canadian authors also celebrated the retelling of Indian and Inuit legends in books for young readers, with the works of Christie Harris (*Once Upon a Totem*) and Dorothy Reid (*Tales of Nanabozho*) being especially noteworthy.

These accomplishments eventually collided with several other events and provided a "tipping point" to mark the birth of Canadian children's literature. The National Library of Canada established the Canadian Children's Literature Service in 1975, acknowledging the literary importance of our country's children's literature. In 1987, the Canada Council for the Arts began awarding Governor General's Literary Awards to children's literature. In the following year, the first annual meeting of the Pacific Rim Conference on Children's Literature was held in Vancouver, attracting speakers from 10 countries to explore the relationship between children and texts.

These events prompted the opening of the Canadian Children's Book Centre, which functioned as a promotional organization and information clearing house. Several small presses, including Kids Can Press, Annick Press, Groundwood Books, and Tundra Books, received grants from the Canada Council for the Arts that enabled them to publish and promote children's literature. New awards for excellence in Canadian writing for children also appeared (e.g., Ruth Schwartz Children's Book Award, Amelia Frances Howard-Gibbon Illustrator's Award). *OWL* magazine for children was launched, and the success of that publication spawned *Chickadee*, a magazine designed for younger children. In short, this was an era when excellence in children's writing was celebrated and embraced.

Current Status

A treasure trove of Canadian literary choices has emerged over the last 35 years. These years have been marked by changes in the content, tone, and positioning of Canadian authors. For instance, the traditional male outdoor survival story has expanded to include female protagonists, and experience of place and community is a frequent theme in Canadian texts (Fitzpatrick, 2005). Canadian authors are widely available to speak to both children and adults, and many Canadian authors have gained international recognition. A multitude of new titles are published annually, and many texts are routinely translated into other languages.

Profiles of Selected Canadian Authors

We maintain that it is incumbent on teachers to be aware of Canadian authors and their works. This knowledge is especially valuable when choosing books for use in the classroom, planning author studies, and advising students about independent reading. While we acknowledge the high quality of work produced by many international authors and the plethora of reading materials available globally, we strongly encourage teachers working in Canadian classrooms to include literary works from among our excellent native writers. To promote the works of Canadian authors, we have listed some of our favourites below, with the caveat that this list is representative rather than exhaustive. Beyond being Canadian, each of the authors featured here has been recognized for excellence in children's literature and has created a significant body of work.

Picture Books

Sheree Fitch (1956–) Fitch was born in Ontario and grew up in the Maritimes. She earned a Master of Arts degree in English, with a focus on children's literature, from Acadia University. She has taught children's literature at St. Thomas University and poetry and writing at the University of New Brunswick. Fitch's earliest texts are often based on family; she wrote her first book, *Toes in my Nose*, for her 2-year-old son when she was 20, and the book was published 10 years later.

Her work as a literacy educator has led her on journeys around the world, and her more recent writings are often informed by her work in education and social justice; for example, *If You Could Wear My Sneakers!* was based on the United Nations Convention on the Rights of the Child. Fitch was instrumental in the implementations of the literacy program called Somebody's Daughter and she continues to work with women and children in the Arctic. She taught writing to college students and teachers to help foster an indigenous literature for the children of Bhutan and her book and library readings have taken her to countries such as Uganda, Tanzania, Kenya, China, Belize, Mexico, Thailand, and Vietnam.

Fitch has received numerous awards for her work, including the Silver Birch Award, Anne Connor Brimer Book Award, Mr. Christie's Book Award, and Atlantic Independent Booksellers' Choice Award. She has also received several awards acknowledging her collective contribution to children's literature. In 1995, Fitch was awarded the Canadian Authors Association Marianna Dempster Award, and in 2000, she won the prestigious Vicky Metcalf Award.

Selected Publications

Picture Books

Sleeping Dragons All Around (1989)

Merry-Go-Day (1991)

There Were Monkeys in My Kitchen (1992)

I Am Small (1994)

Mabel Murple (1995)

If I Were the Moon (1999)

No Two Snowflakes (2001)

Pocket Rocks (2004)

Peek-a-Little Boo (2005)

Kisses Kisses Baby-O (2008)

Chapter Books

The Hullaballoo Bugaboo Day (1998)

The Other Author, Arthur (1999)

Poetry and Plays

Toes in My Nose and Other Poems (1987)

If You Could Wear My Sneakers! (1997)

There's a Mouse in My House (1998)

Persnickety Pete: The Cleanest Boy in the World (2003)

If I Had a Million Onions (2005)

Young Adult

One More Step (2002)

The Gravesavers (2005)

Pluto's Ghost (2010)

Marie-Louise Gay (1952–) Gay was born in Quebec City and currently lives in Montreal. She has received numerous awards for her work, including the Governor General's Literary Award, Vicky Metcalf Award, Ruth Schwartz Children's Book Award, Mr. Christie's Book Award, Elizabeth Mrazik-Cleaver Canadian Picture Book Award, Marilyn Baillie Picture Book Award, and Amelia Frances Howard-Gibbon Illustrator's Award. Her famous Stella and Sam books have been published in more than 12 languages.

Selected Publications

Rainy Day Magic (1987)

Fat Charlie's Circus (1989)

Willy Nilly (1990)

Rabbit Blue (1993)
Stella, Star of the Sea (1999)
Sur Mon Ile (1999)
Stella, Queen of the Snow (2000)
Stella, Fairy of the Forest (2002)
Good Morning Sam (2003)
Good Night Sam (2003)
Stella, Princess of the Sky (2004)
What Are You Doing Sam? (2006)

Phoebe Gilman (1940–2002) Gilman was born in the United States but settled in Canada. She taught at the Ontario College of Art and Design for a number of years and, during that time, started writing and illustrating stories for her children. Her intricate artwork and the accompanying stories have been very popular, including her books about the indomitable Jillian Jiggs. In 1993, she won the Ruth Schwartz Children's Book Award and the Sydney Taylor Book Award for *Something from Nothing*, as well as the Vicky Metcalf Award for a body of work.

Selected Publications

The Balloon Tree (1984)
Jillian Jiggs (1985)
Little Blue Ben (1986)
The Wonderful Pigs of Jillian Jiggs (1987)
Grandma and the Pirates (1990)
Once Upon a Golden Apple (Illustrator) (1991)
Something from Nothing (1992)
Jillian Jiggs to the Rescue (1993)
The Gypsy Princess (1995)
Pirate Pearl (1998)
Jillian Jiggs and the Secret Surprise (1999)
Jillian Jiggs and the Big Snow (2002)

Robert Munsch (1945–) Munsch was born in the United States and studied to be a Jesuit priest. He became increasingly interested in working with children and earned a Master of Education degree in child studies. Munsch moved to Canada in 1975 and was teaching at the University of Guelph when he published his first children's book. He bases his characters on the lives of real children, including his own. He is a renowned storyteller, much loved for his exaggerated expressions and voices. Munsch is a Member of the Order of Canada and earned a position on Canada's Walk of Fame in 2009.

Selected Publications

The Paper Bag Princess (1980)
David's Father (1983)
Mortimer (1984)
Thomas' Snowsuit (1985)
50 Below Zero (1986)

Love You Forever (1986)
I Have to Go! (1987)
Pigs (1989)
Stephanie's Ponytail (1996)
Andrew's Loose Tooth (1999)
Smelly Socks (2004)
I'm So Embarrassed! (2006)
Put Me in a Book (2010)

Student Voice 9.2

My teacher reads a lot of books by Robert Munsch to our class. My favourite book is *One More Goal*. I like the picture where the girl is making the ice rink. I want to play hockey.

Luke
Junior kindergarten student

Ian Wallace (1950–) Wallace was born in southern Ontario. An excellent student, he was drawn to art and attended the Ontario College of Art and Design as a young man. Wallace published his first book when he was 24 years old and continues to publish today. He has received numerous awards, including the Quill & Quire Book of the Year, Smithsonian Notable Books for Children, Elizabeth Mrazik-Cleaver Canadian Picture Book Award, Amelia Frances Howard-Gibbon Illustrator's Award, and Mr. Christie's Book Award (Illustration). Wallace is also an accomplished storyteller and enjoys travelling across Canada and around the world sharing his stories with young children. His writings and illustrations are drawn from his travels abroad as well as from his childhood experiences.

Selected Publications

The Sandwich, with Angela Wood (1975)
Chin Chiang and the Dragon's Dance (1984)
Very Last First Time (Illustrator), written by Jan Andrews (1985)
Morgan the Magnificent (1987)
Architect of the Moon (Illustrator), written by Tim Wynne-Jones (1988)
The Name of the Tree (Illustrator), written by Celia Barker Lottridge (1989)
Mr. Kneebone's New Digs (1991)
The Mummer's Song (Illustrator), written by Bud Davidge (1993)
Sarah and the People of Sand River (Illustrator), written by W.D. Valgardson (1996)
A Winter's Tale (1997)
Duncan's Way (2000)
The True Story of Trapper Jack's Left Big Toe (2002)
The Man Who Walked the Earth (2003)

Chapter Books, Children's Novels, and Young Adult Literature

Brian Doyle (1935–) Doyle was born and resides in Ottawa, Ontario. He submitted several short stories to magazines while in high school, majored in journalism at Carleton University, and spent a brief period working as a journalist for the *Toronto Telegram* before becoming a high school teacher, at which point he published his first short story.

While Doyle situates his works in historical and contemporary periods, much of his writings reflect his experiences growing up and raising his family in urban Ottawa and the Ottawa Valley. Well known for his animated storytelling and use of humour, Doyle's works often depict moral dilemmas faced by young people, including racism, anti-social activities, and violence. He has also included several characters with disabilities in his books, reflecting his experiences growing up with a sister with Down's syndrome.

Doyle is the recipient of many honours and recognitions, including the Canadian Library Association's Book of the Year for Children Award, Mr. Christie's Book Award, Vicky Metcalf Award, Hans Christian Andersen Award short list, and Mr. Christie's Book Award Silver Seal. His books have been translated into seven languages and several have been adopted for radio, stage, and film, including *You Can Pick Me Up at Peggy's Cove* and *Angel Square*.

Selected Publications

Hey, Dad! (1978)
You Can Pick Me Up at Peggy's Cove (1979)
Up to Low (1982)
Angel Square (1987)
Easy Avenue (1988)
Covered Bridge (1990)
Spud Sweetgrass (1992)
Spud in Winter (1995)
The Low Life: Five Great Tales from Up and Down the River (1999)
Mary Ann Alice (2001)
Boy O'Boy (2003)
Uncle Ronald (2004)
Pure Spring (2007)

Deborah Ellis (1960–) Ellis was born in Cochrane, Ontario, and is considered one of the most popular young adult authors today. She grew up loving to read and decided that she wanted to become a writer when she was about 12 years old. She is an anti-war activist and feminist, and many of her writings reflect these orientations. *The Breadwinner* was inspired by an interview with a mother in a refugee camp in Afghanistan, with the following books in the series (*Parvana's Journey* and *Mud City*) sharing the experiences of children in similar circumstances.

She has written about the resilience of children (especially those growing up in developing countries); many of her characters are challenged by poverty, war, sickness (including HIV/AIDS), and discrimination. Ellis has donated more than $1 million of her royalties to non-profit organizations that support international health and education programs.

Her works have been recognized both nationally and internationally. Among her many recognitions, Ellis has received the Governor General's Literary Award, Jane Addams Children's Book Award, Vicky Metcalf Award, Peter Pan Prize, Ruth Schwartz Award, University of California's Middle East Book Award, and Children's Africana Book Award Honor Book for Older Readers. She is a Member of the Order of Ontario.

Selected Publications

Looking for X (1999)
The Breadwinner (2001)
A Company of Fools (2002)
Parvana's Journey (2002)
The Heaven Shop (2004)
Mud City (2004)
Bifocal, with Eric Walters (2007)
Lunch with Lenin and Other Stories (2008)
The Prison Runner (2008)
Beyond the Barricade (2009)

Jean Little (1932–) Little was born in Formosa (now known as Taiwan). As an infant she was diagnosed as legally blind, but despite this her parents read to her regularly and she quickly became an avid reader and writer. When she was 9 years old, Little's family immigrated to Canada, where she published her first work as a teenager. She went on to graduate from Victoria College with a bachelor's degree in English. She subsequently taught in the United States, working with children with physical disabilities.

Sensitive to the needs and struggles of students with exceptionalities, Little bases many of her books on her own life experiences. Her characters often have physical disabilities and learn how to develop resilience to cope with their associated challenges. Little frequently writes about adoption, foster care, life-threatening illness, and emotional disorders and suffering.

She has taught children's literature at the University of Guelph and is a Member of the Order of Canada. Her works have been published internationally and she is the recipient of many literary awards, including the Little, Brown Children's Book Award; Governor General's Literary Award; and Canadian Library Association's Book of the Year for Children Award.

Selected Publications

Picture Books

Jess Was the Brave One (1991)
Revenge of the Small Small (1992)
Bats about Baseball, with Claire Mackay (1995)
Jenny and the Hanukkah Queen (1995)
Gruntle Piggle Takes Off (1996)
I Know an Old Laddie (2003)
The Sweetest One of All (2008)

Children's Novels

Listen for the Singing (1970)
From Anna (1972)
Mama's Going to Buy You a Mockingbird (1984)
His Banner over Me (1995)
Emma's Magic Winter (2000)
Willow and Twig (2000)

Emma's Yucky Brother (2001)
Birdie for Now (2002)
Rescue Pup (2004)
Forward, Shakespeare (2005)
Somebody Else's Summer (2005)
Dancing Through the Snow (2007)

Dear Canada Series

Orphan at My Door: The Home Child Diary of Victoria Cope (2001)
Brothers Far from Home: The World War I Diary of Eliza Bates (2003)
If I Die Before I Wake: The Flu Epidemic Diary of Fiona Macgregor (2007)

Short Stories and Poetry

When the Pie Was Opened (1968)
Hey World, Here I Am! (1986)
What Will The Robin Do Then? (1998)
I Gave My Mom a Castle (2003)

Janet Lunn (1928–) Lunn was born in Dallas, Texas. Even as a child, she describes herself as a writer, claiming to dream up stories before she could write. She came to Canada in 1946 to attend Notre Dame College in Ottawa and then Queen's University in Kingston, Ontario. She met and married Richard Lunn and became a Canadian citizen in 1963.

Lunn published her first children's book, *Double Spell*, in 1968. In part, this book was inspired by memories of her childhood and pine trees outside her family farmhouse. Her love for the countryside is reflected in many of her writings. Lunn was the first children's author to be chair of the Writers' Union of Canada. She has published across several genres, including short stories, picture books, and biographies. However, the majority of her books are historical novels.

Lunn has received numerous awards for her writing, including the Governor General's Literary Award, Mr. Christie's Book Award, California Young Reader Medal, Canada Council Award for Children's Literature, and Young Adult Book of the Year. In 1982, she was awarded the Vicky Metcalf Award for her body of work. She was awarded the Order of Ontario in 1996 and in the following year was made a Member of the Order of Canada. At 81 years of age, she is working on two projects: a picture book about two lonely boys who meet the first prime minister of Canada and her family's history.

Selected Publications

Picture Books

The Twelve Dancing Princesses (1979)
Amos's Sweater (1988)
Duck Cakes for Sale (1989)

Children's Novels

Double Spell (1968)
The Root Cellar (1981)
Shadow in Hawthorn Bay (1986)
The Story of Canada, with Christopher Moore (1995)

The Hollow Tree (1997)

Laura Secord: A Story of Courage (2001)

A Rebel's Daughter: The 1837 Rebellion Diary of Arabella Stevenson, with Christopher Moore (2006)

Kevin Major (1949–) Major was born in Newfoundland and Labrador and currently lives there with his family. He is an accomplished author, writing for both children and adults across several genres including fiction, literary non-fiction, poetry, and plays. Many of his works, especially his early novels, explore issues related to adolescence and family and are usually set in Newfoundland.

After completing high school, he travelled through Europe and parts of the Caribbean. He returned to study education, earning a teaching certificate from Memorial University. While teaching, Major recognized the lack of material reflecting the culture of Newfoundland and edited *Doryloads*, an anthology of Newfoundland writing. He published his first novel, *Hold Fast*, in 1978 while working as a substitute teacher.

Major has received many honours and recognitions for his work, including the Governor General's Literary Award, Young Adult Canadian Book Award, Canadian Association of Children's Librarians' Book of the Year, Mr. Christie's Book Award, and Ann Connor Brimer Award. He was awarded the Vicky Metcalf Award for a body of work in 1992.

Selected Publications

Hold Fast (1978)

Far from Shore (1980)

Thirty-Six Exposures (1984)

Dear Bruce Springsteen (1987)

Blood Red Ochre (1989)

Eating Between the Lines (1991)

Diana: My Autobiography (1993)

No Man's Land (1995)

Gaffer: A Novel of Newfoundland (1997)

The House of Wooden Santas (1997)

Eh? to Zed: A Canadian Abecedarium (2000)

Ann and Seamus (2003)

Aunt Olga's Christmas Postcards (2005)

Gros Morne Time Lines, with Tara Bryan and Anne Meredith Barry (2007)

New Under the Sun (2010)

Carol Matas (1949–) Matas was born in and lives in Winnipeg, Manitoba. Wanting to be an actor, she completed her Bachelor of Arts in English at the University of Western Ontario in 1970, spending much of her free time acting in university productions. After graduation, she moved to England to study acting professionally. She then returned to Toronto, where she worked as an actor for several years. During this time that she took up writing as a recreational hobby after observing several of her acting colleagues writing in their spare time. Years later, Matas considered becoming a professional author and published her first children's book, *The D.N.A. Dimension*, in 1982.

Many of Matas's novels are about World War II and the stories of children during the Holocaust (*The Whirlwind*, *Turned Away*, *In My Enemy's House*, *Jesper*). She hopes that by sharing these stories, she can make the world a better place. Matas has also written about such contemporary subjects as adolescence, science fiction, the supernatural, and politics. When writing, Matas selects topics that she believes are relatively unfamiliar to young people and hopes that she inspires them to consider new ideas and concepts.

Her works are recognized nationally and internationally and her novels have been translated into several languages. She has also received numerous awards, including the Silver Birch Award, Manitoba Young Readers' Choice Award, American Library Association's Best Book for Young Adults, Jewish Book Award, Young Adults' Choice Award, Red Maple Award, and Geoffrey Bilson Award for Historical Fiction for Young People.

Selected Publications

Jesper (1989)
The Race (1991)
Adventure in Legoland (1992)
Sworn Enemies (1993)
The Birth of Israel (1997)
The Garden (1998)
Cloning Miranda (1999)
The Primrose Path (1999)
The War Within (2001)
Footsteps in the Snow: The Red River Diary of Isobel Scott (2002)
In My Enemy's House (2002)
After the War (2004)
Lisa's War (2004)
The Dark Clone (2005)
Past Crimes (2006)
The Freak (2007)
Tales of a Reluctant Psychic (2009)
The Burning Time (2010)
Daniel's Story (2010)
The Hunt for the Haunted Elephant (2010)

Lucy Maud Montgomery (1874–1942) Montgomery was born in Prince Edward Island and is one of Canada's first internationally acclaimed authors. Her mother died of tuberculosis when she was an infant and Montgomery moved to Saskatchewan to live with her grandparents. Although she describes her childhood as a lonely one, she also credits this time with inspiring her creativity, having developed many imaginary friends and worlds during these years. She returned to PEI after publishing her first work in 1890. She went on to obtain her teaching certificate from the Prince of Wales College and published more than 100 stories while working as a teacher. Montgomery returned to school in 1907 to study literature at Dalhousie University. In 1911, she married and moved to Ontario.

Montgomery is perhaps best known for the Anne of Green Gables series. Throughout her lifetime,she published 20 novels as well as more than 500 short stories and poems and an autobiography. Much of her writing is set on Prince Edward Island, making the province a literary landmark, even as her writings were recognized internationally. Montgomery was the first female in Canada to be named a Fellow of the Royal Society of Arts in England and a Member of the Order of the British Empire.

Selected Publications

Novels

Anne of Green Gables (1908)
Anne of Avonlea (1909)
Kilmeny of the Orchard (1910)
The Story Girl (1911)
The Golden Road (1913)
Anne of the Island (1915)
Anne's House of Dreams (1917)
Rainbow Valley (1919)
Rilla of Ingleside (1921)
Emily of New Moon (1923)
Emily Climbs (1925)
The Blue Castle (1926)
Emily's Quest (1927)
Magic for Marigold (1929)
A Tangled Web (1931)
Pat of Silver Bush (1933)
Mistress Pat (1935)
Anne of Windy Poplars (1936)
Jane of Lantern Hill (1937)
Anne of Ingleside (1939)
The Blythes Are Quoted (2009)

Short Story Collections

Chronicles of Avonlea (1912)
Further Chronicles of Avonlea (1920)
The Road to Yesterday (1974)
The Doctor's Sweetheart and Other Stories (1979)
Akin to Anne: Tales of Other Orphans (1988)
Along the Shore: Tales by the Sea (1989)
Among the Shadows: Tales from the Darker Side (1990)
After Many Days: Tales of Time Passed (1991)
Against the Odds: Tales of Achievement (1993)
At the Altar: Matrimonial Tales (1994)
Across the Miles: Tales of Correspondence (1995)
Christmas with Anne and Other Holiday Stories (1995)

Poetry

The Watchman and Other Poems (1916)

The Poetry of Lucy Maud Montgomery (1987)

Kenneth Oppel (1967–) Oppel was born in British Columbia and lived in the western and eastern provinces as a child. While in high school, Oppel wrote his first book, *Colin's Fantastic Video Adventure*,which was published in 1985 when a friend of the family forwarded the manuscript to Roald Dahl, who promoted the book to his publishers. (Although Oppel and Dahl never met or communicated, Oppel credits Dahl for championing his career.)

Oppel went on to study cinema and English at Trinity College in the University of Toronto, where he published his second book, *The Live-Forever Machine*. He lived in England briefly while his wife completed her doctorate, during which time he assumed many part-time jobs, one of which was typing essays and theses for university students. He credits this work as the inspiration for some of his novels and book titles. For instance, the title *Dead Water Zone* was inspired after typing a metallurgy paper. After returning to Canada, Oppel went on to author numerous picture books, chapter books, and young adult novels, including several series. Many of his texts are fantasies featuring the adventures and trials of both animal and human characters.

Oppel has won numerous awards, including the Governor General's Literary Award, Printz Honor Book, Air Canada Award, London Times Children's Novel Award, and American Library Association's Best Book for Young Adults. Oppel currently resides in Ontario, where he now writes screenplays.

Selected Publications

The Silverwing Saga

Silverwing (1997)

Sunwing (1999)

Firewing (2002)

Darkwing (2007)

Airborn Series

Airborn (2004)

Skybreaker (2005)

Starclimber (2008)

Barnes and the Brains

A Bad Case of Ghosts (1993)

A Strange Case of Magic (1994)

A Crazy Case of Robots (1994)

An Incredible Case of Dinosaurs (1994)

A Weird Case of Super-Goo (1997)

A Creepy Case of Vampires (2002)

Children's Novels

Colin's Fantastic Video Adventure (1985)

Cosimo Cat (1990)

The Live-Forever Machine (1990)
Dead Water Zone (1992)
Follow That Star (1992)
Cosmic Snapshots (1993)
Galactic Snapshots (1993)
Emma's Emu (1995)
Peg and the Whale (2000)
Peg and the Yeti (2004)
The King's Taster (2009)

Young Adult

Half Brother (2010)

Kit Pearson (1947–) Pearson was born and continues to live in western Canada. As a young woman, she studied English literature at the University of British Columbia and the University of Alberta. Several years after graduating, she returned to the University of British Columbia to complete a library degree, specializing in children's literature, after which she moved to southern Ontario and worked as a librarian. Enthralled with her work, she pursued a Master of Arts in the study of children's literature at the University of Boston, which included several writing courses. Inspired by her professors, Pearson returned to Canada and published her first book, *The Daring Game*.

Pearson has won numerous awards for her novels, including the prestigious Governor General's Literary Award and the Canadian Library Association's Book of the Year for Children Award. Her best-known novels are a trilogy about British children sent to Canada during World War II: *The Sky Is Falling*, *Looking at the Moon*, and *The Lights Go on Again*. She has also won the Vicky Metcalf Award for a body of work.

Selected Publications

The Daring Game (1986)
A Handful of Time (1987)
The Sky Is Falling (1989)
The Singing Basket (picture book) (1990)
Looking at the Moon (1991)
The Lights Go on Again (1993)
Awake and Dreaming (1996)
This Land (editor) (1998)
Whispers of War: The War of 1812 Diary of Susanna Merritt (2002)
A Perfect Gentle Knight (2007)

Barbara Smucker (1915–2003) Smucker was born in Kansas and studied journalism at Kansas State University. After graduation, she returned to her hometown to work as a reporter. She then married Donovan Smucker, a college professor and ordained minister who pastored the Mennonite Church. The family travelled throughout the United States for his work and Smucker often worked as a teacher. She wrote her first children's novel in Chicago. While teaching in Mississippi in the late 1960s, she was inspired by the civil rights movement.

Smucker and her family came to Canada in 1969, and she accepted an invitation to teach at Conrad Grebel University College. Over the next 15 years, she also worked as the children's librarian at the Kitchener Public Library and as head librarian at Renison University College. She observed that there were relatively few quality children's and young adult books about slavery and, after a trip to a local museum, was inspired to write her first novel. In *Underground to Canada*, she documents the journey of African-American slaves fleeing to Canada. Smucker focused much of her writing on the historical or contemporary plight of minority groups as well as on the universal need for tolerance, respect, and caring.

Smucker's works have been translated into seven languages: French, Swedish, Japanese, German, Dutch, Spanish, and Danish. She has received many national and international honours and recognitions, including the Brotherhood Award of the National Conference on Christians and Jews, Ruth Schwartz Children's Book Award, and Elizabeth Mrazik-Cleaver Canadian Picture Book Award. She also was awarded the Canada Council Children's Literature Prize. In 1988, she received the Vicky Metcalf Award for a distinguished body of writing. She published her last novel when she was 83 years old.

Selected Publications

Henry's Red Sea (1955)
Runaway to Freedom: A Story of the Underground Railway (1979)
Amish Adventure (1984)
Underground to Canada (1986)
Incredible Jumbo (1992)
Selina and the Shoo-Fly Pie (1998)
Selina and the Bear Paw Quilt (1999)
Days of Terror (2008)

Jan Thornhill (1955–) Thornhill was born in northern Ontario and spent her childhood developing a love for art and the natural world. After high school, Thornhill attended the Ontario College of Art and Design, where she majored in experimental film and video. She worked as a freelance illustrator for about a decade. Thornhill began writing after moving to Guatemala in the late 1980s. She hopes that her writings and illustrations will inspire young readers to appreciate art, nature, and the environment. She has published several non-fiction texts and has been awarded the UNICEF Ezra Jack Keats International Award for Excellence in Children's Book Illustration and the Conaculta 7th International Award for the Illustration of a Children's Book. Her books have been translated into several languages, including Korean, Danish, Finnish, and Dutch.

Selected Publications

The Wildlife 1-2-3: A Nature Counting Book (1990)
A Tree in a Forest (1991)
Wild in the City (1995)
Before & After: A Book of Nature Timescapes (1997)
The Rumor: A Jataka Tale from India (2002)
The Wildlife ABC: A Nature Alphabet Book (2004)
I Found a Dead Bird: The Kids' Guide to the Cycle of Life & Death (2006)
This Is My Planet: The Kids' Guide to Global Warming (2007)
Who Wants Pizza? The Kids' Guide to the History, Science & Culture of Food (2010)

Tim Wynne-Jones (1948–) Wynne-Jones was born in England and moved to Canada as a young boy, living in British Columbia and then Ontario. He completed his undergraduate degree at the University of Waterloo and a Master of Arts in visual arts at York University. He wrote his first book, *Odd's End*, in five weeks shortly after graduating. Wynne-Jones currently teaches in the Writing for Children and Young Adults program at Vermont College of Fine Arts.

Wynne-Jones has authored picture books, children's and young adult novels, adult novels, radio dramas, and children's musicals and songs, such as *Fraggle Rock* (a Jim Henson production). Wynne-Jones is probably best known for his children's books, in particular the chronicles of Zoom the cat. His stories often tell the adventures of seemingly average characters; in *Some of the Kinder Planets* he recounts the remarkable journeys made by nine youth from Ontario.

He has been awarded three Governor General's Literary Awards, three Canadian Library Association prizes, the Arthur Ellis Award, the Vicky Metcalf Award, the Ruth Schwartz Children's Book Award, the Edgar Award, and the Boston Globe-Horn Book Award.

Selected Publications

Picture Books

I'll Make You Small (1988)
Boat in the Tree (2007)
On Tumbledown Hill (2008)
Pounce de Leon (2009)
Zoom (2009)

Children's Novels

Madeline and Ermadillo (1976)
Odd's End (1979)
Odd's End No-Name (1980)
The Knot (1982)
Zoom at Sea (1983)
The Hour of the Frog (1985)
Zoom Away (1985)
Mischief City (1986)
Architect of the Moon (1988)
Voices (1990)
Zoom Upstream (1992)
The Last Piece of Sky (1993)
Mouse in the Manger (1993)
The Hunchback of Notre Dame (1996)
Dracula (1997)
On Tumbledown Hill (1998)
Ned Mouse Breaks Away (2002)

Young Adult

The Book of Changes (1994)
Rosie Backstage, with Amanda Lewis (1994)

The Maestro (1995)

Some of the Kinder Planets (1997)

Stephen Fair (1998)

Lord of the Fries and Other Stories (1999)

The Boy in the Burning House (2000)

A Thief in the House of Memory (2004)

Rex Zero and the End of the World (2006)

Click, with David Almond, Eoin Colfer, Roddy Doyle, Deborah Ellis, Nick Hornby, Margo Lanagan, Gregory Maguire, Ruth Ozeki, and Linda Sue Park (2007)

The Uninvited (2009)

Blink & Caution (2011)

REFLECTIVE ACTIVITY 2

Stop for a moment and reflect on your prejudices and biases, or possibly your lack of knowledge about certain racial or cultural groups. Be honest with yourself. To what extent are you likely to make assumptions about your students based on their background, socio-economic status, language differences, physical appearance, health status, and cultural factors? Few people are totally free of prejudice or xenophobia, which tends to prompt emotional responses shaped by upbringing and experiences rather than intellectual responses. If you find that you hold serious biases for whatever reason, remember that anyone can adjust how he or she acts and instructs to ensure that students never see those personal biases.

DIVERSITY IN THE CLASSROOM

Diversity in Children's Literature

Since the 1960s, multicultural literature has emerged as a category of children's literature and has gradually expanded to include books about gender, class, sexual orientation, age, religion, and geographical location (Botelho, 2004). It is more frequently referred to as *diversity literature*. The concept of diversity encompasses tolerance, understanding, acceptance, and respect. It means understanding that each person is unique, recognizing individual differences, and providing equal opportunity for learning (Banks, 1994).

Today, as a natural outcome of our culturally pluralistic society and immigration policies, an increasing number of teachers in Canadian schools have children from a variety of culturally diverse backgrounds in their classrooms, many of whom do not speak English at home. The inclusion of children with special needs in mainstream education has added another potentially enriching form of diversity to the classroom.

Some critics of diversity education have suggested that it has not been very effective because when it was called multiculturalism, it was mandated in a vague way at the federal level but implemented in different ways by each province (Kirova, 2008). Yet despite regional differences, at least three goals are shared: (1) equivalence in achievement, (2) more positive intergroup attitudes, and (3) developing pride in heritage (Kehoe & Mansfield, 1997).

It is a truism that teachers should be fostering an awareness and tolerance of other cultures and minority groups in the Canadian mosaic, enabling their students to understand that people who belong to other groups are real people with feelings, emotions, and needs that are similar to their own. In classrooms with no visible minorities, it is perhaps even more important to foster discussion about these issues. It is increasingly evident that this imperative needs to be more than superficial lip service. We contend that the best ally in serving this goal is children's literature, which broadens children's world views by introducing them to new ways of looking at themselves and others (Luke, 2000; Peterson & Swartz, 2008). However, the way these books are chosen and used in the classroom is what determines the success of these goals.

At the same time, it is necessary to ensure that students do not gain the idea from literature that all members of a certain racial or cultural group are the same as the characters portrayed. Critics caution that merely increasing knowledge of other groups may enhance the feeling of difference and not encourage dialogue that promotes compassion, respect, and understanding (Stables, 2005). For instance, the novel *The Heaven Shop* by Deborah Ellis describes an orphan whose parents and grandmother all died of AIDS in Africa. It would be unfortunate if readers associated black Canadians and Americans exclusively with AIDS. *Very Last First Time* by Jan Andrews is set in the Arctic but it would be equally unfortunate if students associated First Nations peoples exclusively with remote rural living.

If the goal of using a multicultural book is to set the stage for discussion of social justice issues such as how to combat intolerance, how to establish an environment of inclusion, or how to effect positive societal change, it is important to structure the process carefully. Merely reading a book does not necessarily achieve these goals; rather, the questions asked and the assumptions challenged are central to the experience (Peterson & Swartz, 2008).

Choosing Diverse Literature

The metaphor of mirrors and windows is a useful one for teachers to think about when making book selections (Bishop, 1992). Mirrors allow readers to see reflections of their own lives so they can recognize themselves and think about their values and world views, while windows allow them to see the lives of others more clearly. A reading program should encompass both perspectives and avoid didactics in either case.

When choosing literature that will promote discussion and understanding of others in the world, the following should be considered:

- Does the work present diversity authentically? One way to determine authenticity is to ensure that members of the culture who read it feel that their experiences are reflected accurately. Readers outside the culture may not be able to discern this aspect of the text.
- Does the author write from an inside or an outside point of view? The appropriation of voice has become a major issue in diversity literature. A writer from inside the culture writes from a perspective of knowing and thus is more likely to present the culture authentically.
- Does the work promote stereotypes? When a single set of attributes is assigned to a particular group, the result is a stereotype. Many books that present stereotypes are

still in print or on library shelves, and a teacher needs to be wary. A basic rule is: If in doubt, choose something else.

- Which group's perspectives are being described in the work? Identify the perspective or multiple perspectives in the text and become familiar with that group through other reading before sharing with the class.
- Whose voice is not present in the work? When pre-reading the text, be aware of whose perspective is not present. This awareness can lead to a good discussion with the class.
- Is the work well written and plausible? A poorly written book should not be shared in class, no matter what its content.
- Is the book current enough to be representative of today's goals? Check the publication date and be cautious about using older texts that might be presenting diverse issues in a stereotypical or disparaging manner.

The following selections meet the above criteria:

Picture Books

Andrews, J. (1985). *Very Last First Time.*

Badoe, A. (2002). *Nana's Cold Days.*

Cheng, A. (2000). *Grandfather Counts.*

Davidge, B. (1993). *The Mummer's Song*

Gilman, P. (1996). *Something from Nothing.*

Hughes, M. (1993). *A Handful of Seeds.*

Keens-Douglas, R. (1992). *The Nutmeg Princess.*

Lottridge, C. B. (2002). *The Name of the Tree: A Bantu Tale.*

Mollel, T. M. (1990). *The Orphan Boy.*

Mollel, T. M. (1995). *Big Boy.*

Mollel, T. M. (1997). *Kele's Secret.*

Nanji, S. (2000). *Treasure for Lunch.*

Thien, M. (2001). *The Chinese Violin.*

Wallace, I. (1984). *Chin Chiang and the Dragon's Dance.*

Wallace, I. (2000). *Duncan's Way.*

Yee, P. (1991). *Roses Sing on New Snow: A Delicious Tale.*

Yee, P. (1996). *Ghost Train.*

Yee, P. (2007). *Shu-Li and Tamara.*

Yee, P. (2009). *Shu-Li and Diego.*

Novels

Badoe, A. (2010). *Between Sisters.*

Brenna, B, (2005). *Wild Orchid.*

Coerr, E. (1999). *Sadako and the Thousand Paper Cranes.*

Doyle, B. (1992). *Spud Sweetgrass.*

Gilmore, R. (1995). *A Friend Like Zilla.*

Haworth-Attard, B. (2002). *Irish Chain.*

Houston, J. (1990). *Tikta'liktak.*

Keefer, J. K. (2000). *Anna's Goat.*
Khan. R. (1999). *Dahling If You Luv Me, Would You Please, Please Smile.*
Little, J. (2000). *Willow and Twig.*
Matas, C. (1989). *Lisa's War.*
Matas, C. (1993). *Daniel's Story.*
Matas, C. (2007). The Whirlwind.
Phillips, W. (2009). *Fishtailing.*
Smucker, B. (1977). *Underground to Canada.*
Walters, E. (2000). *Caged Eagles.*
Yee, P. (1989). *Tales from Gold Mountain.*
Yee, P. (1998). *The Boy in the Attic.*

SAMPLE ACTIVITY 9.1

Starting a Dialogue about Diversity in the Classroom

Change as a Universal Aspect of Being Human

This activity is suitable for junior or intermediate students and is based on reading the book *Very Last First Time* by Jan Andrews.

Step 1

Ask students to discuss a change in their lives. As the discussion progresses, use prompts such as "Have you ever moved to a new community?" or "Have you ever taken up a new activity?" When students respond, ask further probing questions to help them identify the feelings they had about being new and not being successful initially. Continue the discussion until it is evident that everyone has had changes in their lives. Point out that sometimes we initiate change and sometimes it is beyond our control.

Move the discussion to how the world has changed over the past decade to begin the idea that constant adaptation to change is universal.

Step 2

Ask each student to think of a time when change affected their life. Pass out paper and provide crayons or coloured pencils for drawing. Help students fold their paper into three equal sections and instruct them to write beginning, middle, and end at the top of each section. Then ask them to use pictures to show their change, with the first section being "before the change," the middle section being "during the change," and the last section being "after the change." Finally, ask them to put words in each section to represent how they were feeling during each stage.

Step 3

Ask a few students to describe their changes and read the words they have chosen. These words can be written on the board or on a chart under each of the three sections. Identify common aspects of each stage.

Step 4

Read *Very Last First Time* aloud. (This is a story of an Inuit girl, Eva, who undertakes a new independent activity in Ungava Bay: walking on the ocean floor under the ice while the tide is out to gather mussels. The scary part for Eva is that she will go alone under the ice for the first time.)

Step 5

Ask about Eva's change, her emotions, and the meaning of the experience for her. Ask students to relate Eva's story to their own experience of change and identify common elements. Ask students to identify other stories they have seen or read that fit this pattern.

Step 6

Students can write their own story of change using their diagram as a guide.

SAMPLE ACTIVITY 9.2

Starting a Dialogue about Diversity in the Classroom

Similarities and Differences in Two Canadian Cultures Using a Venn Diagram

This activity is appropriate for primary grades.

Step 1

Over a couple of days, read aloud both *Very Last First Time* by Jan Andrews and *Chin Chiang and the Dragon's Dance* by Ian Wallace. (In *Chin Chiang and the Dragon's Dance*, a young boy living in Chinatown in Vancouver is given the opportunity to participate in the dragon's dance to usher in the Chinese New Year. He is terrified that he will forget the dance steps until he meets an old woman who helps him practise and gives him the confidence to accomplish this important cultural role.)

Step 2

Draw two intersecting circles on the board and tell the class that you are going to compare Eva and Chin Chiang's lives and experiences. The three areas created by the circles should be labelled *Chin Chiang, The Same*, and *Eva*.

Step 3

Through questions and discussion, complete the Venn diagram so that it is evident that although the context for meeting a new adult-like challenge is different, the emotions and sense of accomplishment are the same.

Step 4

Ask students to identify some aspect of their own lives that contains the same elements as those in *The Same* category on the Venn diagram.

Or

Ask students to complete a Venn diagram in the same way by comparing their experiences to those of either Chin Chiang or Eva.

Or

Ask students to compare two other characters from stories with which they are familiar.

Step 5

Allow students to share their work and discuss the fact that there are many shared attributes among people from different cultures.

Aboriginal Literature

Aboriginal peoples in Canada include First Nations, Inuit, and Metis. While the terms *Aboriginal*, *indigenous*, and *First Nations* are used interchangeably in the literature, it is important to remember that the words *Indians* and *Eskimos* have fallen into disuse in Canada and are considered pejorative terms. Some older books and texts may contain these terms and should be avoided. Currently, there are more than 600 separate First Nations governments or bands in Canada with distinct languages, cultures, customs, ceremonies, art, and music. Stories about First Nations identity can be employed to show how these groups helped shape the Canadian identity.

We suggest that when teachers select Aboriginal literature, they choose books that depict the character and culture of a well-defined native nation. There are no generic Aboriginal people, so books that portray these very diverse cultures as identical should be

SAMPLE ACTIVITY 9.3

Starting a Dialogue about Diversity in the Classroom

Developing a Habit of Reading Critically

Texts written in a male-dominated society often reflect a male point of view as if it were the universal one. Likewise, texts written in a white-dominated society reflect a white point of view as if it were universal. Consequently, we need to alert students to look at assumptions about race and ethnicity in the texts they are reading. Remember that a positive stereotype can be just as dangerous and inaccurate as a negative one.

The following questions are appropriate for grades 6 to 8 and can be used with any book featuring minority representation (see Table 9.1 for websites that provide recommendations for texts and materials). These kinds of questions can be used to start a dialogue in your class.

To what degree does the behaviour of the characters represent racial or ethnic stereotypes?

Do the boys do most of the action and identify most of the solutions to problems while the girls merely watch and follow?

Whose voice is heard in the text?

Whose voice or perspective is missing?

Has the author appropriated the voice of a minority group to write this book?

Who solves the problems in the story? Do people from the mainstream culture solve the problems for minority characters?

Table 9.1 Some Websites to Help Select Children's Literature on Diversity

www.rainbowsauce.com
www.comeunity.com
www.librarybooklists.org
http://frankrogers.home.mindspring.com
www.multiculturalchildrenslit.com
www.collectionscanada.gc.ca

avoided. In addition, when selecting Aboriginal literature, try to locate stories written by members of the culture (see Table 9.2 for recommended texts and authors).

Conclusion

Canada, a country of two official languages and with an increasingly pluralistic population, is committed to honouring a notion of community that reflects multiple perspectives. At the same time, we see a pervasive and invasive media portrayal of violence, intolerance, and racism in the evening news that spills over into our schools. Nevertheless, much of our society adheres to the traditional values of quality and respect for diversity and to a belief in the potential of each individual to attain self-fulfillment through growth and understanding. However, it is no simple task for teachers to find practical ways to help children accept and understand the differences among people and simultaneously recognize that, at a basic level human, needs and human nature are universal.

Table 9.2 Some Guidelines to Help Teachers Make Good Choices for Aboriginal Literature

- Seek books that reveal the culture as it exists today.
- Talk about the values that Aboriginal cultures share, such as respect, sharing, and reverence for all living things.
- Avoid books that portray all Aboriginal peoples as either noble or bad. Books that build up one culture at the expense of another serve to keep tensions alive.
- Stress that Aboriginal cultures are vastly different depending on geographical location and historical tradition.

Some Good Choices

Andre, J.-A., & Willett, M. (2008). *We feel good out here.* (Canadian Children's Book Centre Our Choice, 2009)

Bruchac, J. (1998). *The first strawberries:* A Cherokee story.

Bruchac, J. (1999). *The arrow over the door.*

Bruchac, J. (2000). *Pushing up the sky: Seven Native American plays for children.*

Bruchac, J. (2004). *Many nations: An alphabet of native America.*

Bruchac, J. (2005). *Turtle's race with beaver: A traditional Seneca story.*

Courchene, D. (2007). *The seven teachings.*

Jameson, C. (2006). *Zoe and the fawn.*

Kusugak, M. A. (1998). *Arctic stories.*

Loyie, L. (2002). *As long as the rivers flow.*

Loyie, L. (2008). *Goodbye Buffalo Bay.*

Loyie, L., & Brissenden, C. (2006). *The gathering tree.*

Loyie, L., & Brissenden, C. (2006). *When the spirits dance.*

McLeod, E. (2002). *Lessons from Mother Earth.*

Noel, M. (2004). *Good for nothing.* (Geoffrey Bilson Award for Historical Fiction for Young People, 2005).

Rivera, R. (2007). *Arctic adventures: Tales from the lives of Inuit artists.*

Seale, D., & Slapin, B. (Eds.). (2005). *A broken flute: The native experience in books for children.*

Silvey, D. (2005). *The kids book of Aboriginal peoples in Canada.*

Waboose, J. B. (1997). *Morning on the lake.*

We have argued that children's literature is a powerful tool in the hands of a teacher who consciously wants to help students learn more about themselves and others. Stories and texts for students that are sensitive to cultural and racial differences and that can be used to discuss the superficial nature of these differences are vital tools for today's teachers. Canadian authors provide a rich resource of texts suitable for classroom use that can promote inclusivity, understanding, and the best of human nature in everyone. According to Northrop Frye (1988), literature is the language of the imaginative inner life and serves to connect the inner and outer worlds. In other words, literature nourishes life.

POETRY IN THE CLASSROOM

✱ Poetry writing

POETRY IS A POET'S INTUITION OF TRUTH. POETRY COMBINES RICH MEANING WITH sounds of language arranged in an interesting form. Poets select words and arrange them carefully to call attention to experiences we have not known or fully recognized (Galda & Cullinan, 2006).

REFLECTIVE ACTIVITY 3

Think about your experiences with poetry in school.

What poetry do you remember your teachers presenting to you?

What do you remember about your response to this form of literature?

Do you remember enjoying the experiences?

Identify 10 authors of poetry for young people.

Do you read and enjoy poetry today? Why or why not?

Poetry is an art form that surrounds us in our daily lives, from song lyrics to the sounds we overhear in the background of our lives. Parents chant and read poetry to their children, and many individuals recalling Mother Goose rhymes and others as a hallmark of childhood.

Little Miss Muffet
Sat on a tuffet
Eating her curds and whey
Along came a spider
Who sat down beside her
And frightened Miss Muffet away.

Humpty Dumpty sat on a wall,
Humpty Dumpty had a great fall.
All the king's horses
And all the king's men
Couldn't put Humpty together again.

These familiar rhymes are actually very strange, with their meaning being elusive for many children. Indeed, what is important is the way the words are strung together and the rhyme (Nodelman & Reimer, 2002). Early exposure to these rhymes can assist children to develop their sense of rhythm, rhyme, sound, and the playfulness of poetic language (Cumming, 2007). Once at school, they extend their repertoire by engaging in chant-oriented games that are often learned from other children as a rite of passage (Opie & Opie, 2000).

When children arrive at school, many already possess a large repertoire of poems that they recognize, enjoy, and can recite from memory. Many children are also able to compose additional verses to poems using the established poetic pattern. For instance, *Willoughby Wallaby Woo* by Dennis Lee is a nonsense rhyming poem in which children's names can be inserted in successive choruses.

When poetry is introduced into the classroom, it is really a continuation of a love affair with a powerful and evocative way to express feelings, emotions, and ideas. Poetry

also captures the beauty, expressiveness, and playfulness of language that moves beyond the capacity of traditional fiction and non-fiction. Today, more and more poetry is being written for children, providing greater choices for teachers. Teachers need to be careful not to squander the positive experiences and delight in the sound and shape of poetry that their students bring with them intuitively when they enter school.

It is important that teachers at every grade level include poetry in their classes so students can experience this important means of communicating ideas. Students need to recognize that the sound of poetry is often related to music and that this form of literature is highly personal in its creation and interpretation. Poetry contains different types of imagery and can be used to explore or discuss any subject. Students are less likely to benefit from verbal definitions and descriptions of poetry than when provided the opportunity to listen, read, write, and discuss it (Galda & Cullinan, 2006). There are many reasons for introducing students to a wide variety of poetic forms and reinforcing that individuals are entitled to their own opinions and interpretations. A good way to emphasize this latter point is to read the poem "No One Else" from *Free to Be . . . You and Me* by Marlo Thomas.

Students Who Claim to Dislike Poetry

Sadly, the early enjoyment of poetry often wanes as students mature. When students claim to dislike poetry, the following are probably true:

- Enjoyment and playfulness has not been stressed.
- Chosen selections have been inappropriate to experiences, interests, and age.
- Teachers have read aloud poorly.
- There has been an overemphasis on correct analysis, which makes poetry seem like scientific data.
- Students have been asked to write poetry with insufficient preparation (Nodelman & Reimer, 2002).
- Students have been required to memorize poems.

Table 9.3 Some Guidelines for Using Poetry in the Classroom

- Begin by reading the poem aloud.
- Always practise before reading aloud (this applies to both teachers and students).
- Avoid heavy analysis of meaning or rhyme scheme.
- Focus on what students like about the poem and why they like it.
- Do not require memorization.
- Present a large variety of poetry to your students.
- Have books of poetry available in the in-class library and independent reading centre.

More positively, older students can enjoy many forms of poetry when these are taught appropriately. Older students enjoy poetry that is humorous (e.g., anything by Shel Silverstein or Dennis Lee), narrative in format (e.g., "The Cremation of Sam McGee" by Robert W. Service), animal oriented (e.g., "The Wasp," "The Turtle," and "The Termite" by Ogden Nash), or descriptive of familiar experiences (e.g., "Messy Room" by Shel Silverstein). Table 9.3 provides guidelines with respect to using poetry successfully in the classroom.

The enjoyment and comprehension of poetry is an ongoing process that evolves through hearing, reading, discussing, and eventually writing it.

Poetry Genres

While poetry is an art form, like art, it has a number of formal methods of expressing ideas. Below, we have included a few genres that have been favourites for self-expression among students in elementary grades. While the students' ideas are personal, they must be taught the traditions around particular poetic forms.

Couplets and Triplets Playfulness with language, associated ideas, and rhyme produces rhyming couplets and triplets. Rhyme is based on sound rather than appearance (e.g., *day* rhymes with *neigh*, *theme* rhymes with *dream*, and *time* rhymes with *climb*).

Acrostic Poems Acrostic poems are written by choosing a key word or a name and writing it vertically on a piece of paper. Then lines of the poem are written horizontally, with each sentence starting with one of the letters and relating to the vertical word. Frequently, students enjoy using their own names and writing a number of sentences about themselves. This type of poetry can also be used with the names of characters from novels. An example:

Literacy

L – Literacy is about communicating.

I – I love to read good stories.

T – Technology is a tool for communication.

E – Everyone needs to be able to use spelling and grammar skills effectively.

R – Reading comprehension strategies are vital.

A – Assessment and evaluation of literacy skills helps students improve.

C – Children's literature is a wonderful tool for teaching literacy.

Y – Yes! Becoming literate can be fun.

Books that are helpful when teaching acrostic poetry include the Alphabet Acrostic series by Steven Schnur and *African Acrostics: A Word in Edgeways* by Avis Harley.

Concrete Poems Concrete poems involve careful placement of words on a page. Frequently, words, phrases, and sentences are written in the shape of the object described by the poem. For instance, a concrete poem about hockey may be composed on a hockey stick, or a poem about a tornado may be written on a conical shape. A poem about flying a kite may be written across the kite from top to bottom and finally down the string one word at a time. The creativity here is boundless and students are generally very responsive to this genre of poetry, both in terms of reading it and in terms of creating it. Examples of concrete poetry include *Technically It's Not My Fault: Concrete Poems* and *Blue Lipstick: Concrete Poems* by John Grandits and *A Poke in the I: A Collection of Concrete Poems* by Paul Janeczko and Chris Raschka.

Haiku Haiku poetry originated in Japan but is popular around the world. Haiku is very structured and a refined and careful use of language is required to fit the format. This format consists of three lines, with line 1 containing five syllables, line 2 containing seven syllables, and line 3 containing five syllables. Traditionally, haiku is about nature. Books about haiku include *Haiku Poetry: A Children's Collection* by Wilhelm Schule and *Haiku* by Patricia Donegan.

Threatening rain clouds
Rain pounds the startled players
Drenched, ruined game.

An eagle soars high
Floating among the white clouds
A majestic bird.

Cinquain Poetry Cinquain poetry has a specified structure and pattern and, like haiku, requires careful choice of words. Students are required to be flexible and fluent, paying attention to syllabication, word meaning, and parts of speech while being expressively creative.

Format for Cinquain Poetry

Line 1: One word representing the topic of the poem

Line 2: Two words (adjectives) describing the topic

Line 3: Three words representing actions related to the topic

Line 4: Four words that are feelings related to the topic

Line 5: One word that is a synonym for the first line or a reference to the title

Bedbug
Stealthy silent
Creeping, biting, biting
Disgusting, surprising little specs
Marauders

Circus
Exciting, colourful
Soaring, jumping, clapping
Surreal, surprising, enchanting visions
Performers

Diamente Diamente is a seven-line contrast poem and, as the name suggests, reflects the number seven written in the form of a diamond.

Format for Diamente Poetry

Line 1: One noun providing the subject

Line 2: Two adjectives describing the subject

Line 3: Three participles, ending in ing, about the subject

Line 4: Four nouns (the first two related to the subject and the second two related to the opposite of the subject) about the subject

Line 5: Three participles identifying the opposite of the subject

Line 6: Two adjectives describing the opposite

Line 7: One noun that is the opposite of the subject

puppy
soft, gentle
wiggling, snuggling, nipping
kibble, milk, pills, vitamins
relaxing, sleeping, snoring
old, reliable
dog

Limericks Limericks are an old form of light comical verse made popular initially by Edward Lear in the mid-1800s. They are often either humorous or nonsensical with surprise endings and have a rigid format that relies on rhythm and rhyme. Limericks consist of five lines, with lines 1, 2, and 5 rhyming and lines 3 and 4 rhyming (aabba). Lines 3 and 4 are also shorter than the others.

Some students find it easy to create these poems while others find it very challenging. In any case, most students enjoy hearing and reading them. Books about limericks include *Limericks for Children* by Isaac Asimov and *Spikey's Little Book of Limericks* by Raymond Betancourt.

Free Verse Free verse poetry is just that: free, in that there are no structures or boundaries to define it. There is no rhyme or meter, the length of lines can vary, and the number of lines can vary. In free poetry, the emphasis is on the expression of a thought rather than on restrictive conventions. Visual and sound effects can be used as desired and the resultant poem can be simple or complex. Students may want to start with, say, *Sunshine is* . . . Each new idea related to sunshine should then go on a separate line. Books that illustrate the use of free verse include *Swimming Upstream: Middle School Poems* by Kristine O'Connell George and *Girl Coming in for a Landing: A Novel in Poems* by April Halprin Wayland.

Narrative Poetry Narrative poetry has a plot and can vary in format (long or short, simple or complex). Some narrative poetry takes the form of a novel, whereas other narratives are more like short stories. In either case, the story is often far-fetched and rollicking. Many favourite narrative poems have been handed down from the oral tradition and were originally composed to be recited. The following narrative poems can be found in single copies or in anthologies:

"The Cremation of Sam McGee" by Robert W. Service

"Casey at the Bat" by Ernest L. Thayer

"The Night Before Christmas" by Clement Clarke Moore

"There's a Mouse in My House" by Sheree Fitch

"The Highwayman" by Alfred Noyes

Poems for Two Voices A recent phenomenon is the development of poems for two voices by Paul Fleischman. His first book, *Joyful Noise: Poems for Two Voices* (winner of the 1989 Newbery Medal), consists of 14 poems about insects that are intended to be read aloud by two voices. Each poem is written on two pages, with one person reading the left side and the other reading the right side. At times, the voices read together; at other times, they start and finish each other's sentences. These poems can be performed and students must collaborate and practise to provide an engaging interpretation. Other Fleishman poetry books written for multiple voices include *I Am Phoenix: Poems for Two Voices* and *Big Talk: Poems for Four Voices*.

Teacher Voice 9.1

Once, I observed a teacher candidate conducting a poetry lesson around Remembrance Day. She had gathered several large, authentic war pictures and discussed the emotional and physical context that gave rise to war poems. I observed that the students were thoroughly engaged and participated wholeheartedly in the introductory discussion. As the poems were read, students listened intently. The ensuing discussion was thoughtful and reflective, with many students physically leaning forward in their seats. After several students had shared their reactions, the teacher candidate announced that now they would write a war poem of their own to mark Remembrance Day. The students who had been leaning forward were clearly shocked and fell back in their seats as if deflated or shot. The poetic results were very meagre.

Anne Elliott

Teacher Voice 9.1 serves to illustrate that appreciating poetry and writing poetry (although not unrelated) do not have to accompany each other in the same lesson to be valid poetic experiences. Therefore, we address each of these poetry experiences separately.

Poetry Appreciation

Poetry is meant to be heard because it expresses the individual word, the sound of language, and the rhythm of language in a way unique among literary forms. This means that teachers must prepare for a reading so that the beauty of the form and the language can be revealed and emphasized. Teachers' enjoyment can serve as a catalyst for students' appreciation that poetry is pleasurable and worthwhile. Students should feel invited into the world of the imagination, where all is possible and all is unpredictable. Even with older students, it is best to let them hear poetry and avoid having them read it silently (at least initially). As with all Read Aloud activities avoid reading any poem that is not personally enjoyed. Tables 9.4 and 9.5 provide additional ideas for presenting poetry to students in the primary and junior and intermediate grades.

Presenting Poetry to Primary Students Choose appropriate poems, such as those that rhyme, are playful, and address familiar topics. When the poetry has a strong beat, students should be encouraged to clap out the rhythm. Listening to rhyming poetry can help young students build phonemic awareness and prediction skills that will help them as they begin to read. Possible choices for young students include *Willoughby Wallaby Woo* and *Alligator Pie* by Dennis Lee.

Presenting Poetry to Junior and Intermediate Students Junior and intermediate students are ready to read poems that are more sophisticated and abstract in terms of the use of metaphors, similes, allegories, and imagery. It is still important to avoid overanalyzing such poetry so that students can listen to the sound of the language and bring their personal ideas to the reading.

"The Wind" by the classical writer Robert Louis Stevenson is a good example of a poem that would be suitable for a junior class.

The Wind
I saw you toss the kites on high
And blow the birds about the sky;
And all around I heard you pass,
Like ladies' skirts across the grass—

Table 9.4 Steps for Presenting Poetry to Primary Students

1. Set the stage for the reading by introducing a familiar incident, using an object or a picture. If none is available, a simple question related to the topic can suffice.
2. Prior to reading the poem, provide a reason for listening by asking a question or saying, "I want you to listen for . . ."
3. Read the poem at least twice, stopping to discuss the first question and then posing another question for the second reading. Ask questions such as "What is your favourite word?" and "What pictures do you see when listening to the poem?"
4. Show the students a visual copy of the poem. This can be on an overhead, a chart, or a paper copy.
5. Read the poem together with the class.
6. Find a number of ways to read the poem in parts, or in groups, so that students become very familiar with it.
7. Provide extension activities when appropriate, such as creating an illustration for the poem or writing another verse.

Table 9.5 Steps for Discussing "The Wind" with Junior and Intermediate Students

1. Ask students to listen for one thing the wind did in the poem.
2. Read the poem aloud.
3. Ask students to capture an image from the poem.
4. Read the poem aloud again.
5. Show a copy of the poem, in a book or on an overhead, SMART Board, or chart.
6. Read the poem as a class while students review their visual copy.
7. Ask them what the poet is saying in the poem.
8. Ask the class to identify all images of the wind in the poem.
9. Have students describe their feelings about the wind.
10. Read the poem together with some deviation (e.g., designate a couple of students to read the chorus, have one student read each verse while the whole class reads the chorus).

O wind, a-blowing all day long,
O wind, that sings so loud a song!

I saw the different things you did,
But always you yourself you hid.
I felt you push, I heard you call,
I could not see yourself at all—
O wind, a-blowing all day long,
O wind, that sings so loud a song!

O you that are so strong and cold,
O blower, are you young or old?
Are you a beast of field and tree,
Or just a stronger child than me?
O wind, a-blowing all day long,
O wind, that sings so loud a song!

From A *Child's Garden of Verses* by Robert Louis Stevenson

The appreciation lesson could end here or students could write about an experience with wind or a windy day that they remember. Teachers may also end the lesson on a whimsical note by reading "Strange Wind" from Shel Silverstein's *A Light in the Attic* or "Who Has Seen the Wind" by Christina Rossetti.

Writing Poetry

Teaching and encouraging students to express themselves as writers of poetry is a mandate of every curriculum. Students may be daunted by preconceived ideas about poetry, such as that it must rhyme or that it is too challenging. Mini-lessons that share the enjoyment and expressiveness of various poetic forms, including free verse, can alleviate such fears

SAMPLE LESSON 9.1

Teaching Students How to Write a Haiku

Pre-Planning

Select as least five or six examples of haiku poems and prepare them to be seen by the whole class.

Steps (Completed Over Several Days)

1. Read three of the poems aloud, showing students a prepared visual rendition.
2. Read the poems again with students following along. Alternatively, ask a student to read them aloud.
3. Ask students to identify what the poems have in common.
4. Create a chart describing student observations. Provide students with prompts as necessary (e.g., number of lines, number of syllables in line 1 [five], number of syllables in line 2 [seven], number of syllables in line 3 [five], presence of rhyme, number of articles, topic of poem, presence of contrasting ideas).
5. Present one or two more haiku poems visually and ask students to check their observations about format.
6. Create a haiku collaboratively as a class. Present a picture or a word (e.g., rain, wind, snapdragons, irises, roses) to begin the writing process.
7. Think aloud possible words that fit the format and describe the topic, with students contributing ideas.
8. Create a second poem as a class, asking students questions related to its structure (e.g., How can we express that idea in seven syllables?).
9. Create a third poem collaboratively.
10. Provide a topic and sufficient time for students to each try to create a haiku poem independently.
11. Ask for examples and create a compilation poem (or two) using parts of students' poems.
12. Provide students with a sheet of paper with lines suggesting the shape of the haiku, ensuring that there are at least three blank lines on the sheet.

____

____

____

13. Ask students to experiment with composing their own poems.
14. Ask students to select their best example of a haiku poem and rewrite it on rice paper with optional illustrations.
15. Have students share their poems with the class.

This lesson format can be used for any form of poetry, as it provides an understanding of the way in which ideas are expressed. Students' writing experiences are scaffolded so that they better enjoy the writing experience.

and should precede any writing activity. Sample Lesson 9.1 illustrates how teachers can scaffold learning to write poetry so that students feel comfortable and confident expressing themselves using a particular poetic formula. This lesson is inductive in approach and provides scaffolding and experimentation steps to encourage students to play with words and meaning within the context of a structure.

A Teacher's Professional Library

All teachers need at least one good anthology as part of their professional materials. This should be the kind of book in which teachers can locate poems on a variety of topics and for a variety of ages. Some suggestions include the following:

Hale, G. (Ed.). (1997). *Read-aloud poems for young people: Readings from the world's best loved verses*. New York, NY: Black Dog and Leventhal Publishing.

Lithgow, J. (2007). *Poets' corner: The one-and-only poetry book for the whole family*. Boston, MA: Grand Central Publishing.

Paschen, E., & Raccah, D. (Eds.). (2005). *Poetry speaks to children*. Naperville, IL: Sourcebooks Media Fusion. (This comes with a CD of poets reading their poems.)

Prelutsky, J. (Ed.). (1999). *The 20th century children's poetry treasury*. New York, NY: Knopf.

Rubin, R. A. (Ed.). (1995). *Poetry out loud*. New York, NY: Algonquin Books.

Sword, E. H. (2006). *A child's anthology of poetry*. New York, NY: Ecco.

Selected books of poetry by popular authors include the following:

Lee, D. (1977). *Nicholas Knock and other people: Poems*. Boston, MA: Houghton Mifflin.

Lee, D. (1983). *Jelly belly*. Bolton, ON: Key Porter Books.

Lee, D. (2001). *Alligator pie*. Bolton, ON: Key Porter Kids.

Lee, D. (2006). *Garbage delight*. Toronto, ON: Macmillan of Canada.

Little, J. (1990). *Hey world, here I am!* New York, NY: HarperCollins.

Prelutsky, J. (2002). *The frogs wore red suspenders*. New York, NY: Greenwillow Books.

Silverstein, S. (1981). *A light in the attic*. New York, NY: Harper and Row Publishers.

Silverstein, S. (1996). *Falling up*. New York, NY: HarperCollins.

Silverstein, S. (2004). *Where the sidewalk ends*. New York, NY: HarperCollins.

STORYTELLING

From ancient to present times, cultures around the world have practised the art of storytelling. Storytelling is an oral art form that relies on expression and words to place the images and storyline into the mind of the listener (see Table 9.6 for a description of storytelling techniques). It takes both a listener and a teller to make the magic happen (Abbott & Godinho, 2001; Roney, 1996). When students are guided to explore this art form in the classroom, both the listener and the teller can benefit in many ways. The teller builds self-confidence, memory recall, visual imagery, vocal and gestural expression, and an enjoyment of and appreciation for language. The listener develops skills for memory recall, visual imagery, listening for detail, and interpretation of body language, and builds an enjoyment of and appreciation for language (Barton, 1986; Hodgson, 2007; Miyata, 2001; Rosen, 1988). Research has demonstrated additional benefits for both listeners and tellers, which include developing sequencing skills, internalizing narrative form, understanding and using descriptive detail, and vocabulary building (Campbell & Hlusek, 2009; Rooks, 1998; Rosen, 1986).

Different Types of Storytelling

Storytelling is not new to students, as they practise it quite naturally while sharing a favourite ghost story they may have heard at camp or relaying something that happened over the weekend. Essentially, these are the two simple categories into which storytelling falls: retellings and sharing personal narrative. Each type offers unique potential for students to develop speaking and critical listening skills (Miyata, 2001).

Real or personal stories are highly significant stories for students to share, as the characters are frequently family members and the setting is familiar. The situation is

Table 9.6 Storytelling Techniques

Students need to see a storyteller perform before performing themselves. The teacher can model storytelling by sharing a favourite story or fable. These stories are quick to learn and usually contain interesting animal characters that are easy to portray. Alternatively, a parent can be invited to share a story. There are also professional storytellers in every province; contact Storytellers of Canada (www.sc-cc.com) for a list of storytellers and storytelling guilds, both English and French

After students have experienced storytelling, ask them to brainstorm a list of all of the techniques the teller used to keep the storytelling interesting. Here are a few examples for reference:

- Remembered the story (but didn't memorize it)
- Eye contact
- Hand gestures
- Facial expression (eyes, mouth)
- Vocal expression (pace: fast or slow, volume: loud or soft, pitch: high or low, silence, accents)
- Stance (posture: sitting in a chair or standing)
- Audience participation (call and response games, inviting audience to echo chants, repeat lines, or make sounds)
- Props
- Descriptive detail
- Created an image
- Improvisation (adding events or names that were not part of the original story but reflect something an audience member said or did)
- Selected an exciting and interesting story

often compelling because students tend to select highly emotional events to relate. The investment in these stories is enormous and the results of telling such stories can be highly rewarding, especially in preparation for writing (Campbell & Hlusek, 2009). However, personal stories that have not been shaped tend to lack the polish that make the telling as exciting for the listener as it is for the teller. Therefore, sharing personal stories well takes some guidance and practice.

Retellings, on the other hand, do not need to be shaped. In a retelling, a student is simply remembering a story he or she has heard from oral tradition or read in a printed source and sharing that story orally with a listener. The story has already been shaped and polished either by a professional editor or through years and years of retellings in the oral tradition. Some of the most effective stories to retell come from folklore, which includes folk tales, fairy tales, myths, legends, parables, and fables. Every culture around the world possesses a body of these wonderful tales. Since Canada is a diverse society, the sharing of these stories honours the rich tapestry of Canadian culture. Reading aloud stories from various cultures for students to retell, as well as encouraging students to select stories from their cultural heritage to share as a storytelling performance, validates students' heritage and encourages cultural respect and acceptance among peers.

Retellings of folklore in the junior and intermediate grades also offer students the opportunity to develop speaking skills without the responsibility of writing the content themselves. Typically, teachers of the junior and intermediate grades work on techniques of speaking when developing speech writing, but most of the emphasis is placed on writing the speech and the skills for effective delivery may be overlooked. A unit on storytelling prior to speech writing enables students to develop presentation skills separate from the writing of the material. Similarly, students who are expected to write their own stories to tell must write, revise, and edit their stories before they can prepare to tell them. Often a student is tired of the story by the time he or she must learn it, or the story is not strong enough to hold the interest of an audience. If the story selected to present is from traditional folklore, students are guaranteed interesting content and are free to focus primarily on delivery skills.

Sources for Retellings Stories from folklore are unique because they are usually so old that the author is unknown. Often, children who are raised hearing these stories do not realize that they are unique to their culture until they come to school. These stories are found in anthologies such as *Peach Boy and Other Japanese Children's Favorite Stories* or *The Magic Orange Tree and Other Haitian Folktales*. A list of anthologies that represent some of the cultures in a typical Canadian classroom can be found in Table 9.7. Some folk tales are also published in picture books such as *Strega Nona* (an Italian folk tale) and *Lon Po Po* (a Chinese folk tale).

Several Aboriginal, African, and Caribbean cultures still share stories orally with family and friends. These stories are not in books, but are passed from one generation to another by word of mouth. This sharing through the oral tradition represents storytelling in its purest form. A classroom survey will determine how many students are steeped in this oral tradition.

Traditional folk tales from either a printed source or the oral tradition were designed to be fast-paced and to fascinate the listener. They were also designed to stimulate visual imagery, unlike modern picture books, which usually rely on illustrations to tell part of the story. A student trying to retell a story from a modern picture book may have to edit, revise, or add to the story so it will make sense to the listener. This does not imply that students should never use contemporary stories, as some are terrific sources for retellings, but the content has to be scrutinized more carefully by both the teller and the teacher.

Preparing for a Retelling

There are many ways to prepare students for retellings, depending, of course, on their age and awareness of self-expression. A teacher may wish to simply have students retell a story to a partner after hearing the story read aloud, so that the teacher can assess whether students can sequence a story and remember some descriptive detail. Retelling in small groups, round robin style, also works well (Barton & Booth, 1990). The teacher may also wish to prepare students for a more formal presentation to the whole class or an even larger audience involving the entire school at a storytelling festival (Miyata, 2001). Each student needs his or her own form of preparation. Visual cues such as story maps (see Table 9.8), picture cards, stuffed animals, or props that represent items or characters in the story work well as prompts to assist primary grade children in remembering a story.

Table 9.7 Storytelling Resources for Students

Multicultural Collections

Asian Cultural Centre for UNESCO. (1976). *Folk tales from Asia for children everywhere.*

DeSpain, P. (2005). *Thirty-three multicultural tales to tell.*

Forest, H. (1996). *Wisdom tales from around the world.*

Lottridge, C. B. (1994). *Ten small tales: Stories from around the world.*

Yolan, J. (1988). *Favorite folktales from around the world.*

Collections by Culture

Caduto, M., & Bruchac, J. (1989). *Keepers of the Earth.* (American Aboriginal)

Calvino, I. (1992). *Italian folktales.* (Italian)

Canadian Library Association. (1979). *Storytellers' rendezvous: Canadian stories to tell to children.* (Canadian)

Carle, E. (1984). *Twelve tales from Aesop.* (Greek)

Chang, I. C. (1976). *Tales from old China.* (Chinese)

Fairman, T. (1993). *Bury my bones but keep my words: African tales for retelling.* (African)

Grimm, J., & Grimm, W. (1998). *The Brothers Grimm: The complete fairy tales.* (German)

Haviland, V. (1961). *Favorite fairy tales told in Russia.* (Russian) (also Favorite fairy tales told in Germany, England, France, Norway, and Ireland)

Jacobs, J. (1890). *English fairy tales.* (British)

Lang, A. (2009) *Stories from 1001 Arabian Nights.* (Arabic)

Ramanujan, A. K. (1994). *Folktales from India.* (Indian)

Riordan, J. (1998). *The sun maiden and the crescent moon: Serbian folktales.* (Serbian)

Sakade, F. (1989). *Peach boy and other Japanese children's favorite stories.* (Japanese)

Wolkstein, D. (1997). *The magic orange tree and other Haitian folktales.* (Haitian)

Scary Stories

San Souci, R. (1989). *Short & shivery: Thirty chilling tales.*

Yashinsky, D. (1997). *Ghostwise: A book of midnight stories.*

Canadian Books for Retelling

Davis, A. (1995). *Bone button borscht.*

Gilman, P. (1993). *Something from nothing.*

Munsch, R. (1985). *Mortimer.*

Stinson, K. (1992). *Red is best.*

Toye, W., & Cleaver, E. (1988). *The loon's necklace.*

Zimmerman, H. W. (1996). *Henny penny.*

Note: This is a small offering of what is available. Ask parents for recommended books on a particular culture or invite them to read (or tell) a story to your students.

Table 9.8 Retelling Using Story Mapping (Primary Activity)

Step 1: Gather students in a large open space and arrange them so they are sitting next to a partner for the retelling.
Step 2: Introduce the story to be told. In this example, the story is an Anishinabe tale, *Why Bears Have Short Tails* (from *Storytellers' Rendezvous* by Canadian Library Association). Ask students to watch carefully how the teacher makes the story sound interesting.
Step 3: Tell the first half of the story (up to where the fox hides behind a tree to watch the bear put his tail in the hole). If you are reading the story and not telling it, do not show any pictures that may be in the book. Instead, encourage the students to see the story in their imagination. Model the techniques of a good storyteller by using a lot of vocal and facial expression (change voices for the fox and the bear, make voice louder and softer, look directly at listeners during the story, make gestures to express the words, use eyes to express surprise and suspicion).
Step 4: (Do step 4 only if you want your students to develop delivery techniques. If they are not ready, skip to step 5. This step can then be added at a later date, when students are comfortable with partner retelling and story mapping.) Stop the story and invite students to brainstorm all of the techniques you used to express the story. Write the techniques on an anchor chart to reference later.
Step 5: Invite students to retell the first part of the story together as a class. Ask what happened at the very beginning of the story. On a piece of chart paper, make a simple pictorial representation, or symbol, or use a word to represent that part of the story. Ask the students what happened next and draw another representation close to the first drawing. Ask students how they can show on the map that this drawing comes after the first drawing. Students may suggest drawing an arrow or using numbers. Add whatever is suggested to the map.
Step 6: Explain that students will be creating their own story map of the first half of the tale with a partner. Assign partners and have them sit side by side. Give each pair a large piece of paper and a marker. Instruct students to create a story map that includes important events and special details they thought were important to the story. They will need to take turns with the marker. (Note: Creating a story map is a different exercise than storyboarding. With storyboards, story events are sequenced in a linear fashion and usually a limited number of squares are used, which forces students to summarize and prioritize the events in the story. Each square also usually depicts a picture of what happened. Story mapping represents ideas of what happened and leaves the descriptive process to the teller. It is a much more open-ended process. The mapping is not limited and new ideas and details can be added as students progress through the retelling.)
Step 7: Once students have created their map, encourage them to take turns retelling the story to each other. The pair can keep the map beside them to follow the sequence of the story. Next, encourage students to retell using a technique of a good storyteller from the anchor chart. Instruct the listeners to watch for a moment when their tellers use a technique and encourage the listeners to praise their teller. Finally, join two pairs and instruct the tellers to sit in chairs to tell the story while the listeners sit on the floor. As the students retell the story, circulate among them and praise the tellers for using any techniques you observe. Constantly encourage the listeners to give feedback to the tellers regarding the techniques they observe as well. This develops a critical eye for storytelling technique and gives the listeners responsibility toward the development of the tellers.
Step 8: Tell the second half of the story and repeat the steps as needed. Eventually, students will be able to put the two halves of the story map together and retell the whole story.

These strategies also work well for English language learners and junior and intermediate students who are hesitant to recall story events.

Formal Retellings (Junior and Intermediate)

Begin by asking students to retell stories to a partner and then gently increase the size of the listening audience to allow the tellers to develop suitable techniques before subjecting them to criticism or judgment. Allow several weeks for students to develop their delivery

Table 9.9 Strategies for Learning a Story to Retell (Junior and Intermediate Activity)
■ Read Aloud: Read the story out loud several times with a lot of expression.
■ Draw: Think of the story as a cartoon and draw the different parts of the story.
■ Map: Create a map of the story using symbols and words.
■ Sing: Sing the story to a familiar song.
■ Listen: Record the story on an MP3 player and play it back to yourself.
■ Summarize: Shrink the story to 16 lines. Then shrink those lines to 8, and then to 4.

technique and work through their apprehension about publicly presenting a story, especially if you expect students to present to a class of their peers. In the first week, use the retelling to work on memory recall of the story and eye contact. In the second week, work on adding gestures, vocal expression, and facial expression. In the third week (and possibly fourth, depending on how much time you can devote to this unit), join partnerships so students can retell to a slightly larger audience. The book *Speaking Rules!* by Canadian storyteller Cathy Miyata outlines many exercises and games for junior and intermediate students that develop specific techniques such as eye contact, memory, and gesturing. If your class is weak in a particular technique, it may be wise to spend some time on that area using one or several of the exercises suggested.

Students Selecting Stories to Retell

Students in the junior and intermediate divisions can retell a story told to them by the teacher when first exploring retellings, but subsequently need to be allowed to select their own material. Provide a wide variety of stories from which they can choose, including stories of different lengths and styles and about different cultures. A five-minute telling is long enough at this level. Generally, we speak about 150 words per minute, so stories should not be longer than 750 words. If students wish to tell a story they know from their experiences, allow this, but the students should either have a printed copy of the story or already know it so well that they can easily create a story map of the sequence (Table 9.9 lists strategies for helping students learn stories for retelling).

Telling to a Younger Audience

Older students experience great success when they are given the task of presenting their retellings to small groups of younger children. Ghost stories are popular with junior and intermediate students but this content brings with it a responsibility to the audience. Students must choose the material carefully to suit their audience (Swartz, 1989). A simple rule of thumb is to agree that ghost stories can be presented only to grades 4 and up.

The junior or intermediate classroom becomes the practice arena when students are presenting to a younger audience, and the partner they retell to as they practise becomes their guide and peer critic (Miyata, 2001; Rooks, 1998). Encourage students to practise remembering the story and to practise different delivery techniques to a partner for about the first week. The listening partner is responsible for giving feedback and praise. Slowly

Table 9.10 Self-Evaluation of Storytelling (Junior and Intermediate Activity)

- Voice: Did I speak clearly, loudly, and slowly enough?
- Stance: Did I sit or stand tall and hold my head up?
- Composure: Did I look calm, not fidget, and hide my nervousness?
- Expression: Did my words sound interesting and exciting?
- Gestures: Did I express the words using hand and arm movements?
- Eye contact: Did I look at my audience?
- Audience awareness: Did my audience look at me and appear to enjoy the story?
- How did I feel about this experience?

join partnerships together until students are rehearsing their stories to a group of eight. This audience size is sufficient, without being too intimidating, to require students to increase the volume of their voice and exaggerate their gestures and facial expressions. When students can successfully retell to a peer audience of this size, they are ready to perform their story to the real audience of younger students (Miyata, 2001).

Send the students to their audiences in pairs or threes, so that the tellers have a support team and the peers can give the tellers feedback. Self-evaluation is critical to the growth of students during this experience, as it allows them to observe the success of the project and determine how they might improve (see Table 9.10).

Sharing Personal Narratives

Personal narratives are important because they are real. The storytelling experience needs to be set up for success because it represents the student in every way. An oral telling of a personal story also makes a wonderful first draft for the same story in written form (Campbell & Hlusek, 2009). Students often need prompts to stimulate memories

Table 9.11 Prompts for Personal Storytelling (All Ages)

1. Have you ever been so lost you almost started to cry?
2. Have you ever been in a search party looking for someone who was lost?
3. Have you ever been so embarrassed by something your mother (or someone else) did that you wanted to die?
4. Have you ever waited and waited, expecting the very best present ever, only to open it and find it wasn't the present you wanted?
5. Have you ever experienced a pet dying?
6. Have you ever been so frightened you were shaking?
7. Have you ever had a really terrifying dream that you thought was real?
8. Have you ever laughed so hard you could hardly control yourself?
9. Were you ever in an accident?
10. Have you got a scar?

of personal stories. Table 9.11 provides a list of prompts that will stir up many memories. Remind students that if a particular story is too sad or uncomfortable to share publicly, they should choose a different story to tell.

Whether the personal narrative will be an oral draft or remain an oral telling, it needs to be structured so the pace and excitement of the story can unfold and keep the listener engaged. When sharing a personal narrative, students often want to jump right in and tell the most exciting part first. Or, they share the whole story in one sentence. For instance, "I was driving down the street on my bicycle and fell off and cracked my head open." This is a very dramatic story to be sure, but it needs some shaping to draw out the descriptive details and allow the listeners to enjoy the climax. The kite organizer described in Table 9.12 offers structure to guide both the teller and the listener, while Table 9.13 lists relevant Canadian children's literature services.

Table 9.12 The Kite Model (Junior and Intermediate Activity)

Step 1: Demonstrate the kite organizer by first drawing a picture of a kite on chart paper. Explain: "All good stories are shaped like a kite. The head of the kite is the attention getter. In a story it's the where and who." (Print *where* and *who* in the head of the kite.) "As soon as the audience hears the where and the who, they get a picture in their imagination and that holds their attention. What happens in the story is the what. It is the action or the wind that drives the kite forward." (Draw little x's on the kite tail representing the action.) "The action in any good story builds up to one great big emotional moment." (Draw a big X on the kite tail three-quarters of the way down.) "That's the climax of the story and that is what we will build toward today."

Step 2: Explain that students will be working in pairs when it is their turn to tell their story. It will be the teller's job to tell the story following the kite model, placing the who and the where first, and then the action. It will be the listener's job to help the teller by asking many questions, just as you are about to demonstrate. The goal during the telling is for the picture in the listener's imagination to be just as vivid as the picture in the teller's mind.

Step 3: Invite a volunteer from the class to share a personal story. State: "We are going to follow this kite model to sequence the story. Teller, start by telling me only where you are." The teller describes the scene. You, as the listener, pull more and more details about the where from the teller by asking questions. For example: Where exactly are you? What time of day is it? What season is it? What are you wearing? Ask the class if it has a question it wants clarified by the teller.

Step 4: The teller continues with the story and adds the who. You, as the listener, continue to ask probing questions about the characters in the story. For example: How many friends are there? Is your brother older or younger? Are you completely alone or is someone nearby?

Step 5: The when may need to be investigated. Ask if this happened recently or several years ago. (If the incident happened when the teller was 4 years old, the mental image of the main character changes dramatically for the listener.) Point this out to the audience.

(continued)

Table 9.12 The Kite Model (Junior and Intermediate Activity) *(continued)*

Step 6: Prompt the teller to begin to describe the what, or the action. Continue to ask probing questions. For example: How fast were you going? Where were the other characters? How did you feel at that moment?

Step 7: When the teller reaches the most emotional moment, ask the teller to describe it almost as if it is happening in slow motion. Ask for a very detailed description of how things unfolded, so you can picture it happening. (This part often causes an audible and physical reaction from the listening audience, which is good for the teller since it proves to him or her that the story is exciting and interesting.) For example: Did you flip over the handle bars? What part of you hit the ground first? Did you scream? Did you see any blood? How much?

Step 8: At this point in the story there is a character reaction or a cause-and-effect sequence that often can lend well to humour. Ask the teller how each character reacted. Students begin to see the who's in their story as actual characters that do unexpected things, especially parents. For example: Did your mother become hysterical or remain calm? How fast did your dad drive you to the hospital? What did your friends (or family) say? Did your brother faint? What did you do or say in response?

Step 9: Ask the teller to wind up or resolve the story. If the story looks as if it will continue (perhaps the teller is now going to have stitches), suggest that the teller end the story for now and consider the next part as Chapter 2. If students are going to write their stories down, this story can be a chapter book. Invite applause for the volunteer.

Step 10: Instruct students to consider the personal incident prompts and select a personal incident to share.

Step 11: Assign partners. Pairs can find a private place to share their stories. Remind listeners to ask many questions to help the tellers be more descriptive. Circulate among the students as they tell their stories and encourage the listeners to ask questions.

Step 12: If this exercise is an oral draft, students can begin writing their stories down, remembering to include all of the descriptive detail prompted by the listeners. If this will remain an oral exercise, students can tell their partner's story to another partner, making it sound as if it happened to them.

Teacher Voice 9.2

As a professional storyteller, I have performed, conducted residencies, and taught workshops in almost every province across Canada from kindergarten to grade 12 and facilitated workshops for educators in nine countries. My repertoire now includes multi-modal and digital storytelling, but the basic art form is the same. For any age, in any language, storytelling is an empowering and literacy-enhancing experience for all involved. I also instruct teacher candidates at Brock University and integrate storytelling into all of our literacy practices. Many of my teacher candidates have discovered for themselves that a simple storytelling can transform a chaotic classroom into a focused literacy experience in a matter of seconds.

Cathy Miyata
Storyteller and literacy instructor

Table 9.13 Canadian Children's Literature Services

1. Pika—Canadian Children's Literature Database, www.collectionscanada.gc.ca/pika/index-e.html
2. Canadian Children's Book Centre, which includes Our Choice, an annual listing of the best in Canadian children's books, www.bookcentre.ca
3. Children's Literature service at Library and Archives Canada, www.collectionscanada.gc.ca/childrenliterature/index-e.html
4. *Children's Literature in Education*, www.springer.com/education+%26+language/linguistics/journal/10583

SUGGESTIONS FOR PROFESSIONAL DEVELOPMENT

1. Watch a movie adaptation of a children's novel you have read (or read the novel as well). Consider the film interpretation of the text and compare it to your own interpretation. Good examples are *The Tale of Despereaux, The Secret Garden, Mrs. Frisby and the Rats of NIMH* (book) and *The Secret of NIMH* (movie), *Stuart Little*, and *Charlotte's Web.*
2. Ask some children to show you their book collections. Preview the selections and watch for patterns indicating interest. Talk to the children about their favourite books, how they got them, and why they like them.
3. Investigate the culture of a minority group that is represented in a class you are teaching now or have taught in the past. Research the literature associated with that culture, as well as the culture's customs and language. If possible, plan a lesson about that culture, teach it, and evaluate its effectiveness.
4. Begin a card index or computer file of children's literature with which you are familiar. Organize it according to genre and diversity and add at least one book to each category.

CHILDREN'S LITERATURE REFERENCES

Andrews, J. (2003). *Very last first time.* Toronto, ON: Groundwood Books.

Barrie, J. M. (1902). *Peter Pan.* New York, NY: Sterling Publishing.

Baum, L. F. (1900). *The wonderful wizard of Oz.* Chicago, IL: George M. Hill.

Becker, H. (2009). *Insecto-files.* Toronto: Maple Tree Press.

Burnett, F. H. (1911). *The secret garden.* London, UK: Heinemann.

Carroll, L. (1865). *Alice's adventures in Wonderland.* London, UK: Macmillan.

Clark, A. N. (1952). *Secret of the Andes.* New York, NY: Puffin Books.

Collodi, C. (1983). *The adventures of Pinocchio.* Radford, VA: Wilder Publications.

Dahl, R. (1961). *James and the giant peach.* New York, NY: Alfred A. Knopf Inc.

Dahl, R. (1964). *Charlie and the chocolate factory.* New York, NY: Alfred A. Knopf Inc.

dePaola, T. (1979). *Strega nona.* Fullerton, CA: Aladdin Books.

Ellis, D. (2001). *The Breadwinner*. Toronto, ON: Groundwood Books.
Godkin, C. (1991). *Ladybug garden*. Markham, ON: Fitzhenry and Whiteside.
Haig-Brown, R. (1944). *Starbuck valley winter*. Madeira Park, BC: Harbour Publishing.
Haig-Brown, R. (1948). *Saltwater summer*. Madeira Park, BC: Harbour Publishing.
Harris, C. (1900). *Once upon a totem*. Toronto, ON: McClelland & Stewart.
Houston, J. (1977). *Frozen fire: A tale of courage*. Fullerton, CA: Aladdin Books.
Houston, J. (1979). *River runners: A tale of hardship and bravery*. Boston, MA: Atheneum Books.
Kipling. R. (1889). *The jungle book*. London, UK: Macmillan.
Lowrey, L. (1989). *Number the stars*. Boston, MA: Houghton Mifflin, Random House.
Milne, A.A. (1926). *Winnie-the-Pooh*. London, UK: Methuen & Co. Ltd.
Mowat, F. (1956). *Lost in the barrens*. Boston, MA: Little Brown & Co.
Mowat, F. (1961). *Owls in the family*. Boston, MA: Little Brown & Co.
Potter, B. (1883). *The tale of Peter Rabbit*. London, UK: Frederick Warne & Co.
Ransome, A. (1930). *Swallows and amazons*. London, UK: Jonathan Cape.
Reid, D. M. (1963). *Tales of Nanabozho*. Toronto, ON: Oxford University Press.
Sendak, M. (1964). *Where the wild things are*. New York, NY: HarperCollins.
Snicket, L. (1999). *A series of unfortunate events*. New York, NY: HarperCollins.
Stevenson, R. L. (1883). *Treasure island*. London, UK: Cossell & Company.
Swanson, D. (1997). *Bug bites*. North Vancouver, BC: Whitecap Books.
Swift, J. (1726). *Gulliver's travels*. London, UK: Benjamin Motte.
Twain, M. (1876). *The adventures of Tom Sawyer*. American Publishing Company.
White, E. B. (1952). *Charlotte's web*. New York, NY: HarperCollins.
Winters, K-L. (2010). *When chickens fly*. Vancouver, BC: Gumboot Books.
Young, E. (1989). *Lon po po*. New York, NY: Philomel.

CHILDREN'S POETRY REFERENCES

Asimov, I. (1984). *Isaac Asimov's limericks for children*. New York, NY: Caldmon Children's Books.
Betancourt, R. (2010). *Spikey's little book of limericks*. Raymond Betancourt Publishing.
Donegan, P. (2003). *Haiku*. Reno, NV: Turtle Publishing.
Fitch, S. (1999). *There's a mouse in my house*. Washington, DC: Turtleback Books.
Fleischman, P. (1988). *Joyful noise: Poems for two voices*. New York, NY: HarperCollins.
Fleischman, P. (1989). *I am phoenix: Poems for two voices*. New York, NY: HarperCollins.
Fleischman, P. (2004). *Big talk: Poems for four voices*. Sommerville, MA: Candlewick.
George, K. O. (2002). *Swimming upstream: Middle school poems*. New York, NY: Clarion Books.
Grandits, J. (2004). *Technically it's not my fault: Concrete poems*. London, UK: Sandpiper.
Grandits, J. (2005). *Blue lipstick: Concrete poems*. London, UK: Sandpiper.
Halprin Wayland, A. (2004). *Girl coming in for a landing: A novel in poems*. New York, NY: Dell Yearling Book.
Harley, A. (2009). *African acrostics: A word in edgeways*. Sommerville, MA: Candlewick Press.

Janeczko, P. B., & Raschka, C. (2005). *A poke in the I: A collection of concrete poems*. Sommerville, MA: Candlewick Press.
Lee, D. (2006). *Alligator pie*. Toronto, ON: Scholastic Canada.
Lee, D. (2006). *Willoughby wallaby woo*. Toronto, ON: Key Porter Kids.
Moore. C. C. (1998). *The night before Christmas*. New York, NY: Putnam Juvenile.
Noyes, A. (1999). *The Highwayman*. Oxford, UK: Oxford University Press.
Schnur, S. (2002). *Winter: An alphabet acrostic*. New York, NY: Clarion Books.
Schnur, S. (2001). *Summer: An alphabet acrostic*. New York, NY: Clarion Books.
Schnur, S. (1999). *Spring: An alphabet acrostic*. New York, NY: Clarion Books.
Schnur, S. (1997). *Autumn: An alphabet acrostic*. New York, NY: Clarion Books.
Schule, W. (1978). *Haiku poetry: A children's collection*. New York, NY: Bantam Books.
Service, R. W. (1986). *The cremation of Sam McGee*. Toronto, ON: Kids Can Press.
Silverstein, S. (1981). *A light in the attic*. New York, NY: Harper & Row Publishers.
Thayer, E. L. (2000). *Casey at the bat: A ballad of the republic sung in 1888*. San Francisco, CA: Chronicle Books.
Thomas, M. (1997). *Free to be . . . you and me*. Philadelphia, PA: Running Press.

MyEducationLab

MyEducationLab is an interactive, virtual learning tool that will help improve your understanding of the concepts taught in this textbook and in your course. Through this engaging resource, you will have access to simulations of real classroom experiences, exercises that will help you improve your knowledge of key concepts, and additional resources that will help you in your teaching career. Use this online tool with your textbook to help you succeed in your studies and beyond!

Chapter 10

Redefining Literacy: Integrating the New Literacies and a Critical Response to Popular Culture in Your Classroom

Learning Objectives

In this chapter you will discover

- How to understand the scope of the "multiliteracies."
- How to think about literacy in the future.
- How to use digital tools for learning literacy in the classroom.
- How to conduct webquests.
- How to bring critical literacy into the classroom.
- How to help students become critical consumers.
- How to use graphic novels in the classroom.

JOHN HOWEY: EXPLORING TECHNOLOGY AND PROMOTING CRITICAL LITERACY

For John Howey, teaching is a career that allows him to learn with his students. John's school has about 20 teachers with varying years of teaching experience. He believes that this mix creates an excellent learning environment, as teachers are encouraged to share experiences and develop together professionally. He is also completing his Master of Education, where he is exploring the potential for using technology and critical literacy in the classroom. Recently, he wrote a paper about establishing blogs and wikis in the classroom. For John, the theoretical issues he studies are best confirmed when applied in the classroom setting. "You have to keep growing. I think that is important because that is what we are asking students to do."

John's grade 5 classroom is built on a series of educational concepts and constructs, including Gardner's theory of multiple intelligences. He carefully assigns students to collaborative groups based on their individual learning styles and abilities. For John's students, learning almost always begins with talk. Think, Pair, Share is a favourite discussion strategy in which students are encouraged to consider various perspectives on a topic. This kind of talk and larger class discussions are precursors to writing.

The reading and writing connection is an important part of John's language arts program and he recently incorporated picture books and graphic novels to provide additional visuals in his instruction. He often uses the document camera and SMART Board to feature visual images, followed by a brainstorming session of related vocabulary and concepts. In their most recent project, the class read

The Arrival by Shaun Tan. This graphic novel contains only images and John charged his class with collaboratively writing text to accompany the images. Prior to having students begin their own chapters, they wrote some text based on pictures from the book, "bumping it up" to a high level. John believes that this writing approach is especially effective, as it involves an individual as well as a collaborative component. Students then posted their chapters on a wiki located on John's school webpage and their peers provided commentary and editorial suggestions. John finds that the novelty of the wiki engages students in the revision process while leaving an assessment "trail."

The class is now experiencing Deborah Ellis's *The Breadwinner* as a Read Aloud. John selected this novel after the Canadian author visited his school last year. He has recently created a blog on which students can post their responses to *The Breadwinner* from home. He has provided them with critical questions and challenged them to be reflective and to use higher-order thinking when responding. He also encourages students to revisit the blog to monitor how their thinking has changed and progressed as a result of the ongoing discussions.

It is important to John that his students understand that the text and the world do not have to be accepted at "face value." He wants them to realize that they can change it and that they can create their own text. He focuses discussion on why texts are constructed as they are and why authors made particular choices related to the text:

> All texts are constructions, so they present an intentional viewpoint and purpose. Readers also bring their background to the reading process and that influences the meaning they derive from the text. Reading of text is never neutral.

John feels that *The Breadwinner* is perfect for this approach. He asks students to consider why Ellis focused on certain themes and what she is trying to tell her readers. He asks students to consider the text in light of what they hear and see in the media, emphasizing that these constructions are made through a Western lens.

John believes that many teachers are using critical literacy instructional techniques, but that they need to be more "intentional" or explicit in their practices. He cautions that shifts in classroom practices require time. Professional dialogue with colleagues, attending workshops, and completing the Master of Education program have provided John with greater opportunities and impetus to include technology and critical literacy in the classroom.

REFLECTIVE ACTIVITY 1

Take a moment to think about all of the literacy activities you have completed in the last week.

Estimate how long you spent on each of the following:

- Reading books, magazines, or newspapers in hard copies
- Reading menus
- Reading mail

- Completing crosswords, word searches, or other related games
- Writing letters and lists or making diary entries

Now estimate how long you spent on each of the following:

- Browsing internet sites
- Watching television or movies
- Playing video games
- Listening to music
- Reading a digital reader
- Writing on Facebook, Twitter, email, or a blog

Compare your estimates of time spent on these literacy activities. How many of these activities involved writing and reading using a hard copy or a pen or pencil? How many of these literacy activities involved technology?

Share your results with a peer and discuss the implications.

REFLECTIVE ACTIVITY 2

Brainstorm all of the different literacy spaces young people inhabit (think of literacy in its broadest sense, including popular culture, artifacts, viewing media, and interactive media).

When you have completed your list, put a check mark beside the activities that are part of traditional literacy programs in schools. Note the literacy activities that did not receive check marks. Consider the gap between literacy activities at home and literacy activities in schools.

Teacher Voice 10.1

Not long ago, I was in a grade 5 classroom watching a teacher candidate conduct a language lesson. As part of the lesson, the teacher candidate directed the students to read a chapter in an assigned novel that I knew to be well written and generally popular with young readers. I became intrigued with watching one of students. He spent an inordinate amount of time finding and opening the book. Then, instead of reading it, he searched for someone nearby with whom he could interact. Finding no one, he twisted in his seat and watched the teacher candidate interact in a private conference with another student at the back of the room. Over the 20-minute period, he never put his eyes on the page in front of him. Finally, he asked if he could go to the washroom and disappeared from the classroom for a lengthy period of time. He returned just prior to a recess break and then suddenly came to life. He asked if he could sit at the computer (there were three at the back of the room). He proceeded to search the web intently, moving through a variety of websites that he appeared to read voraciously.

I was struck that he was thoroughly engaged and motivated in this reading activity and could not help but reflect on the differences between the two reading experiences. On the computer, he was responding as I do when I am reading a book that thoroughly captures me. The only difference was the medium. The experience made me question the relevance and limitations of what we were doing in traditional language classrooms.

Anne Elliott

THE NEW LITERACIES

> Literacy is about more than reading or writing—it is about how we communicate in society. It is about social practices and relationships, about knowledge, language and culture.
>
> Those who use literacy take it for granted—but those who cannot use it are excluded from much communication in today's world. Indeed, it is the excluded who can best appreciate the notion of "literacy as freedom."
>
> UNESCO, Statement for the United Nations Decade, 2003–2012

In 1996, a group of 10 international literacy academics gathered to discuss the rapidly changing social, economic, and environmental realities and the multiplicity of communication methods in the world today. The group, now referred to as the New London Group, argued that the new ways of communicating and the increasingly cultural and linguistic diversity of the world called for a much broader view of literacy. They called the new approach to literacy pedagogy *multiliteracies*, a term they believed overcame the limitations of traditional approaches to literacy. The goal of the multiliteracies approach is to enable students to attain access to the evolving language and communication methods of work, power, and community and to achieve success in engaging critically in designing and understanding their social and economic futures (Cope & Kalantzis, 2000; New London Group, 1996).

The multiliteracies movement recognizes that communication forums are changing as a result of readily available technologies and shifts in English-language usage within different cultures. It acknowledges that the world is becoming smaller in terms of communication between cultures and languages, and that the ability to communicate effectively both on the world stage and locally is an essential skill. Technology and multimedia are providing individuals with greater choices with respect to how they communicate. Consider that the 2011 Arab spring revolutions were fostered and sustained peacefully via a deluge of communication through such relatively new technologies as Twitter, Facebook, and YouTube.

"Screen" activity has become a fact of life for Canadian students and is causing concern in some spheres. In 2011, the Canadian Society for Exercise Physiology recommended that children spend no more than two hours a day in sedentary "screen" activity; a sharp contrast to the current average of 10 hours per day (www.parentcentral.ca, 2011). These statistics are further substantiated by the Kaiser Family Foundation, which found that young people aged 8 to 18 are packing 10.75 hours of screen time into a typical day (www.kff.org).

While these numbers have implications for health and obesity, they also have implications for schooling. Students need to develop the skills to select, comprehend, interpret, and evaluate messages that they encounter in print, sound, and visual formats. Their considerations need to include the social, political, and economic contexts of these messages and they need to develop an appreciation that literacy is a form of social power that provides individuals with control over the circulation and interpretations of messages in society (Giroux & Simon, 1989; Hobbs, 2006; Luke, 1997). They need to understand and critique the role that media play in constructing or mediating reality, identity, and self (De Zengotia, 2005). Lack of literacy in this broader sense may prevent students from participating fully in a dynamic and changing world.

The multiliteracies challenge educators to include multi-modal communications across all school subjects, including language arts (Knobel & Lankshear, 2007; Rowsell, 2005). The New London Group proposed the teaching of all representations of meaning, including linguistic, visual, audio, spatial, and gestural, through a balanced classroom program of situated practice, overt instruction, critical framing, and transformed practice. Overall, this instruction reflects the literacy practices of the wider community and is collaborative in nature.

Situated practice builds on students' life experiences and situates meaning-making in the real world.

Overt instruction guides students to use an explicit metalanguage.

Critical framing encourages students to interpret the social context and purpose of information.

Transformed practice encourages students to transform existing meanings to design new ones (Mills, 2006).

This is not so say that everything we currently know about literacy needs to be discarded; rather, existing programs need to expand to embrace the realities of new communication practices (Beck, 2005; Hull & Schultz, 2002; Kist, 2005). Basic literacy skills must still be taught, and taught well. However, teachers also must ensure that students have the opportunity to develop the skills they will need to secure access to new forms of work and play. Students must acquire and gain proficiency in the use of various forms of media to engage critically with their work and world environments.

Differences between Traditional Literacies and Multiliteracies

Initially, the multiliteracies approach was equated primarily with computers and other communication technologies (Henderson, 2004). In reality, multiliteracy encompasses much more. Consider how our public lives have changed since the end of the Cold War. Many public institutions such as schools and universities now operate in response to market variables. Schools are no longer an arm of the state that standardizes the national language and culture. Instead, schools are now expected to honour cultural and linguistic diversity.

Our private lives have undergone similar changes, with gender, ethnicity, cultural background, sexual orientation, and generation being acknowledged as critical elements in the definition of self. Acknowledging such individual differences also suggests that we are less likely to possess a common culture, with Canada's human rights laws underlining the national acceptance of diversity. Increasing media choices and growing divergence are inconsistent with a homogeneous community. Simultaneously and paradoxically, private lives are becoming more public as technology provides a space for discourse of global ideas and events as well as the minutiae of individual lives. As a result, people are members of many groups and their identities have multiple layers.

Essential Components of the Multiliteracies

Visual literacy involves interpreting, negotiating, and making meaning with images. It is based on the premise that pictures carry meaning that can be "read." The ability to read images is indispensible to life in the information age. Visual and linguistic literacies typically complement each other and enhance the meaning-making process (e.g., graphic novels). The meaning of the words associated with visual images is different from the meaning of the same words without images. Originating in prehistoric times (animal drawings in caves), visual literacy skills require the ability to apply, create, and evaluate visual representations in order to communicate knowledge or represent insights. One issue related to visual literacy is that while texts are clearly only "representations" of reality, people are more likely to process visual texts as if they were veridical, or coinciding with reality (Hobbs, 2006).

Auditory literacy refers to the ability to understand, interpret, and create mood and sound in order to support vision and dialogue through music. For instance, students learn to analyze musical styles and the messages conveyed through the use of style and instruments. They also learn how to interpret sound effects provided by voice-over, background noise, and the use of silence.

Gestural literacy involves recognizing and interpreting facial, body, and other expressions as well as the relationship between these and other factors such as culture, attitude, position, and power. It also involves the ability to recognize mood and feelings as expressed through voice and accompanying body language. It is especially important to recognize that gestures can assume different meanings across cultures.

Spatial literacy refers to angles, distances, foreground and background, left and right, framing, space, place, and shape in relation to objects. Spatial thinking is malleable and can be improved through practice of specific tasks, including playing computer games in which players are required to keep track of their location and the location of other objects (Newcombe, 2006).

Multi-modal literacy describes any combination of the above four literacies, encompassing all of the different ways and combinations in which meaning can be created and communicated in the world today. Lemke (2006, p. 4) calls these interconnections "multimedia constellations."

The pedagogy of multiliteracies, or textual multiplicity, is based on the following understandings and complexities:

- Appreciating that we are a culturally and linguistically diverse global society
- Recognizing the plurality of texts from around the globe
- Understanding the variety of text forms associated with information and multimedia technologies
- Developing competent functionality with new representational language forms that are increasingly accepted around the world
- Interpreting visual images and understanding their relationship to the print
- Recognizing that differences in culture, language, age, and gender are not barriers to educational success
- Understanding that literacy moves beyond the text (paper, electronic, live, multimedia) to include semiotic codes, including auditory (e.g., music, sound effects,

silence), gestural (e.g., facial expressions, body language), spatial (e.g., organization of objects), and visual (e.g., still or moving images, layout, colour)

- Understanding that critical literacy is central to understanding and interpreting the new literacies

Educational Implications

The educational implications of the multiliteracies are huge! Students today, whom Gee (2002) refers to as "millennials" and whom Prensky (2001) calls "digital natives," appear to think and process information differently than their parents and teachers. In some instances, students' existing literacy skills as related to information and communication technologies (ICTs) may exceed or differ from those of their teachers (Chandler-Olcott & Mahar, 2003). Effective teachers take advantage of students' knowledge and skills by constructing learning contexts in which students can share their expertise. Such classrooms tend to be student-centred and emphasize inquiry-based learning (Buckingham, 2003). In this context, teachers are no longer the providers of "knowledge" per se. Rather they provide critical questions and guide the learning process so students can construct their own knowledge and understandings.

The Quebec-based Centre for Literacy (2008) identified the new literacies as focusing on individuals' capacities to use and make critical judgments about information that they encounter daily. Literacy is an essential foundation for learning throughout life and must be valued and treated as a human right.

The International Reading Association (2009) holds a similar position regarding new literacies and twenty-first century technologies, stating that students have the right to:

- Teachers who use ICTs skilfully for teaching and learning
- Peers who use ICTs responsibly and who share their knowledge
- A literacy curriculum that offers opportunities for collaboration with peers around the world
- Instruction that embeds critical and culturally sensitive thinking into practice
- Standards and assessments that include new literacies
- Leaders and policy-makers who are committed advocates of ICTs for teaching and learning
- Equal access to ICTs

The necessary multiliteracy skills for today's students include:

- The ability to locate information
- The ability to organize information
- The ability to narrow the focus of a topic by selecting key words so that information retrieved is on topic and manageable
- The ability to determine which information is important and which is extraneous
- The ability to be critical of conflicting information
- How to store data electronically and to retrieve it

- How to communicate effectively on social networks such as MSN and Facebook and via email.
- How to demonstrate understanding using visual communication such as photographs and other visual images

Teachers must identify where they can benefit from professional development, which is generally available through provincial initiatives, the school board, online, or at universities. The practice of being a lifelong learner becomes more than mere rhetoric and is a prerequisite for teaching.

Provincial Responses to the New Literacies

The way in which multiliteracy is taught in schools in part reflects our orientation to citizenship, including the knowledge and responsibilities we expect citizens to demonstrate and use. For instance, inclusive classrooms ensure that our students are aware of diversity as a natural component of any society.

In British Columbia, the Ministry of Education has designated information technology as a separate course, and all of the prescribed learning outcomes in this area are now integrated across the curriculum. This is seen as a positive shift from computers being viewed as a separate subject to being viewed as a technological tool for learning across the curriculum.

In Alberta, the English language arts curriculum encourages the study and creation of a wide variety of text types and forms, including oral, print, visual, and multimedia formats. The program also incorporates ICT outcomes. The ICT curriculums work as a "curriculum within a curriculum" for core subjects such as English, language arts, social studies, and science.

Media Literacy Saskatchewan holds that language is the basis for communicating, learning, and thinking. Opportunities for media studies are integrated throughout units and modules of the overall curriculum. Teachers are provided with extensive resources on the Evergreen website (www.sasked.gov.sk.ca/branches/curr/evergreen/index.shtml).

Media literacy within the Manitoba English language arts curriculum is based on the Western and Northern Canadian Protocol. Students are expected not only to comprehend but also to respond personally and critically to texts. These responses include reflecting, creating, analyzing, synthesizing, and evaluating. As they become proficient language learners, they are expected to employ these strategies to construct meaning from oral, literary, and media texts.

In Ontario, teachers are provided with an extensive support system of elearning programs to ensure that they possess the necessary information to teach the curriculum. The language arts curriculum was revised in 2006 and includes critical thinking and "using language to interact and connect with individuals and communities for personal growth and for active participation as world citizens" (Ontario Ministry of Education, 2006b, p. 4). Further, the role of technology in the language arts curriculum includes encouraging students to use ICTs to support and communicate their learning. Teachers are also encouraged to use ICTs to support their teaching practice.

In 2000, Quebec undertook its broadest educational reform in 30 years, which included developing cross-curricular competencies, interdisciplinary teacher strategies, and collaborative student-centred instruction. Media literacy goals are to develop critical and ethical judgments with respect to popular culture and to provide students with opportunities to produce media documents that respect individual and collective rights.

In 1995, New Brunswick, Nova Scotia, Prince Edward Island, and Newfoundland and Labrador formed a curriculum consortium called the Atlantic Provinces Education Foundation (APEF). Media literacy figures prominently in the APEF's English language arts curriculum, which states that literacy includes the ability to use and understand visual and technological methods of communication. It also states that media literacy needs to address the interplay between students and popular culture.

Digital Tools That Can Be Used in the Multiliteracies Classroom

Students, especially those in the intermediate grades, are increasingly engaged with digital tools and media, including blogs, wikis, social networking sites, instant messaging, online chats, website production, video production, digital music tools, and video games. Through these experiences they are acquiring diverse literacies, forging connections between texts and self, using problem-solving and inquiry skills, and communicating with a multitude of others. These are very different literacy skills from traditional reading and writing. Students are now able to make connections among a number of different texts to construct new knowledge (Myers & Beach, 2004). Consider the connections that students can form between text, images, and sound while working through a website. These same tools can be adapted to classroom instruction in a variety of creative and engaging ways. For instance, blogs and wikis are powerful digital tools that can be particularly helpful in teaching writing (also see Chapter 7, Writing: Exploring the Reading and Writing Connection). It behooves teachers to use these tools to enhance their classroom instruction if they are to bridge the gap between home and school and to prepare students for the future of communication.

Blogs Blogs can be used in the classroom as a forum for responding to specific writing prompts or as a method of sharing personal reflections (Glogoff, 2005). When using blogs, teachers are advised to establish some "ground rules," including the purpose of the site as well as the required minimum number of posts and comments on other students' blogs. Students also must be provided with clear and explicit guidelines for appropriate use of language and referencing.

Decisions also need to be made about who will have access to the blogs. Generally, it is advisable to restrict the readership to the class, especially if the blogs are used as reflective journals. If the purpose is to address world issues, it may be helpful to extend the readership so students can receive input from readers worldwide and participate in dialogue that is broader than the classroom (Ferdig & Trammell, 2004). In this way, students learn to create text that is part of a network.

In general, students are motivated to use blogs and blogs provide teachers with alternatives to standard essay or journal writing. Blogs are cost efficient and relatively easy to set up in the classroom.

Wikis A wikiinvolves multiple writers collaboratively composing, revising, and editing online text. Possibilities for classroom use include collaborative writing projects, creating a class statement, composing a letter to an editor, or developing a service learning or inquiry report (Moxley, Morgan, Barton, & Hanak, 2005). A primary characteristic of wikis is that writing is organized around specific topics that students are required to use to organize their thinking. This tool also provides a trail of all revisions and changes, which provides teachers with the opportunity to evaluate the writing process as well as the contributions of individual group members.

Students must negotiate their roles in the collaboration before beginning to write, agreeing on what material they will contribute to the text or the topic for which they will assume responsibility. Students also take responsibility for editing and revising each other's work. As well, they can create hypertext links to other websites. This process mimics successful collaborations in higher education and the workplace and eliminates difficulties associated with finding a time and place to work face to face.

It is not difficult to set up a wiki in the classroom and many free wiki-hosting sites are available to teachers (some schools may provide a wiki as part of the school server). It is important to note that each wiki program has a particular style guide for creating, formatting, and revising the text that students will need to learn (Beach, 2007).

Video and Electronic Games Video and electronic games are the most advanced form of multi-sensory, multi-modal media used successfully by large numbers of people (Gee, 2003). They are more interactive than television or movies and provide opportunities for creative exploration, decision making, movement, and artifact use. Of greater concern, they are also the most prevalent source of screen-based violence, with some students allocating vast amounts of time to their use. While controversial in nature, the positive side of this phenomenon is that students can hone many skills through game playing and that the problem solving associated with some game playing can extend to such real-world activities as scientific research or architectural construction (Lemke, 2006).

Games vary greatly from first-person shooters to so-called "god games" (Beach, 2007), in which players are provided with some form of challenge (e.g., to design a safe amusement park). Some researchers believe that by participating in these games, students can acquire different narratives for coping with challenges or conflict (Gee, 2003; Jenkins, 2006). Thus, their social skills can be enhanced by experiencing these challenges, particularly when they are working or playing online as part of a group in collaborative problem-solving situations.

We are not suggesting that teachers bring violent games or any other kind of video game into the classroom. Rather, we believe that the skills students are developing outside school through gaming can be effectively called on when addressing an issue or conflict in the school or community. For instance, a school may be considering adopting a balanced nutrition break day as opposed to the traditional morning, lunch, and afternoon recess. Experienced gamers could construct a gamelike simulation in which roles are assigned to those in favour and those against the proposal. Students can be assigned different roles (e.g., students, administrators, teachers, parents, school board members) as they participate in online discussions about the proposal.

Other ways to integrate home and school learning through gaming involve asking students to reflect explicitly on the specific problem-solving strategies they are learning in their favourite games. Drawing on these skills, teachers can challenge students to create a gamelike simulation for a curriculum-based issue or conflict. For instance, such simulations could be created for use in history class (e.g., Was Louis Riel a rebel or a hero?) or current events (e.g., Should Canada continue to maintain troops in Afghanistan?). Avid gamers can help those who are less familiar with playing.

Social Networking Social networking sites are a fact of life for most students in grade 6 and above. Many young people, in part, create their self-esteem and emotional responses to life through networking technologies, and the web has become a central social meeting and gathering zone (Turkle, 2011). Indeed, these technologies are such important components of so many students' lives that they quickly learn the necessary social literacies to use them. Teachers can tap in to these skills and incorporate them constructively in the classroom by setting up online class discussions. Before beginning a discussion, however, it is important to establish boundaries on being judgmental and unduly opinionated, appropriate use of language and images, respect for the ideas of others, and participation. It is also essential to monitor the discussion carefully and provide support for positive and productive participation. At times it may be necessary to intervene if students have trouble working together fairly and equally (Beach, 2007). Teachers can also address issues related to the ethics associated with the construction of personal identity and authenticity (Turkle, 1995).

Webquests Webquests are teacher-designed activities that enable groups of three to four students to use the web to inquire critically about an issue, question, or topic related to the curriculum. To complete webquests successfully, teachers must ensure that students possess the following foundational skills:

1. Ability to define and conceptualize issues
2. Ability to collect, examine, and critique information from the internet
3. Ability to formulate a report or solution appropriate for the task at hand (Beach, 2007)

Teachers must also ensure that students understand the task and that supporting resources are in place. Teachers must therefore provide the following information and resources prior to having students begin a webquest:

1. Introduction, which includes purpose of the webquest and expected outcomes
2. Clearly defined tasks that describe the overall final product, such as problem solution, final report, narrative, and media product
3. Activities linked to websites that provide relevant materials
4. Supporting materials and guides for collecting and organizing material related to the final outcome (some teachers provide structured worksheets)
5. Assessment, typically in the form of a rubric (when appropriate, students can participate in the development of the rubric and associated criteria)
6. A reflective summary in which students think about the content they have learned and the skills they have used while completing the webquest; teachers can use a variety of formats when guiding students through this process, ranging from group discussion to individual reflection

Even young students can complete webquests successfully when provided with appropriate guidance from their teachers. Some school boards may provide a template for

Table 10.1 Teaching Students to Review Websites Critically

- Use Think Aloud to model how to assess websites and how to record information.
- Show students how to open two websites simultaneously and how to navigate between them.
- Provide time for exploration of the websites and associated links.
- Have students respond to the following questions:
  a. Why was this website created?
  b. Why did the author include all of the parts?
  c. How is this website similar to and different from other websites?
  d. What can you learn from this website?
  e. What is missing from this website that you need to learn? (Jupiter, 2009).
- Provide a sheet on which students can make notes and record thoughts and new questions.
- Remind students to assess the accuracy of information they locate in one website by checking other sites.

creating webquests. Alternatively, templates can be found at http://educationaltechnology.ca/resources/webquest/index.php, www.ga.K12.pa.us/curtech/WEBQPRE/tempques.htm, and http://webquest.org/index-resources.php. Perhaps one of the greatest challenges for students when completing webquests and other internet-related activities involves being able to review information critically and narrow their selections accordingly. Teachers can follow the steps outlined in Table 10.1 when guiding students through the process of selecting information critically from a website.

Student Voice 10.1

Usually we just go on to Google and we enter a question, phrase, or term. We then read the little bits of information that are underneath each of the links. If we think that the information is important for our topic, we then go to the website and search for more facts. We "copy and paste" the information into a file and then write it up using our own words. It can be hard work looking for research on the computer.

Liam
Grade 5 student

CRITICAL LITERACY

According to *Literacy for Learning* (Ontario Ministry of Education, 2004), critical literacy is:

> A process of looking beyond the literal meaning of texts to observe what is present and what is missing, in order to analyze and evaluate the meaning and the author's intent. Critical Literacy goes beyond conventional critical thinking because it focuses

> on issues related to fairness, equity and social justice. Students take a critical attitude by asking what view of the world the text advances and whether they find this view acceptable. (p. 9)

Critical literacy challenges the perception that language arts can be taught using a neutral text that merely requires technical competencies to decode (Freebody & Freiberg, 2011). Rather, critical literacy is the ability to read texts actively and reflectively in order to understand the nature of human relationships. These relations often include the concepts of justice, equity, gender, ability, and societal norms (Shor & Freire, 1986). This stance posits that students can become more socially aware by critically examining information and constructing new knowledge accordingly. As they develop this approach to reading text and other multiliteracies, students are better able to question social conventions and norms, especially in the context of socio-economic status, ethnicity, gender, and sexual orientation (to name a few). Such instruction helps students identify the hidden agendas and biases embedded in text and other media. When students are able to review messages critically, they are better prepared to assume an advocacy role and participate in the transformation of discriminatory societal institutions and structures (McLaren & Lankshear, 1994).

Students are exposed to a constant barrage of concepts, facts, and ideas and they need to possess higher-level thinking skills to process, select, interpret, and respond to these messages appropriately. Teachers need to help students move beyond literal translations of these multitudinous texts to becoming critical thinkers about the messages, their sources, and their purposes. Students need to possess these skills so they have the confidence to develop their own perspectives on world issues and to build their own world view in a conscious manner (Behrman, 2006).

The ultimate purpose of critical literacy is to empower individuals to take a critical stance toward all sources of information (Lemke, 2006). This is particularly important since individuals are now more influenced by what they see and hear than by what they read. For instance, websites are "texts" characterized by the integration of print, images, music, voice, animation, video, and sound effects. The various kinds of "texts" that students encounter in their lives, both in and out of school, are cultural in nature and contribute strongly to the development of their identities, beliefs, values, and world views (Luke, 2000). Through these encounters, they seek to interpret the world and to determine their place in it (Anstey & Bull, 2006; Hobbs, 2006). While we may wish to believe that our constructs of the world are our own, in reality they are formed, in part, by others to influence, persuade, and control us. Critical literacy skills help individuals maintain some autonomy when making choices about whom and what to believe, admire, emulate, or challenge.

Current definitions of critical literacy share four dimensions (Lewison, Flint, & Van Sluys, 2002):

1. Disrupting the commonplace
2. Interrogating multiple viewpoints
3. Focusing on socio-political issues
4. Taking action and promoting social justice

These four dimensions can be addressed by selecting texts to help students identify, discuss, and ultimately challenge commonly held beliefs and assumptions about the roles of power, culture, class, and gender. Useful guiding questions include the following:

In whose interest is this text written?

What is the purpose behind this text?

Who benefits from this message?

Teaching Critical Literacy

Bringing students' cultures into the classroom

The following describe the most commonly used critical literacy instructional techniques and practices:

- **Reading supplementary texts.** It is often helpful to have students consult other texts when discussing a topic from the curriculum or an assigned reading. For instance, students can be directed to review relevant internet sites, song lyrics, advertisements, or television programs.
- **Reading multiple texts.** Students should have access to multiple texts that share a common theme when completing a novel study or similar activity. Access to multiple texts provides students with the opportunity to critique the theme from a variety of perspectives and values. Such analysis confirms that meaning is not a single entity but can be derived in a multitude of ways by different people in varying circumstances.
- **Reading from a resistant perspective.** While reading, students should be challenged to consider how students from different backgrounds may read and interpret a text as well as how they may be affected by the reading. Such perspectives can include consideration of race, culture, gender, religion, and socio-economic status. One example would be having students read (or Read Aloud) Prime Minister Stephen Harper's 2008 apology to Aboriginal peoples regarding residential schools. Following that activity and subsequent discussion, young students could read *Shin-Chi's Canoe* or *Shi-shi-etko* by Nicola Campbell, illustrated by Kim LaFave. Older students could read *As Long as the Rivers Flow* and its sequel *Goodbye Buffalo Bay* by Larry Loyie. They can then discuss the impact of residential schools on the Aboriginal children who attended them. Encouraging students to read in this way can broaden their understanding of the world.
- **Producing counter-text.** Students can create counter-texts, which involves writing a complete text from the perspective of an underrepresented or non-represented group. The product can take the form of a printed text or a multimedia creation. This task can be accomplished by rewriting a story from the perspective of a minority character or by adding a minority character to an existing story. Again, this shift in perspective helps broaden students' views of the world.
- **Having students conduct research.** Providing opportunities for students to conduct research on the internet is a common technique used by teachers who want to empower students to participate in the construction of new knowledge. A key component to completing such research activities is to have students select topics of

interest. If it is to be a critical study, however, students need to select and evaluate topics that are problematic and explore the societal conditions that created the problem and consider ways to solve the problem.

- **Challenging students to take social action.** Critical literacy is also related to engaging students in social action projects that improve their school, community, or world. For instance, environmental projects frequently involve setting unifying goals that motivate students to take social action. Other activities, such as fundraising or collecting for local food banks, are also feasible. Such projects generally involve moving outside the confines of the classroom and establishing the relationship between literacy and social action in a larger context.

A primary component of critical literacy pedagogy is its focus on identifying and examining multiple perspectives and viewpoints while exploring themes such as power and identity. Luke and Freebody (1999) have developed a Four Resources Model that outlines the four families of practices that are used by literate individuals when they interact with a text. While these four resources are presented sequentially, in reality they are interconnected and used simultaneously.

- **Code breaker.** Practices that enable individuals to understand the code of written texts in order to decode what they read and encode while they write.
- **Text participant.** Practices that enable individuals to obtain meaning when they read and to communicate meaning when they write.
- **Text user.** Practices that enable individuals to understand the different functions of text and appreciate how the structure and language of texts are determined and shaped by these functions.
- **Text analyst.** Practices that enable individuals to examine, evaluate, and transform texts critically. Critically literate readers and writers understand that texts are never neutral. Instead, they are value laden and simultaneously promote and marginalize different points of view (Luke & Freebody, 1999).

Teachers often place greater emphasis on similarities than they do on differences, inadvertently ignoring the unique sets of cultural and social norms and values that students bring to the classrooms. Students, however, construct new knowledge based on their previous cultural experiences, values, and beliefs (Bandura, 1986; Bruner, 1986; Piaget, 1932).Through the successful implementation of critical literacy skills, students are encouraged to identify and challenge their previous experiences when constructing new meanings and when applying their new understandings to practice.

Currently, the meaning of the term *text* has moved beyond the printed word to include digital text, which is non-linear, multi-modal, and visual. Children have become frequent users of digital text through such information and communication technologies as MSN, Twitter, Facebook, email, and blogs. This shift poses a challenge for educators since printed text, which is still pervasive in schools, is sequential and linear whereas digital text, which is pervasive in media, is non-linear and interactive and governed by space, display, and simultaneity (Kress, 2003; Kress & Leeuwen, 2001).Lemke (2006) argues that these new meanings in multimedia are flexible, in that word meaning and picture meaning are constantly intertwined. Word meaning is transformed by image context and image meaning is transformed by textual context. Many images can be very powerful and are

Table 10.2 Thoughtful Questions That Promote Critical Thinking

1. How do people from diverse backgrounds interpret images or video in relation to text or narrative?
2. How do texts that we hear or read change in meaning when images or videos are integrated with the words?
3. What visual messages are less readily available for critical analysis (e.g., life values embedded in product advertising)?
4. What messages presented in popular culture media are designed to further the commercial or political interests of those who control the media?
5. How critical are we and how critical do we need to be?

presented as part of the popular culture. They also can be misleading. For instance, clever manipulation of images by manufacturers, advertisers, and designers often presents images that can mould young children's perception of reality. See Table 10.2 for some thoughtful questions that promote critical thinking in students.

Teachers need to encourage students to read and interpret text in a way that moves beyond comprehending the text to understanding the power relationships revealed through it. Students need to understand that the author created the text from a particular perspective and for a particular purpose and that the reader has a responsibility and right to critique, question, and analyze these ideas and concepts from multiple perspectives (Fresch, 2007). Specifically, students need to understand that:

- All texts (regardless of format) are written from a particular perspective and with a specific voice
- Other perspectives can be brought to the text
- Individual texts address the same issues differently
- Authors use specific methods to present point of view

Students must be taught to prompt themselves to ask specific questions while they read or view text. As discussed in Chapter 5, Comprehension of Narrative Text, such questions include:

- Whose point of view is represented in the text? Whose point of view is not represented in the text?
- What is the author's point of view?
- Do I agree or disagree with the author's point of view, and why?

When introducing students of any level to critical thinking, it is useful to begin with familiar texts that have relatively obvious messages (see suggestions in Table 10.3). Another possibility is to use magazine advertisements or other texts that have strong visual components.

Learning to Live in a Consumer Society

Society is frequently manipulated and misled by and permeated with product propaganda largely related to advertising media (Heath & Potter, 2004). From a very young

Table 10.3 Suggested Texts for Developing Students' Critical Literacy Skills

Bunting, E. (1993). *Fly away home*. London, UK: Sandpiper. (Primary)

Coleman, E. (1996). *White socks only*. Park Ridge, IL: Albert Whitman & Company. (Junior)

Ellis, D. (2000). *The breadwinner*. Toronto, ON: Groundwood. (Junior)

Ellis, D. (2002). *Parvana's journey*. Toronto, ON: Groundwood. (Junior)

Ellis, D. (2003). *Mud city*. Toronto, ON: Groundwood. (Junior)

Ellis, D. (2004). *The heaven shop*. Markham, ON: Fitzhenry & Whiteside. (Junior)

Ellis, D. (2004). *Three wishes: Palestinian and Israeli children speak*. Toronto, ON: Groundwood. (Intermediate)

Joseph, L. (2000). *The color of my words*. New York, NY: HarperCollins. (Junior)

Lyon, G. E., & Anderson, S. (2009). *You and me and home sweet home*. New York, NY: Atheneum/Richard Jackson Books. (Primary)

Polacco, P. (2000). *The butterfly*. New York, NY: Philomel. (Primary)

Stead, R. (2010). *When you reach me*. New York, NY: Yearling. (Junior and intermediate)

Stone, T. L. (2009). *Almost astronauts: 13 women who dared to dream*. Sommerville, MA: Candlewick. (Junior and intermediate)

Williams, K. L., & Mohammad, K. (2007). *Four feet, two sandals*. Grand Rapids, MI: Eerdmans Books for Young Readers. (Primary)

Winter, J. (2009). *Nasreen's secret school: A true story from Afghanistan*. San Diego, CA: Beach Lane Books. (Primary)

Woodson, J. (2001). *The other side*. New York, NY: Putnam Juvenile. (Primary)

age, children are inundated with advertisements, many of which focus on making them aware of brand names so that their desire for material goods is enhanced (Gladwell, 2002; Lindstrom, 2003; Linn, 2004; Schor, 2004). This consumer culture includes internet shopping, branding, consumer credit, and selling "cool" (mostly to children and teenagers).

"Cool" is an interesting and elusive concept that holds a great deal of cultural power, particularly among the young. According to Heath and Potter (2004), being cool represents a dominant status hierarchy in current urban society and serves as a form of distinction. Equivalent terms include *edgy*, *alternate*, *hip*, *awesome*, *great*, and *sick*. In some ways, "cool" has replaced the old notion of class (Heath & Potter, 2004). "Cool" is also a slippery concept in that it is constantly changing, creating tension for those with cool aspirations. Being cool requires individuals to attend to the media vigilantly and then acquire the necessary clothing, technologies, and gadgets (Gladwell, 2002). Children are particularly susceptible to these messages, as their identities and self-esteem are developing.

Some argue that media activities and images are created largely in the boardrooms of the United States, with a focus on profit (Kline, Dyer-Witheford, & De Peuter, 2005). This is worrying because the ideas, stories, and values presented through popular media are seen as being endorsed by society, or at least by some parts of society. As a result, these messages can contribute to maintaining or creating injustices or inequities (Freire & Macedo, 1987). Students need to read and understand these texts as informed critical consumers (Dalton & Proctor, 2008). The skills needed to navigate these confusing

messages must be taught explicitly if students are to develop a personal concept of social equity and justice. Students need to recognize how authors use techniques such as point of view and information omission to foster specific interpretations and purposes (Freebody & Freiberg, 2011).

Knowledge and curiosity are important and empowering aspects of learning to analyze popular culture critically. Teachers can bring a number of critical perspectives to analysis of the advertising media by viewing existing advertisements and having students create their own advertising media productions. Examples of critical perspectives that can be taught explicitly are presented in Table 10.4.

The sample lessons that follow provide students with opportunities to develop a critical lens through which they can view popular culture.

Table 10.4 Critical Perspectives That Can Be Taught Explicitly

- Study how language, signs, and images are used to encourage viewers to adopt a desired response, belief, or practice. Present a series of advertisements and ask the following questions:
    1. For whom is this ad created?
    2. What do the creators want me to think about what is being sold?
    3. What beliefs does this ad want me to accept?

    After considering these questions, students can decide whether they accept or reject the ideas and the product. This activity can be done in groups, as a grand conversation with the whole class, or individually and then shared.

- Study how audiences are socialized by the media to believe that consumption of a product ensures "cool."
    1. Discuss what it means to be cool and popular.
    2. Ask students to identify (or bring to class) ads that suggest "cool." Alternatively, view video clips for a series of products that appeal to students.
    3. Ask students to analyze how the products can help consumers become cool.

- Study how gender is portrayed in the media.
  1. Discuss traditional gender roles and how they have changed over time. Reference can be made to fairy tales, *The Paper Bag Princess*, the Harry Potter series, or the Dear Canada series (e.g., *Days of Toil and Tears, A Trail of Broken Dreams*).
  2. Ask students to analyze how gender is portrayed in advertisements, television, music, news, and video games. Assign various media forms to small groups of students and have them report back to the class.
  3. Alternatively, have the entire class watch prime-time television for two hours one night, recording and analyzing the representation of males and females. Criteria for analysis could include hair colour and length, body size and shape, and activities in which characters engage. Have students present their findings.
- Study how products are endorsed.
  1. Have students collect samples of celebrity and professional (e.g., doctor, dentist) endorsements.
  2. Place students in groups to critique the logic and validity of the endorsements using such questions as:
     a. Who is the intended or target audience?
     b. What language is used by the person doing the endorsement?
     c. What values or underlying assumptions does this reveal? (Beach, 2007)
  3. Have students share their ideas as a class.
  4. Have students to create their own advertisement, their own magazine, or their own description of a television series. Have students critique each other's products using the same criteria that were used when analyzing product endorsements in the media.

SAMPLE LESSON 10.1A

A Critical Perspective on Advertising

Possible materials for this activity include advertisements for clothing, sportswear, toys, food, or technologies such as cellphones. This activity is suitable for students in the junior and intermediate grades.

Steps

1. Place students in pairs or triads and provide each group with a series of advertisements.
2. Provide students with a worksheet (or a series of question prompts) for each advertisement that requires them to consider the following:
   a. Brand name and product
   b. Visual image
   c. Catchy words and slogans
   d. Techniques used and why. Provide students with adequate time to complete activity.
3. Ask each group to select one (or more) of their advertisements to discuss from a critical perspective. Invite the whole class to share additional insights or thoughts concerning the advertisements.
4. List overall conclusions reached by the class. Have students tally identified marketing techniques, including the following:
   a. *Consumer compliments* such as "The lady has taste!" or "If you do what is right for you, no matter what others do, then ____ is right for you."

(continued)

(continued)

b. *Rhetorical questions* such as "What do you want most from _____? That's what you get from ____." or "Shouldn't you be drinking (wearing, eating) _______?"

c. *Vague claims* such as "_____ makes sensible eating delicious." or "Its deep rich lather makes hair feel good again."

d. *Celebrity or medical endorsements.*

e. *Scientific or statistical claims* such as "____ has more power than our leading competitor." or "_____ has 33% more nutrition."

SAMPLE LESSON 10.1B

A Critical Perspective on Literature

This activity follows Sample Lesson 10.1a.

Steps

1. Choose a familiar short story or article from popular culture.
2. Allow sufficient time for students to read the text.
3. Begin a whole-class discussion by asking the following key questions:

   a. What is the topic?

   b. What is the theme?

   c. Who is the author anticipating will read this story or article?

   d. Whose position is being expressed?

4. Continue the discussion by providing the students with higher-level critical thinking questions, including the following:

   a. Whose voices and positions are not being expressed?

   b. What ideas might another author express about this topic?

   c. What was not being stated about the topic?

   d. What do you think about this topic?

   e. What parts of this story or article are consistent with your beliefs and opinions?

   f. What parts of this story or article are inconsistent with your beliefs and opinions?

Teachers need to be especially patient with students when first introducing these questions, as they may be unfamiliar with the process of questioning what they read or expressing alternative opinions. With continued practice, however, students will be able to apply such questions when viewing and reading texts.

SAMPLE LESSON 10.2

A Critical Perspective on Media Images

This activity is appropriate for students in grades 6, 7, and 8. In this activity, students are required to view popular images critically in terms of intent and impact, relevance to their own lives, marketing techniques, and equity.

Teachers should select at least three popular teen magazines, removing every picture of young males and young females.

Steps

1. Display each picture to students without comment. Show pictures of males and females separately. Ask students to identify any defining or shared characteristics among the images, including body shape, attitude, and clothing.

2. Hold a grand conversation about students' observations and reactions. Record student responses for each gender. Tally or organize student responses into common themes.
3. Ask students to record their responses to the following questions:
   a. How are these images being "sold"?
   b. Do these images reflect my personal style in any way?
   c. What influences my choice of style?
   d. What qualities do I look for in a friend?
   e. Which of these qualities are related to how the person looks?
   f. Who may feel left out or even despondent when they view these images in a magazine?
4. Hold another conversation, letting those who wish to respond do so. Focus part of the discussion on equality with respect to the socio-economic ability to purchase "cool" products, those whose body image is different from the North American ideal, those who are racially or culturally different, the self-esteem of those who cannot participate in the "cool" culture, those for whom parental approval poses problems, etc.
5. Place students in small groups to consider the impact of these images on the identity and self-esteem of the magazines' intended readers.
6. Have students record their thoughts about the impact of popular culture on young people's emerging identity and self-esteem. Suggest that they consider issues related to equity as well as personal experiences.

SAMPLE LESSON 10.3

A Critical Perspective on Stories

The purpose of this activity is to develop a critical attitude toward familiar and unfamiliar stories by examining the portrayal of wolves in fairy tales (adapted from Sinfield & Hawkins, 2005). This activity is suitable for students in grades 1 and 2 but can be adapted for those in the junior grades.

Teachers need to select a series of fairy tales featuring wolves, such as *The Three Little Pigs, Little Red Riding Hood, Peter and the Wolf*, and *The Boy Who Cried Wolf*. They also need to select one to three websites that feature accurate information about wolves.

Steps

1. Read the selected fairy tales aloud over the course of a few days.
2. Ask students what they have learned about wolves from these stories. Record student responses and compile a list of descriptors and characteristics of wolves as revealed through fairy tales.
3. Ask students to think about why the authors of fairy tales have portrayed wolves in this manner.
4. Have students review the selected websites for information about wolves. Teachers may need to read aloud information from websites when working with students in the primary grades. Older students may be able to gather information about wolves independently.
5. As a class, create a new list of descriptors and characteristics of wolves, stressing that all ideas should be confirmed in at least two websites.
6. Discuss the differences between the two lists and ask students to speculate about why wolves are depicted inaccurately in fairy tales.
7. Discuss how authors frequently depict ideas that suit the purpose of their stories but may not be accurate.
8. Ask students to write a story with a wolf as the main character, incorporating the characteristics gathered from the websites. Students can write the story as a class or individually.
9. Have students read their stories aloud and ask the rest of the class to consider how wolves are portrayed in these stories.

MEANING-MAKING USING MULTILITERACIES

THE TEACHER'S ROLE HAS SHIFTED FROM TRANSMITTING KNOWLEDGE TO ORCHESTRATING learning opportunities among students and providing support for the final application of new learning. Another objective of critical literacy is to help students understand how their prior experiences influence their ability to deconstruct words and ideas and reconstruct their own world views (Freire, 1978; Freire & Macedo, 1987). This means that teachers need to provide and support multiple modes of communication to enable students to express their learning. Whatever the topic, learning can be displayed by creating a poster, a model, a PowerPoint presentation, a video, or a combination of these ways of communicating. These choices allow for cultural, linguistic, and technological differences, with students actively engaged with new ideas and values and connecting these ideas and values to current social dynamics (Freebody, 2005). A good example of multiliteracies in the classroom is the increasingly popular graphic novel, which combines language and images to tell a story.

Graphic Novels: An Example of Multiliteracies in the Classroom

The term *graphic novel* refers to a specific writing form. Like comic books, graphic novels contain words and pictures organized sequentially to tell a story. The stories presented in graphic novels, however, are markedly different from those presented in traditional comic books. While some graphic novels feature superheroes, many more are written in the genres of history, historical fiction, biography, fiction, science fiction, and realistic fiction. They usually are about 170 pages in length and contain about 12 500 words (although some can be longer). The majority of the story is presented through graphics, drawings, and other visuals. To comprehend graphic novels, readers must be able to interpret the images with respect to character, mood, and plot as well as to decode the text.

Graphic novels are becoming increasingly entrenched in popular culture. Students of all ages appear eager to read them, with these texts being especially motivating for students who struggle with the reading process or for whom English is a subsequent language. Timeless classics are now available in this more accessible mode for all students. For instance, *Oliver Twist*, *Frankenstein*, *Macbeth*, and *Romeo and Juliet* have all been transformed into graphic novels. Other graphic novels are recognized as serious literature and works of art; Art Spiegelman received the Pulitzer Prize in 1992 for his graphic novel *Maus: A Survivor's Tale* about a Holocaust survivor.

Well-written graphic novels contain many standard literary devices, including point of view, irony, flashbacks, symbolism, satire, allegory, and allusion; however, others contain profanity and feature sexual and violent content. Accordingly, care must be taken when selecting graphic novels for the classroom. It is probably best to alert principals and parents when using graphic novels in the classroom and provide a sound rationale for the text selection (Table 10.5). Table 10.6 provides a list of some potential titles for use in the classroom.

Creating Graphic Novels in the Classroom

Many students enjoy the challenge of creating a graphic novel and generally work best with at least one self-selected

Table 10.5 Rationale for Using Graphic Novels

1. Students can be introduced to literature they might never encounter otherwise, such as Franz Kafka as interpreted by Peter Kuper in *Give It Up! And Other Short Stories* (1995).
2. Reading graphic novels may require more complex cognitive skills than reading text alone (Lavin, 1998).
3. Graphic novels may be used to teach literary terms and techniques (Schwarz, 2002).
4. Graphic novels present alternative views of culture, history, and human life in accessible ways.
5. Graphic novels give voice to minorities and to those with diverse points of view.

partner. There are many ways in which students can complete the novel. For instance, they can author the story together and create separate illustrations. Alternatively, one student can assume responsibility for the illustrations and the other can assume responsibility for the text. It is usually best to allow students to determine the nature of their collaboration during their assignment. Table 10.7 lists specific steps associated with having students author graphic novels.

Table 10.6 Suggested Graphic Novels

Avi. (2004). *City of light, city of dark.* Markham, ON: Scholastic. (Junior)

Busiek, K. (2001). *Marvels.* New York, NY: Marvel. (Junior)

Cibos, L., & Hodges, J. (2008). *Peach fuzz.* Madison, NC: Spotlight. (Primary)

Crilley, M. Akiko series. New York, NY: Delacourt Books for Young Readers. (Junior)

Eisner, W. (2003). *Sundiata: A legend of Africa.* New York, NY: NBM Publishing. (Junior)

Espinosa, R. (2004). *The courageous princess.* San Antonio, TX: Antarctic Press. (Primary)

Gaff, J. (2008). *Aquaman's guide to the oceans.* Toronto, ON: DK Publishing. (Primary)

Grownley, J. Amelia Rules! series. Arlington, MA: Renaissance Press. (Junior)

Kesel, B. (2003). *Meridian: Flying solo.* Oldsmar, FL: Cross Generational Comics. (Intermediate)

Kouno, F. (2007). *Town of evening calm, country of cherry blossoms.* San Francisco, CA: Last Gasp Publications. (Intermediate)

Moore, A. (1995). *Watchmen.* New York, NY: DC Comics. (Intermediate)

Satrapi, M. (2004). *Persepoli: The story of a childhood.* Rome, Italy: Pantheon. (Intermediate)

Smith, J. (2004). *Bone.* Somerset, UK: Cartoon Books Publishing. (Intermediate)

Ware, C. (2003). *Jimmy Corrigan: The smartest kid on Earth.* Rome, Italy: Pantheon. (Intermediate)

Colonial village map

Table 10.7 Having Students Author Graphic Novels

Step 1: Provide students with a number of age-appropriate graphic novels as reference to help them determine length, topic, and style. Students also may wish to consult "how to draw" books such as:

Coope, K. (2002). *How to draw manga.* New York, NY: Tangerine Press.

Hablitzel, M., & Stitzer, K. (1994). *Draw write now.* Poulsbo, WA: Barker Creek.

Hart, C. (2008). *Manga for the beginner: Everything you need to start drawing right away!* New York, NY: Watson-Guptill.

Roche, A. (2010). *Cartooning: The only cartooning book you'll ever need to be the artist you've always wanted to be.* New York, NY: Sterling.

Temple, K. (2005). *Drawing: The only drawing book you'll ever need to be the artist you've always wanted to be.* Asheville, NC: Lark Books.

Step 2: Help students develop a list of characters. Direct them to think of their characters' appearances, personalities, and histories. Encourage them to draw the characters in several ways to ensure that their appearances suit their personalities. A simple character chart that lists aspects of appearance, personality traits, and emotional traits can be helpful at this point.

Step 3: Have students brainstorm potential story events. Remind them that graphic novels require less text and space than traditional stories.

Step 4: Ask students to create a fully developed plot line with all events organized sequentially. Teacher-student conferences can be an effective format for checking students' work at this point.

Step 5: Have students complete a rough sketch of their ideas. Assist them to determine the paper size, number of pages, and number of boxes they will need for their final product. For instance, if using letter-sized paper, boxes of 3.75 × 5 cm are best. These "thumbnails" can be changed as necessary as students complete the planning process. Remind students to keep about 1 cm from the edges "clean" to allow for binding and general appearance. Again, group sharing and teacher conferences are effective here.

Step 6: Have students "pencil" the pictures and the text for each page. They will need a good eraser.

Step 7: Once students are satisfied with their penciling, have them begin the inking stage using a black pen or marker. Teachers should make available black pens or marker tools of different sizes to allow for different line widths. Students should ink the lettering as well.

Step 8: Have students erase pencil lines. It is a good idea to photocopy the inked novel and have a couple of copies available in case of errors before adding colour.

Step 9: Encourage students to select from a variety of media when colouring their artwork.

Step 10: Have students bind their pages. Again, encourage students to be creative when binding their novels. Have students share their novels with their classmates, parents, and other classes.

Student Voice 10.2

We wanted to write something different than the other class so we decided to do a graphic novel. I saw one in the library and now I have one of my own. I really like them because they have speech bubbles and pictures. Me and my friend really like drawing pictures so I asked my teacher if I could make one and then I asked my friend if she wanted to do it with me. So we are writing the same thing—we put the same thing in our speech bubbles but we are each drawing our own pictures. Our handwriting is also different but we collaborate on the ideas. I think of something and she thinks of something and then we put it together. It is going to be a pretty long story but I love doing it. My teacher likes it too, and when we are finished we will present it to the class.

Zoya
Grade 3 student

The following resources provide additional ideas about how to use graphic novels in the classroom:

- *Getting Graphic! Using Graphic Novels to Promote Literacy with Preteens and Teens* by Michelle Gorman (2003)
- *The 101 Best Graphic Novels* by Stephen Weiner (2001), found at www.adherents.com/lit/comics/101_best_graphic_ novels.html
- *Graphic Storytelling and Visual Narrative* by Will Eisner (1996)

Concerns and Cautions Regarding the New Literacies

Generation Gap Since many teachers were educated prior to the proliferation of modern ICTs, they think differently about information and communication. As a result, at times educators may have some difficulty establishing appropriate criteria to assess the dynamic, creative, and possibly edgy work produced by their students (Tierney & Rogers, 2004).

Sources As students access digital environments, there is moral concern about the risk of accessing (by accident or by design) sources that disseminate non-factual, distorted, or potentially harmful information and attitudes. Teachers need to be vigilant about such eventualities and remind students that not all information in the public domain is accurate or culturally appropriate.

Equity The technological tools that facilitate the new literacies are relatively expensive. All school boards are not equally solvent and all homes are not able to access the most current technologies. For instance, students in Aboriginal homes may have less access to the internet and use computers less than other students (Downing, 2002). Additionally, there is also a lack of technical support and user skills in many rural Aboriginal communities (Hui, 2009).

Teacher Education To provide effective classroom instruction, teacher education programs must move beyond operational skills training. That is, they need to focus on a critical approach to socio-cultural, global, and political issues as well as changing educational epistemologies (Luke, 2003). There is a need for teachers and teacher educators to take responsibility for seeking additional professional development if they feel they are not current in terms of technology.

SUGGESTIONS FOR PROFESSIONAL DEVELOPMENT

1. Graphic novels have come of age for children, young adults, and adults. If you have never done so, search for an adult graphic novel and read it for your own pleasure. Well-reviewed selections include *Stuck Rubber Baby* (2010) by Howard Cruse, *Blacksad* (2010) by Juan Diaz Canales and Juanjo Guarnido, and *The Night Bookmobile* (2010) by Audrey Niffenegger. However, do not feel constrained by these suggestions and consider consulting graphic novels for young adults as well.
2. Consider your technological skills. If you know that you have fallen behind, search for a course (brief or more extensive) that you can attend to hone your skills. Failing that, ask one of your more technologically advanced friends to be your "go-to person" when you have questions or ideas that you would like to implement in your class.
3. When you are in schools, ask primary, junior, and intermediate students about their technological patterns and habits. Make notes about what you hear and watch for changes across the grades.
4. Ask teachers at the primary, junior, and intermediate level how they use technology in their classroom. Make notes and compare the results with what you learned from students at each level.

CHILDREN'S LITERATURE REFERENCES

Campbell, N., & LaFave, K. (2005). *Shi-shi-etko*. Toronto, ON: Groundwood Books.

Campbell, N., & LaFave, K. (2008). *Shin-chi's canoe*. Toronto, ON: Groundwood Books.

Ellis, S. (2008). *Days of toil and tears: The child labour diary of Flora Rutherford*. Markham, ON: Scholastic.

Haworth-Attard, B. (2004). *A trail of broken dreams: The Gold Rush diary of Harriet Palmer*. Markham, ON: Scholastic.

Kuper, P., & Kafka, F. (2003). *Give it up! And other short stories*. Syracuse, NY: NBM Publishing.

Loyie, L. (2005). *As long as the rivers flow*. Toronto, ON: Groundwood Books.

Loyie, L. (2008). *Goodbye Buffalo Bay*. Penticton, BC: Theytus Books.

Munsch, R. (1992). *The paper bag princess*. Toronto, ON: Annick Press.

Spiegelman, A. (1986). *Maus: A survivor's tale*. New York, NY: Pantheon.

Tan, S. (2007). *The arrival*. Toronto, ON: Arthur A. Levine Books.

MyEducationLab

MyEducationLab is an interactive, virtual learning tool that will help improve your understanding of the concepts taught in this textbook and in your course. Through this engaging resource, you will have access to simulations of real classroom experiences, exercises that will help you improve your knowledge of key concepts, and additional resources that will help you in your teaching career. Use this online tool with your textbook to help you succeed in your studies and beyond!

Chapter 11

Working with Students with Diverse Learning Needs

Learning Objectives

In this chapter you will discover

- How some Aboriginal communities have overcome traditional educational limitations.
- How to identify the characteristics of inclusive classrooms.
- How to provide instruction for students who are learning English as a subsequent language.
- How to work with students who are at risk.
- How to work with students who are living in poverty.
- How to program for students with learning exceptionalities.
- How to work with students with attention deficit hyperactivity disorder (ADHD).
- How to work with slow and reluctant learners.
- How to differentiate instruction to meet the needs of all students in the classroom.

NICOLE MAHEU AND TIEHA McGEE: WORKING COLLABORATIVELY TO ASSIST STUDENTS WITH LEARNING DIFFICULTIES

Nicole Maheu and Tieha McGee work collaboratively as learning resource teachers at a large school with about 600 students in southern Ontario. Nicole is responsible for working with students with special learning needs in the primary and junior grades, while Tieha is responsible for working with the junior and intermediate grades. Nicole is the more experienced member of the team, with just over 15 years of experience. She has experience teaching most grade levels and has held her current position for the past four years. She has completed numerous professional development courses, including specialist in English as a second language. Tieha has completed a number of long-term occasional positions in grades 1 to 7 over the past five years, including working in a high-needs segregated classroom. She has a Master of Education degree with an emphasis on literacy and using assistive technologies when working with students who have reading and writing difficulties. Nicole and Tieha both are adamant that all students can succeed if provided with the proper instruction and opportunities to demonstrate their learning: "It's just the different ways that they need to access the work and be able to show what they know."

When they are not providing individual students with supplemental instruction, Nicole and Tieha work collaboratively with their colleagues in regular classrooms to help develop and implement programming for students with reading, writing, and other learning difficulties. Accordingly, they are advocates for differentiated instruction and believe strongly in its potential to improve learning for all students in the classroom.

Tieha recalls an instance when she provided differentiated instruction in a grade 7 classroom. Like many classrooms across the country, she had close to 30 students who differed vastly in their abilities. While about half of the students were performing at or above grade level and were capable of working independently, the remaining students either were formally identified as having learning challenges or were struggling learners. Tieha and her students were working on a descriptive writing unit, focusing on character development. Initially, Tieha provided the whole class with writing examples by several authors. Together, they explored the strengths of the compositions and deconstructed the elements of descriptive writing that they could transfer to their work. They also worked together to develop a rubric that would be used to assess their final compositions, with Tieha providing students with a related checklist that they could consult throughout the writing process.

Providing students with these models and the rubric helped to concretize the task for all learners. Tieha also provided all students with graphic organizers to use for brainstorming and planning their character descriptions. While she made use of the graphic organizer optional, she was able to use it to provide extra, small-group support to those students who struggled with beginning the writing process. She also provided students with choice about how they would write their character descriptions, with some students working on computers, some using pen and paper, and others having their ideas scribed: "Some of the students were on the computer, some were sitting with me while I wrote their ideas, and others worked independently writing their descriptions—it just depends on what works best for them as individuals." Regardless of how they produced their descriptions, all students were responsible for presenting their drafts and discussing them with Tieha. For students who struggled, these discussions focused on whether they had fulfilled all of the criteria outlined in the assessment rubric and associated checklist. In this way, students who struggled were held to the same criteria as their peers but were provided with greater support and options with respect to how they would demonstrate their learning.

Nicole agrees about the potential of technology to help create differentiated learning environments and remembers an instance when she worked collaboratively with a grade 4 teacher to plan and deliver a unit on medieval times. Assigned to work with a student reading at a grade 1 level, Nicole was able to use text-to-speech software to help the student access reading materials for the unit that otherwise were beyond his reading level. However, having the student listen to the material was insufficient, so Nicole followed up by reading and discussing selected sections of the text with him. They also worked together to write the report using assistive technology, which provided a unique opportunity for Nicole to cue and prompt word-writing strategies that the student was learning as part of the pull-out supplemental program to his language arts program: "Because those strategies were introduced as part of our remediation program, I could prompt him to use them here . . . it fit in very well with what the class was doing."

Nicole and Tieha explain that most students with special learning needs appreciate the extra support provided to them by their teachers and the resource staff. Over time, many students are able to identify their learning needs and the environments that best support their growth as learners. Nicole and Tieha also explain that other students are very accepting about the various programming options provided to them and their peers.

In fact, many students seek support when the two learning resource teachers are present in the classroom. Nicole and Tieha concur that this type of seamless or "invisible" support is ideal and represents the concept of inclusion well.

When asked what advice they can provide to teachers who are working with students with special needs, they comment that it is important for all teachers to be "open-minded." Being open-minded means, in part, being willing to work collaboratively with other teachers and staff. While they acknowledge that having others in the classroom can be intimidating to teachers, they point out the many benefits associated with the additional resources and programming ideas that come from working collaboratively.

> When you are student centred, it's not about you. It's about what we all can do for students. Essentially, we are bringing people together to help problem solve. Students benefit when we are open-minded and willing to try new approaches.

REFLECTIVE ACTIVITY 1

Take a moment to consider your ancestors on both of your parents' sides. (Remember that, unless you have a First Nations background, you have immigrant ancestors somewhere in your background.) Answer the following questions:

- From how many countries did they originate? Which ones?
- Who is the earliest ancestor you can identify coming to Canada?
- Who came most recently?
- What challenges did each of the newcomers face?
- How is your current family culture affected by your ancestors?
- Are there any customs, values, or attitudes evident today that you can trace to the immigrant experiences of your ancestors?
- Do you have any beliefs or orientations that result from your family's background or immigrant experiences? If so, try to confront them explicitly and think about them logically.

Share your thoughts about these questions and their answers with others.

DIVERSITY AND INCLUSION

Globalization is a phenomenon that integrates people from different cultural backgrounds and traditions for a variety of social or economic purposes. Economic and natural disasters, wars, and a search for a better standard of living prompt people to emigrate, with Canada being a favoured destination. Canada's population of visible minorities more than tripled in only two decades, increasing from 1.1 million in 1981 to almost 4 million in 2001 (or about 13 percent of the total population). By 2016, visible minorities are expected to comprise about 20 percent of the adult population and about 25 percent of the student population in Canada (Antunes, MacBride-King, & Swettenham, 2004), with these percentages being higher in urban centres such as Toronto, Vancouver, and Montreal. Because of our democratic tradition of accepting differences, cultural and ethnic diversity will continue to define us as Canadians. It is imperative, then, that teachers work with their students to develop respect and tolerance for people from different cultural and ethnic backgrounds (Banks, 2008; James, 2005; James & Wood, 2005).

Canada is officially a bilingual country, with English and French reflecting our historical roots. The two official languages have been augmented by German, Italian, Ukrainian, Dutch, and Polish. Beyond these, a multitude of other languages are spoken in Canada, with the Chinese languages being the third most frequently spoken since 2001. Recently, there have been substantial increases in other languages, including Punjabi, Arabic, Urdu, Tagalog, and Tamil (Statistics Canada, 2006). Cree was identified as the largest Aboriginal language group, followed by Inuktitut and Ojibway (Statistics Canada, 2006).

One of the most important educational issues in Canada today is how to meet the needs of all students regardless of culture, race, socio-economic level, linguistic background, and ability (Gollnick & Chinn, 2002). These differences can affect achievement on standardized tests, particularly those relating to language and mathematics, with gaps usually widening as students progress through the grades (Anderson, Medrich, & Fowler, 2007; Haycock, 2001). Therefore, rather than stating that all students must come to school ready to learn, we would suggest that all schools must be ready to teach all students. This view reflects a very different orientation to learning outcomes than one that assumes that students of a similar age or grade form a homogeneous group. Effective teachers are those who are able to develop and implement pedagogy that is culturally sensitive and responsive to individual differences (Richards, Brown, & Forde, 2007).

Characteristics of Inclusive Classrooms

Standards and accountability

Teachers' attitudes and beliefs about the nature of cultural and ethnic differences, as well as the nature of students' abilities and disabilities, are key components of successful inclusive classrooms. Teachers who believe that they are responsible for the programming for all students in their classrooms, including those with special needs, are more effective than teachers who view their students as a homogeneous group that learns at about the same rate (Jordan, Schwartz, & McGhie-Richmond, 2009). Teachers who accept this responsibility are more likely to use a variety of accommodations and modifications in the classroom and to acquire a broader repertoire of instructional strategies than those who leave the responsibility to others (Darling-Hammond & Bransford, 2005; Stanovich & Jordan, 2004).

The following are some characteristics of successful inclusive classrooms:

- Students are active rather than passive learners.
- Teachers provide students with choices with respect to completing learning activities. For instance, young students may choose a spelling activity that involves cutting and pasting letters from a magazine, creating words using magnetic letters, or using new words in sentences. Older students may choose between writing a diary of the Vikings' journey to Newfoundland, creating a map showing the likely Viking voyage to Newfoundland, or conducting a webquest activity documenting the trials the Vikings encountered while attempting to colonize a harsh environment.
- Parents are involved in their children's learning in a variety of ways, including regular volunteering. Teachers promote an open classroom policy and communicate regularly with parents (e.g., newsletters, phone calls, website).

- Students are free to learn at their own pace, allowing for differences between those who learn quickly and those who require additional time and assistance. The traditional practice of teaching a single class as if it were a homogeneous unit is not part of the inclusive environment.
- Learning goals vary among students so that each student has specific, attainable, and measurable challenges. This differentiation allows teachers to provide praise and encouragement that has real meaning for students at different stages of learning.
- Teachers manage their time and their classroom efficiently. They constantly observe students, watching for individuals who are struggling with a task. Individual interviews with students are completed regularly.

Cultural and Linguistic Diversity

Cultural and linguistic differences apply to those students whose culture and language differ from those dominant in the school. Multiculturalism has evolved from a narrow definition that describes only a few people to a global and inclusive concept that honours equity, social justice, and exceptionality. Multiculturalism is a concept and a process that affects school leaders, parents, community, and society as a unit (Banks, 2008; James, 2005). It recognizes that all cultures have resources and value (Freire & Macedo, 1987). Teachers are charged with modelling and encouraging positive interactions among all students as well as with raising their own social and global awareness. The picture of Earth from space provides a powerful image to broaden our thinking from an "us" versus "them" perspective to an "us" perspective, as it becomes clear that we are all on this planet together. The image, which shows no delineation of national boundaries, reinforces the universality of what it means to be a human being living on Earth in the twenty-first century.

Promoting Tolerance and Understanding of Cultural Differences

Multicultural education has the lofty goal of countering discriminatory attitudes and actions in Canadian schools and promoting the development of a tolerance and appreciation of cultural differences (Lund, 2006). Multicultural education has five dimensions that can be used to implement and assess educational programs: (1) content integration, (2) knowledge construction, (3) prejudice rejection, (4) equitable pedagogy, and (5) an empowering school culture and social structure (Banks, 2008). Although these dimensions can be discussed separately, they are interconnected and overlap in practice.

Content integration involves the study of diverse cultures, which can be accomplished in a variety of ways, including contributions, additions, transformations, and social action.

Contributions are explicit studies and acknowledgment of the heroes and holidays valued by specific cultures. Appropriate choices here depend on the cultural makeup of the class and often can involve parental input. For example, the Chinese New Year or Martin Luther King, Jr.'s birthday could be celebrated. Alternatively, a unit on influential women could be introduced. Regardless of the topic, the focus would be to enable students to consider concepts, issues, and events from multiple perspectives.

Additions are units that are added to the curriculum but do not substantially change it. Examples are a study of Haitian people after the earthquake in 2010 or a study of Russian culture during the 2014 Winter Olympics.

Transformations occur when the curriculum is altered so that the perspectives of others are present and the material is not expressed exclusively from a North American or Eurocentric point of view. In this case, teachers need to infuse diverse materials, alternative frames of reference, and content material from various groups to extend students' understanding of other cultures (Sadker & Sadker, 2002).

Social action originates from the studies or issues that emerge in class discussions. Students can make decisions to take action related to the concepts, issues, or problems they have studied. This approach encourages decision making and social action to achieve multicultural goals and constructive social change at the school, community, or global level.

Knowledge construction refers to helping students understand that texts are written from the perspective of the author and that multiple perspectives and interpretations can be made of the same text. For instance, when the Hudson Bay and North West Trading companies moved "west" to develop the fur trade, their notion of "west" was not the same as that of the Aboriginal peoples living on the western coast of Canada. They considered themselves as being at the centre and "west" was toward the sunset. Similarly, when Europeans discovered the New World and began to establish settlements, they believed that there were no people of consequence already living there. In reality, these settlers displaced highly developed societies living all over North America. The key to knowledge construction is to provide a setting in which students can draw their own conclusions and become critical of what they read. Table 11.1 lists sample activities that promote multicultural awareness and Table 11.2 lists selected texts that can be used as part of multicultural instruction. For an extended discussion, see also Chapter 10, Redefining Literacy: Integrating the New Literacies and a Critical Response to Popular Culture in Your Classroom.

Table 11.1 Sample Activities That Promote Multicultural Awareness

Activity 1: The Story of My Name

The purpose of this activity is to help build intercultural respect and understanding and, if they are unacquainted with each other, help students become acquainted in an equitable way. This simple activity can be adapted for almost any grade and is most appropriate at the beginning of the school year. It can be done with just first names or both first and last names.

Pre-planning

At least a day before the activity is scheduled, inform students that they are going to be asked to share information about their names. Ask them to think about stories they have heard about their naming or find out the meaning of their names by asking parents and grandparents, by using a name book, or by searching the internet. Remind them that everyone's name has an interesting origin.

Steps

1. Consider beginning the session by sharing information about your own name.
2. Place students in triads and tell them to take turns sharing the information they have learned about their names.
3. When sufficient time has elapsed, return students to a large group and ask each student to tell the group about the name of one of the members in his or her triad.
4. Conclude with an informal discussion of nicknames, names of pets, or names they would like to call their children in the future.

(continued)

Table 11.1 Sample Activities That Promote Multicultural Awareness (*continued*)

Activity 2: Sharing Perspectives

This self-reflective activity is designed for intermediate students but can be adapted for students in the junior grades. This activity requires that students write and share short reflections about how their "gender identities" or "gender expressions" were established through childhood messages about what it meant to be a boy or a girl (this can be used for other identifiers where appropriate). This writing activity prepares students to engage in a whole-class discussion during which they will need to recognize that their experiences and perspectives may be different from those of their peers.

Steps

1. Ask students to write a short (maximum one page) reflection on childhood memories that helped shape their gender identity. Ask them to address messages they received about what it meant to be a "boy" or a "girl." Ask them to discuss who provided those messages (teachers, parents, grandparents, caregivers, coaches, peers).
2. Place students in small groups (triads are easiest) and have them read their reflections or share them orally. Stress that each person should have an equal opportunity to share his or her experiences. This step may be done the next day if necessary.
3. Return students to a large group for a grand conversation. Ask for volunteers who will share their ideas and experiences. Questions that may be asked to enhance the discussion include the following:
   - Is your gender identity and expression affected by these early experiences? How?
   - Have you ever been ridiculed or denied an opportunity to do or say something based on your gender? How did you feel? How did you react?
   - Have you ever ridiculed someone else for doing something that you did not consider gender-appropriate?
   - What messages do you send to others about your gender identity?
   - Did the perceptions of others affect your experiences?
   - What did you learn about the perspective of others that surprised you?

Activity 3: Hosting an International Day (or Evening) in Your Classroom

The nature of this activity varies depending on the cultural makeup of the class and the cultures that the class has studied in literature studies, social studies, or current events. This activity may be extended by consulting with other teachers and making it a schoolwide event. Such an event could include stations set up around the classroom (or throughout the school) reflecting and featuring the following:

Food

Traditional games

Geographical information

Music

National costumes

Traditional holidays and celebrations

Videos of the countryside

Weblinks for Further Activities

www.archaeolink.com/multiculturalism_tolerance_lesso.htm

www.funderstanding.com/v2/educators/multiculturalism-at-school

www.sincerelyyourspenpals.com/home.html

Table 11.2 Selected Texts for Multicultural Instruction

Bell, W. (1995). *The golden disk*. Toronto, ON: Doubleday Canada.

Ming-Yue discovers something about the world and reaches a new understanding of herself during a Chinese New Year celebration. Primary and junior.

Baylor, B. (1985). *Everybody needs a rock.* New York, NY: Aladdin.

This book illustrates that making a decision of any kind, be it big or small (even choosing a rock), takes time, thought, and concentration. It is a celebration of the world of nature. Primary.

Harrison, T. (2002). *Courage to fly.* Markham, ON: Red Deer Press.

Meg, an island girl adjusting to a new home in a faraway city, finds friendship with the help of a wounded bird and an old man who does exercises in the park. Primary.

Bourdeau Waboose, J. (1997). *Morning on the lake*. Toronto, ON: Kids Can Press.

A First Nations boy and his grandfather spend a full day in the wilderness. From a morning encounter with a family of loons on the lake to an evening faceoff with some wolves, the child is reassured by his grandfather's presence and wisdom. Quiet in tone, the contemplative first-person narrative brings the Ojibway view of the world into focus. The idea that people are part of nature and must respect both land and animals is never directly stated but is clearly shown. Primary.

Gilman, P. (1994). *Something from nothing.* Markham, ON: Scholastic Canada.

When Joseph was a baby, his grandfather made him a shimmering blue blanket adorned with the moon and stars. As the boy grows and the blanket wears out, the old tailor recycles it, in succession fashioning a jacket, a vest, a tie, and finally a cloth-covered button. But when Joseph loses the button, even his grandfather cannot make something from nothing. Primary.

Meuse-Dallien, T. (2003). *The medicine pouch.* Halifax, NS: Nimbus Publishing.

When Matthew and his family go on a camping trip, Matthew remembers to bring his medicine pouch. His grandfather gave him the pouch and told him to fill it with things that were special to him. Matthew put in sacred herbs for prayer, a small feather, and a sparkly stone. At their campsite, Matthew finds a beautiful bush that he wants to protect. He takes his sacred herbs out of his pouch and says a prayer to protect the bush. For many years the bush thrives. One year, Matthew sees a smaller bush growing next to it. Primary.

Kertes, J. (1998). *The red corduroy shirt.* Markham, ON: Fitzhenry & Whiteside.

Jerry, an immigrant from China, and Jake, who has recently come from Hungary, encounter barriers as they become friends. Primary and junior.

Langston, L. (1994). *No such thing as far away*. Victoria, BC: Orca Books.

Michael is upset about leaving Chinatown, the only home he has known. The words of his best friend, Grandpa Doc, help him adjust: "There is no such thing as far away when you carry a place with you." Junior.

Wallace, I. (1992). *Chin Chiang and the dragon's dance*. Toronto, ON: Groundwood.

Chin Chiang is apprehensive about performing the dragon dance with his grandfather on the first day of the year of the dragon until he meets an old woman who performed the dance in her youth. Primary and junior.

Meuse-Dallien, T. (2000). *The dream catcher*. Halifax, NS: Nimbus Publishing.

Matthew presents his friend Dustin with a dream catcher for his birthday so it will bring him good dreams instead of the bad ones he has been experiencing recently. It was made specially for Dustin by Matthew's father using stones and feathers in Dustin's favourite colour, blue. Dustin is glad that Matthew has shared a part of his culture with him. Primary and junior.

(continued)

Table 11.2 Selected Texts for Multicultural Instruction (*continued*)

Wiebe, R. (2003). *Hidden buffalo.* Markham, ON: Red Deer Press. 🍁

The Cree of the Canadian West always hunted bison for their survival. But during this particular summer, no one sees any herds on the horizon. With the arrival of the fall, the very survival of the tribe is in danger if no bison are found. Junior.

Buttery, J. (2000). *Mei Ling discovers Jack Miner.* Truelight. 🍁

Mei Ling, a new immigrant to Canada, shares a school project about a Canada goose with a new Canadian school friend. At the end of the project, she becomes happier in her new home. Junior and intermediate.

Doyle, B. (1992). *Spud Sweetgrass.* Toronto, ON: Groundwood Books. 🍁

Set in contemporary Ottawa, this book tells of Spud's attempts to solve the problems of the world, including racism, multiculturalism, and pollution. Junior and intermediate.

Doyle, B. (1995). *Spud in winter.* Toronto, ON: Groundwood Books. 🍁

A sequel to *Spud Sweetgrass.* When Spud witnesses a murder and recognizes an accomplice, he fears for himself and for his friend Connie Pan. Junior and intermediate.

Ye, T.-X., & Bell, W. (2003). *Throwaway daughter.* Toronto: ON: Doubleday Canada. 🍁

Grace Dong-mei Parker, a Canadian teenager, is determined to learn about her Chinese ancestry after watching the Tiananmen Square massacre on television. Supported by her adoptive parents, Grace journeys to China where she studies the culture and searches for her birth mother. Junior and intermediate.

Wheeler, J., & Jackson, D. (2006). *Christmas at Wapos Bay*. Regina, SK: Coteau Books.

This is a modern story about Aboriginal culture. The authors describe the struggle between the pull of the modern and the importance of the "old ways" with sensitivity. This multi-generational story, written by two Aboriginal authors, raises many topical issues and introduces young readers to a different culture and its customs. Intermediate.

Gordon, M. (2001). *Daughter of strangers.* Ottawa, ON: Oberon Press.

Thirteen-year-old Amy is not happy with herself and she also dislikes being part of her adoptive parents' summer archaeology digs in the Barrenlands. She has thought for a while about asking her mom to help her find her birth mother but has never gone through with it. She feels like a daughter of strangers. Some people give away puppies and kittens, she tells herself, but her parents gave *her* away. Intermediate.

Prejudice reduction involves confronting and negating stereotypes that students may hold concerning people or events that appear in the media (Phinney & Rotheram, 1987). If offensive comments are made by students, it is incumbent on teachers to make it clear that such comments are not acceptable. Naturally, this requires a sensitive decision-making process to determine the best course of action. However addressed, it is imperative that teachers convey that prejudicial and hurtful racial or cultural comments are not acceptable. Teachers are also wise to remember that encouraging collaborative learning in the class has been shown to promote respectful dialogue where students consider and accommodate the perspectives of others (Payne, Monk-Turner, Smith, & Sumter, 2006).

Equitable pedagogy requires teachers to modify the instructional program so that all students have the possibility of meeting their fullest potential. This implies that teachers are adept problem solvers who possess large repertoires of teaching strategies and techniques that can be used to create modifications for diverse students.

Empowering school culture requires that the principal and staff consciously consider the school's activities in light of equity. It also requires the creation of qualitatively different relationships among various groups in the school that are based on mutual respect for cultural differences as reflected in schoolwide goals and cultural practices. Teachers need to be provided with opportunities for collaborative planning and instruction and all parents and school staff should have the opportunity to assume some responsibility for school governance.

This orientation of conscious awareness means revisiting grouping and labelling practices, participation rates related to extracurricular activities, achievement gaps, enrolment in gifted and special education programs, and interactions between staff and students (Banks, 2008). Essentially, school staff need to know what is happening, care about what is happening, and act appropriately with this knowledge.

Teachers can also broaden their perspectives by reading the following texts:

Abuelaish, I. (2011). *I shall not hate: A Gaza doctor's journey*. London, UK: Pluto Press.

Ali, A. H. (2010). *Nomad*. Toronto: ON: Knopf Canada.

Choy, W. (2005). *All that matters*. Toronto, ON: Anchor Canada.

Gowda, S. S. (2010). *Secret daughter*. New York, NY: William Morrow.

Grennan, C. (2010). *Little princes: One man's promise to bring home the lost children of Nepal*. New York, NY: HarperCollins.

Highway, T. (2005). *The kiss of the fur queen*. Toronto, ON: Anchor Publishing.

Kamboureli, S. (2006). *Making a difference: Canadian multicultural literature*. Don Mills, ON: Oxford University Press.

King, T. (2005). *The truth about stories: A Native narrative*. Minneapolis, MN: University of Minnesota Press.

Kogawa, J. (1983). *Obasan*. Toronto, ON: Penguin Books.

Nafisi, A. (2003). *Reading Lolita in Tehran: A memoir in books*. New York, NY: Random House Trade.

Ondaatje, M. (1993). *Running in the family*. Toronto, ON: Vintage Canada.

Philps, A., & Lahutsky, J. (2011). *The boy from Baby House 10: From the nightmare of a Russian orphanage to a new life in America*. New York, NY: St. Martin's Press.

Tan, A. (2010). *The hundred secret senses*. New York, NY: Penguin Books.

Toews, M. (2005). *Swing low: A life*. Toronto, ON: Vintage Canada.

Wagamese, R. (2006). *Keeper'n me*. Toronto, ON: Anchor Canada.

Caution The need to address culture and ethnic diversity is likely to be evident in many schools, especially those in urban settings. It is important, however, to remember that issues of cultural and ethnic diversity are just as important in seemingly homogeneous classrooms, as these students will be working and living in an increasingly diverse world. Teachers will need to consciously introduce these ideas.

First Nations Students: Confronting the Legacy of Residential Schools

While our current policies honour and celebrate individual differences, it was not always so in Canada. It should be acknowledged that Canadians have come to this inclusionary position in part because of a painful past, including the establishment of residential schools for First Nations students. The creation of these residential schools was based on the belief that the best chance for successful assimilation of First Nations peoples into mainstream Canadian culture was to force the learning of English and the adoption of Christianity and to remove First Nations children from the home environment. Indeed, the expectation was that within a few generations all First Nations cultures would disappear (www.irsss.ca/history). This policy of "aggressive assimilation" was enforced by removing Aboriginal children from their families and placing them in boarding schools. These schools were run by the federal government under the Department of Indian Affairs and were administered largely by the Catholic, Anglican, and United churches. The first residential schools were established in the 1840s, with the last one closing in 1996 after about 150 000 Inuit, Metis, and Aboriginal students had been forced to attend. This punitive policy was a debilitating and cruel experience for these children and the acrimonious policy has been condemned, with the Canadian government officially apologizing to our Aboriginal peoples in 2008. Not surprisingly, the pain associated with this policy reverberates in the lives of Aboriginal peoples today.

Today, many Aboriginal students are "at risk" for school failure. Almost 50 percent of students attending one of the 518 reserve schools will not complete high school. According to the Assembly of First Nations, there is a large discrepancy (of about $2000 to $3000) in funding provided to Aboriginal students who attend reserve schools versus non-Aboriginal students (Laboucane, 2010). Aboriginal students attending mainstream schools are likely to be challenged by a curriculum that has little cultural relevance. Unequal funding, curriculum, and low expectations all contribute to a poor success rate on provincial and national standardized tests.

More positively, a number of schools have demonstrated that these kinds of results do not have to be a foregone conclusion. For example, in a small school in Bella Coola, British Columbia, the majority of Aboriginal students have elected to remain in school and have demonstrated superior performance scores on provincial examinations compared to other non-Aboriginal students. Similar outcomes have been achieved at a First Nations school in Fort Nelson, British Columbia. In 1982, 90 percent of students were below grade level. Today, the K–12 school has more than 80 percent of its students achieve the provincial standards for their grade level (*The Globe and Mail*, April 15, 2011).

These excellent results have been accomplished by incorporating a number of changes in the education system in these small and remote towns. First, the communities have taken advantage of distance learning programs and new provincial programs that have enabled students to opt for Aboriginal-influenced credits. Second, they have prioritized literacy support programs and have provided a place for students to complete their homework and receive additional help. Most importantly, Aboriginal experiences and culture form the centre of the curriculum. This kind of experience has encouraged the national chief of the Assembly of First Nations, Shawn Atleo, to assert that First Nations need to control their own education (Henderson & Wakeham, 2009).

Students Who Speak English as a Subsequent Language

Students who first learned to speak in a language other than English are referred to as English as a second language students, English as a subsequent language students, or ESL students. These students are either born into a family that does not speak English at home or live in a home where English deviates significantly from the language structures used for instruction in schools. These children may have arrived recently from other countries or may have been born in Canada but experience only their native language at home. An example of the latter would be First Nations students who speak one of the official native languages at home. Both groups need focused support to help them attain proficiency in English. Over time, many children learn English fluently at school and continue to speak their original language at home, becoming completely bilingual. Naturally, when the first language is close to English, it is easier to become bilingual, with the average time for achieving this goal being between four and seven years.

According to the 2006 census, 98 percent of Canadians can speak one or both of the two official languages. In addition, English or French is spoken at least regularly at home by 94 percent of Canadians and most often at home by 89 percent of the population, sometimes in combination with a non-official language. Since 2001, the Chinese languages have become the third largest language group in Canada, with 3 percent of the population reporting a Chinese language as their mother tongue (Statistics Canada, 2006). Obviously, students learning English as a second or subsequent language are a diverse group and it is difficult to isolate all of the variables related to success and speed of learning English. It is also clear that schools are providing an important linguistic function by helping children become fluent users of English.

In the past, students were immersed in English-speaking classrooms and left to learn the new language at their own pace. Unfortunately, this proved ineffective over the long run, as many of these students did not graduate from high school (Spangenberg-Urbaschat & Pritchard, 1994). Research has shown that it is important to acknowledge and respect the first language of students, as it is part of their identity and their culture. Respecting a student's need and desire to maintain his or her native language is key to their successfully learning a new language (Anderson-Mejias, 2002). It is believed that better results come from respecting students' first language by helping them develop proficiency in that language while simultaneously learning English (Freeman & Freeman, 1993). Methods of maintaining pride in heritage language skills include communicating with parents, valuing students' first language, and engaging in early reading.

Teacher Voice 11.1

Second or subsequent language learners have unique needs in terms of the language arts. They may have knowledge of several other languages beside their mother tongue, although language acquisition may not have occurred in a formal setting. These students may have inconsistent schooling because of war, natural disasters, or displacement, and any gaps in their first language literacy need to be addressed. These students also bring different approaches and expectations about learning that will influence their classroom experiences in Canada.

Kim Henrie
M.Ed. candidate and LINC instructor

The following are some suggestions for communicating with parents:

- To include parents of all cultures in activities, schools can host welcoming events (such as a picnic) early in the school year. Encourage the extended family to attend and enjoy the event in an informal setting (Anderson-Mejias, 2002).

- Teachers may wish to arrange home visits with reticent parents who do not attend functions at the school.
- Invite parents or other family members to the classroom to observe their children. A system of rotating visits can help build respectful relationships. It helps students who are learning English to see their classmates and teachers interact positively with their parents.
- Reassure parents that their children are making progress.
- It can be helpful to invite parents of ESL students to come to the school an hour early on an event night. The teacher can demonstrate a typical ESL lesson for them to help them understand the current approach to language learning, which is probably very different from their expectations or their own experiences.
- In some instances, it may be necessary to have a translator participate in parent-teacher meetings. It is generally wise to use an adult rather than a child as a translator, if possible. If not possible, try to use an older sibling rather than the child who is enrolled in the class (Anderson-Mejias, 2002).
- Inform parents and students that the ability to speak a heritage language is a positive rather than a negative. Recognize that teaching English in school may imply that it is "better" than the student's first language.
- Try to have a "language awareness" minute. Ask ESL students to share a puzzle or expressions from their language to help build understanding of different language structures (Anderson-Mejias, 2002). Alternatively, have students write in their first language so they can share their "other voice" (Anderson-Mejias, 2002). Keep these alternate activities short, remembering that the intention is to show respect for the multitude of languages in the world.
- Invite parents or students themselves to share special events from their culture.
- Contrast the sounds of English with the sounds of the native language. Have older students consult the internet for vocal tracks that illustrate the sounds of various languages (Hornberger, 1998).
- Show compassion for the emotional and personal aspects that accompany learning to express ideas in a new language (Kouritzin, 2000).

Students' ability to read and write in their first language can be an important foundation for second or subsequent language learning. It is equally helpful for ESL students to see that the teacher and the class value the language they have already acquired. Suggestions of ways to convey this valuing include the following:

- Post signs and other print written in students' first language in the classroom.
- Ask students to bring in favourite books written in their first language and add these to the classroom library.
- Try to locate a tutor who speaks the first language of the students so he or she can talk to the students and read to them in their first language when necessary. This can be a parent volunteer, a community member, or an older student.
- If another student in the class speaks the language of the newcomer, place their seats together and allow discussion to occur during work periods.

- Encourage students to write in their first language using the same writing process as the rest of the class. Encourage them to share their writing with the class and, if necessary, ask a tutor to translate.
- View videos or documentaries of the students' previous home.

The key to successful bilingual reading programs is teaching students to read in their first language initially. Next, we provide additional information about how schools can implement such programming.

Strategies for Teaching Linguistically Diverse Students Since instructional programs work best when they create opportunities for students to develop proficiency in their first language, schools must try to make provisions for this type of instruction. Studies that compare bilingual instruction and English-only instruction demonstrate that language-minority students instructed in their native language as well as in English perform better, on average, on measures of English reading proficiency than do language-minority students instructed in English only (August & Shanahan, 2006). The International Reading Association (www.reading.org/General/CurrentResearch/Standards/LanguageArtsStandards.aspx) asserts that literacy learning is easiest for students when schools provide initial literacy instruction in their first language. Such instruction is consistent with the learning principles of building on students' strengths and connecting unfamiliar material to the familiar. Literacy skills developed in the first language can then be applied to learning to read and write in a second language, which generally results in students becoming literate and gaining proficiency in two languages.

Proficiency in the dominant language (English) is the goal of language and literacy instruction, but bilingualism or multilingualism is also a desirable outcome. Instruction in another language initially must be accompanied by the learning of oral English, as English is essential to success in every other subject as well as to economic and educational opportunities beyond schooling (August & Shanahan, 2006; Snow, Burns, & Griffin, 1998). Once they have a sufficient grasp of oral English and of basic reading in their first language, they can transfer that knowledge to learning to read in English. The key lies in knowing when to start reading instruction in English. Research suggests that students should be able to read relatively proficiently in their native language, being able to interpret and draw inferences from text (Fillmore & Valdez, 1986; Gunning, 2005). English literacy development, however, is a dynamic process and is strongly influenced by individual differences in general language proficiency, age, English oral proficiency, cognitive abilities, previous learning, and the similarities and differences between the first language and English.

While instruction in the key components of reading (phonemic awareness, phonics, fluency, vocabulary, and text comprehension) is necessary and important, oral language is also critical. Concerns have been expressed that at times the oral language component of language learning is either overlooked or insufficiently stressed (August & Shanahan, 2006). Well-developed oral proficiency in English is associated with stronger comprehension and writing skills among ESL students. Thus, oral proficiency and the ability to read in the first language can be used as a strong foundation to facilitate literacy development in English.

There are, of course, some difficulties and uncertainties associated with teaching ESL students to read in their native language. There may be no qualified teacher who speaks the first language of the students. If a teacher is available, the regular classroom teacher must spend time planning activities to enhance the students' progress based on themes and units being studied in other areas of the curriculum. There are many variables that affect the progress ESL students can reasonably make. For instance, ESL students with learning disabilities often struggle; in other cases, shyness can prevent some students from trying to speak English in public. As a general guideline, it takes about two years for students to become socially proficient in English, with younger students requiring less time than older ones (Cummins, 2001). However, it may take much longer for students to catch up to native English speakers in their ability to use English effectively for academic purposes. The research on the development of English literacy strongly suggests that adequate assessments are essential to gauge the individual strengths and weaknesses of language-minority students, making placement decisions and tailoring instruction to meet students' needs. Unfortunately, existing assessments are frequently inadequate in terms of providing accurate information (August & Shanahan, 2006). Table 11.3 lists some strategies that teachers can use when working with students who are acquiring English as a subsequent language. Table 11.4 lists strategies that are specific to the reading process.

Table 11.3 Strategies to Enhance English Language Learning

1. Increase the amount of oral language in the classroom. Teachers can structure conversations about the weather, sports, current events, out-of-school activities, and anything else of interest. Encourage students to question each other and to share opinions and experiences. Thoughtful teacher participation can ensure that new vocabulary is introduced and reinforced in a natural context.
2. Establish multiple opportunities for students to work collaboratively with peers. ESL students are generally less reluctant to speak when in a smaller group and can more readily make themselves understood in this context. Explicitly develop a class spirit of mutual support and group work.
3. When holding discussions or lessons or when reading a book, try to use pictures, maps, demonstrations, role plays, and models to enhance comprehension. For instance, use pictures of the tundra and a map of Canada to introduce a story about being lost in the North.
4. Use print to expand oral language learning by labelling items in the room and writing directions, schedules, and homework on the board. Repeat information aloud while writing. Keep information clear and concise when providing instructions. Demonstrate homework examples.
5. Make use of field trips and planning sessions during which language is clearly contextualized. Write all conclusions on the board while saying them aloud.
6. Make use of existing knowledge that ESL students may have about the computer and the media.
7. Establish a peer coaching system in which students have a "go to" person they can consult prior to asking the teacher for clarification or assistance.
8. When a new ESL student enters your room, accept the "silent period" while remaining positive, receptive, and encouraging.

Table 11.4 Selected Reading Strategies for ESL Students

1. Use the Language Experience Approach (LEA)

This approach to reading is especially suited to ESL students since the reading materials are created from the students' own background and experiences using their existing language patterns. Students read the sections that they dictate, so unfamiliar syntax and vocabulary should be less constraining. The pre-writing discussion plays an especially significant role in extending learning. Specifically, the discussion provides an opportunity to use new vocabulary that will require clarification and repetition. Vocabulary learning and comprehension are also enhanced by the use of pictures or models. Immediately after the discussion of new vocabulary, when the students are creating the story that the teacher is writing, students are likely to incorporate some of these words into the creation of the group story. Below is an example of an adapted LEA lesson, with readers referred to Chapter 5, Comprehension of Narrative Text, for additional information about LEA.

Sample Adapted LEA Lesson

Introduce a large picture of a winter scene in which many typical winter activities are happening.

Discuss the picture in a very simple way, using concrete terms such as *skating*, *tobogganing*, *shovelling snow*, and *building a snow house.*

Connect the discussion to students' personal experiences. Do not correct their language but always use a strong model of Standard English and repeat terms and vocabulary regularly while pointing to the activity in the picture.

2. Use Materials with Predictable Language Patterns

These materials are designed to be readily understood and are best read aloud, with students participating in choral reading of the patterned component. Some of these materials can be found as picture books. It can be helpful to vary the type of pattern employed when using these materials regularly.

Types of Predictable Books

Cumulative story Each time a new event occurs, all previous events in the story are repeated (e.g., *Little Pink Pig, The Rose in My Garden*).

Familiar sequence Organized by recognizable themes such as days of the week, seasons, or numbers (e.g., *Today is Monday, Come Out and Play, Little Mouse*).

Pattern stories Scenes are repeated with some variation (e.g., *The Three Billy Goats Gruff, The Little Red Hen*).

Question and answer The same or similar questions are repeated throughout the story (e.g., Whose Footprints? *Brown Bear, Brown Bear, What Do You See?*).

Repetition of phrase Word order in a phrase or sentence is repeated (e.g., *Goodnight Moon, Chicken Soup with Rice*).

Rhyme Rhyming words, refrains, or patterns are used throughout the story (e.g., *Jake Baked the Cake, Flap Your Wings*).

3. Use Wordless Picture Books to Create Stories

Wordless picture books in which a strong storyline is delivered through illustrations enable ESL students to draw from their personal experiences and create a story at their ability level using personal vocabulary, no matter how limited. This approach allows students to use self-expression and creative thinking skills in an authentic language development activity. These materials provide the teacher with a degree of flexibility that can be used to fit the needs of ESL students. The choice of book is critical, as it needs to be interesting and generate a good deal of oral language. The picture books listed below can be "read" with varying degrees of depth and breadth, which makes them appropriate for many ESL students. A sample lesson for creating stories using wordless picture books is included below.

(continued)

Table 11.4 Selected Reading Strategies for ESL Students (*continued*)

A Selection of Wordless Picture Books

Briggs, R. (2011). *The snowman*. New York, NY: Random House Books.

Carle, E. (1991). *Do you want to be my friend?* Toronto, ON: HarperCollins Publishers.

Cottin, M. (2008). *The black book of colors.* Toronto, ON: Groundwood Books.

DePaola, T. (2001). *Pancakes for breakfast.* Boston, MA: Houghton Mifflin Harcourt.

Graham, A. (2003). *Full moon soup: A wordless book that's brimful of stories!* London, UK: Chrysalis Children's Books.

Hutchins, P. (1971). *Rosie's walk*. New York, NY: Aladdin.

Mayer, M. (2003). *A boy, a dog, a frog, and a friend.* New York, NY: Puffin.

Mayer, M. (2005). *There are monsters everywhere.*New York, NY: Penguin Group.

Mayer, M. (2011). *Octopus soup*. Tarrytown, NY: Marshall Cavendish Children's Books.

Tan, S. (2007). *The arrival.* New York, NY: Arthur A. Levine Books.

Sample Lesson for Creating Stories Using Wordless Picture Books

Choose the book and preview it with students. Let them observe what is happening in the pictures. Encourage them to listen to each other.

Identify core vocabulary for the story.

Compose the story together. Let students name the characters and ask questions to prompt them to dictate the story. It may be necessary to modify the answers to conform to Standard English. After each sentence is written, read it aloud. This task does not necessarily have to be accomplished in a single lesson. In fact, it is helpful to come back the next day and reiterate the story and what has already been written.

Read the story several times. First the teacher reads, then students read along with the teacher, and then students take turns reading individually.

Involve family members by typing the story and sending it home for students to read aloud to them. Ask parents to sign the story, provide a comment, and send it back to the school.

Follow-up activities can include the following:

- Asking comprehension questions
- Making flashcards of sight words
- Teaching grammatical structures (e.g., past-tense verbs)
- Reviewing phonics (e.g., finding all words that begin with a target sound)
- Teaching antonyms and synonyms for words in the story

4. Use Listening Comprehension Activities

The teacher reads a selection and the students follow the printed word either on an individual copy or on a screen. During the reading, the teacher pauses so students can ask questions and discuss the story. The story can be above students' independent reading level but not above their listening level. The discussion should improve comprehension of text, enhance vocabulary acquisition, and provide more confidence with expression in English.

Caution It is problematic to accept any diagnosis of learning disabilities or cognitive exceptionality for students who have been learning English for less than five years, as any genuine learning problems are probably masked by students' inadequately developed proficiency in English. Verbal and achievement tests also are likely to

seriously underestimate minority students' academic potential. Accepting such results can be very damaging to minority students' future academic prospects as well as to their self-esteem. Beware of the cycle of poor achievement → poor self-esteem → poor achievement.

WORKING WITH STUDENTS WHO ARE AT RISK

THE TERM *AT RISK* REFERS TO STUDENTS WHO ARE LIKELY TO STRUGGLE OR "FAIL" in school or their future life because of life circumstances. Many factors may contribute to students being at risk, including poverty, family violence or instability, and cognitive difficulties. While for some students only one of these challenges is sufficient to place them at risk, others may experience several challenges. When more than one factor is present, there is a compounding effect and the likelihood for difficulty increases significantly. Students who are struggling with their sexual orientation can also be considered at risk, as anxiety can compromise their ability to learn. Teachers can play an important role in countering the negative impact of these factors. Next, we describe specific instructional approaches and techniques that can be used when working with students who live in poverty and who may be struggling with their sexual orientation.

Working with Students Who Live in Poverty

The number of Canadians who live in poverty is difficult to define in absolute terms, as there is no standard measure. Some disturbing statistics are available, however. According to the 2010 Report Card on Child and Family Poverty in Canada, more than 1 million (or nearly 1 in 10) children live in poverty. Another widely accepted measure is the low income cut-off (LICO). According to the LICO, families who spend 70 percent or more of their gross income on food, shelter, and clothing live in poverty. Data show that the rate of child and family poverty in Canada declined slightly to 9.1 percent in 2008 from 11.9 percent in 1989. This change is less than expected given the high level of income growth for the wealthy from 1998 to 2008. In addition, these numbers do not adequately demonstrate the shameful situation of First Nations communities, where the young are a high proportion of the population and 1 in every 4 children is growing up in poverty (Report Card on Child and Family Poverty in Canada, 2010).

Since the recession of 2008–2009, even more economic pressure and insecurity have been placed on lower-income families. During this period, the employment numbers plummeted and the number of unemployed (including those who do and do not receive employment insurance) rose. There were rising debt loads and bankruptcies and increased use of food banks across the country. Today, the cost of basic food, housing, and fuel continues to rise in Canada and around the world. When families experience such economic pressures, students can be at risk (Leroy & Symes, 2001). Not surprisingly, students who live in poverty systematically tend to rank lower than their wealthier peers on all measures of school success (Flessa, 2007; Statistics Canada, 2002).

Some of the factors related to poverty that may place students at risk academically include parents who are very young or single or who have a low level of education, unemployment, family abuse, neglect, substance abuse in the home, dangerous neighbourhoods, transiency, and inadequate or inappropriate educational experiences. Students who live in these circumstances often demonstrate behaviours that may help identify them as being at risk. These behaviours may include one or more of the following: delayed language or reading development, aggression, violence, social withdrawal, substance abuse, irregular school attendance, and depression. These students may not complete assignments, study for tests, or appear able to concentrate or focus. In addition, they may be unwilling or unable to interact with peers and adults in an effective manner. Such behaviours not only affect the learning of the specific student in question, but also may affect the learning of other students.

Without conscious efforts to break the achievement gap, schools become institutions where social inequalities are maintained by systematically reinforcing and reproducing social and academic advantages for the wealthy and disadvantages for the poor (Bowles, Gintis, & Groves, 2005; Flessa, 2007). Some schools have experienced success working with students who live in poverty. We describe some of the schoolwide efforts and the instructional approaches used in these schools next.

Positive Attitudes and Building Self-Esteem in an Environment of Success Teachers and schools can help provide students who live in poverty with a sense of warmth, care, and stability. Students tend to thrive in consistent environments where they know exactly what to expect from their teachers and class community. Being poor can be a source of embarrassment at best and a debilitating factor for self-esteem at worst. Teachers need to be very sensitive and careful to avoid addressing economic capability or incapability in front of the class.

Some research has suggested that when students feel a sense of school community, their achievement is enhanced (Battistich et al., 1995). Rather than focusing on what students lack, the focus should be on what they possess. Such a resolution may be difficult to achieve for predominantly middle-class teachers.

Teacher Voice 11.2

> When I was teaching in an inner-city school in the early years of my career, I had a student who had to go to court for an out-of-school infraction. The boy was about 12 years old and had difficulty focusing in the classroom. Some might refer to him as a "behaviour problem" although he was likeable overall. After his court date, I was surprised when the social worker came to school to tell me that on the witness stand the boy had stated that, "The only person who cares about me is my teacher." Although I cared, I was humbled because I often went home at night exhausted from working with him. His home life, however, contained abuse and poverty and his nights were as difficult as his days.
>
> Anne Elliott

Early Education Programs In the fight against poverty, there is growing recognition of the importance of early childhood education, through which students can have an early start in developing critical background knowledge and learning skills. Experience with these skill sets is especially important for children from economically disadvantaged homes (O'Connor & Fernandez, 2006). Children who participate in high-quality early intervention programs are more likely to graduate high school and enter university or college (Sawhill & McLananan, 2006).

Connecting to the Community Schools do not operate effectively independently. Rather, they need interact, exchange, and consult with the environments in which they operate. Successful schools have a clearly defined and stated school mission as well as a secure and safe environment for learning. They communicate their goals effectively within the school as well as with parents so that a sense of partnership and respectful community relations are established. Such schools believe that raising and educating children is a shared and complementary endeavour. This approach requires a strong school principal who sets high expectations for students and teachers alike. Such a leader also establishes and conveys to teachers that the "no excuses, it's my job" belief must prevail (Corbett, Wilson, & Williams, 2002). The focus needs to be on student learning rather than on instruction per se (Payne, 2005; Pellino, 2007). In other words, teachers are not permitted to blame students when they fail to achieve. Instead, they are expected to find solutions to do whatever is necessary to ensure that every last child achieves at his or her highest potential (Kannapel & Clements, 2005).

Providing a Balanced Program Economically disadvantaged students tend to do poorly on norm-referenced skill tests (Flessa, 2007, Statistics Canada, 2002), tempting some teachers to "teach to the test." This can occur quite easily in Canada, where schools and teachers are under pressure to demonstrate strong results on standardized mathematics, reading, and writing tests. These skills, however, are most effectively taught in context, with authentic tasks and extended practice. It is also important to avoid neglecting higher-order thinking skills in favour of very basic skills. It is imperative that students from disadvantaged homes receive excellent teaching, especially in light of their sometimes limited background experiences and home supports.

Children living in poverty tend to have different schema than those who are considered "mainstream" as a result of different societal norms and rules (Payne, 2005). Three primary areas appear to be affected by poverty: writing skills, planning and predicting, and organizational skills. Payne suggests using constructivist principles while teaching with explicit instruction focusing on the following three stages of the learning process:

Input strategies for addressing the quality and quantity of information (i.e., thinking and organizing material that is often taken for granted)

1. Setting appropriate goals
2. Setting timelines
3. Identifying parts of the task
4. Reflecting and planning before doing
5. Exploring data systematically

Elaboration strategies for processing and applying new information

1. Summarizing
2. Creating a précis
3. Making connections between prior knowledge and new material

Output strategies for communicating acquired information

1. Writing formats
2. Multi-modal presentations (see Chapter 10, Redefining Literacy: Integrating the New Literacies and a Critical Response to Popular Culture in Your Classroom)

Counteracting the Grade 4 Slump

Sometimes students perform quite well in language skills in grades 1 to 3 yet "slump" in grade 4 (Chall, Jacobs, & Baldwin, 1990). At this time, they begin to have difficulty understanding, writing, and spelling some of the more abstract words they encounter. This inability begins a downward spiral, as these skills underlie achievement in reading and writing. While the reason for the slump is not entirely clear, there is speculation that some poorly educated parents are no longer able to provide their children with assistance and support at home (Gunning, 2005).

Schools must fill this gap by teaching vocabulary and concepts that are needed to cope with various units of study. While all students require this instruction, it is particularly important for those students with limited background knowledge and academic support at home. Since students from disadvantaged homes tend not to read at home for pleasure, the opportunity to do so at school and to sense the power of story as a source of pleasure is also very helpful (Price, 2010). Additional opportunities for reading in the content areas are also recommended for producing higher vocabulary scores (Gunning, 2005). Teachers who are aware of the grade 4 slump can make concerted efforts to prevent a downward spiral from starting, which is likely to be more successful than subsequent efforts to reverse it!

Diversity in Sexual Orientation

Teachers must help students develop sensitivity to those whose sexual orientation is different from theirs. Students typically become aware of their sexual orientation around 11 or 12 years of age and some discover an alliance with the LGBT (lesbian, gay, bisexual, transsexual) group. Puberty is often a difficult time for many students, but can be especially so for those who must also sort through feelings of sexual diversity in what are often perceived to be unsupportive and hostile school environments. Many of these students also feel that they cannot discuss issues of sexual diversity with their parents (Ueno, 2005). This anxiety may be exacerbated by the bullying and social isolation that can occur in a homophobic environment. Indeed, these students may experience emotional and social repercussions that are so distressing that their ability to learn becomes severely limited.

For some students, verbal harassment, ostracism, and even physical abuse can become a daily routine resulting in isolation and depression. Disparaging terms such as *gay* or *fag* are often used to taunt individuals. Homophobia and its accompanying behaviours are an extremely destructive force in any learning environment; in extreme cases, victims engage in self-harming behaviours, including suicide (Hatzenbuehler, 2011; Marshal et al., 2008).

Some school boards in Canada have adopted proactive measures to confront and hopefully eliminate homophobia among students. For instance, the Vancouver School Board held an anti-homophobia conference in 2010 to address homophobia and gender stereotypes in their schools (LifeSiteNews.com, April 6, 2010). It is imperative that teachers respond to homophobia and ensure that all students be able to learn in a physically and emotionally safe environment (Eisenberg & Resnick, 2006). Positive behaviours that teachers can adopt include the following:

- Refuse to accept bullying or intolerance in the classroom.
- Explicitly discuss and demystify the disparaging language that degrades LGBT groups and forbid the use of these terms in the classroom.
- Assist students in establishing classroom rules for name-calling and bullying and agree on the consequences associated with breaking these rules.
- Discuss the fact that sexuality is not something people choose but rather an innate orientation.
- Signal support for LGBT students (e.g., post a rainbow flag or pink triangle).
- Initiate discussions about homophobia with colleagues and establishing a school-wide position.
- Refer students to appropriate specialists (counsellor, psychologist) if there is a suspicion that they may harm themselves or hold suicidal thoughts.
- Avoid language that assumes that all students come from two-gendered families.
- Provide students with access to literature and other resources that promote understanding and acceptance of LGBT individuals (see Table 11.5).

Table 11.5 Resources to Promote Understanding and Acceptance of LGBT Individuals

Films

Sticks and Stones (17 minutes). Features students between ages 5 and 12 years talking about their experiences with name-calling and bullying, as well as a short animated sequence about the history of derogatory slang. National Film Board of Canada (www.nfb.ca).

One of Them (25 minutes). A group of teenagers is planning a Human Rights Day. Controversy around the inclusion of the issue of homophobia emerges in this short drama. National Film Board of Canada (www.nfb.ca).

In Other Words (25 minutes). Explores the origins of homophobic words, how young people feel about them, and how to overcome the hurt and anger they cause. Alberta Teachers' Association (www.teachers.ab.ca).

Books

Bantle, L. (2009). *David inside out.* New York, NY: Henry Holt and Company.

Brand, D. (2005). *What we all long for.* New York, NY: Vintage Books.

Holland, I. (1993). *The man without a face*. Newport Beach, CA: Tween Publishing.

Moore, P. (2007). *Hero*. New York, NY: Hyperion.

Ryan, S. (2003*). Empress of the world*. New York, NY: Speak.

WORKING WITH STUDENTS WITH LEARNING EXCEPTIONALITIES

REFLECTIVE ACTIVITY 2

Think about your previous interactions with students with special learning needs.

- How did these students' learning needs affect their ability to participate in the language arts?
- What programming or other provisions were made for these students?
- What additional accommodations or modifications might you suggest for these students?
- How did the other students respond to these individuals?

Working with students with learning exceptionalities is an important consideration for all classroom teachers. The term *exceptionality* refers to students with disabilities as well as to those who are gifted. However, the proportion of students with disabilities—including those with sensory and physical handicaps, learning and intellectual challenges, and emotional and behavioural disorders—is greater than the proportion of those who are gifted. Approximately 4.6 percent of all elementary school students in Canada have some form of disability (Statistics Canada, 2006).

Inclusion in mainstream schools is based on the principle of normalization established by Wolfensberger (1975), which emphasizes that all people, regardless of ability, should live and work in environments that are as "normal" as possible. According to the Centre for Inclusive Education, people with disabilities should be viewed through a lens of sameness rather than through a lens that focuses on differences (www.edu.uwo.ca/inclusive_education).

In Canada, the majority of students with disabilities (approximately 57 percent) are situated in regular classroom settings. The remaining students will receive some form of special education, with many (27 percent) being withdrawn on a part-time basis to a special education classroom or resource room (Statistics Canada, 2006). Accordingly, working with students with disabilities is an important consideration for all classroom teachers. Research supports the positive and supportive role of the principal and other school administrators as being significant in ensuring the success of inclusion practices (DiPetta et al., 2010; Praisner, 2003). Below, we review evidence-based instructional approaches and teaching techniques for working with students with high-frequency disabilities as well as with those who are gifted.

Students with Learning Disabilities

Learning disabilities comprise the largest proportion of exceptionality, accounting for the majority of all students identified as exceptional in Canada. More boys than girls are identified as having learning disabilities. Learning disabilities can range in severity, resulting in varied learning profiles across students. Learning disabilities affect the acquisition, organization, retention, understanding, or use of verbal and non-verbal information. Accordingly, students with learning disabilities often experience difficulties with the acquisition and use of oral language (e.g., listening comprehension, speaking), reading (e.g., decoding, comprehension), written language (e.g., spelling, written expression), and mathematics (e.g., computation, problem solving). Some students with learning disabilities may demonstrate poor social skills and experience difficulties interacting with their peers. Learning disabilities are distinct from intellectual disabilities such as mild intellectual disability (MID). Specifically, students with learning disabilities demonstrate at least average abilities essential for thinking and reasoning (Fletcher, Lyon, Fuchs, & Barnes, 2007; Hallahan, Kauffman, McIntyre, & Mykota, 2010; Hutchinson, 2010; Learning Disabilities Association of Ontario, 2009).

The term *dyslexia* is sometimes used to refer to a severe impairment in the ability to read (Mathes & Fletcher, 2008; Learning Disabilities Association of Ontario, 2009). Most students with learning disabilities demonstrate significant difficulties with reading, especially with respect to developing the phonological skills needed to understand letter-sound associations. Other students demonstrate difficulties comprehending materials. While some of these students also struggle with decoding, a smaller number are proficient decoders but demonstrate little understanding or memory for the text. These students often read without any prosody—that is, without change of tone, logical phrasing, pacing, or rhythm. Reading and writing are interrelated skills.

Students who experience reading difficulties often experience writing ones as well. The term *dysgraphia* is sometimes used to refer to difficulties in handwriting, spelling, or composition (Learning Disabilities Association of Ontario, 2009). Students with dysgraphia may present extremely slow or illegible printing or handwriting with numerous spelling errors (in part, reflecting difficulties with letter-sound associations).

Students with learning disabilities can experience academic success when provided with appropriate supports and interventions, especially when intervention is provided in the primary grades (National Reading Panel, 2000; Ontario Ministry of Education, 2005; Snow et al., 1998). Without appropriate intervention, reading and learning difficulties tend to plague students throughout their school years and be exponential in nature, perpetuating a continuum of negative reading experiences (i.e., the Matthew effect; Stanovich, 1986). In these cases, individuals with learning disabilities experience higher rates of dropout, unemployment and underemployment, incarceration, and social-emotional difficulties (Berninger, 2006).

Not surprisingly, there is no single program or intervention that is effective for all students with learning disabilities, requiring teachers to be reflective of individual students' learning needs and vigilant in monitoring their response to intervention. In general, programs are most effective when they include explicit or direct strategy instruction as well as the provision of metacognitive information (O'Conner & Vadasy, 2011). Many of the reading interventions used with students with learning disabilities mirror those used routinely in the classroom, with the exception that the instruction is slower and more intense. For example, students with reading disabilities can benefit from intensive phonological awareness training (Chapter 2, Listening, Speaking, and Beyond), reading by analogy training (Chapter 4, Word Learning), and instruction in evidence-based comprehension strategies (Chapter 5, Comprehension of Narrative Text, and Chapter 6, Reading Comprehension Strategies for Non-Fiction: Reading in the Content Areas). Other times, these students may benefit from participating in supplemental programs such as Reading Recovery (Clay, 1987, 1993), Book Buddies (Invernizzi, 2000), and cross-age peer tutoring (Topping & Bryce, 2004), all of which are described in Table 11.6.

Students with Attention Deficit Hyperactivity Disorder

Attention deficit hyperactivity disorder (ADHD) is one of the most commonly diagnosed disorders in children today, involving between 3 and 5 percent of all students, with boys representing more than half of all diagnoses (Arns, de Ridder, Strehl, Breteler, & Coenen, 2009; Radar, McCauley, & Callen, 2009). The primary symptoms of ADHD are difficulty in focusing and sustaining attention, impulsivity, and difficult social interactions and peer relations. Although ADHD is distinct from that of a learning disability, some students may present both disorders. Students with any combination of these disorders require special assistance, patience, and understanding to learn in the inclusive classroom. It is critical that teaches refrain from "blaming" students with ADHD when they are acting in ways that are symptomatic of the disorder. It is much more productive to find ways to work with these children rather than try to change them (Edmunds & Edmunds, 2008; Hutchinson, 2010). Table 11.7 provides some general teaching techniques that teachers can implement when working with students with learning disabilities and ADHD.

Student Voice 11.1

There is a boy in my class with attention deficit disorder and he finds it hard to concentrate and read. It is a good idea to have students with different learning abilities in the classroom because it can help everyone learn. When the teacher needs to explain something to a student who doesn't understand, she might explain something that you do not understand too. The boy in my class is also really good at thinking about ideas for writing—he is very creative and that is his learning strength.

Neha
Grade 6 student

Table 11.6 Sample Reading Intervention Programs

Program	Description	Instructional Process
Reading Recovery	Empirically supported and used worldwide (Schwartz, Askew, & Gómez-Bellengé, 2007) Intended for lowest 20 percent of grade 1 students Students receive 30 minutes of individual, supplemental instruction for 12 to 20 weeks Reading Recovery teachers are trained specialists Demonstrated learning gains until the end of grade 2 and beyond (D'Agostino & Murphy, 2004) Increasing evidence of application in classroom instruction (Iverson, Tunmer, & Chapman, 2005)	Student reads familiar book (enhancing fluency and confidence) Student reads less familiar book (usually introduced in previous session) Teacher completes running record (Chapter 3, Assessing and Evaluating Your Students as Language Users) Student completes word study using evidence-based strategies such as reading by analogy (based on error analysis) Teacher assists student in writing response to story New text is introduced
Book Buddies	Empirically supported (Meier & Invernizzi, 2001) Community members assist struggling grade 1 and 2 readers Also effective for students who are learning English as a subsequent language Tutors receive concentrated training by teachers or Book Buddies coordinators (reading specialists) in the use of evidence-based reading strategies Students participate in two 45-minute tutoring sessions per week Sessions are usually held after school Older students may also serve as book buddies	Book Buddies coordinator or teacher recruits volunteers from community Tutors receive training before and during reading program Sessions consist of reading, writing, and phonics activities in which students (a) reread 3 to 4 familiar books, (b) participate in word study, (c) write dictated sentences from text or provide reader response, and (d) read a new book (buddy may use choral or echo reading to support initial attempts) Coordinators provide tutors with ongoing feedback and instructional guidance
Peer Tutoring	Empirically supported (Jacobson et al., 2001) Intended for struggling kindergarten to grade 8 readers and English language learners Requires advance preparation and teacher supervision and feedback Cross-age peer tutoring with older peer is more effective than same-age peer tutoring Tutors receive advanced instruction Sessions are usually 20 to 40 minutes in duration and occur three (or more) times per week.	Student tutors meet with teachers to plan instructional sessions (Monday–Tuesday) Teachers model effective reading and instructional strategies to tutors (e.g., question answering, imagery, reading by analogy) Tutors practise target reading strategies and review identified texts for younger students Tutors meet with younger students to read text (Wednesday–Friday) Tutors submit outcome of tutoring sessions (Friday) Teachers provide tutors with directed feedback for subsequent sessions (Monday–Tuesday)

Table 11.7 Teaching Techniques for Working with Students with Learning Disabilities and ADHD

- Provide interesting and meaningful tasks and assignments.
- Provide choice of materials and activities.
- Allow mobility in the classroom.
- Encourage students to confer with each other.
- Provide directions carefully (i.e., speak slowly while writing them on the board, have one or more students read them aloud, discuss directions, maintain eye contact with students).
- Break tasks into small sequential parts.
- Provide students with schedules for assignments and help them maintain them.
- Ensure that students have the necessary materials for rotary classes, homework, and in-class activities before starting.
- Communicate with parents on a regular basis (e.g., weekly letters, regular phone calls about successes, webpage for homework and assignments).
- Get sufficient rest so you can be patient during the day!

Slow Learners

It is well known that students learn at different rates and present varied abilities. Slower learners generally need extra time to complete tasks and benefit when school tasks are augmented at home. These students also tend to respond positively when appropriate incentives are provided to persevere with tasks (Skaalvik, 2004). Finally, it is imperative that all children, but especially those who are slow learners, have a nutritional breakfast before coming to school.

Typically, slow learners are immature in their relations with others. They have difficulty solving complex problems and cannot readily transfer what they have learned from one task to another. They also have difficulty following multi-step directions. These students acquire reading abilities at a much slower rate (Cooter & Cooter, 2004). Long-term goals are challenging, as are time management and sustained concentration. For some students, these challenges may be accentuated in particular subject areas. These students consistently score low on achievement tests and may display anxiety related to poor self-image.

Caution Slow learners differ from reluctant learners in that they genuinely want to succeed but experience difficulties with the learning process. Reluctant learners are often unmotivated and unco-operative. Teachers need to be careful to distinguish between these two types of learners, as common symptoms represent distinct underlying differences.

Assisting Slow Learners Three major components emerge for teaching slow learners: (1) making the abstract concrete, (2) fostering generalization, and (3) facilitating automatization.

According to Gunning (2005), it is helpful to remember that these students are "more so" students who need the same instruction as their peers but to a greater extent. Some methods that will help include the following:

- Provide a quiet place for work where teachers can observe students and provide regular motivation and support (do not isolate these students at the back of the classroom or behind a barrier).
- Make information as concrete as possible so they can "see it," "touch it," and complete it independently.
- Ask questions of students while they are completing a task.
- Allow for success and praise it.
- Assign students to collaborative groups carefully, ensuring that partners are patient and positive.
- Learn about the students' interests.
- Keep in-class tasks and homework assignments manageable and brief.
- Provide additional time to accomplish tasks when appropriate.
- Suggest to parents that there be activity times before and after homework.
- Teach students how to use a calendar or day planner and help them maintain it.

Reluctant Learners and Reluctant Readers

Reluctant learners are satisfied with just "getting by" and seemingly do not care about achieving in school (Protheroe, 2004), although they may appear to have the potential to excel. Generally, they fail to complete tasks, do not respond to challenges, and believe themselves to be poor students. There are several beliefs that hinder the self-efficacy students need to achieve (Dicintio & Gee, 1999). These include a belief that school work is irrelevant to their lives, a belief that assignments are below their ability level, and frustration about keeping pace with their peers and simply giving up. Other factors include a fear of failure, a desire to appear "cool," and a desire for teacher attention. Also of concern are reluctance issues related to emotional distress such as anxiety or depression (Protheroe, 2004). In extreme cases, the reluctance can be related to rebellion against parents who are pressing students to excel (Shore, 2001).

Teachers can help reluctant readers by:

- Teaching them how to study effectively, how to manage time well, and how to summarize reading material
- Providing them with materials they like to read, such as scary stories, comics or graphic novels, magazines about popular culture, funny books, series books, and books about animals (Worthy, Moorman, & Turner, 1999)
- Reading dynamic Read Aloud books to the whole class and then offering to find a similar book for reluctant readers (Jobe & Dayton-Sakari, 1999)
- Encouraging parents to read aloud to their children at home
- Encouraging school library acquisitions of popular materials (Worthy, Moorman, & Turner, 1999).

Assistive Technology

Teachers should be aware of the benefits associated with assistive technology when working with students who experience difficulties with reading or writing. Assistive technology includes any technology—whether acquired commercially off the shelf, modified, or customized—that increases, maintains, or improves the functional capabilities of individuals with exceptionalities or enables them to access previously inaccessible learning opportunities (Ontario Ministry of Education, 2005). It is most often implemented with students in the junior and intermediate grades as a form of accommodation or modification (Edyburn, 2003, 2004; MacArthur, Ferretti, Okolo, & Cavalier, 2001). For instance, students with reading disabilities can use text recognition software such as Kurzweil 3000 or Premier to decode text, while speech-to-text programs such as Dragon Naturally Speaking or graphic programs such as Kidspiration can assist students in developing their compositions. Research supports the promise of these technologies in assisting students to experience academic success, independence, and confidence (Hecker, Elkind, Elkind, & Katz, 2002).

To promote maximal learning gains, however, students (and their teachers) must receive appropriate training in the use of these assistive technologies as well as the associated strategic processes associated with proficient reading and writing (e.g., comprehension strategies, writing process). Table 11.8 provides a list of available assistive technologies for students with reading and writing difficulties.

Assistive technology should not be viewed as a panacea for all students with exceptionalities, and decisions regarding its use need to be considered carefully in the context of intervention efficiency and cost effectiveness. When making such decisions, teachers should also explore whether their school board has adopted specific technologies and the support services associated with individual products. To assist teachers and school administrators in this decision-making process, agencies such as the Ontario Software Acquisition Program Advisory Committee (OSAPAC) have developed a database of licensed software available for classroom use (www.osapac.org).

Gifted and Talented Students

Approximately 3 to 5 percent of students in Canadian schools are gifted (Hutchinson, 2010). Giftedness has been defined in many ways over the years, generally referring to superior intellectual ability. More recently, the term has been broadened to include special talents as well as high intellect (Gunning, 2005). Thus, giftedness now includes those students who are capable of higher performance in areas such as intelligence, creative and artistic endeavours, or leadership and who require extra services or programming to develop their capacities to the fullest (Shaughnessy, Siegel, & Stanley, 1994). Sometimes, teachers of young students may incorrectly assume that mature girls (i.e., those born in the first four months of the year) are gifted. Gifted students are often identified through IQ tests, norm-referenced achievement tests, and teacher observation. They may display behaviours that differ qualitatively and quantitatively from those of their same-age peers in several ways, including the following:

- Learning to read early (50 percent of gifted students learn to read before entering school)
- Reading widely and quickly and possessing large vocabularies

Table 11.8 Assistive Technologies for Students with Reading and Writing Difficulties

Technology	Function	Program or Software
Reading		
Text-to-speech	Reads selected text and documents aloud Combines optical character recognition (scanned documents) with speech synthesizer (Read Aloud) Assists students with decoding difficulties Requires students to demonstrate proficient listening comprehension	Kurzweil 3000 Premier Reading Pen 2 ReadPlease 2000 Hear It MacUser Reading Mouse HELP Read Talk to Me TextHelp Screen Reader TextHelp Wordsmith
Talking web browsers	Web browsers with built-in text-to-speech Reads information on webpages aloud Assists students with decoding difficulties Requires students to demonstrate proficient listening comprehension	WeMedia Talking Browser MyKidster Web Talkster iCab Talking Web Browser-Pro for iPad
Audiobooks	Audio recorded books Trade books may be purchased commercially or available through non-profit organizations (e.g., CNIB) Commercial recordings may be "too fast" for students who wish to follow with hard copy Variable speech control audiobooks allow students to adjust rate of Read Aloud Assists students with decoding difficulties Requires students to demonstrate proficient listening comprehension	Audible.com Books Aloud, Inc. National Library Service (NLS) Recording for the Blind and Dyslexic Talking Books
Writing		
Word prediction	Lists high-frequency words in response to students' composition Word prediction improves as function of second, third letters, etc. Assists students with written expression, spelling, and motivation for writing	Word Q & Speak Q Version 3 Co:Writer 6 Penfriend XL Version 3 SoothSayer Word Prediction Version 4 Typing Assistant 5.4
Planning and organizing	Generates semantic webs Numerous templates that can be manipulated and rearranged readily Assists students in structuring their writing	Inspiration Kidspiration VisiMap StoryWeaver Centron's Lesson Power Freemind WriteOnline Brainstorm Version 3 Premier Talking Word Processor

(continued)

Table 11.8 Assistive Technologies for Students with Reading and Writing Difficulties *(continued)*

Writing *(continued)*		
Speech recognition	Students dictate compositions Assists students who experience difficulties with writing mechanics, including grammar and spelling May be faster than paper and pen or typing May require students to complete several training sessions Students tend to experience greater accuracy with increased use; however, proofreading is always required Students require proficient oral language	Dragon Naturally Speaking MacSpeech Dictate Windows 7 Built-in Speech Recognition SpeechMagic iPhone and BlackBerry Built-in Speech Recognition Dragon Search (for mobile devices) Shoutout (for mobile devices)
Screen readers	Reads selected text and documents aloud Combines computer screen and speech synthesis Especially helpful when reviewing compositions—students may be better able to "hear" errors or edits than "read" them Requires students to demonstrate proficient listening comprehension	Browsealoud eReader HearIt Help Read Screen Reader NETalker TextAloud MP3

Note: Many programs provide multiple functions. For instance, many text readers also provide word prediction functions or semantic organizers.

- Learning basic skills quickly and with less practice
- Constructing and comprehending abstract ideas and concepts quickly
- Asking "how" and "why" questions frequently
- Working well independently
- Sustaining focus for long periods of time
- Demonstrating boundless energy
- Enjoying learning new facts and concepts
- Displaying curiosity and intrinsic motivation (Winner, 1996, 2000).

Programs for Gifted Students Since most gifted students have the ability to read above grade level, provisions needs to be made to ensure that they read material in class that challenges them. They also may need early instruction in how to research a topic and organize the findings to communicate what they have learned to others (Karnes & Bean, 2001). When they reach the older grades, gifted students suddenly may appear to have difficulty completing tasks, as they may not have developed the study skills and habits that enable them to function at their highest level. When that occurs, teachers need to take the time to provide them with additional help in learning these strategies. Reading and writing workshops are suitable activities for these students, as they can select their own topics and reading materials and proceed at an accelerated pace. Teachers may have to provide these students with additional or alternative expectations for task completion (Maker & Neilson, 1996).

Caution Gifted students can have hidden learning disabilities that are undiscovered in earlier grades. Without proper challenges, they can become bored and behavioural problems can emerge. Giftedness can caused students to feel embarrassed, socially isolated, and generally misunderstood.

Some Interesting Facts

- Albert Einstein did not speak until he was 4 years old and could not read until he was 7 years old.
- Isaac Newton did poorly in grade school.
- Enrico Caruso's music teacher told him he could not sing.
- Wernher von Braun failed grade 9 algebra.
- Leo Tolstoy failed university.
- Winston Churchill failed grade 6.

DIFFERENTIATED INSTRUCTION

STUDENTS ARE UNIQUE INDIVIDUALS, AND THIS UNIQUENESS OFTEN CREATES ONE of the greatest joys of teaching. At the same time, this sense of uniqueness creates one of the greatest dilemmas for teachers in the classroom in that they cannot, in good conscience, teach to the "middle of the road." Rather, they need to accept the challenge of differentiating instruction so that all students can learn to the best of their ability (Hammeken, 2007).

Originally developed for working with gifted students, differentiated instruction is a teaching philosophy based on the foundational belief that teachers must adapt instruction to the diversity of their students (Tomlinson, 1999, 2003). In other words, the focus of differentiated instruction is on the knowledge and skills that learners bring forward versus the instructional approaches adopted by teachers (Noble, 2004; Tomlinson, 2003). Of course, this concept is not a new one but one that warrants teachers' continued consideration and efforts.

Differentiated instruction requires teachers to provide students with instruction that is responsive to their prior knowledge, interests, and preferred leaning styles (e.g., auditory, visual, kinesthetic) (Willis & Mann, 2000), thus providing them with multiple pathways to achieve targeted learning outcomes and maximize learning success (Smutny, 2003). These pathways are neither "good" nor "bad" but instead reflect the issue of "fit" between learners and teachers and learners and materials. These pathways are not "fixed" and can vary across tasks and circumstances (Sternberg & Zhang, 2005).

The following are some characteristics of classrooms that incorporate differentiated instruction:

- The classroom is a physically safe and emotionally secure learning space. Students are encouraged to take learning risks. Each student is respected.
- The classroom is physically comfortable (appropriate lighting, seating) and contains a variety of engaging materials and resources.
- Teachers know their students' abilities, skills, talents, strengths, and weaknesses. Students' learning efforts are acknowledged and their accomplishments are celebrated.
- Instruction is presented in different learning modalities.
- Competition among students is de-emphasized and collaboration among students is emphasized. Students are encouraged to compete against themselves.
- Students receive individualized instruction. Students acknowledge that learning is a process and that each student learns in a unique manner (Gregory & Chapman, 2007; Holloway, 2000).

Differentiated instruction requires teachers to modify or adjust their programming across three dimensions: content, process, and product.

Content

Teachers should address the same concepts with all students but adjust the degree of complexity associated with these topics (Tomlinson, 1999). Concepts can be explained in a highly abstract manner or by using simple everyday metaphors or hands-on experiences. Teachers who differentiate instruction provide students with access to skills and knowledge through texts, lectures, demonstrations, field trips, and manipulatives. Advanced learners may be expected to read complex tests, consult websites, and interview experts while less advanced learners may use reading buddies and easier material and view videos that make information more accessible. Teachers may work directly with slow learners, spending additional time clarifying target concepts.

Process

Process refers to a series of activities that enable students to make sense of ideas by becoming facile with the necessary skills for learning. These activities can be modified so that some students are able to reach independence quickly whereas others need more scaffolding before they can become independent. Scaffolding includes teacher modelling, step-by-step instructions (repeated as many times as necessary), and repeated practice. If a skill is being taught, teachers can use student interest as the vehicle for instruction.

Product

Learning products are usually represented in culminating projects through which students demonstrate their knowledge and skills. Through the completion of these projects, students demonstrate their abilities to apply their new skills or knowledge, as well as their problem solving and creativity. Students can create different products based on interests, skill attainment, and learning preferences. The success of this stage depends on the teacher providing open-ended instructions that allow for individual ways of responding (Hammeken, 2007; Tomlinson, 1999).

Strategies Associated with Differentiated Learning

Teachers can employ a number of specific strategies to differentiate learning opportunities in the classroom. Most of these strategies modify the pace of learning and the level of instruction (Kingore, 2004; Tomlinson, 2003), including:

- Establishing collaborative learning
- Employing multi-age grouping
- Addressing multiple intelligences
- Using flexible grouping (interest-based groups, homogeneous groups, heterogeneous groups)
- Moving from whole-class instruction to small-group instruction to individual instruction
- Establishing stations where students can complete different tasks
- Using multiple levels of texts and a variety of learning materials
- Using agendas so students maintain personalized lists of tasks that they are accountable for completing within a defined time frame
- Establishing open-ended tasks so students can respond at their level of understanding and skill development
- Forming problem-solving groups
- Ensuring choice for task completion
- Coaching and facilitating students' learning
- Promoting active learning

Assessing and Evaluating

Standards and accountability

A genuine balance between educational standards and differentiated instruction in teaching and learning is both possible and necessary if classrooms are to be inclusive (McTighe & Brown, 2005). Multi-faceted and continual assessment practices must be employed to guide instructional decisions. Ensure that students as individuals and as group members participate actively in assessing their own learning. Observational notes are helpful when students are working in groups on shared learning goals and outcomes. Be certain to have a lot of learning data to be able to report accurately.

The backward design planning process enhances teachers' abilities to consider content and learners throughout the planning stage. Stage 1 requires the identification of desired results. First, it is necessary to focus on content standards: the big ideas and essential questions to be asked and answered by all students. In backward design, evidence of successful learning is derived from these establish learning goals. In stage 2, teachers match assessment measures with the goals in a culminating performance, task, or project. These tasks allow students to engage in decision making, problem solving, investigation, experimental inquiry, creative expression, and other higher-order thinking processes. This is when much of the learning occurs. Finally, in stage 3, teachers develop teaching and learning plans that enable students to achieve the learning goals identified in stage 1 and the understandings to accomplish the tasks identified in stage 2 (McTighe & Brown, 2005).

Each student should adhere to high standards and show progress toward genuine understanding of the new learning. However, the pathway to understanding and attaining the standards involves differentiated approach to content, process, and product. Teachers need to be vigilant in ensuring that students are achieving at a maximum level and that they understand associated expectations.

The following example indicates three different levels of achievement related to a unit about the Riel Rebellion:

Struggling Students

- Students are expected to meet three main objectives of the lesson (e.g., identify two causes of the rebellion, understand the rebellion outcome)
- Accommodations or modifications may be necessary

Average Students

- Students are expected to master all objectives of the lesson (e.g., identify three causes of the rebellion, explain the dilemma regarding the trial, understand the rebellion outcome)
- Performance is at grade level

Gifted Students

Cultural and linguistic differences: What teachers should know

- Students are expected to master all objectives of the lesson (e.g., identify three causes of the rebellion, explain the dilemma regarding the trial, understand the rebellion outcome) and demonstrate extended learning (e.g., study the trial transcript, develop and discuss an opinion related to the outcome, consider the lives of Metis today)
- Performance is beyond grade level expectations.

SUGGESTIONS FOR PROFESSIONAL DEVELOPMENT

1. Select one of the suggested culturally diverse books for teachers (page 423) and read it for pleasure. Reflect on what you may have learned and share the book with a friend.
2. Helen Keller once said, "The highest result of education is tolerance."
   - Think about whether you agree with the statement. Explain your position.
   - Consider associated implications for your classroom teaching.
   - Discuss your thoughts with at least one other person.
3. Arrange to observe or speak with a resource teacher or special education teacher.
   - What are the greatest challenges and rewards associated with their position?
   - What specific programs or instructional techniques do they use when working with students who struggle with reading or writing?

4. Gather information about the following:
   a. Local support programs and organizations (schools, libraries, learning disabilities association) that assist students and their families with reading and writing difficulties. If possible, volunteer to participate or make arrangements to observe the program. Reflect on the training provided to volunteers, program structure, and instructional approach.
   b. Local support programs and organizations that assist students and their families who have immigrated to Canada.
      - What types of programs are available?
      - If possible, volunteer to participate or make arrangements to observe a program session.
      - Reflect on the training provided to volunteers, program structure, and instructional approach.

CHILDREN'S LITERATURE REFERENCES

Brown, M. W. (2005). *Goodnight moon.* New York, NY: HarperCollins.
Carle, E. (1997). *Today is Monday*. New York, NY: Puffin.
Coxe, M. (1990). *Whose footprints?* Ty Crowell Co.
Eastman, P. D. (2000). *Flap your wings*. New York, NY: Random House for Young Readers.
Galdone, P. (2008). *The three billy goats gruff*. Boston, MA: Sandpiper.
Galdone, P. (2011). *The little red hen*. Boston, MA: HMH Publishers.
Hennessy, B. G. (1992). *Jake baked the cake*. New York, NY: Puffin.
Hutchins, P. (1994). *Little pink pig*. New York, NY: Greenwillow Books.
Kraus, R. (1995). *Come out and play, little mouse*. New York, NY: Greenwillow Books.
Lobel, A. (1993). *The rose in my garden*. New York, NY: Greenwillow Books.
Martin, B., & Carle, E. (1996). *Brown bear, brown bear, what do you see?* New York, NY: Henry Holt and Co.
Sendack, M. (1991). *Chicken soup with rice*. New York, NY: HarperCollins.

MyEducationLab

MyEducationLab is an interactive, virtual learning tool that will help improve your understanding of the concepts taught in this textbook and in your course. Through this engaging resource, you will have access to simulations of real classroom experiences, exercises that will help you improve your knowledge of key concepts, and additional resources that will help you in your teaching career. Use this online tool with your textbook to help you succeed in your studies and beyond!

Chapter 12

Creating Your Language Arts Classroom: How Do You Begin?

Learning Objectives

In this chapter you will discover

- How to plan the physical set-up of your classroom.
- How to set up special spaces in the classroom associated with language arts.
- How to set up an in-class library.
- How to create independent reading centres using levelled texts.
- How to plan the daily and weekly schedule.
- How to plan a balanced program.
- How to create a positive classroom atmosphere that enhances learning.
- How to get started in September.
- How to be an effective substitute teacher.
- How to communicate with parents.
- How to continue your professional development.

JAMIE TAYLOR: SUPPLY AND LONG-TERM CONTRACT TEACHER LOOKING FOR A PERMANENT POSITION

Jamie Taylor is completing his third year as a supply and long-term contract teacher and hopes to attain a permanent position next year. He has a positive attitude about these early teaching experiences, stating that he is "pretty lucky, as many people have trouble obtaining any work—only some of my graduating class secured a job and the rest went back to school." His "luck" started early when he was able to begin his career with a seven-week supply contract after completing the final practicum in his teacher education program.

Through his practicum and contract placements, Jamie has developed a philosophy of individualized instruction with an emphasis on literacy across the subject areas. Jamie believes that supply teaching and his contract experiences have provided a solid foundation for his career and helped him become a committed professional. His current role enables him to observe various teachers' instructional approaches and teaching techniques. After each new teaching experience, he reflects on what worked well and what was less successful, confirming his teaching philosophy.

Since the majority of his experiences have been at the intermediate level, Jamie considers himself to be a grades 7 and 8 teacher. He attributes his successes with preadolescents, in part, to his youthfulness, informality, and perceived "coolness." He also believes that his focus on providing a strong, hands-on literacy program, which allows for individual differences and choice, is appreciated by his students. Jamie includes Read Aloud, guided reading, and silent reading as part of his language arts program. He believes that these strategies enhance intermediate students' reading skills, just as they do with junior and primary students. He admits, however, that implementing such a program requires some "winning over" when working in schools where this type of programming is not routine. When he succeeds, he is gratified to see students' engagement and motivation improve.

> It can be difficult when you parachute in for a term only. When the students have never seen such a practice before, it can be challenging to meet your teaching goals. It takes time and effort but the kids generally respond and like what I am doing with them.

Jamie integrates his literacy program into history, geography, and science units. He describes an instance when he taught a unit on conflict and change in history focusing on William Lyon McKenzie and the rebellion of Upper Canada. To help students comprehend the concepts of revolt, conflict, and government change, he read *Among the Hidden* by Margaret Peterson Haddix (a futuristic novel that focuses on a totalitarian regime and the internet). The students loved the book and were able to generalize their new learning to the history unit.

Jamie also instituted an individualized silent reading program in which students choose their books and, selecting from several possible formats, write a weekly journal response. When collecting the journals, Jamie assessed the students' book selection, comprehension, and overall response to the text. He also participated in written dialogues with the students and held teacher-student conferences, meeting frequently with those who struggled with reading and writing.

To vary his program, Jamie also had students participate in literature circles. After each student had selected a book, he grouped them according to their shared interest. Working in groups of about four, students were then charged with making an "arts-based" presentation (i.e., visually representing). Student responses were varied, ranging from puppet shows to graphic novels to dramatic presentations.

As a supply and long-term contract teacher, Jamie recognizes that there are some compromises he must make based on what has been implemented in the classroom and what he believes are best practices. For instance, he does not believe in using reward-based systems, such as candy. Recently, he worked in a school where external rewards had been used routinely for many years. His grade 7 class was the only one in the school with no extrinsic reward system in place, as Jamie was reluctant to compromise his beliefs. He found that he was forced to compromise with the grade 7 students, but that the grade 8 students were more receptive to his position and he was able to hold his ground. He declared, "I would never compromise with the grade 7s if they were my class throughout the year."

Jamie looks forward to being assigned his own classroom and has faith that this will happen shortly. In the interim, he enjoys experiencing different schools and grade levels, believing that these encounters help him to develop strong classroom management skills and instructional practices. Reflecting on his initial positions, Jamie acknowledges that he was "just surviving." More positively, he also acknowledges that he moved quickly beyond this survival mode and is now confident that he can respond to any situation with flexibility and the ability to develop meaningful lessons and learning activities for the students.

> After three long-term contracts and many supply days, I still love the profession. Every day, I get excited to go to work. It is the best thing I have ever done! I have never lost that passion. I like the dynamic, non-stop nature of the way I need to adjust, work on the fly, and problem-solve.

INTRODUCTION

THE INITIAL PLANNING IS AN ABSOLUTELY CRITICAL COMPONENT OF A SUCCESSFUL year. When thoughtful planning is completed prior to the beginning of the school year, the year has a good chance of being successful. Effective teachers are highly organized and care about their students, believing that they can learn (Pressley, Allington, Wharton-McDonald, Block, & Morrow, 2001). Failure to establish expectations, standards, routines, and a good motivational atmosphere can lead to confusion and frustration on the part of students and teachers alike. Therefore, teachers need to make decisions about how the classroom will function (in this case, we will focus on the language arts program) and then communicate those decisions clearly to the class. There may be some areas of negotiation that can be introduced during the first few days so that ownership of the classroom atmosphere is a shared responsibility. Therefore, we emphasize the importance of thinking carefully about what kind of classroom you want to establish in terms of the following:

- Physical arrangement
- Routines
- Language program
- Community building
- Communication with parents

For many new teachers, the first few years of their professional careers are spent either supply teaching on a daily basis or teaching on a long-term contract that can begin at any time throughout the year. These kinds of teaching assignments require a special set of skills that are related to classroom planning and management but also have to consider the routines, atmosphere, and physical set-up that have already been established in the classroom. This second type of teaching requires flexibility and the ability to think and act quickly based on a set of personal teaching principles. In this chapter, we attempt to identify some strategies and methods for establishing an environment in which learning can be pleasant and self-actualizing for everyone.

Caution It is critical to remember that when planning for a new year there are three main goals that direct much of the initial instructional activity. The following three goals dominate the first month or six weeks of the school year:

1. To become well acquainted with the students in terms of their abilities, interests, and personalities
2. To establish basic routines that will provide a firm foundation for developing a community of learners
3. To establish high standards for tasks and projects

PLANNING THE PHYSICAL ARRANGEMENT OF THE CLASSROOM

PLANNING THE PHYSICAL ARRANGEMENT OF THE CLASSROOM MAY BE COMPLETED most effectively when actually sitting in the classroom. The first consideration is to assess the physical limitations of the room and, where possible, make changes to reduce these limitations. For instance, teachers can control the lighting by replacing flickering lights and ensuring that the room can be darkened sufficiently for media presentations. Although teachers have little control over the size of the classroom or student numbers, decisions can be made about how to maximize space. When physical space is well used, considerable differences in student learning and behaviour can result (Andrews & Lupart, 2000; Jankowska & Atlay, 2008).

Seating Arrangements

Seating arrangements should be flexible enough to facilitate movement that supports various learning activities. If the primary learning focus will be group work, desks can be grouped in sets of four or even six. If teacher-directed lessons will be dominant and much work will be completed individually, a more traditional seating in rows may be best. Teachers should also consider how the language arts program will be conducted at this time. In any case, teachers should be able to move easily around the room to interact with individual students without disrupting others. It is worth remembering that seating arrangements in which high- and lower-achieving students are interspersed can increase involvement and participation. Also, when lower-ability students are seated closer to the front of the room, their achievement may improve (Jones & Jones, 2009).

Consideration needs to be given to leaving adequate space around high-use areas such as pencil sharpeners, sinks, and computers. Decisions must also be made about where space will be allocated for learning centres, work tables, Read Aloud, and informal oral language. Appropriate consideration of these aspects helps the classroom physically reflect the excitement associated with a variety of learning formats. There also needs to be a semi-invisible organizational structure that allows for easy access to supplies, submitted work, and storage of books and unfinished projects. A messy classroom suggests to students that disorganization and sloppiness are acceptable. For examples of classroom layout designs, try an online search using the following keywords: *classroom layout design*, *seating*, and *physical arrangements*.

Bulletin Boards

Bulletin boards can be used for a variety of reasons and usually reflect many different purposes over the school year. Bulletin boards are a way to recognize students' achievements publicly and allow them to participate in the appearance of their classroom. They can also be used to introduce a unit of study or provide background knowledge. For instance, if the class is about to study *The Breadwinner* by Deborah Ellis, a bulletin board may be posted (either by the teacher or the students) showing a map of Afghanistan and its location in the world as well as some pictures of the terrain, cities, typical dress, and transportation. It may be possible to include some information about Canadian military involvement. This information could facilitate a dialogue that would provide relevant prior knowledge necessary to read the book. Similarly, posting anchor charts outlining strategy steps can enhance students' memory for the new skill and help them transfer it across different learning contexts.

Teachers should set up the first bulletin boards of the year to make the classroom attractive and interesting to entering students. Teachers can set up a word wall as part of the wall display, which can then become a dynamic focus for word learning. After that, student work should dominate. While bulletin boards can serve several purposes, they will fail to accomplish any of these goals if they are not changed regularly. It sends a very bad message to students about their environment if the faded bulletin boards from Halloween are still up after Christmas.

Special Spaces Associated with the Language Arts

The beginning of the year is the time to plan spaces for any centres that will operate on a regular basis in a language arts classroom; these include the listening centre, the writing centre, and (in the case of young students) the play centre. This planning does not prohibit adding new centres that are associated with curriculum topics periodically throughout the year. All such centres should be dynamic and encourage students' interests and motivation. It is critical that teachers remember that each centre has its own set of routines that must be taught and learned. For instance, space will determine how many students can participate in the centre at any given time. Students may also need to submit completed tasks in a particular place. Therefore, it is best to introduce such centres slowly over the first few weeks of school, ensuring that students understand the associated routines and procedures.

Zone of proximal development

Classrooms that focus on literacy and language require designated spaces designed to encourage and facilitate students' literacy skills. In Chapter 2, Listening, Speaking, and Beyond, we discussed the foundational role of oral language and listening in developing students' language skills. With this in mind, many primary and junior grade teachers designate an area (carpeting is optional) where either the whole class or groups of students can gather for conversation, Read Aloud, and discussions. Routines also may be unique to this setting, as many teachers call students to the carpeted area as a signal for informal dialogue. Hand-raising may or may not be suspended and students need to understand the parameters of the personal space they occupy at that time.

Most classrooms require a designated circle area or table for small-group discussion about novels or other texts. The table may also serve as a gathering place for guided reading and writing lessons. Some of these spaces are organized around smaller tables and chairs depending on the age of the students.

Similarly, teachers need to consider how students will access computers in the classroom and what protocols will be associated with their use. Access to computers can be especially challenging when associated with the use of assistive technologies for students who may be experiencing reading or writing difficulties. In these instances, teachers will need to balance individual educational needs with issues related to general access for all students.

In-Class Library

Another focus of the classroom should be the in-class library, which must include a sufficient number of books to provide students with plenty of choice. According to Tompkins, Bright, Pollard, and Winsor (2011), the minimum number of books in the library should be four times the number of students. Another important criterion is that it include narratives, expository texts, and poetry. As the year progresses, books written by students can be included. Choices can also include magazines and graphic novels. Teachers generally try to establish a "cozy" environment with rocking chairs or beanbag chairs, large pillows, and carpets. There should be a flat surface where particular books can be featured to entice students. It is a good idea to vary the positioning of books on the shelves, with most books displayed spine-out while others are featured so that the front cover is displayed. The following are some suggestions for beginning an in-class library:

- Build a personal collection of appropriate books by visiting garage sales and second-hand bookstores.
- Check with the school library about borrowing theme-based materials.
- Introduce yourself as a teacher at the local library and inquire about how many books can be borrowed at one time and if extended borrowing privileges are possible. It is worthwhile to exchange books every three weeks or so. Librarians will often help with selections once it is evident that books are being returned on time.
- Ask friends if they have any good books that they or their children have outgrown.
- Ask students to bring in their favourite books from home. Keep close track of them and ensure that a list of ownership is established and posted.

It is generally wise to establish a rule that no in-class library books leave the classroom. Otherwise, fines and lost books are inevitable. Finally, teachers need to remember that in-class libraries work well if they are dynamic and students know that new books will appear regularly. Students will avoid in-class libraries that have not been updated or changed. In such cases, the library may look good to the casual eye but it serves no real purpose in the literacy program.

Independent Reading Centres with Levelled Texts

Independent reading is a critical component of all language arts programs. The independent reading centre holds a collection of books that are systematically coded according to their readability. Coding systems used to identify the level of text difficulty vary across classrooms, with some teachers making reference to the alphabet (levels A to Z), numbers (levels 10 to 15), or animal names (dolphins, fish, and elephants). Books belonging to each level are then stored in plastic bins or other containers that allow students to retrieve and return them easily.

As discussed in Chapter 3, Assessing and Evaluating Your Students as Language Users, one of the most immediate questions held by many language arts teachers concerns their students' current reading abilities. To this end, teachers can complete any combination of formal and informal assessment measures, including miscue analysis, running records, informal reading inventories, and standardized tests (see Chapter 3). One critical outcome of these assessments is to determine students' independent, instructional, and frustration reading levels.

Independent level. Students can read text without any assistance, demonstrating 90 percent or greater accuracy with comprehension. Students recognize 99 percent of all words correctly.

Instructional level. Students require teacher assistance to gain meaning from the text. Students read with about 95 to 98 percent word accuracy and at a comprehension level between 75 and 89 percent or greater.

Frustration level. Students are unable to read these texts successfully, even with assistance. Students demonstrate poor accuracy with word recognition at less than 90 percent and with a comprehension level of less than 70 percent.

Effective language arts teachers then use this information to develop a collection of corresponding classroom texts. These texts are then ranked in order of ascending difficulty (e.g., A through Z) or with reference to grade level and position in the school year (e.g., winter, grade 2; spring, grade 6; fall, grade 8). Teachers then provide students with specific information related to the categorical range (e.g., levels D to F; dolphins to fish) in which they should select text when reading independently or with a buddy. Teachers need to conference with students regularly to monitor their ability to decode and comprehend text. When students demonstrate repeated competency in reading text at a prescribed level, they can graduate to the next level of difficulty. Teachers can also use this information when implementing guided reading activities.

Independent Reading Giving students access to levelled texts provides them with opportunities to select books that correspond to their independent reading levels as well as to their interests. In general, teachers should stock reading centres with books that vary by at least two grade levels below and above the current grade placement (e.g., reading materials ranging from grades 1 to 5 for a grade 3 classroom). Resources such as *The Fountas and Pinnell Leveled Book List* (Fountas & Pinnell, 2010–2011) provide teachers with reference tables that include specific suggestions about the level and number of texts that should be contained in an independent reading centre at each grade level. Students should also be presented with substantial choice in reading materials, including a selection of narrative and expository texts and associated genres.

Shared and Guided Reading Students require access to reading materials at their instructional levels when mixed-ability grouping is used to partner students for shared reading (with reading materials reflecting the poor readers' ability level) and when teachers lead students in small-group (approximately 4 to 6 students) guided reading sessions. Texts at these levels challenge students to refine their use of strategic processes and extend their vocabulary (see Chapter 5, Comprehension of Narrative Text).

Read Aloud Students often enjoy and are able to listen successfully to texts written beyond their instructional levels. This ability, in part, reflects the reality that students' listening comprehension levels usually exceed their reading comprehension levels, providing teachers with even greater choice when selecting texts for Read Aloud (Chapter 5 lists specific recommendations on how to select texts to read aloud).

Researchers have demonstrated that students learn to read best when they are provided with reading materials that correspond to their independent or instructional levels (Allington, 2006; Allington & Cunningham, 2001; Cunningham & Allington, 2006). However, this can be a challenge for teachers since students differ vastly in their reading levels in any one classroom. While this variability partly reflects differences in students' reading ability, differences also exist among students in their interest and prior knowledge of specific topics. For instance, remember how difficult it was to read the passage titled "Contrast between Moral and Aesthetic Values" found at the beginning of Chapter 6, Reading Comprehension Strategies for Non-Fiction: Reading in the Content Areas, without having the appropriate prior knowledge.

Estimating Text Complexity

Levelling Systems There are several packaged programs available to teachers who wish to use commercially prepared levelled readers in their classrooms. Many factors are considered when determining text complexity, including word count and length, sentence length, repetition, syntax, vocabulary, and inclusion of visuals (see Table 12.1 for a description of levelled books for kindergarten and grade 1). Examples of levelled reading programs include:

- Reading Recovery
- Reading A–Z
- Accelerated Reading
- Reading Counts!
- Rigby
- Guided Reading
- Houghton Mifflin Online Leveled Books K–6
- Fountas and Pinnell Guided Graded Levels

There are also several commercial products available to help teachers estimate the reading levels of authentic texts (making them ideal for library use). While some of these

Table 12.1 Description of Levelled Text Characteristics in Kindergarten and Grade 1

Level	Characteristics
Levels A and B	■ Simple storyline ■ Direct correspondence between pictures and text ■ Familiar topic ■ Familiar language structures ■ Print is at same place on each page ■ Print is easy to see and words are repeated ■ Level A has about four lines of text per page ■ Level B has more lines of text and a slightly larger vocabulary range
Level C	■ Simple storyline ■ Familiar topics ■ More words and longer sentences ■ Familiar language structures ■ Storyline is carried by the text ■ Although a direct correlation exists between text and pictures, more information is carried by the text
Level D	■ Stories are more complex and longer ■ Familiar experiences

	■ More attention to print is required ■ Illustrations are present to support text ■ Between two and six lines of text per page ■ Full range of punctuation
Level E	■ Stories are more complex and longer ■ Familiar experiences but concepts are more subtle and may require interpretation ■ Language patterns repeat but are also varied ■ Illustrations support the story but may contain several ideas ■ From three to eight lines of text per page ■ Words are longer and may require analysis ■ Full variety of punctuation is evident
Level F	■ Texts are longer than in previous levels ■ Print may be smaller ■ Usually three to eight lines of text per page ■ Meaning is carried more by text than by pictures ■ Variety of words expands ■ Many opportunities for word analysis ■ Stories have more episodes ■ Dialogue has greater variety ■ Punctuation indicates phrasing and meaning
Levels G and H	■ Books contain more challenging ideas and vocabulary ■ Content may move beyond individual student's experience ■ Typically four to eight lines of text per page ■ Literary language and natural language intermingle ■ Stories have more events ■ Language and vocabulary becomes more complex ■ Less likely to be episodic repetition
Level I	■ Greater variety of texts represented ■ Longer, with more sentences per page ■ Story structure is more complex ■ Episodes are more elaborate ■ Illustrations extend the text but are less supportive of main ideas ■ Vocabulary is more specialized and unusual

Source: Adapted from Fountas and Pinnell (1996, 2010–2011).

Table 12.2 Sample of a Reading Levels Correlation Chart

<table>
<tr><th>Grade Level</th><th>Fountas-Pinnell Guided Reading</th><th>Reading Recovery</th><th>PM Benchmark Assessment Level</th><th>DRA</th><th>Reading A-Z Level</th></tr>
<tr><td rowspan="4">Kindergarten</td><td rowspan="2">A</td><td>A,B</td><td></td><td>A</td><td>aa</td></tr>
<tr><td>1</td><td>1</td><td>1</td><td>A</td></tr>
<tr><td>B</td><td>2</td><td>2</td><td>2</td><td>B</td></tr>
<tr><td rowspan="2">C</td><td>3</td><td>3,4</td><td>3</td><td>C</td></tr>
<tr><td rowspan="13">Grade 1</td><td>4</td><td>5,6</td><td>4</td><td rowspan="2">D</td></tr>
<tr><td rowspan="2">D</td><td>5</td><td rowspan="2">7</td><td rowspan="2">6</td></tr>
<tr><td>6</td><td rowspan="2">E</td></tr>
<tr><td rowspan="2">E</td><td>7</td><td rowspan="2">8</td><td rowspan="2">8</td></tr>
<tr><td>8</td><td rowspan="2">F</td></tr>
<tr><td rowspan="2">F</td><td>9</td><td rowspan="2">9,10</td><td rowspan="2">10</td></tr>
<tr><td>10</td><td rowspan="2">G</td></tr>
<tr><td rowspan="2">G</td><td>11</td><td></td><td rowspan="2">12</td></tr>
<tr><td>12</td><td>11,12</td><td rowspan="2">H</td></tr>
<tr><td rowspan="2">H</td><td>13</td><td rowspan="2">13,14</td><td rowspan="2">14</td></tr>
<tr><td>14</td><td rowspan="2">I</td></tr>
<tr><td rowspan="2">I</td><td>15</td><td>15,16</td><td rowspan="2">16</td></tr>
<tr><td>16</td><td>17,18</td><td>J</td></tr>
<tr><td rowspan="2">Grade 2</td><td>J,K</td><td>18</td><td>19,21</td><td>20</td><td>K,L,M</td></tr>
<tr><td>L,M</td><td>20</td><td>22</td><td>28</td><td>N,O,P</td></tr>
<tr><td rowspan="3">Grade 3</td><td rowspan="2">N</td><td rowspan="2">22</td><td>23</td><td>30</td><td>Q</td></tr>
<tr><td>24</td><td>34</td><td>R</td></tr>
<tr><td>O,P</td><td>24</td><td>25,26</td><td>38</td><td>S,T</td></tr>
<tr><td>Grade 4</td><td>Q,R,S</td><td>26</td><td>27</td><td>40</td><td>U,V,W</td></tr>
<tr><td>Grade 5</td><td>T,U,V</td><td>28</td><td></td><td>44</td><td>X,Y</td></tr>
<tr><td>Grade 6</td><td>W,X,Y</td><td>30</td><td></td><td></td><td></td></tr>
<tr><td>Grade 7</td><td>Z</td><td>32</td><td></td><td></td><td></td></tr>
<tr><td>Grade 8</td><td>Z</td><td>34</td><td></td><td></td><td></td></tr>
</table>

resources appear in print, many are available online. Examples of frequently used print-based and internet resources include the following:

Books

Fountas and Pinnell Leveled Book List, K–8+ (Fountas & Pinnell, 2010–2011)

Best Books for Building Literacy for Elementary School Children (Gunning, 2000)

Best Books for Beginning Readers (Gunning, 1997)

Internet

Scholastic Book Wizard (http://bookwizard.scholastic.com)
Leveled Book Lists (www.home.comcast.net/~ngiansante)
440 Book Titles (http://faculty.tamu-commerce.edu/espinoza/s/ellis-b-rdlevl.html)
A–Z Teacher Stuff Leveled Book Database (http://books.atozteacherstuff.com/leveled-books)
Fountas and Pinnell Leveled Books K–8 (www.fountasandpinnellleveledbooks.com)
Scholastic Canada Book Clubs (www.scholastic.ca/readinglevels)

Comparison Charts While access to resources that assist teachers in estimating the readability of text is extremely helpful in creating an in-class reading centre and is foundational to promoting students' reading abilities, this information can be confusing, especially when teachers are provided with information from varied sources. For example, consider a teacher who wishes to create a reading centre consisting of commercially created levelled readers (e.g., Reading Recovery, Reading A–Z) and authentic texts levelled according to *Fountas and Pinnell Leveled Book List*. While each text has an assigned reading level, this level is only relevant with direct reference to the corresponding program. Relationships between the levelling systems are not apparent. Fortunately, several comparison charts are available to teachers, such as the one illustrated in Table 12.2. There are also resources online, such as the following:

www.readinga-z.com/correlation-chart.php
http://library.springbranchisd.com/sbisd_library/reading_levels_comparison_chart.htm
http://pathways.nadeducation.org/files/managed/comparison-1200885940.pdf
www.suu.edu/faculty/lundd/readingsite/readingresources/bookleveling.htm
http://steckvaughn.hmhco.com/HA/correlations/pdf/l/LevelingChart.pdf

Levelling Formulas There will be times when readability levels for authentic texts are not provided in the resources described above, or when teachers will wish to calculate the readability estimates for content-specific text books or their lesson materials. Readability formulas can provide such estimates, with software programs like Readability Calculations (www.readabilityformulas.com/readability-calculations.php) and Readability Plus (www.micropowerandlight.com/rdplus.html) providing automated reading estimates for scanned documents. See Table 12.3 for some of the more commonly used readability formulas.

The **Fry Readability Graph** is designed to provide a measure of reading level for most materials ranging from primary through secondary grades. Three 100-word passages from within the same text are required to use the graph correctly. The formula includes a measure of average number of sentences per 100 words and average number of syllables per 100 words (see Figure 12.1). After calculating each of these measures, teachers then

Table 12.3 Common Readability Formulas

The Spache Readability Formula is best suited for use with primary materials (grades 2 and below; Gunning, 2000). Using passages between 100 and 150 words in length, the formula includes measures of the total number of words and total number of sentences, average sentence length (total number of words divided by total number of sentences), and number of difficult words (low-frequency words). The Powers-Sumner-Kearl Readability Formula is similar in format and can also be used to assess primary level materials (grades 3 and below).

The New Dale-Chall Reading Formula is best suited for use with junior and intermediate level materials (grades 3 and above) and provides two-year estimates of reading level (e.g., grades 4 to 6, grades 4 and below; Allington, 2006; Gunning, 2000). Following the principle that students are better able to read text that contains familiar words, the formula includes measures of the number of "hard or low-frequency words" contained in the text and the average sentence length.

The Flesch–Kincaid Grade Level Readability and Flesch Reading Ease Formulas are two of the oldest and most reliable estimates of reading level (Allington, 2006). The formulas include measures of the average sentence length (number of words divided by the number of sentences) and the average number of syllables per word (number of syllables divided by the number of words). Resulting scores range from 0 to 100, with higher numbers representing easier-to-read texts (Flesch Reading Ease) and lower grade levels (Flesch–Kincaid Grade Level Readability).

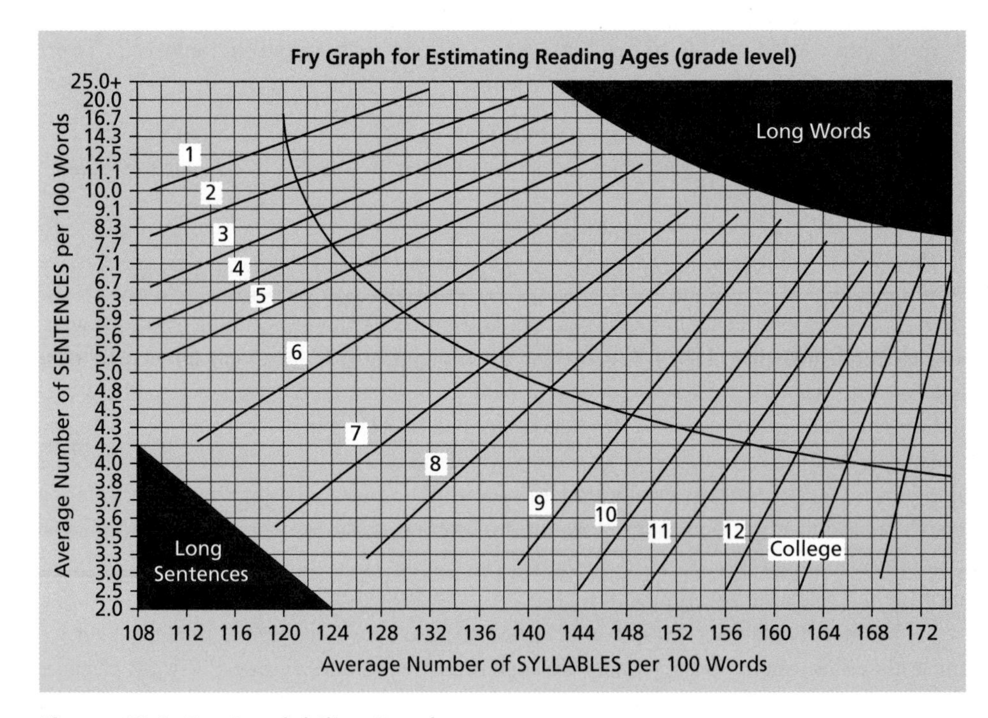

Figure 12.1 Fry Readability Graph

Source: From *Elementary Reading Instruction* by Edward Fry. © The McGraw-Hill Companies, Inc. Reproduced by permission.

plot the numbers on the corresponding axes to estimate reading level. For example, a text that contains an average of 4.5 sentences per 100 words and 136 syllables per 100 words is estimated to be at a mid grade 8 reading level.

Where to Begin: Consulting Others The prospect of levelling texts for a classroom may be an overwhelming one. Therefore, we recommend that new teachers consult with other teachers, resource staff, and administrators prior to creating a levelled reading program. In many instances, schools and school boards will have adopted a specific levelling system and reading program. Other times, teachers may be able to pool knowledge about the reading levels of specific texts. Ideally, teachers will want to level at least one-third of the texts in their classrooms, with the goal of levelling as many texts as possible over time. However, teachers (especially beginning teachers) need to be aware that creating a levelled reading collection requires substantial time and energy and that it may take several years to acquire and develop such a collection.

PLANNING THE DAILY AND WEEKLY SCHEDULE

Beginning the day

Daily news

MANAGING A CLASSROOM HAS MANY COMPONENTS BUT NONE IS AS VITAL AS planning for effective instruction (Mastropieri & Scruggs, 2005). This includes careful thought about everything from time management to conducting a balanced literacy program to planning a variety of lessons complete with student choices. For a beginning teacher, this planning must be accomplished prior to the school year. While curriculum expectations are clearly defined by provincial and territorial ministries of education, the amount of time needed to achieve those expectations is largely left to teachers' discretion. However, many school boards have specific guidelines about the amount of time required for instruction in the subject areas, including the language arts. Effective teachers can also integrate the language arts across the curriculum to increase language time while achieving curriculum expectations in other subjects such as social studies and science.

Time Allocation and Maximizing Time on Task

Time allocations need to be determined with the goal of maximizing learning time and meeting curriculum expectations. Teachers should plan to have students actively engaged in relevant academic assignments, minimizing transitions and time spent waiting to begin (Brophy, 1988). Guidelines for increasing student engagement and time on task follow.

- Use substantive interactions when presenting information, ask questions to assess students' comprehension, provide feedback, and monitor student work. This instructional format usually results in higher student engagement than independent or small-group work that is not teacher-led.
- Monitor the entire class during the beginning and ending portions of an activity as well as throughout the activity. Such monitoring results in higher engagement rates.
- Ensure that students understand what is required to complete the activity at hand and that they possess the necessary skills and materials to complete the task successfully.
- Provide students with oral and written directions about how to complete an activity and what to do when they have finished it.

- Communicate teacher awareness of student behaviour.
- Provide students with a variety of activities to help keep them on task and minimize interruptions while working with small groups (Evertson, 1989).
- Include breaks with physical movement such as stretching or chatting with a partner to enhance students' energy and engagement (Marzano, 2007).
- Use games that focus on academic content but that have low-level stakes and are perceived to be "fun."
- Model enthusiasm and high energy that is focused on academic content (Marzano, 2007).

Planning a Balanced Language Program

According to *Webster's Dictionary*, the pertinent definition of *balance* is "A harmonious or satisfying arrangement or proportion of parts or elements, as in a design." The term has been appropriated by educators to emphasize that all areas of the language arts (listening, speaking, reading, writing, viewing, and visually representing) require systematic attention. This approach becomes an organizing principle for teachers to work collaboratively to ensure that students' skill development in all areas of the language arts are incorporated within and between grades.

A balanced program also requires that students' work be grounded in authentic tasks such as writing for real audiences and purposes and engaging in book club–like discussions with teachers and peers (Cappello, 2009; Schultz, 2009). In a balanced program, literacy development is linked very strongly with oral language and the classroom discourse that students experience (Gee, 2008). While turn taking and the nature of the discourse need to be directed by teachers, there should be plenty of student interaction (Frey, Lee, Tollefson, Pass, & Massengill, 2005). Content balance is important so that students experience different print genres such as poetry, personal stories, essays, narratives, and expository materials (Nodelman & Reimer, 2002). Teachers also need to balance these resources with media texts that reflect the new literacies (Anstey & Bull 2009; Cope & Kalantzis, 2000). These activities must be balanced with learning about language and how it operates in different contexts. For instance, punctuation still needs to be taught explicitly (Morrow & Gambrell, 2011).

Organizational Frameworks for Conducting a Balanced Language Program

Three distinct frameworks assist in planning a balanced language program: resource-based units, thematic units, and inquiry-based units. The three approaches are similar in that they provide students with opportunities to be engaged in meaningful, genuine activities. Student-to-student and teacher-to-student discourses are powerful forums for learning. Using the three frameworks in a rotating manner optimizes students' language development and provides them with opportunities to experience teacher-directed and student-directed instructional activities.

Resource-Based Units Resource-based instruction is organized around either a single selection or several related texts or media materials. Students read, view, or listen to the selection and then prepare, respond, explore, and extend their knowledge as a result of this experience. Throughout the unit, students work together either as a whole class or in small groups as a community of learners. In this context, they share their interpretations of the text. Teachers organize, participate, and provide mini-lessons on pertinent language concepts, strategies, and skills. Teachers also need to assist students in making connections with their personal experiences and directing their thinking to extend their comprehension. One good example of such a unit is the novel study, described in Chapter 5, Comprehension of Narrative Text.

Caution During the initial long-range planning for the year, it is suggested that teachers select the novels and other resources they plan to use throughout the year. These selections can then be removed from the classroom library to prevent students from reading them ahead of the planned unit of study.

Thematic Units Thematic units are interdisciplinary in nature and integrate language in one or more curriculum areas, such as social studies, science, mathematics, and health. They are especially time efficient since multiple expectations in one or more subject areas are being addressed simultaneously. When determining the topics for thematic units, it is helpful to keep them broad so that there are many possible avenues for exploration and focus. For instance, environmental issues, civilization, transportation, and celebration are broad topics that provide multiple foci. When students explore thematic topics, they use all strands of the language arts, including reading and viewing texts, writing, and oral skills (e.g., conducting interviews or making presentations that may be oral, dramatic, or multi-modal). The skills of critical analysis, questioning, synthesizing and summarizing, and locating information are also necessary in thematic units.

Inquiry-Based Units Inquiry-based units are sometimes less structured in their preparation and planning. They usually emerge from student interests or from a media event or shared book. They reflect genuine unexplored areas of interest that engage both students and teacher so that the classroom truly becomes a community of learners. The strength of such inquiry is that it is generally motivational for students. Teachers need to provide students with adequate time and resources to explore topics either individually, in pairs, or in small groups. The planning for the inquiry should be made as a whole class, with the teacher participating as mediator and organizer when necessary but not dominating students' sense of ownership and choices for implementation. Elements common to all inquiry-based units include the following:

- Clarifying the focus of the inquiry together. This may require some preliminary exploration on the internet, teacher-led Read Aloud, or ongoing dialogue and quick writes.
- Multiple sources of data must be readily available, including texts (both fiction and expository), reputable internet sites, and other sources (e.g., interviews with relevant individuals). Field trips for data gathering may also be appropriate.
- The sharing of results is a vital component and students should be provided with a variety of options, including dramatic presentations, multimedia presentations, musical productions, oral presentations, bulletin boards, compositions, and artistic presentations.
- A reflective session at the conclusion of the unit is useful for identifying what has been learned and exploring new questions. The important message for students is that inquiry is an ongoing process in which questions result from the acquisition of new knowledge and experience.

ATMOSPHERE

WHILE EFFECTIVE TEACHERS DO WORK WITH THEIR STUDENTS TO CREATE A CLASSROOM atmosphere, they must make many initial decisions to guide this process. The ultimate goal is to create a positive sense of being a community of learners and to motivate students to participate in all activities, including the language arts (see Table 12.4). Teachers must walk a fine line of becoming co-learners and partners with their students while retaining all of their roles as guide, teacher, monitor, coach, mentor, and grader (Tompkins, 2004).

Self-Esteem

The essence of self-esteem is the sense of self-worth, which individuals strive continually to attain. When students feel good about themselves, they are usually motivated to learn. When they successfully demonstrate new understandings and skills, they are usually provided with extrinsic reinforcement, accompanied by an intrinsic sense of satisfaction about their ability to learn. This cycle leads to the development of self-esteem and self-respect that Maslow (1943) refers to as self-actualization. The cycle of self-esteem, learning, and self-actualization can occur if home and school environments provide students with lower-level needs: physiological needs, safety and security, and a sense

Creating word walls

Table 12.4 Characteristics of Language Learning Communities

- Students have a sense of responsibility for their own behaviour and learning. They view themselves as valued members who contribute to the community.
- There are many authentic and genuine opportunities to read and write.
- Motivation is strong and maintained by providing students with choice (e.g., books to read, activities to complete, partners for collaborative projects).
- Teachers teach literacy skills explicitly, modelling and scaffolding instruction until students can apply skills independently.
- Students are encouraged to take risks associated with asking questions, exploring areas of interest, and making guesses.
- Teachers model an enjoyment for reading and writing.
- Teachers are able to provide quick mini-lessons on skills and strategies for individuals, small groups, or the whole class.
- Students help each other by participating in classroom dialogues and sharing drafts and final products.
- Students are provided with opportunities to make choices about activities, reading materials, and writing topics.
- The language arts are given a large block of time that is not interrupted for small component tasks.
- Students provide some of the criteria for assessment so they can monitor their progress (Tompkins, 2004).
- There is shared humour, with "in-class jokes" that mark membership in the group.

of belonging and affection (Novak & Purkey, 2001). Teachers need to be alert to signs of bullying, which can be either overt or covert in the classroom or schoolyard, and respond firmly to expunge it. They also need to be aware of students who may be sleep deprived or nutritionally deprived or who seem depressed.

Classroom Management

It is well known that social interactions enhance students' cognitive development (Vygotsky, 1978). The implication of this is that social interactions must include positive and meaningful language opportunities, which also implies that teachers need to structure the classroom and manage it effectively so that learning can be maximized (Dixon-Krauss, 1996; Wessler & Preble, 2003).

It is inevitable that, at times, some students will exhibit behaviours that seriously interfere with teaching and learning (Haberman, 1995; Horner, Sugai, Lewis-Palmer, & Todd, 2001). Teachers are more likely to engage in effective management of such behaviours when they have determined in advance how they will respond to various scenarios and when they believe that they are able maintain a positive learning environment (Bembenutty & Chen, 2005). Thinking in advance is especially important for beginning teachers who may experience difficulty in making good decisions on the spot. Teachers should consult practices within the school or the code of conduct (if one exists) as part of this preliminary thinking and decision-making process. While the response to misbehaviour is often highly personal and strongly influenced by grade level, there are a number of professional principles to consider when planning for such eventualities:

1. An awareness of the causes of misbehaviour helps teachers to use positive techniques rather than negative ones and avoids the trap of taking misbehaviour as a personal affront.
2. Instructional competence can lessen negative student behaviour.
3. Communicating clearly with students about expectations and guidelines and obtaining their commitment to following them enhances appropriate classroom behaviour.
4. Deciding on natural and logical consequences helps students to learn that they are responsible for the consequences of their behaviour and thus for controlling it.
5. When teachers hold private conferences with students who have chronic behavioural issues, the likelihood of resolving the problem within the classroom increases.
6. When students act inappropriately, teachers should review the following questions before determining an appropriate response:
   - Does this behaviour disrupt the classroom learning environment? If the answer is yes, a decision to act is made. If it is no, a decision is made about whether to address the misbehaviour later or to ignore it.
   - How can I minimize or lessen the disruptive factor so I do not draw undue attention to the disruptive behaviour?
   - How can I manage the situation to return to an effective learning environment?
7. In all circumstances, it is important for teachers to remain calm.
   (Adapted from Levin, Levin, Kerr, & Elliott, 2011.)

Motivation

Motivation is the internal drive that causes students to be persistent in trying to achieve a goal, solve a problem, or complete a task successfully and it contributes strongly to the atmosphere of the classroom. Studies on effective instruction have concluded that motivation has a significant impact on student learning (Brophy, 2004). Teachers have always attempted to foster motivation in students because it is one of the best ways to achieve a strong learning environment and prevent classroom behaviour problems from arising (see Chapter 5, Comprehension of Narrative Text, and Chapter 6, Reading Comprehension for Non-Fiction: Reading in the Content Areas, for a more extensive discussion of motivation for reading). There are many variables that teachers can employ to increase student motivation, including the following:

- Heighten student interest by relating learning to life outside of school. For instance, relate poetry to the lyrics of popular music or have students compose lyrics.
- Create an environment in which students' opinions are heard and valued. Plan group work that creates a sense of belonging and acceptance.
- Employ a variety of teaching techniques and match them to students' needs.
- Plan lessons that are novel or use multimedia. Do not extend direct instruction beyond students' concentration and schedule regular breaks.
- Ensure that all students achieve a sense of success by developing clear goals and programming for individual differences.
- Make the classroom tension free. Avoid making threats or nagging.
- Strive for a pleasant, firm, and friendly attitude that is focused on completing the task at hand.
- Provide specific feedback soon after the performance or task is completed. It is helpful to use students' names when providing written feedback (e.g., "Good improvement in paragraph structure, Carol! Try to vary the types of sentences you use in your story.")
- Encourage students as a method of increasing their motivation and validating their efforts. Encouragement also works well one-on-one.

Connecting with Colleagues

Classrooms exist within a larger social community. It is important for beginning teachers to make an effort to connect with the larger school community by collaborating with colleagues and participating in school initiatives and programs. A very good time to make initial connections with colleagues is during those few days before school starts when people come to work dressed casually and well rested from the summer. While beginning teachers may feel inclined to focus on their classroom, it is a mistake not to reach out to become part of the school staff at this time. During these early encounters, it is a good practice to seek out someone with whom a connection is felt and ask if he or she would serve as a sort of mentor. It is also important to have someone to consult about school routines. At all times, it is vital to remember to be professional when discussing students, parents, administrators, and other teachers.

Building a Community of Learners: Starting in September

Building a positive classroom atmosphere begins the instant students enter the classroom in September. There is only one chance to make a positive first impression (with the next chance occurring in the following year). Day 1 needs to be planned carefully, with nothing left to chance. Tips for the first day include the following:

- Provide students with the opportunity to select a book from a prearranged book display as soon as they enter the room. Use only books from the school library that are relatively new in appearance to signify new beginnings (leave the old favourites that are dog-eared until later). This gives students something to do if they complete a task early that day.
- Share and follow the prearranged schedule, as students tend to feel confident and comfortable when they understand what is expected and that the day is well organized.
- Teach something new in the morning and in the afternoon. These can be stand-alone lessons that do not relate directly to the curriculum.
- Conclude the lesson with some sort of written assignment. Use paper rather than new notebooks for the first few days. Observe students closely during the work period and review their work to determine their areas of strength and need.
- Name tags can be placed on desks before class or students can be permitted to find their own seats and create name tags (clarify that this is a temporary seating arrangement).
- Learn and use students' names immediately.
- Avoid sharing inexperience in a classroom (although, if asked, this should not be denied). Acknowledge relevant experiences in classrooms.
- Start the Read Aloud program using a motivational book. Have a second selection ready in case the majority of students have read the book previously.

- Discuss pencil sharpening and other routines when distributing materials and supplies.
- Indicate whether hand-raising is an expected routine for question answering.
- Use genuine praise for sincere efforts and appropriate answers and behaviours throughout the day.

Caution Do not assume that students will understand what is expected of them. Provide specific and clear instructions throughout the day. Remember that establishing routines requires considerable time and rushing through instructions may negate retention. The first few days and weeks represent a "honeymoon" period when much can be accomplished toward establishing an orderly environment in which learning can flourish.

COMMUNICATING WITH PARENTS

STUDENTS ACHIEVE BETTER WHEN THEIR PARENTS ARE INVOLVED IN THEIR EDUCATION. They are more likely to be motivated, to earn higher grades, to exhibit better behaviour and social skills, and to seek higher education when their parents support their success at school (Epstein, 2001; Sui-Chu & Willms, 1999). Of paramount importance are parental expectations as well as the oral language discourse and reading shared by parents with their children over time (Jeynes, 2005). Therefore, it is imperative that teachers view family-school partnerships as an integral part of good teaching and student success. Parents should be kept informed about what students are studying and how their children are performing. This goal is often difficult to achieve, as parents sometimes have relatively little time to spend with their children. In many cases, therefore, the onus is on teachers to communicate frequently with the parents, remembering that most parents, regardless of socio-economic background, hold high aspirations for their children's success (Jeynes, 2005). It is a good idea to consult with other teachers about how they communicate with parents, as this may indicate what is expected in the community.

A teacher's communication needs to be systematic. For instance, many teachers send newsletters home each month describing what aspects of the curriculum will be studied as well as other pertinent information. Other teachers maintain a classroom webpage located on the school's website so parents can check daily for homework expectations and assignment and test due dates. Other events such as field trips, projects, and classroom celebrations can also be featured.

There are other ways to maintain a two-way dialogue with parents. Many teachers like to invite parents to participate as classroom volunteers, especially at the primary level, as students are generally very happy to have a parent visit the classroom. Phone calls regarding particular classroom problems or celebrating individual successes are generally appreciated and result in a stronger home-school connection. Teachers should also let parents know that they are willing to meet on their request.

There should never be surprises for parents about any difficulties their children may be experiencing. Tasks and projects—accompanied by criteria and teacher comments, and, if relevant, teacher marks—should be sent home regularly. If there is doubt about parents receiving and reviewing these materials, teachers can ask that they be returned with a signature to indicate that they have been read.

It is useful to have a parent meeting early in the school year to describe the curriculum plan, introduce the teacher's philosophy of education, and set up methods of systematic communication. At the same time, it is a good plan to ask parents for preferred methods of communication. It is important to project positive messages about students' achievement throughout the year and an openness to meeting whenever requested. Dates for regular teacher-parent conferences can also be shared.

SUBSTITUTE TEACHING

THE TERM *SUBSTITUTE TEACHER* IS COMMONLY USED IN CANADA AND THE UNITED States when referring to individuals who teach classes when regular teachers are absent because of illness, personal leave (e.g., maternity leave), or professional development (e.g., conferences, meetings). Other terms to describe this role include *teacher on call* (British Columbia) and *occasional* or *supply teacher* (Ontario). While the terms differ, the duties and responsibilities associated with the position remain essentially constant. Qualified teachers are registered on a list that is held centrally by local school boards, with school administrators calling on individuals as required.

In Canada, substitute teaching frequently represents the typical path for beginning a teaching career. This trend, in part, reflects declining student enrolments in many school boards, making it less likely that newly qualified teachers will be hired immediately. In a sense, an additional period of hands-on teaching has been added to the completion of teacher preparation programs. Many beginning teachers believe that substitute teaching is an effective way to hone skills and develop a personal philosophy of teaching.

There are three types of assignments for substitute teachers. First, there is the long-term placement where the substitute teaches a subject or grade level. This is generally the preferred assignment. Second, there is the pre-booked assignment where the substitute teacher has advanced planning time, even speaking with the teacher of record in some cases. The third type is the most challenging and involves no advance notice and teaching with little preparation. This last form supports the creation of an emergency activity folder for each grade level (Duebber, 2000). Table 12.5 lists suggestions for successful substitute teaching.

There are many resources available to assist substitute teachers. Many useful resources can be found on the internet, including ETFO Occasional Teachers (www.etfo-ot.net) and EducationWorld (www.educationworld.com). The online *Substitute Teacher Magazine* (www.substituteteachermagazine.com) similarly provides tips and recommendations.

Teacher Voice 12.1

Supply teaching can be very unpredictable; you never know when you will be working or what type of classroom you will be going into. I can typically tell within the first 10 minutes of being in a classroom what type of day I will have and if I need to implement a reward system such as "good work tickets" for a prize at the end of the period or day or if a list of "star students" on the board will suffice. It helps if you can get to know one or two schools really well so that, in time, you can become just another regular teacher to the students as opposed to an unknown supply teacher.

Jessica Dunn, B.Ed.
Supply teacher

Table 12.5 Tips for Successful Substitute Teaching

- Be punctual, sending a positive message to administration and to students that you are in control of the situation and environment.
- Be prepared to be flexible. Teaching assignments may change from the time of receiving the call and arriving at the school.
- Be prepared to teach. Bring some lessons you have prepared for various grade levels, complete with resources.
- Use the internet to find lesson plans, worksheets, and information about curriculum topics.
- Be proactive about discipline and inform students of your expectations and boundaries. Begin by indicating that you intend to have a productive day. Use all of the classroom management strategies and techniques you have learned (e.g., position yourself in the classroom to encourage attention and move about as needed, ensure that students stay on task by checking that they understand all instructions). It is a good idea to check with another teacher or the administrator about procedures for students who persistently disrupt the class, following through on this information as a last resort.
- Praise students for sincere efforts and good behaviours.
- Grade work that you assign.
- Leave the classroom tidy.
- Dress professionally. While the dress code is very casual in some schools (especially at the end of the week), it is wise to be professionally attired and groomed.
- Volunteer to assist with school plays, field days, or field trips whenever possible to network with staff and administrators and demonstrate teaching and relationship skills.
- Be friendly and professional with staff and administration. Leave a detailed note for the returning teacher (some substitute teachers use a customized reporting form) with itemized comments about what was taught, how students responded, which students did well, and which ones experienced difficulties. Some substitute teachers prepare business cards and take a moment to present these to the principal or vice-principal in the hopes of being called again or considered for permanent or long-term positions.

PROFESSIONAL DEVELOPMENT: AN ESSENTIAL COMPONENT OF A SUCCESSFUL TEACHING CAREER

Continuous learning has become an essential professional expectation (Webster-Wright, 2009). Effective teachers build skills and knowledge continuously throughout their career. As an example, there is always more to learn about language arts since a great deal of research is conducted in the area and new instructional methods and techniques emerge frequently. Professional learning can take many forms, with teachers having preferred learning formats. Opportunities exist for informal, formal, and independent learning and many are provided within the school, the school board, or the provincial jurisdiction. Additionally, much learning can be accomplished collaboratively among colleagues and with mentors who also serve to increase collegiality. See Table 12.6 for other suggestions about continued learning and professional development activities that are especially relevant for language arts teachers.

Teacher Voice 12.2

It is important to engage in additional activities to continue your growth as a teacher. Over time, you should challenge yourself to consider topics that do not relate directly to your current position or school. That is, consider topics that will be relevant for the future. For instance, I work in a school with a relatively low proportion of students who are learning English as second language. But I know that these demographics will change in the future, so I am completing courses in this area now.

Nicole Maheu
Learning resource teacher

Table 12.6 Suggestions for Continued Learning and Professional Development

- Attend all after-school workshops sponsored by your school board.
- Join a national literacy organization (organizations exist for other curriculum areas as well). The International Reading Association has affiliate organizations in many provinces and school boards across Canada and generally offers several informative meetings over the course of the school year.
- Join an international literacy organization such as the International Reading Association (www.reading.org) or National Council of Teachers of English (www.ncte.org). Both of these organizations offer an annual conference and a wealth of publications and online information.
- Visit local children's bookstores and libraries to keep current with newly published and acclaimed books. Read at least one or two new children's books each year so that your repertoire expands.
- Consider taking specialized credit curriculum courses through the school board or a local university.
- Think about what interests you professionally and become an expert.
- Consider completing a Master of Education degree.
- Read both for pleasure and from a wide range of excellent professional materials to enhance your understanding of methodology, assessment, and classroom management. Most school libraries have a good selection of professional books.
- Attend at least one conference per year, if possible.
- Observe an admired professional in the classroom.

SUGGESTIONS FOR PROFESSIONAL DEVELOPMENT

1. Seek out two or three experienced teachers and ask them how they prepare for the school year. Ask them how they set up their daily and weekly schedules and establish their long-range plans. Ask if they would be willing to share copies of their plans to provide you with a template for constructing your own. Ensure that at least one of the teachers with whom you consult is from the school at which you will be teaching.
2. Make arrangements to spend a morning or afternoon observing a classroom (or, if possible, observe several classrooms over a series of visits). Reflect on the physical

arrangement of the classroom as well as the patterns and routines. As part of your observations consider questions such as:

- How are reading and writing spaces defined?
- How are books and other materials presented and stored?
- What routines are in place for students to hand in assignments?
- How do students transition between activities?
- How does the teacher obtain students' attention?
- Does the physical arrangement of chairs allow for students to collaborate readily?

Share and discuss your observations with the teacher.

3. Make arrangements to attend either a literacy-related conference or a school board–sponsored professional development event. If you cannot attend, make arrangements to speak to a teacher who was able to attend. Consider the following questions:
   - How did the focus of the topic connect to your teaching and teaching philosophy?
   - What information could be transferred to your classroom practice?
   - Which other individuals attended the session? What insights did they provide? How did they contribute to your growth as an educator?
4. Reflect on your experiences as a student. What type of information did you provide to your parents about your school day? How did your parents receive information about your performance as a student? Did your parents visit your classrooms? Did they meet with your teachers? What was the relationship between your parents, your teachers, and your school?

   Seek out two or three experienced teachers and ask them how they communicate with parents. How frequently do they communicate and what methods and tools do they use when providing parents with information (ask to see any written communications)? What are their policies about having parents in the classroom and meeting with them outside of school hours?

   Consider and discuss how your parents' experiences while you were a student compare with those whose children are currently attending school.

CHILDREN'S LITERATURE REFERENCES

Ellis, D. (2003). *The breadwinner*. Toronto, ON: Groundwood Books.
Haddix, M. P. (2000). *Among the hidden*. New York, NY: Simon & Schuster Publishing.

MyEducationLab

MyEducationLab is an interactive, virtual learning tool that will help improve your understanding of the concepts taught in this textbook and in your course. Through this engaging resource, you will have access to simulations of real classroom experiences, exercises that will help you improve your knowledge of key concepts, and additional resources that will help you in your teaching career. Use this online tool with your textbook to help you succeed in your studies and beyond!

References

Abbott, C., & Godinho, S. (2001). *Speak, listen and learn: Building speaking, discussion and presentation skills in every classroom*. Toronto, ON: Pembroke.

Adams, M. J. (1990). *Beginning to read: Thinking and learning about print*. Cambridge, MA: MIT Press.

Afferbach, P. (2007). *Understanding and using reading assessment, K–12*. Newark, DE: International Reading Association.

Agrey, L. (2004). The pressure cooker in education: Standardized assessment and high-stakes. *Canadian Social Studies, 38*(3). Retrieved from **http://www.quasar.ualberta.ca/css/Css_38_3/ ARagrey_pressure_cooker_education.htm**

Airasian, P. W., Engemann, J. F., & Gallagher, T. L. (2007). *Classroom assessment: Concepts and applications*. Toronto, ON: McGraw-Hill.

Alderman, M. K. (1999). *Motivation for achievement: Possibilities for teaching and learning*. Mahwah, NJ: Lawrence Erlbaum Associates Inc.

Al-Fartousi, M., & Woloshyn, V. E. (2009). Promoting Arabic-heritage students' use of question answering while reading. *The Reading Teacher, 32*(1), 20–28.

Alfassi, M. (2004). Reading to learn: Effects of combined strategy instruction on high school students. *Journal of Educational Research, 97*(4), 171–184.

Al-Hilawani, Y.A. (2003). Clinical examination of three methods of teaching reading comprehension to deaf and hard-of-hearing students: From research to classroom application. *Journal of Deaf Studies and Deaf Education, 8*(2), 146–156.

Allen, G. (2003). *Roland Barthes*. New York, NY: Routledge.

Allington, R. L. (2006). *What really matters for struggling readers: Designing research-based interventions* (2nd ed.). New York: NY: Longman.

Allington R. L., & Cunningham P. M. (2001). *School sthat work: Where all children read and write* (2nd ed.). Needham Heights MA: Allyn & Bacon.

Almasi, J. F. (2003). *Teaching strategic processes in reading*. New York, NY: The Guilford Press.

Alvermann, D. E., & Phelps, S. F. (1998). *Content reading and literacy: Succeeding in today's diverse classrooms Second edition*. Toronto, ON: Allyn and Bacon.

Alvermann, D. E., & Phelps, S. F. (2001). *Content reading and literacy: Succeeding in today's diverse classrooms* (3rd ed.). Toronto, ON: Allyn and Bacon.

Amaral, O. M., Garrison, L., & Klentschy, M. (2002). Helping English learners increase achievement through inquiry-based science instruction. *Bilingual Research Journal, 26*(2), 213–239.

Anderson, L. W., & Krathwohl, D. R. (2001). *A taxonomy for learning, teaching and assessing*. New York, NY: Longman.

Anderson, M. (2003). Reading violence in boys' writing. *Language Arts, 80*(3), 223–230.

Anderson, R. C., Hiebert, E. H., Scott, J. A., & Wilkinson, I. A. G. (1985). *Becoming a nation of readers: The report on the commission on reading*. Washington, DC: National Academy of Education, Commission on Education & Public Policy.

Anderson, S., Medrich, E., & Fowler, D. (2007). Which achievement gap? *Phi Delta Kappan, 88*(7), 547–550.

Anderson-Mejias, P. L. (2002). The ESL teacher's role in heritage language maintenance. *The Internet Journal, 8*(10).

Andersson, U., & Lyxell, B. (2007). Working memory deficit in children with mathematical difficulties: A general or specific deficit? *Journal of Experimental Child Psychology*, 96, 197–228.

Andrews, J., & Lupart, J. L. (2000). *The inclusive classroom: Educating exceptional children* (2nd ed.). Scarborough, ON: Nelson Canada.

Anstey, M., & Bull, G. (2006). *Teaching and learning multiliteracies: Changing times, changing literacies*. Newark, DE: International Reading Association.

Anstey, M., & Bull, G. (2009). Helping teachers to explore multimodal texts. *Curriculum Leadership, 8*(16).

Antunes, P. J., MacBride-King, J., & Swettenham, J. (2004). *Making a visible difference: The contribution of visible minorities to Canadian economic growth*. Ottawa, ON: Conference Board of Canada. Retrieved from **http://www.conferenceboard.ca/documents.aspx?did=705**

Applebee, A. N. (1978). *The child's concept of story*. Chicago, IL: University of Chicago Press.

Applebee, A. N., Langer, J. A., Nystrand, M., & Gamoran, A. (2003). Discussion-based approaches to developing understanding: Classroom instruction and student performance in middle and high school English. *American Educational Research Journal, 40*(3), 685–730.

Armstrong, J. (2002). *What is an accountability model?* Denver, CO: Education Commission of the States.

Arns, M., de Ridder, S., Strehl, U., Breteler, M., & Coenen, M. (2009). Efficacy of neuro feedback treatment in ADHD: The effects on attention, impulsivity & hyperactivity: A meta-analysis. *Clinical EEG & Neuroscience, 40*, 180–189.

Ash, G. E. (2002). Teaching readers who struggle: A pragmatic middle school framework. *Reading Online: The Online Journal of the International Reading Association, 5*(7). Retrieved from **http://www.readingonline.org/articles/art_index.asp?href=ash/index/html**

Atkinson, R. C., & Shiffrin, R. M. (1968). Human memory: A proposed system and its control processes. In K. W. Spence & J. T. Spence (Eds.), *The psychology of learning and motivation* (Vol. 2, pp. 89–195). San Diego, CA: Academic Press.

Atwell, N. (1998). *In the middle: New understandings about writing, reading and learning*. Portsmouth, NH: Heinemann.

August, D., & Shanahan, T. (2006). *Developing literacy in second language learners: Report of the National Literacy Panel on Language, Minority Children and Youth*. Mahwah, NJ: Lawrence Erlbaum Associates Publishers.

Ayersman, D. J. (1996). The effects of computer instruction, learning styles, gender and experience on computer anxiety. *Computers in the Schools, 12*(30), 15–30.

Baddeley, A. (2000). Short-term and working memory. In E. Tulving & F. I. M. Craik (Eds.), *The Oxford handbook of memory* (pp. 77–92). New York, NY: Oxford University Press.

Baddeley, A. D. (2006). Working memory: An overview. In S. Pickering (Ed.), *Working memory and education* (pp. 1–32). New York, NY: Academic Press.

Baddeley, A. D. (2007). *Working memory, thought and action*. New York, NY: Oxford University Press.

Bainbridge, J., Oberg, D. & Carbonaro, M. (2005). No text is innocent: Canadian children's books in the classroom. *The Journal of Teaching and Learning, 3*(2), 1–14.

Ball, E. W., & Blachman, B. A. (1991). Does phoneme segmentation training in kindergarten make a difference in early word recognition and developmental spelling? *Reading Research Quarterly, 26*, 49–66.

Bandura, A. (1977). Self-efficacy: Toward a unifying theory of behavioural change. *Psychological Review, 84*(2), 191–215.

Bandura, A. (1986). *Social foundations of thought and action: A social cognitive theory*. Englewood Cliffs, NJ: Prentice Hall.

Bandura, A. (1989). Regulation of cognitive processes through perceived self-efficacy. *Developmental Psychology, 25*(5), 729–735.

Banks, J. (2008). *An introduction to multicultural education* (4th ed.) New York, NY: Allyn & Bacon.

Banks, J. A. (1994). Transforming the mainstream culture. *Educational Leadership, 51*(8), 4–8.

Barchers, S. I. (1994). *Teaching language arts: An integrated approach*. New York, NY: West Publishing Company.

Barnett, W. S. (1995). Long-term effects of early childhood programs on cognitive and school outcomes. *The Future of Children, 5*, 25–50.

Barton, B. (1986). *Tell me another: Storytelling and reading aloud at home, at school and in the community*. Portsmouth, NH: Heinemann.

Barton, B., & Booth, D. (1990). *Stories in the classroom*. Toronto, ON: Pembroke.

Battistich, V., Solomon, D., Kim, D., Watson, M., & Schaps, E. (1995). Schools as communities, poverty levels of student populations, and students' attitudes, motives, and performance: A multilevel analysis. *American Educational Research Journal, 32*, 627–658.

Baumann, J. F. (2009). Vocabulary and reading comprehension: The nexus of meaning. In S. E. Israel & G. G. Duffy (Eds.), *Handbook of research on reading comprehension* (pp. 323–346). New York: NY: Routledge.

Baumann, J. F., & Kame'enui, E. J. (2004). *Vocabulary instruction: Research to practice*. New York, NY: Guilford.

Beach, R. (2007). *A web-linked guide to resources and activities*. New York, NY: Teachers College Press.

Beach, R., & Friedrich, T. (2006). Response to writing. In C. A. MacArthur, S. Graham, & J. Fitzgerald (Eds.), *Handbook of writing research* (pp. 222–234). New York, NY: Guilford Publications.

Beals, D. E. (2001). Eating and reading: Links between family conversations with preschoolers and later language and literacy. In O. K. Dickinson & P. O. Tabors (Eds.), *Beginning literacy with language: Young children learning at home and school* (pp. 75–92). Baltimore, MD: Paul H. Brooks.

Bean, T., & Rigoni, N. (2001). Exploring the intergenerational dialogue journals discussion of a multicultural young adult novel. *Reading Research Quarterly, 36*(3), 232–248.

Bear, D., Invernizzi, M., Templeton, S., & Johnston, F. (2003). *Words their way: Word study for phonics, vocabulary, and spelling instruction* (3rd ed.). Upper Saddle River, NJ: Pearson.

Beck, C. (2005). Language arts teaching meets new literacy studies. *Orbit, 36*(1), 2–4.

Beck, I. L., McKeown, M. G., Hamilton, R. L., & Kucan, L. (1997). *Questioning the author: An approach for enhancing student engagement with text.* Newark, DE: International Reading Association.

Beck, I. L., McKeown, M. G., & Kucan, L. (2002). *Bringing words to life: Robust vocabulary instruction*. New York, NY: Guilford Press.

Beck, I. L., McKeown, M. G., & Omanson, R. C. (1987). The effects and uses of diverse vocabulary instruction techniques. In M. G. McKeown & M. E. Curtis (Eds.), *The nature of vocabulary acquisition* (pp. 147–163). Hillsdale, NY: Lawrence Erlbaum.

Beech, J. (2004). Using a dictionary: Its influence on children's reading, spelling, and phonology. *Reading Psychology, 25*, 19–36.

Behrman, E. (2006). Teaching about language, power and text: A review of classroom practices that support critical literacy. *Journal of Adolescent & Adult Literacy, 49*(6) 498–498.

Bembenutty, H., & Chen, P. P. (2005). Self-efficacy and delay of gratification. *Academic Exchange Quarterly, 9*(4), 78–86.

Ben Jaafar, S., & Earl, L. (2008). Comparing performance-based accountability models: A Canadian example. *Canadian Journal of Education, 31*(3), 697–726.

Benchmark School. (1998). *Benchmark word identification/ Vocabulary development program*. Media, PA: Benchmark Press.

Bennett, L., & Ottley, P. (2011). *Launch into reading success (book 2)*. Bloomington, IN: Trafford Publishing.

Berko Gleason, J. B. (2009). *The development of language* (7th ed.). New York, NY: Allyn & Bacon.

Berko Gleason, J. B. & Ratner, N. B. (2009). *The development of language* (7th ed.). New York, NY: Allyn & Bacon.

Berninger, V. W. (2006). A developmental approach to learning disabilities. In W. Damon & R. Lerner (Eds.), *Handbook of child psychology* (6th ed.). New York, NY: Wiley.

Berrill, D., & Gall, M. (1999). On the carpet: Emergent writer/readers' letter sharing in a penpal program. *Language Arts, 75*(6), 470–478.

Berrill, D., & Gall, M. (2000). *Pen pal programs in primary grades*. Markham, ON: Pembroke Publishing.

Bettelheim, B. (1976). *The uses of enchantment: The meaning and importance of fairy tales*. New York, NY: Vintage Books.

Biemiller, A. (2007). *The influence of vocabulary on reading acquisition*. In Canadian Language and Literacy Centre, *Encyclopaedia of language and literacy development*. Retrieved from **http://www.softwaregroup.ca/encyclopedia./index.php?fa=items.show&topicid=19**

Biemiller, A. & Boote, C. (2006). An effective method for building vocabulary in primary grades. *Journal of Educational Psychology*, 98, 44–62.

Bishop, R. S. (1992). Mirrors, windows and sliding glass doors. *Perspectives: Choosing and using books for the classroom*, 6(3), ix–xi.

Bjorklund, D. E. (2000). Middle childhood: Cognitive development. In A. Kazdin (Ed.), *Encyclopedia of psychology*. Washington, DC, and New York, NY: American Psychological Association and Oxford University Press.

Blachmann, B. (2000). Phonolocial awareness. In M. L. Kamil, P. B. Mosenthal, P. D. Pearson, & R. Barr (Eds.), *Handbook of reading research* (Vol. III, pp. 483–502). Mahwah, NJ: Lawrence Erlbaum.

Blachowicz, C. L. Z., & Fisher, P. (2000). *Vocabulary instruction*. In M. L. Kamil, R. Mossenthal, P. D. Pearson, & R. Barr (Eds.), *Handbook of reading research* (Vol. III, pp. 503–523). Mahwah, NJ: Lawrence Erlbaum Associates.

Blachowicz, C., & Fisher, P. (2010). *Teaching vocabulary in all classrooms* (4th ed.). Columbus, OH: Prentice Hall.

Blachowicz, C., Fisher, P., & Ogle, D. (2006). Vocabulary: Questions from the classroom. *Reading Research Quarterly, 41*(4), 524–539.

Black, P., & Wiliam, D. (2009). Developing the theory of formative assessment. *Educational Assessment Evaluation and Accountability, 21*, 5–31.

Bodrova, E., & Leong, D. J. (2007). *Tools of the mind* (2nd ed.). Upper Saddle River, NJ: Prentice Hall.

Boling, E., Castek, J., Zawillinski, L., Barton, K., & Nierlich, T. (2008). Collaborative literacy: Blogs and internet projects. *The Reading Teacher, 61*(6), 504–506.

Bomer, R. (2006). *Girls, social class and literacy*. Oxford, UK: Heinemann.

Booth, D. (2005). *Story drama: Creating stories through role playing, improvising and reading aloud*. Markham, ON: Pembroke Publishers.

Booth, D., & Swartz, L. (2004). *Literacy techniques: For building successful readers and writers*. Markham, ON: Pembroke Publishing.

Boscolo, P. (2008). Writing in primary school. In C. Bazerman (Ed.), *Handbook of research on writing: History, society, school, individual, text* (pp. 293–310). New York: NY: Lawrence Erlbaum Associates.

Botelho, M. J. (2004). *Reading class: Disrupting power in children's literature*. (Unpublished doctoral dissertation). University of Massachusetts, Amherst, MA.

Boushey, G., & Moser, J. (2006). *The daily five*. Markham, ON: Stenhouse Publishers.

Bowles, S., Gintis, H., & Groves, M. O. (Eds.). (2005). *Unequal chances: Family background and economic success*. Princeton, NJ: Princeton University Press and Russell Sage Foundation.

Brabham, E. G., & Villaume, S. K. (2000). Questions and answers: Continuing conversations about literature circles. *The Reading Teacher, 54*(3), 278–280.

Bradley, D. H. (2001). How beginning writers articulate and demonstrate their understanding of the act of writing. *Reading Research and Instruction, 40*(4), 273–296.

Bradley, L., & Bryant, R. E. (1999). Categorizing sounds and learning to read: A causal connection. In A. Slater & D. Muir (Eds.), *The Blackwell reader in developmental psychology* (pp. 335–340). Malden, MA: Blackwell Publishing.

Bravo, M. A., & Cervetti, G. N. (2009). Teaching vocabulary through text and experience in content areas. In M. F. Graves (Ed.), *Essential readings on vocabulary instruction* (pp. 141–152). Newark, DE: International Reading Association.

Bredekamp, S. (2002). Language and early childhood programs. In C. T. Temple Adger, C. E. Snow, & D. Christian (Eds.), *What teachers need to know about language* (pp. 52–69). McHenry, IL: Delta Systems Co. Inc.

Brookhart, S. M. (2003). Developing measurement theory for classroom assessment purposes and uses. *Educational Measurement: Issues and Practice, 22*(4), 5–12.

Brookhart, S. M. (2004). Classroom assessment: Tensions and intersections in theory and practice. *Teachers College Record, 106*, 429–458.

Brophy, J. (2004). *Motivating students to learn* (2nd ed.). Mahwah, NJ: Lawrence Erlbaum Associates.

Brophy, J. E. (1988). Research linking teacher behaviour to student achievement: Potential implications for instruction of Chapter I students. *Educational Psychologist, 23*, 235–312.

Brown, A. (1982). Learning how to read from reading. In J. A. Langer & M. T. Smith-Burke (Eds.), *Reader meets author: Bridging the gap* (pp. 26–54). Newark, DE: International Reading Association.

Brown, A. L., & Day, J. D. (1983). Macrorules for summarizing texts: The development of expertise. *Journal of Verbal Learning and Verbal Behaviour, 22*, 1–14.

Bruner, J. (1986). *Actual minds, possible worlds*. Cambridge, MA: Harvard University Press

Brusilovsky, P., & Maybury, M. T. (2002) From adaptive hypermedia to adaptive web. In P. Brusilovsky & M. T. Maybury (Eds.), *Communications of the ACM, 45*(5, Special Issue on the Adaptive Web), 31–33.

Buckingham, D. (2001). After the death of childhood: Growing up in the age of electronic media. *Journal of Early Childhood Literacy, 1*(3), 331–334.

Buckingham, D. (2003). *Media education*. London, UK: Policy Press.

Budra, P. (2010). The case for teaching grammar. *Education Canada, 50*(4).

Burns, M. (2007). *About teaching mathematics: A K–8 Resource*. Sausalito, CA: Math Solutions Publications.

Burns, M. S., Griffin, P., & Snow, C. E. (1999). *Starting out right: A guide to promoting children's reading success*. Washington, DC: National Academy Press.

Burns, T. J. (2001). Being "social": Expanding our view of social interaction in writing workshops. *Language Arts, 78*(5), 458–466.

Butovsky, L., & Moscoe, T. (1985). *Spell well*. Scarborough, ON: Prentice-Hall Canada.

Caldwell, J. S., & Leslie, L. (2005). *Intervention strategies to follow informal reading inventory assessment: So what do I do now?* Boston, MA: Pearson Allyn & Bacon.

Caldwell, J. S., & Leslie, L. (2009). *Intervention strategies to follow informal reading inventory assessment: So what should I do now?* (2nd ed.). Boston, MA: Pearson Education Inc.

Calfee, R. C., & Wilson, K. M. (2004). A classroom-based writing assessment framework. In C. Addison Stone, E. R., Silliman, B. J. Ehren, & K. Apel (Eds.), *Handbook of language and literacy* (pp. 583–599). New York: NY: The Guilford Press.

Calkins, L. M. (1994). *The act of teaching writing* (2nd ed.). Portsmouth, NH: Heineman.

Calkins, L. M. (2009). *A quick guide to teaching second-grade writers with units of study*. Portsmouth, NH: Firsthand.

Campbell, J. (1949). *The hero with a thousand faces*. Princeton, NJ: Princeton University Press.

Campbell, T. A., & Hlusek, M. (2009). Storytelling and story writing: "Using a different kind of pencil." *What Works? Research into Practice*. The Literacy and Numeracy Secretariat, Research Monograph #20.

Campbell Hill, B., Johnson, N. J., & Schlick Noe, K. L. (1995). *Literature circles and response*. Norwood, CA: Christopher-Gordon Publishers.

Canadian Teachers' Federation. (2009). Standardized Testing + High-Stakes Decisions = Educational Inequity. Retrieved from **http://www.ctf-fce.ca/archive/docs/en/issues/assessment/high-stakes.htm**

Cappello, M. (2009). *Contemporary reading in literacy education*. Thousand Oaks, CA: Sage.

Carlisle, J. F. (2010). Review of research: Effects of instruction in morphological awareness on literacy achievement: An integrative review. *Reading Research Quarterly, 45*(4), 464–487.

Case, R. (2000). Conceptual structures. In M. Bennett (Ed.), *Developmental psychology*. Philadelphia, PA: Psychology Press.

Casey, H. K. (2008–2009). Engaging the disengaged: Using learning clubs to motivate struggling adolescent readers and writers. *Journal of Adolescent & Adult Literacy, 52*(4), 284–294.

Centre for Literacy, Quebec, Canada. (2008). Retrieved from **http://www.centreforliteracy.qc.ca/**

Certo, J., Moxley, K., Reffitt, K., & Miller, J. A. (2010). I learned how to talk about a book: Children's perceptions of literature circles across grade and ability levels. *Literacy Research and Instruction, 49*(3), 243–263.

Chall, J. S. (1983). Stages of reading development. New York, NY: McGraw-Hill Book Company.

Chall, J. S. (1996). *Learning to read: The great debate*. Fort Worth, TX: Harcourt Brace College Publishers.

Chall, J. S., Jacobs, J. A., & Baldwin, L. E. (1990). *The reading crisis: Why poor children fall behind*. Cambridge, MA: Harvard University Press.

Chandler-Olcott, K., & Mahar, D. (2003). "Tech-savviness" meets multiliteracies: Exploring adolescent girls' technology-related literacy practices. *Reading Research Quarterly, 39*, 356–385.

Chapman, J. W., & Tunmer, W. E. (2003). Reading difficulties, reading-related self-perceptions, and strategies for overcoming negative self-beliefs. *Reading and Writing Quarterly, 19*(1), 5–24.

Chen, K., & Bradshaw, A. C. (2007). The effect of web-based question prompts on scaffolding knowledge integration and ill-structured problem solving. *Journal of Research on Technology in Education, 39*(4), 359–375.

Chomsky, N. (1955). Systems of syntax and semantics: Their linguistic relevance. *Language, 31*(1–2).

Chomsky, N. (1975). *Reflections on language*. New York, NY: Random House.

Chomsky, N. (1987). Language, language development and reading: Review by Lillian R. Putnam. *Reading Instruction Journal*. Retrieved from **http://www.chomsky.info/interviews/1987**

Clay, M. (1987). *The early detection of reading difficulties* (3rd ed.). Auckland, New Zealand: Heinemann.

Clay, M. (1993). *Reading Recovery: A guidebook for teachers in training*. Portsmouth, NH: Heinemann.

Clay, M. (2001). *Change over time in children's literacy development*. Auckland, New Zealand: Heinemann.

Clay, M. M., & Cazden, C. B. (1990). A Vygotskian interpretation of Reading Recovery. In L. Moll (Ed.), *Vygotsky and education*. New York, NY: Oxford University Press.

Collins-Black, D., Gambrell, L. B., & Pressley, M. (2003). *Improving comprehension instruction: Advances in research, theory and classroom practice*. San Francisco, CA: Jossey-Bass.

Connelly, V. Dockrell, J., & Barnett, J. (2005). The slow handwriting of undergraduate students constrains overall performance in exam essays. *Educational Psychology, 25*, 99–107.

Cooter, K. S., & Cooter Jr., R. B. (2004). One size doesn't fit all: Slow learners in the read! *The Reading Teacher, 5*(7).

Cooter, R. B., & Reutzel, D. R. (2004). *Teaching children to read: Putting the pieces together*. Upper Saddle River, NJ: Pearson Education Inc.

Cope, B., & Kalantzis, M. (2000). *Multiliteracies: Literacy learning and the design of social futures*. New York, NY: Routledge.

Corbett, D., Wilson, B., & Williams, B. (2002). *Effort and excellence in urban schools*. New York, NY: Teachers College Press.

Cornett, C. E., & Smithrim, K. L. (2001). *The arts as meaning makers: Integrating literature and the arts throughout the curriculum* (Canadian ed.). Toronto, ON: Prentice Hall.

Cott, J. (1981). *Pipers at the gates of dawn*. Toronto, ON: McGraw-Hill.

Cox, T. (2000). *Combating educational disadvantage: Meeting the needs of vulnerable children*. London, UK: Falmer Press.

Craik, F. I. M., & Lockhart, R. S. (1972). Levels of processing: A framework for memory research. *Journal of Verbal Learning and Verbal Behavior, 11*, 671–684.

Csikszentmihalyi, M. (1997). *Finding flow*. New York, NY: Basic Books.

Culham, R. (1995). *6 + 1 traits of writing: The complete guide for grades 3 and up*. New York, NY: Scholastic Teaching Resources.

Culham, R. (2005). *6 + 1 traits of writing: The complete guide for the primary grades*. New York, NY: Scholastic Teaching Resources.

Cumming, R. (2007). Language play in the classroom: Encouraging children's intuitive creativity with words through poetry. *Literacy, 41*(2), 93–101.

Cummins, J. (2001) *Negotiating identities: Education for empowerment in a diverse society* (2nd ed.). Los Angeles, CA: California Association for Bilingual Education.

Cunningham, A. E. (2005). Vocabulary growth through independent reading and reading aloud to children. In E. H. Hiebert & M. L. Kamil (Eds.), *Teaching and learning vocabulary: Bringing research to practice* (pp. 45–68). Mahwah, NJ: Erlbaum.

Cunningham, P., & Hall, D. (1998). *Month-by-month PHONICS for upper grades*. Greensboro, NC: Carson-Dellosa.

Cunningham, P. M. (2000). Big words for big kids. In K. Wood & T. S. Dickinson (Eds.), *Promoting literacy in grades 4–9: A handbook for teachers and administrators* (pp. 282–294). Needham Heights, MA: Allyn & Bacon.

Cunningham, P. M. (2007). Best practices in teaching phonological awareness and phonics. In L. B. Gambrell, L. M. Morrow, & M. Pressley (Eds.), *Best practices in literacy instruction* (3rd ed., pp. 159–177). New York, NY: Guilford Press

Cunningham P. M., & Allington, R. L. (2006). *Classrooms that work: They can all read and write* (4th ed.). New York, NY: Allyn & Bacon.

Cunningham, P. M., Hall, D. P., & Cunningham, J. W. (2000). *Guided reading the four-blocks way*. Greensboro, NC: Carson-Dellosa.

Cunningham, P. M., Hall, D. P., & Sigmon, C. M. (1998). *The teacher's guide to the four-blocks literacy model: A multimethod, multilevel literacy framework*. Greenboro, NC: Carson-Dellosa.

D'Agostino, J. V., & Murphy, J. A (2004). A meta-analysis of Reading Recovery in the United States schools. *Educational Evaluation and Policy Analysis, 26*(1), 23–38.

Dahl, K., Barto, B., Bonfils, A., Carasello, M., Christopher, J., Davis, R., . . . Williams, J. (2004). Connecting developmental word study with classroom writing: Children's descriptions of spelling strategies. *The Reading Teacher, 57*, 310–319.

Dalton, B., & Proctor, C. P. (2008). The changing landscape of text and comprehension in the age of new literacies. In J. Coiro, M. Knobel, C. Lankshear, & D. Leu (Eds.), *Handbook of research on new literacies* (pp. 297–324). Mahweh, NJ: Lawrence Earlbaum Publishers.

Daniels, H. (1994). *Literature circles: Voice and choice in the student-centered classroom*. Markham, ON: Pembroke Publishers.

Daniels, H. (2002). *Literature circles: Voice and choice in book clubs and reading groups*. Portland, ME: Stenhouse Publishers.

Daniels, H. (2007). Pedagogy. In H. Daniels, J. Wertsch, & M. Cole (Eds.), *The Cambridge companion to Vygotsky*. New York, NY: Cambridge University Press.

Daniels, H., & Steineke, N. (2004). *Mini-lessons for literature circles*. Portsmouth, NH: Heinemann.

Danielson, C., & Abrulyn, L. (1997). *An introduction to using portfolios in the classroom*. Alexandria, VA: Association for Supervision and Curriculum Development.

Darling-Hammond, L., & Bransford, J. (2005). *Preparing teachers for a changing world*. San Francisco, CA: Jossey-Bass.

De La Paz, S., & Graham, S. (2002). Explicitly teaching strategies, skills and knowledge: Writing instruction in middle school classrooms. *Journal of Educational Psychology, 94*, 687–698.

De Zengotia, T. (2005). *Mediated: How the media shapes your world and the way you live in it*. New York, NY: Bloomsbury.

Dean, D. (2007). *Bringing grammar to life*. Newark, DE: International Reading Association.

DeVries, R. (2000). Vygotsky, Piaget, and education: A reciprocal assimilation of theories and educational practices. *New Ideas in Psychology, 18*, 187–213.

Dicintio, M. J., & Gee, S. (1999). Control is the key: Unlocking the motivation of at-risk students. *Psychology in the Schools, 36*(3), 231–237.

Dickinson, D. K., McCabe, A., Anastasopoulos, L., Peisner-Feinberg, E. S., & Poe, M. D. (2003). The comprehensive language approach to early literacy: The interrelationships among vocabulary, phonological sensitivity, and print knowledge among preschool-aged children. *Journal of Educational Psychology*, 95(3), 465–481.

Dickinson, O. K., & Tabors, P. O. (Eds.). (2001). *Beginning literacy with language: Young children learning at home and school*. Baltimore, MD: Paul H. Brooks.

DiPetta, T., Woloshyn, V. E., Gallagher, T., DiBiase, A. E., Hyatt, M., Dworet, D., & Bennett, S. (2010). Lessons from the field: Recommendations for education leaders planning. In A. Edmunds & B. McMillan (Eds.), *Leadership for inclusion: A practical guide* (pp. 131–150). Rotterdam, Taipei, SENSE Publishers.

Dixon-Krauss, L. (1996). *Vgyotsky in the classroom: Mediated literacy instruction and assessment*. White Plains, NY: Longman.

Dougherty Stahl, K. A. (2009). Assessing the comprehension of young children. In S. E., Israel & G. G. Duffy (Eds.), *Handbook of research on reading comprehension* (pp. 428–448). New York, NY: Routledge.

Downing, R. (2002). *Bridging Aboriginal digital and learning divides*. Retrieved from **http://www.hrsdc.gc.ca/eng/hip/lld/olt/skills_development/oltresearch/bridging-aboriginal-divide_e.pdf**

Duebber, D. (2000). Substitute teaching: Sink or swim. *Educational Leadership, 57*(8), 73–74.

Duffy, G. G. (2009). *Explaining reading: A resource for teaching concepts, skills, and strategies* (2nd ed.). New York, NY: The Guilford Press.

Duke, N. L., & Pearson, D. P. (2002). Effective practices for developing reading comprehension In A. E. Farstrup & S. J. Samuels (Eds.), *What research has to say about reading instruction* (3rd ed., pp. 205–242). Newark, DE: International Reading Association.

Dunn, P. A., & Lindblom, K. (2003). Why revitalize grammar? *The English Journal, 92*(3), 43–50.

Durkin, D. (1978). What classroom observations reveal about reading comprehension instruction. *Reading Research Quarterly, 14*(4), 482–533.

Duursmal, E., Augustyn, M., & Zuckerman, B. (2008). Reading aloud to children: The evidence. *Archives of Disease in Childhood, 93*, 554–557.

Earl, L. (2003). *Assessment as learning: Using classroom assessment to maximise student learning*. Thousand Oaks, CA: Corwin Press.

Earl, L. (2006). Rethinking classroom assessment with purpose in mind. Retrieved from **http://www.curicuum.org/secretariate/april 27.shtml**

Edmunds, A., & Edmunds, G. (2008). *Special education in Canada*. Toronto, ON: McGraw-Hill Ryerson.

Edwards, P. A., & Turner, J. D. (2009). Family literacy and reading comprehension. In S. E., Israel & G. G. Duffy (Eds.), *Handbook of research on reading comprehension* (pp. 622–642). New York: NY: Routledge.

Edyburn, D. L. (2003). Insights into the effective and appropriate use of technology in special education. *Remedial and Special Education, 24*, 130–131.

Edyburn, D. L. (2004). Assistive technology and evidence-based practice. *The ConnSENSE Bulletin*. Retrieved from **http://www.connsensebulletin.com/edyatevidence.html**

Ehri, L. C., & Nunes, S. R. (2002). The role of phonemic awareness in learning to read. In A. E. Farstrup & S. Samuels (Eds.), *What research has to say about reading instruction* (pp. 110–139). Newark, DE: International Reading Association.

Eisenberg, M. E. & Resnick, M. D. (2006). Suicidality among gay, lesbian and bisexual youth: The role of protective factors. *Journal of Adolescent Health, 39*(5), 682–668.

Elbow, P. (1998). *Writing with power: Techniques for mastering the writing process* (2nd ed.) New York, NY: Oxford University Press.

Elliott, A., Bosacki, S., Woloshyn, V., & Richards, M. (2002). Exploring preadolescents' media and literacy choices. *Language & Literacy, 3*(2), 1–13.

Ellison, N., & Wu, N. (2008). Blogging in the classroom: A preliminary exploration of student attitude and impact on comprehension. *Journal of Educational Multimedia and Hypermedia, 17*(1), 99–122.

Englert, C., Hiebert, E., & Stewart, S. (1985). Spelling unfamiliar words by an analogy strategy. *The Journal of Special Education, 19*, 291–306.

Epstein, J. (2001). *School, family and community partnerships*. Boulder, CO: Westview Press.

Evans, G. W. (2004). The environment of childhood poverty. *American Psychologist, 59*, 77–92.

Evertson, C. M. (1989). Classroom organization and management. In M. C. Reynolds (Ed.), *Knowledge base for the beginning teacher*. Oxford, UK: Pergamon Press.

Facer, K., Furlong, J., Furlong, R., & Sutherland, R. (2004). *Screenplay: Children and computing in the home*. London, UK: Routledge.

Felton, R. H., & Miller, L. L. (2001). "It's one of them . . . I don't know": Case study of a student with phonological, rapid naming, and word-finding deficits. *The Journal of Special Education, 35*(3), 125–133.

Ferdig, R. E., & Trammell, K. D. (2004). Content delivery in the "blogosphere." *THE Journal*. Retrieved from **http://www.thejournal.com/articles/16626**

Fillmore, L. W. & Valdez, C. (1986). Teaching bilingual learners. In M. E. Wittrock (Ed.), *Handbook of research on teaching* (pp. 648–685). New York, NY: Macmillan.

Fitzpatrick, B. (2005). Young adult literature. *School Libraries in Canada, 25*(1), 3–8.

Flavell, J. H. (2004). Theory-of-mind development: Retrospect and prospect. *Merrill-Palmer Quarterly, 50*, 274–290.

Flessa, J. J. (2007). *Poverty and education: Towards effective action: A review of the literature*. Toronto, ON: Elementary Teachers' Federation of Ontario.

Fletcher, J. M., Lyon, G. R., Fuchs, L. S., & Barnes, M. (2007). *Learning disabilities: From instruction to identification*. New York: NY: The Guilford Press.

Flower, L. S., & Hayes, J. R. (1981). Problem-solving and the cognitive processes in writing. In C. Frederiksen & J. F. Dominic (Eds.), *Writing: The nature, development, and teaching of written communication*. Mahwah, NJ: Erlbaum.

Foregrave, K. (2003). Exploring the use of prediction and summarization to increase students' reading comprehension. (M.Ed. dissertation). Brock University, St. Catharines, ON.

Fountas, I. C., & Pinnell, G. S. (2010–2011). *Leveled book list K–8+*. Portsmouth, NH: Heinemann.

Fountas, I. C., & Pinnell, G. S. (1996). *Guiding readers and writers (grades 3–6)*. Portsmouth, NH: Heinemann.

Fountas, I. C., & Pinnell, G. U. (2009). *Leveled literacy intervention (LLI)*. Portsmouth, NH: Heinemann

Freebody, P. (2005). Critical literacy. In R. Beach, J. Green, M. Michael, & T. Shanahan (Eds.), *Multidisciplinary perspectives on literacy research* (pp. 433–454). New York, NY: Hampton Press.

Freebody, P., & Freiberg, J. (2011). Teaching and learning critical literacy: Beyond the "show of wisdom." In M. Kamil, P. D. Pearson, E. B. Moje, & P. Afflerbach (Eds.), *International handbook of reading research* (pp. 432–453). Mahwah, NJ: Routledge.

Freeman, D. E., & Freeman, Y. S. (1993). Strategies for promoting the primary languages of all students. *The Reading Teacher, 46*, 552–558.

Freire, P. (1978). *Pedagogy in process: The letters to Guinea-Bissau*. New York, NY: Seabury Press.

Freire, P., & Macedo, D. (1987). *Literacy: Reading the word and the world*. Boston, MA: Virgin and Garvey.

Fresch, M. J. (2007). *An essential history of current reading practices*. Newark, DE: International Reading Association.

Frey, B. B., Lee, S. W., Tollefson, N., Pass, L., & Massengill, D. (2005). Balanced literacy in an urban school district. *Journal of Educational Research, 98*(5), 272–280.

Frye, N. (1957). *Anatomy of criticism: Four essays*. Princeton, NJ: Princeton University Press.

Frye, N. (1988). *On education*. Markham, ON: Fitzhenry & Whiteside.

Frye, N. (1991). *The double vision*. Toronto, ON: University of Toronto Press.

Fuchs, D., & Fuchs, L. S. (2006). Introduction to response to intervention: What, why, and how valid is it? *Reading Research Quarterly, 41*(1), 93–99.

Fuchs, D., Fuchs, L. S., & Burish, P. (2000). Peer-assisted learning strategies: An evidence-based practice to promote reading achievement. *Learning Disabilities Research & Practice, 15*, 85–91.

Fuchs, D., Fuchs, L. S., & Vaughn, S. (2008). *Response to intervention: A framework for reading teachers*. Newark, DE: International Reading Association.

Fung, I. Y. Y., Wilkinson, I. A. G., & Moore, D. W. (2002). L-1-assisted reciprocal teaching to improve ESL students' comprehension of English expository text. *Learning and Instruction, 13*(1), 1–31.

Galda, L., & Cullinan, B. E. (2002). *Literature and the child*. Belmont, CA: Wadsworth/Thompson Learning.

Galda, L., & Cullinan, E. (2006). *Literature and the child* (6th ed.). Belmont, CA: Wadsworth Thomson Learning.

Gambell, T., & Hunter, D. (2000). Surveying gender differences in Canadian school literacy. *Journal of Curriculum Studies, 32*, 689–719.

Gambrell, L., & Koskinen, P. S. (2002). Imagery: A strategy for enhancing comprehension. In C. B. Block & M. Pressley (Eds.), *Comprehension instruction: Research-based best practices*. New York, NY: Guilford Publications.

Gammill, D. M. (2006). Learning the *write* way. *The Reading Teacher, 59*(8), 754–762.

Ganske, K (1999). The developmental spelling analysis: A measure of orthographic knowledge. *Educational Assessment, 6*, 41–70.

Ganske, K. (2000). Word journeys: Assessment-guided phonics, spelling, and vocabulary instruction. *Educational Assessment, 6*, 41–70.

Ganske, K. (2008). *Mindful of words: Spelling and vocabulary explorations 4–8*. New York, NY: The Guilford Press

Gardner, S. (2008). Changing approaches to teaching grammar. *English Language Teacher Education and Development, 11*(4), 39–44.

Gaskins, I. W. (2005). Strategies for reading words: Teaching phonemic awareness, decoding, and fluency. In I. W. Gaskins (Ed.), *Success with struggling readers: The benchmark school approach* (pp. 155–176). New York, NY: The Guilford Press.

Gauvain, M., & Perez, S. M. (2007). The socialization of cognition. In J. E. Grusec & P. D. Hastings (Eds.), *Handbook of socialization*. New York, NY: Guilford Press.

Gee, J. P. (2002). Millennials and Bobos, Blue's Clues and Sesame Street: A story for our times. In D. E. Alverman (Ed.), *Adolescents and literacies in a digital world* (pp. 51–67). New York, NY: Peter Lang Publishing Inc.

Gee, J., P. (2003). *What video games have to teach us about language and literacy*. New York, NY: ACM Press.
Gee, J. P. (2008). *What video games have to teach us about learning and literacy*. Basingstoke, NH: Palgrave Macmillan.
Gentry, J. R. (1982). Developmental spelling: Assessment. *Diagnostique, 8*(1), 52–61.
Gentry, J. R. (1985). *You can analyze development spelling . . . And here's how to do it*. Retrieved from **http://www.gse.uci.edu/docs/DEVELOPMENTAL_SPELLING.pdf**
Gentry, J. R. (2004). *The science of spelling: The explicit specifics that make great readers and writers (and spellers!)*. Portsmouth, NH: Heinemann
Gentry, J. R. (2010). *Raising confident readers: How to teach your child to read and write from baby to age 7*. Jackson, TN: De Capo Lifelong Books.
Gentry, J. R., & Gillet, J. W. (1992). *Teaching kids to spell*. Portsmouth, NH: Heinemann.
Gerber, M. (1984). Techniques to teach generalizable spelling skills. *Academic Therapy, 20*, 49–58.
Gerber, M. (1986). Generalization of spelling strategies by LD students as a result of contingent imitation/modeling and mastery criteria. *Journal of Learning Disabilities, 19*, 530–537.
Gersten, R., Fuchs L. S., Williams, J. P., & Baker, S. (2001). Teaching reading comprehension strategies to students with learning disabilities: A review of the research. *Review of Educational Research, 71*(2), 279–320.
Gillies, R. M. (2007). *Cooperative learning: Integrating theory and practice*. Thousand Oaks, CA: SAGE Publications, Inc.
Giroux, H., & Simon, R. (1989). *Popular culture, schooling and everyday life*. New York, NY: Bergin & Garvey.
Gladwell, M. (2002). *The tipping point*. New York, NY: Back Bay Books.
Glogoff, S. (2005). Instructional blogging: Promoting interactivity, student-centered learning and peer input. *Innovate: Journal of Online Education, 1*(5).
Golden, J. M. (1984). Children's concept of story in reading and writing. *The Reading Teacher, 37*, 578–584.
Golden, J. M., Meiners, A., & Lewis, S. (1992). The growth of story meaning. *Language Arts, 69*, 22–27.
Goldenberg, C. (2004). *Successful school change: Creating settings to improve teaching and learning*. New York, NY: Teachers College.
Gollnick, D. M., & Chinn, R. C. (2002). *Multicultural education in a pluralistic society* (6th ed.). New York, NY: Merrill.
Gonzalez-DeHass, A. R., Willems, P. P., & Doan Holbein, M. F. (2005). Examining the relationship between parental involvement and student motivation. *Educational Psychology Review, 17*(2), 99–123.
Gordon, C., & Donnon, T. (2003). Early literacy: A success story. *Education Canada, 43*(3), 16–19.
Gose, E. (1988) *Mere creatures: A study of modern fantasy tales for children*. Toronto, ON: University of Toronto Press.
Goswami, I. (2000). Phonological and lexical processes. In M. L. Kamil, P. B. Mosenthal, P. D. Pearson, & R. Barr (Eds.), *Handbook of reading research* (Vol. III, pp. 174–200). Mahwah, NJ: Lawrence Erlbaum.
Goswami, U. C., & Bryant, P. (2000). *Phonological skills and learning to read*. London, UK: Psychology Press.
Graham, S. (1983). Effective spelling instruction. *Elementary School Journal, 83*, 560–568.
Graham, S. (2006). Strategy instruction and the teaching of writing: A meta-analysis. In C. A. MacArthur, S. Graham, and J. Fitzgerald (Eds.), *Handbook of writing research*. New York, NY: Guilford Publications.
Graham, S., & Harris, K. R. (2001). The role of self-evaluation and transcription skills in writing and writing development. *Educational Psychologist, 35*, 3–12.
Graham, S., & Harris, K. R. (2009). Evidence-based writing practices: Drawing recommendations from multiple sources. British Journal of Educational Psychology Monograph Series II, Number 6. *Teaching and Learning Writing, 1*(1), 95–111.
Graham, S., & Miller, L. (1979). Spelling research and practice: A unified approach. *Focus on Exceptional Children, 12*, 1–16.
Graham, S., Struck, M., Richardson, J., & Berninger, V. (2006). Dimensions of good and poor handwriting legibility in first and second graders. *Developmental Neuropsychology*, 29, 43–60.
Graves, D. H. (1983). *Writing: Teachers and children at work*. Portsmouth, NH: Heinemann.
Graves, D. H. (1994). *A fresh look at writing*. Portsmouth, NH: Heinemann.
Graves, D. H. (2003). *Writing: Children and teachers at work* (20th anniversary ed.). Portsmouth, NH: Heinemann.
Graves, M., & Slater, W. (1996). Vocabulary instruction in content areas. In D. Lapp, J. Flood, & N. Farnan (Eds.), *Content area reading and learning: Instructional strategies*. Boston, MA: Allyn & Bacon.
Graves, M. F. (2006). *The vocabulary book*. New York, NY: Teachers College Press.
Graves, M. F., Juel, C., & Graves, B. B. (1998). *Teaching reading in the 21st century*. Toronto, ON: Allyn and Bacon.
Gredler, M. E. (2008). Vygotsky's cultural-historical theory of development. In N. J. Salkind (Ed.), *Encyclopedia of educational psychology*. Thousand Oaks, CA: Sage.
Greenfield, P. M. (2000). Three approaches to the psychology of culture: Where do they come from? Where can they go? *Asian Journal of Social Psychology, 3*, 223–240.
Gregory, G. H., & Chapman, C. (2007). *Differentiated instruction strategies: One size doesn't fill all* (2nd ed). Thousand Oaks, CA: Corwin Press.
Grierson, A., Gallagher, T., & Woloshyn, V. E. (2007). Special educators' experiences implementing a "scientifically based" remedial reading program: All that glitters is not gold. *Policy and Practice in Education, 13*(1–2), 25–45.
Gronlund, N. E. (2006). *Assessment of student achievement* (8th ed.). Boston, MA: Allyn & Bacon.

Guerian, M. (2006). *The wonder of boys*. New York, NY: Tarcher.

Guerian, M. (2010). *Boys and girls learn differently* (10th ed.). Toronto, ON: Jossey-Bass.

Gunning, T. (2000). *Best books for building literacy for elementary school children*. Needham Heights, MA: Allyn & Bacon.

Gunning, T. (2005). *Creating literacy instruction for students* (5th ed.). Toronto, ON: Pearson Education.

Gunning, T. G. (1997). *Best books for beginning readers*. New York, NY: Allyn & Bacon.

Gurian, M. (2001). *Boys and girls learn differently: A guide for teachers and parents*. San Francisco, CA: Jossey-Bass.

Guthrie, J. T., & Cox, K. E. (2001). Classroom conditions for motivation. *Educational Psychology Review, 13*(3), 283–302.

Guthrie, J. T., & Ozgungor, S. (2002). Instructional contexts for reading engagement. In C. C. Block & M. Pressley (Eds.), *Comprehension instruction: Research-based best practices* (pp. 275–288). New York, NY: Guilford.

Haberman, M. (1995). *Star teachers of children in poverty*. West Lafayette, IN: Kappa Delta Pi.

Hacker, D. J. (2004). Self-regulated comprehension during normal reading. In R. B. Ruddell & N. J. Unrau (Eds.), *Theoretical models and processes of reading* (5th ed., pp. 755–779). Newark, DE: International Reading Association.

Hacker, D. J., & Tenent, A. (2002). Implementing reciprocal teaching in the classroom: Overcoming obstacles and making modifications. *Journal of Educational Psychology, 94*(4), 699–718.

Hackney, C. S. (1991). *Standard manuscript or modified italic? A critical evaluation of letter forms for initial handwriting instruction*. Columbus, OH: Zaner-Bloser Inc.

Hallahan, D. P., Kauffman, J. M., McIntyre, L. J., & Mykota, D. (2010). *Exceptional learners: An introduction to special education* (Canadian ed.). Toronto, ON: Pearson.

Hamilton, L. S. & Koretz, D. M. (2002). Tests and their use in test-based accountability systems. In L. S. Hamilton, B. M. Stecher, & S. P. Klein (Eds.), *Making sense of test-based accountability in education* (pp. 13–49). Santa Monica, CA: RAND Education.

Hammeken, P. A. (2007). *A teacher's guide to inclusive education: 750 strategies for success*. Thousand Oaks, CA: Corwin Press.

Haney, M., & Hill, J. (2004). Relationships between parent-teaching activities and emergent literacy in preschool children. *Early Child Development and Care, 174*, 215–228.

Hargraves, A., Earl, L., Moore, S., & Manning, S. (2001). *Learning to change: Teaching beyond subjects and standards* (1st ed.). San Francisco, CA: Jossey-Bass.

Hart, B., & Risley, T. R. (1995). *Meaningful experiences in the everyday lives of young American children*. Baltimore, MD: Paul H. Brookes Publishing Co.

Hart, P., & Teeter, R. (2001). *A measured response: Americans speak on education reform*. Princeton, NJ: Educational Testing Service.

Harvey, S., & Goudvis, A. (2000). *Strategies that work*. Markham, ON: Pembroke Publishers.

Harvey, S., & Goudris, A. (2007). *Strategies that work: Teaching comprehension to enhance understanding* (2nd ed.). York, ME: Stenhouse.

Hatzenbuehler, M. L. (2011). The social environment and suicide attempts in lesbian, gay and bisexual youth. *Pediatrics, 127*(5), 896–903.

Hauerwas, L., & Walker, J. (2004). What can children's spelling of running and jumped tell us about their need for spelling instruction? *The Reading Teacher, 58*(2), 168–176.

Haycock, K. (2001). Closing the achievement gap. *Educational Leadership, 58*(6), 6–11.

Heath, J., & Potter, A. (2004). *The rebel sell*. New York, NY: HarperCollins Publishers Ltd.

Hecker, L., Elkind, J., Elkind, K., & Katz, L. (2002). Benefits of assistive reading software for students with attention disorders. *Annals of Dyslexia, 52*, 243–272.

Heilman, H., Blair, T. R., & Rupley, W. H. (2001). *Principles and practices of teaching* (10th ed.). Upper Saddle River, NJ: Pearson Education.

Henderson, R. (2004). Recognizing difference: One of the challenges of using a multiliteracies approach? *Practically Primary, 9*(2), 11–14.

Henderson, J., & Wakeham, P. (2009). Colonial reckoning, national reconciliation? Aboriginal peoples and the culture of redress in Canada. *ESC: English Studies in Canada, 35*(1), 1–26.

Hess, F. M. (2002). Reform, resistance, . . . retreat? The predictable politics of accountability in Virginia. In D. Ravitch (Ed.), *Brookings papers on education policy* (pp. 69–104). Washington, DC: Brookings Institute Press.

Hibbing, A. N., & Rankin-Erickson, J. L. (2003). A picture is worth a thousand words: Using visual images to improve comprehension for middle school struggling readers. *The Reading Teacher, 56*(8), 758–770.

Hidi, S., Berndorff, D., & Ainley, M. (2002). Children's argument writing, interest and self-efficacy: An intervention study. *Leaning Instruction, 12*(4), 429–446.

Hiebert, E. H., & Raphael, T. E. (1998). *Early literacy instruction*. Orlando, FL: Holt, Rinehart and Winston.

Hill, S. E., & Nichols, S. (2006). Emergent literacy: Symbols at work. In B. Spodek & O. N. Saracho (Eds.), *Handbook of research on the education of young children* (pp. 153–165). Mahwah, NY: Lawrence Erlbaum Associates.

Hillman, J. (1995). *Discovering children's literature*. Columbus, OH: Merrill.

Hillocks, G. (2008). Writing in secondary schools. In C. Bazerman (Ed.), *Handbook of research on writing: History, society, school, individual, text* (pp. 311–330). New York: NY. Lawrence Erlbaum Associates.

Hirsch, E. D., Jr. (2003). Reading comprehension requires knowledge of words and the world: specific insights into the fourth grade slump and the nation's stagnant comprehension scores. *American Educator*, Spring, 10–29.

Hobbs, R. (2006). Multiple visions of multimedia literacy. In M. C. Kenna, L. D. Labbo, R. D. Kieffer, & D. Reinking (Eds.), *International handbook of literacy and technology* (Vol. 2, pp. 15–28). Mahwah, NJ: Lawrence Erlbaum Associates Publishers.

Hodgson, C. (2007). Assessing oracy: Storytelling. *Literacy Today*, December, 24–26.

Hoff, E. (2006). How social contexts support and shape language development. *Developmental Review, 26*, 55–88.

Hoff, E. (2009). *Language development* (4th ed.) Belmont, CA: Wadsworth.

Hoffman, M. J. (2003). Grammar for teachers: Attitudes and aptitudes. *Academic Exchange Quarterly, 7*(4).

Holder, M. K. (2003). *Teaching left-handers to write*. Bloomington, IN: Handedness Research Institute. Retrieved from **http://handedness.org/action/leftwrite.html**

Holloway, J. H. (2000). Preparing teachers for differentiated Instruction. *Educational Leadership, 58*(1), 82–83.

Horn, T. (1969). Research critiques. *Elementary English, 46*, 210–212.

Hornberger, N. H. (1998). Language, policy, language education, language rights: Indigenous, immigrant and international perspectives. *Language in Society, 27*, 439–458.

Horner, R. H., Sugai, G., Lewis-Palmer, T., and Todd, A. W. (2001). Teaching school-wide behavioral expectations. *Report on Emotional and Behavioral Disorders in Youth, 1*(4), 77–79, 93–96.

Hudson, R. (2004). Why education needs linguistics (and vice versa). *Journal of Linguistics, 40*(1), 105–130.

Huffaker, D. (2004). Spinning yarns around a digital fire: Storytelling and dialogue among youth on the internet. *First Monday, 9*(1).

Huffaker, D. (2005). The educated blogger: Using weblogs to promote literacy in the classroom. *AACE Journal, 13*(2), 91–98.

Hui, S. (2009). *First nations seeking to cross digital divided.* Retrieved from **http://www.straight.com/article-240587/first-nations-seeking-cross-digital-divide**

Hull, G., & Schultz, K. (2002). *School's out! Bridging out-of-school literacies with classroom practice*. New York, NY: Teachers College Press.

Hutchinson, N. (2010). *Inclusion of exceptional learners in Canadian schools: A practical handbook for teachers* (3rd Canadian ed.). Toronto, ON: Pearson Education Canada.

International Reading Association. (2009). *New literacies and 21st century technologies*. Retrieved from **http://www.reading.org.General/About IRA/PositionStatements/21stCentruyLiteracies.aspx**

Invernizzi, M. (2000). Book buddies: A community volunteer tutorial. In L. Morrow & D.G. Woo (Eds.), *Tutoring programs for struggling readers: The America reads challenge*. New York, NY: Guilford Press.

Invernizzi, M., & Hayes, L. (2004). Developmental-spelling research: A systematic imperative. *Reading Research Quarterly, 39*(2), 216–228.

Israel, S. E., & Duffy, G. G. (2009). *Handbook of research on reading comprehension*. New York, NY: Routledge.

Iverson, S., Tunmer, W. E., & Chapman, J. W. (2005). The effects of varying group size on the Reading Recovery approach to preventative early intervention. *Journal of Learning Disabilities, 38*, 456–472.

Jackson, N. E., & Coltheart, M. (2001). *Routes to reading success and failure*. Ann Arbor, MI: Sheridan Books.

Jacobs, J. E., & Paris, S. G. (1987). Children's metacognition about reading: Issues in definition, measurement, and instruction. *Education Psychology, 22*, 255–278.

Jacobson, J., Thrope, L., Fisher, D., Lapp, D., Frey, N., & Flood, J. (2001). Cross-age tutoring: A literacy improvement approach for struggling adolescent readers. *Journal of Adolescent & Adult Literacy, 44*(6), 528–536.

Jacobus, L. A. (1986). *A world of ideas*. New York, NY: St. Martin's Press.

Jalongo, M. R. (2000). *Early childhood language arts* (2nd ed.). Boston, MA: Allyn & Bacon.

James, C. (2005). Canadian multiculturalism. In C. James (Ed.), *Possibilities and limitations: Multicultural policies and programs in Canada* (pp. 21–33). Halifax, NS: Fernwood Publishing.

James, C., & Wood, M. (2005). Multicultural education in Canada: Opportunities, limitations and contradictions. In C. James (Ed.), *Possibilities and limitations: Multicultural policies and programs in Canada* (pp. 93–107). Halifax, NS: Fernwood Publishing.

Jankowska, M., and Atlay, M. (2008). Use of creative space in enhancing students' engagement. *Innovations in Education and Teaching International, 45*(3), 271–279.

Jenkins, H. (2006). *Fans, bloggers, and gamers: Exploring participatory culture*. New York, NY: New York University Press.

Jeynes, W. H. (2005). A meta-analysis of the relation of parental involvement to urban elementary school student academic achievement. *Urban Education, 40*(3), 237–269.

Jobe, R., & Dayton-Sakari, M. (1999). *Reluctant readers: Connecting students and books for successful reading.* Markham, ON: Pembroke Publishers.

John-Steiner, V. (2007). Vygotsky on thinking and speaking. In H. Daniels, J. Wertsch, & M. Cole (Eds.), *The Cambridge companion to Vygotsky*. New York, NY: Cambridge University Press.

Johns, J. L., & Berglund, R. L. (2010). *Fluency: Differentiated interventions and progress-monitoring assessments* (4th ed.). Dubuque, IA: Kendall Hunt Publishing Company.

Johnson, D. D. (2001). *Vocabulary in the elementary and middle school*. Needham Heights, MA: Allyn & Bacon.

Johnson, D. W., & Johnson, F. (2009). *Joining together: Group theory and group skills* (10th ed.). Boston, MA: Allyn & Bacon.

Johnson, D. W., Johnson, R. T., & Stanne, M. B. (2000). *Cooperative learning methods: A meta analysis*. Retrieved from **http://www.tabellearning.com**

Jones, I. (2003). Collaborative writing and children's use of literate language: A sequential analysis of social interaction. *Journal of Early Childhood Literacy*, *3*(2), 165–178.

Jones, V., & Jones, L. (2009). *Comprehensive classroom management: Creating communities of support and solving problems* (9th ed.). New York, NY: Prentice Hall.

Jordan, A., Schwartz, E., & McGhie-Richmond, D. (2009). Preparing teachers for inclusive classrooms. *Teaching and Teacher Education*, *25*(4), 535–542.

Juel, C. (1988). Learning to read and write: A longitudinal study of 54 children from first through fourth grades. *Journal of Educational Psychology*, *80*, 437–447.

Jupiter, C. (2009). Debugging texts with metacognition. In S. S. Peterson, D. Booth, & C. Jupiter (Eds.), *Books, media & the internet*. Winnipeg, MB: Portage & Main Press.

Justice, L. H. (2003). Promising interventions for promoting emergent literacy skills. *Topics in early childhood special education*, *23*(3), 99–113.

Kagan, S. (1994). *Cooperative learning*. San Clemente, CA: Kagan Publishing.

Kagan, S. (2001). *Cooperative learning*. San Clemente, CA: Kagan Cooperative Learning.

Kajder, S., & Bull, G. (2003). Scaffolding for struggling students: Reading and writing with blogs. *Learning and Leading with Technology*, *31*(2), 32–35.

Kamil, M. L., Pearson, P. D., Moje, E. B., & Afferbach, P. P. (Eds.). *2011 handbook of reading research* (Vol. 4). New York, NY: Routledge, Taylor & Francis Group.

Kannapel, P. J., & Clements, S. K. (2005). *Inside the black box of high-performing high-poverty schools*. Lexington, KY: The Prichard Committee for Academic Excellence.

Kanfer, R. P. L., Ackerman, T., Murtha, C., Dugdale, B., & Nelson, L. (1994). Goal setting, conditions of practice, and task performance: A resource allocation perspective. *Journal of Applied Psychology*, *79*, 826–835.

Kavale, K. A., Holdnack, J. A., & Mostert, M. P. (2005). Responsiveness to intervention and the identification of specific learning disability: A critique and alternative proposal. *Learning Disability Quarterly*, *28*(1), 2.

Karchmer, R. (2001). The journey head: Thirteen teachers report how the internet influences literacy instruction in their K–12 classrooms. *Reading Research Quarterly*, *36*(4), 442–456.

Karnes, F. A., & Bean, S. M. (2001). *Methods and materials for teaching the gifted*. Waco, TX: Prufrock Press Inc.

Kassow, D. Z. (2006). Parent-child shared book reading: Quality versus quantity of reading interactions between parents and young children. *Talaris Research Institute*, *1*(1), 1–7.

Keene, E. K., & Zimmerman, S. (1997). *Mosaic of thought: Teaching comprehension in a reading workshop*. Portsmouth, NH: Heinemann.

Kehoe, J., & Masfield, E. (1997). *The limitations of multicultural education and anti-racist education*. Retrieved from **http://casit.org?reserach/multicult.htm**

Kellogg, R. T. (2000). Writing. In A. Kazdin (Ed.), *Encyclopaedia of psychology*. Washington, DC, and New York, NY: American Psychological Association and Oxford University Press.

Kelly, H. (1967). Attribution theory in social psychology. In D. Levine (Ed.), *Nebraska symposium on motivation* (pp. 192–238). Lincoln, NE: University of Nebraska Press.

Kennedy, K. (2003). *Writing weblogs*. Retrieved from **http://www.techlearning.com/db area/archives/TL/ 2003/02/blogs.php**

Kernaghan, K., & Woloshyn, V. E. (1995). Providing grade one students with multiple spelling strategies: Comparisons between strategy instruction, strategy instruction with metacognitive information and traditional language arts. *Applied Cognitive Psychology*, *9*, 157–166.

Kindlon, D., & Thompson, M. (1999). *Raising Cain: Protecting the emotional life of boys*. New York, NY: Ballantine Publishing Group.

Kindlon, D., & Thompson, M. (2000). *Raising Cain: Protecting the emotional life of boys*. New York, NY: Ballantine Books.

King, A. (1995). Cognitive strategies for learning from direct teaching. In E. Wood, V. Woloshyn, & T. Willoughby (Eds.), *Cognitive strategy instruction for middle and high schools* (pp. 18–65). Cambridge, MA: Brookline Books.

King, A., & Rosenshine, B. (1993). Effects of guided cooperative-questioning on children's knowledge construction. *Journal of Experimental Education*, 6, 127–148.

Kingore, B. (2004). *Differentiation: simplified, realistic and effective*. Austin, TX: Professional Association Publishing.

Kirova, A. (2008). Critical and emerging discourses in multicultural education: A review. *Canadian Ethnic Studies*, *40*(1), 101–124.

Kist, W. (2005). *New literacies in action: Teaching and learning in multiple media*. New York, NY: Teachers College Press.

Kline, S., Dyer-Witheford, N., & Peuter, G. (2005). *Digital play*. Montreal & Kingston: McGill-Queen's University Press.

Klingner, J. K., & Vaughn, S. (1999). Promoting reading comprehension, content learning, and English acquisition though collaborative strategic reading (CSR). *The Reading Teacher*, *52*(7), 738–747.

Knobel, M., & Lankshear, C. (2007). *A new literacies sampler*. New York, NY: Peter Lang.

Kostos, K., & Shin, E. (2010). Using math journals to enhance second graders' communication of mathematical thinking. *Early Childhood Education Journal*, *38*, 223–231.

Kouritzin, S. (2000). A mother's tongue. *TESOL Quarterly*, *34*, 311–324.

Kramarski, B., & Gutman, M. (2006). How can self-regulated learning be supported in mathematical in learning environments? *Journal of Computer Assisted Learning*, *22*(1), 24–33.

Krashen, S. (2002). More smoke and mirrors: A critique of the National Reading Panel report on fluency. In R. L. Allington (Ed.), *Big brother and the national reading curriculum: How ideology trumped evidence* (pp. 112–124). Portsmouth, NH: Heinemann.

Krashen, S. (2006). SSR is a very good idea: A response to Shanahan. *Reading Today, 24*(1), 16.

Kress, G. (2003). *Literacy in the new media age*. New York, NY: Routledge.

Kress, G., & van Leeuwen, T. (2001). *Multimodal discourse: The modes and media of contemporary communication*. London, UK: Arnold.

Laboucane, R. (2010). Canada's Aboriginal education crisis. *Windspeaker, 28*(7).

Lavin, M. R. (1998). Comic books and graphic novels for libraries: What to buy. *Serials Review, 24*(2), 31–46.

Learning Disabilities Association of Ontario. (2009). Retrieved from **https://www.access.wbtt.ldao.ca/**

Lederer, J. M. (2000). Reciprocal teaching of social studies in inclusive elementary classrooms. *Journal of Learning Disabilities, 33*(1), 91–106.

Lehman, B. A. (1991. Children's choice and critical acclaim: A united perspective for children's literature. *Reading Research and Illustration, 30*, 1–20.

Lemke, J. (2006). Toward critical multimedia literacy: Technology, research, and politics. In M. C. McKenna, L. D. Labbo, R. D. Kieffer, & D. Reinking (Eds.), *International handbook of literacy and technology* (Vol. II, pp. 3–14). Mahwah, NJ: Lawrence Erlbaum Associates Inc.

Lenchner, O., & Podhajski, B. (1997). *Sound start: Teaching phonological awareness in the classroom*. Williston, VT: Stern Center for Language.

Lenski, S. D., Wham, M. A., & Johns, J. L. (1999). *Reading and learning strategies for middle and high school students*. Dubuque, IA: Kendall/Hunt.

Leroy, C., & Symes, B. (2001). Teachers' perspectives on the family backgrounds of children at risk. *McGill Journal of Education, 36*, 45–60.

Leslie, L., & Caldwell, J. (2006). *Qualitative reading inventory 4*. New York, NY: Longman.

Leslie, L., & Caldwell, J. (2009). Formal and informal measures of reading comprehension. In S. E. Israel & G. G. Duffy (Eds.), *Handbook of research on reading comprehension* (pp. 403–427). New York: NY: Routledge.

Leslie, L., & Caldwell, J. S. (2010). *Qualitative reading inventory* (5th ed.). Boston, MA: Allyn & Bacon.

Levin, J., Levin, J. F., Kerr. J. W., & Elliott, A. E. (2011). *Principles of classroom management* (3rd Canadian ed.) Toronto, ON: Pearson Education.

Levin, J., Nolan, J. F., Kerr, J. W., & Elliott, A. E. (2011). *Principles of classroom management*. Toronto, ON: Pearson.

Lewison, M., Flint, A. S., & Van Sluys, K. (2002). Taking on critical literacy: The journey of newcomers and novices. *Language Arts, 79*(5), 382–392.

Linan-Thompson, S., & Vaughn, S. (2007). *Research-based methods of reading instruction for English language learners K–4*. Alexandria, VA: Association for Supervision and Curriculum Development.

Lindstrom, M. (2003). *Brand child.* Sterling, VA: Milward Brown.

Linn, S. (2004). *Consuming kids: The hostile takeover of childhood.* New York, NY: New Press.

Livingstone, S. (2003). *Children's use of the internet: Reflections on the emerging research agenda*. London, UK: Sage Publications.

Loban, W. D. (1976). *Language development: Kindergarten through grade twelve* (Research Report No. 18). Urbana, IL: National Council of Teachers of English.

Lonigan, C. J., Shanahan, T., & Cunningham, A. (2008). Impact of shared-reading interventions on young children's early literacy skills. In *Developing early literacy: Report of the National Early Literacy Panel* (pp. 153–171). Washington, DC: National Institute for Literacy.

Luke, A. (2000). Critical literacy in Australia: A matter of context and standpoint. *Journal of Adolescent & Adult Literacy*, 43(5), 448–461.

Luke, A., & Freebody, P. (1999). A map of possible practice: Further notes on the four resources model. *Practically Primary*, 4(2), 5–8.

Luke, C. (1997). Media literacy and cultural studies. In S. Muspratt, A. Luke, & P. Freeman (Eds.), *Constructing critical literacies: Teaching and learning textual practice* (pp. 19–49). Cresskill, NJ: Hampton.

Luke, C. (2003). Pedagogy, connectivity, multimodality and interdisciplinarity. *Reading Research Quarterly*, 38(3), 397–403.

Lund, D. E. (2006). Waking up the neighbors: Surveying multicultural and antiracist education in Canada, the United Kingdom and the United States. *Multicultural Perspectives*, 8(1), 35–43.

Lynch-Brown, D., & Tomlinson, C. M. (1998). *Essentials of children's literature* (3rd ed.) Toronto, ON: Allyn & Bacon.

MacArthur, C. A., Ferretti, R. P., Okolo, C. M., & Cavalier, A. R. (2001). Technology applications for students with literacy problems: A critical review. *The Elementary School Journal, 101*(3), 273–301.

MacArthur, C. A., Graham, S., & Harris, K. H. (2004). Insights from instructional research on revision with struggling writers. In L. Allal, L. Chanquoy, & P. Largy (Eds.), *Revision: Cognition and instructional processes* (pp. 125–137). Dordrecht, The Netherlands: Kluwer.

Mackie, J. (1976). *Problems from Locke*. Oxford, UK: Oxford University Press.

Maker, C. J., & Nielson, A. B. (1996). *Curriculum development and teaching strategies for gifted learners* (2nd ed.). Austin, TX: PRO-ED.

Manitoba Education, Citizenship and Youth. (2006). Rethinking classroom assessment with purpose in mind: Assessment for learning, assessment as learning, assessment of learning. Retrieved from **http://www.edu.gov.mb.ca/k12/assess/wncp/rethinking_assess_mb.pdf**

Manitoba Education, Citizenship and Youth. (2008). *Listening and speaking: First steps into literacy*. Winnipeg, MB: Manitoba Education and Training.

Manyak, P. C. (2008). Phonemes in use: Multiple activities for a critical process. *The Reading Teacher*, 61(8), 659–662.

Manzo, A. V. (1969). The ReQuest procedure. *Journal of Reading, 12*, 123–126.

Manzo, U. C., Manzo, A. V., & Thomas, M. M. (2009). *Content area literacy: A framework for reading-based instruction* (5th ed.). Hoboken, NJ: John Wiley & Sons Inc.

Mariotti, A. S., & Homan, S. P. (2005). *Linking reading assessment to instruction*. Mahwah, NJ: Lawrence Erlbaum Associates.

Marshal, M. P., Friedman, M. S., Stall, R., King, K. M., Miles, J., Gold, M. A., . . . Morse, J. Q. (2008). Sexual orientation and adolescent substance use: A meta-analysis and methodological review. *Addiction, 103*(4), 546–556.

Martin, S. (2010). *Take a look* (5th ed.) Toronto, ON: Pearson Canada.

Martinez, M. G., & Roser, N. L. (Eds.). (1995). *Book talk and beyond: Children andteachers respond to literature*. Newark, DE: International Reading Association.

Martino, W., & Kehler, M. (2007). Gender-based literacy reform: A question of challenging or recuperating gender binaries. *Canadian Journal of Education, 30*(2), 406–431.

Marzano, J. M. (2007). *The art and science of teaching: A comprehensive framework for effective instruction*. Alexandria, VA: ASCD.

Maslow, A. (1943). A theory of human motivation. *Psychological Review, 50*(4), 370–396.

Mastropieri, M. A., & Scruggs, T. E. (2005). Feasibility and consequences of response to intervention: Examination of the issues and scientific evidence as a model for the identification of individuals with learning disabilities. *Journal of Learning Disabilities, 38*, 525–532.

Mathes, P. G., & Fletcher, J. M. (2008). Dyslexia. In N. J. Salkind (Ed.), *Encyclopedia of educational psychology*. Thousand Oaks, CA: Sage.

May, F. B., & Rizarrdi, L. (2002). *Reading for communication*. Upper Saddle River, NJ: Prentice Hall.

Mayer, R. E. (2008). *Learning and instruction* (2nd ed.). Upper Saddle River, NJ: Prentice Hall.

McCarthy, P. A. (2008). Using sound boxes systematically to develop phonemic awareness. *The Reading Teacher, 62*(4), 346–349.

McCutchen, D. (2006). Cognitive factors in the development of children's writing. In C. A. MacArthur, S. Graham, & J. Fitzgerald (Eds.), *Handbook of writing research* (pp. 115–130). New York, NY: Guilford Publications.

McGuinness, D. (2004). *Early reading instruction: What science really tells us about how to teach reading*. Cambridge, MA: MIT Press.

McKenna, M. C., & Dougherty Stahl, K. A. (2009). *Assessment for reading instruction* (2nd ed.). New York, NY: Guilford Press.

McLaren, P., & Lankshear, C. (Eds.). (1994). *Politics of liberation: Paths from Freire*. New York NY: Routledge.

McMaster, K. L. N, Fuchs, D., Fuchs, L. S. & Compton, D. L. (2005). Responding to nonresponders: An experimental field trial of identification and intervention methods. *Exceptional Children, 71*(4), 445–463.

McMillan J. H. (2008). *Assessment essentials for standards-based education* (2nd ed.). Thousand Oaks, CA: Sage.

McQuirter, S. R., & Siamon, S. (2004). *Spelling: Connecting the pieces*. Katonah, NY: Richard C. Owen Publisher Inc.

McQuirter, S. R., & Siamon, S. (2005). *Sharing the secrets: Teach your child to spell* (2nd ed.) Victoria, BC: Trafford.

McTavish, M. (2008). "What were you thinking?": The use of metacognitive strategy during engagement with reading narrative and informational genres. *Canadian Journal of Education, 31*(2), 405–430.

McTighe, J., & Brown, J. L. (2005). Differentiated instruction and educational standards: Is détente possible? *Theory into Practice, 44*(3), 234–244.

Meier, J. D., & Invernizzi, M. (2001). Book buddies in the Bronx: Testing a model for America reads. *Journal of Education for Students Placed at Risk, 6*, 319–333.

Merali N. (2008). Immigration. In N. J. Salkind (Ed.), *Encyclopedia of educational psychology*. Thousand Oaks, CA: Sage.

Millard, E. (1997). *Differently literate: Boys, girls and the schooling of literacy*. London, UK: Falmer Press.

Miller, S. D., & Faircloth, B. S. (2009). Motivation and dreading comprehension. In S. E. Israel & G. G. Duffy (Eds.), *Handbook of research on reading comprehension* (pp. 307–322). New York, NY: Routledge.

Mills, K. (2006). Discovering design possibilities through a pedagogy of multiliteracies. *Journal of Learning Design, 1*(3), 61–72.

Miyata, C. (2001). *Speaking rules!* Toronto, ON: Pembroke Publishing.

Moloney, J. (2002). Ideas for getting boys to read. Retrieved from **http://www.home.gil.com.au/~cbcqld/moloney/books7.htm**

Moore, D., & Moore, S. (1992). Possible sentences: An update. In E. Dishner, T. Bean, J. Readence, & D. Moore (Eds.), *Reading in content areas: Improving classroom instruction* (3rd ed., pp. 196–201). Dubuque, IA: Kendall/Hunt.

Morra, S., Gobbo, C., Marini, Z., & Sheese, R. (2008). *Cognitive development: Neo-Piagetian perspectives*. Mahwah, NJ: Lawrence Erlbaum Associates.

Morrow, L. M., & Gambrell, L. B. (2001). Literature-based instruction in the early years. In S. B. Neuman & D. K. Dickinson (Eds.), *Handbook of early literacy research* (pp. 348–360). New York, NY: Guilford Press.

Morrow, L. M., & Gambrell, L. B. (Eds.). (2011). *Best practices in literacy instruction* (4th ed.). New York, NY: Guilford Publications.

Moxley, J., Morgan, M. C., Barton, M., & Hanak, D. (2005). For teachers new to wikis. Retrieved from **http://writingwiki-org/default.aspx/writing Wiki/For teachers new to Wikis.html**

Munakata, Y. (2006). Information processing: Approaches to development. In W. Damon & R. Lerner (Eds.),

Handbook of educational psychology. New York, NY: Wiley.

Murphy, S., & Yancey, Y. B. (2008). Construct and consequence: Validity in writing assessment. In C. Bazerman (Ed.), *Handbook of research on writing: History, society, school, individual, text* (pp. 365–386). New York: NY. Lawrence Erlbaum Associates.

Murray, M. (2001). *A teacher teaches writing*. Portsmouth, NH: Heinemann.

Myers, J., & Beach, R. (2004). Constructing critical literacy practices through technology tools and inquiry. *Contemporary Issues in Technology and Teacher Education*, 4(3), 257–268.

Nagy, W. E., Berninger, V. W., & Abbott, R. D. (2006). Contribution of morphology beyond phonology to literacy outcomes of upper elementary and middle-school students. *Journal of Educational Psychology*, 98(1), 134–147.

National Early Literacy Panel. (2008). Retrieved from **http://www.nifl.gov/archive/pfr/aboutHtm/**

National Reading Panel. (2000). *Teaching children to read: An evidence-based assessment of the scientific research literature on reading and its implications for reading instruction*. Bethesda, MD: National Institute of Child Health and Human Development.

National Research Council. (2001). *Knowing what students know: The science and design of educational assessment*. Washington, DC: National Academy Press.

National Writing Project & Nagin, C. (2006). *Because writing matters: Improving students writing in our schools*. San Francisco, CA: Jossey-Bass.

Neuman, S. B., & Celano, D. (2001). Access to print in low-income and middle-income communities: An ecological study of four neighborhoods. *Reading Research Quarterly*, 36, 8–26.

New London Group. (1996). A pedagogy of multiliteracies: Designing social futures. *Harvard Educational Review*, 66(1), 60–92.

Newcombe, N. (2006). A plea for spatial literacy. *The Chronicle Review*, 52(26).

Newkirk, T. (2000). Misreading masculinity: Speculations on the great gender gap in writing. *Language Arts*, 77(4), 294–300.

Nilsson, N. L. (2008). A critical analysis of eight informal reading inventories. *The Reading Teacher*, 61(7), 526–536.

Noble, T. (2004). Integrating the revised Bloom's taxonomy with multiple intelligences: A planning tool for curriculum differentiation. *Teachers College Record*, 106(1), 193–211.

Nodelman, P., & Reimer, M. (2002). *The pleasures of children's literature* (3rd ed.) Toronto, ON: Allyn & Bacon.

Noguchi, R. R. (1991). *Grammar and the teaching of writing: Limits and possibilities*. Urbana, IL: National Council of Teachers of English.

Novak, J. M., & Purkey, W. W. (2001). Invitational education. Bloomington, IN: Phi Delta Kappa Educational Foundation Fastback.

O'Connor, C., & Fernandez, S. D. (2006). Race, class and disproportionality: Reevaluating the relationship. *Educational Researcher*, 35(6), 6–11.

O'Connor, R. E., & Vadasy, P. F. (2011). *Handbook of reading interventions*. New York, NY: Guilford Press.

Oczkus, L. (2003). *Reciprocal teaching at work: Strategies for improving reading comprehension*. Newark, DE: International Reading Association.

Oczkus, L. D. (2007). *Guided writing: Practical lessons, powerful results*. Portsmouth, NH: Heinemann.

Ogle, D. (1986). K-W-L: A teaching model that develops active reading of expository text. *The Reading Teacher*, 39, 563–570.

The Ontario Curriculum, Grades 1–8. (2006). *Language*. Toronto, ON: Queen's Printer for Ontario.

Ontario Ministry of Education. (2003). *A guide to effective instruction in reading in kindergarten to grade 3*. Toronto, ON: Author.

Ontario Ministry of Education. (2004). *Literacy for learning: The report of the expert panel on literacy in grades 4 to 6 in Ontario*. Toronto, ON: Author.

Ontario Ministry of Education. (2005). *Education for all: Literacy and numeracy instruction for special education students: The report of the expert panel*. Toronto, ON: Ontario Ministry of Education, Special Education Policy and Programs Branch.

Ontario Ministry of Education. (2006a). *The kindergarten program*. Toronto, ON: Author.

Ontario Ministry of Education. (2006b). *The Ontario language curriculum*. Toronto, ON: Author.

Opie, I. A., & Opie, P. (2000). *The love and language of school children* (New ed.). New York, NY: NYRB Classics.

Pajares, F., & Valiante, G. (1999). Grade level and gender differences in the writing self-beliefs of middle school students. *Contemporary Educational Psychology*, 24, 390–405.

Palincsar, A. S. (1986). Metacognitive strategy instruction. *Exceptional children*, 53(2), 118–124.

Palincsar, A. S. (1986). Reciprocal teaching. In *Teaching reading as thinking*. Oak Brook, IL: North Central Regional Educational Laboratory.

Palincsar, A. S. (2003). Collaborative approaches to reading comprehension. In A. Sweet & C. Snow (Eds.), *Rethinking reading comprehension* (pp. 99–115). New York, NY: Guilford Press.

Palincsar, A. S., & Brown, A. L. (1983). Reciprocal teaching of comprehension-fostering and comprehension-monitoring activities. *Cognition and Instruction*, 1(2), 117–175.

Palincsar, A. S., & Klenk, L. J. (1991). Dialogues promoting reading comprehension. In B. Means, C. Chelemer, & M. S. Knapp (Eds.), *Teaching advanced skills to at-risk students*. San Francisco, CA: Jossey-Bass.

Palm, T. (2008). Performance assessment and authentic assessment: A conceptual analysis of the literature. *Practical Assessment Research & Evaluation*, 13(4), 1–11.

Palumbo, T., & Willcutt, J. (2006). Perspectives on fluency: English-language learners and students with dyslexia. In S. J. Samuels & A. E. Farstrup (Eds.), *What research has to say about fluency instruction* (pp. 159–178). Newark, DE: International Reading Association.

Paris, A. H., & Paris, S. G. (2003). Assessing narrative comprehension in young children. *Reading Research Quarterly*, *38*, 36–76.

Paris, S. G., & Stahl, S. A. (2005). *Children's reading comprehension and assessment*. Mahwah, NJ: Lawrence Erlbaum Associates.

Parr, M., & Campbell, T. (2007). *Teaching the language arts*. Mississauga, ON: John Wiley & Sons Canada.

Payne, B. K., Monk-Turner, E., Smith, D., & Sumter, M. (2006). Improving group work: Voices of students. *Education*, *126*(3), 441–448.

Payne, R. K. (2005). *A framework for understanding poverty* (4th rev. ed.). Highlands, TX: Ahai Process Inc.

Pellino, K. (2007). *The effects of poverty on teaching and learning*. Retrieved from **http://www.teachnology.com/tutorials/teaching/poverty/print.htm**

Perez, S. (2001). Revising during writing in a second grade classroom. *Educational Research Quarterly*, *25*(1), 27–32.

Perry, N., & Drummond, L. (2002). Helping young students become regulated researchers and writers. *Reading Teacher*, *56*(3), 298–310.

Peterson, S. (2006). Influence of gender on writing. In C. A. MacArthur, S. Graham, & J. Fitzgerald (Eds.), *Handbook of writing research* (pp. 311–323). New York, NY: Guilford Publications.

Peterson, S. S., & Swartz, L. (2008). *Good books matter*. Markham, ON: Pembroke Publishers.

Phelps-Gunn, T., & Phelps-Terasaki, D. (1982). *Written language instruction*. Rockville, MD: Aspen Systems Corporation.

Phenix, J. (2003). *The spelling teacher's book of lists: Words to illustrate spelling patterns . . . and tips for teaching them* (2nd ed.). Markham, ON: Pembroke Publishers.

Phinney, J. S., & Rotheram, M. J. (Eds.). (1987). *Children's ethnicity, pluralism and development*. Beverly Hills, CA: Sage Publications.

Piaget, J. (1932). *The moral judgement of the child*. New York, NY: Harcourt Brace Jovanovich.

Piaget, J. (1959). *The psychology of intelligence*. Totowa, NJ: Littlefield Adams.

Pintrich, P. R., & Schunk, D. H. (2002). *Motivation in education: Theory, research and applications*. Columbus, OH: Merrill.

PIRLS. (2001). Retrieved from **http://nces.ed.gov/pubs2004/pirlspub3.asp**

PISA. (2001). Retrieved from **http://wwwAllc.org/content/pubs/pisa_2001.html**

Popham, W. J. (2008). *Classroom assessment* (5th ed.). Boston, MA: Allyn & Bacon.

Postman, N. (1979). *Teaching as a conserving activity*. New York, NY: Laurel Press, Dell.

Powell, D. A., & Aram, R. (2008). Spelling in parts: A strategy for spelling and decoding polysyllabic words. *The Reading Teacher*, *61*(7), 567–570.

Pragnell, M. V., Roselli, T., & Rossano, V. (2006). Can a hypermedia cooperative e-learning environment stimulate constructive collaboration? *Educational Technology & Society*, 9(2), 119–132.

Praisner, C. L. (2003). Attitudes of elementary school principals toward the inclusion of students with disabilities. *Exceptional Children*, 69(2), 135–145.

Prensky, M. (2001). Digital natives, digital immigrants. *On the Horizon*, 9(5).

Pressley, M. (2000). What should comprehension instruction be the instruction of? In N. L. Kamil, P. B. Mosenthal, P. D. Pearson, & D. Barr (Eds.), *Handbook of reading research* (Vol. III, pp. 545–561). Mahwah, NJ: Erlbaum.

Pressley, M. (2006). *Reading instruction that WORKS: The case for balanced teaching* (3rd ed.). New York, NY: Guilford.

Pressley, M. (2007). Achieving best practices. In L. B. Gambrell, L. M. Morrow, & M. Pressley (Eds.), *Best practices in literacy instruction*. New York, NY: Guilford Press.

Pressley, M., Allington, R. L., Wharton-McDonald, R., Block, C. C., & Morrow, L. (2001). *Learning to read: Lessons from exemplary first-grade classrooms*. New York, NY: Guilford Press.

Pressley, M., Gaskins, I., Cunicelli, E. A., Burdick, N. J., Schaub-Matt, M., Lee, D. S., & Powell, N. (1992). Beyond direct explanation: Transactional instruction of reading comprehension strategies. *Elementary School Journal*, *92*, 511–554.

Pressley, M., & Harris, K. R. (2006). Cognitive strategies instruction: From basic research to classroom instruction. In P. A. Alexander & P. H. Winne (Eds.), *Handbook of educational psychology* (2nd ed.). Mahwah, NJ: Erlbaum.

Pressley, M., & McCormick, C. B. (2007). *Child and adolescent development for educators*. New York, NY: Guilford Press.

Pressley, M., & Woloshyn, V. E. (Eds.). (1995). *Cognitive strategy instruction that really improves children's academic performance*. Cambridge, MA: Brookline Books.

Price, K. L. (2010). Teaching reading comprehension to children of poverty. *Academic Leadership*, 8(3).

Pritchard, R., & Honeycutt, R. (2006). The process approach to writing instruction: Examining its effectiveness. In C. MacArthur, S. Graham, & J. Fitzgerald (Eds.), *Handbook of writing research*. New York, NY: Guilford Press.

Protheroe, N. (2004). Motivating reluctant learners. *Principal Magazine*, 84(1).

Provost, M. C. & Lambert, M. A. (2010). Informal reading inventories: Creating teacher-designed literature-based assessments. *Intervention in Schools and Clinic*, *45*(4), 211–220.

Quebec Ministère de l'Éducation. (2000). *Quebec preschool education*. Quebec City, QC: Gouvernement du Québec.

Radar, R., McCauley, L. & Callen, E. C. (2009). Current strategies in the diagnosis and treatment of childhood attention-deficit/hyperactivity disorder. *American Family Physician, 79*(8), 657–665.

RAND Reading Study Group. (2002). *Reading for understanding: Toward an R&D program in reading comprehension* (pp. 61–72). Santa Monica, CA: Rand Corporation.

Raphael, T. E., George, M., Weber, C. M., & Nies, A. (2009). Approaches to teaching reading comprehension. In S. E. Israel & G. G. Duffy (Eds.), *Handbook of research on reading comprehension* (pp. 449–469). New York, NY: Routledge.

Rasinski, T. V. (2001). *Making and writing words: Grades 3–6*. Greensboro, NC: Carson-Dellosa Publishing Company.

Rasinski, T. V. (2004). *Assessing reading fluency*. Honolulu, HI: Pacific Resources for Education and Learning. Retrieved from **http://www.prel.org/products/re_/assessing-fluency.htm**

Rasinski, T. V. (2009). Fluency: The essential link from phonics to comprehension. In T. V. Rasinski (Ed.), *Essential readings on fluency* (pp. 1–10). Newark, DE: International Reading Association.

Ray, B. B., & Coulter, G. A. (2008). Reflective practice among language arts teachers: The use of weblogs. *Contemporary Issues in Technology and Teacher Education, 8*(1), 6–26.

Reed, W. M., Ayersman, D. J., & Kraus, L. A. (1997). The effects of learning type and task type on hypermedia-based mental models. *Journal of Educational Multimedia and Hypermedia, 6*(3–4).

Report Card on Child and Family Poverty in Canada: 1989–2010. (2010). Retrieved from **http://www.campaign2000.ca/reportCards/national/2010EnglishC2000NationalReportCard.pdf**

Reutzel, D. R., & Cooter Jr., R. B. (2004). *The essentials of teaching children to read*. Upper Saddle River, NJ: Pearson Prentice Hall.

Reutzel, D. R., & Cooter Jr., R. B. (2004). *Teaching children to read: Putting the pieces together* (4th ed.). Upper Saddle River, NJ: Pearson Education.

Reutzel, D. R., & Cooter Jr., R. B. (2005). *The essentials of teaching children to read*. Upper Saddle River, NJ: Pearson Prentice Hall.

Reutzel, D. R., Jones, C. D., Fawson, P. C., & Smith, J. A. (2008). Scaffolded silent reading: A complement to guided repeated oral reading that works! *The Reading Teacher, 62*(3), 194–207.

Reutzel, D. R., Smith, J. A., & Fawson, P. C. (2005). An evaluation of two approaches for teaching reading comprehension strategies in the primary years using science information texts. *Early Childhood Research Quarterly, 20*, 276–305.

Richards, H. V., Brown, A. F., & Forde, T. B. (2007). Addressing diversity in schools: Culturally responsive pedagogy. *Teaching Exceptional Children, 39*(3), 64–68.

Richardson, W. (2005). Blog revolution: Expanding classroom horizons with web logs. *Technology & Learning, 26*(4), 48.

Richek, M. A., Caldwell, J. S., Holt Jennings, J., & Lerner, J. W. (2005). *Reading problems: Assessment and teaching strategies* (5th ed.). Boston, MA: Allyn & Bacon.

Risley, T. (2003). Meaningful experiences in the everyday experiences of young American children. Paper presented at the annual convention of the International Reading Association, Orlando, FL, May.

Robertson, C., & Salter, W. (2007). *Phonological awareness test (PAT2)*. East Moline, IL: LinguiSystems.

Robinson, F. P. (1962). *Effective reading*. New York, NY: Harper and Row.

Romero F., Paris, S. G., & Brem, S. K. (2005). Children's comprehension and local-to-global recall of narrative and expository texts. *Current Issues in Education, 8*(25). Retrieved from **http://cie.ed.asu.edu/volume8/number25/**

Roney, R. C. (1996, Winter–Spring). Storytelling in the classroom: Some theoretical thoughts. *Storytelling World, 9*, 7–9.

Rooks, D. (1998). Can I tell you my story? How storytelling contributes to pupils' achievements in other aspects of speaking and listening to their understanding of how language works. *Reading, 32*(1), 24–28.

Rosen, B. (1988). *And none of it was nonsense: The power of storytelling in the school*. Portsmouth, NH: Heinemann.

Rosen, H. (1986). The importance of story. *Language Arts, 63*(3), 226–237.

Rosenblatt, L. (1978). *The reader, the text, the poem: The transactional theory of the literary work*. Carbondale, IL: Southern Illinois Press.

Rosner, J. (1975). *Test of auditory analysis*. Novato, CA: Academic Therapy.

Ross, J. A. (2004). Effects of running records assessment on early literacy achievement. *The Journal of Educational Research, 92*(4), 186–195.

Rowe, D. W. (2008). Development of writing abilities in childhood. In C. Bazerman (Ed.), *Handbook of research on writing: History, society, school, individual, text* (pp. 401–420). New York, NY: Lawrence Erlbaum Associates.

Rowsell, J. (2005). Editorial introduction: New directions in literacy education. In J. Rowsell & D. Booth (Eds.), *Orbit, 36*(1).

Rozelle, R. (2005). *Write great fiction: Description & setting*. Cincinnati, OH: Writer's Digest Book.

Sadker, M. P., & Sadker, D. M. (2002). *Teachers, schools, and society*. Boston, MA: McGraw-Hill.

Sadoski, M., & Paivio, A. (2001). *Imagery and text: A dual coding theory of reading and writing*. Mahwah, NJ: Lawrence Erlbaum Associates.

Sadoski, M., & Paivio, A. (2004). A dual coding theoretical model of reading. In R. R. Ruddell & N. J. Unrau, (Eds.), *Theoretical models and processes of reading* (5th ed., pp. 1329–1362). Newark, DE: International Reading Association.

Samuels, S. J. (1979). The method of repeated reading. *The Reading Teacher, 32*, 403–408.

Samuels, S. J. (2002). Reading fluency: Its development and assessment. In A. E. Farstrup & S. Samuels (Eds.), *What research has to say about reading instruction* (pp. 110–139). Newark, DE: International Reading Association.

Samuels, S. J. (2006). Reading fluency: Its past, present, and future. In T. Rasinski, C. Blachowicz, & K. Lems (Eds.), *Fluency instruction: Research-based best practices* (pp. 7–20). New York, NY: Guilford Press.

Santrock, J. W., & Halonen, J. S. (1999). *The guide to college success*. Belmont, CA: Wadsworth.

Santrock, J. W., Woloshyn, V. E., Levy-Gallagher, T., Di Petta, T., & Marini, Z. (2010). *Educational psychology* (3rd Canadian ed.). Toronto, ON: McGraw-Hill.

Sawhill, I. V., & McLananan, S. (2006). Introducing the issue. *The Future of Children, 16*(2), 3–17.

Sawyer, D. J. (1987). *Test of awareness of language segments (TALS)*. Rockville, MD: Aspen Publication.

Scardamalia, M. (1981). How children cope with the cognitive demands of writing. In C. Frederiksen & J. F. Dominic (Eds.), *Writing: The nature, development, and teaching of written communication*. Mahwah, NJ: Erlbaum.

Schlechty, P. C. (2009). *Leading for learning: How to transform schools into learning organizations*. San Francisco, CA: John Wiley & Sons.

Schmitt, J. T. (1990). A questionnaire to measure children's awareness of strategic reading processes. *The Reading Teacher, 43*(7), 454–461.

SchoolNet News Network. (2001). Speaking publicly! News report by Lillian. *Student Magazine, 7*(March). Retrieved from **http://www.snn-rdr.ca/snn/march2001/speeches.html**

Schor, J. B. (2004). *Born to buy*. Toronto, ON: Scribner.

Schultz, B. D. (2009). Social action curriculum projects: Power and potential of school in the public sphere. *Journal of Curriculum and Pedagogy, 6*(1).

Schwarz, G. (2002). Graphic novels for multiple literacies. *Journal of Adolescent & Adult Literacy* (November). Retrieved form **http://www.readingonline.org/newliteracies/jaal/11-02_column/**

Schwartz, R. M., Askew, B. J., & Gómez-Bellengé, F. X. (2007). What works? Reading Recovery: An analysis of the What Works Clearinghouse Intervention Report issued March 19, 2007. Worthington, OH: Reading Recovery Council of North America.

Scott, J. A., & Nagy, W. E. (1997). Understanding the definitions of unfamiliar verbs. *Reading Research Quarterly, 32*, 184–200.

Scott, R., Siamon, S., & Thomas, V. (1999). *The Canadian spelling program*. Scarborough, ON: Gage Educational Publishing Company.

Shanahan, T. (2006). Does he really think kids shouldn't read? *Reading Today, 23*(6), 12.

Sharan, Y. (2010). Cooperative learning for academic and social gains: Valued pedagogy, problematic practice. *European Journal of Education, 45*(2), 300–313.

Shaughnessy, M. F., Siegel, J., & Stanley, N. Y. (1994). *Gifted and reading: Handicapped and gifted children* (ERIC Accession No. ED 368145). U.S. Information Analyses.

Shaywitz, S. (2003). *Overcoming dyslexia: A new and complete science-based program for reading problems at any level*. New York, NY: Alfred A. Knopf.

Shor, I., & Freire, P. (1986). *A pedagogy for liberation: Dialogue on transforming education*. Westport, CT: J. F. Berger & Garrey.

Shore, K. (2001). Success for ESL students. *Instructor, 110*(6), 30–32.

Short, E. J., & Ryan, E. B. (1984). Metacognitive differences between skilled and less skilled readers: Remediating deficits through story grammar and attribution training. *Journal of Educational Psychology, 76*, 225–235.

Short, K., & Harste, J., with Burke, C. (1995). *Creating classrooms for authors & inquirers*. Portsmouth, NH: Heinemann.

Siegler, R. S. (2007). Cognitive variability. *Developmental Science, 10*, 104–109.

Simner, M. L. (2000). A joint position statement by the Canadian Psychological Association and the Canadian Association of School Psychologists on the Canadian press coverage of the province-wide achievement test results. Retrieved from **http://www.cpa.ca/documents/joint_position.html**

Simmons, J. (2003). Responders are taught, not born. *Journal of Adolescent and Adult Literacy, 46*(8), 684–693.

Sinfield, I., & Hawkins, L. (2005). Critical literacy: Policy and practice. *Orbit, 36*(1), 27–29.

Singer, H., & Donlan, D. (1989). *Reading and learning from text* (2nd ed.). Hillsdale, NJ: Erlbaum.

Skaalvik, S. (2004). Reading problems in school children and adults: Experiences, self-perceptions and strategies. *Social Psychology of Education, 7*, 105–125.

Smith, M., & Wilhelm, J. (2002). *Reading don't fix no Chevys: Literacy in the lives of young men*. Portsmouth, NH: Heinemann.

Smutny, J. F. (2003). Differentiated instruction. *Phi Delta Kappa Fastbacks, 506*, 7–47.

Snow, C. E., Burns, M. S., & Griffin, P. (Eds.). (1998). *Preventing difficulties in young children*. Washington, DC: National Institute for Child Health and Human Development.

Soven, M. I. (1999). *Teaching & writing in middle and secondary schools: Theory, research and practice*. Toronto, ON: Allyn & Bacon.

Spangenberg-Urbschat, K., & Pritchard, R. (Eds.). (1994). *Kids come in all languages: Reading instruction for ESL students*. Newark, DE: International Reading Association.

Spear-Swerling, L. (2006). Children's reading comprehension and oral reading fluency in easy text. *Reading & Writing: An Interdisciplinary Journal, 19*, 199–220.

Stables, A. (2005). Multiculturalism and moral education: Individual positioning, dialogue and cultural practice. *Journal of Moral Education, 34*(2), 185–197.

Stahl, S. (2004). What do we know about fluency? In P. McCardle & V. Chhabra (Eds.), *The voice of evidence in reading research* (pp. 187–211). Baltimore, MD: Paul H. Brookes.

Stahl, S. A. (1986). Three principles of effective vocabulary instruction. *Journal of Reading, 29*(7), 662–668.

Stahl, S. A. (2002). Teaching phonics and phonological awareness. In S. B. Heuman & D. K. Dickinson (Eds.), *The handbook of early literacy research*. New York, NY: Guilford Press.

Stahl, S. A., & Kapinus, B. A. (1991). Possible sentences: Predicting word meanings to teach content area vocabulary. *The Reading Teacher, 45*(1), 36–43.

Stahl, S. A., & Nagy, W. E. (2006). *Teaching word meanings*. Mahwah, NJ: Lawrence Erlbaum Associates.

Stanovich, K. E. (1986). Matthew effects in reading: Some consequences of individual differences in the acquisition of literacy. *Reading Research Quarterly, 21*, 360–407.

Stanovich, K. E. (1988). *Children's reading and the development of phonological awareness*. Detroit, MI: Wayne State University Press.

Stanovich, K. E. (2004). Matthew effects in reading: Some consequences of individual differences in the acquisition of literacy. In R. B. Ruddell & N. J. Unrau (Eds.), *Theoretical models and processes of reading*. Newark, DE: International Reading Association.

Stanovich, P. J., & Jordan, A. (2004). Inclusion as professional development. *Exceptionality Education Canada, 14*(2 & 3), 169–188.

Statistics Canada. (2002). *Measuring up: The performance of Canada's youth in reading, mathematics and science. OECD PISA study—First results for Canadians aged 15* (Catalogue no. 81-590-XPE). Ottawa, ON: Council of Ministries of Education and Human Resources Development Canada.

Statistics Canada. (2006). *Participation and activity limitation survey of 2006: A profile of education for children with disabilities in Canada*. Retrieved from **http://www.statcan.gc.ca/pub/89-628-x/89-628-x2008004-eng.htm**

Sternberg, R. J., & Zhang, L. (2005). Styles of thinking as a basis of differentiated instruction. *Theory into Practice, 44*(3), 245–253.

Stewig, J. W., & Nordberg, B. (1994). *Exploring language arts in the elementary classroom*. Belmont, CA: Wadsworth Publishing Co.

Stiggins, R. J. (2008). *Assessment manifesto: A call for the development of balanced assessment systems*. Portland, OR: ETS Assessment Training Institute.

Stipek, D. (1998). *Motivation to learn: From theory to practice*. Toronto, ON; Allyn & Bacon.

Stipek, D., & MacIver, D. (1989). Development of change in children's assessment of intellectual competence. *Child Development, 60*, 521–538.

Stoodt-Hill, B., & Amspaugh-Corson, L. (2001). *Children's literature: Discovery for a lifetime*. Upper Saddle River, NJ: Prentice-Hall.

Stoodt-Hill, B. D., & Amspaugh-Corson, L. B. (2008). *Children's literature: Discovery for a lifetime* (4th ed.). Toronto, ON: Pearson Education.

Sudweeks, R. R., Glissmeyer, C. B., Morrison, T. G., Wilcox, B. R., & Tanner, M. W. (2004). Establishing reliable procedures for rating ELL students' reading comprehension using oral retellings. *Reading Research and Instruction, 43*(2), 65–86.

Sui-Chu, E. H., & Willms, D. J. (1999). Effects of parental involvement on eighth grade achievement. *Sociology of Education, 69*(2), 126–141.

Swanson, E., & Vaughn, S. (2011). Implementing a response to intervention model to improve reading outcomes for all students. In S. J. Samuels & A. E. Farstrup (Eds.), *What research has to say about reading instruction* (4th ed., pp. 379–405). Newark, DE: International Reading Association.

Swanson, H. L. (1999). What develops in working memory? A life-span perspective. *Developmental Psychology, 35*, 986–1000.

Swartz, M. (1989). Storytelling: A way to look deeper. *The English Journal, 78*(1), 42–46.

Tager-Flusberg, H. (2008). Cognitive neuroscience of autism. *Journal of International Neuropsychological Society, 14*, 917–921.

Tamis-LeMonda, C. S., Bornstein, M. H., & Baumwell, L. (2001). Maternal responsiveness and children's achievement of language milestones. *Child Development, 72*, 748–767.

Tappan, M. B. (1998). Sociocultural psychology and caring psychology: Exploring Vygotsky's "hidden curriculum." *Educational Psychology, 33*, 23–33.

Taylor, C., & Nolen, S. B. (2008). *Classroom assessment* (2nd ed.). Upper Saddle River, NJ: Prentice Hall

Temple, C., Martinez, M., Yokota, J., & Naylor, A. (1998). *Children's books in the hands of children: An introduction to their literature*. Toronto, ON: Allyn & Bacon.

Templeton, S., & Morris, D. (1999). Questions teachers ask about spelling. *Reading Research Quarterly, 34*(1), 102–112.

Templeton, S., & Morris, D. (2000). Spelling. In M. L. Kamil, P. B. Mosenthal, P. D. Pearson, & R. Barr (Eds.), *Handbook of reading research* (Vol. III, pp. 525–544). Mahwah, NJ: Lawrence Erlbaum Associates.

Terry, W. S. (2006). *Learning and memory* (3rd ed.). Boston, MA: Allyn & Bacon.

Thomas, A. (1998). *Family literacy in Canada: Profiles of effective practices*. Welland, ON: Soleil.

Thomas, V. (1979). *Teaching spelling: Canadian word lists and instructional techniques* (2nd ed.). Crescent City, FL: Gage Publishing Limited.

Thompson, M., & Barker, T. (2008). *It's a boy!Your son's development from birth to age 18*. New York, NY: Ballantine Books.

Thornbury, S. (1999). *How to teach grammar*. Essex, UK: Longman.

Tierney, R. J., & Readence, J. E. (2005). *Reading strategies and practices: A compendium*. New York, NY: Pearson.

Tierney, R. J., & Rogers, T. (2004). Process/content/design/critique: Generative and dynamic evaluation in a digital world. *Reading Teacher, 58*(2), 218–221.

Tomasello, M. (1992). *First verbs: A case study of early grammatical development*. Cambridge, MA: Cambridge University Press.

Tomasello, M. (2003). *Constructing a language: A usage-based approach to child language acquisition*. Cambridge, MA: Harvard University Press.

Tomlinson, C. (2003). *Fulfilling the promise of the differentiated classroom: Strategies and tools for responsive teaching*. Alexandria, VA: Association for Supervision and Curriculum Development.

Tomlinson, C. A. (1999). *The differentiated classroom: Responding to the needs of all*. Alexandria, VA: Association for Supervision and Curriculum Development.

Tomlinson, C. A. (2003). Differentiating instruction for academic diversity. In J. M. Cooper (Ed.), *Classroom teaching skills* (7th ed., pp. 149–180). Boston, MA: Houghton Mifflin.

Tompkins, G. E. (1998). *50 literacy strategies*. Upper Saddle River, NY: Merrill.

Tompkins, G. E. (2004). *Literacy for the 21st century*. Upper Saddle River, NJ: Pearson Education.

Tompkins, G. E., Bright, R. M., Pollard, M. J., & Winsor, P. J. (2005). *Language arts content and teaching strategies* (3rd ed.). Toronto, ON: Pearson Education.

Tompkins, G. E., Bright, R. M., Pollard, M. J., & Winsor, P. J. T. (2008). *Language arts: Content and teaching strategies* (4th Canadian ed.). Toronto, ON: Pearson Education.

Tompkins, G. E., Bright, P. M., Pollard, M. J., & Winsor, P. J. T. (2011). *Language arts: Content and teaching strategies*.Toronto, ON: Pearson Education.

Topping, K., & Bryce, A. (2004) Cross age peer tutoring of reading and thinking: Influence on thinking skills. *Educational Psychology, 24*(5), 595–622.

Topping, K. J. (2006a). Building reading fluency: Cognitive, behavioral, and socioemotional factors and the role of peer-mediated learning. In S. J. Samuels & A. E. Farstrup (Eds.), *What research has to say about fluency instruction* (pp. 106–129). Newark, DE: International Reading Association.

Topping, K. J. (2006b). Paired reading: Impact of a tutoring method on reading accuracy, comprehension and fluency. In T. Rasinski, C. Blachowicz, & K. Lems (Eds.), *Fluency instruction: Research-based best practices* (pp. 173–191). New York, NY: Guilford Press.

Torgesen, J., & Bryant, B. (1994). *Phonological awareness training for reading*. Austin, TX: Pro-Ed.

Tovani, C. (2000). *I read it, but I don't get it. Comprehension strategies for adolescent readers*. Portland, ME: Stenhouse.

Trabasso, T., & Magliano, J. P. (1996). How do children understand what they read and what we can do to help them? In M. Graves, P. van den Broek, & T. Taylor (Eds.), *The first R: A right of all children* (pp. 158–181). New York, NY: Teachers College, Columbia University Press.

Troia, G. A. (2006). Writing instruction for students with learning disabilities. In C. A. MacArthur, S. Graham, & J. Fitzgerald (Eds.), *Handbook of writing research* (pp. 324–336). New York, NY: Guilford Publications.

Turkle, S. (1995). *Life on the screen: Identity in the age of the internet*. New York, NY: Simon & Schuster.

Turkle, S. (2011). *Alone together*. New York, NY: Basic Books.

Tuttle, C. L. (2005). Writing in the mathematics classroom. In J. M. Kenny (Ed.), *Literacy strategies for improving mathematics instruction* (pp. 24–50). Alexandria, VA: Association for Supervision and Curriculum Development.

Ueno, K. (2005). Sexual orientation and psychological distress in adolescence: Examining interpersonal stressors and social support processes. *Social Psychology Quarterly, 68*(3), 258–277.

Vacca, J. L., Vacca, R. T., Gove, M. K., Burkey, L. B., Lenhart, L. A., & McKeon, C. A. (2006). *Reading & learning to read* (6th ed.). New York, NY: Allyn & Bacon.

Valencia, S. W. (2011). Using assessments to improve teaching and learning. In S. J. Samuels & A. E. Farstrup (Eds.), *What research has to say about reading instruction* (4th ed., pp. 379–405). Newark, DE: International Reading Association.

Vellutino, F., & Scanlon, D. (1987). Phonological coding, phonological awareness, and reading ability: Evidence from a longitudinal and experimental study. *Merrill-Palmer Quarterly, 33*, 321–363.

Vygotsky, L. (1978). *Mind in society*. Cambridge, MA: Harvard University Press.

Vygotsky L. (1986). *Thought and language*. Cambridge, MA: Massachusetts Institute of Technology.

Wagner, R. K., Torgesen, J. K., & Rashotte, C. A. (1999) *Comprehensive test of phonological processing (CTOPP)*. Austin, TX: Pro-Ed.

Walpole, S., & McKenna, M. C. (2006). The role of informal reading inventories in assessing word recognition. *The Reading Teacher, 59*(6), 591–594.

Warner, M. (1994). *Managing monsters: The 1994 Reith lectures*. London, UK: Vintage Books.

Wasik, B. H., & Hendrickson, J. D. (2004). Family literacy practices. In A. Stone, B. Schulman, K. Apel, & C. Silliuman (Eds.), *Handbook of language and development and disorder*. New York, NY: Guilford Press.

Weaver, C. (1996). *Teaching grammar in context*. Portsmouth, NH: Heinemann.

Weaver, C. (1998). Teaching grammar in the context of writing. In C. Weaver (Ed.), *Lessons to share: On teaching grammar in context* (pp. 18–38). Portsmouth, NH; Heinemann.

Webster-Wright, A. (2009). Reframing professional development through understanding authentic professional learning. *Review of Educational Research, 79*(2), 702–739.

Weiner, B. (1992). *Human motivation: Metaphors, theories and research.* Beverley Hills, CA: Sage Publications.

Wells, G. (2007). Semiotic mediation, dialogue and the construction of knowledge. *Human Development, 50*(5), 244–274.

Wertsch, J. V. (2007). Mediation. In H. Daniels, J. Wertsch, & M. Cole (Eds.), *The Cambridge companion to Vygotsky.* New York, NY: Cambridge University Press.

Wessler, S., & Preble, W. (2003). *The respectful school.* Alexandria, VA: Association for Supervision & Curriculum Development.

Westwood, P. (2005). *Spelling: Approaches to teaching and assessment.* London, UK: David Fulton Publishers.

Wharton-McDonald, R., & Swiger, S. (2009). Developing higher order comprehension in middle grades. In S. Israel & G. Duffy (Eds.), *Handbook of research on reading comprehension* (pp. 510–530). New York, NY, and London, UK: Routledge.

Whittingham, J. L., & Huffman, S. (2009). The effects of book clubs on the reading attitudes of middle school students. *Reading Improvement, 46*(3), 130–136.

Wiggins, J. P., & McTighe, J. (2005). *Understanding by design.* Upper Saddle River, NJ: Prentice Hall.

William, D. (2010). An integrative summary of the research literature and implications for a new theory of formative assessment. In H. L. Andrade & G. J. Cizek (Eds.), *Handbook of formative assessment* (pp. 18–40). New York, NY: Routledge.

Williams, C., & Lundstrom, R. P. (2007). Strategy instruction during word study and interactive writing activities. *The Reading Teacher, 61*(3), 204–212.

Williams, J. (1980). Teaching decoding with an emphasis on phoneme analysis and phoneme blending. *Journal of Educational Psychology, 72,* 1–15.

Willis, S., & Mann, L. (2000). Differentiating instruction: Finding manageable ways to meet individual needs. *Curriculum Update* (Winter).

Willms, J. D. (2003). *Ten hypotheses about socioeconomic gradients and community differences in children's developmental outcomes.* Ottawa, ON: Applied Research Branch of Human Resources Development Canada.

Winner, E. (1996). *Gifted children: Myths and realities.* New York, NY: Basic Books.

Winner, E. (2000). Giftedness: Current theory and research. *Current Directions in Psychological Science, 9*(5), 153–156.

Wittrock, M. C., & Alesandrini, K. (1990). Generation of summaries and analogies and analytic and holistic abilities. *American Educational Research Journal, 27*(3), 489–502.

Wixson, K. K., & Carlisle, J. F. (2005). The influence of large-scale assessment of reading comprehension on classroom practice: A commentary. In S. G. Paris & S. A. Stahl (Eds.), *Children's reading comprehension and assessment.* Mahwah, NJ: Lawrence Erlbaum.

Wolfensberger, W. (1975). *The origin and nature of our institutional models.* Syracuse, NY: Human Policy Press.

Wolfson, B., Manning, G., & Manning, M. (1984). Revisiting what children say their reading interests are. *The Reading World, 14,* 81–82.

Woloshyn, V. E., Elliott, A., & Kaucho, S. (2001). So what exactly is explicit strategy instruction? A review of eight critical teaching steps. *The Reading Professor, 24*(1), 66–114.

Woloshyn, V. E., Elliott, A., & Riordon, M. (1998). Seven teachers' experiences using explicit strategy instruction in the classroom. *Journal of Professional Studies, 5,* 18–28.

Woloshyn, V. E., & Foregrave, K. (2003). Creating effective strategy repertoires: Exploring the use of predictive story frames. Paper presented at Hawaii International Conference on Education, Honolulu, HI.

Woloshyn, V. E., & Pressley, M. (1995). Spelling. In M. Pressley, V. Woloshyn, & Associates (Eds.), *Cognitive strategy instruction that really improves children's academic performances* (2nd ed.) Cambridge, MA: Brookline Books.

Woolfolk, A. (2009). *Educational psychology.* Upper Saddle River, NJ: Prentice Hall.

Worthy, J., Moorman, M., & Turner, M. (1999). What Johnny likes to read is hard to find in school. *Reading Research Quarterly, 34*(10), 12–27.

Wyatt, V. (2001). *The kids book of Canadian firsts.* Toronto, ON: Kids Can Press.

Yolan, J. (1981). *Touch magic.* New York, NY: Philomel Books.

Yopp, H. K. (1992). Developing phonemic awareness in young children. *The Reading Teacher, 45,* 696–703.

Yopp, H. (1995a). A test for assessing phonemic awareness in young children. *The Reading Teacher, 49,* 20–29.

Yopp, H. (1995b). Yopp-Singer test of phonemic segmentation. *The Reading Teacher, 49*(1), 20–29.

Yopp, H., & Yopp, R. (2000). Supporting phonemic awareness development in the classroom. *The Reading Teacher, 54,* 130–143.

Yopp, H., & Yopp, R. (2002). Supporting phonemic awareness development in the classroom. In *Evidence-based reading instruction* (pp. 5–18). Newark, DE: International Reading Association.

Younger, M., Warrington, M., & McLellan, R. (2005). *Raising boys' achievement.* Maidenhead, UK: Open University Press.

Zbaracki, M. D., Opitz, M. F., & Ford, M. P. (2006). *Books and beyond.* Oxford, UK: Heinemann.

Zipes, J. (1991). *Spells of enchantment: The wondrous fairy tales of western culture.* New York NY: Viking Penguin.

Zuckerman, B. (2009). Promoting early literacy in pediatric practice: Twenty years of reach out and read. *Pediatrics, 124*(6), 1660–1665.

Index

Note: Entries for tables and figures are followed by "*t*" and "*f*," respectively.

D

E

O

P

Q

R

S

T

U

V

W

Y

Z

Photo Credits

Chapter 1 Page 1: © Dmitriy Shironosov/Shutterstock.com; **2:** Courtesy of Liz McAnanama; **15:** © Morgan Lane Photography/ Shutterstock.com.

Chapter 2 Page 32: © Monkey Business Images/Shutterstock. com; **33:** Courtesy of Brent Cross; **42:** © Andrew Lundquis/ Shutterstock.com.

Chapter 3 Page 72: © iofoto/Shutterstock.com; **73:** Courtesy of Todd Robinson; **92:** © Matt Antonino/Shutterstock.com.

Chapter 4 Page 109: © Matka Wariatka/Shutterstock. com; **110:** Courtesy of Marilee Lamond; **128:** © privilege/ Shutterstock.com

Chapter 5 Page 154: © Sonya Etchison/Shutterstock.com; **155:** Courtesy of Karen Evangelista; **166:** Guys Read Program; **199:** © Benis Arapovic/Shutterstock.com.

Chapter 6 Page 208: © Dmitriy Shironosov/Shutterstock.com; **209:** Courtesy of Dave Chuchman; **224:** © iofoto/Shutterstock. com.

Chapter 7 Page 255: © Monkey Business Images/Shutterstock. com; **256:** Courtesy of Linda Out; **270:** © Fred Sweet/ Shutterstock.com.

Chapter 8 Page 292: © Dmitriy Shironosov/Shutterstock.com; **293:** Courtesy of Milica Veljic; **311:** © Gladskikh Tatiana/ Shutterstock.com.

Chapter 9 Page 334: © lightpoet/Shutterstock.com; **335:** Courtesy of Kari-Lynn Winters; **366:** © Ingrid Balabanova/ Shutterstock.com.

Chapter 10 Page 386: © Podfoto/Shutterstock.com; **387:** Courtesy of John Howey; **404:** © Krivosheev Vitaly/ Shutterstock.com.

Chapter 11 Page 413: © ZouZou/Shutterstock.com; **414:** Courtesy of Nicole Maheu and Tieha McGee; **431:** © Zuritjeta/ Shutterstock.com.

Chapter 12 Page 450: © Dmitriy Shironosov/Shutterstock. com; **451:** Courtesy of Jamie Taylor; **469:** © Dean Mitchell/ Shutterstock.com.